REACH OUT

An illustrated edition of
The Living New Testament
as developed by
the editors of
CAMPUS LIFE Magazine,
Youth for Christ International

Paraphrase: Ken Taylor
Additional Text: Harold Myra
Layout: Joan Nickerson
Cover Photos: Tom Schmerler

Tyndale House Publishers
Wheaton, Illinois

SBN 8423-5200-7, cloth
SBN 8423-5201-5, kivar

The Living New Testament
Copyright © 1967 by Tyndale House Foundation
Wheaton, Illinois 60187

Additional text
Copyright © 1969 by Youth for Christ International
Wheaton, Illinois 60187

Fifth printing, July 1970
365,000 copies now in print

REACH OUT

Alienation: of blacks from whites, of students from parents, of Arab from Jew . . . all around us and throughout our world we see the need to reach out in love toward our fellow humans . . . to love people as they are.

In a little Jewish town years ago, God did just this. He reached out in love to every human through His own Son, Jesus Christ. This book is the story of that Man, the extension

Students discuss the HOW of putting love into action (see page 354b).

The grim realities of war—which man has lived with since history's beginning— and questions about the future for a girl named Brigitte: how, specifically, does God enter in? (see pages 471a and 594b).

of God's love and at the same time God Himself, who in flesh-and-blood reached out to fishermen, toddlers and businessmen alike.

It was a rugged world He entered. Men were sold like lobsters to die for others' amusement. Rumors of insurrection buzzed in cities and towns, and at times when walking along the road one could see the results of mass executions. It was a sordid world—of poverty contrasted with opulence, of men literally used as fish food while their masters considered themselves aristocracy, of women degraded, of racial strife and hatreds.

Into this world He came . . . not as an emperor, but as a low-born person, to taste of the poverty, the sorrow, the anguish, to be just one man in a system in which men exploited men, Jew hated Samaritan, Roman hated Jew, and religion was usually phony.

He entered as a baby and grew up to become a revolutionary. He, who had created both tiny flowers and distant stars, entered the cor-

A rough ride on cowhide and a strain
for an Olympic world record are the kind of
jolts and triumphs which God wants
to be part of (see pages 569a; 515a).

ruption of His once perfect creation, and, in His reaching out to people with the *truth*, He revolutionized it by transforming individuals.

How? Read through the Gospels. Why are there four Gospels? Is it repetitious? Not when you consider how crucial are these factual, eyewitness accounts of what Jesus said and did! Here is the base on which all other Scripture rests. Here are the documents by which all knowledge can be seen from a clear perspective.

Read through *Acts*—the story of the young church in action. See how men and women filled with the incredible fact that *He* had literally walked out of His grave, reached out to others with this God-love within them and turned their world upside down.

Read through the letters circulated in that early church and study the depth of how these people were making this new Christ-life part of their very beings, enabling them to do that world-changing.

Read, too, *The Revelation*, which gives us a glimpse of another facet of Jesus Christ, the awesome Creator-God, with the fury of His wrath contrasted with the expanse of His love.

As you read, allow your mind to be expanded by the God behind these words. Let Him reach out to your thoughts, your emotions, your will. Then, as He fills you with Himself, reach out to others with the fantastic good news!

CONTENTS

IT'S
A STRANGE
WORLD
WE
LIVE
IN

BOB COMBS

A New England high-school junior, bored, took off from home with a few extra clothes, a guitar and $12 and thumbed his way to Pittsburgh, Nashville, then west through Texas, New Mexico, Arizona, California. The $12 gone, he sang for his supper —often just a cup of coffee or two. Months later, forty pounds lighter, finding that "people are much the same wherever you go," he returned home. Reason: boredom.

You've probably felt the same emotions which triggered his trip. He had wanted to get alone to think. What a strange world to face up to . . . so many conflicting ideas . . . so many incomprehensible things. . . .

Actually, it was much the same kind of world Jesus entered on the first Christmas. As you read His story in this book written by His follower, Matthew, you see how Jesus introduced a totally new perspective, a jolting set of different ideas and dynamics which many flatly rejected and others allowed to change their lives. There was no middle ground with this Man Jesus—who came as the fulfillment of hundreds of facts the prophets had foretold about Him centuries before. He came into a bewildering world of hatreds and confusion with a message and a power available to anybody wanting to listen. . . .

MATTHEW

CHAPTER 1

THESE are the ancestors of Jesus Christ, a descendant of King David and of Abraham:

2 Abraham was the father of Isaac; Isaac was the father of Jacob; Jacob was the father of Judah and his brothers.

3 Judah was the father of Perez and Zerah (Tamar was their mother); Perez was the father of Hezron; Hezron was the father of Aram;

4 Aram was the father of Amminadab; Amminadab was the father of Nahshon; Nahshon was the father of Salmon;

5 Salmon was the father of Boaz (Rahab was his mother); Boaz was the father of Obed (Ruth was his mother); Obed was the father of Jesse;

6 Jesse was the father of King David. David was the father of Solomon (his mother was the ex-wife of Uriah);

7 Solomon was the father of Rehoboam; Rehoboam was the father of Abijah; Abijah was the father of Asa;

8 Asa was the father of Jehoshaphat; Jehoshaphat was the father of Joram; Joram was the father of Uzziah;

9 Uzziah was the father of Jotham; Jotham was the father of Ahaz; Ahaz was the father of Hezekiah;

10 Hezekiah was the father of Manasseh; Manasseh was the father of Amos; Amos was the father of Josiah;

11   Josiah was the father of Jechoniah and his brothers
      (born at the time of the exile to Babylon).
12   After the exile:
      Jechoniah was the father of Shealtiel; Shealtiel was
         the father of Zerubbabel;
13   Zerubbabel was the father of Abiud; Abiud was the
         father of Eliakim; Eliakim was the father of Azor;
14   Azor was the father of Zadok; Zadok was the father of
         Achim; Achim was the father of Eliud;
15   Eliud was the father of Eleazar; Eleazar was the father
         of Matthan; Matthan was the father of Jacob;
16   Jacob was the father of Joseph (who was the husband
         of Mary, the mother of Jesus Christ the Messiah).
17   These are[1] fourteen of the generations from Abraham
         to King David; and fourteen from King David's
         time to the exile; and fourteen from the exile to
         Christ.

                    *   *   *   *   *

18   These are the facts concerning the birth of Jesus Christ:
His mother, Mary, was engaged to be married to Joseph. But
while she was still a virgin she became pregnant by the Holy
Spirit.

19   Then Joseph, her fiancé,[2] being a man of stern principle,[3] decided to break the engagement but to do it quietly, as
he didn't want to publicly disgrace her.

20   As he lay awake[4] considering this, he fell into a dream,
and saw an angel standing beside him. "Joseph, son of David,"
the angel said, "don't hesitate to take Mary as your wife! For
the child within her has been conceived by the Holy Spirit!

21   And she will have a Son, and you shall name Him Jesus
(meaning 'Savior'), for He will save His people from their sins.

22   This will fulfill God's message through His prophets—

23   *'Listen! The virgin shall conceive a child!* She shall
         give birth to a Son, and He shall be called "Emmanuel"
         (meaning "God is with us").' "

---

[1]Literally, "So all the generations from Abraham unto David are fourteen."
[2]Literally, "her husband."
[3]Literally, "a just man."
[4]Implied in remainder of verse.

24 When Joseph awoke, he did as the angel commanded, and brought Mary home to be his wife,

25 But she remained a virgin until her Son was born; and Joseph named Him "Jesus."

CHAPTER 2

JESUS was born in the town of Bethlehem, in Judea, during the reign of King Herod. At about that time some astrologers from eastern lands arrived in Jerusalem, asking,

2 "Where is the newborn King of the Jews? for we have seen His star in far-off eastern lands, and have come to worship Him."

3 King Herod was deeply disturbed by their question, and all Jerusalem was filled with rumors.[1]

4 He called a meeting of the Jewish religious leaders. "Did the prophets tell us where the Messiah would be born?" he asked.

5 "Yes, in Bethlehem," they said, "for this is what the prophet Micah[2] wrote:

6 'O little town of Bethlehem, you are not just an unimportant Judean village, for a Governor shall rise from you to rule My people Israel.' "

7 Then Herod sent a private message to the astrologers, asking them to come to see him; at this meeting he found out from them the exact time when they first saw the star. Then he told them,

8 "Go to Bethlehem and search for the child. And when you find him, come back and tell me so that I can go and worship him too!"

9 After this interview the astrologers started out again. And look! The star appeared to them again, standing over Bethlehem.[3]

10 Their joy knew no bounds!

---

[1]Literally, "and all Jerusalem with him."
[2]Implied. Micah 5:2.
[3]Literally, "went before them until it came and stood over where the baby was."

11   Entering the house where the baby and Mary His mother were, they threw themselves down before Him, worshiping. Then they opened their presents and gave Him gold, frankincense and myrrh.

12   But when they returned to their own land, they didn't go through Jerusalem to report to Herod, for God had warned them in a dream to go home another way.

13   After they were gone, an angel of the Lord appeared to Joseph in a dream. "Get up and flee to Egypt with the baby and His mother," the angel said, "and stay there until I tell you to return, for King Herod is going to try to kill the child."

14   That same night[4] he left for Egypt with Mary and the baby,

15   And stayed there until King Herod's death. This fulfilled the prophet's prediction,
"I have called My Son from Egypt."[5]

16   Herod was furious when he learned that the astrologers had disobeyed him. Sending soldiers to Bethlehem, he ordered them to kill every baby boy two years old and under, both in the town and on the nearby farms, for the astrologers had told him the star first appeared to them two years before.

17   This brutal action of Herod's fulfilled the prophecy of Jeremiah,[6]

18   "Screams of anguish come from Ramah,[7]
Weeping unrestrained;
Rachel weeping for her children,
Uncomforted—
For they are dead."

19   When Herod died, an angel of the Lord appeared in a dream to Joseph in Egypt, and told him,

20   "Get up and take the baby and His mother back to Israel, for those who were trying to kill the child are dead."

21   So he returned immediately to Israel with Jesus and His mother.

22   But on the way he was frightened to learn that the new

---

[4]Implied.
[5]Hosea 11:1.
[6]Jeremiah 31:15.
[7]Or, "the region of Ramah."

4

king was Herod's son, Archelaus. Then, in another dream, he was warned not to go to Judea, so they went to Galilee instead,

23 And lived in Nazareth. This fulfilled the prediction of the prophets concerning the Messiah,

"He shall be called a Nazarene."

CHAPTER 3

WHILE they were living in Nazareth,[1] John the Baptist began preaching out in the Judean wilderness. His constant theme was,

2 "Turn from your sins . . . turn to God . . . for the Kingdom of Heaven is coming soon."[2]

3 Isaiah the prophet had told about John's ministry centuries before! He had written,

"I hear[3] a shout from the wilderness, 'Prepare a road for the Lord—straighten out the path where He will walk.' "

4 John's clothing was woven from camel's hair and he wore a leather belt; his food was locusts and wild honey.

5 People from Jerusalem and from all over the Jordan Valley, and, in fact, from every section of Judea went out to the wilderness to hear him preach,

6 And when they confessed their sins, he baptized them in the Jordan River.

7 But when he saw many Pharisees[4] and Sadducees[5] coming to be baptized, he denounced them. "You sons of snakes!" he warned. "Who said that you could escape the coming wrath of God?

8 Before being baptized, prove that you have turned from sin by doing worthy deeds.

9 Don't try to get by as you are, thinking, 'We are safe for we are Jews—descendants of Abraham.' That proves nothing.

[1]Literally, "in those days."
[2]Or, "has arrived." Literally, "is at hand."
[3]Implied. Isaiah 40:3.
[4]Jewish religious leaders who strictly followed the letter of the law but often violated its intent.
[5]Jewish political leaders.

God can change these stones here into Jews![6]

10   And even now the axe of God's judgment is poised to chop down every unproductive tree. They will be chopped and burned.

11   With[7] water I baptize those who repent of their sins; but Someone else is coming, far greater than I am, so great that I am not worthy to carry His shoes! He shall baptize you with[8] the Holy Spirit and with fire.

12   He will separate the chaff from the grain, burning the chaff with never-ending fire, and storing away the grain."

13   Then Jesus went from His home[9] in Galilee to the Jordan River to be baptized there by John.

14   John didn't want to do it. "This isn't proper," he said. "I am the one who needs to be baptized by You."

15   But Jesus said, "Please do it, for I must do all that is right."[10] So then John baptized Him.

16   After His baptism, as soon as Jesus came up out of the water, the heavens were opened to Him and He saw the Spirit of God coming down in the form of a dove.

17   And a voice from heaven said, "This is My beloved Son, and I am wonderfully pleased with Him."

CHAPTER 4

THEN Jesus was led out into the wilderness by the Holy Spirit, to be tempted there by Satan.

2   For forty days and forty nights He ate nothing and became very hungry.

3   Then Satan tempted Him to get food by changing stones into loaves of bread. "It will prove You are the Son of God," he said.

4   But Jesus told him, "No! For the Scriptures tell us that bread won't feed men's souls: obedience to every word of God is what we need."

[6]Literally, "God is able of these stones to raise up children unto Abraham."
[7]Or, "in water."
[8]Or, "in the Holy Spirit and in fire."
[9]Implied.
[10]Literally, "to fulfill all righteousness."

5 Then Satan took Him to Jerusalem to the roof of the Temple.

6 "Jump off," he said, "and prove You are the Son of God; for the Scriptures declare, 'God will send His angels to keep you from harm,' . . . they will prevent You from smashing on the rocks below."

7 Jesus retorted, "It also says not to put the Lord God to a foolish test!"[1]

8 Next Satan took Him to the peak of a very high mountain and showed Him the nations of the world and all their glory.

9 "I'll give it all to You," he said, "if You will only kneel and worship me."

10 "Get out of here, Satan," Jesus told him. "The Scriptures say, 'Worship only the Lord God. Obey only Him.' "

11 Then Satan went away, and angels came and cared for Jesus.

* * * * * *

12, 13 When Jesus heard that John had been arrested, He left Judea and returned [home[2]] to Nazareth in Galilee; but soon He moved to Capernaum, beside the Lake of Galilee, close to Zebulun and Naphtali.

14 This fulfilled Isaiah's prophecy:

15 "The land of Zebulun and the land of Naphtali, beside the Lake, and the countryside beyond the Jordan River, and Upper Galilee where so many foreigners live—

16 There the people who sat in darkness have seen a great Light; they sat in the land of death, and the Light broke through upon them."[3]

17 From then on, Jesus began to preach, "Turn from sin, and turn to God, for the Kingdom of Heaven is near."[4]

18 One day as He was walking along the beach beside the Lake of Galilee, He saw two brothers—Simon, also called Peter, and Andrew—[out in a boat[5]] fishing with a net, for they were commercial fishermen.

---

[1]Literally, "you must not make trial of the Lord your God."
[2]Implied.
[3]Isaiah 9:1, 2.
[4]Or, "is at hand," or, "has arrived."
[5]Implied.

19   Jesus called out, "Come along with Me and I will show you how to fish for the souls of men!"

20   And they left their nets at once and went with Him!

21   A little farther up the beach He saw two other brothers, James and John, sitting in a boat with their father Zebedee, mending their nets; and He called to them to come too.

22   At once they stopped their work and, leaving their father behind, went with Him.

23   Jesus traveled all through Galilee teaching in the Jewish synagogues, everywhere preaching the Good News about the Kingdom of Heaven. And He healed every kind of sickness and disease.

24   The report of His miracles spread far beyond the borders of Galilee so that sick folk were soon coming to be healed from as far away as Syria. And whatever their illness and pain, or if they were possessed by demons, or were insane, or paralyzed—He healed them all.

25   Enormous crowds followed Him wherever He went— people from Galilee, and the Ten Cities, and Jerusalem, and from all over Judea, and even from across the Jordan River.

CHAPTER 5

ONE day as the crowds were gathering, He went up the hillside with His disciples and sat down and taught them there.

3   "Humble men are very fortunate!" He told them, "for the Kingdom of Heaven is given to them.

4   Those who mourn are fortunate! for they shall be comforted.

5   The meek and lowly are fortunate! for the whole wide world belongs to them.

6   Happy are those who long for justice, for they shall surely have it.

7   Happy are the kind and merciful, for they shall be shown mercy.

8   Happy are those whose hearts are pure, for they shall see God.

9   Happy are those who strive for peace—they shall be called the sons of God.

10   Happy are those who are persecuted because they are good, for the Kingdom of Heaven is theirs.

11   When you are reviled and persecuted and lied about because you are My followers—wonderful!

12   Be *happy* about it! Be *very glad!* for a *tremendous reward* awaits you up in heaven. And remember, the ancient prophets were persecuted too.

13   You are the world's seasoning, to make it tolerable. If you lose your flavor, what will happen to the world? And you yourselves will be thrown out and trampled underfoot as worthless.

14   You are the world's light—a city on a hill, glowing in the night for all to see.

15, 16   Don't hide your light! Let it shine for all; let your good deeds glow for all to see, so that they will praise your heavenly Father.

17   Don't misunderstand why I have come—it isn't to cancel the laws of Moses and the warnings of the prophets. No, I came to fulfill them, and to make them all come true.

18   With all the earnestness I have I say: Every law in the Book will continue until its purpose is achieved.[1]

19   And so if anyone breaks the least commandment, and teaches others to, he shall be the least in the Kingdom of Heaven. But those who teach God's laws *and obey them* shall be great in the Kingdom of Heaven.

20   But I warn you—unless your goodness[2] is greater than that of the Pharisees and other Jewish leaders, you can't get into the Kingdom of Heaven at all!

21   Under the laws of Moses the rule was, 'If you kill, you must die.'

22   But I have added to that rule,[3] and tell you that if you

---

[1]Literally, "until all things be accomplished."
[2]Literally, "righteousness."
[3]Literally, "But I say."

are only *angry,* even in your own home,[4] you are in danger of judgment! If you call your friend an idiot, you are in danger of being brought before the court. And if you curse him, you are in danger of the fires of hell.[5]

23 So if you are standing before the altar in the Temple, offering a sacrifice to God, and suddenly remember that a friend has something against you,

24 Leave your sacrifice there beside the altar and go and apologize and be reconciled to him, and then come and offer your sacrifice to God.

25 Come to terms quickly with your enemy before it is too late and he drags you into court and you are thrown into a debtor's cell,

26 For you will stay there until you have paid the last penny.

27 The laws of Moses said, 'You shall not commit adultery.'

28 But I say: Anyone who even looks at a woman with lust in his eye has already committed adultery with her in his heart.

29 So if your eye—even if it is your best[6] eye!—causes you to lust, gouge it out and throw it away. Better for part of you to be destroyed than for all of you to be cast into hell.

30 And if your hand—even your right hand—causes you to sin, cut it off and throw it away. Better that than find yourself in hell.

31 The law of Moses says, 'If anyone wants to be rid of his wife, he can divorce her merely by giving her a letter of dismissal.'

32 But I say that a man who divorces his wife, except for unfaithfulness, causes her to commit adultery. And he who marries her commits adultery.

33 Again, the law of Moses says, 'You shall not break your vows to God, but must fulfill them all.'

34 But I say: Don't make any vows! And even to say, 'By

---

[4]Literally, "with your brother."
[5]Literally, "the hell of fire."
[6]Literally, "your right eye."

heavens!' is a sacred vow to God, for the heavens are God's throne.

35   And if you say 'By the earth!' it is a sacred vow, for the earth is His footstool. And don't swear 'By Jerusalem!' for Jerusalem is the capital of the great King.

36   Don't even swear 'By my head!' for you can't turn one hair white or black.

37   Say just a simple 'Yes, I will' or 'No, I won't.' Your word is enough. To strengthen your promise with a vow shows that something is wrong.

38   The law of Moses says, 'If a man gouges out another's eye, he must pay with his own eye. If a tooth gets knocked out, knock out the tooth of the one who did it.'⁷

39   But I say: Don't resist violence! If you are slapped on one cheek, turn the other too.

40   If you are ordered to court, and your shirt is taken from you, give your coat too.

41   If the military demand that you carry their gear for a mile, carry it two.

42   Give to those who ask, and don't turn away from those who want to borrow.

43   There is a saying, 'Love your *friends* and hate your enemies.'

44   But I say: Love your *enemies!* Pray for those who *persecute* you!

45   In that way you will be acting as true sons of your Father in heaven. For He gives His sunlight to both the evil and the good, and sends rain on the just and on the unjust too.

46   If you love only those who love you, what good is that? Even scoundrels do that much.

47   If you are friendly only to your friends, how are you different from anyone else? Even the heathen do that.

48   But you are to be perfect, even as your Father in heaven is perfect.

---

⁷Literally, "an eye for an eye and a tooth for a tooth."

CHAPTER 6

TAKE care! Don't do your good deeds publicly, to be admired, for then you will lose the reward from your Father in heaven.

2 When you give a gift to a beggar, don't shout about it as the hypocrites do—blowing trumpets in the synagogues and streets to call attention to their acts of charity! I tell you in all earnestness, they have received all the reward they will ever get.

3 But when you do a kindness to someone, do it secretly— don't tell your left hand what your right hand is doing.

4 And your Father who knows all secrets will reward you.

5 And now about prayer. When you pray, don't be like the hypocrites who pretend piety by praying publicly on street corners and in the synagogues where everyone can see them. Truly, that is all the reward they will ever get.

6 But when you pray, go away by yourself, all alone, and shut the door behind you and pray to your Father secretly, and your Father, who knows your secrets, will reward you.

7, 8 Don't recite the same prayer over and over as the heathen do, who think prayers are answered only by repeating them again and again. Remember, your Father knows exactly what you need even before you ask Him!

9 Pray along these lines: 'Our Father in heaven, we honor Your holy name.

10 We ask that Your kingdom will come soon. May Your will be done here on earth, just as it is in heaven.

11 Give us our food again today, as usual,

12 And forgive us our sins, just as we have forgiven those who have sinned against us.

13 Don't bring us into temptation, but deliver us from the Evil One.[1] Amen.'

14, 15 Your heavenly Father will forgive you if you forgive those who sin against you; but if *you* refuse to forgive *them, He* will not forgive *you.*

---

[1]Or, "from evil." Some manuscripts add here, "For yours is the kingdom and the power and the glory forever. Amen."

16 And now about fasting. When you fast, declining your food for a spiritual purpose, don't do it publicly, as the hypocrites do, who try to look wan and disheveled so people will feel sorry for them! Truly, that is the only reward they will ever get.

17 But when you fast, put on festive clothing,

18 So that no one will suspect you are hungry, except your Father who knows every secret. And He will reward you.

19 Don't store your profits here on earth where they can erode away or may be stolen.

20 Store them in heaven where they will never lose their value, and are safe from thieves!

21 If your profits are in heaven your heart will be there too.

22 If your eye is pure, there will be sunshine in your soul.

23 But if your eye is clouded with evil thoughts and desires, you are in deep spiritual darkness. And oh, how deep that darkness can be!

24 You cannot serve two masters: God and money. For you will hate one and love the other, or else the other way around.

25 So my counsel is: Don't worry about *things*—food, drink, money,[2] and clothes. For you already have life and a body—and they are far more important than what to eat and wear.

26 Look at the birds! They don't worry about what to eat—they don't need to sow or reap or store up food—for your heavenly Father feeds them. And you are far more valuable to Him than they are.

27 Will all your worries add a single moment to your life?

28 And why worry about your clothes? Look at the field lilies! They don't worry about theirs.

29 Yet King Solomon in all his glory was not clothed as beautifully as they.

30 And if God cares so wonderfully for flowers that are here today and gone tomorrow, won't He more surely care for you, O men of little faith?

[2]Implied.

31, 32   So don't worry at all about having enough food and clothing. Why be like the heathen? For they take pride in all these things and are deeply concerned about them. But your heavenly Father already knows perfectly well that you need them,

33   And He will gladly give them to you if you give Him first place in your life.

34   So don't be anxious about tomorrow. God will take care of your tomorrow too. Live one day at a time.[3]

CHAPTER 7

DON'T criticize, and then you won't be criticized!   2   For others will treat you as you treat them.

3   And why worry about a speck in the eye of a brother when you have a board in your own?

4   Should you say, 'Friend, let me help you get that speck out of your eye,' when you can't even see because of the board in your own?

5   Hypocrite! First get rid of the board. Then you can see to help your brother.

6   Don't give pearls to swine! They will trample the pearls and turn and attack you.

7   Ask, and you will be given what you ask for. Seek, and you will find. Knock, and the door will be opened.

8   For everyone who asks, receives. Anyone who seeks, finds. If only you will knock, the door will open.

9   If a child asks his father for a loaf of bread, will he be given a stone instead?

10   If he asks for fish, will he be given a poisonous snake? Of course not!

11   And if you hardhearted, sinful men know how to give good gifts to your children, won't your Father in heaven even more certainly give good gifts to those who ask Him for them?

12   Do for others what you want them to do for you. This is the teaching of the laws of Moses in a nutshell.[1]

---

[3]Literally, "sufficient unto the day is the evil thereof."
[1]Literally, "this is the law and the prophets."

13   Heaven can be entered only through the narrow gate! The highway to hell[2] is broad, and its gate is wide enough for all the multitudes who choose its easy way.

14   But the Gateway to Life is small, and the road is narrow, and only a few ever find it.

15   Beware of false teachers who come disguised as harmless sheep, but are wolves and will tear you apart.

16   You can detect them by the way they act, just as you can identify a tree by its fruit. You need never confuse grapevines with thorn bushes! Or figs with thistles!

17   Different kinds of fruit trees can quickly be identified by examining their fruit.

18   A variety that produces delicious fruit never produces an inedible kind! And a tree producing an inedible kind can't produce what is good!

19   So the trees having the inedible fruit are chopped down and thrown on the fire.

20   Yes, the way to identify a tree or a person[3] is by the kind of fruit produced.

21   Not all who talk like godly people are. They may refer to Me as 'Lord,' but still won't get to heaven. For the decisive question is whether they obey My Father in heaven.

22   At the Judgment[4] many will tell Me, 'Lord, Lord, we told others about You and used Your name to cast out demons and to do many other great miracles.'

23   But I will reply, 'You have never been Mine.[5] Go away, for your deeds are evil.'

24   All who listen to My instructions and follow them are wise, like a man who builds his house on solid rock.

25   Though the rain comes in torrents, and the floods rise and the storm winds beat against his house, it won't collapse, for it is built on rock.

26   But those who hear My instructions and ignore them are foolish, like a man who builds his house on sand.

---

[2]Literally, "the way that leads to destruction."
[3]Implied.
[4]Literally, "in that day."
[5]Literally, "I never knew you."

27 For when the rains and floods come, and storm winds beat against his house, it will fall with a mighty crash."

28 The crowds were amazed at Jesus' sermons,

29 For He taught as one who had great authority, and not as their Jewish leaders.[6]

CHAPTER 8

L ARGE crowds followed Jesus as He came down the hill-side.

2 *Look! A leper is approaching. He kneels before Him, worshiping. "Sir," the leper pleads, "if You want to, You can heal me."*

3 *Jesus touches the man. "I want to," He says; "be healed." And instantly the leprosy disappears!*

4 *Then Jesus says to him, "Don't stop to talk[1] to anyone; go right over to the priest to be examined; and take with you the offering required by Moses' law for lepers who are healed, —a public testimony of your cure."*

5, 6 When Jesus arrived in Capernaum, a Roman army captain came and pled with Him to come to his home and heal his servant boy who was in bed paralyzed and racked with pain.

7 "Yes," Jesus said, "I will come and heal him."

8, 9 Then the officer said, "Sir, I am not worthy to have You in my home; [and it isn't necessary for You to come[2]]. If You will only stand here and say, 'Be healed,' my servant will get well! I know, because I am under the authority of my superior officers and I have authority over my soldiers, and I say to one, 'Go,' and he goes, and to another, 'Come,' and he comes, and to my slave boy, 'Do this or that,' and he does it. And I know You have authority to tell his sickness to go—and it will go!"

10 Jesus stood there amazed! Turning to the crowd He said, "I haven't seen faith like this in all the land of Israel!

11 And I tell you this, that many Gentiles [like this Roman

---

[6]Literally, "not as the scribes." These leaders only quoted others, and did not presume to present any fresh revelation.
[1]Literally, "See you tell no man."
[2]Implied.

officer[2]], shall come from all over the world and sit down in the Kingdom of Heaven with Abraham, Isaac, and Jacob.

12   And many an Israelite—those for whom the Kingdom was prepared—shall be cast into outer darkness, into the place of weeping and torment."

13   Then Jesus said to the Roman officer, "Go on home. What you have believed has happened!" And the boy was healed that same hour!

14   When Jesus arrived at Peter's house, Peter's mother-in-law was in bed with a high fever.

15   But when Jesus touched her hand, the fever left her; and she got up and prepared a meal[3] for them!

16   That evening several demon-possessed people were brought to Jesus; and when He spoke a single word, all the demons fled; and all the sick were healed.

17   This fulfilled the prophecy of Isaiah, "He took our sicknesses and bore our diseases."[4]

18   When Jesus noticed how large the crowd was growing, He instructed His disciples to get ready to cross to the other side of the lake.

19   Just then[5] one of the Jewish religious teachers[6] said to Him, "Teacher, I will follow You no matter where You go!"

20   But Jesus said, "Foxes have dens and birds have nests, but I, the Son of Mankind, have no home of My own—no place to lay My head."

21   Another of His followers said, "Sir, let me first go and bury my father."[7]

22   But Jesus told him, "Follow Me *now!*[8] Let those who are spiritually[8] dead care for their own dead."

23   Then He got into a boat and started across the lake with His disciples.

24   Suddenly a terrible storm came up, with waves higher than the boat. But Jesus was asleep.

---

[2]Implied.
[3]Literally, "ministered unto them."
[4]Isaiah 53:4.
[5]Implied.
[6]Literally, "a scribe."
[7]This probably does not mean his father was awaiting burial. A possible paraphrase would be, "Let me wait until my father dies."
[8]Implied.

25 The disciples went to Him and wakened Him, shouting, "Lord, save us! We're sinking!"

26 But Jesus answered, "O you men of little faith! Why are you so frightened?" Then He stood up and rebuked the wind and waves, and the storm subsided and all was calm!

27 The disciples just sat there, awed! "Who is this," they asked themselves, "that even the winds and the sea obey Him?"

28 When they arrived on the other side of the lake, in the country of the Gadarenes, two men with demons in them met Him. They lived in a cemetery and were so dangerous that no one could go through that area.

29 They began screaming at Him, "What do You want with us, O Son of God? You have no right to torment us yet."[9]

30 A herd of pigs was feeding in the distance,

31 So the demons begged, "If You cast us out, send us into that herd of pigs."

32 "All right," Jesus told them. "Begone." And they came out of the men and entered the pigs, and the whole herd rushed over a cliff and drowned in the water below.

33 The herdsmen fled to the nearest city with the story of what had happened,

34 And the entire population came rushing out to see Jesus, and begged Him to go away and leave them alone.

CHAPTER 9

SO Jesus climbed into a boat and went across the lake to Capernaum, His home[1] town.

2 Soon some men brought Him a paralyzed boy on a mat. When Jesus saw their faith, He said to the sick boy, "Cheer up, son! For I have forgiven your sins!"

3 "Blasphemy! This man is saying he is God!" exclaimed some of the religious leaders to themselves.

4 Jesus knew what they were thinking and asked them, "Why are you thinking such evil thoughts?

---

[9]Literally, "Have you come here to torment us before the time?"
[1]Literally, "His own city."

5 Is it any harder to forgive his sins than to heal him?

6 Consequently, to prove that I[2] have authority here on earth to forgive sins"—turning to the paralyzed boy He said, "Get up, roll up your mat and walk home!"

7 And the boy jumped up and left!

8 A chill of fear swept through the crowd as they saw this happen right before their eyes. How they praised God for giving such authority to a man!

9 As Jesus was going on down the road, He saw a tax collector, Matthew,[3] sitting at a tax collection booth. "Come and be My disciple," Jesus said to him, and Matthew jumped up and went along with Him.

10 Later, as Jesus and His disciples were eating dinner [at Matthew's house[4]], there were many notorious swindlers there as guests!

11 The Pharisees were indignant. "Why does your teacher associate with men like that?"

12 "Because people who are well don't need a doctor! It's the sick people who do!" was Jesus' reply.

13 Then He added, "Go away and learn the meaning of this verse of Scripture,

'It isn't your sacrifices and your gifts I care about—it's that you have some pity.'[5]

My job down here on earth is to get sinners back to God— not to worry about the good people."

14 One day the disciples of John the Baptist came to Jesus and asked Him, "Why don't your disciples fast as we do and as the Pharisees do?"

15 "Should the bridegroom's friends mourn and go without food while he is with them?" Jesus asked. "But the time is coming when I[6] will be taken from them. Time enough then for them to refuse to eat.

16 And who would patch an old garment with unshrunk cloth? For the patch would tear away and make the hole worse.

---

[2]Literally, "that the Son of Man."
[3]The Matthew who wrote this book.
[4]Implied.
[5]Hosea 6:6.
[6]Literally, "the Bridegroom."

17 And who would use old wineskins[7] to store new wine? For the old skins would burst with the pressure, and the wine would be spilled and the skins ruined. Only new wineskins are used to store new wine. That way both are preserved."

18 As He was saying this, the rabbi of the local synagogue came and worshiped Him, "My little daughter has just died," he said, "but You can bring her back to life again if You will only come and touch her."

19 As Jesus and the disciples were going to the rabbi's home,

20 A woman who had been sick for twelve years with internal bleeding came up behind Him and touched a tassel of His robe,

21 For she thought, "If I only touch Him, I will be healed."

22 Jesus turned around and spoke to her. "Daughter," He said, "all is well! Your faith has healed you." And the woman was well from that moment.

23 When Jesus arrived at the rabbi's home and saw the noisy crowds and heard the funeral music,

24 He said, "Get them out, for the little girl isn't dead; she is only sleeping!" Then how they all scoffed and sneered at Him!

25 When the crowd was finally outside, Jesus went in where the little girl was lying and took her by the hand, and she jumped up and was all right again!

26 The report of this wonderful miracle swept the entire countryside.

27 As Jesus was leaving her home, two blind men followed along behind, shouting, "O Son of King David, have mercy on us."

28 They went right into the house where He was staying, and Jesus asked them, "Do you believe I can make you see?" "Yes, Lord," they told Him, "we do."

29 Then He touched their eyes and said, "Because of your faith it will happen!"

---

[7]These were leather bags for storing wine.

30   And suddenly they could see! Jesus sternly warned them not to tell anyone about it,

31   But instead they spread His fame all over the town.[8]

32   Leaving that place, Jesus met a man who couldn't speak because a demon was inside him.

33   So Jesus cast out the demon, and instantly the man could talk. How the crowds marveled! "Never in all our lives have we seen anything like this," they exclaimed.

34   But the Pharisees said, "The reason he can cast out demons is that he is demon-possessed himself—possessed by Satan, the demon king!"

35   Jesus traveled around through all the cities and villages of that area, teaching in the Jewish synagogues and announcing the Good News about the Kingdom. And wherever He went He healed people of every sort of illness.

36   And what pity He felt for the crowds that came, because their problems were so great and they didn't know what to do or where to go for help. They were like sheep without a shepherd.

37   "The harvest is so great, and the workers are so few," He told His disciples.

38   "So pray to the one in charge of the harvesting, and ask Him to recruit more workers for His harvest fields."

CHAPTER 10

JESUS called His twelve disciples to Him, and gave them authority to cast out evil spirits and to heal every kind of sickness and disease.

2   Here are the names of His twelve disciples:
Simon (also called Peter),
Andrew (Peter's brother),
James (Zebedee's son),
John (James' brother),

3   Philip,
Bartholomew,

---

[8]Literally, "in all that land."

Thomas,

Matthew (the tax collector),

James (Alphaeus' son),

Thaddaeus,

4   Simon (a member of "The Zealots," a subversive political party),

Judas Iscariot (the one who betrayed Him).

5   Jesus sent them out with these instructions: "Don't go to the Gentiles or the Samaritans,

6   But only to the people of Israel—God's lost sheep.

7   Go and announce to them that the Kingdom of Heaven is near.[1]

8   Heal the sick, raise the dead, cure the lepers, and cast out demons. Give as freely as you have received!

9   Don't take any money with you;

10   Don't even carry a duffle bag with extra clothes and shoes, or even a walking stick; for those you help should feed and care for you.

11   Whenever you enter a city or village, search for a godly man and stay in his home until you leave for the next town.

12   When you ask permission to stay, be friendly,

13   And if it turns out to be a godly home, give it your blessing; if not, keep the blessing.

14   Any city or home that doesn't welcome you—shake off the dust of that place from your feet as you leave.

15   Truly, the wicked cities of Sodom and Gomorrah will be better off at Judgment Day than they.

16   I am sending you out as sheep among wolves. Be as wary as serpents and harmless as doves.

17   But beware! For you will be arrested and tried, and whipped in the synagogues.

18   Yes, and you must stand trial before governors and kings for My sake. This will give you the opportunity to tell them about Me, yes, to witness to the world.

19   When you are arrested, don't worry about what to say at your trial, for you will be given the right words at the right time.

[1]Or, "at hand," or, "has arrived."

20 For it won't be you doing the talking—it will be the Spirit of your heavenly Father speaking through you!

21 Brother shall betray brother to death, and fathers shall betray their own children. And children shall rise against their parents and cause their deaths.

22 Everyone shall hate you because you belong to Me. But all of you who endure to the end shall be saved.

23 When you are persecuted in one city, flee to the next! I[2] will return before you have reached them all!

24 A student is not greater than his teacher. A servant is not above his master.

25 The student shares his teacher's fate. The servant shares his master's! And since I, the master of the household, have been called 'Satan,'[3] how much more will you!

26 But don't be afraid of those who threaten you. For the time is coming when the truth will be revealed: their secret plots will become public information.

27 What I tell you now in the gloom, shout abroad when daybreak comes. What I whisper in your ears, proclaim from the housetops!

28 Don't be afraid of those who can kill only your bodies —but can't touch your souls! Fear only God who can destroy both soul and body in hell.

29 Not one sparrow (What do they cost? Two for a penny?) can fall to the ground without your Father knowing it.

30 And the very hairs of your head are all numbered.

31 So don't worry! You are more valuable to Him than many sparrows.

32 If anyone publicly acknowledges Me as his friend, I will openly acknowledge him as My friend before My Father in heaven.

33 But if anyone publicly denies Me, I will openly deny him before My Father in heaven.

34 Don't imagine that I came to bring peace to the earth! No, rather, a sword.

35 I have come to set a man against his father, and a

---

[2]Literally, "the Son of Man."
[3]See Matthew 9:34, where they called Him this.

daughter against her mother, and a daughter-in-law against her mother-in-law—

36　A man's worst enemies will be right in his own home!

37　If you love your father and mother more than you love Me, you are not worthy of being Mine; or if you love your son or daughter more than Me, you are not worthy of being Mine.

38　If you refuse to take up your cross and follow Me, you are not worthy of being Mine.

39　If you cling to your life, you will lose it; but if you give it up for Me, you will save it.

40　Those who welcome you are welcoming Me. And when they welcome Me they are welcoming God who sent Me.

41　If you welcome a prophet because he is a man of God, you will be given the same reward a prophet gets. And if you welcome good and godly men because of their godliness, you will be given a reward like theirs.

42　And if, as My representatives, you give even a cup of cold water to a little child, you will surely be rewarded."

CHAPTER 11

WHEN Jesus had finished giving these instructions to His twelve disciples, He went off preaching in the cities where they were scheduled to go.[1]

2　John the Baptist, who was now in prison, heard about all the miracles the Messiah was doing, so he sent his disciples to ask Jesus,

3　"Are you really the one we are waiting for, or shall we keep on looking?"

4　Jesus told them, "Go back to John and tell him about the miracles you've seen Me do—

5　The blind people I've healed, and the lame people now walking without help, and the cured lepers, and the deaf who hear, and the dead raised to life; and tell him about My preaching the Good News to the poor.

---

[1] Literally, "to teach and preach in their cities." Luke 10:1 remarks, "The Lord appointed 70 others and sent them two and two before His face, into every city and place where He Himself was about to come."

6   Then give him this message, 'Blessed are those who don't doubt Me.' "

7   When John's disciples had gone, Jesus began talking about him to the crowds. "When you went out into the barren wilderness to see John, what did you expect him to be like? Grass blowing in the wind?

8   Or were you expecting to see a man dressed as a prince in a palace?

9   Or a prophet of God? Yes, and he is more than just a prophet.

10   For John is the man mentioned in the Scriptures—a messenger to precede Me, to announce My coming, and prepare people to receive Me.[2]

11   Truly, of all men ever born, none shines more brightly than John the Baptist. And yet, even the lesser lights in the Kingdom of Heaven will be greater than he is!

12   And from the time John the Baptist began preaching and baptizing until now, ardent multitudes have been crowding toward the Kingdom of Heaven,[3]

13   For all the laws and prophets looked forward [to the Messiah[4]]. Then John appeared,

14   And if you are willing to understand what I mean, he is Elijah, the one the prophets said would come [at the time the Kingdom begins[4]].

15   If ever you were willing to listen, listen now!

16   What shall I say about this nation? These people are like children playing, who say to their little friends,

17   'We played wedding and you weren't happy, so we played funeral but you weren't sad.'

18   For John the Baptist doesn't even drink wine and often goes without food, and you say, 'He's crazy.'[5]

19   And I, the Son of Mankind, feast and drink, and you complain that I am 'a glutton and a drinking man, and hang around with the worst sort of sinners!' But brilliant men like you can justify your every inconsistency!"[6]

---

[2]Implied.
[3]Literally, "the kingdom of heaven suffers violence and men of violence take it by force."
[4]Implied.
[5]Literally, "he has a demon."
[6]Literally, "wisdom is justified by her children."

20   Then He began to pour out His denunciations against the cities where He had done most of His miracles, because they hadn't turned to God.

21   "Woe to you, Chorazin, and woe to you, Bethsaida! For if the miracles I did in your streets had been done in wicked Tyre and Sidon[7] their people would have repented long ago in shame and humility.

22   Truly, Tyre and Sidon will be better off on the Judgment Day than you!

23   And Capernaum, though highly honored,[8] shall go down to hell! For if the marvelous miracles I did in you had been done in Sodom,[9] it would still be here today.

24   Truly, Sodom will be better off at the Judgment Day than you."

25   And Jesus prayed this prayer: "O Father, Lord of heaven and earth, thank You for hiding the truth from those who think themselves so wise, and for revealing it to little children!

26   Yes, Father, for it pleased You to do it this way!"

*   *   *   *   *

27   "All truth[10] has been entrusted to Me by My Father. Only the Father knows the Son, and the Father is known only by the Son and by those to whom the Son reveals Him.

28   Come to Me and I will give you rest—all of you who work so hard beneath a heavy yoke.

29, 30   Wear My yoke—for it fits perfectly—and let Me teach you; for I am gentle and humble, and you shall find rest for your souls; for I give you only light burdens."

CHAPTER 12

ABOUT that time, Jesus was walking one day through some grainfields with His disciples. It was on the Sabbath, the Jewish day of worship, and His disciples were hungry; so they began breaking off heads of wheat and eating the grain.

---

[7]Cities destroyed by God for their wickedness.
[8]Highly honored by Christ's being there.
[9]See footnote 7.
[10]Literally, "all things."

2   But some Pharisees saw them do it and protested, "Your disciples are breaking the law. They are harvesting on the Sabbath!"[1]

3   But Jesus said to them, "Haven't you ever read what King David did when he and his friends were hungry?

4   He went into the Temple and they ate the special bread[2] permitted to the priests alone. That was breaking the law too!

5   And haven't you ever read in the law of Moses how the priests on duty in the Temple may work on the Sabbath?

6   And truly, one is here who is greater than the Temple!

7   But if you had known the meaning of this Scripture verse, 'I want you to be merciful more than I want your offerings,' you would not have condemned those who aren't guilty!

8   For I, the Son of Mankind, am master even of the Sabbath."

9   Then He went over to the synagogue,

10   And noticed there a man with a deformed hand. The Pharisees[3] asked Jesus, "Is it legal to work by healing on the Sabbath day?" (They were, of course, hoping He would say "yes," so they could arrest[4] Him!)

11   This was His answer: "If you had just one sheep, and it fell into a well on the Sabbath, would you work to rescue it that day? Of course you would.[5]

12   And how much more valuable is a person than a sheep! Yes, it is right to do good on the Sabbath!"

13   Then He said to the man, "Stretch out your arm." And as he did, his hand became normal, just like the other one!

14   Then the Pharisees called a meeting to plot Jesus' arrest and death.

15   But He knew what they were planning, and left the synagogue, with many following Him. He healed all the sick among them,

16   But He cautioned them against spreading the news about His miracles.

17   This fulfilled the prophecy of Isaiah concerning Him:

[1]Implied.
[2]Literally, "the shewbread."
[3]Implied.
[4]Literally, "accuse."
[5]Implied.

18   "Look at My Servant.
See My Chosen One.
He is My Beloved, in whom My soul delights.
I will put My Spirit upon Him,
And He will judge the nations.

19   He does not fight nor shout;
He does not raise His voice!

20   He does not crush the weak,
Or quench the smallest hope;
He will end all conflict with His final victory,

21   And His name shall be the hope
Of all the world."[6]

22   Then a demon-possessed man—he was both blind and unable to talk—was brought to Jesus, and Jesus healed him so that he could both speak and see.

23   The crowd was amazed. "Maybe Jesus is the Messiah!"[7] they exclaimed.

24   But when the Pharisees heard about the miracle they said, "He can cast out demons because he is Satan,[8] king of devils."

25   Jesus knew their thoughts and replied, "A divided kingdom ends in ruin. A city or home divided against itself cannot stand.

26   And if Satan is casting out Satan, he is fighting himself, and destroying his own kingdom.

27   And if, as you claim, I am casting out demons by invoking the powers of Satan, then what power do your own people use when they cast them out? Let them answer your accusation!

28   But if I am casting out demons by the Spirit of God, then the Kingdom of God has arrived among you.

29   One cannot rob Satan's kingdom without first binding Satan.[9] Only then can his demons be cast out![10]

30   Anyone who isn't helping Me is harming Me.

---

[6]Isaiah 42:1-4.
[7]Literally, "the Son of David."
[8]Literally, "Beelzebub."
[9]Literally, "the strong."
[10]Literally, "then will he spoil his house."

31, 32   Even blasphemy against Me[11] or any other sin, can be forgiven—all except one: speaking against the Holy Spirit shall never be forgiven, either in this world or in the world to come.

33   A tree is identified by its fruit. A tree from a select variety produces good fruit; poor varieties don't.

34   You brood of snakes! How could evil men like you speak what is good and right? For a man's heart determines his speech.

35   A good man's speech reveals the rich treasures within him. An evil-hearted man is filled with venom, and his speech reveals it.

36   And I tell you this, that you must give account on Judgment Day for every idle word you speak.

37   Your words now reflect your fate then: either you will be justified by them or you will be condemned."

*   *   *   *   *

38   One day some of the Jewish leaders, including some Pharisees, came to Jesus asking to see a miracle[12] to prove that He was really the Messiah.[13]

39, 40   But Jesus replied, "Only an evil, faithless nation would ask for further proof; and none will be given except what happened to Jonah the prophet! For as Jonah was in the great fish for three days and three nights, so I, the Son of Mankind, shall be in the heart of the earth three days and three nights.

41   The men of Nineveh shall arise against this nation at the judgment and condemn you. For when Jonah preached to them, they repented and turned to God from all their evil ways. And now a greater than Jonah is here—and you refuse to believe Him.[13]

42   The Queen of Sheba shall rise against this nation in the judgment, and condemn it; for she came from a distant land to hear the wisdom of Solomon; and now a greater than Solomon is here—and you refuse to believe Him.[13]

43, 44, 45   This evil nation is like a man possessed by a

[11]Literally, "the Son of Man."
[12]Literally, "to see a sign."
[13]Implied.

demon. For if the demon leaves, it goes into the deserts [14] for a while, seeking rest but finding none. Then it says, 'I will return to the man I came from.' So it returns and finds the man's heart clean but empty! Then the demon finds seven other spirits more evil than itself, and all enter the man and live in him. And so he is worse off than before."

46, 47   As Jesus was speaking in a crowded house[15] His mother and brothers were outside, wanting to talk with Him. When someone told Him they were there,

48   He remarked, "Who is My mother? Who are My brothers?"

49   He pointed to His disciples. "Look!" He said, "these are My mother and brothers."

50   Then He added, "Anyone who obeys My Father in heaven is My brother, sister and mother!"

CHAPTER 13

L ATER that same day, Jesus left the house and went down to the shore,

2, 3   Where an immense crowd soon gathered. He got into a boat and taught from it while the people listened on the beach. He used many illustrations such as this one in His sermon: "A farmer was sowing grain in his fields.

4   As he scattered the seed across the ground, some fell beside a path, and the birds came and ate it.

5   And some fell on rocky soil where there was little depth of earth; the plants sprang up quickly enough in the shallow soil,

6   But the hot sun soon scorched them and they withered and died, for they had so little root.

7   Other seeds fell among thorns, and the thorns choked out the tender blades.

8   But some fell on good soil, and produced a crop that was 30, 60 and even 100 times as much as he had planted.

9   If you have ears, listen!"

[14]Literally, "passes through waterless places."
[15]Implied.

10   His disciples came and asked Him, "Why do you always use these hard-to-understand[1] illustrations?"

11   Then He explained to them that only they were permitted to understand about the Kingdom of Heaven, and others were not.

12, 13   "For to him who has will more be given," He told them, "and he will have great plenty; but from him who has not, even the little he has will be taken away. That is why I use these illustrations, so people will hear and see but not understand.[2]

14   This fulfills the prophecy of Isaiah,
    'They hear, but don't understand; they look, but don't see!

15   For their hearts are fat and heavy, and their ears are dull, and they have closed their eyes in sleep,

16   So they won't see and hear and understand and turn to God again, and let Me heal them.'

But blessed are your eyes, for they see; and your ears, for they hear.

17   Many a prophet and godly man has longed to see what you have seen, and hear what you have heard, but couldn't.

18   Now here is the explanation of the story I told about the farmer planting grain:

19   The hard path where some of the seeds fell represents the heart of a person who hears the Good News about the Kingdom and doesn't understand it; then Satan[3] comes and snatches away the seeds from his heart.

20   The shallow, rocky soil represents the heart of a man who hears the message and receives it with real joy,

21   But he doesn't have much depth in his life, and the seeds don't root very deeply, and after a while when trouble comes, or persecution begins because of his beliefs, his enthusiasm fades, and he drops out.

22   The ground covered with thistles represents a man who hears the message, but the cares of this life and his longing for

---

[1]Implied.
[2]Those who were receptive to spiritual truth understood the illustrations. To others they were only stories without meaning.
[3]Literally, "the evil."

money choke out God's Word, and he does less and less for God.

23   The good ground represents the heart of a man who listens to the message and understands it and goes out and brings 30, 60, or even 100 others into the Kingdom."[4]

24   Here is another illustration Jesus used: "The Kingdom of Heaven is like a farmer sowing good seed in his field;

25   But one night as he slept, his enemy came and sowed thistles among the wheat.

26   When the crop began to grow, the thistles grew too.

27   The farmer's men came and told him, 'Sir, the field where you planted that choice seed is full of thistles!'

28   'An enemy has done it,' he explained.

'Shall we pull out the thistles?' they asked.

29   'No,' he replied. 'You'll hurt the wheat if you do.

30   Let both grow together until the harvest, and I will tell the reapers to sort out the thistles and burn them, and put the wheat in the barn.' "

31, 32   Here is another of His illustrations: "The Kingdom of Heaven is like a tiny mustard seed planted in a field. It is the smallest of all seeds, but becomes the largest of plants, and grows into a tree where birds can come and find shelter."

33   He also used this example: "The Kingdom of Heaven can be compared to a woman making bread. She takes a measure of flour and mixes in the yeast until it permeates every part of the dough."

34, 35   Jesus constantly used these illustrations when speaking to the crowds. In fact, because the prophets said that He would use so many, He never spoke to them without at least one illustration. For it had been prophesied, "I will talk in parables; I will explain mysteries hidden since the beginning of time."[5]

36   Then, leaving the crowds outside, He went into the house. His disciples asked Him to explain to them the illustration of the thistles and the wheat.

---

[4]Literally, "produces a crop many times greater than the amount planted—30, 60, or even 100 times as much."
[5]Psalm 78:2.

37 "All right," He said, "I[6] am the farmer who sows the choice seed.

38 The field is the world, and the seed represents the people of the Kingdom; the thistles are the people belonging to Satan.

39 The enemy who sowed the thistles among the wheat is the devil; the harvest is the end of the world,[7] and the reapers are the angels.

40 Just as in this story the thistles are separated and burned, so shall it be at the end of the world:[7]

41 I[6] will send My angels and they will separate out of the Kingdom every temptation and all who are evil,

42 And throw them into the furnace and burn them. There shall be weeping and gnashing of teeth.

43 Then the godly shall shine as the sun in their Father's Kingdom. Let those with ears, listen!

44 The Kingdom of Heaven is like a treasure a man discovered in a field. In his excitement, he sold everything he owned to get enough money to buy the field—and get the treasure, too!

45 Again, the Kingdom of Heaven is like a pearl merchant on the lookout for choice pearls.

46 He discovered a real bargain—a pearl of great value—and sold everything he owned to purchase it!

47, 48 Again, the Kingdom of Heaven can be illustrated by a fisherman—he casts a net into the water and gathers in fish of every kind, valuable and worthless. When the net is full, he drags it up onto the beach and sits down and sorts out the edible ones into crates and throws the others away.

49 That is the way it will be at the end of the world[7]—the angels will come and separate the wicked people from the godly,

50 Casting the wicked into the fire; there shall be weeping and gnashing of teeth.

51 Do you understand?"

"Yes," they said, "we do."

---

[6]Literally, "the Son of Man."
[7]Or, "age."

52   Then He added, "Those experts in Jewish law who are now My disciples have double treasures—from the Old Testament as well as from the New!"[8]

53, 54   When Jesus had finished giving these illustrations, He returned to His home town, Nazareth in Galilee,[9] and taught there in the synagogue and astonished everyone with His wisdom and His miracles.

55   "How is this possible?" the people exclaimed. "He's just a carpenter's son, and we know Mary his mother and his brothers—James, Joseph, Simon, and Judas.

56   And His sisters—they all live here. How can He be so great?"

57   And they became angry with Him! Then Jesus told them, "A prophet is honored everywhere except in his own country, and among his own people!"

58   And so He did only a few great miracles there, because of their unbelief.

CHAPTER 14

WHEN King[1] Herod heard about Jesus,

2   He said to his men, "This must be John the Baptist, come back to life again. That is why He can do these miracles."

3   For Herod had arrested John and chained him in prison at the demand of[2] his wife Herodias, his brother Philip's ex-wife,

4   Because John had told him it was wrong for him to marry her.

5   He would have killed John but was afraid of a riot, for all the people believed John was a prophet.

6   But at a birthday party for Herod, Herodias' daughter performed a dance that greatly pleased him,

---

[8]Literally, "brings back out of his treasure things both new and old." The paraphrase is of course highly anachronistic!
[9]Implied.
[1]Literally, "the Tetrarch"—he was one of four "kings" over the area, his sovereignty being Galilee and Peraea.
[2]Literally, "on account of."

7   So he vowed to give her anything she wanted!

8   Consequently, at her mother's urging, the girl asked for John the Baptist's head on a tray!

9   The king was grieved, but because of his oath, and because he didn't want to back down in front of his guests, he issued the necessary orders.

10   So John was beheaded in the prison,

11   And his head was brought on a tray and given to the girl, who took it to her mother.

12   Then John's disciples came for his body and buried it, and came to tell Jesus what had happened.

13   As soon as Jesus heard the news, He went off by Himself in a boat to a remote area to be alone. But the crowds saw where He was headed, and followed by land from many villages.

14   So when Jesus came out of the wilderness, a vast crowd was waiting for Him and He pitied them and healed their sick.

15   That evening the disciples came to Him and said, "It is already past time for supper, and there is nothing to eat here in the desert; send the crowds away so they can go to the villages and buy some food."

16   But Jesus replied, "That isn't necessary—you feed them!"

17   "What!" they exclaimed. "We have exactly five small loaves of bread and two fish!"

18   "Bring them here," He said.

19   Then He told the people to sit down on the grass; and He took the five loaves and two fish, looked up into the sky and asked God's blessing on the meal, then broke the loaves apart and gave them to the disciples to place before the people.

20   And everyone ate until full! And when the scraps were picked up afterwards, there were twelve basketfuls left over!

21   (About 5,000 men were in the crowd that day, besides all the women and children.)

22   Immediately after this, Jesus told His disciples to get into their boat and cross to the other side of the lake while He stayed to get the people started home.

23, 24   Then afterwards He went up into the hills to pray. Night fell, and out on the lake the disciples were in trouble. For the wind had risen and they were fighting heavy seas.

25   About four o'clock in the morning Jesus came to them, walking on the water!

26   They screamed in terror, for they thought He was a ghost.

27   But Jesus immediately spoke to them, reassuring them. "Don't be afraid!" He said.

28   Then Peter called to Him: "Sir, if it is really You, tell me to come over to You, walking on the water."

29   "All right," the Lord said, "come along!" So Peter went over the side of the boat and walked on the water toward Jesus.

30   But when he looked around at the high waves, he was terrified and began to sink. "Save me, Lord!" he shouted.

31   Instantly Jesus reached out His hand and rescued him. "O man of little faith," Jesus said. "Why did you doubt?"

32   And when they had climbed back into the boat, the wind stopped.

33   The others sat there, awestruck. "You really are the Son of God!" they exclaimed.

34   They landed at Gennesaret.

35   The news of their arrival spread quickly throughout the city, and soon people were rushing around, telling everyone to bring in their sick to be healed.

36   The sick begged Him to let them touch even the tassel of His robe, and all who did were healed.

CHAPTER 15

SOME Pharisees and other Jewish leaders now arrived from Jerusalem to interview Jesus.

2   "Why do Your disciples disobey the ancient Jewish traditions?" they demanded. "For they ignore our ritual of ceremonial handwashing before they eat."

3 He replied, "And why do your traditions violate the direct commandments of God?

4 For instance, God's law is 'Honor your father and mother; anyone who reviles his parents must die.'

5, 6 But you say, 'Even if your parents are in need, you may give their support money to the church[1] instead.' And so, by your man-made rule, you nullify the direct command of God to honor and care for your parents.

7 You hypocrites! Well did Isaiah prophesy of you,

8 'These people say they honor Me, but their hearts are far away.

9 Their worship is worthless, for they teach their man-made laws instead of those from God.' "[2]

10 Then Jesus called to the crowds and said, "Listen to what I say and try to understand:

11 You aren't made unholy by eating non-kosher food! It is what you *say* and *think*[3] that makes you unclean."

12 Then the disciples came and told Him, "You offended the Pharisees by that remark."

13, 14 Jesus replied, "Every plant not planted by My Father shall be rooted up, so ignore them. They are blind guides leading the blind, and both will fall into a ditch."

15 Then Peter asked Jesus to explain what He meant when He said that people are not defiled by non-kosher food.

16 "Don't you understand?" Jesus asked him.

17 "Don't you see that anything you eat passes through the digestive tract and out again?

18 But evil words come from an evil heart, and defile the man who says them.

19 For from the heart come evil thoughts, murder, adultery, fornication, theft, lying and slander.

20 These are what defile; but there is no spiritual defilement from eating without first going through the ritual of ceremonial handwashing!"

21 Jesus then left that part of the country and walked the fifty miles[4] to Tyre and Sidon.

---

[1]Literally, "to God."
[2]Isaiah 29:13.
[3]Implied.
[4]Implied. Literally, "withdrew into the parts of Tyre and Sidon."

22   A woman from Canaan who was living there came to Him, pleading, "Have mercy on me, O Lord, King David's Son! For my daughter has a demon within her, and it torments her constantly."

23   But Jesus gave her no reply—not even a word! Then His disciples urged Him to send her away. "Tell her to get going," they said, "for she is bothering us with all her begging."

24   Then He said to the woman, "I was sent to help the Jews, not the Gentiles."

25   But she came and worshiped Him and pled again, "Sir, help me!"

26   "It doesn't seem right to take bread from the children and throw it to the dogs," He said.

27   "Yes, it is!" she replied, "for even the puppies beneath the table are permitted to eat the crumbs that fall."

28   "Woman," Jesus told her, "your faith is large, and your request is granted." And her daughter was healed right then.

29   Jesus now returned to the Sea of Galilee, and climbed a hill and sat there.

30   And a vast crowd brought Him their lame, blind, maimed, and those who couldn't speak, and many others, and laid them before Jesus, and He healed them all.

31   What a spectacle it was! Those who hadn't been able to say a word before were talking excitedly, and those with missing arms and legs had new ones; the crippled were walking and jumping around, and those who had been blind were gazing about them! The crowds just marveled, and praised the God of Israel.

32   Then Jesus called His disciples to Him and said, "I pity these people—they've been here with Me for three days now, and have nothing left to eat; I don't want to send them away hungry or they will faint along the road."

33   The disciples replied, "And where would we get enough here in the desert for all this mob to eat?"

34   Jesus asked them, "How much food do you have?" And they replied, "Seven loaves of bread and a few small fish!"

35   Then Jesus told all of the people to sit down on the ground,

36   And He took the seven loaves and the fish, and gave thanks to God for them, and divided them into pieces, and gave them to the disciples who presented them to the crowd.

37, 38   And everyone ate until full—4,000 men besides the women and children! And afterwards, when the scraps were picked up, there were seven basketfuls left over!

39   Then Jesus sent the people home and got into the boat and crossed to Magadan.

CHAPTER 16

ONE day the Pharisees and Sadducees[1] came to test Jesus' claim of being the Messiah by asking Him to show them some great demonstrations in the skies.

2, 3   He replied, "You are good at reading the weather signs of the skies—red sky tonight means fair weather tomorrow; red sky in the morning means foul weather all day—but you can't read the obvious signs of the times!

4   This evil, unbelieving nation is asking for some strange sign in the heavens, but no further proof will be given except the kind given to Jonah." Then Jesus walked out on them.

5   Arriving across the lake, the disciples discovered they had forgotten to bring any food.

6   "Watch out!" Jesus warned them; "beware of the yeast of the Pharisees and Sadducees."

7   They thought He was saying this because they had forgotten to bring bread.

8   Jesus knew what they were thinking and told them, "O men of little faith! Why are you so worried about having no food?

9   Won't you ever understand? Don't you remember at all the 5,000 I fed with five loaves, and the basketfuls left over?

[1]Jewish politico-religious leaders of two different parties.

10   Don't you remember the 4,000 I fed, and all that was left?

11   How could you even think I was talking about food? But again I say, 'Beware of the yeast of the Pharisees and Sadducees.' "

12   Then at last they understood that by "yeast" he meant the *wrong teaching* of the Pharisees and Sadducees.

13   When Jesus came to Caesarea Philippi, He asked His disciples, "Who are the people saying I[2] am?"

14   "Well," they replied, "some say John the Baptist; some, Elijah; some, Jeremiah or one of the other prophets."

15   Then He asked them, "Who do *you* think I am?"

16   Simon Peter answered, "The Christ, the Messiah, the Son of the living God."

17   "God has blessed you, Simon, son of Jonah," Jesus said, "for My Father in heaven has personally revealed this to you—this is not from any human source.

18   You are Peter, a stone; and upon this rock I will build My church; and all the powers of hell shall not prevail against it.

19   And I will give you the keys of the Kingdom of Heaven; whatever doors you lock on earth shall be locked in heaven; and whatever doors you open on earth shall be open in heaven!"

20   Then He warned the disciples against telling others that He was the Messiah.

21   From then on Jesus began to speak plainly to His disciples about going to Jerusalem, and what would happen to Him there—that He would suffer at the hands of the Jewish leaders,[3] that He would be killed, and that three days later He would be raised to life again.

22   But Peter took Him aside to remonstrate with Him. "Heaven forbid, sir," he said. "This is not going to happen to You!"

23   Jesus turned on Peter and said, "Get away from Me, you Satan! You are a dangerous trap to Me. You are thinking merely from a human point of view, and not from God's."

---

[2]Literally, "the Son of Man."
[3]Literally, "of the elders, and chief priests, and scribes."

40

24 Then Jesus said to the disciples, "If anyone wants to be a follower of Mine, let him deny himself and take up his cross and follow Me.

25 For anyone who keeps his life for himself shall lose it; and anyone who loses his life for Me shall find it again.

26 What profit is there if you gain the whole world—and lose eternal life? What can be compared with the value of eternal life?

27 For I, the Son of Mankind, shall come with My angels in the glory of My Father and judge each person according to his deeds.

28 And some of you standing right here now will certainly live to see Me coming in My Kingdom."

CHAPTER 17

SIX days later Jesus took Peter, James, and his brother John to the top of a high and lonely hill,

2 And as they watched, His appearance changed so that His face shone like the sun and His clothing became dazzling white.

3 Suddenly Moses and Elijah appeared and were talking with Him.

4 Peter blurted out, "Sir, it's wonderful that we can be here! If you want me to, I'll make three shelters,[1] one for You and one for Moses and one for Elijah."

5 But even as he said it, a bright cloud came over them, and a voice from the cloud said, "*This* is My beloved Son, and I am wonderfully pleased with Him. Obey[2] *Him.*"

6 At this the disciples fell face downward to the ground, terribly frightened.

7 Jesus came over and touched them. "Get up," He said, "don't be afraid."

8 And when they looked, only Jesus was with them.

9 As they were going down the mountain, Jesus com-

[1]Literally, "three tabernacles" or "tents." What was in Peter's mind is not explained.
[2]Literally, "hear Him."

manded them not to tell anyone what they had seen until after He had risen from the dead.

10   His disciples asked, "Why do the Jewish leaders insist Elijah must return before the Messiah comes?"[3]

11   Jesus replied, "They are right. Elijah must come and set everything in order.

12   And, in fact, he has already come, but he wasn't recognized, and was badly mistreated by many. And I, the Son of Mankind, shall also suffer at their hands."

13   Then the disciples realized He was speaking of John the Baptist.

14   When they arrived at the bottom of the hill, a huge crowd was waiting for them. A man came and knelt before Jesus and said,

15   "Sir, have mercy on my son, for he is mentally deranged, and in great trouble, for he often falls into the fire or into the water;

16   So I brought him to Your disciples, but they couldn't cure him."

17   Jesus replied, "Oh, you stubborn, faithless people! How long shall I bear with you? Bring him here to Me."

18   Then Jesus rebuked the demon in the boy and it left him, and from that moment the boy was well.

19   Afterwards the disciples asked Jesus privately, "Why couldn't we cast that demon out?"

20   "Because of your little faith," Jesus told them. "For if you had faith even as small as a tiny mustard seed you could say to this mountain, 'Move!' and it would go far away. Nothing would be impossible.

21   But this kind of demon won't leave unless you have prayed and gone without food."[4]

22, 23   One day while they were still in Galilee, Jesus told them, "I am going to be betrayed into the power of those who will kill Me, and on the third day afterwards I will be brought back to life again." And the disciples' hearts were filled with sorrow and dread.

---

[3]Implied.
[4]This verse is omitted in many of the ancient manuscripts.

24   On their arrival in Capernaum, the Temple tax collectors came to Peter and asked him, "Doesn't your master pay taxes?"

25   "Of course He does," Peter replied. Then he went into the house to talk to Jesus about it, but before he had a chance to speak, Jesus asked him, "What do you think, Peter? Do kings levy assessments against their own people, or against conquered foreigners?"

26, 27   "Against the foreigners," Peter replied.

"Well, then," Jesus said, "the citizens are free! However, we don't want to offend them, so go down to the shore and throw in a line, and open the mouth of the first fish you catch. You will find a coin to cover the taxes for both of us; take it and pay them."

CHAPTER 18

ABOUT that time the disciples came to Jesus to ask which of them would be greatest in the Kingdom of Heaven!

2   Jesus called a small child over to Him and set the little fellow down among them,

3   And said, "Unless you turn to God from your sins and become as little children, you will never get into the Kingdom of Heaven.

4   Therefore anyone who humbles himself as this little child, is the greatest in the Kingdom of Heaven.

5   And any of you who welcomes a little child like this because you are Mine, is welcoming Me and caring for Me.

6   But if any of you causes one of these little ones who trusts in Me to lose his faith,[1] it would be better for you to have a rock tied to your neck and be thrown into the sea.

7   Woe upon the world for all its evils.[2] Temptation to do wrong is inevitable, but woe to the man who does the tempting.

8   So if your hand or foot causes you to sin, cut it off and throw it away. Better to enter heaven crippled than to be in hell with both of your hands and feet.

[1]Literally, "cause to stumble."
[2]Literally, "because of occasions of stumbling."

9   And if your eye causes you to sin, gouge it out and throw it away. Better to enter heaven with one eye than to be in hell with two.

10   Beware that you don't look down upon a single one of these little children. For I tell you that in heaven their angels have constant access[3] to My Father.

11   And I, the Son of Mankind, came to save the lost.[4]

12   If a man has a hundred sheep, and one wanders away and is lost, what will he do? Won't he leave the ninety-nine others and go out into the hills to search for the lost one?

13   And if he finds it, he will rejoice over it more than over the ninety-nine others safe at home!

14   Just so, it is not My Father's will that even one of these little ones should perish.

15   If a brother sins against you, go to him privately and confront him with his fault. If he listens and confesses it, you have won back a brother.

16   But if not, then take one or two others with you and go back to him again, proving everything you say by these witnesses.

17   If he still refuses to listen, then take your case to the church, and if the church's verdict favors you, but he won't accept it, then the church should excommunicate him.[5]

18   And I tell you this—whatever you bind on earth is bound in heaven, and whatever you free on earth will be freed in heaven.

19   I also tell you this—if two of you agree down here on earth concerning anything you ask for, My Father in heaven will do it for you.

20   For where two or three gather together because they are Mine, I will be right there among them.

21   Then Peter came to Him and asked, "Sir, how often should I forgive a brother who sins against me? Seven times?"

22   "No!" Jesus replied, "seventy times seven!

23   The Kingdom of Heaven can be compared to a king who decided to bring his accounts up to date.

---

[3]"Do always behold . . ."
[4]This verse is omitted in many manuscripts, some ancient.
[5]Literally, "let him be to you as the Gentile and the publican."

24   In the process, one of his debtors was brought in who owed him $10,000,000![6]

25   He couldn't pay, so the king ordered him sold for the debt, also his wife and children and everything he had.

26   But the man fell down before the king, his face in the dust, and said, 'Oh, sir, be patient with me and I will pay it all.'

27   Then the king was filled with pity for him and released him and forgave his debt.

28   But when the man left the king, he went to a man who owed him $2,000[7] and grabbed him by the throat and demanded instant payment.

29   The man fell down before him and begged him to give him a little time. 'Be patient and I will pay it,' he pled.

30   But his creditor wouldn't wait. He had the man arrested and jailed until the debt would be paid in full.

31   Then the man's friends went to the king and told him what had happened.

32   And the king called before him the man he had forgiven and said, 'You evil-hearted wretch! Here I forgave you all that tremendous debt, just because you asked me to—

33   Shouldn't you have mercy on others, just as I had mercy on you?'

34   Then the angry king sent the man to the torture chamber until he had paid every last penny due.

35   So shall My heavenly Father do to you if you refuse to truly forgive your brothers."

CHAPTER 19

A FTER Jesus had finished this address, He left Galilee and circled back to Judea from across the Jordan River.

2   Vast crowds followed Him, and He healed their sick.

3   Some Pharisees came to interview Him, and tried to trap

---

[6]Literally, "10,000 talents." Approximately £3,000,000.
[7]Approximately £700.

Him into saying something that would ruin Him. "Do you permit divorce?" they asked.

4   "Don't you read the Scriptures?" He replied, "In them it is written that at the beginning God created man and woman,

5, 6   And that a man should leave his father and mother, and be forever united to his wife. The two shall become one— no longer two, but one! And no man may divorce what God has joined together."

7   "Then, why," they asked, "did Moses say a man may divorce his wife by merely writing her a letter of dismissal?"

8   Jesus replied, "Moses did that in recognition of your hard and evil hearts, but it was not what God had originally intended.

9   And I tell you this, that anyone who divorces his wife, except for fornication, and marries another, commits adultery."[1]

10   Jesus' disciples then said to Him, "If that is how it is, it is better not to marry!"

11   "Not everyone can accept this statement," Jesus said. "Only those whom God helps.

12   Some are born without the ability to marry,[2] and some are disabled by men, and some refuse to marry for the sake of the Kingdom of Heaven. Let anyone who can, accept My statement."

*   *   *   *   *

13   Little children were brought for Jesus to lay His hands on them and pray. But the disciples scolded those who brought them. "Don't bother Him," they said.

14   But Jesus said, "Let the little children come to Me, and don't prevent them. For of such is the Kingdom of Heaven."

15   And He put His hands on their heads and blessed them before He left.

*   *   *   *   *

16   Someone came to Jesus with this question: "Good sir, what good thing shall I do to get eternal life?"

17   "Good?" He asked. "There is only one who is truly

---

[1]"And the man who marries a divorced woman commits adultery." This sentence is added in some ancient manuscripts.
[2]Literally, "born eunuchs," or, "born emasculated."

46

good—and that is God.[3] But to answer your question, you can get to heaven if you keep the commandments."

18   "Which ones?" the man asked.

And Jesus replied, "Don't kill, don't commit adultery, don't steal, don't lie,

19   Honor your father and mother, and love your neighbor as yourself!"

20   "I've always obeyed every one of them," the youth replied. "What else must I do?"

21   Jesus told him, "If you want to be perfect, go and sell everything you have and give the money to the poor, and you will have treasure in heaven; and come, follow Me."

22   But when the young man heard this, he went away sadly, for he was very rich.

23   Then Jesus said to His disciples, "It is almost impossible for a rich man to get into the Kingdom of Heaven.

24   I say it again—it is easier for a camel to go through the eye of a needle than for a rich man to enter the Kingdom of God!"

25   This remark confounded the disciples. "Then who in the world can be saved?" they asked.

26   Jesus looked at them intently and said, "Humanly speaking, no one. But with God, everything is possible."

27   Then Peter said to Him, "We left everything to follow You. What will we get out of it?"

28   And Jesus replied, "When I, the Son of Mankind, shall sit upon My glorious throne in the Kingdom,[4] you My disciples shall certainly sit on twelve thrones judging the twelve tribes of Israel.

29   And anyone who gives up his home, brothers, sisters, father, mother, wife,[5] children, or property, to follow Me, shall receive a hundred times as much in return, and shall have eternal life.

30   But many who are first now will be last then; and some who are last now will be first then."

---

[3]Implied from Luke 18:19.
[4]Literally, "in the regeneration."
[5]Omitted in many manuscripts, but included in Luke 18:29.

CHAPTER 20

HERE is another illustration of the Kingdom of Heaven. "The owner of an estate went out early one morning to hire workers for his harvest field.[1]

2   He agreed to pay them $20 a day[2] and sent them off to work.

3   A couple of hours later he was passing a hiring hall and saw some men standing around waiting for jobs,

4   So he sent them also into his fields, telling them he would pay them whatever was right at the end of the day.

5   At noon and again around three o'clock in the afternoon he did the same thing.

6   At five o'clock that evening he was in town again and saw some more men standing around and asked them, 'Why have you been idle all day?'

7   'Because no one has hired us,' they replied. 'Then go on out and join the others in my fields,' he told them.

8   That evening he told the paymaster to call the men in and pay them, beginning with the last men first.

9   When the men hired at five o'clock were paid, each received $20.

10   So when the men hired earlier came to get theirs, they assumed they would receive much more. But they, too, were paid $20.

11, 12   They protested, 'Those fellows worked only one hour, and yet you've paid them just as much as those of us who worked all day in the scorching heat.'

13   'Friend,' he answered one of them, 'I did you no wrong! Didn't you agree to work all day for $20?

14   Take it and go. It is my desire to pay all the same;

15   Is it against the law to give away my money if I want to? Should you be angry because I am kind?'

16   And so it is that the last shall be first, and the first, last."

---

[1] Literally, "vineyard."
[2] Literally, "a denarius," the payment for a day's labor; equivalent to $20 in modern times, or £7.

*   *   *   *   *

17 As Jesus was on the way to Jerusalem, He took the twelve disciples aside,

18 And talked to them about what would happen to Him when they arrived. "I[3] will be betrayed to the chief priests and other Jewish leaders, and they will condemn Me to die.

19 And they will hand Me over to the Roman government, and I will be mocked and crucified, and the third day I will rise to life again."

20 Then the mother of James and John, the sons of Zebedee, brought them to Jesus, bowed, and asked a favor.

21 "What is your request?" He asked.

She replied, "In Your Kingdom, will You let my two sons sit on two thrones[4] next to Yours?"

22 But Jesus told her, "You don't know what you are asking!" Then He turned to James and John and asked them, "Are you able to drink from the terrible cup I am about to drink from?"

"Yes," they replied, "we are able!"

23 "You shall indeed drink from it," He told them. "But I have no right to say who will sit on the thrones[4] next to Mine. Those places are reserved for the persons My Father selects."

24 The other ten disciples were indignant when they heard what James and John had asked for.

25 But Jesus called them together and said, "Among the heathen, kings are tyrants and each minor official lords it over those beneath him.

26 But among you it is quite different. Anyone wanting to be a leader among you must be your servant.

27 And if you want to be right at the top, you must serve like a slave.

28 Your attitude[4] must be like My own, for I, the Son of Mankind, did not come to be served, but to serve, and to give My life as a ransom for many."

29 As Jesus and the disciples left the city of Jericho, a vast crowd surged along behind.

[3]Literally, "the Son of Man."
[4]Implied.

30   Two blind men were sitting beside the road and when they heard that Jesus was coming that way, they began shouting, "Sir, King David's Son, have mercy on us!"

31   The crowd told them to be quiet, but they only yelled the louder.

32, 33   When Jesus came to the place where they were He stopped in the road and called, "What do you want Me to do for you?"

"Sir," they said, "we want to see!"

34   Jesus was moved with pity for them and touched their eyes. And instantly they could see, and followed Him.

CHAPTER 21

AS Jesus and the disciples approached Jerusalem, and were near the town of Bethphage on the Mount of Olives, Jesus sent two of them into the village ahead.

2   "Just as you enter," He said, "you will see a donkey tied there, with its colt beside it. Untie them and bring them here.

3   If anyone asks you what you are doing, just say, 'The Master needs them,' and there will be no trouble."

4   This was done to fulfill the ancient prophecy,

5   "Tell Jerusalem her King is coming to her, riding humbly on a donkey's colt!"

6   The two disciples did as Jesus said,

7   And brought the animals to Him and threw their garments over the colt[1] for Him to ride on.

8   And some in the crowd threw down their coats along the road ahead of Him, and others cut branches from the trees and spread them out before Him.

9   Then the crowds surged on ahead and pressed along behind, shouting, "God bless King David's Son!" . . . "Praise Him!" . . . "God's Man is here!"[2] . . . "Bless Him, Lord!"

---

[1]Implied.
[2]Literally, "Blessed is He who comes in the name of the Lord."

50

10   The entire city of Jerusalem was stirred as He entered. "Who is this?" they asked.

11   And the crowds replied, "It's Jesus, the prophet from Nazareth up in Galilee."

*   *   *   *   *

12   Jesus went into the Temple, drove out the merchants, and knocked over the money-changers' tables and the stalls of those selling doves.

13   "The Scriptures say My Temple is a place of prayer," He declared, "but you have turned it into a den of thieves."

14   And now the blind and crippled came to Him and He healed them there in the Temple.

15   But when the chief priests and other Jewish leaders saw these wonderful miracles, and heard even the little children in the Temple shouting, "God bless the Son of David," they were disturbed and indignant and asked Him, "Do you hear what these children are saying?"

16   "Yes," Jesus replied. "Didn't you ever read the Scriptures? For they say, 'Even little babies shall praise Him!' "

17   Then He returned to Bethany, where He stayed overnight.

18   In the morning, as He was returning to Jerusalem, He was hungry,

19   And noticed a fig tree beside the road. He went over to see if there were any figs, but there were only leaves. Then He said to it, "Never bear fruit again!" And soon[3] the fig tree withered up.

20   The disciples were utterly amazed and asked, "How did the fig tree wither so quickly?"

21   Then Jesus told them, "Truly, if you have faith, and don't doubt, you can do things like this and much more. You can even say to this Mount of Olives, 'Move over into the ocean,' and it will.

22   You can get anything—*anything* you ask for in prayer —if you believe."

23   When He had returned to the Temple and was teaching, the chief priests and other Jewish leaders came up to Him and

---

[3]Or, "immediately."

demanded to know by whose authority He had thrown out the merchants the day before.[4]

24 "I'll tell you if you answer one question first," Jesus replied.

25 "Was John the Baptist sent from God, or not?"

They talked it over among themselves. "If we say, 'From God.' " they said, "then He will ask why we didn't believe what John said.

26 And if we deny that God sent him, we'll be mobbed, for the crowd all think he was a prophet."

27 So they finally replied, "We don't know!"

And Jesus said, "Then I won't answer your question either.

28 But what do you think about this? A man with two sons told the older boy, 'Son, go out and work on the farm today.'

29 'I won't,' he answered, but later he changed his mind and went.

30 Then the father told the youngest, 'You go!' and he said 'Yes, sir, I will.' But he didn't.

31 Which of the two was obeying his father?"

They replied, "The first, of course."

Then Jesus explained His meaning: "Surely evil men and prostitutes will get into the Kingdom before you do.

32 For John the Baptist told you to repent and turn to God, and you wouldn't, while very evil men and prostitutes did. And even when you saw this happening, you refused to repent, and so you couldn't believe.

33 Now listen to this story: A certain landowner planted a vineyard with a hedge around it, and built a platform for the watchman, then leased the vineyard to some farmers on a sharecrop basis, and went away to live in another country.

34 At the time of the grape harvest he sent his agents to the farmers to collect his share.

35 But the farmers attacked his men, beat one, killed one and stoned another.

36 Then he sent a larger group of his men to collect for him, but the results were the same.

---

[4]Literally, "By what authority do you do these things?"

37 Finally the owner sent his son, thinking they would, surely respect him.

38 But when these farmers saw the son coming they said among themselves, 'Here comes the heir to this estate; come on, let's kill him and get it for ourselves!'

39 So they dragged him out of the vineyard and killed him.

40 When the owner returns, what do you think he will do to those farmers?"

41 The Jewish leaders replied, "He will put the wicked men to a horrible death, and lease the vineyard to others who will pay him promptly."

42 Then Jesus asked them, "Didn't you ever read in the Scriptures: 'The stone rejected by the builders has been made the honored cornerstone;[5] how remarkable! what an amazing thing the Lord has done'?

43 What I mean is that the Kingdom of God shall be taken away from you, and given to a nation that will give God His share of the crop.[6]

44 All who stumble on this rock of truth[7] shall be broken, but those it falls on will be scattered as dust."

45 When the chief priests and other Jewish leaders realized that Jesus was talking about them—that they were the farmers in His story—

46 They wanted to get rid of Him, but were afraid to try because of the crowds, for they accepted Jesus as a prophet.

CHAPTER 22

JESUS told several other stories to show what the Kingdom of Heaven is like. "For instance," He said, "it can be illustrated by the story of a king who prepared a great wedding dinner for his son.

3 Many guests were invited, and when the banquet was ready he sent messengers to notify everyone that it was time to come. But all refused!

---

[5]Literally, "the head of the corner."
[6]Literally, "bringing forth the fruits."
[7]Literally, "on this stone."

4   So he sent other servants to tell them, 'Everything is ready and the roast is in the oven. Hurry!'[1]

5   But the guests he had invited merely laughed and went on about their business, one to his farm, another to his store;

6   Others beat up his messengers and treated them shamefully, even killing some of them.

7   Then the angry king sent out his army and destroyed the murderers and burned their city.

8   And he said to his servants, 'The wedding feast is ready, and the guests I invited aren't worthy of the honor.

9   Now go out to the street corners and invite everyone you see.'

10   So the servants did, and brought in all they could find, good and bad alike; and the banquet hall was filled with guests.

11   But when the king came in to meet the guests he noticed a man who wasn't wearing the wedding robe [provided for him[2]].

12   'Friend,' he asked, 'how does it happen that you are here without a wedding robe?' And the man had no reply.

13   Then the king said to his aides, 'Bind him hand and foot and throw him out into the outer darkness where there is weeping and gnashing of teeth.'

14   For many are called, but few are chosen."

15   Then the Pharisees met together to try to think of some way to trap Jesus into saying something for which they could arrest Him.

16   They decided to send some of their men along with the Herodians[3] to ask Him this question: "Sir, we know you are very honest and teach the truth regardless of the consequences, without fear or favor.

17   Now tell us, is it right to pay taxes to the Roman government or not?"

18   But Jesus saw what they were after. "You hypocrites!" He exclaimed, "who are you trying to fool with your trick questions?

19   Here, show Me a coin." And they handed Him a penny.

[1]Literally, "come to the wedding feast."
[2]Implied.
[3]The Herodians were a Jewish political party.

20   "Whose picture is stamped on it?" He asked them. "And whose name is this beneath the picture?"

21   "Caesar's," they replied.

"Well, then," He said, "give it to Caesar if it is his, and give God everything that belongs to God."

22   His reply surprised and baffled them and they went away.

23   But that same day some of the Sadducees, who say there is no resurrection after death, came to Him and asked,

24   "Sir, Moses said that if a man died without children, his brother should marry the widow and their children would get all the dead man's property.

25   Well, we had among us a family of seven brothers. The first of these men married and then died, without children, so his widow became the second brother's wife.

26   This brother also died without children, and the wife was passed to the next brother, and so on until she had been the wife of each of them.

27   And then she also died.

28   So whose wife will she be in the resurrection? For she was the wife of all seven of them!"

29   But Jesus said, "Your error is caused by your ignorance of the Scriptures and of God's power!

30   For in the resurrection there is no marriage; everyone is as the angels in heaven.

31   But now, as to whether there is a resurrection of the dead—don't you ever read the Scriptures? Don't you realize that God was speaking directly to you when He said,

32   'I *am* the God of Abraham, Isaac, and Jacob'? So God is not the God of the dead, but of the *living*."[4]

33   The crowds were profoundly impressed by His answers—

34, 35   But not the Pharisees! When they heard that He had routed the Sadducees with His reply, they thought up a fresh question of their own to ask Him. One of them, a lawyer, spoke up:

---

[4] i.e., if Abraham, Isaac, and Jacob, long dead, were not alive in the presence of God, then God would have said, "I *was* the God of Abraham, etc."

36 "Sir, which is the most important command in the laws of Moses?"

37 Jesus replied, " 'Love the Lord your God with all your heart, soul, and mind.'

38, 39 This is the first and greatest commandment.

The second most important is similar: 'Love your neighbor as much as you love yourself.'

40 All the other commandments and all the demands of the prophets stem from these two laws and are fulfilled if you obey them. Keep only these and you will find that you are obeying all the others."

41 Then, surrounded by the Pharisees, He asked them a question:

42 "What about the Messiah? Whose son is He?"

"The son of David," they replied.

43 "Then why does David, speaking under the inspiration of the Holy Spirit, call Him 'Lord'?" Jesus asked. "For David said,

44 'God said to my Lord, Sit at My right hand until I put Your enemies beneath Your feet.'

45 Since David called Him 'Lord,' how can He be merely his son?"

46 They had no answer. And after that no one dared ask Him any more questions.

CHAPTER 23

THEN Jesus said to the crowds, and to His disciples,

2 "You would think these Jewish leaders and these Pharisees were Moses,[1] the way they keep making up so many laws!

3 And of course you should obey their every whim! It may be all right to do what they say, but above anything else, *don't follow their example*. For they don't do what they tell you to do.

[1]Literally, "sit on Moses' seat."

4   They load you with impossible demands that they themselves don't even try to keep.

5   Everything they do is done for show. They act holy[2] by wearing on their arms large prayer boxes with Scripture verses inside,[3] and by lengthening the memorial fringes of their robes.

6   And how they love to sit at the head table at banquets, and in the reserved pews in the synagogue!

7   How they enjoy the deference paid them on the streets, and to be called 'Rabbi' and 'Master'!

8   Don't ever let anyone call you that. For only God is your Rabbi and all of you are on the same level, as brothers.

9   And don't address anyone here on earth as 'Father,' for only God in heaven should be addressed like that.

10   And don't be called 'Master,' for only one is your master, even the Messiah.

11   The more lowly your service to others, the greater you are. To be the greatest, be a servant.

12   But those who think themselves great shall be disappointed and humbled; and those who humble themselves shall be exalted.

13, 14   Woe to you, Pharisees, and you other religious leaders. Hypocrites! For you won't let others enter the Kingdom of Heaven, and won't go in yourselves. And you pretend to be holy, with all your long, public prayers in the streets, while you are evicting widows from their homes. Hypocrites!

15   Yes, woe upon you hypocrites. For you go to all lengths to make one convert, and then turn him into twice the son of hell you are yourselves.

16   Blind guides! Woe upon you! For your rule is that to swear 'By God's Temple' means nothing—you can break that oath, but to swear 'By the gold in the Temple' is binding!

17   Blind fools! Which is greater, the gold, or the Temple that sanctifies the gold?

18   And you say that to take an oath 'By the altar' can be broken, but to swear 'By the gifts on the altar' is binding!

---

[2]Implied.
[3]Literally, "enlarge their phylacteries."

19 Blind! For which is greater, the gift on the altar, or the altar itself that sanctifies the gift?

20 When you swear 'By the altar' you are swearing by it and everything on it,

21 And when you swear 'By the Temple' you are swearing by it, and by God who lives in it.

22 And when you swear 'By heavens' you are swearing by the Throne of God and by God Himself.

23 Yes, woe upon you, Pharisees, and you other religious leaders—hypocrites! For you tithe down to the last mint leaf in your garden, but ignore the important things—justice and mercy and faith. Yes, you should tithe, but you shouldn't leave the more important things undone.

24 Blind guides! You strain out a gnat and swallow a camel.

25 Woe to you, Pharisees, and you religious leaders—hypocrites! You are so careful to polish the outside of the cup, but the inside is foul with extortion and greed.

26 Blind Pharisees! First cleanse the inside of the cup, and then the whole cup will be clean.

27 Woe to you, Pharisees, and you religious leaders! You are like beautiful mausoleums—full of dead men's bones, and of foulness and corruption.

28 You try to look like saintly men, but underneath those pious robes of yours are hearts besmirched with every sort of hypocrisy and sin.

29, 30 Yes, woe to you, Pharisees, and you religious leaders—hypocrites! For you build monuments to the prophets killed by your fathers and lay flowers on the graves of the godly men they destroyed, and say, 'We certainly would never have acted as our fathers did.'

31 In saying that, you are accusing yourselves of being the sons of wicked men.

32 And you are following in their steps, filling up the full measure of their evil.

33 Snakes! Sons of vipers! How shall you escape the judgment of hell?

34 I will send you prophets, and Spirit-filled men, and inspired writers, and you will kill some by crucifixion, and rip open the backs of others with whips in your synagogues, and hound them from city to city,

35 So that you will become guilty of all the blood of murdered godly men from righteous Abel to Zechariah (son of Barachiah), slain by you in the Temple between the altar and the sanctuary.

36 Yes, all the accumulated judgment of the centuries shall break upon the heads of this very generation.

37 O Jerusalem, Jerusalem, the city that kills the prophets, and stones all those God sends to her! How often I have wanted to gather your children together as a hen gathers her chicks beneath her wings, but you wouldn't let Me.

38 And now your house is left to you, desolate.

39 For I tell you this, you will never see Me again until you are ready to welcome the one sent to you from God."[4]

CHAPTER 24

AS Jesus was leaving the Temple grounds, His disciples came along and wanted to take Him on a tour of the various Temple buildings.

2 But He told them, "All these buildings will be knocked down, with not one stone left on top of another!"

3 "When will this happen?" the disciples asked Him later, as He sat on the slopes of the Mount of Olives. "What events will signal Your return, and the end of the world?"[1]

4 Jesus told them, "Don't let anyone fool you.

5 For many will come claiming to be the Messiah, and will lead many astray.

6 When you hear of wars beginning, this does not signal My return; these must come, but the end is not yet.

7 The nations and kingdoms of the earth will rise against

---

[4]Literally, "in the name of the Lord."
[1]Literally, "age."

each other and there will be famines and earthquakes in many places.

8   But all this will be only the beginning of the horrors to come.

9   Then you will be tortured and killed and hated all over the world because you are Mine,

10   And many of you shall fall back into sin and betray and hate each other.

11   And many false prophets will appear and lead many astray.

12   Sin will be rampant everywhere and will cool the love of many.

13   But those enduring to the end shall be saved.

14   And the Good News about the Kingdom will be preached throughout the whole world, so that all nations will hear it, and then, finally, the end will come.

15   So, when you see the horrible thing[2] (told about by Daniel[3] the prophet) standing in a holy place (Note to the reader: You know what is meant!),[4]

16   Then those in Judea must flee into the Judean hills.

17   Those on their porches[5] must not even go inside to pack before they flee.

18   Those in the fields should not return to their homes for their clothes.

19   And woe to pregnant women and to those with babies in those days.

20   And pray that your flight will not be in winter, or on the Sabbath.[6]

21   For there will be persecution such as the world has never before seen in all its history, and will never see again.

22   In fact, unless those days are shortened, all mankind will perish. But they will be shortened for the sake of God's chosen[7] people.

23   Then if anyone tells you, 'The Messiah has arrived at

2Literally, "the abomination of desolation."
3Daniel 9:27, 11:31, 12:11.
4Literally, "Let the reader take note."
5Literally, "roof tops" which, being flat, were used as porches at that time. See Acts 10:9.
6The city gates were closed on the Sabbath.
7Literally, "the elect."

such and such a place, or has appeared here or there, or in the village yonder,' don't believe it.

24   For false Christs shall arise, and false prophets, and will do wonderful miracles, so that if it were possible, even God's chosen[7] ones would be deceived.

25   See, I have warned you.

26   So if someone tells you the Messiah has returned and is out in the desert, don't bother to go and look. Or, that He is hiding at a certain place, don't believe it!

27   For as the lightning flashes across the sky from east to west, so shall My coming be, when I, the Son of all Mankind, return.

28   And wherever the carcass is, there the vultures will gather.

29   Immediately after the persecution of those days the sun will be darkened, and the moon will turn black, and the stars will seem[8] to fall from the heavens, and the powers overshadowing the earth will be convulsed.[9]

30   And then at last the signal of My coming[10] will appear in the heavens and there will be deep mourning all around the earth. And the nations of the world will see Me arrive in the clouds of heaven, with power and great glory.

31   And I shall send forth My angels with the sound of a mighty trumpet blast, and they shall gather My chosen ones from the farthest ends of the earth and heaven.[11]

32   Now learn a lesson from the fig tree. When her branch is tender and the leaves begin to sprout, you know that summer is almost here.

33   Just so, when you see all these things beginning to happen, you can know that My[12] return is near, even at the doors.

34   Then at last this age will come to its close.

35   Heaven and earth will disappear, but My words remain forever.

---

[7]Literally, "the elect."
[8]Literally, "the stars shall fall from heaven."
[9]Literally, "the powers of the heavens shall be shaken." See Eph. 6:12.
[10]Literally, "of the coming of the Son of Man."
[11]"From the four winds, from one end of heaven to the other."
[12]Literally, "He is nigh."

36   But no one knows the date and hour when the end will be—not even the angels. No, nor even God's Son.[13] Only the Father knows.

37, 38   The world will be at ease[14]—banquets and parties and weddings—just as it was in Noah's time before the sudden coming of the flood;

39   People wouldn't believe[15] what was going to happen until the flood actually arrived and took them all away. So shall My coming be.

40   Two men will be working together in the fields, and one will be taken, the other left.

41   Two women will be going about their household tasks; one will be taken, the other left.

42   So be prepared, for you don't know what day your Lord is coming.

43   Just as a man can prevent trouble from thieves by keeping watch for them,

44   So you can avoid trouble by always being ready for My unannounced return.

45   Are you a wise and faithful servant of the Lord? Have I given you the task of managing My household, to feed My children day by day?

46   Blessings on you if I return and find you faithfully doing your work.

47   I will put such faithful ones in charge of everything I own!

48   But if you are evil and say to yourself, 'My Lord won't be coming for a while,'

49   And begin oppressing your fellow servants, partying and getting drunk,

50   Your Lord will arrive unannounced and unexpected,

51   And severely whip you and send you off to the judgment of the hypocrites; there will be weeping and gnashing of teeth.

---

[13]Literally, "neither the Son." Many ancient manuscripts omit this phrase.
[14]Implied.
[15]Literally, "knew not."

CHAPTER 25

THE Kingdom of Heaven can be illustrated by the story of ten bridesmaids[1] who took their lamps and went to meet the bridegroom.

2, 3, 4 But only five of them were wise enough to fill their lamps with oil, while the other five were foolish and forgot.

5, 6 So, when the bridegroom was delayed, they lay down to rest until midnight, when they were roused by the shout, 'The bridegroom is coming! Come out and welcome him!'

7, 8 All the girls jumped up and trimmed their lamps. Then the five who hadn't any oil begged the others to share with them, for their lamps were going out.

9 But the others replied, 'We haven't enough. Go instead to the shops and buy some for yourselves.'

10 But while they were gone, the bridegroom came, and those who were ready went in with him to the marriage feast, and the door was locked.

11 Later, when the other five returned, they stood outside, calling, 'Sir, open the door for us!'

12 But he called back, 'Go away! It is too late!'[2]

13 So stay awake and be prepared, for you do not know the date or moment of My return.[3]

14 Again, the Kingdom of Heaven can be illustrated by the story of a man going into another country, who called together his servants and loaned them money to invest for him while he was gone.

15 He gave $5,000 to one, $2,000 to another, and $1,000 to the last—dividing it in proportion to their abilities—and then left on his trip.

16 The man who received the $5,000 began immediately to buy and sell with it and soon earned another $5,000.

17 The man with $2,000 went right to work, too, and earned another $2,000.

[1]Literally, "virgins."
[2]Literally, "I know you not!"
[3]Implied.

18   But the man who received the $1,000 dug a hole in the ground and hid the money for safekeeping.

19   After a long time their master returned from his trip and called them to him to account for his money.

20   The man to whom he had entrusted the $5,000 brought him $10,000.

21   His master praised him for good work. 'You have been faithful in handling this small amount,' he told him, 'so now I will give you many more responsibilities. Begin the joyous tasks I have assigned to you.'

22   Next came the man who had received the $2,000, with the report, 'Sir, you gave me $2,000 to use, and I have doubled it.'

23   'Good work,' his master said, 'You are a good and faithful servant. You have been faithful over this small amount, so now I will give you much more.'

24, 25   Then the man with the $1,000 came and said, 'Sir, I knew you were a hard man, and I was afraid you would rob me of what I earned,[4] so I hid your money in the earth and here it is!'

26   But his master replied, 'Wicked man! Lazy slave! Since you knew I would demand your profit,

27   You should at least have put my money into the bank so I could have some interest.

28   Take the money from this man and give it to the man with the $10,000.

29   For the man who uses well what he is given shall be given more, and he shall have abundance. But from the man who is unfaithful, even what little responsibility he has shall be taken from him.

30   And throw the useless[5] servant out into outer darkness: there shall be weeping and gnashing of teeth.'

31   But when I, the Son of Mankind, shall come in My glory, and all the angels with Me, then I shall sit upon My throne of glory.

32   And all the nations shall be gathered before Me. And I

---

[4]Literally, "reaping where you didn't sow, and gathering where you didn't scatter, and I was afraid . . ."
[5]Literally, "unprofitable servant."

will separate the people[6] as a shepherd separates the sheep from the goats,

33   And place the sheep at My right hand, and the goats at My left.

34   Then I, the King, shall say to those at My right, 'Come, blessed of My Father, into the Kingdom prepared for you from the founding of the world.

35   For I was hungry and you fed Me; I was thirsty and you gave Me water; I was a stranger and you invited Me into your homes;

36   Naked and you clothed Me; sick and in prison, and you visited Me.'

37   Then these righteous ones will reply, 'Sir, when did we ever see You hungry and feed You? Or thirsty and give You anything to drink?

38   Or a stranger, and help You? Or naked, and clothe You?

39   When did we ever see You sick or in prison, and visit You?'

40   And I, the King, will tell them, 'When you did it to these My brothers you were doing it to Me!'

41   Then I will turn to those on My left and say, 'Away with you, you cursed ones, into the eternal fire prepared for the devil and his demons.

42   For I was hungry and you wouldn't feed Me; thirsty, and you wouldn't give Me anything to drink;

43   A stranger, and you refused Me hospitality; naked, and you wouldn't clothe Me; sick, and in prison, and you didn't visit Me.'

44   Then they will reply, 'Lord, when did we ever see You hungry or thirsty or a stranger or naked or sick or in prison, and not help You?'

45   And I will answer, 'When you refused to help the least of these My brothers, you were refusing help to Me.'

46   And they shall go away into eternal punishment; but the righteous into everlasting life."

---

[6]Or, "separate the nations."

CHAPTER 26

WHEN Jesus had finished this talk with His disciples, He told them,

2 "As you know, the Passover celebration begins in two days, and I[1] shall be betrayed and crucified."

3 At that very moment the chief priests and other Jewish officials were meeting at the residence of Caiaphas the High Priest,

4 To discuss ways of capturing Jesus quietly, and killing Him.

5 "But not during the Passover celebration," they agreed, "for there would be a riot."

6 Jesus now proceeded to Bethany, to the home of Simon the leper.

7 While He was eating, a woman came in with a bottle of very expensive perfume, and poured it over His head.

8, 9 The disciples were indignant. "What a waste of good money," they said. "Why, she could have sold it for a fortune and given it to the poor."

10 Jesus knew what they were thinking, and said, "Why are you criticizing her? For she has done a good thing to Me.

11 You will always have the poor among you, but you won't always have Me.

12 She has poured this perfume on Me to prepare My body for burial.

13 And she will always be remembered for this deed. The story of what she has done will be told throughout the whole world, wherever the Good News is preached."

14 Then Judas Iscariot, one of the twelve apostles, went to the chief priests,

15 And asked, "How much will you pay me to get Jesus into your hands?" And they gave him thirty silver coins.

16 From that time on, Judas watched for an opportunity to betray Jesus to them.

17 On the first day of the Passover ceremonies, when

---

[1]Literally, "the Son of Man."

bread made with yeast was purged from every Jewish home, the disciples came to Jesus and asked, "Where shall we plan to eat the Passover?"

18 He replied, "Go into the city and see Mr. So-and-So, and tell him, 'Our Master says, My time has come, and I will eat the Passover meal with My disciples at your house.' "

19 So the disciples did as He told them, and prepared the supper there.

20, 21 That evening as He sat eating with the Twelve, He said, "One of you will betray Me."

22 Sorrow chilled their hearts, and each one asked, "Am I the one?"

23 He replied, "It is the one I served first.[2]

24 For I must die[3] just as was prophesied, but woe to the man by whom I am betrayed. Far better for that one if he had never been born."

25 Judas, too, had asked him, "Rabbi, am I the one?" And Jesus had told him, "Yes."

26 As they were eating, Jesus took a small loaf of bread and blessed it and broke it apart and gave it to the disciples and said, "Take it and eat it, for this is My body."

27 And He took a cup of wine and gave thanks for it and gave it to them and said, "Each one drink from it,

28 For this is My blood, sealing the New Covenant. It is poured out to forgive the sins of multitudes.

29 Mark My words—I will not drink this wine again until the day I drink it new with you in My Father's Kingdom."

30 And when they had sung a hymn, they went out to the Mount of Olives.

31 Then Jesus said to them, "Tonight you will all desert Me. For it is written in the Scriptures[4] that God will smite the Shepherd, and the sheep of the flock will be scattered.

32 But after I have been brought back to life again I will go to Galilee, and meet you there."

33 Peter declared, "If everyone else deserts You, I won't."

---

[2]Literally, "he that dipped his hand with me in the dish."
[3]Literally, "the Son of Man goes."
[4]Zechariah 13:7.

34   Jesus told him, "The truth is that this very night, before the cock crows at dawn, you will deny Me three times!"

35   "I would die first!" Peter insisted. And all the other disciples said the same thing.

36   Then Jesus brought them to a garden grove, Gethsemane, and told them to sit down and wait while He went on ahead to pray.

37   He took Peter with him and Zebedee's two sons James and John, and began to be filled with anguish and despair.

38   Then He told them, "My soul is crushed with horror and sadness to the point of death . . . stay here . . . stay awake with Me."

39   He went forward a little, and fell face downward on the ground, and prayed, "My Father! If it is possible, let this cup be taken away from Me. But I want Your will, not Mine."

40   Then He returned to the three disciples and found them asleep. "Peter," He called, "couldn't you even stay awake with Me one hour?

41   Keep alert and pray. Otherwise temptation will overpower you. For the spirit indeed is willing, but how weak the body is!"

42   Again He left them and prayed, "My Father! If this cup cannot go away until I drink it all, Your will be done."

43   He returned to them again and found them sleeping, for their eyes were heavy,

44   So He went back to prayer the third time, saying the same things again.

45   Then He came to the disciples and said, "Sleep on now and take your rest . . . but no! The time has come! I[5] am betrayed into the hands of evil men!

46   Up! Let's be going! Look! Here comes the man who is betraying Me!"

47   At that very moment while He was still speaking, Judas, one of the Twelve, arrived with a great crowd armed with swords and clubs, sent by the Jewish leaders.

48   Judas had told them to arrest the man he greeted, for that would be the one they were after.

[5]Literally, "the Son of Man."

49   So now Judas came straight to Jesus and said, "Hello, Master!" and embraced[6] Him in friendly fashion.

50   Jesus said, "My friend, go ahead and do what you have come for." Then the others grabbed Him.

51   One of the men with Jesus pulled a sword and slashed off the ear of the High Priest's servant.

52   "Put away your sword," Jesus told him. "Those using swords will get killed.

53   Don't you realize that I could ask My Father for thousands of angels to protect us, and He would send them instantly?

54   But if I did, how would the Scriptures be fulfilled that describe what is happening now?"

55   Then Jesus spoke to the crowd. "Am I some dangerous criminal," He asked, "that you had to arm yourselves with swords and clubs before you could arrest Me? I was with you teaching daily in the Temple and you didn't stop Me then.

56   But this is all happening to fulfill the words of the prophets as recorded in the Scriptures."

At that point, all the disciples deserted Him and fled.

57   Then the mob led Him to the home of Caiaphas the High Priest, where all the Jewish leaders were gathering.

58   Meanwhile, Peter was following far to the rear, and came to the courtyard of the High Priest's house and went in and sat with the soldiers, and waited to see what was going to be done to Jesus.

59   The chief priests and, in fact, the entire Jewish Supreme Court assembled there and looked for witnesses who would lie about Jesus, in order to build a case against Him that would result in a death sentence.

60, 61   But even though they found many who agreed to be false witnesses, these always contradicted each other. Finally two men were found who declared, "This man said, 'I am able to destroy the Temple of God and rebuild it in three days.' "

---

[6]Literally, "kissed," the greeting still used among men in Eastern lands.

62   Then the High Priest stood up and said to Jesus, "Well, what about it? Did you say that, or didn't you?"

63   But Jesus remained silent. Then the High Priest said to Him, "I demand in the name of the living God that you tell us whether you claim to be the Messiah, the Son of God."

64   "Yes," Jesus said, "I am. And in the future you will see Me, the Son of Mankind, sitting at the right hand of God and returning on the clouds of heaven."

65, 66   Then the High Priest tore at his own clothing, shouting, "Blasphemy! What need have we for other witnesses? You have all heard him say it! What is your verdict?"

They shouted, "Death!—Death!—Death!"

67   Then they spat in His face and struck Him and some slapped Him,

68   Saying, "Prophesy to us, you Messiah! Who struck you that time?"

69   Meanwhile, as Peter was sitting in the courtyard a girl came over and said to him, "You were with Jesus, for both of you are from Galilee."[7]

70   But Peter denied it loudly. "I don't even know what you are talking about," he angrily declared.

71   Later, out by the gate, another girl noticed him and said to those standing around, "This man was with Jesus—from Nazareth."

72   Again Peter denied it, this time with an oath. "I don't even know the man," he said.

73   But after a while the men who had been standing there came over to him and said, "We know you are one of His disciples, for we can tell by your Galilean[8] accent."

74   Peter began to curse and swear. "I don't even know the man," he said. And immediately the cock crowed.

75   Then Peter remembered what Jesus had said, "Before the cock crows, you will deny Me three times." And he went away, crying bitterly.

---

[7] Literally, "with Jesus the Galilean."
[8] Implied.

CHAPTER 27

WHEN it was morning, the chief priests and Jewish leaders met again to discuss how to induce the Roman government to sentence Jesus to death.[1]

2   Then they sent Him in chains to Pilate, the Roman governor.

3   About that time Judas, who betrayed Him, when he saw that Jesus had been condemned to die, changed his mind and deeply regretted what he had done,[2] and brought back the money to the chief priests and other Jewish leaders.

4   "I have sinned," he declared, "for I have betrayed an innocent man."

"That's your problem," they retorted.

5   Then he threw the money onto the floor of the Temple and went out and hanged himself.

6   The chief priests picked the money up. "We can't put it in the collection," they said, "since it's against our laws to accept money paid for murder."

7   They talked it over and finally decided to buy a certain field where the clay was used by potters, and to make it into a cemetery for foreigners who died in Jerusalem.

8   That is why the cemetery is still called "The Field of Blood."

9   This fulfilled the prophecy of Jeremiah which says, "They took the thirty pieces of silver—the price at which He was valued by the people of Israel—

10   And purchased a field from the potters as the Lord directed me."

11   Now Jesus was standing before Pilate, the Roman governor. "Are you the Jews' Messiah?"[3] the governor asked Him.

"Yes," Jesus replied.

12   But when the chief priests and other Jewish leaders made their many accusations against Him, Jesus remained silent.

---

[1]Literally, "took counsel against Jesus to put Him to death." They did not have the authority themselves.
[2]Literally, "repented himself."
[3]Literally, " 'King' of the Jews."

71

13   "Don't you hear what they are saying?" Pilate demanded.

14   But Jesus said nothing, much to the governor's surprise.

15   Now the governor's custom was to release one Jewish prisoner each year during the Passover celebration—anyone they wanted.

16   This year there was a particularly notorious criminal in jail named Barabbas,

17   And as the crowds gathered before Pilate's house that morning he asked them, "Which shall I release to you—Barabbas, or Jesus, your Messiah?"[4]

18   For he knew very well that the Jewish leaders had arrested Jesus out of envy because of His popularity with the people.

19   Just then, as he was presiding over the court, Pilate's wife sent him this message: "Leave that good man alone; for I had a terrible nightmare concerning him last night."

20   Meanwhile the chief priests and Jewish officials persuaded the crowds to ask for Barabbas' release, and for Jesus' death.

21   So when the governor asked again,[5] "Which of these two shall I release to you?" the crowd shouted back their reply: "Barabbas!"

22   "Then what shall I do with Jesus, your Messiah?" Pilate asked.

And they shouted, "Crucify him!"

23   "Why?" Pilate demanded. "What has he done wrong?"

But they kept shouting, "Crucify! Crucify!"

24   When Pilate saw that he wasn't getting anywhere, and that a riot was developing, he sent for a bowl of water and washed his hands before the crowd, saying, "I am innocent of the blood of this good man. The responsibility is yours!"

25   And the mob yelled back, "His blood be on us and on our children!"

26   Then Pilate released Barabbas to them. And after he

---

[4]Literally, "Jesus who is called Christ."
[5]Implied.

had whipped Jesus, he gave Him to the Roman soldiers to take away and crucify.

27   But first they took Him into the armory and called out the entire contingent.

28   They stripped Him and put a scarlet robe on Him,

29   And made a crown from long thorns and put it on His head, and placed a stick in His right hand as a scepter and knelt before Him in mockery. "Hail, King of the Jews," they yelled.

30   And they spat on Him and grabbed the stick and beat Him on the head with it.

31   After the mockery, they took off the robe and put His own garment on Him again, and took Him out to crucify Him.

32   As they were on the way to the execution grounds they came across a man from Cyrene, in Africa—Simon was his name—and forced him to carry Jesus' cross.

33   Then they went out to an area known as Golgotha, that is, "Skull Hill,"[6]

34   Where the soldiers gave Him drugged wine to drink; but when He had tasted it, He refused.

*   *   *   *   *

35   After the crucifixion, the soldiers threw dice to divide up His clothes among themselves.

36   Then they sat around and watched Him as He hung there.

37   And they put a sign above His head, "This is Jesus, the King of the Jews."

38   Two robbers were also crucified there that morning, one on either side of Him.

39   And the people passing by hurled abuse, shaking their heads at Him and saying,

40   "So! You can destroy the Temple and build it again in three days, can you? Well, then, come on down from the cross if you are the Son of God!"

41, 42, 43   And the chief priests and Jewish leaders also mocked Him. "He saved others," they scoffed, "but he can't save himself! So you are the King of Israel, are you? Come

---

[6]Literally, "the place of a skull."

down from the cross and we'll believe you! He trusted God—let God show His approval by delivering him! Didn't he say, 'I am God's Son'?"

*   *   *   *   *

44   And the robbers also threw the same in His teeth.

*   *   *   *   *

45   That afternoon, the whole earth[7] was covered with darkness for three hours, from noon until three o'clock.

*   *   *   *   *

46   About three o'clock, Jesus shouted, "Eli, Eli, lama sabachthani," which means, "My God, My God, why have You forsaken Me?"

47   Some of the bystanders misunderstood and thought He was calling for Elijah.

48   One of them ran and filled a sponge with sour wine and put it on a stick and held it up to Him to drink.

49   But the rest said, "Leave Him alone. Let's see whether Elijah will come and save Him."

*   *   *   *   *

50   Then Jesus shouted out again, dismissed His spirit, and died.

51   And look! The curtain secluding the Holiest Place[8] in the Temple was split apart from top to bottom; and the earth shook, and rocks broke,

52   And tombs opened, and many godly men and women who had died came back to life again.

53   After Jesus' resurrection, they left the cemetery and went into Jerusalem, and appeared to many people there.

*   *   *   *   *

54   The soldiers at the crucifixion and their sergeant were terribly frightened by the earthquake and all that happened. They exclaimed, "Surely this was God's Son."[9]

*   *   *   *   *

55   And many women who had come down from Galilee with Jesus to care for Him were watching from a distance.

---

[7]Or, "land."
[8]Implied.
[9]Or, "a godly man."

74

56   Among them were Mary Magdalene and Mary the mother of James and Joseph, and the mother of James and John (the sons of Zebedee).

*   *   *   *   *

57   When evening came, a rich man from Arimathea named Joseph, one of Jesus' followers,

58   Went to Pilate and asked for Jesus' body. And Pilate issued an order to release it to him.

59   Joseph took the body and wrapped it in a clean linen cloth,

60   And placed it in his own new rock-hewn tomb, and rolled a great stone across the entrance as he left.

61   Both Mary Magdalene and the other Mary were sitting nearby watching.

*   *   *   *   *

62   The next day—at the close of the first day of the Passover ceremonies[10]—the chief priests and Pharisees went to Pilate,

63   And told him, "Sir, that liar once said, 'After three days I will come back to life again.'

64   So we request an order from you sealing the tomb until the third day, to prevent his disciples from coming and stealing his body and then telling everyone he came back to life! If that happens we'll be worse off than we were at first."

65   "Use your own Temple police," Pilate told them. "They can guard it safely enough."

66   So they sealed[11] the stone and posted guards to protect it from intrusion.

CHAPTER 28

EARLY the next morning,[1] as the new day was dawning, Mary Magdalene and the other Mary went out to the tomb.

[10]Implied; literally, "on the morrow, which is after the Preparation."
[11]This was done by stringing a cord across the rock, the cord being sealed at each end with clay.
[1]Literally, "late on the Sabbath day as it began to dawn . . ."

2 Suddenly there was a great earthquake; for an angel of the Lord came down from heaven and rolled aside the stone and sat on it.

3 His face shone like lightning and his clothing was a brilliant white.[2]

4 The guards shook with fear when they saw him, and fell into a dead faint.

5 Then the angel spoke to the women. "Don't be frightened!" he said, "I know you are looking for Jesus, who was crucified,

6 But He isn't here! For He has come back to life again, just as He said He would. Come in and see where His body was lying . . . .

7 And now, go quickly and tell His disciples that He has risen from the dead, and that He is going to Galilee to meet them there. That is my message to them."

8 The women ran from the tomb, badly frightened, but also filled with joy, and rushed to find the disciples to give them the angel's message.

9 And as they were running, suddenly Jesus was there in front of them! "Good morning!"[3] He said. And they fell to the ground before Him, holding His feet and worshiping Him.

10 Then Jesus said to them, "Don't be frightened! Go tell My brothers to leave at once for Galilee, to meet Me there."

*   *   *   *   *

11 As the women were on the way into the city, some of the Temple police who had been guarding the tomb went to the chief priests and told them what had happened.

12, 13 A meeting of all the Jewish leaders was called, and it was decided to bribe the police to say they had all been asleep when Jesus' disciples came during the night and stole His body.

14 "If the governor hears about it," the Council promised, "we'll stand up for you and everything will be all right."

15 So the police accepted the bribe and said what they

---

[2]Literally, "white as snow."
[3]Literally, "All hail!"

were told to. Their story spread widely among the Jews, and is still believed by them to this very day.

16 Then the eleven disciples left for Galilee, going to the mountain where Jesus had said they would find Him.

17 There they met Him and worshiped Him—but some of them weren't sure it really was Jesus!

18 He told His disciples, "I have been given all authority in heaven and earth.

19 Therefore go and make disciples in[4] all the nations, baptizing them into the name of the Father and of the Son and of the Holy Spirit,

20 And then teach these new disciples to obey all the commands I have given you; and be sure of this—that I am with you always, even to the end of the world."[5]

[4]Literally, "of."
[5]Or, "age."

BE A REBEL—

As never before, the young world is one of activism and involvement.

Some object to the "rebels" of our day and think they should just be quiet and conform. In fact, the word "rebel" has pretty well fallen into disrepute.

Yet, is it necessarily bad to rebel?

One band of rebels in tattered clothes at Valley Forge helped create a magnificent "nation under God."

Others, shoved by the rough hands of Roman soldiers to hungry beasts, had rebelled against edicts denying their freedom to worship—and their bravery in death spread the dynamic of Christianity.

And the God-Man born on the first Christmas, Jesus Christ, rebelled against the hypocrisy and evil of His day to show the way of love and truth and life in God. From His "one solitary life," a world was changed and millions found meaning and hope.

So, when is it right to rebel? And against what? Some rebel against the established order, but offer little to take its place. Others rebel against the misery and injustice of this world and offer valid solutions.

Be a rebel! Be the kind of young person who won't be content with the hypocrisies, the cheating, the immorality of a world that often rejects God. But in your rebellion—in your uprooting of the evils and inequities of contemporary society—replace them with integrity, reality, and God's love flowing through your life.

There is only one way to really do this—through the power of a close relationship with the Lord Jesus Christ. Here is the story of the greatest Activist who ever lived, the One who supplies every need of everyone who is concerned enough to seek Him out.

WITH A CAUSE

URUGUAY SPOKESMAN *Fanny Schnur of Uruguay speaks out in a round-table discussion at Williamsburg, Va., with 100 teens from 50 states and 34 foreign countries. The topic under discussion: "Protest: a Right and a Responsibility!"*

MARK

CHAPTER 1

HERE begins the wonderful story of Jesus the Messiah, the Son of God.

2 In the book written by the prophet Isaiah, God announced that He would send His Son[1] to earth, and that a special messenger would arrive first to prepare the world for His coming.

3 "This messenger will live out in the barren wilderness," Isaiah[2] said, "and will proclaim that everyone must straighten out his life to be ready for the Lord's arrival."[3]

4 This messenger was John the Baptist. He lived in the wilderness and taught that all should be baptized as a public announcement of their decision to turn their backs on sin, so that God could forgive them.[4]

5 People from Jerusalem and from all over Judea traveled out into the Judean wastelands to see and hear John, and when they confessed their sins he baptized them in the Jordan River.

6 His clothes were woven from camel's hair and he wore a leather belt; locusts and wild honey were his food.

7 Here is a sample of his preaching: "Someone is coming soon who is far greater than I am, so much greater that I am not even worthy to be His slave.[5]

8 I baptize you with[6] water but He will baptize you with[6] God's Holy Spirit!"

[1]Implied.
[2]Some ancient manuscripts read, "the prophets said." This quotation, unrecorded in the book of Isaiah, also appears in Malachi 3:1.
[3]Literally, "make ready the way of the Lord; make His paths straight."
[4]Literally, "preaching a baptism of repentance for the forgiveness of sins."
[5]Literally, "Whose shoes I am not worthy to unloose."
[6]Or, "in." The Greek word is not clear on this controversial point.

9   Then one day Jesus came from Nazareth in Galilee, and was baptized by John there in the Jordan River.

10   The moment Jesus came up out of the water, He saw the heavens open and the Holy Spirit in the form of a dove descending on Him,

11   And a voice from heaven said, "You are My beloved Son; You are My Delight."

12, 13   Immediately the Holy Spirit urged Jesus into the desert. There, for 40 days, alone except for desert animals, He was subjected to Satan's temptations to sin. And afterwards the angels came and cared for Him.

14   Later on, after John was arrested by King Herod,[7] Jesus went to Galilee to preach God's Good News.

15   "At last the time has come!" He announced. "God's Kingdom is near! Turn from your sins and act on this glorious news!"

16   One day as Jesus was walking along the shores of the Sea of Galilee, He saw Simon and his brother Andrew fishing with nets, for they were commercial fishermen.

17   Jesus called out to them, "Come, follow Me! And I will make you fishermen for the souls of men!"

18   At once they left their nets and went along with Him.

19   A little farther up the beach, He saw Zebedee's sons, James and John, in a boat mending their nets.

20   He called them, too, and immediately they left their father Zebedee in the boat with the hired men and went with Him.

21   Jesus and His companions now arrived at the town of Capernaum and on Saturday[8] morning went into the Jewish place of worship—the synagogue—where He preached.

22   The congregation was surprised at His sermon because He spoke as an authority, and didn't try to prove His points by quoting others—quite unlike what they were used to hearing![9]

23   A man possessed by a demon was present and began shouting,

---

[7]Implied.
[8]Sabbath.
[9]Literally, "not as the scribes."

24   "Why are You bothering us, Jesus of Nazareth—have You come to destroy us demons? I know who You are—the holy Son of God!"

25   Jesus curtly commanded the demon to say no more and to come out of the man.

26   At that the evil spirit screamed and convulsed the man violently and left him.

27   Amazement gripped the audience and they began discussing what had happened. "What sort of new religion is this?" they asked excitedly. "Why, even evil spirits obey His orders!"

28   The news of what He had done spread quickly through that entire area of Galilee.

29, 30   Then, leaving the synagogue, He and His disciples went over to Simon and Andrew's home, where they found Simon's mother-in-law sick in bed with a high fever. They told Jesus about her right away.

31   He went to her bedside, and as He took her by the hand and helped her to sit up, the fever suddenly left, and she got up and prepared dinner for them!

32, 33   By sunset the courtyard was filled with the sick and demon-possessed, brought to Him for healing; and a huge crowd of people from all over the city of Capernaum gathered outside the door to watch.

34   So Jesus healed great numbers of sick folk that evening and ordered many demons to come out of their victims. (But He refused to allow the demons to speak, because they knew who He was.)

35   The next morning He was up long before daybreak and went out alone into the wilderness to pray.

36, 37   Later, Simon and the others went out to find Him, and told Him, "Everyone is asking for You."

38   But He replied, "We must go on to other towns as well, and give My message to them too, for that is why I came."

39   So He traveled throughout the province of Galilee, preaching in the synagogues and releasing many from the power of demons.

80

40 Once a leper came and knelt in front of Him and begged to be healed. "If You want to, You can make me well again," he pled.

41 And Jesus, moved with pity, touched him and said, "I want to! Be healed!"

42 Immediately the leprosy was gone—the man was healed!

43, 44 Jesus then told him sternly, "Go and be examined immediately by the Jewish priest. Don't stop to speak to anyone along the way. Take along the offering prescribed by Moses for a leper who is healed, so that everyone will have proof that you are well again."

45 But as the man went on his way he began to shout the good news that he was healed; as a result, such throngs soon surrounded Jesus that He couldn't publicly enter a city anywhere, but had to stay out in the barren wastelands. And people from everywhere came to Him there.

CHAPTER 2

SEVERAL days later He returned to Capernaum, and the news of His arrival spread quickly through the city.

2 Soon the house where He was staying was so packed with visitors that there wasn't room for a single person more, not even outside the door. And He preached the Word to them.

3 Four men arrived carrying a paralyzed man on a stretcher.

4 They couldn't get to Jesus through the crowd, so they dug through the clay roof above His head and lowered the sick man on his stretcher, right down in front of Jesus.[1]

5 When Jesus saw how strongly they believed that He would help their friend, Jesus said to the sick man, "Son, your sins are forgiven!"

6 But some of the Jewish religious leaders[2] said to themselves as they sat there,

[1]Implied.
[2]Literally, "teachers of the law."

81

7 "What? This is blasphemy! Does he think he is God? For only God can forgive sins."

8 Jesus could read their minds and said to them at once, "Why does this bother you?

9 Is it any harder to forgive his sins than to heal him?

10, 11 So, to prove that I, the Man from Heaven,[3] have forgiven his sins,"—turning to the paralyzed man He said, "You are healed.[4] Pick up your stretcher and go home!"

12 The man jumped up, took the stretcher, and pushed his way through the stunned onlookers! Then how they praised God. "We've never seen anything like this before!" they all exclaimed.

13 Then Jesus went out to the seashore again, and preached to the crowds that gathered around Him.

14 As He was walking up the beach He saw Levi, the son of Alphaeus, sitting at his tax collection booth. "Come with Me," Jesus told him. "Come be My disciple." And Levi jumped to his feet and went along.

15 That night Levi invited his fellow tax collectors and many other notorious sinners to be his dinner guests so that they could meet Jesus and His disciples. (There were many men of this type among the crowds that followed Him.)

16 But when some of the Jewish religious leaders[5] saw Him eating with these men of ill repute, they said to His disciples, "How can he stand it, to eat with such scum?"

17 When Jesus heard what they were saying, He told them, "Sick people need the doctor, not healthy ones! I haven't come to tell good people to repent, but the bad ones."

*   *   *   *   *

18 John's disciples and the Jewish leaders sometimes fasted, that is, went without food as part of their religion. One day they came to Jesus and asked why His disciples didn't do this too.

19 Jesus replied, "Do friends of the bridegroom refuse to

---

[3]Literally, "Son of Man"—a term full of meaning to Jesus and His contemparies, but very difficult for us today. "Man from Heaven" is one part of its connotation.
[4]Literally, "Stand up, pick up your mat and walk."
[5]Literally, "the scribes and Pharisees."

eat at the wedding feast? Should they be sad while he is with them?

20 But some day he will be taken away from them, and then they will mourn.

21 [Besides, going without food is part of the old way of doing things.[6]] It is like patching an old garment with un-shrunk cloth! What happens? The patch pulls away and leaves the hole worse than before.

22 You know better than to put new wine into old wine-skins. They would burst. The wine would be spilled out and the wineskins ruined. New wine needs fresh wineskins."

23 Another time, on a Sabbath day as Jesus and His disciples were walking through the fields, the disciples were breaking off heads of wheat and eating the grain.[6]

24 Some of the Jewish religious leaders said to Jesus, "They shouldn't be doing that! It's against our laws to harvest grain on the Sabbath."

25, 26 But Jesus replied, "Didn't you ever hear about the time King David and his companions were hungry, and he went into the house of God—Abiathar was high priest then—and they ate the special bread[7] only priests were allowed to eat? That was against the law too.

27 But the Sabbath was made to benefit man, and not man to benefit the Sabbath.

28 And I, the Man from Heaven,[8] have authority even to decide what men can do on Sabbath days!"

CHAPTER 3

WHILE in Capernaum Jesus went over to the synagogue again, and noticed a man there with a deformed hand.

2 Since it was the Sabbath, Jesus' enemies watched Him closely. Would He heal the man's hand? If He did, they planned to arrest Him!

---

[6]Implied.
[7]Literally, "shewbread."
[8]Literally, "the Son of Man," a term of highest honor and acclaim.

3   Jesus asked the man to come and stand in front of the congregation.

4   Then turning to His enemies He asked, "Is it all right to do kind deeds on Sabbath days? Or is this a day for doing harm? Is it a day to save lives or to destroy them?" But they wouldn't answer Him.

5   Looking around at them angrily, for He was deeply disturbed by their indifference to human need, He said to the man, "Reach out your hand." He did, and instantly his hand was healed!

6   At once the Pharisees[1] went away and met with the Herodians[2] to discuss plans for killing Jesus.

7, 8   Meanwhile, Jesus and His disciples withdrew to the beach, followed by a huge crowd from all over Galilee, Judea, Jerusalem, Idumea, from beyond the Jordan River, and even from as far away as Tyre and Sidon. For the news about His miracles had spread far and wide and vast numbers came to see Him for themselves.

9   He instructed His disciples to bring around a boat and to have it standing ready to rescue Him in case He was crowded off the beach.

10   For there had been many healings that day and as a result great numbers of sick people were crowding around Him, trying to touch Him.

11   And whenever those possessed by demons caught sight of Him they would fall down before Him shrieking, "You are the Son of God!"

12   But He strictly warned them not to make Him known.

13   Afterwards He went up into the hills and summoned certain ones He chose, inviting them to come and join Him there; and they did.

14, 15   Then He selected twelve of them to be His regular companions and to go out to preach and to cast out demons.

16, 17, 18, 19   These are the names of the twelve He chose: Simon (He renamed him "Peter"),

---

[1]The Pharisees were a religious sect of the Jews.
[2]A pro-Roman political party.

James and John (the sons of Zebedee, but Jesus called them "Sons of Thunder"),
Andrew,
Philip,
Bartholomew,
Matthew,
Thomas,
James (the son of Alphaeus),
Thaddaeus,
Simon (a member of a political party advocating violent overthrow of the Roman government),
Judas Iscariot (who later betrayed Him).

20 When He returned to the house where He was staying, the crowds began to gather again, and soon it was so full of visitors that He couldn't even find time to eat.

21 When His friends heard what was happening they came to try to take Him home with them. "He's out of his mind," they said.

22 But the Jewish teachers of religion who had arrived from Jerusalem said, "His trouble is that he's possessed by Satan, king of demons. That's why demons obey him."

23 Jesus summoned these men and asked them (using proverbs they all understood), "How can Satan cast out Satan?

24 A kingdom divided against itself will collapse.

25 A home filled with strife and division destroys itself.

26 And if Satan is fighting against himself, how can he accomplish anything? He would never survive.

27 [Satan must be bound before his demons are cast out[3]], just as a strong man must be tied up before his house can be ransacked and his property robbed.

28 I solemnly declare that any sin of man can be forgiven, even blasphemy against My Father,

29 But blasphemy against the Holy Spirit can never be forgiven. It is an eternal sin."

30 He told them this because they were saying He did His

---

[3]Implied.

miracles by Satan's power [instead of acknowledging it was by the Holy Spirit's power[4]].

31, 32   Now His mother and brothers arrived at the crowded house where He was teaching, and they sent word for Him to come out and talk with them. "Your mother and brothers are outside and want to see You," He was told.

33   He replied, "Who is My mother? Who are My brothers?"

34   Looking at those around Him He said, "These are My mother and brothers!

35   Anyone who does God's will is My brother, and My sister, and My mother."

CHAPTER 4

ONCE again an immense crowd gathered around Him on the beach as He was teaching, so He got into a boat and sat down and talked from there.

2   His usual method of teaching was to tell the people stories. One of them went like this:

3   "Listen! A farmer decided to sow some grain. As he scattered it across his field

4   Some of it fell on a path, and the birds came and picked it off the hard ground and ate it.

5, 6   Some fell on thin soil with underlying rock. It grew up quickly enough, but soon wilted beneath the hot sun and died because the roots had no nourishment in the shallow soil.

7   Other seeds fell among thorns that shot up and crowded the young plants so that they produced no grain.

8   But some of the seeds fell into good soil and yielded 30 times as much as he had planted—some of it even 60 or 100 times as much!

9   If you have ears, listen!"

10   Afterwards, when He was alone with the Twelve and with His other disciples, they asked Him, "What does Your story mean?"

[4]Implied.

11, 12   He replied, "You are permitted to know some truths about the Kingdom of God that are hidden to those outside the Kingdom. As Isaiah[1] the prophet says:

'Though they see and hear, they will not understand or turn to God, or be forgiven for their sins.'

13   But if you can't understand *this* simple illustration, what will you do about all the others I am going to tell?

14   The farmer I talked about is anyone who brings God's message to others, trying to plant good seed within their lives.

15   The hard pathway, where some of the seed fell, represents the hard hearts of some of those who hear God's message; Satan comes at once to try to make them forget it.

16   The rocky soil represents the hearts of those who hear the message with joy,

17   But, like young plants in such soil, their roots don't go very deep, and though at first they get along fine, as soon as persecution begins, they wilt.

18   The thorny ground represents the hearts of people who listen to the Good News and receive it,

19   But all too quickly the attractions of this world and the delights of wealth, and the search for success and lure of nice things come in and crowd out God's message from their hearts, so that no crop is produced.

20   But the good soil represents the hearts of those who truly accept God's message and produce a plentiful harvest for God—30, 60, or even 100 times as much as was planted in their hearts."

21   Then He asked them, "When someone lights a lamp, does he put a box over it to shut out the light? Of course not! The light couldn't be seen or used. A lamp is placed on a stand to shine and be useful.

22   All that is now hidden will someday come to light.

23   If you have ears, listen!

24   And be sure to put into practice what you hear. The more you do this, the more you will understand what I tell you.

25   To him who has shall be given; from him who has not shall be taken away even what he has.

---

[1]Implied.

26   Here is another story illustrating what the Kingdom of God is like: A farmer sowed his field,

27   And went away, and as the days went by, the seeds grew and grew without his help.

28   For the soil made the seeds grow. First a leaf-blade pushed through, and later the wheat-heads formed and finally the grain ripened,

29   And then the farmer came at once with his sickle and harvested it."

30   Jesus asked, "How can I describe the Kingdom of God? What story shall I use to illustrate it?

31, 32   It is like a tiny mustard seed! Though this is one of the smallest of seeds, yet it grows to become one of the largest of plants, with long branches where birds can build their nests and be sheltered."

33   He used many such illustrations to teach the people as much as they were ready to understand.[2]

34   In fact, He taught only by illustrations in His public teaching, but afterwards, when He was alone with His disciples, He would explain His meaning to them.

*   *   *   *   *

35   As evening fell, Jesus said to His disciples, "Let's cross to the other side of the lake."

36   So they took Him just as He was and started out, leaving the crowds behind (though other boats followed).

37   But soon a terrible storm arose. High waves began to break into the boat until it was nearly full of water and about to sink.

38   Jesus was asleep at the back of the boat with His head on a cushion. Frantically they wakened Him, shouting, "Teacher, don't You even care that we are all about to drown?"

39   Then He rebuked the wind and said to the sea, "Quiet down!" And the wind fell, and there was a great calm!

40   And He asked them, "Why were you so fearful? Don't you even yet have confidence in Me?"

41   And they were filled with awe and said among them-

---

[2]Literally, "as they were able to hear."

selves, "Who is this man, that even the winds and seas obey Him?"

CHAPTER 5

WHEN they arrived at the other side of the lake a demon-possessed man ran out from a graveyard, just as Jesus was climbing from the boat.

3, 4   This man lived among the gravestones, and had such strength that whenever he was put into handcuffs and shackles —as he often was—he snapped the handcuffs from his wrists and smashed the shackles and walked away. No one was strong enough to control him.

5   All day long and through the night he would wander among the tombs and in the wild hills, screaming and cutting himself with sharp pieces of stone.

6   When Jesus was still far out on the water, the man had seen Him and had run to meet Him, and fell down before Him.

7, 8   Then Jesus spoke to the demon within the man and said, "Come out, you evil spirit." It gave a terrible scream, shrieking, "What are You going to do to me, Jesus, Son of the Most High God? For God's sake, don't torture me!"

9   "What is your name?" Jesus asked, and the demon replied, "Legion, for there are many of us here within this man."

10   Then the demons begged Him again and again not to send them to some distant land.

11   Now as it happened there was a huge herd of hogs rooting around on the hill above the lake.

12   "Send us into those hogs," the demons begged.

13   And Jesus gave them permission. Then the evil spirits came out of the man and entered the hogs, and the entire herd plunged down the steep hillside into the lake and drowned.

14   The herdsmen fled to the nearby towns and countryside, spreading the news as they ran. Everyone rushed out to see for themselves.

15   And a large crowd soon gathered where Jesus was; but

as they saw the man sitting there, fully clothed and perfectly sane, they were frightened.

16   Those who saw what happened were telling everyone about it,

17   And the crowd began pleading with Jesus to go away and leave them alone!

18   So He got back into the boat. The man who had been possessed by the demons begged Jesus to let him go along.

19   But Jesus said no. "Go home to your friends," He told him, "and tell them what wonderful things God has done for you; and how merciful He has been."

20   So the man started off to visit the Ten Towns[1] of that region and began to tell everyone about the great things Jesus had done for him; and they were awestruck by his story.

*   *   *   *   *

21   When Jesus had gone across by boat to the other side of the lake, a vast crowd gathered around Him on the shore.

22   The leader of the local synagogue, whose name was Jairus, came and fell down before Him,

23   Pleading with Him to heal his little daughter. "She is at the point of death," he said in desperation. "Please come and place Your hands on her and make her live."

24   Jesus went with him, and the crowd thronged behind.

25   In the crowd was a woman who had been sick for twelve years with a hemorrhage.

26   She had suffered much from many doctors through the years and had become poor from paying them, and was no better but, in fact, was worse.

27   She had heard all about the wonderful miracles Jesus did, and that is why she came up behind Him through the crowd and touched His clothes.

28   For she thought to herself, "If I can just touch His clothing, I will be healed."

29   And sure enough, as soon as she had touched Him, the bleeding stopped and she knew she was well!

30   Jesus realized at once that healing power had gone out

[1]Or, "to visit Decapolis."

from Him, so He turned around in the crowd and asked, "Who touched My clothes?"

31   His disciples said to Him, "All this crowd pressing around You, and You ask who touched You?"

32   But He kept on looking around to see who it was who had done it.

33   Then the frightened woman, trembling at the realization of what had happened to her, came and fell at His feet and told Him what she had done.

34   And He said to her, "Daughter, your faith has made you well; go in peace, healed of your disease."

35   While He was still talking to her, messengers arrived from Jairus' home with the news that it was too late—his daughter was dead and there was no point in Jesus' coming now.

36   But Jesus ignored their comments and said to Jairus, "Don't be afraid. Just trust Me."

37   Then Jesus halted the crowd and wouldn't let anyone go on with Him to Jairus' home except Peter and James and John.

38   When they arrived, Jesus saw that all was in great confusion, with unrestrained weeping and wailing.

39   He went inside and spoke to the people. "Why all this weeping and commotion?" He asked. "The child isn't dead; she is only asleep!"

40   They laughed at Him in bitter derision, but He told them all to leave, and taking the little girl's father and mother and His three disciples, He went into the room where she was lying.

41, 42   Taking her by the hand He said to her, "Get up, little girl!" (She was twelve years old.) And she jumped up and walked around! Her parents just couldn't get over it.

43   Jesus instructed them very earnestly not to tell what had happened, and told them to give her something to eat.

CHAPTER 6

SOON afterwards He left that section of the country and returned with His disciples to Nazareth, His home town.

2, 3   The next Sabbath He went to the synagogue to teach, and the people were astonished at His wisdom and His miracles because He was just a local man like themselves. "He's no better than we are," they said. "He's just a carpenter, Mary's boy, and a brother of James and Joseph, Judas and Simon. And his sisters live right here among us." And they were offended!

4   Then Jesus told them, "A prophet is honored everywhere except in his home town and among his relatives and by his own family."

5   And because of their unbelief He couldn't do any mighty miracles among them except to place His hands on a few sick people and heal them.

6   And He could hardly accept the fact that they wouldn't believe in Him. Then He went out among the villages, teaching.

7   And He called His twelve disciples together and sent them out two by two, with power to cast out demons.

8, 9   He told them to take nothing with them except their walking sticks—no food, no knapsack, no money, not even an extra pair of shoes or a change of clothes.

10   "Stay at one home in each village—don't shift around from house to house while you are there," He said.

11   "And whenever a village won't accept you or listen to you, shake off the dust from your feet as you leave; it is a sign that you have abandoned it to its fate."

12   So the disciples went out, telling everyone they met to turn from sin.

13   And they cast out many demons, and healed many sick people, anointing them with olive oil.

14   King Herod soon heard about Jesus, for His miracles were talked about everywhere. The king thought Jesus was John the Baptist come back to life again. So the people were saying, "No wonder He can do such miracles."

15   Others thought Jesus was Elijah the ancient prophet, now returned to life again; still others claimed He was a new prophet like the great ones of the past.

16   "No," Herod said, "it is John, the man I beheaded. He has come back from the dead."

17, 18   For Herod had sent soldiers to arrest and imprison John because he kept saying it was wrong for the king to marry Herodias, his brother Philip's wife.

19   Herodias wanted John killed in revenge, but without Herod's approval she was powerless.

20   And Herod respected John, knowing that he was a good and holy man, and so he kept him under his protection. Herod was disturbed whenever he talked with John, but even so he liked to listen to him.

21   Herodias' chance finally came. It was Herod's birthday and he gave a stag party for his palace aides, army officers, and the leading citizens of Galilee.

22, 23   Then Herodias' daughter came in and danced before them and greatly pleased them all. "Ask me for anything you like," the king vowed, "even half of my kingdom, and I will give it to you!"

24   She went out and consulted her mother, who told her, "Ask for John the Baptist's head!"

25   So she hurried back to the king and told him, "I want the head of John the Baptist—right now—on a tray!"

26   Then the king was sorry, but he was embarrassed to break his oath in front of his guests.

27   So he sent one of his bodyguards to the prison to cut off John's head and bring it to him. The soldier killed John in the prison,

28   And brought back his head on a tray, and gave it to the girl and she took it to her mother.

29   When John's disciples heard what had happened, they came for his body and buried it in a tomb.

*   *   *   *   *

30   The apostles now returned to Jesus from their tour and told Him all they had done and what they had said to the people they visited.

31   Then Jesus suggested, "Let's get away from the crowds

93

for a while and rest." For so many people were coming and going that they scarcely had time to eat.

32   So they left by boat for a quieter spot.

33   But many people saw them leaving and ran on ahead along the shore and met them as they landed.

34   So the usual vast crowd was there as He stepped from the boat; and He had pity on them because they were like sheep without a shepherd, and He taught them many things they needed to know.

35, 36   Late in the afternoon His disciples came to Him and said, "Tell the people to go away to the nearby villages and farms and buy themselves some food, for there is nothing to eat here in this desolate spot, and it is getting late."

37   But Jesus said, *"You* feed them."

"With what?" they asked. "It would take a fortune[1] to buy food for all this crowd!"

38   "How much food do we have?" He asked. "Go and find out." They came back to report that there were five loaves of bread and two fish.

39, 40   Then Jesus told the crowd to sit down, and soon colorful groups of 50 or 100 each were sitting on the green grass.

41   He took the five loaves and two fish and looking up to heaven, gave thanks for the food. Breaking the loaves into pieces, He gave some of the bread and fish to each disciple to place before the people.

42   And the crowd ate until they could hold no more!

43, 44   There were about 5,000 men there for that meal, and afterwards twelve basketfuls of scraps were picked up off the grass!

45   Immediately after this Jesus instructed His disciples to get back into the boat and strike out across the lake to Bethsaida, where He would join them later. He Himself would stay and tell the crowds good-bye and get them started home.

46   Afterwards He went up into the hills to pray.

47   During the night, as the disciples in their boat were out in the middle of the lake, and He was alone on land,

---

[1]Literally, "200 denarii," a year's wage.

48   He saw that they were in serious trouble, rowing hard and struggling against the wind and waves. About three o'clock in the morning He walked out to them on the water. He started past them,

49   But when they saw something walking along beside them they screamed in terror, thinking it was a ghost,

50   For they all saw Him. But He spoke to them at once. "It's all right," He said. "It is I! Don't be afraid."

51   Then He climbed into the boat and the wind stopped! They just sat there, unable to take it in!

52   For they still didn't realize who He was, even after the miracle the evening before! For they didn't want to believe![2]

53   When they arrived at Gennesaret on the other side of the lake they moored the boat,

54   And climbed out. The people standing around there recognized Him at once,

55   And ran throughout the whole area to spread the news of His arrival, and began carrying sick folks to Him on mats and stretchers.

56   Wherever He went—in villages and cities, and out on the farms—they laid the sick in the market plazas and streets, and begged Him to let them at least touch the fringes of His clothes; and as many as touched Him were healed.

CHAPTER 7

ONE day some Jewish religious leaders arrived from Jerusalem to investigate Him,

2   And noticed that some of His disciples failed to follow the usual Jewish rituals before eating.

3   (For the Jews, especially the Pharisees, will never eat until they have sprinkled their arms to the elbows,[1] as required by their ancient traditions.

4   So when they come home from the market they must

---

[2]Literally, "for their hearts were hardened," perhaps implying jealousy, as in Mark 6:2-6.
[1]Literally, "to wash with the fist."

always sprinkle themselves in this way before touching any food. This is but one of many examples of laws and regulations they have clung to for centuries, and still follow, such as their ceremony of cleansing for pots, pans and dishes.)

5 So the religious leaders asked Him, "Why don't your disciples follow our age-old customs? For they eat without first performing the washing ceremony."

6, 7 Jesus replied, "You bunch of hypocrites! Isaiah the prophet described you very well when he said, 'These people speak very prettily about the Lord but they have no love for Him at all. Their worship is a farce, for they claim that God commands the people to obey their petty rules.' How right Isaiah was!

8 For you ignore God's specific orders and substitute your own traditions.

9 You are simply rejecting God's laws and trampling them under your feet for the sake of tradition.

10 For instance, Moses gave you this law from God: 'Honor your father and mother.' And he said that anyone who speaks against his father or mother must die.

11 But you say it is perfectly all right for a man to disregard his needy parents, telling them, 'Sorry, I can't help you! for I have given to God what I could have given to you.'

12, 13 And so you break the law of God in order to protect your man-made tradition. And this is only one example. There are many, many others."

14 Then Jesus called to the crowd to come and hear. "All of you listen," He said, "and try to understand.

15, 16[2] Your souls aren't harmed by what you eat, but by what you think and say!"[3]

17 Then He went into a house to get away from the crowds, and His disciples asked Him what He meant by the statement He had just made.

18 "Don't you understand either?" He asked. "Can't you see that what you eat won't harm your soul?

---

[2]Verse 16 is omitted in many of the ancient manuscripts. "If any man has ears to hear, let him hear."
[3]Literally, "what proceeds out of the man defiles the man."

19 For food doesn't come in contact with your heart, but only passes through the digestive system." (By saying this He showed that every kind of food is kosher.)

20 And then He added, "It is the thought-life that pollutes.

21 For from within, out of men's hearts, come evil thoughts of lust, theft, murder, adultery,

22 Wanting what belongs to others, wickedness, deceit, lewdness, envy, slander, pride, and all other folly.

23 All these vile things come from within; they are what pollute you and make you unfit for God."

*   *   *   *   *

24 Then He left Galilee and went to the region of Tyre and Sidon,[4] and tried to keep it a secret that He was there, but couldn't. For as usual the news of His arrival spread fast.

25 Right away a woman came to Him whose little girl was possessed by a demon. She had heard about Jesus and now she came and fell at His feet,

26 And pled with Him to release her child from the demon's control. (But she was Syrophoenician—a "despised Gentile!")

27 Jesus told her, "First I should help My own family—the Jews.[5] It isn't right to take the children's food and throw it to the dogs."

28 She replied, "That's true, sir, but even the puppies under the table are given some scraps from the children's plates."

29 "Good!" He said, "You have answered well—so well that I have healed your little girl. Go on home, for the demon has left her!"

30 And when she arrived home, her little girl was lying quietly in bed, and the demon was gone.

31 From Tyre He went to Sidon, then back to the Sea of Galilee by way of the Ten Towns.

32 A deaf man with a speech impediment was brought to Him, and everyone begged Jesus to lay His hands on the man and heal him.

---

[4]About 50 miles away.
[5]Literally, "Let the children eat first."

33 Jesus led him away from the crowd and put His fingers into the man's ears, then spat and touched the man's tongue with the spittle.

34 Then, looking up to heaven, He sighed and commanded, "Open!"

35 Instantly the man could hear perfectly and speak plainly!

36 Jesus told the crowd not to spread the news, but the more He forbade them, the more they made it known,

37 For they were overcome with utter amazement. Again and again they said, "Everything He does is wonderful; He even corrects deafness and stammering!"

CHAPTER 8

ONE day about this time as another great crowd gathered, the people ran out of food again. Jesus called His disciples to discuss the situation. "I pity these people," He said, "for they have been here three days, and have nothing left to eat.

3 And if I send them home without feeding them, they will faint along the road! For some of them have come a long distance."

4 "Are we supposed to find food for them here in the desert?" His disciples scoffed.

5 "How many loaves of bread do you have?" He asked. "Seven," they replied.

6 So He told the crowd to sit down on the ground. Then He took the seven loaves, thanked God for them, broke them into pieces and passed them to His disciples; and the disciples placed them before the people.

7 A few small fish were found, too, so Jesus also blessed these and told the disciples to serve them.

8, 9 And the whole crowd ate until they were full, and afterwards He sent them home. There were about 4,000 people in the crowd that day and when the scraps were picked up after the meal, there were seven very large basketfuls left over!

10   Immediately after this He got into a boat with His disciples and came to the region of Dalmanutha.

11   When the local Jewish leaders learned of His arrival they came to argue with Him. "Do a miracle for us," they said. "Make something happen in the sky. Then we will believe in you."[1]

12   His heart fell[2] when He heard this and He said, "Certainly not. How many more miracles do you people need?"[3]

13   So He got back into the boat and left them, and crossed to the other side of the lake.

14   But the disciples had forgotten to stock up on food before they left, and had only one loaf of bread in the boat.

15   As they were crossing, Jesus said to them very solemnly, "Beware of the yeast of King Herod and of the Pharisees."

16   "What does He mean?" the disciples asked each other. They finally decided that He must be talking about their forgetting to bring bread.

17   Jesus realized what they were discussing and said, "No, that isn't it at all! Can't you understand? Are your hearts too hard to take it in?

18   As Isaiah[4] declared, 'Your eyes are to see with—why don't you look? Why don't you open your ears and listen?' Don't you remember anything at all?

19   What about the 5,000 men I fed with five loaves of bread? How many basketfuls of scraps did you pick up afterwards?"

"Twelve," they said.

20   "And when I fed the 4,000 with seven loaves, how much was left?"

"Seven basketfuls," they said.

21   "And yet you think I'm worried that we have no bread?"[5]

---

[1]Literally, "to test Him."
[2]Literally, "He sighed deeply."
[3]Literally, "Why does this generation seek a sign?"
[4]Implied.
[5]Literally, "Do you not yet understand?"

22   When they arrived at Bethsaida, some people brought a blind man to Him and begged Him to touch and heal him.

23   Jesus took the blind man by the hand and led him out of the village, and spat upon his eyes, and laid His hands over them. "Can you see anything now?" Jesus asked him.

24   The man looked around. "Yes!" he said, "I see men! But I can't see them very clearly; they look like tree trunks walking around!"

25   Then Jesus placed His hands over the man's eyes again and as the man stared intently, his sight was completely restored, and he saw everything clearly, drinking in the sights around him.

26   Jesus sent him home to his family. "Don't even go back to the village first," He said.

*   *   *   *   *

27   Jesus and His disciples now left Galilee and went out to the villages of Caesarea Philippi. As they were walking along He asked them, "Who do the people think I am? What are they saying about Me?"

28   "Some of them think You are John the Baptist," the disciples replied, "and others say You are Elijah or some other ancient prophet come back to life again."

29   Then He asked, "Who do you think I am?" Peter replied, "You are the Messiah."

30   But Jesus warned them not to tell anyone!

31   Then He began to tell them about the terrible things He[6] would suffer, and that He would be rejected by the elders and the Chief Priests and the other Jewish leaders—and be killed, and that He would rise again three days afterwards.

32   He talked about it quite frankly with them, so Peter took Him aside and chided Him.[7] "You shouldn't say things like that," He told Jesus.

33   Jesus turned and looked at His disciples and then said to Peter very sternly, "Satan, get behind Me! You are looking at this only from a human point of view and not from God's."

34   Then He called His disciples and the crowds to come

---

[6]Literally, "the Son of Man."
[7]Literally, "Peter began to rebuke Him."

over and listen. "If any of you wants to be My follower," He told them, "you must put aside your own pleasures and shoulder your cross, and follow Me closely.

35   If you insist on saving your life, you will lose it. Only those who throw away their lives for My sake and for the sake of the Good News will ever know what it means to really live.

36   And how does a man benefit if he gains the whole world and loses his soul in the process?

37   For is anything worth more than his soul?

38   And anyone who is ashamed of Me and My message in these days of unbelief and sin, I, the Man of Glory,[8] will be ashamed of him when I return in the glory of My Father, with the holy angels."

CHAPTER 9

JESUS went on to say to His disciples, "Some of you who are standing here right now will live to see the Kingdom of God arrive in great power!"

2   Six days later Jesus took Peter, James and John to the top of a mountain. No one else was there. Suddenly His face began to shine with glory,

3   And His clothing became dazzling white, far more glorious than any earthly process could ever make it!

4   Then Elijah and Moses appeared and began talking with Jesus!

5   "Teacher, this is wonderful!" Peter exclaimed. "We will make three shelters here, one for each of you . . . ."

6   He said this just to be talking, for he didn't know what else to say and they were all terribly frightened.

7   But while he was still speaking these words, a cloud covered them, blotting out the sun, and a voice from the cloud said, "*This* is My beloved Son. Listen to *Him.*"

8   Then suddenly they looked around and Moses and Elijah were gone, and only Jesus was with them.

---

[8]Literally, "Son of Man." The above paraphrase reveals another facet of this interesting term.

9   As they descended the mountainside He told them never to mention what they had seen until after He[1] had risen from the dead.

10   So they kept it to themselves, but often talked about it, and wondered what He meant by "rising from the dead."

11   Now they began asking Him about something the Jewish religious leaders often spoke of, that Elijah must return [before the Messiah could come[2]].

12, 13   Jesus agreed that Elijah must come first and prepare the way—and that he had, in fact, already come! And that he had been terribly mistreated, just as the prophets had predicted. Then Jesus asked them what the prophets could have been talking about when they predicted that the Messiah[1] would suffer and be treated with utter contempt.

14   At the bottom of the mountain they found a great crowd surrounding the other nine disciples, as some Jewish leaders argued with them.

15   The crowd watched Jesus in awe as He came toward them, and then ran to greet Him.

16   "What's all the argument about?" He asked.

17   One of the men in the crowd spoke up and said, "Teacher, I brought my son for You to heal—he can't talk because he is possessed by a demon.

18   And whenever the demon is in control of him it dashes him to the ground and makes him foam at the mouth and grind his teeth and become rigid.[3] So I begged your disciples to cast out the demon, but they couldn't do it."

19   Jesus said [to His disciples[4]], "Oh, what tiny faith you have;[5] how much longer must I be with you until you believe? How much longer must I be patient with you? Bring the boy to Me."

20   So they brought the boy, but when he saw Jesus the demon convulsed the child horribly, and he fell to the ground writhing and foaming at the mouth.

---

[1]Literally, "the Son of Man."
[2]Implied.
[3]Or, "is growing weaker day by day."
[4]Implied.
[5]Literally, "O unbelieving generation."

21 "How long has he been this way?" Jesus asked the father.

And he replied, "Since he was very small,

22 And the demon often makes him fall into the fire or into water to kill him. Oh, have mercy on us and do something if You can."

23 "If I can?" Jesus asked. *"Anything* is possible if you have faith."

24 The father instantly replied, "I *do* have faith; oh, help me to have *more!"*

25 When Jesus saw that the crowd was growing He rebuked the demon. "O demon of deafness and dumbness," He said, "I command you to come out of this child and enter him no more!"

26 Then the demon screamed terribly and convulsed the boy again and left him; and the boy lay there limp and motionless, to all appearance dead. A murmur ran through the crowd —"He is dead."

27 But Jesus took him by the hand and helped him to his feet and he stood up and was all right!

28 Afterwards, when Jesus was alone in the house with His disciples, they asked Him, "Why couldn't we cast that demon out?"

29 Jesus replied, "Cases like this require prayer."[6]

30, 31 Leaving that region they traveled through Galilee where He tried to avoid all publicity in order to spend more time with His disciples, teaching them. He would say to them, "I, the Son of Mankind, am going to be betrayed and killed and three days later I will return to life again."

32 But they didn't understand and were afraid to ask Him what He meant.

33 And so they arrived at Capernaum. When they were settled in the house where they were to stay He asked them, "What were you discussing out on the road?"

34 But they were ashamed to answer, for they had been arguing about which of them was the greatest!

---

[6]"And fasting" is added in some manuscripts, but not the most ancient.

35 He sat down and called them around Him and said, "Anyone wanting to be the greatest must be the least—the servant of all!"

36 Then He placed a little child among them; and taking the child in His arms He said to them,

37 "Anyone who welcomes a little child like this in My name is welcoming Me, and anyone who welcomes Me is welcoming My Father who sent Me!"

*   *   *   *   *

38 One of His disciples, John, told Him one day, "Teacher, we saw a man using Your name to cast out demons; but we told him not to, for he isn't one of our group."

39 "Don't forbid him!" Jesus said. "For no one doing miracles in My name will quickly turn against Me.[7]

40 Anyone who isn't against us is for us.

41 If anyone so much as gives you a cup of water because you are Christ's—I say this solemnly—he won't lose his reward.

42 But if someone causes one of these little ones who believe in Me to lose faith—it would be better for that man if a huge millstone were tied around his neck and he were thrown into the sea.

*   *   *   *   *

43, 44[8] If your hand does wrong, cut it off. Better live forever with one hand than be thrown into the unquenchable fires of hell with two!

45, 46[8] If your foot carries you toward evil, cut it off! Better be lame and live forever than have two feet that carry you to hell.

47 And if your eye is sinful, gouge it out. Better enter the Kingdom of God half blind than have two eyes and see the fires of hell,

48 Where the worm never dies, and the fire never goes out—

49 Where all are salted with fire.[9]

50 Good salt is worthless if it loses its saltiness; it can't

[7]Literally, "will be able to speak evil of Me."
[8]Verses 44 and 46 (which are identical with verse 48) are omitted in some of the ancient manuscripts.
[9]Literally, "For everyone shall be salted with fire."

season anything. So don't lose your flavor! Live in peace with each other."

CHAPTER 10

THEN He left Capernaum[1] and went southward to the Judean borders and into the area east of the Jordan River. And as always there were the crowds; and as usual He taught them.

2 Some Pharisees came and asked Him, "Do you permit divorce?" Of course they were trying to trap Him.

3 "What did Moses say about divorce?" Jesus asked them.

4 "He said it was all right," they replied. "He said that all a man has to do is write his wife a letter of dismissal."

5 "And why did he say that?" Jesus asked. "I'll tell you why—it was a concession to your hard-hearted wickedness.

6, 7 But it certainly isn't God's way. For from the very first He made man and woman to be joined together permanently in marriage; therefore a man is to leave his father and mother,

8 And he and his wife are united so that they are no longer two, but one.

9 And no man may separate what God has joined together."

10 Later, when He was alone with His disciples in the house, they brought up the subject again.

11 He told them, "When a man divorces his wife to marry someone else, he commits adultery against her.

12 And if a wife divorces her husband and remarries, she, too, commits adultery."

*   *   *   *   *

13 Once when some mothers[2] were bringing their children to Jesus to bless them, the disciples shooed them away, telling them not to bother Him.

---

[1]Literally, "and rising up, He went from there." Mentioned here so quietly, this was His final farewell to Galilee. He never returned until after His death and resurrection.
[2]Implied.

14   But when Jesus saw what was happening He was very much displeased with His disciples and said to them, "Let the children come to Me, for the Kingdom of God belongs to such as they. Don't send them away!

15   I tell you as seriously as I know how that anyone who refuses to come to God as a little child will never be allowed into His Kingdom."

16   Then He took the children into His arms and placed His hands on their heads and He blessed them.

*   *   *   *   *

17   As He was starting out on a trip, a man came running to Him and knelt down and asked, "Good Teacher, what must I do to get to heaven?"

18   "Why do you call Me good?" Jesus asked. "Only God is truly good!

19   But as for your question—you know the commandments: don't kill, don't commit adultery, don't steal, don't lie, don't cheat, respect your father and mother."

20   "Teacher," the man replied, "I've never once[3] broken a single one of those laws."

21   Jesus felt genuine love for this man as He looked at him. "You lack only one thing," He told him; "go and sell all you have and give the money to the poor—and you shall have treasure in heaven—and come, follow Me."

22   Then the man's face fell, and he went sadly away, for he was very rich.

23   Jesus watched him go, then turned around and said to His disciples, "It's almost impossible for the rich to get into the Kingdom of God!"

24   This amazed them. So Jesus said it again: "Dear children, how hard it is for those who trust in riches[4] to enter the Kingdom of God.

25   It is easier for a camel to go through the eye of a needle than for a rich man to enter the Kingdom of God."

26   The disciples were incredulous! "Then who in the world can be saved, if not a rich man?" they asked.

---

[3]Literally, "from my youth."
[4]Some of the ancient manuscripts do not contain the words, "for those who trust in riches."

27   Jesus looked at them intently, then said, "Without God, it is utterly impossible. But with God everything is possible."

28   Then Peter began to mention all that he and the other disciples had left behind. "We've given up everything to follow You," he said.

29   And Jesus replied, "Let Me assure you that no one has ever given up anything—home, brothers, sisters, mother, father, children, or property—for love of Me and to tell others the Good News,

30   Who won't be given back, a hundred times over, homes, brothers, sisters, mothers, children, and land—with persecutions! All these will be his here on earth, and in the world to come he shall have eternal life.

31   But many people who seem to be important now will be the least important then; and many who are considered least here shall be greatest there."

                    *   *   *   *   *

32   Now they were on the way to Jesusalem, and Jesus was walking along ahead; and as the disciples were following they were filled with terror and dread. Taking them aside, Jesus once more began describing all that was going to happen to Him when they arrived at Jerusalem.

33   "When we get there," He told them, "I, the Son of Mankind, will be arrested and taken before the chief priests and the Jewish leaders, who will sentence Me to die and hand Me over to the Romans to be killed.

34   They will mock Me and spit on Me and flog Me with their whips and kill Me; but after three days I will come back to life again."

35   Then James and John, the sons of Zebedee, came over and spoke to Him in a low voice.[5] "Master," they said, "we want You to do us a favor."

36   "What is it?" He asked.

37   "We want to sit on the thrones next to Yours in Your kingdom," they said, "one at Your right and the other at Your left!"

38   But Jesus answered, "You don't know what you are

---

[5]Literally, "came up to Him."

asking! Are you able to drink from the bitter cup of sorrow I must drink from? Or to be baptized with the baptism of suffering I must be baptized with?"

39   "Oh, yes," they said, "we are!" And Jesus said, "You shall indeed drink from My cup and be baptized with My baptism,

40   But I do not have the right to place you on thrones next to Mine. Those appointments have already been made."

41   When the other disciples discovered what James and John had asked, they were very indignant.

42   So Jesus called them to Him and said, "As you know, the kings and great men of the earth lord it over the people;

43   But among you it is different. Whoever wants to be great among you must be your servant.

44   And whoever wants to be greatest of all must be the slave of all.

45   For even I, the Man from Heaven,[6] am not here to be served, but to help others, and to give My life as a ransom for many."

46   And so they reached Jericho. Later, as they left town, a great crowd was following. Now it happened that a blind beggar named Bartimaeus (the son of Timaeus) was sitting beside the road as Jesus was going by.

47   When Bartimaeus heard that Jesus from Nazareth was near, he began to shout out, "Jesus, Son of David, have mercy on me!"

48   "Shut up!" some of the people yelled at him.

But he only shouted the louder, again and again, "O Son of David, have mercy on me!"

49   When Jesus heard him He stopped there in the road and said, "Tell him to come here."

So they called the blind man. "You lucky fellow,"[7] they said, "come on, He's calling you!"

50   Bartimaeus yanked off his old coat and flung it aside, jumped up and came to Jesus.

---

[6]Literally, "the Son of Man."
[7]Literally, "Be of good cheer.' '

51 "What do you want Me to do for you?" Jesus asked.

"O Teacher," the blind man said, "I want to see!"

52 And Jesus said to him, "All right, it's done.[8] Your faith has healed you." And instantly the blind man could see, and followed Jesus down the road!

CHAPTER 11

A S they neared Bethphage and Bethany on the outskirts of Jerusalem and came to the Mount of Olives, Jesus sent two of His disciples on ahead.

2 "Go into that village over there," He told them, "and just as you enter you will see a colt tied up that has never been ridden. Untie him and bring him here.

3 And if anyone asks you what you are doing, just say, 'Our Master needs him and will return him soon.' "

4, 5 Off went the two men and found the colt standing in the street, tied outside a house. As they were untying it, some who were standing there demanded, "What are you doing, untying that colt?"

6 So they said what Jesus had told them to, and then the men agreed.

7 So the colt was brought to Jesus and the disciples threw their cloaks across its back for Him to ride on.

8 Then many in the crowd spread out their coats along the road before Him, while others threw down leafy branches from the fields.

9 He was in the center of the procession with crowds ahead and behind, and all of them shouting, "Long live the King!"[1] "Blessed is He who comes in the name of the Lord!" . . .

10 "Blessed is the Kingdom He is bringing, the Kingdom of our father David!" . . . "God save the King!"[2]

11 And so He entered Jerusalem and went into the Temple. He looked around carefully at everything and then left—for

[8]Literally, "Go your way."
[1]Literally, "Hosanna."
[2]Literally, "Hosanna in the highest."

now it was late in the afternoon—and went out to Bethany with the twelve disciples.

12   The next morning as they left Bethany, He felt hungry.

13   A little way off He noticed a fig tree in full leaf, so He went over to see if He could find any figs on it. But no, there were only leaves, for it was too early in the season for fruit.

14   Then Jesus said to the tree, "You shall never bear fruit again!" And the disciples heard Him say it.

15   When they arrived back to Jerusalem He went to the Temple and began to drive out the merchants and their customers, and knocked over the tables of the moneychangers and the stalls of of those selling doves,

16   And stopped everyone from bringing in loads of merchandise.

17   He told them, "It is written in the Scriptures, 'My Temple is to be a place of prayer for all nations,' but you have turned it into a den of robbers."

18   When the chief priests and other Jewish leaders heard what He had done they began planning how best to get rid of Him. Their problem was their fear of riots because the people were so enthusiastic about Jesus' teaching.

19   That evening as usual they left the city.

20   Next morning, as the disciples passed the fig tree He had cursed, they saw that it was withered from the roots!

21   Then Peter remembered what Jesus had said to the tree on the previous day, and exclaimed, "Look, Teacher! The fig tree You cursed has withered!"

22, 23   In reply Jesus said to the disciples, "If you only have faith in God—this is the absolute truth—you can say to this Mount of Olives, 'Rise up and fall into the Mediterranean,' and your command will be obeyed. All that's required is that you really believe and have no doubt!

24   Listen to Me! You can pray for *anything,* and *if you believe, you have it;* it's yours!

25   But when you are praying, first forgive anyone you are holding a grudge against, so that your Father in heaven will forgive you your sins too."

26,[3] 27, 28 By this time they had arrived in Jerusalem again, and as He was walking through the Temple area, the chief priests and other Jewish leaders[4] came up to Him demanding, "What's going on here? Who gave you the authority to drive out the merchants?"

29 Jesus replied, "I'll tell you if you answer one question!

30 What about John the Baptist? Was he sent by God, or not? Answer Me!"

31 They talked it over among themselves. "If we reply that God sent him, then he will say, 'All right, why didn't you accept him?'

32 But if we say God didn't send him, then the people will start a riot." (For the people all believed strongly that John was a prophet.)

33 So they said, "We can't answer. We don't know." To which Jesus replied, "Then I won't answer your question either!"

CHAPTER 12

HERE are some of the story-illustrations Jesus gave to the people at that time:

"A man planted a vineyard and built a wall around it and dug a pit for pressing out the grape juice, and built a watchman's tower. Then he leased the farm to tenant farmers and went on a trip to a distant[1] land.

2 At grape-picking time he sent one of his men to collect his share of the crop.

3 But the farmers beat up the man and sent him back empty-handed.

4 The owner then sent another of his men, who received the same treatment, only worse, for his head was seriously injured.

---

[3]Many ancient authorities add verse 26, "but if you do not forgive, neither will your Father who is in heaven forgive your trespasses." All include this in Matthew 6:15.
[4]Literally, "scribes and elders."
[1]Implied.

5 The next man he sent was killed; and later, others were either beaten or killed, until

6 There was only one left—his only son. He finally sent him, thinking they would surely give him their full respect.

7 But when the farmers saw him coming they said, 'He will own the farm when his father dies. Come on, let's kill him—and then the farm will be ours!'

8 So they caught him and murdered him and threw his body out of the vineyard.

9 What do you suppose the owner will do when he hears what happened? He will come and kill them all, and lease the vineyard to others.

10 Don't you remember reading this verse in the Scriptures? 'The Cornerstone—the most honored stone in the building—is a Rock the builders threw away!

11 This is the Lord's doing and it is an amazing thing to see.' "

12 The Jewish leaders wanted to arrest Him then and there for using this illustration, for they knew He was pointing at them—they were the wicked farmers in His story. But they were afraid to touch Him for fear of a mob. So they left Him and went away.

13 But they sent other religious and political leaders[2] to talk with Him and try to trap Him into saying something He could be arrested for.

14 "Teacher," these spies said, "we know you tell the truth no matter what! You aren't influenced by the opinions and desires of men, but sincerely teach the ways of God. Now tell us, is it right to pay taxes to Rome, or not?"

15 Jesus saw their trick and said, "Show Me a coin and I'll tell you."

16 When they handed it to Him He asked, "Whose picture and title is this on the coin?"

They replied, "The emperor's."

17 "All right," he said, "if it is his, give it to him. But everything that belongs to God must be given to God!" And

[2]Literally, "Pharisees and Herodians."

they scratched their heads in bafflement at His reply.

18 Then the Sadducees stepped forward—a group of men who say there is no resurrection. Here was their question:

19 "Teacher, Moses gave us a law that when a man dies without children, the man's brother should marry his widow and have children in his brother's name.

20, 21, 22 Well, there were seven brothers and the oldest married and died, and left no children. So the second brother married the widow, but soon he died too, and left no children. Then the next brother married her, and died without children, and so on until all were dead, and still there were no children; and last of all, the woman died too.

23 What we want to know is this:[3] In the resurrection, whose wife will she be, for she had been the wife of each of them?"

24 Jesus replied, "Your trouble is that you don't know the Scriptures, and don't know the power of God.

25 For when these seven brothers and the woman rise from the dead, they won't be married—they will be like the angels.

26 But now as to whether there will be a resurrection— have you never read in the book of Exodus about Moses and the burning bush? God said to Moses, 'I *am* the God of Abraham, and I *am* the God of Isaac, and I *am* the God of Jacob.'

27 God was telling Moses that these men, though dead for hundreds of years,[3] were still very much alive, for He would not have said, 'I *am* the God' of those who don't exist! You have made a serious error."

28 One of the teachers of religion who was standing there listening to the discussion realized that Jesus had answered well. So he asked, "Of all the commandments, which is the most important?"

29 Jesus replied, "The one that says, 'Hear, O Israel! The Lord our God is the one and only God.

30 And you must love Him with all your heart and soul and mind and strength.'

[3]Implied.

31   The second is: 'You must love others as much as yourself.' No other commandments are greater than these."

32   The teacher of religion replied, "Sir, You have spoken a true word in saying that there is only one God and no other.

33   And I know it is far more important to love Him with all my heart and understanding and strength, and to love others as myself, than to offer all kinds of sacrifices on the altar of the Temple."

34   Realizing this man's understanding, Jesus said to him, "You are not far from the Kingdom of God." And after that, no one dared ask Him any more questions.

35   Later, as Jesus was teaching the people in the Temple area, He asked them this question: "Why do your religious teachers claim that the Messiah must be a descendant of King David?

36   For David himself said—and the Holy Spirit was speaking through him when he said it—'God said to my Lord, sit at My right hand until I make Your enemies Your footstool.'

37   Since David called Him his Lord, how can He be his *son?*" (This sort of reasoning delighted the crowd and they listened to Him with great interest.)

38   Here are some of the other things He taught them at this time: "Beware of the teachers of religion! For they love to wear the robes of the rich and scholarly, and to have everyone bow to them as they walk through the markets.

39   They love to sit in the best seats in the synagogues, and at the places of honor at banquets—

40   But they shamelessly cheat widows out of their homes and then, to cover up the kind of men they really are, they pretend to be pious by praying long prayers in public. Because of this, their punishment will be the greater."

41   Then He went over to the collection boxes in the Temple and sat and watched as the crowds dropped in their money. Some who were rich put in large amounts.

42   Then a poor widow came and dropped in two pennies.

43, 44   He called His disciples to Him and remarked, "That poor widow has given more than all those rich men put together! For they gave a little of their extra fat,[4] while she gave up her last penny."

CHAPTER 13

AS He was leaving the Temple that day, one of His disciples said, "Teacher, what beautiful buildings these are! Look at the decorated stonework on the walls."

2   Jesus replied, "Yes, look! For not one stone will be left upon another, except as ruins."

3, 4   And as He sat on the slopes of the Mount of Olives across the valley from Jerusalem, Peter, James, John, and Andrew got alone with Him and asked Him, "Just when is all this going to happen to the Temple? Will there be some warning ahead of time?"

5   So Jesus launched into an extended reply. "Don't let anyone mislead you," He said,

6   "For many will come declaring themselves to be your Messiah, and will lead many astray.

7   And wars will break out near and far, but this is not the signal of the end-time.

8   For nations and kingdoms will proclaim war against each other, and there will be earthquakes in many lands, and famines. These herald only the early stages of the anguish ahead.

9   But when these things begin to happen, watch out! For you will be in great danger. You will be dragged before the courts, and beaten in the synagogues, and accused before governors and kings of being My followers. This is your opportunity to tell them the Good News.

10   And the Good News must first be made known in every nation before the end-time finally comes.[1]

11   But when you are arrested and stand trial, don't worry about what to say in your defense. Just say what God tells you to. Then you will not be speaking, but the Holy Spirit will.

12   Brothers will betray each other to death, fathers will

---

[4]Literally, "out of their surplus."
[1]Implied.

betray their own children, and children will betray their parents to be killed.

13   And everyone will hate you because you are Mine. But all who endure to the end without renouncing Me shall be saved.

14   When you see the horrible thing standing in the Temple[2]—reader, pay attention!—flee, if you can, to the Judean hills.

15, 16   Hurry! If you are on your rooftop porch, don't even go back into the house. If you are out in the fields, don't even return for your money or clothes.

17   Woe to pregnant women in those days, and to mothers nursing their children.

18   And pray that your flight will not be in winter.

19   For those will be days of such horror as have never been since the beginning of God's creation, nor will ever be again.

20   And unless the Lord shortens that time of calamity, not a soul in all the earth will survive. But for the sake of His chosen ones He will limit those days.

21   And then if anyone tells you, 'This is the Messiah,' or, 'That one is,' don't pay any attention.

22   For there will be many false Messiahs and false prophets who will do wonderful miracles that would deceive, if possible, even God's own children.[3]

23   Take care! I have warned you!

24   After the tribulation ends, then the sun will grow dim and the moon will not shine,

25   And the stars will fall—the heavens will convulse.

26   Then all mankind will see Me, the Son of Mankind, coming in the clouds with great power and glory.

27   And I will send out the angels to gather together My chosen ones from all over the world—from the farthest bounds of earth and heaven.

28   Now, here is a lesson from a fig tree. When its buds

---

[2]Literally, "standing where it ought not."
[3]Literally, "elect of God."

become tender and its leaves begin to sprout, you know that spring has come.

29 And when you see these things happening that I've described, you can be sure that My return is very near, that I am right at the door.

30 Yes, these are the events that will signal the end of the age.[4]

31 Heaven and earth shall disappear, but My words stand sure forever.

32 However, no one, not even the angels in heaven, nor I Myself,[5] knows the day or hour when these things will happen; only the Father knows.

33 And since you don't know when it will happen, stay alert. Be on the watch [for My return[6]].

34 My coming[7] can be compared with that of a man who went on a trip to another country. He laid out his employees' work for them to do while he was gone, and told the gatekeeper to watch for his return.

35, 36, 37 Keep a sharp lookout! For you do not know when I[6] will come, at evening, at midnight, early dawn or late daybreak. Don't let Me find you sleeping. *Watch for My return!* This is My message to you and to everyone else."

CHAPTER 14

THE Passover observance began two days later—an annual Jewish holiday when no bread made with yeast was eaten. The chief priests and other Jewish leaders were still looking for an opportunity to arrest Jesus secretly and put Him to death.

2 "But we can't do it during the Passover," they said, "or there will be a riot."

3 Meanwhile Jesus was in Bethany, at the home of Simon the leper; during supper a woman came in with a beautiful flask

---

[4]Literally, "this generation."
[5]Literally, "the Son."
[6]Implied.
[7]Literally, "the Lord of the house."

of expensive perfume. Then, breaking the seal, she poured it over His head.

4, 5   Some of those at the table were indignant among themselves about this "waste," as they called it. "Why, she could have sold that perfume for a fortune and given the money to the poor!" they snarled.

6   But Jesus said, "Let her alone; why berate her for doing a good thing?

7   You always have the poor among you, and they badly need your help, and you can aid them whenever you want to; but I won't be here much longer.

8   She has done what she could, and has anointed My body ahead of time for burial.

9   And I tell you this in solemn truth, that wherever the Good News is preached throughout the world, this woman's deed will be remembered and praised."

10   Then Judas Iscariot, one of His disciples, went to the chief priests to arrange to betray Jesus to them.

11   When the chief priests heard why he had come, they were excited and happy and promised him a reward. So he began looking for the right time and place to betray Jesus.

12   On the first day of the Passover, the day the lambs were sacrificed, His disciples asked Him where He wanted to go to eat the traditional Passover supper.

13   He sent two of them into Jerusalem to make the arrangements. "As you are walking along," He told them, "you will see a man coming towards you carrying a pot of water. Follow him.

14   At the house he enters, tell the man in charge, 'Our Master sent us to see the room you have ready for us, where we will eat the Passover supper this evening!'

15   He will take you upstairs to a large room all set up. Prepare our supper there."

16   So the two disciples went on ahead into the city and found everything as Jesus had said, and prepared the Passover.

17   In the evening Jesus arrived with the other disciples,

18   And as they were sitting around the table eating, Jesus said, "I solemnly declare that one of you will betray Me, one of you who is here eating with Me."

19   A great sadness swept over them, and one by one they asked Him, "Am I the one?"

20   He replied, "It is one of you twelve eating with Me now.

21   I[1] must die, as the prophets declared long ago; but, oh, the misery ahead for the man by whom I[1] am betrayed. Oh, that he had never been born!"

22   As they were eating, Jesus took a small loaf of bread and asked God's blessing on it and broke it in pieces and gave it to them and said, "Eat it—this is My body."

23   Then He took a cup of wine and gave thanks to God for it and gave it to them; and they all drank from it.

24   And He said to them, "This is My blood, poured out for many, sealing[2] the new agreement between God and man.

25   I solemnly declare that I shall never again taste wine until the day I drink a far better kind[3] in the Kingdom of God."

26   Then they sang a hymn and went out to the Mount of Olives.

27   "All of you will desert Me," Jesus told them, "for God has declared through the prophets, 'I will kill the Shepherd, and the sheep will scatter.'

28   But after I am raised to life again, I will go to Galilee and meet you there."

29   Peter said to Him, "I will never desert You no matter what the others do!"

30   "Peter," Jesus said, "before the cock crows a second time tomorrow morning you will deny Me three times."

31   "No!" Peter exploded. "Not even if I have to die with You! I'll *never* deny You!" And all the others vowed the same.

32   And now they came to an olive grove called the Garden

---

[1]Literally, "the Son of Man."
[2]Literally, "This is My blood of the covenant." Some ancient manuscripts read, "new covenant."
[3]Literally, "drink it new."

of Gethsemane, and He instructed His disciples, "Sit here, while I go and pray."

33   He took Peter, James and John with Him and began to be filled with horror and deepest distress.

34   And He said to them, "My soul is crushed by sorrow to the point of death; stay here and watch with Me."

35   He went on a little further and fell to the ground and prayed that if it were possible the awful hour awaiting Him might never come.[4]

36   "Father, Father," He said, "everything is possible for You. Take away this cup from Me. Yet I want Your will, not Mine."

37   Then He returned to the three disciples and found them asleep. "Simon!" He said. "Asleep? Couldn't you watch with Me even one hour?

38   Watch with Me and pray lest the Tempter overpower you. For though the spirit is willing enough, the body is weak."

39   And He went away again and prayed, repeating His pleadings.

40   Again He returned to them and found them sleeping, for they were very tired. And they didn't know what to say.

41   The third time when He returned to them He said, "Sleep on; get your rest! But no! The time for sleep has ended! Look! I[5] am betrayed into the hands of wicked men.

42   Come! Get up! We must go! Look! My betrayer is here!"

43   And immediately, while He was still speaking, Judas (one of His disciples) arrived with a mob equipped with swords and clubs, sent out by the chief priests and other Jewish leaders.

44   Judas had told them, "You will know which one to arrest when I go over and greet[6] Him. Then you can take Him easily."

45   So as soon as they arrived he walked up to Jesus. "Master!" he exclaimed, and embraced Him with a great show of friendliness.

---

[4]Literally, "that the hour might pass away from Him."
[5]Literally, "the Son of Man."
[6]Literally, "kiss"—the usual oriental greeting, even to this day.

46 Then the mob arrested Jesus and held Him fast.

47 But someone[7] pulled a sword and slashed at the high priest's servant, cutting off his ear.

48 Jesus asked them, "Am I some dangerous robber, that you come like this, armed to the teeth to capture Me?

49 Why didn't you arrest Me in the Temple? I was there teaching every day. But these things are happening to fulfill the prophecies about Me."

50 Meanwhile, all His disciples had fled.

51, 52 There was, however, a young man following along behind, clothed only in a linen nightshirt.[8] When the mob tried to grab him, he escaped, though his clothes were torn off in the process, so that he ran away completely naked.

53 Jesus was led to the High Priest's home where all of the chief priests and other Jewish leaders soon gathered.

54 Peter followed far behind and then slipped inside the gates of the High Priest's residence and crouched beside a fire among the servants.

55 Inside, the chief priests and the whole Jewish Supreme Court were trying to find something against Jesus that would be sufficient to condemn Him to death. But their efforts were in vain.

56 Many false witnesses volunteered, but they contradicted each other.

57 Finally some men stood up to lie about Him and said,

58 "We heard him say, 'I will destroy this Temple made with human hands and in three days I will build another, made without human hands!' "

59 But even then they didn't get their stories straight!

60 Then the High Priest stood up before the Court and asked Jesus, "Do you refuse to answer this charge? What do you have to say for yourself?"

61 To this Jesus made no reply. Then the High Priest asked Him, "Are you the Messiah, the Son of God?"

62 Jesus said, "I am, and you will see Me[9] sitting at the

---

[7]It was Peter. John 18:10.
[8]Implied. Literally, "wearing only a linen cloth."
[9]Literally, "the Son of Man."

right hand of God, and returning to earth in the clouds of heaven."

63, 64 Then the High Priest tore at his clothes and said, "What more do we need? Why wait for witnesses? You have heard his blasphemy. What is your verdict?" And the vote for the death sentence was unanimous.

65 Then some of them began to spit at Him, and they blindfolded Him and began to hammer His face with their fists. "Who hit you that time, you prophet?" they jeered. And even the bailiffs were using their fists on Him as they led Him away.

66, 67 Meanwhile Peter was below in the courtyard. One of the maids who worked for the High Priest noticed Peter warming himself at the fire. She looked at him closely and then announced, *"You* were with Jesus, the Nazarene."

68 Peter denied it. "I don't know what you're talking about!" he said, and walked over to the edge of the courtyard. Just then, a rooster crowed.[10]

69 The maid saw him standing there and began telling the others, "There he is! There's that disciple of Jesus!"

70 Peter denied it again. A little later others standing around the fire began saying to Peter, "You are, too, one of them, for you are from Galilee!"

71 He began to curse and swear. "I don't even know this fellow you are talking about," he said.

72 And immediately the rooster crowed the second time. Suddenly Jesus' words flashed through Peter's mind: "Before the cock crows twice, you will deny Me three times." And he began to cry.

CHAPTER 15

EARLY in the morning the chief priests, elders and teachers of religion—the entire Supreme Court—met to discuss their next steps. Their decision was to send Jesus under armed guard to Pilate, the Roman governor.[1]

---

[10]This statement is found in only some of the manuscripts.
[1]Implied.

122

2   Pilate asked Him, "Are you the King of the Jews?"

"Yes," Jesus replied, "it is as you say."

3, 4   Then the chief priests accused Him of many crimes, and Pilate asked Him, "Why don't you say something? What about all these charges against you?"

5   But Jesus said no more, much to Pilate's amazement.

6   Now, it was Pilate's custom to release one Jewish prisoner each year at Passover time—any prisoner the people requested.

7   One of the prisoners at that time was Barabbas, convicted along with others for murder during an insurrection.

8   Now a mob began to crowd in toward Pilate, asking him to release a prisoner as usual.

9   "How about giving you the 'King of Jews'?" Pilate asked. "Is he the one you want released?"

10   (For he realized by now that this was a frameup, backed by the chief priests because they envied Jesus' popularity.)

11   But at this point the chief priests whipped up the mob to demand the release of Barabbas instead of Jesus.

12   "But if I release Barabbas," Pilate asked them, "what shall I do with this man you call your king?"

13   They shouted back, "Crucify him!"

14   "But why?" Pilate demanded. "What has he done wrong?" They only roared the louder, "Crucify him!"

15   Then Pilate, afraid of a riot and anxious to please the people, released Barabbas to them. And he ordered Jesus flogged with a leaded whip, and handed Him over to be crucified.

16, 17   Then the Roman soldiers took Him into the barracks of the palace, called out the entire palace guard, dressed Him in a purple robe, and made a crown of long, sharp thorns and put it on His head.

18   Then they saluted, yelling, "Yea! King of the Jews!"

19   And they beat Him on the head with a cane, and spit on Him and went down on their knees to "worship" Him.

20   When they finally tired of their sport, they took off the

purple robe and put His own clothes on Him again, and led Him away to be crucified.

21 Simon of Cyrene, who was coming in from the country just then, was pressed into service to carry Jesus' cross. (Simon is the father of Alexander and Rufus.)

22 And they brought Jesus to a place called Golgotha. (Golgotha means skull.)

23 Wine drugged with bitter herbs was offered to Him there, but He refused it.

24 And then they crucified Him—and threw dice for His clothes.

*   *   *   *   *

25 It was about nine o'clock in the morning when the crucifixion took place.

*   *   *   *   *

26 A signboard was fastened to the cross above His head, announcing His crime. It read, "The King of the Jews."

*   *   *   *   *

27 Two robbers were also crucified that morning, their crosses on either side of His.

28[2] And so the Scripture was fulfilled that said, "He was counted among evil men."

*   *   *   *   *

29, 30 The people jeered at Him as they walked by, and wagged their heads in mockery. "Ha! Look at you now!" they yelled at Him. "Sure, you can destroy the Temple and rebuild it in three days! If you're so wonderful, save yourself and come down from the cross."

*   *   *   *   *

31 The chief priests and religious leaders were also standing around joking about Jesus. "He's quite clever at 'saving' others," they said, "but he can't save himself!"

32 "Hey there, Messiah!" they yelled at Him. "You 'King of Israel'! Come on down from the cross and we'll believe you!" And even the two robbers dying with Him, cursed Him.

*   *   *   *   *

---

[2]Verse 28 is omitted in some of the ancient manuscripts. The quotation is from Isaiah 53:12.

33   About noon, darkness fell across the entire land,[3] lasting until three o'clock that afternoon.

*   *   *   *   *

34   Then Jesus called out with a loud voice, "Eli, Eli, lama sabachthani?"[4] ("My God, My God, why have You deserted Me?")

35   Some of the people standing there thought He was calling for the prophet Elijah.

36   So one man ran and got a sponge and filled it with sour wine and held it up to Him on a stick. "Let's see if Elijah will come and take him down!" he said.

*   *   *   *   *

37   Then Jesus uttered another loud cry, and dismissed His spirit.

*   *   *   *   *

38   And the curtain[5] in the Temple was split apart from top to bottom.

*   *   *   *   *

39   When the Roman officer standing beside His cross saw how He dismissed His spirit, he exclaimed, "Truly, this was a son of God!"

*   *   *   *   *

40   Some women were there watching from a distance— Mary Magdalene, Mary (the mother of James the Younger and of Joses), Salome, and others.

41   They and many other Galilean women who were His followers had ministered to Him when He was up in Galilee, and had come with Him to Jerusalem.

*   *   *   *   *

42, 43   This all happened the day before the Sabbath. Late that afternoon Joseph from Arimathea, an honored member of the Jewish Supreme Court (who personally was eagerly expect-

---

[3]Or, "over the entire world."
[4]He spake here in Aramaic. The onlookers, who spoke Greek and Latin, misunderstood His first two words ("Eloi, Eloi") and thought He was calling for the prophet Elijah.
[5]A heavy veil hung in front of the room in the Temple called "The Holy of Holies," a place reserved by God for Himself; the veil separated Him from sinful mankind. Now this veil was split from above, showing that Christ's death, for man's sin, had opened up access to the holy God.

ing the arrival of God's Kingdom), gathered his courage and
went to Pilate and asked for Jesus' body.

44   Pilate couldn't believe that Jesus was already dead so
he called for the Roman officer in charge and asked him.

45   The officer confirmed the fact, and Pilate told Joseph
he could have the body.

46   Joseph bought a long sheet of linen cloth and, taking
Jesus' body down from the cross, wound it in the cloth and laid
it in a rock-hewn tomb, and rolled a stone in front of the
entrance.

47   (Mary Magdalene and Mary the mother of Jesus were
watching as Jesus was laid away.)

CHAPTER 16

THE next evening, when the Sabbath ended, Mary Magdalene and Salome and Mary the mother of James went
out and purchased embalming spices. Early the following morning, just at sunrise, they carried them out to the tomb.

3   On the way they were discussing how they could ever roll
aside the huge stone from the entrance.

4   But when they arrived they looked up and saw that the
stone—a *very* heavy one—was already moved away and the
entrance was open!

5   So they entered the tomb—and there on the right sat a
young man clothed in white. The women were startled,

6   But the angel said, "Don't be so surprised. Aren't you
looking for Jesus, the Nazarene who was crucified? He isn't
here! He has come back to life! Look, that's where His body
was lying.

7   Now go and give this message to His disciples including
Peter: 'Jesus is going ahead of you to Galilee. You will see Him
there, just as He told you before He died!' "

8   The women fled from the tomb, trembling and bewildered, too frightened to talk.

*   *   *   *   *

9¹ It was early on Sunday morning when Jesus came back to life, and the first person who saw Him was Mary Magdalene— the woman from whom He had cast out seven demons.

10, 11 She found the disciples wet-eyed with grief and exclaimed that she had seen Jesus, and He was alive! But they didn't believe her!

* * * * *

12 Later that day² He appeared to two men walking from Jerusalem into the country, but they didn't recognize Him at first because He had changed His appearance.

13 When they finally realized who He was, they rushed back to Jerusalem to tell the others, but no one believed them.

* * * * *

14 Still later He appeared to the eleven disciples as they were eating together. He rebuked them for their unbelief—their stubborn refusal to believe those who had seen Him alive from the dead.

15 And then He told them, "You are to go into all the world and preach the Good News to everyone, everywhere.

16 Those who believe and are baptized will be saved. But those who refuse to believe will be condemned.

17 And those who believe shall use My authority to cast out demons, and they shall speak new languages.³

18 They will be able even to handle snakes with safety, and if they drink anything poisonous, it won't hurt them; and they will be able to place their hands on the sick and heal them."

19 When the Lord Jesus had finished talking with them, He was taken up into heaven and sat down at God's right hand.

20 And the disciples went everywhere preaching, and the Lord was with them and confirmed what they said by the miracles that followed their messages.

---

¹Verses 9 through 20 are not found in the most ancient manuscripts, but may be considered an appendix giving additional facts.
²Literally, "after these things."
³Literally, "tongues." Some ancient manuscripts omit "new."

GO!
GO!
GO!

Cheerleaders in San Jose, Calif., warm up for CAMPUS LIFE's city-wide competition to select the best cheerleading squad. In the snap and sizzle, emotions soar, excitement grabs everybody—and one squad will win! Some, of course, will lose. Victory, defeat, joy, pain, birth, death—life is all of these. Jesus knew joy—and tears. He knew birth and life—and death! But after He was murdered, He rose from the dead! And that's what His life was all about. He lived so we could live —*really* live—and that's why He said we can know joy which runs so deep that no disappointment can fully squelch it. All through Luke's account of Christ's life, you'll see Him "fleshing out" this kind of living—the integrity and depth and power all of us want, so that when our successes and accomplishments disappear like smoke and all we have left is sand in our mouths, we still have what *He* had. *Life.*

ROGER KOSKELA

LUKE

CHAPTER 1

DEAR Friend who loves God:[1]

1, 2   Several biographies of Christ have already been written using as their source material the reports circulating among us from the early disciples and other eyewitnesses.

3   However, it occurred to me that it would be well to recheck all these accounts from first to last and after thorough investigation to pass this summary on to you,[2]

4   To reassure you of the truth of all you were taught.

*   *   *   *   *

5   My story begins with a Jewish priest, Zacharias, who lived when Herod was king of Judea. Zacharias was a member of the Abijah division of the Temple service corps. (His wife Elizabeth was, like himself, a member of the priest tribe of the Jews, a descendant of Aaron.)

6   Zacharias and Elizabeth were godly folk, careful to obey all of God's laws in spirit as well as in letter.

7   But they had no children, for Elizabeth was barren; and now they were both very old.

8, 9   One day as Zacharias was going about his work in the Temple—for his division was on duty that week—the honor fell to him by lot[3] to enter the inner sanctuary and burn incense before the Lord.

10   Meanwhile, a great crowd stood outside in the Temple

---

[1]From verse 3. Literally, "most excellent Theophilus." The name means "one who loves God."
[2]Literally, "an account of the things accomplished among us."
[3]Probably by throwing dice or something similar—"drawing straws" would be a modern equivalent.

court, praying as they always did during that part of the service when the incense was being burned.

11, 12   Zacharias was in the sanctuary when suddenly an angel appeared, standing to the right of the altar of incense! Zacharias was startled and terrified.

13   But the angel said, "Don't be afraid, Zacharias! For I have come to tell you that God has heard your prayer, and your wife Elizabeth will bear you a son! And you are to name him John.

14   You will both have great joy and gladness at his birth, and many will rejoice with you.

15   For he will be one of the Lord's great men. He must never touch wine or hard liquor—and he will be filled with the Holy Spirit, even from before his birth!

16   And he will persuade many a Jew to turn to the Lord his God.

17   He will be a man of rugged[4] spirit and power like Elijah, the prophet of old; and he will precede the coming of the Messiah, preparing the people for His arrival. He will teach them to love the Lord just as their ancestors did, and to live as godly men."

18   Zacharias said to the angel, "But this is impossible! I'm an old man now, and my wife is also well along in years."

19   Then the angel said, "I am Gabriel! I stand in the very presence of God. It was He who sent me to you with this good news!

20   And now, because you haven't believed me, you are to be stricken silent, unable to speak until the child is born. For my words will certainly come true at the proper time."

21   Meanwhile the crowds outside were waiting for Zacharias to appear and wondered why he was taking so long.

22   When he finally came out, he couldn't speak to them, and they realized from his gestures that he must have seen a vision in the Temple.

23   He stayed on at the Temple for the remaining days of his Temple duties and then returned home.

---

[4]Implied.

24 Soon afterwards Elizabeth his wife became pregnant and went into seclusion for five months.

25 "How kind the Lord is," she exclaimed, "to take away my disgrace of having no children!"

26 The following month God sent the angel Gabriel to Nazareth, a village in Galilee,

27 To a virgin, Mary, engaged to be married to a man named Joseph, a descendant of King David.

28 Gabriel appeared to her and said, "Congratulations, favored lady! The Lord is with you!"[5]

29 Confused and disturbed, Mary tried to think what the angel could mean.

30 "Don't be frightened, Mary," the angel told her, "for God has decided to wonderfully bless you!

31 Very soon now, you will become pregnant and have a baby boy, and you are to name Him 'Jesus.'

32 He shall be very great and shall be called the Son of God. And the Lord God shall give Him the throne of His ancestor David.

33 And He shall reign over Israel forever; His Kingdom shall never end!"

34 Mary asked the angel, "But how can I have a baby? I am a virgin."

35 The angel replied, "The Holy Spirit shall come upon you, and the power of God shall overshadow you; so the baby born to you will be utterly holy—the Son of God.

36 Furthermore, six months ago your cousin[6] Elizabeth— 'the barren one,' they called her—became pregnant in her old age!

37 For every promise from God shall surely come true."

38 Mary said, "I am the Lord's servant, and I am willing to do whatever He wants. May everything you said come true." And then the angel disappeared.

39, 40 A few days later Mary hurried to the highlands of Judea to the town where Zacharias lived, to visit Elizabeth.

---

[5]Some ancient versions add, "Blessed are you among women," as in verse 42 which appears in all the manuscripts.
[6]Literally, "relative."

41 At the sound of Mary's greeting, Elizabeth's child leaped within her and she was filled with the Holy Spirit.

42 She gave a glad cry and exclaimed to Mary, "You are favored by God above all other women, and your child is destined for God's mightiest praise.

43 What an honor this is, that the mother of my Lord should visit me!

44 When you came in and greeted me, the instant I heard your voice, my baby moved in me for joy!

45 You believed that God would do what He said; that is why He has given you this wonderful blessing."

46 Mary responded, "Oh, how I praise the Lord.

47 How I rejoice in God my Savior!

48 For He took notice of His lowly servant girl, and now generation after generation forever shall call me blest of God.

49 For He, the mighty Holy One, has done great things to me.

50 His mercy goes on from generation to generation, to all who reverence Him.

51 How powerful is His mighty arm! How He scatters the proud and haughty ones!

52 He has torn princes from their thrones and exalted the lowly.

53 He has satisfied the hungry hearts and sent the rich away with empty hands.

54 And how He has helped His servant Israel! He has not forgotten His promise to be merciful.

55 For He promised our fathers—Abraham and his children—to be merciful to them forever."

56 Mary stayed with Elizabeth about three months and then went back to her own home.

57 By now Elizabeth's waiting was over, for the time had come for the baby to be born—and it was a boy.

58 The word spread quickly to her neighbors and relatives of how kind the Lord had been to her, and everyone rejoiced.

59 When the baby was eight days old, all the relatives and

friends came for the circumcision ceremony. They all assumed the baby's name would be Zacharias, after his father.

60   But Elizabeth said, "No! He must be named John!"

61   "What?" they exclaimed. "There is no one in all your family by that name."

62   So they asked the baby's father, talking to him by gestures.[7]

63   He motioned for a piece of paper and to everyone's surprise wrote, "His name is JOHN!"

64   Instantly Zacharias could speak again, and he began praising God.

65   Wonder fell upon the whole neighborhood, and the news of what had happened spread through the Judean hills.

66   And everyone who heard about it thought long thoughts and asked, "I wonder what this child will turn out to be? For the hand of the Lord is surely upon him in some special way."

67   Then his father Zacharias was filled with the Holy Spirit and gave this prophecy:

68   "Praise the Lord, the God of Israel, for He has come to visit His people and has redeemed them.

69   He is sending us a Mighty Savior from the royal line of His servant David,

70   Just as He promised through His holy prophets long ago—

71   Someone to save us from our enemies, from all who hate us;

72, 73   He has been merciful to our ancestors, yes, to Abraham himself, by remembering His sacred promise to him,

74   And by granting us the privilege of serving God fearlessly, freed from our enemies,

75   And by making us holy and acceptable, ready to stand in His presence forever.

76   And you, my little son, shall be called the prophet of the glorious God, for you will prepare the way for the Messiah.

77   You will tell His people how to find salvation through forgiveness of their sins.

---

[7]Zacharias was apparently stone deaf as well as speechless, and had not heard what his wife had said.

132

78   All this will be because the mercy of our God is very tender, and heaven's dawn is about to break upon us,

79   To give light to those who sit in darkness and death's shadow, and to guide us to the path of peace."

80   The little boy greatly loved God and when he grew up he lived out in the lonely wilderness until he began his public ministry to Israel.

CHAPTER 2

ABOUT this time Caesar Augustus, the Roman Emperor, decreed that a census should be taken throughout the nation.[1]

2   (This census was taken when Quirinius was governor of Syria.)

3   Everyone was required to return to his ancestral home for this registration.

4   And because Joseph was a member of the royal line, he had to go to Bethlehem in Judea, King David's ancient home—journeying there from the Galilean province of Nazareth.

5   He took with him Mary, his fiancée, who was obviously pregnant by this time.

6   And while they were there, the time came for her baby to be born;

7   And she gave birth to her first child, a son. She wrapped Him in a blanket[2] and laid Him in a manger, because there was no room for them in the village inn.

8   That night some shepherds were in the fields outside the village, guarding their flocks of sheep.

9   Suddenly an angel appeared among them, and the landscape shone bright with the glory of the Lord. They were badly frightened,

10   But the angel reassured them. "Don't be afraid!" he said. "I bring you the most joyful news ever announced, and it is for everyone!

[1]Literally, "all the land."
[2]Literally, "swaddling clothes."

11   The Savior—yes, the Messiah, the Lord—has been born tonight in Bethlehem![3]

12   How will you recognize Him? You will find a baby wrapped in a blanket,[4] lying in a manger!"

13   Suddenly, the angel was joined by a vast host of others—the armies of heaven—praising God:

14   "Glory to God in the highest heaven," they sang,[5] "and peace on earth for all those pleasing Him."

15   When this great army of angels had returned again to heaven, the shepherds said to each other, "Come on! Let's go to Bethlehem! Let's see this wonderful thing that has happened, which the Lord has told us about."

16   They ran to the village and found their way to Mary and Joseph. And there was the baby, lying in the manger.

17   The shepherds told everyone what had happened and what the angel had said to them about this child.

18   All who heard the shepherds' story expressed astonishment,

19   But Mary quietly treasured these things in her heart and often thought about them.

20   Then the shepherds went back again to their fields and flocks, praising God for the visit of the angels, and because they had seen the child, just as the angel had told them.

21   Eight days later, at the baby's circumcision ceremony, He was named Jesus, the name given Him by the angel before He was even conceived.

22   When the time came for Mary's purification offering at the Temple, as required by the laws of Moses after the birth of a child, His parents took Him to Jerusalem to present Him to the Lord;

23   For in these laws God had said, "If a woman's first child is a boy, he shall be dedicated to the Lord."

24   At that time Jesus' parents also offered their sacrifice for purification—"either a pair of turtledoves or two young pigeons" was the legal requirement.

25   That day a man named Simeon, a Jerusalem resident,

---

[3]Literally, "in the City of David."
[4]Literally, "swaddling clothes."
[5]Literally, "said."

was in the Temple. He was a good man, very devout, filled with the Holy Spirit and constantly expecting the Messiah[6] to come soon.

26 For the Holy Spirit had revealed to him that he would not die until he had seen Him—God's anointed King.

27 The Holy Spirit had impelled him to go to the Temple that day; and so, when Mary and Joseph arrived to present the baby Jesus to the Lord in obedience to the law,

28 Simeon was there and took the child in his arms, praising God.

29, 30, 31 "Lord," he said, "now I can die content! For I have seen Him as You promised me I would. I have seen the Savior You have given to the world.

32 He is the Light that will shine upon the nations, and He will be the glory of Your people Israel!"

33 Joseph and Mary just stood there, marveling at what was being said about Jesus.

34, 35 Simeon blessed them but then said to Mary, "A sword shall pierce your soul, for this child shall be rejected by many in Israel, and this to their undoing. But He will be the greatest joy of many others.

And the deepest thoughts of many hearts shall be revealed."

*   *   *   *   *

36, 37 Anna, a prophetess, was also there in the Temple that day. She was the daughter of Phanuel, of the Jewish tribe of Asher, and was very old, for she had been a widow for 84 years following seven years of marriage. She never left the Temple but stayed there night and day, worshiping God by praying and often going without food.

38 She came along just as Simeon was talking with Mary and Joseph, and she also began thanking God and publicly proclaiming the Messiah's arrival to everyone in Jerusalem who had been awaiting the coming of the Savior.[7]

39 When Jesus' parents had fulfilled all the requirements of the Law of God they returned home to Nazareth in Galilee.

40 There the child became a strong, robust lad, and was

[6]Literally, "the Consolation of Israel."
[7]Literally, "looking for the redemption of Jerusalem."

known for wisdom beyond His years; and God poured out His blessings on Him.

      *   *   *   *   *

41, 42   When Jesus was 12 years old He accompanied His parents to Jerusalem for the annual Passover Festival, which they attended each year.

43   After the celebration was over they started home to Nazareth, but Jesus stayed behind in Jerusalem. His parents didn't miss Him the first day,

44   For they assumed He was with friends among the other travelers. But when He didn't show up that evening, they started to look for Him among their relatives and friends;

45   And when they couldn't find Him, they went back to Jerusalem to search for Him there.

46, 47   Three days later they finally discovered Him. He was in the Temple, sitting among the teachers of Law, discussing deep questions with them and amazing everyone with His understanding and answers.

48   His parents didn't know what to think when they saw Him sitting there so calmly.[8] "Son!" His mother said to Him, "Why have You done this to us? Your father and I have been frantic, searching for You everywhere."

49   "But why did you need to search?" He asked. "Didn't you realize that I would be here at the Temple, in My Father's House?"

50   But they didn't understand what He meant.

51   Then He returned to Nazareth with them and was obedient to them; and His mother stored away all these things in her heart.

52   So Jesus grew both tall and wise, and was loved by God and man.

CHAPTER 3

IN the fifteenth year of the reign of Emperor Tiberius Caesar, a message came from God to John (the son of

[8]Implied.

Zacharias), as he was living out in the deserts. (Pilate was governor over Judea at that time; Herod, over Galilee; his brother Philip, over Iturea and Trachonitis; Lysanias, over Abilene; and Annas and Caiaphas were the Jewish High Priests.)

3   Then John went from place to place on both sides of the Jordan River, preaching that people should be baptized to show that they had turned to God and away from their sins, in order to be forgiven.[1]

4   In the words of Isaiah the prophet, John was "a voice shouting from the barren wilderness, 'Prepare a road for the Lord to travel on! Widen the pathway before Him!

5   Level the mountains! Fill up the valleys! Straighten the curves! Smooth out the ruts!

6   And then all mankind shall see the Savior sent from God.'"

7   Here is a sample of John's preaching to the crowds that came for baptism: "You brood of snakes! You are trying to escape hell without truly turning to God! That is why you want to be baptized!

8   First go and prove by the way you live that you really have repented. And don't think you are safe because you are descendants of Abraham. That isn't enough. God can produce children of Abraham from these desert stones!

9   The axe of His judgment is poised over you, ready to sever your roots and cut you down. Yes, every tree that does not produce good fruit will be chopped down and thrown into the fire."

10   The crowd replied, "What do you want us to do?"

11   "If you have two coats," he replied, "give one to the poor. If you have extra food, give it away to those who are hungry."

12   Even tax collectors—notorious for their corruption—came to be baptized and asked, "How shall we prove to you that we have abandoned our sins?"

13   "By your honesty," he replied. "Make sure you collect no more taxes than the Roman[2] government requires you to."

---

[1]Or, "preaching the baptism of repentance for remission of sins."
[2]Implied.

14 "And us," asked some soldiers, "what about us?" John replied, "Don't extort money by threats and violence; don't accuse anyone of what you know he didn't do; and be content with your pay!"

15 Everyone was expecting the Messiah to come soon, and eager to know whether or not John was He. This was the question of the hour, and was being discussed everywhere.

16 John answered the question by saying, "I baptize only with water; but someone is coming soon who has far higher authority than mine; in fact, I am not even worthy of being His slave.[3] He will baptize you with fire—with the Holy Spirit.

17 He will separate chaff from grain, and burn up the chaff with eternal fire and store away the grain."

18 He used many such warnings as he announced the Good News to the people.

19, 20 (But after John had publicly criticized Herod, governor of Galilee, for marrying Herodias, his brother's wife, and for many other wrongs he had done, Herod put John in prison, thus adding this sin to all his many others.)

21 Then one day Jesus Himself joined the crowds being baptized by John. And after He was baptized, and was praying, the heavens opened,

22 And the Holy Spirit in the form of a dove settled upon Him, and a voice from heaven said, "You are My much loved Son, yes, My delight."

23 Jesus was about 30 years old when He began His public ministry.

> Jesus was known as the son of Joseph.
> Joseph's father was Heli;

24   Heli's father was Matthat;
> Matthat's father was Levi;
> Levi's father was Melchi;
> Melchi's father was Jannai;
> Jannai's father was Joseph;

---

[3]Literally, "of loosing (the sandal strap of) His shoe."

138

25 Joseph's father was Mattathias;
Mattathias' father was Amos;
Amos' father was Nahum;
Nahum's father was Esli;
Esli's father was Naggai;
26 Naggai's father was Maath;
Maath's father was Mattathias;
Mattathias' father was Semein;
Semein's father was Josech;
Josech's father was Joda;
27 Joda's father was Joanan;
Joanan's father was Rhesa;
Rhesa's father was Zerubbabel;
Zerubbabel's father was Shealtiel;
Shealtiel's father was Neri;
28 Neri's father was Melchi;
Melchi's father was Addi;
Addi's father was Cosam;
Cosam's father was Elmadam;
Elmadam's father was Er;
29 Er's father was Joshua;
Joshua's father was Eliezer;
Eliezer's father was Jorim;
Jorim's father was Matthat;
Matthat's father was Levi;
30 Levi's father was Simeon;
Simeon's father was Judah;
Judah's father was Joseph;
Joseph's father was Jonam;
Jonam's father was Eliakim;
31 Eliakim's father was Melea;
Melea's father was Menna;
Menna's father was Mattatha;
Mattatha's father was Nathan;
Nathan's father was David;

32 David's father was Jesse;
    Jesse's father was Obed;
    Obed's father was Boaz;
    Boaz' father was Salmon;[4]
    Salmon's father was Nahshon;
33 Nahshon's father was Amminadab;
    Amminadab's father was Admin;
    Admin's father was Arni;
    Arni's father was Hezron;
    Hezron's father was Perez;
    Perez' father was Judah;
34 Judah's father was Jacob;
    Jacob's father was Isaac;
    Isaac's father was Abraham;
    Abraham's father was Terah;
    Terah's father was Nahor;
35 Nahor's father was Serug;
    Serug's father was Reu;
    Reu's father was Peleg;
    Peleg's father was Eber;
    Eber's father was Shelah;
36 Shelah's father was Cainan;
    Cainan's father was Arphaxad;
    Arphaxad's father was Shem;
    Shem's father was Noah;
    Noah's father was Lamech;
37 Lamech's father was Methuselah;
    Methuselah's father was Enoch;
    Enoch's father was Jared;
    Jared's father was Mahalaleel;
    Mahalaleel's father was Cainan;
38 Cainan's father was Enos;
    Enos' father was Seth;
    Seth's father was Adam;
    Adam's father was God.

---

[4]"Sala."

CHAPTER 4

THEN Jesus, full of the Holy Spirit, left the Jordan River, being urged by the Spirit out into the barren wastelands of Judea, where Satan tempted Him for 40 days. He ate nothing all that time, and was very hungry.

3 Satan said, "If You are God's Son, tell this stone to become a loaf of bread."

4 But Jesus replied, "It is written in the Scriptures, 'Other things in life are much more important than bread!' "[1]

5 Then Satan took Him up and revealed to Him all the kingdoms of the world in a moment of time;

6, 7 And the Devil told Him, "I will give You all these splendid kingdoms and their glory—for they are mine to give to anyone I wish—if You will only get down on Your knees and worship me."

8 Jesus replied, "We must worship God, and Him alone. So it is written in the Scriptures."

9, 10, 11 Then Satan took Him to Jerusalem to a high roof of the Temple and said, "If You are the Son of God, jump off! For the Scriptures say that God will send His angels to guard You and to keep You from crashing to the pavement below!"

12 Jesus replied, "The Scriptures also say, 'Don't experiment with God's patience.' "[2]

13 When the Devil had ended all the temptations, he left Jesus for a while and went away.

14 Then Jesus returned to Galilee, full of the Holy Spirit's power. Soon He became well known throughout all that region

15 For His sermons in the synagogues; everyone praised Him.

16 When He came to the village of Nazareth, His boyhood home, He went as usual to the synagogue on Saturday,[3] and stood up to read the Scriptures.

17 The book of Isaiah the prophet was handed to Him, and He opened it to the place where it says:

[1]Literally, "Man shall not live by bread alone." Deuteronomy 8:3.
[2]Literally, "Do not make trial of the Lord your God."
[3]Literally, "the Sabbath day."

18, 19 "The Spirit of the Lord is upon Me; He has appointed Me to preach Good News to the poor; He has sent Me to announce that captives shall be released and the blind shall see, that the downtrodden shall be freed from their oppressors, and that God is ready to give blessings to all who come to Him."[4]

20 He closed the book and handed it back to the attendant and sat down, while everyone in the synagogue gazed at Him intently.

21 Then He added, "These Scriptures came true today!"

22 All who were there spoke well of Him and were amazed by the beautiful words that fell from His lips. "How can this be?" they asked. "Isn't this Joseph's son?"

23 Then He said, "Probably you will quote Me that proverb, 'Physician, heal yourself'—meaning, 'Why don't you do miracles here in your home town like those you did in Capernaum?'

24 But I solemnly declare to you that no prophet is accepted in his own home town!

25, 26 For example, remember how Elijah the prophet used a miracle to help the widow of Zarephath—a foreigner from the land of Sidon. There were many Jewish widows needing help in those days of famine, for there had been no rain for three and one-half years, and hunger stalked the land; yet Elijah was not sent to them.

27 Or think of the prophet Elisha, who healed Naaman, a Syrian, rather than the many Jewish lepers needing help."

28 These remarks stung them to fury;

29 And jumping up, they mobbed Him and took Him to the edge of the hill on which the city was built, to push Him over the cliff.

30 But He walked away through the crowd and left them.

31 Then He returned to Capernaum, a city in Galilee, and preached there in the synagogue every Saturday.

32 Here, too, the people were amazed at the things He said. For He spoke as one who knew the truth, instead of merely quoting the opinions of others as His authority.

---

[4]Literally, "to proclaim the acceptable year of the Lord."

142

33   Once as He was teaching in the synagogue, a man possessed by a demon began shouting at Jesus,

34   "Go away! We want nothing to do with You, Jesus from Nazareth. You have come to destroy us. I know who You are—the Holy Son of God."

35   Jesus cut him short. "Be silent!" He told the demon. "Come out!" The demon threw the man to the floor as the crowd watched, and then left him without hurting him further.

36   Amazed, the people asked, "What is in this man's words that even demons obey Him?"

37   The story of what He had done spread like wildfire throughout the whole region.

38   After leaving the synagogue that day, He went to Simon's home where He found Simon's mother-in-law very sick with a high fever. "Please heal her," everyone begged.

39   Standing at her bedside He spoke to the fever, rebuking it, and immediately her temperature returned to normal and she got up and prepared a meal[5] for them!

40   As the sun went down that evening, all the villagers who had any sick people in their homes, no matter what their diseases were, brought them to Jesus; and the touch of His hands healed every one!

41   Some were possessed by demons; and the demons came out at His command, shouting, "You are the Son of God." But because they knew He was the Christ, He stopped them and told them to be silent.

42   Early the next morning He went out into the desert. The crowds searched everywhere for Him and when they finally found Him they begged Him not to leave them, but to stay at Capernaum.

43   But He replied, "I must preach the Good News of the Kingdom of God in other places too, for that is why I was sent."

44   So He continued to travel around preaching in synagogues throughout Judea.

_____
[5]Literally, "ministered unto them."

CHAPTER 5

ONE day as He was preaching on the shore of Lake Gennesaret, great crowds pressed in on Him to listen to the Word of God.

2   He noticed two empty boats standing at the water's edge while the fishermen washed their nets.

3   Stepping into one of the boats, Jesus asked Simon, its owner, to push out a little into the water, so that He could sit in the boat and speak to the crowds from there.

4   When He had finished speaking, He said to Simon, "Now go out where it is deeper and let down your nets and you will catch a lot of fish!"

5   "Sir," Simon replied, "we worked hard all last night and didn't catch a thing. But if You say so, we'll try again."

6   And this time their nets were so full that they began to tear!

7   A shout for help brought their partners in the other boat and soon both boats were filled with fish and on the verge of sinking.

8   When Simon Peter realized what had happened, he fell to his knees before Jesus and said, "Oh, sir, please leave us—I'm too much of a sinner for You to have around."

9   For he was awestruck by the size of their catch, as were the others with him,

10   And his partners too—James and John, the sons of Zebedee.

Jesus replied, "Don't worry! From now on you'll be fishing for the souls of men!"

11   And as soon as they landed, they left everything and went with Him.

12   One day in a certain village He was visiting, there was a man with an advanced case of leprosy. When he saw Jesus he fell to the ground before Him, face downward in the dust, begging to be healed. "Sir," he said, "if You only will, You can clear me of every trace of my disease."

13 Jesus reached out and touched the man and said, "Of course I will. Be healed." And the leprosy left him instantly!

14 Then Jesus instructed him to go at once without telling anyone what had happened and be examined by the Jewish priest. "Offer the sacrifice Moses' law requires for lepers who are healed," He said. "This will prove to everyone that you are well."

15 Now the report of His power spread even faster and vast crowds came to hear Him preach and to be healed of their diseases.

16 But He often withdrew to the wilderness for prayer.

17 One day while He was teaching, some Jewish religious leaders[1] and teachers of the Law were sitting nearby. (It seemed that these men showed up from every village in all Galilee and Judea, as well as from Jerusalem.) And the Lord's healing power was upon Him.

18, 19 Then—look! Some men came carrying a paralyzed man on a sleeping mat. They tried to push through the crowd to Jesus but couldn't reach Him. So they went up on the roof above Him, took off some tiles and lowered the sick man down into the crowd, still on his sleeping mat, right in front of Jesus.

20 Seeing their faith, Jesus said to the man, "My friend, your sins are forgiven!"

21 "Who does this fellow think he is?" the Pharisees and teachers of the Law exclaimed among themselves. "This is blasphemy! Who but God can forgive sins?"

22 Jesus knew what they were thinking, and He replied, "Why is it blasphemy?

23 Is it any harder to forgive his sins than to heal him?

24 Now I will prove My[2] authority to forgive sin by demonstrating My power to heal disease." Then He said to the paralyzed man, "Get up, roll up your sleeping mat and go on home."

25 And immediately, as everyone watched, the man jumped to his feet, picked up his mat and went home praising God!

[1]Literally, "Pharisees."
[2]Literally, "the Son of Man's."

26   Everyone present was gripped with awe and fear. And they praised God, remarking over and over again, "We have seen strange things today."

27   Later on as Jesus left the town He saw a tax collector—with the usual reputation for cheating—sitting at a tax collection booth. The man's name was Levi. Jesus said to him, "Come and be one of My disciples!"

28   So Levi left everything, sprang up and went with Him!

29   Soon Levi held a reception in his home with Jesus as the guest of honor. Many of Levi's fellow tax collectors and other guests were there.

30   But the Pharisees and teachers of the Law complained bitterly to Jesus' disciples about His eating with such notorious sinners.

31   Jesus answered them, "It is the sick who need a doctor, not those in good health.

32   My purpose is to invite sinners to turn from their sins, not to spend My time with those who think themselves already good enough."

33   Their next complaint was that Jesus' disciples were feasting instead of fasting. "John the Baptist's disciples are constantly going without food, and praying," they declared, "and so do the disciples of the Pharisees. Why are yours wining and dining?"

34   Jesus asked, "Do happy men fast? Do wedding guests go hungry while celebrating with the groom?

35   But the time will come when the bridegroom will be killed;[3] then they won't want to eat."

36   Then Jesus used this illustration: "No one tears up unshrunk cloth to make patches for old clothes, for the new garment is ruined and the old one isn't helped when the patch tears out again.

37   And no one puts new wine into old wineskins, for the new wine bursts the old skins, ruining the skins and spilling the wine.

38   New wine must be put into new wineskins.

---

[3]Literally, "taken away from them."

146

39   But no one after drinking the old wine seems to want the fresh and the new. 'The old ways are best,' they say."

CHAPTER 6

O NE Sabbath as Jesus and His disciples were walking through some grainfields, they were breaking off the heads of wheat, rubbing off the husks in their hands and eating the grains.

2   But some Pharisees said, "That's illegal! Your disciples are harvesting grain, and it's against the Jewish law to work on the Sabbath."

3   Jesus replied, "Don't you read the Scriptures? Haven't you ever read what King David did when he and his men were hungry?

4   He went into the Temple and took the shewbread, the special bread that was placed before the Lord, and ate it— illegal as this was—and shared it with others."

5   And Jesus added, "I[1] am master even of the Sabbath."

6   On another Sabbath He was in the synagogue teaching, and a man was present whose right hand was deformed.

7   The teachers of the Law and the Pharisees watched closely to see whether He would heal the man that day, since it was the Sabbath. For they were eager to find some charge to bring against Him.

8   How well He knew their thoughts! But He said to the man with the deformed hand, "Come and stand here where everyone can see." So he did.

9   Then Jesus said to the Pharisees and teachers of the Law, "I have a question for you. Is it right to do good on the Sabbath day, or to do harm? To save life, or to destroy it?"

10   He looked around at them one by one and then said to the man, "Reach out your hand." And as he did, it became completely normal again!

---

[1]Literally, "the Son of Man."

11   At this, the enemies of Jesus were wild with rage, and began to plot His murder.

*   *   *   *   *

12   One day soon afterwards He went out into the mountains to pray, and prayed all night.

13   At daybreak He called together His followers and chose twelve of them to be the inner circle of His disciples. (They were appointed as His "apostles," or "missionaries.")

14, 15, 16   Here are their names:

Simon (He also called him Peter),
Andrew (Simon's brother),
James,
John,
Philip,
Bartholomew,
Matthew,
Thomas,
James (the son of Alphaeus),
Simon (also called "Zealotes"),
Judas (son of James),
Judas Iscariot (who later betrayed Him).

17, 18   When they came down from the slopes of the mountain, they stood with Jesus on a large, level area, surrounded by many of His followers who, in turn, were surrounded by the crowds. For people from all over Judea and from Jerusalem and from as far north as the seacoasts of Tyre and Sidon had come to hear Him or to be healed. And He cast out many demons.

19   Everyone was trying to touch Him, for when they did healing power went out from Him and they were cured.

20   Then He turned to His disciples and said, "What happiness there is for you who are poor, for the Kingdom of God is yours!

21   What happiness there is for you who are now hungry, for you are going to be satisfied! What happiness there is for you who weep, for the time will come when you shall laugh with joy!

22   What happiness it is when others hate you and exclude you and insult you and smear your name because you are Mine![2]

23   When that happens, rejoice! Yes, leap for joy! For you will have a great reward awaiting you in heaven. And you will be in good company—the ancient prophets were treated that way too!

24   But, oh, the sorrows that await the rich. For they have their only happiness down here.

25   They are fat and prosperous now, but a time of awful hunger is before them. Their careless laughter now means sorrow then.

26   And what sadness is ahead for those praised by the crowds—for *false* prophets have *always* been praised.

27   Listen, all of you. Love your *enemies*. Do *good* to those who *hate* you.

28   Pray for the happiness of those who *curse* you; implore God's blessing on those who *hurt* you.

29   If someone slaps you on one cheek, let him slap the other too! If someone demands your coat, give him your shirt besides.

30   Give what you have to anyone who asks you for it; and when things are taken away from you, don't worry about getting them back.

31   Treat others as you want them to treat you.

32   Do you think you deserve credit for merely loving those who love you? Even the godless do that!

33   And if you do good only to those who do you good—is that so wonderful? Even sinners do that much!

34   And if you lend money only to those who can repay you, what good is that? Even the most wicked will lend to their own kind for full return!

35   Love your *enemies!* Do good to *them!* Lend to *them!* And don't be concerned about the fact that they won't repay. Then your reward from heaven will be very great, and you will truly be acting as sons of God: for He is kind to the *unthankful* and to those who are *very wicked*.

---

[2]Literally, "the Son of Man."

36 Try to show as much compassion as your Father does.

37 Never criticize or condemn—or it will all come back on you. Go easy on others; then they will do the same for you.[3]

38 For if you give, you will get! Your gift will return to you in full and overflowing measure, pressed down, shaken together to make room for more, and running over. Whatever measure you use to give—large or small—will be used to measure what is given back to you."

39 Here are some of the story-illustrations Jesus used in His sermons: "What good is it for one blind man to lead another? He will fall into a ditch and pull the other down with him.

40 How can a student know more than his teacher? But if he works hard, he may learn as much.

41 And why quibble about the speck in someone else's eye—his little fault[4]—when a board is in your own?

42 How can you think of saying to him, 'Brother, let me help you get rid of that speck in your eye,' when you can't see past the board in yours? Hypocrite! First get rid of the board, and then perhaps you can see well enough to deal with his speck!

43 A tree from good stock doesn't produce scrub fruit nor do trees from poor stock produce choice fruit.

44 A tree is identified by the kind of fruit it produces. Figs never grow on thorns, or grapes on bramble bushes!

45 A good man produces good deeds from a good heart. And an evil man produces evil deeds from his hidden wickedness. Whatever is in the heart overflows into speech.

46 So why do you call Me 'Lord' when you won't obey Me?

47, 48 But all those who come and listen and obey Me are like a man who builds a house on a strong foundation laid upon the underlying rock. When the floodwaters rise and break against the house, it stands firm, for it is strongly built.

49 But those who listen and don't obey are like a man who

---

[3]Literally, "release, and you shall be released."
[4]Implied.

150

builds a house without a foundation. When the floods sweep down against that house, it crumbles into a heap of ruins."

CHAPTER 7

WHEN Jesus had finished His sermon He went back into the city of Capernaum.

2 Just at that time the highly prized slave of a Roman[1] army captain was sick and near death.

3 When the captain heard about Jesus, he sent some respected Jewish elders to ask Him to come and heal his slave.

4 So they began pleading earnestly with Jesus to come with them and help the man. They told Him what a wonderful person the captain was. "If anyone deserves your help, it is he," they said,

5 "For he loves the Jews and even paid personally to build us a synagogue!"

6, 7 Jesus went with them; but just before arriving at the house, the captain sent some friends to say, "Sir, don't inconvenience Yourself by coming to my home, for I am not worthy of any such honor or even to come and meet You. Just speak a word from where You are, and my servant boy will be healed!

8 I know, because I am under the authority of my superior officers, and I have authority over my men. I only need to say 'Go!' and they go; or 'Come!' and they come; and to my slave, 'Do this or that,' and he does it. [So just say, 'Be healed!' and my servant will be well again!"[2]]

9 Jesus was amazed. Turning to the crowd He said, "Never among all the Jews in Israel have I met a man with faith like this."

10 And when the captain's friends returned to his house, they found the slave completely healed!

11 Not long afterwards Jesus went with His disciples to the village of Nain, with the usual great crowd at His heels.

12 A funeral procession was coming out as He approached

---

[1]Implied
[2]This sentence implied in the previous verse.

the village gate. The boy who had died was the only son of his widowed mother, and many mourners from the village were with her.

13   When the Lord saw her, His heart overflowed with sympathy. "Don't cry!" He said.

14   Then He walked over to the coffin and touched it, and the bearers stopped. "Laddie," He said, "come back to life again."

15   Then the boy sat up and began to talk to those around him! And Jesus gave him back to his mother.

16   A great fear swept the crowd, and they exclaimed with praises to God, "A mighty prophet has risen among us," and, "We have seen the hand of God at work today."

17   The report of what He did that day raced from end to end of Judea and even out across the borders.

18   The disciples of John the Baptist soon heard of all that Jesus was doing. When they told John about it,

19   He sent two of his disciples to Jesus to ask Him, "Are You really the Messiah?[3] Or shall we keep on looking for Him?"

20, 21, 22   The two disciples found Jesus while He was curing many sick people of their various diseases—healing the lame and the blind and casting out evil spirits. When they asked Him John's question, this was His reply: "Go back to John and tell him all you have seen and heard here today: how those who were blind can see! The lame are walking without a limp! The lepers are completely healed! The deaf can hear again! The dead come back to life! And the poor are hearing the Good News!

23   And tell him, 'Blessed is the one who does not lose his faith in Me.' "[4]

24   After they left, Jesus talked to the crowd about John. "Who is this man you went out into the Judean wilderness to see?" He asked. "Did you find him weak as grass, moved by every breath of wind?

25   Did you find him dressed in expensive clothes? No!

[3]Literally, "the one who is coming."
[4]Literally, "Blessed is he who keeps from stumbling over Me."

Men who live in luxury are found in palaces, not out in the wilderness.

26 But did you find a prophet? Yes! And more than a prophet.

27 He is the one to whom the Scriptures refer when they say, 'Look! I am sending My messenger ahead of You, to prepare the way before You.'

28 In all humanity there is no one greater than John. And yet the least citizen of the Kingdom of God is greater than he."

29 And all who heard John preach—even the most wicked of them[5]—agreed that God's requirements were right, and they were baptized by him.

30 All, that is, except the Pharisees and teachers of Moses' Law. They rejected God's plan for them and refused John's baptism.

31 "What can I say about such men?" Jesus asked. "With what shall I compare them?

32 They are like a group of children who complain to their friends, 'You don't like it if we play "wedding" and you don't like it if we play "funeral" '![6]

33 For John the Baptist used to go without food and never took a drop of liquor all his life, and you said, 'He must be crazy!'[7]

34 But I eat My food and drink My wine, and you say, 'What a glutton Jesus is! And He drinks! And has the lowest sort of friends!'[8]

35 But I am sure you can always justify your inconsistencies."[9]

36 One of the Pharisees asked Jesus to come to his home for lunch and Jesus accepted the invitation. As they sat down to eat,

37 A woman of the streets—a prostitute—heard He was there and brought an exquisite flask filled with expensive perfume.

[5]Literally, "even the tax collectors"; i.e., the publicans.
[6]Literally, "We played the flute for you and you didn't dance; we sang a dirge and you didn't weep."
[7]Literally, "He has a demon."
[8]Literally, "is a friend of tax gatherers and sinners."
[9]Literally, "but wisdom is justified of all her children."

38 Going in, she knelt behind Him at His feet, weeping, until His feet were wet with her tears; and she wiped them off with her hair and kissed them and poured the perfume on them.

39 When Jesus' host, a Pharisee, saw what was happening and who the woman was, he said to himself, "This proves that Jesus is no prophet, for if God had really sent him, he would know what kind of woman this one is!"

40 Then Jesus spoke up and answered his thoughts. "Simon," He said to the Pharisee, "I have something to say to you."

"All right, Teacher," Simon replied, "go ahead."

41 Then Jesus told him this story: "A man loaned money to two people—$5,000 to one and $500 to the other.

42 But neither of them could pay him back, so he kindly forgave them both, letting them keep the money! Which do you suppose loved him most after that?"

43 "I suppose the one who had owed him the most," Simon answered. "Correct," Jesus agreed.

44 Then He turned to the woman and said to Simon, "Look! See this woman kneeling here! When I entered your home, you didn't bother to offer Me water to wash the dust from my feet, but she has washed them with her tears and wiped them with her hair!

45 You refused Me the customary kiss of greeting, but she has kissed My feet again and again from the time I first came in.

46 You neglected the usual courtesy of olive oil to anoint My head, but she has covered My feet with rare perfume.

47 Therefore her sins—and they are many—are forgiven, for she loved Me much; but one who is forgiven little, shows little love."

48 And He said to her, "Your sins are forgiven."

49 Then the men at the table said to themselves, "Who does this man think He is, going around forgiving sins?"

50 And Jesus said to the woman, "Your faith has saved you; go in peace."

CHAPTER 8

NOT long afterwards He began a tour of the cities and villages of Galilee[1] to announce the coming of the Kingdom of God, and took His twelve disciples with Him.

2 Some women went along, from whom He had cast out demons or whom He had healed; among them were Mary Magdalene (Jesus had cast out seven demons from her),

3 Joanna, Chuza's wife (Chuza was King Herod's business manager and was in charge of his palace and domestic affairs), Susanna, and many others who were contributing from their private means to the support of Jesus and His disciples.

4 One day He gave this illustration to a large crowd that was gathering to hear Him—while many others were still on the way, coming from other towns.

5 "A farmer went out to his field to sow grain. As he scattered the seed on the ground, some of it fell on a footpath and was trampled on; and the birds came and ate it as it lay exposed.

6 Other seed fell on shallow soil with rock beneath. This seed began to grow, but soon withered and died for lack of moisture.

7 Other seed landed in thistle patches, and the young grain stalks were soon choked out.

8 Still other fell on fertile soil; this seed grew and produced a crop 100 times as large as he had planted." (As He was giving this illustration He said, "If anyone has listening ears, use them now!")

9 His apostles asked Him what the story meant.

10 He replied, "God has granted you to know the meaning of these parables, for they tell a great deal about the Kingdom of God. But these crowds hear the words and do not understand, just as the ancient prophets predicted.

11 This is its meaning: The seed is God's message to men.

[1]Implied.

12   The hard path where some seed fell represents the hard hearts of those who hear the words of God, but then the devil comes and steals the words away and prevents people from believing and being saved.

13   The stony ground represents those who enjoy listening to sermons, but somehow the message never really gets through to them and doesn't take root and grow. They know the message is true, and sort of believe for awhile; but when the hot winds of persecution blow, they lose interest.

14   The seed among the thorns represents those who listen and believe God's words but whose faith afterwards is choked out by worry and riches and the responsibilities and pleasures of life. And so they are never able to help anyone else to believe the Good News.

15   But the good soil represents honest, good-hearted people. They listen to God's words and cling to them and steadily spread them to others who also soon believe."

*   *   *   *   *

16   [Another time He asked,[2]] "Who ever heard of someone lighting a lamp and then covering it up to keep it from shining? No, lamps are mounted in the open where they can be seen.

17   This illustrates the fact that someday everything [in men's hearts[2]] shall be brought to light and made plain to all.

18   So be careful how you listen; for whoever has, to him shall be given more; and whoever does not have, even what he thinks he has shall be taken away from him."

*   *   *   *   *

19   Once when His mother and brothers came to see Him, they couldn't get into the house where He was teaching, because of the crowds.

20   When Jesus heard they were standing outside and wanted to see Him,

21   He remarked, "My mother and My brothers are all those who hear the message of God and obey it."

*   *   *   *   *

[2]Implied. See Matthew 5:16.

22   One day about that time, as He and His disciples were
out in a boat, He suggested that they cross to the other side of
the lake.

23   On the way across He lay down for a nap, and while He
was sleeping the wind began to rise. A fierce storm developed
that threatened to swamp them, and they were in real danger.

24   They rushed over and woke Him up. "Master, Master,
we are sinking!" they screamed. So He spoke to the storm:
"Quiet down," He said, and the wind and waves subsided and
all was calm!

25   Then He asked them, "Where is your faith?" And they
were filled with awe and fear of Him and said to one another,
"Who is this man, that even the winds and waves obey Him?"

26   So they arrived at the other side, in the Gerasene country across the lake from Galilee.

27   As He was climbing out of the boat a man from the city
of Gadara came to meet Him, a man who had been demon-
possessed for a long time. Homeless and naked, he lived in a
cemetery among the tombs.

28   As soon as he saw Jesus he shrieked and fell to the
ground before Him, screaming, "What do You want with me,
Jesus, Son of God Most High? Please, I beg You, oh, don't
torment me!"

29   For Jesus was already commanding the demon to leave
him. This demon had often taken control of the man so that
even when shackled with chains he simply broke them and
rushed out into the desert, completely under the demon's
power.

30   "What is your name?" Jesus asked the demon.
"Legion," they replied—for the man was filled with thousands[3]
of them!

31   They kept begging Him not to order them into the
Bottomless Pit.

32   A herd of pigs was feeding on the mountainside nearby,
and the demons pled with Him to let them enter into the pigs.
And Jesus said they could.

---

[3]Implied; a legion consisted of 6,000 troops. Whether the demons were speaking
literally is, of course, unknown.

33 So they left the man and went into the pigs, and immediately the whole herd rushed down the mountainside and fell over a cliff into the lake below, where they drowned.

34 The herdsmen rushed away to the nearby city, spreading the news as they ran.

35 Soon a crowd came out to see for themselves what had happened and saw the man who had been demon-possessed sitting quietly at Jesus' feet, clothed and sane! And the whole crowd was badly frightened.

36 Then those who had seen it happen told how the demon-possessed man had been healed.

37 And everyone begged Jesus to go away and leave them alone (for a deep wave of fear had swept over them). So He returned to the boat and left, crossing back to the other side of the lake.

38 The man who had been demon-possessed begged to go too, but Jesus said no.

39 "Go back to your family," He told him, "and tell them what a wonderful thing God has done for you." So he went all through the city telling everyone about Jesus' mighty miracle.

40 On the other side of the lake the crowds received Him with open arms, for they had been waiting for Him.

41 And now a man named Jairus, a leader of a Jewish synagogue, came and fell down at Jesus' feet and begged Him to come home with him,

42 For his only child was dying, a little girl twelve years old. Jesus went with him, pushing through the crowds.

43, 44 As they went a woman who wanted to be healed came up behind and touched Him, for she had been slowly bleeding for twelve years, and could find no cure (though she had spent everything she had on doctors[4]). But the instant she touched the edge of His robe, the bleeding stopped.

45 "Who touched Me?" Jesus asked.

Everyone denied it, and Peter said, "Master, so many are crowding against You . . . ."

46 But Jesus told him, "No, it was someone who deliber-

---

[4]This clause is not included in some of the ancient manuscripts.

ately touched Me, for I felt healing power go out from Me."

47   When the woman realized that Jesus knew, she began to tremble and fell to her knees before Him and told why she had touched Him and that now she was well.

48   "Daughter," He said to her, "your faith has healed you. Go in peace."

49   While He was still speaking to her, a messenger arrived from the Jairus' home with the news that the little girl was dead. "She's gone," he told her father; "there's no use troubling the Teacher now."

50   But when Jesus heard what had happened, He said to the father, "Don't be afraid! Just trust Me, and she'll be all right."

51   When they arrived at the house Jesus wouldn't let anyone into the room except Peter, James, John, and the little girl's father and mother.

52   The home was filled with mourning people, but He said, "Stop the weeping! She isn't dead; she is only asleep!"

53   This brought scoffing and laughter, for they all knew she was dead.

54   Then He took her by the hand and called, "Get up, little girl!"

55   And at that moment her life returned and she jumped up! "Give her something to eat!" He said.

56   Her parents were overcome with happiness, but Jesus insisted that they not tell anyone the details of what had happened.

CHAPTER 9

ONE day Jesus called together His twelve apostles and gave them authority over all demons—power to cast them out —and to heal all diseases.

2   Then He sent them away to tell everyone about the coming of the Kingdom of God and to heal the sick.

3   "Don't even take along a walking stick," He instructed

them, "nor a beggar's bag, nor food, nor money. Not even an extra coat.

4   Be a guest in only one home at each village.

5   If the people of a town won't listen to you when you enter it, turn around and leave, demonstrating God's anger against it by shaking its dust from your feet as you go."[1]

6   So they began their circuit of the villages, preaching the Good News and healing the sick.

7   When reports of Jesus' miracles reached Herod,[2] the governor, he was worried and puzzled, for some were saying, "This is John the Baptist come back to life again";

8   And others, "It is Elijah or some other ancient prophet risen from the dead." These rumors were circulating all over the land.

9   "I beheaded John," Herod said, "so who is this man about whom I hear such strange stories?" And he tried to see Him.

10   After the apostles returned to Jesus and reported what they had done, He slipped quietly away with them to the city of Bethsaida.

11   But the crowds found out where He was going, and followed. And He welcomed them, teaching them again about the Kingdom of God and curing those who were ill.

12   Late in the afternoon all twelve of the disciples came and urged Him to send the people away to the nearby villages and farms, to find food and lodging for the night. "For there is nothing to eat here in this deserted spot," they said.

13   But Jesus replied, "*You* feed them!"

"Why, we have only five loaves of bread and two fish among the lot of us," they protested; "or are You expecting us to go and buy enough for this whole mob?"

14   For there were about 5,000 men there! "Just tell them to sit down on the ground in groups of about fifty each," Jesus replied.

15   So they did.

16   Jesus took the five loaves and two fish and looked up

[1]Literally, "as a testimony against them."
[2]Literally, "Herod the Tetrarch."

into the sky and gave thanks; then he broke off pieces for His disciples to set before the crowd.

17 And everyone ate and ate; still, twelve basketfuls of scraps were picked up afterwards!

* * * * *

18 One day as He was alone, praying, with His disciples nearby, He came over and asked them, "Who are the people saying I am?"

19 "John the Baptist," they told Him, "or perhaps Elijah or one of the other ancient prophets risen from the dead."

20 Then He asked them, "Who do you think I am?"

Peter replied, "The Messiah—the Christ of God!"

21 He gave them strict orders not to speak of this to anyone.

22 "For I[3] must suffer much," He said, "and be rejected by the Jewish leaders—the elders, chief priests, and teachers of the Law—and be killed; and three days later I will come back to life again!"

23 Then He said to all, "Anyone who wants to follow Me must put aside his own desires and conveniences and carry his cross with him every day and *keep close to Me!*

24 Whoever loses his life for My sake will save it, but whoever insists on keeping his life will lose it;

25 And what profit is there in gaining the whole world when it means forfeiting one's self?

26 When I, the Man of Glory,[4] come in My glory and in the glory of the Father and the holy angels, I will be ashamed then of all who are ashamed of Me and of My words now.

27 But this is the simple truth—some of you who are standing here right now will not die until you have seen the Kingdom of God!"

28 Eight days later He took Peter, James, and John with Him into the hills to pray.

29 And as He was praying, His face began to shine,[5] and His clothes became dazzling white and blazed with light.

---

[3]Literally, "the Son of Man," a term filled with exalted meanings as well as describing His perfect humanity.
[4]Literally, "the Son of Man."
[5]Literally, "the appearance of His face changed."

30   Then two men appeared and began talking with Him—Moses and Elijah!

31   They were splendid in appearance, glorious to see; and they were speaking of His death at Jerusalem, to be carried out in accordance with God's plan.

32   Peter and the others had been very drowsy and had fallen asleep. Now they woke up and saw Jesus covered with brightness and glory, and the two men standing with Him.

33   As Moses and Elijah were starting to leave, Peter, all confused and not even knowing what he was saying, blurted out, "Master, this is wonderful! We'll put up three shelters—one for You and one for Moses and one for Elijah!"

34   But even as he was saying this, a bright[6] cloud formed above them; and terror gripped them as it covered them.

35   And a voice from the cloud said, *"This* is My Son, My Chosen One; listen to *Him."*

36   Then, as the voice died away, Jesus was there alone with His disciples. They didn't tell anyone what they had seen until long afterwards.

37   The next day as they descended from the hill, a huge crowd met Him,

38   And a man in the crowd called out to Him, "Teacher, this boy here is my only son,

39   And a demon keeps seizing him, making him scream; and it throws him into convulsions so that he foams at the mouth; it is always hitting him and hardly ever leaves him alone.

40   I begged Your disciples to cast the demon out, but they couldn't."

41   "O you stubborn faithless people," Jesus said [to His disciples[6]], "How long should I put up with you? Bring him here."

42   As the boy was coming the demon knocked him to the ground and threw him into a violent convulsion. But Jesus ordered the demon to come out, and healed the boy and handed him over to his father.

---

[6]Implied.

43   Awe gripped the people as they saw this display of the power of God. Meanwhile, as they were exclaiming over all the wonderful things He was doing, Jesus said to His disciples,

44   "Listen to Me and remember what I say. I, the Son of Mankind, am going to be betrayed."

45   But the disciples didn't know what He meant, for their minds had been sealed and they were afraid to ask Him.

46   Now came an argument among them as to which of them would be greatest [in the coming Kingdom[7]]!

47   But Jesus knew their thoughts, so He stood a little child beside Him

48   And said to them, "Anyone who takes care of a little child like this is caring for Me! And whoever cares for Me is caring for God who sent Me. Your care for others is the measure of your greatness."

49   His disciple John came to Him and said, "Master, we saw someone using Your name to cast out demons. And we told him not to. After all, he isn't in our group."

50   But Jesus said, "You shouldn't have done that! For anyone who is not against you is for you."

51   As the time drew near for His return to heaven, He moved steadily onward towards Jerusalem with an iron will.

52   One day He sent messengers ahead to reserve rooms for them in a Samaritan village.

53   But they were turned away! The people of the village refused to have anything to do with them because they were headed for Jerusalem.[8]

54   When word came back of what had happened, James and John said to Jesus, "Master, shall we order fire down from heaven to burn them up?"

55   But Jesus turned and rebuked them,[9].

56   And they went on to another village.

57   As they were walking along someone said to Jesus, "I will always follow You no matter where You go."

---

[7]Implied.

[8]A typical case of discrimination. (cf. John 4:9). The Jews called the Samaritans "half-breeds," so the Samaritans naturally hated the Jews.

[9]Later manuscripts add to verses 55 and 56, "And Jesus said, You don't realize what your hearts are like. For the Son of Man has not come to destroy men's lives, but to save them."

58 But Jesus replied, "Remember, I don't even own a place to lay My head. Foxes have dens to live in, and birds have nests, but I, the Man from Heaven,[10] have no earthly home at all."

59 Another time, when He invited a man to come with Him and to be His disciple, the man agreed—but wanted to wait until his father's death.[11]

60 Jesus replied, "Let those without eternal life concern themselves with things like that.[12] Your duty is to come and preach the coming of the Kingdom of God to all the world."

61 Another said, "Yes, Lord, I will come, but first let me ask permission of those at home."[13]

62 But Jesus told him, "Anyone who lets himself be distracted from the work I plan for him is not fit for the Kingdom of God."

CHAPTER 10

THE Lord now chose 70 other disciples and sent them on ahead in pairs to all the towns and villages He planned to visit later.

2 These were His instructions to them: "Plead with the Lord of the harvest to send out more laborers to help you, for the harvest is so plentiful and the workers so few.

3 Go now, and remember that I am sending you out as lambs among wolves.

4 Don't take any money with you, or a beggar's bag, or even an extra pair of shoes. And don't waste time along the way.[1]

5 Whenever you enter a home, give it your blessing.

6 If it is worthy of the blessing, the blessing will stand; if not, the blessing will return to you.

[10]Literally, "the Son of Man."
[11]Literally, "But he said, 'Lord, suffer me first to go and bury my father,"—perhaps meaning that the man could, when his father died, collect the inheritance and have some security.
[12]Literally, "let the dead bury their dead."
[13]Literally, "bid them farewell at home."
[1]Literally, "Salute no one in the way."

7 When you enter a village, don't shift around from home to home, but stay in one place, eating and drinking without question whatever is set before you. And don't hesitate to accept hospitality, for the workman is worthy of his wages!

8, 9 If a town welcomes you, follow these two rules:
    (1) Eat whatever is set before you.
    (2) Heal the sick; and as you heal them, say, 'The Kingdom of God is very near you now.'

10 But if a town refuses you, go out into its streets and say,

11 'We wipe the dust of your town from our feet as a public announcement of your doom. Never forget how close you were to the Kingdom of God!'

12 Even wicked Sodom will be better off than such a city on the Judgment Day.

13 What horrors await you, you cities of Chorazin and Bethsaida! For if the miracles I did for you had been done in the cities of Tyre and Sidon,[2] their people would have sat in deep repentance long ago, clothed in sackcloth and throwing ashes on their heads to show their remorse.

14 Yes, Tyre and Sidon will receive less punishment on the Judgment Day than you.

15 And you people of Capernaum, what shall I say about you? Will you be exalted to heaven? No, you shall be brought down to hell."

16 Then He said to the disciples, "Those who welcome you are welcoming Me. And those who reject you are rejecting Me. And those who reject Me are rejecting God who sent Me."

17 When the 70 disciples returned, they joyfully reported to Him, "Even the demons obey us when we use Your name."

18 "Yes," He told them, "I saw Satan falling from heaven as a flash of lightning!

19 And I have given you authority over all the power of the Enemy, and to walk among serpents and scorpions and to crush them! Nothing shall injure you!

20 However, the important thing is not that demons obey

---

[2]Cities destroyed by God in judgment for their wickedness. For a description of this event, see Ezekiel, chapters 26-28.

you, but that your names are registered as citizens of heaven."

21   Then He was filled with the joy of the Holy Spirit and said, "I praise You, O Father, Lord of heaven and earth, for hiding these things from the intellectuals and worldly wise and for revealing them to those who are as trusting as little children.[3] Yes, thank You, Father, for that is the way You wanted it.

22   I am the Agent of My Father in everything; and no one really knows the Son except the Father, and no one really knows the Father except the Son and those to whom the Son chooses to reveal Him."

23   Then, turning to the twelve disciples, He said quietly, "How privileged you are to see what you have seen.

24   Many a prophet and king of old has longed for these days, to see and hear what you have seen and heard!"

25   One day an expert on Moses' laws came to test Jesus' orthodoxy by asking Him this question: "Teacher, what does a man need to do to live forever in heaven?"

26   Jesus replied, "What does Moses' law say about it?"

27   "It says," he replied, "that you must love the Lord your God with all your heart, and with all your soul, and with all your strength, and with all your mind. And you must love your neighbor just as much as you love yourself."

28   "Right!" Jesus told him. "*Do* this and *you* shall live!"

29   The man wanted to justify (his lack of love for some kinds of people),[4] so he asked, "Which neighbors?"

30   Jesus replied with an illustration: "A Jew going on a trip from Jerusalem to Jericho was attacked by bandits. They stripped him of his clothes and money and beat him up and left him lying half dead beside the road.

31   By chance a Jewish priest came along; and when he saw the man lying there, he crossed to the other side of the road and passed him by.

---

[3]Literally, "babies."
[4]Literally, "wanting to justify himself."

32   A Jewish Temple-assistant[5] did the same thing; he, too, left him lying there.

33   But a despised Samaritan[6] came along, and when he saw him, he felt deep pity.

34   Kneeling beside him the Samaritan soothed his wounds with medicine and bandaged them. Then he put the man on his donkey and walked along beside him till they came to an inn, where he nursed him through the night.

35   The next day he handed the innkeeper two twenty-dollar bills[7] and told him to take care of the man. 'If his bill runs higher than that,' he said, 'I'll pay the difference the next time I am here.'

36   Now which of these three would you say was a neighbor to the bandits' victim?"

37   The man replied, "The one who showed him some pity."

Then Jesus said, "Yes, now go and do the same."

38   As Jesus and the disciples continued on their way to Jerusalem[8] they came to a village where a woman named Martha welcomed them into her home.

39   Her sister Mary sat on the floor, listening to Jesus as He talked.

40   But Martha was the jittery type, and was worrying over the big dinner she was preparing. She came to Jesus and said, "Sir, doesn't it seem unfair to You that my sister just sits here while I do all the work? Tell her to come and help me."

41   But the Lord said to her, "Martha, dear friend,[9] you are so upset over all these details!

42   There is really only one thing worth being concerned about. Mary has discovered it—and I won't take it away from her!"

---

[5]Literally, "Levite."
[6]Literally, "a Samaritan." All Samaritans were despised by Jews, and the feeling was mutual, due to historic reasons.
[7]Literally, "two denarii," each the equivalent of a modern day's wage.
[8]Implied.
[9]Literally, "Martha, Martha."

CHAPTER 11

ONCE when Jesus had been out praying, one of His disciples came to Him as He finished and said, "Lord, teach us a prayer to recite[1] just as John taught one to his disciples."

2 And this is the prayer He taught them: "Father, may Your name be honored for its holiness; send Your Kingdom soon.

3 Give us our food day by day.

4 And forgive our sins—for we have forgiven those who sinned against us. And don't allow us to be tempted."

5, 6 Then, teaching them more about prayer,[2] He used this illustration: "Suppose you went to a friend's house at midnight, wanting to borrow three loaves of bread. You would shout up to him, 'A friend of mine has just arrived for a visit and I've nothing to give him to eat.'

7 He would call down from his bedroom, 'Please don't ask me to get up. The door is locked for the night and we are all in bed. I just can't help you this time.'

8 But I'll tell you this—though he won't do it as a friend, if you keep knocking long enough he will get up and give you everything you want—just because of your persistence.

9 And so it is with prayer—keep on asking and you will keep on getting; keep on looking and you will keep on finding; knock and the door will be opened.

10 Everyone who asks, receives; all who seek, find; and the door is opened to everyone who knocks.

11 You men who are fathers—if your boy asks for bread, do you give him a stone? If he asks for fish, do you give him a snake?

12 If he asks for an egg, do you give him a scorpion? [Of course not![3]]

---

[1]Implied.
[2]Some ancient manuscripts add at this point additional portions of the Lord's Prayer as recorded in Matthew 6:9-13.
[3]Implied.

13   And if even sinful persons like yourselves give children what they need, don't you realize that your heavenly Father will do at least as much, and give the Holy Spirit to those who ask for Him?"

14   Once, when Jesus cast out a demon from a man who couldn't speak, his voice returned to him. The crowd was excited and enthusiastic,

15   But some said, "No wonder he can cast them out. He gets his power from Satan,[4] the king of demons!"

16   Others asked for something to happen in the sky to prove His claim of being the Messiah.[5]

17   He knew the thoughts of each of them, so He said, "Any kingdom filled with civil war is doomed; so is a home filled with argument and strife.

18   Therefore, if what you say is true, that Satan is fighting against himself by empowering Me to cast out his demons, how can his kingdom survive?

19   And if I am empowered by Satan, what about your own followers? For they cast out demons! Do you think this proves they are possessed by Satan? Ask *them* if you are right!

20   But if I am casting out demons because of power from God, it proves that the Kingdom of God has arrived.

21   For when Satan,[6] strong and fully armed, guards his palace, it is safe—

22   Until someone stronger and better-armed attacks and overcomes him and strips him of his weapons and carries off his belongings.

23   Anyone who is not for Me is against Me; if he isn't helping Me, he is hurting My cause.

24   When a demon is cast out of a man, it goes to the deserts, searching there for rest; but finding none, it returns to the person it left,

25   And finds that its former home is all swept and clean.[7]

26   Then it goes and gets seven other demons more evil than

---

[4]Literally, "from Beelzebub."
[5]Implied; literally, "Others, tempting, sought of Him a sign from heaven."
[6]Literally, "the Strong."
[7]But empty, since the person is neutral about Christ.

169

itself, and they all enter the man. And so the poor fellow is seven times[8] worse off than he was before."

27   As He was speaking, a woman in the crowd called out, "God bless Your mother—the womb from which You came, and the breasts that gave You suck!"

28   He replied, "Yes, but even more blessed are all who hear the Word of God and put it into practice."

29, 30   As the crowd pressed in upon Him, He preached them this sermon: "These are evil times, with evil people. They keep asking for some strange happening in the skies [to prove I am the Messiah[8]], but the only proof I will give them is a miracle like that of Jonah, whose experiences proved to the people of Nineveh that God had sent him. My similar experience will prove that God has sent Me to these people.

31   And at the Judgment Day the Queen of Sheba[9] shall arise and point her finger at this generation, condemning it, for she went on a long, hard journey to listen to the wisdom of Solomon; but one far greater than Solomon is here [and few pay any attention[10]].

32   The men of Nineveh, too, shall arise and condemn this nation, for they repented at the preaching of Jonah; and someone far greater than Jonah is here [but this nation won't listen[10]].

*   *   *   *   *

33   No one lights a lamp and hides it! Instead, he puts it on a lampstand to give light to all who enter the room.

34   Your eyes light up your inward being.

A pure eye lets sunshine into your soul. A lustful eye shuts out the light and plunges you into darkness.

35   So watch out that the sunshine isn't blotted out.

36   If you are filled with light within, with no dark corners, then the outside will be radiant too, as though a floodlight is beamed upon you."

37, 38   As He was speaking, one of the Pharisees asked Him home for a meal. When Jesus arrived, He sat down to eat

[8]Implied.
[9]Literally, "Queen of the South." See 1 Kings, Chapter 10.
[10]Implied.

without first performing the ceremonial washing required by Jewish custom. This greatly surprised His host.

39 Then Jesus said to him, "You Pharisees wash the outside, but inside you are still dirty—full of greed and wickedness!

40 Fools! Didn't God make the inside as well as the outside?

41 Purity is best demonstrated by generosity!

42 But woe to you Pharisees! For though you are careful to tithe even the smallest part of your income, you completely forget about justice and the love of God. You should tithe, yes, but you should not leave these other things undone.

43 Woe to you Pharisees! For how you love the seats of honor in the synagogues and the respectful greetings from everyone as you walk through the markets!

44 Yes, awesome judgment is awaiting you. For you are like hidden graves in a field. Men go by you with no knowledge of the corruption they are passing."

45 "Sir," said an expert in religious law who was standing there, "You have insulted my profession, too, in what you just said."

46 "Yes," said Jesus, "the same horrors await you! For you crush men beneath impossible religious demands—demands that you yourselves would never think of trying to keep.

47 Woe to you! For you are exactly like your ancestors who killed the prophets long ago.

48 Murderers! You agree with your fathers that what they did was right—you would have done the same yourselves.

49 This is what God says about you: 'I will send prophets and apostles to you, and you will kill some of them and chase away the others.'

50 And you of this generation will be held responsible for the murder of God's servants from the founding of the world—

51 From the murder of Abel to the murder of Zechariah who perished between the altar and the sanctuary. Yes, it will surely be charged against you.

52 Woe to you experts in religion! For you hide the truth

from the people. You won't accept it for yourselves, and you prevent others from having a chance to believe it."

53, 54   The Pharisees and legal experts were furious; and from that time on they plied Him fiercely with a host of questions, trying to trap Him into saying something for which they could have Him arrested.

CHAPTER 12

MEANWHILE the crowds grew until thousands upon thousands were milling about and crushing each other. He turned now to His disciples and warned them, "More than anything else, beware of these Pharisees and the way they pretend to be good when they aren't. But such hypocrisy cannot be hidden forever.

2   It will become as evident as yeast in dough.

3   Whatever they[1] have said in the dark shall be heard in the light, and what you have whispered in the inner rooms shall be broadcast from the housetops for all to hear!

4   Dear friends, don't be afraid of these who want to murder you. They can only kill the body; they have no power over your souls.

5   But I'll tell you whom to fear—fear God who has the power to kill and then cast into hell.

6   What is the price of five sparrows? A couple of pennies? Not much more than that. Yet God does not forget a single one of them.

7   And He knows the number of hairs on your head! Never fear, you are far more valuable to Him than a whole flock of sparrows.

8   And I assure you of this: I, the Man from Heaven,[2] will publicly honor you in the presence of God's angels if you publicly acknowledge Me here on earth as your Friend.

9   But I will deny before the angels those who deny Me here among men.

[1]Literally, "you."
[2]Literally, "the Son of Man."

10   (Yet those who speak against Me³ may be forgiven—while those who speak against the Holy Spirit shall never be forgiven.)

11   And when you are brought to trial before these Jewish rulers and authorities in the synagogues, don't be concerned about what to say in your defense,

12   For the Holy Spirit will give you the right words even as you are standing there."

13   Then someone called from the crowd, "Sir, please tell my brother to divide my father's estate with me."

14   But Jesus replied, "Man, who made Me a judge over you to decide such things as that?

15   Beware! Don't always be wishing for what you don't have."

16   Then He gave an illustration: "A rich man had a fertile farm that produced fine crops.

17   In fact, his barns were full to overflowing—he couldn't get everything in. He thought about his problem,

18   And finally exclaimed, 'I know—I'll tear down my barns and build bigger ones! Then I'll have room enough.

19   And I'll sit back and say to myself, "Friend, you have enough stored away for years to come. Now take it easy! Wine, women, and song for you!" '⁴

20   But God said to him, 'Fool! Tonight you die. Then who will get it all?'

21   Yes, every man is a fool who gets rich on earth but not in heaven."

22   Then turning to His disciples He said, "Don't worry about whether you have enough food to eat or clothes to wear.

23   For life consists of far more than food and clothes.

24   Look at the ravens—they don't plant or harvest or have barns to store away their food, and yet they get along all right—for God feeds them. And you are far more valuable to Him than any birds!

25   And besides, what's the use of worrying? What good does it do? Will it add a single day to your life? Of course not!

³Literally, "the Son of Man."
⁴Literally, "Eat, drink, and be merry."

26   And if worry can't even do such little things as that, what's the use of worrying over bigger things?

27   Look at the lilies! They don't toil and spin, and yet Solomon in all his glory was not robed as well as they are.

28   And if God provides clothing for the flowers that are here today and gone tomorrow, don't you suppose that He will provide clothing for you, you doubters?

29   And don't worry about food—what to eat and drink; don't worry at all that God will provide it for you.

30   All mankind scratches for its daily bread, but your heavenly Father knows your needs.

31   He will always give you all you need from day to day if you will make the Kingdom of God your primary concern.

32   So don't be afraid, little flock. For it gives your Father great happiness to give you the Kingdom.

33   Sell what you have and give to those in need. This will fatten your purses in heaven! And the purses of heaven have no rips or holes in them. Your treasures there will never disappear; no thief can steal them; no moth can destroy them.

34   Wherever your treasure is, there your heart and thoughts will also be.

35   Be prepared—all dressed and ready—

36   For your Lord's return from the wedding feast. Then you will be ready to open the door and let Him in the moment He arrives and knocks.

37   There will be great joy for those who are ready and waiting for His return. He Himself will seat them and put on a waiter's uniform and serve them as they sit and eat!

38   He may come at nine o'clock at night—or even at midnight. But whenever He comes there will be joy for His servants who are ready!

39   Everyone would be ready for Him if they knew the exact hour of His return—just as they would be ready for a thief if they knew when he was coming.

40   So be ready all the time. For I, the Man of Glory,[5] will come when least expected."

---

[5]Literally, "the Son of Man."

41   Peter asked, "Lord, are You talking just to us or to everyone?"

42, 43, 44   And the Lord replied, "I'm talking to any faithful, sensible man whose master gives him the responsibility of feeding the other servants. If his master returns and finds that he has done a good job, there will be a reward—his master will put him in charge of all he owns.

45   But if the man begins to think, 'My Lord won't be back for a long time,' and begins to whip the men and women he is supposed to protect, and to spend his time at drinking parties and in drunkenness—

46   Well, his master will return without notice and remove him from his position of trust and assign him to the place of the unfaithful.

47   He will be severely punished, for though he knew his duty he refused to do it.

48   But anyone who is not aware that he is doing wrong will be punished only lightly. Much is required from those to whom much is given, for their responsibility is greater.

49   I have come to bring fire to the earth, and, oh, that My task were completed!

50   There is a terrible baptism ahead of Me, and how I am pent up until it is accomplished!

51   Do you think I have come to give peace to the earth? *No!* Rather, strife and division!

52   From now on families will be split apart, three in favor of Me, and two against—or perhaps the other way around.

53   A father will decide one way about Me; his son, the other; mother and daughter will disagree; and the decision of an honored[6] mother-in-law will be spurned by her daughter-in-law."

54   Then He turned to the crowd and said, "When you see clouds beginning to form in the west, you say, 'Here comes a shower.' And you are right.

55   When the south wind blows you say, 'Today will be a scorcher.' And it is.

---

[6]Implied by ancient custom.

56   Hypocrites! You interpret the sky well enough, but you refuse to notice the warnings all around you about the crisis ahead.

57   Why do you refuse to see for yourselves what is right?

58   If you meet your accuser on the way to court, try to settle the matter before it reaches the judge, lest he sentence you to jail;

59   For if that happens you won't be free again until the last penny is paid in full."

CHAPTER 13

ABOUT this time He was informed that Pilate had butchered some Jews from Galilee as they were sacrificing at the Temple in Jerusalem.

2   "Do you think they were worse sinners than other men from Galilee?" He asked. "Is that why they suffered?

3   Not at all! And don't you realize that you also will perish unless you leave your evil ways and turn to God?

4   And what about the 18 men who died when the Tower of Siloam fell on them? Were they the worst sinners in Jerusalem?

5   Not at all! And you, too, will perish unless you repent."

6   Then He used this illustration: "A man planted a fig tree in his garden and came again and again to see if he could find any fruit on it, but he was always disappointed.

7   Finally he told his gardener to cut it down. 'I've waited three years and there hasn't been a single fig!' he said. 'Why bother with it any longer? It's taking up space we can use for something else.'

8   'Give it one more chance,' the gardener answered. 'Leave it another year, and I'll give it special attention and plenty of fertilizer.

9   If we get figs next year, fine; if not, I'll cut it down.'"

*   *   *   *   *

10   One Sabbath as He was teaching in a synagogue,

11 He saw a seriously handicapped woman who had been bent double for 18 years and was unable to straighten herself.

12 Calling her over to Him Jesus said, "Woman, you are healed of your sickness!"

13 He touched her, and instantly she could stand straight. How she praised and thanked God!

14 But the local Jewish leader in charge of the synagogue was very angry about it because Jesus had healed her on the Sabbath day. "There are six days of the week to work," he shouted to the crowd. "Those are the days to come for healing, not on the Sabbath!"

15 But the Lord replied, "You hypocrite! You work on the Sabbath! Don't you untie your cattle from their stalls on the Sabbath and lead them out for water?

16 And is it wrong for Me, just because it is the Sabbath day, to free this Jewish woman from Satan's 18 years of bondage?"

17 This shamed His enemies. And all the people rejoiced at the wonderful things He did.

18 Now He began teaching them again about the Kingdom of God: "What is the Kingdom like?" He asked. "How can I illustrate it?

19 It is like a tiny mustard seed planted in a garden; soon it grows into a tall bush, and the birds live among its branches.

20, 21 It is like yeast kneaded into dough, which works unseen until it has risen high and light."

22 He went from city to city and village to village, teaching as He went, always pressing onward toward Jerusalem.

23 Someone asked Him, "Will only a few be saved?" And He replied,

24, 25 "The door to heaven is narrow. Work hard to get in, for the truth is that many will try to enter but when the head of the house has locked the door, it will be too late. Then if you stand outside knocking, and pleading, 'Lord, open the door for us,' He will reply, 'I do not know you.'

26 'But we ate with You, and You taught in our streets,' you will say.

27   And He will reply, 'I tell you, I don't know you. You can't come in here, guilty as you are. Go away.'

28   And there will be great weeping and gnashing of teeth as you stand outside and see Abraham, Isaac, Jacob, and all the prophets within the Kingdom of God—

29   For people will come from all over the world to take their places there.

30   And note this: some who are despised now will be greatly honored then; and some who are highly thought of now will be least important then."

31   A few minutes later some Pharisees said to Him, "Get out of here if you want to live, for King Herod is after you!"

32   Jesus replied, "Go tell that fox that I will keep on casting out demons and doing miracles of healing today and tomorrow; and the third day I will reach my destination.

33   Yes, today, tomorrow, and the next day! For it wouldn't do for a prophet of God to be killed except in Jerusalem!

34   O Jerusalem, Jerusalem! The city that murders the prophets. The city that stones those sent to help her. How often I have wanted to gather your children together even as a hen protects her brood under her wings, but you wouldn't let Me.

35   And now—now your house is left desolate. And you will never again see Me until you say, 'Welcome to Him who comes in the name of the Lord.'"

CHAPTER 14

O NE Sabbath as He was in the home of a member of the Jewish Council, the Pharisees were watching Him like hawks to see if He would heal a man who was present who was suffering from dropsy.

3   Jesus said to the Pharisees and legal experts standing around, "Well, is it within the Law to heal a man on the Sabbath day, or not?"

4   And when they refused to answer, Jesus took the sick man by the hand and healed him and sent him away.

5   Then He turned to them: "Which of you doesn't work on the Sabbath?" He asked. "If your cow falls into a pit, don't you proceed at once to get it out?"

6   Again they had no answer.

*   *   *   *   *

7   When He noticed that all who came to the dinner were trying to sit near the head of the table, He gave them this advice:

8   "If you are invited to a wedding feast, don't always head for the best seat. For if someone more respected than you shows up,

9   The host will bring him over to where you are sitting and say, 'Let this man sit here instead.' And you, embarrassed, will have to take whatever seat is left at the foot of the table!

10   Do this instead—start at the foot; and when your host sees you he will come and say, 'Friend, we have a better place than this for you!' Thus you will be honored in front of all the other guests!

11   For everyone who tries to honor himself shall be humbled; and he who humbles himself shall be honored."

12   Then He turned to His host. "When you put on a dinner," He said, "don't invite friends, brothers, relatives, and rich neighbors! For they will return the invitation.

13   Instead, invite the poor, the crippled, the lame, and the blind.

14   Then at the resurrection of the godly, God will reward you for inviting those who can't repay you."

15   Hearing this, a man sitting at the table with Jesus exclaimed, "What a privilege it would be to get into the Kingdom of God!"

16   Jesus replied with this illustration: "A man prepared a great feast and sent out many invitations.

17   When all was ready, he sent his servant around to notify the guests that it was time for them to arrive.

18   But they all began making excuses. One said he had just

bought a field and wanted to inspect it, and asked to be excused.

19   Another said he had just bought five pair of oxen and wanted to try them out.

20   Another had just been married and for that reason couldn't come.

21   The servant returned and reported to his master what they had said. His master was angry and told him to go quickly into the streets and alleys of the city and to invite the beggars, crippled, lame, and blind.

22   But even then, there was still room!

23   'Well, then,' said his master, 'go out into the country lanes and out behind the hedges and urge anyone you find to come, so that the house will be full.

24   For none of those I invited first will get even the smallest taste of what I had prepared for them.' "

*   *   *   *   *

25   Great crowds were following Him. He turned around and addressed them as follows:

26   "Anyone who wants to be My follower must love Me far more than[1] he does his own father, mother, wife, children, brothers, or sisters—yes, more than his own life—otherwise he cannot be My disciple.

27   And no one can be My disciple who does not carry his own cross and follow Me.

28   But don't begin until you count the cost.[2] For who would begin construction of a building without first getting estimates and then checking to see if he has enough money to pay the bills?

29   Otherwise he might complete only the foundation before running out of funds. And then how everyone would laugh!

30   'See that fellow there?' they would mock. 'He started that building and ran out of money before it was finished!'

31   Or what king would ever dream of going to war without first sitting down with his counselors and discussing whether his

---

[1]Literally, "if anyone comes to me and does not hate his father and mother. . . ."
[2]Implied in verse 33.

army of 10,000 is strong enough to defeat the 20,000 men who are marching against him?

32   If the decision is negative, then while the enemy troops are still far away, he will send a truce team to discuss terms of peace.

33   So no one can become My disciple unless he first sits down and counts his blessings—and then renounces them all for Me!

34   What good is salt that has lost its saltiness?[3]

35   Flavorless salt is fit for nothing—not even for fertilizer. It is worthless and must be thrown out. Listen well, if you would understand My meaning."

CHAPTER 15

DISHONEST tax collectors and other notorious sinners often came to listen to Jesus' sermons;

2   But this caused complaints from the Jewish religious leaders and the experts on Jewish law because He was associating with such despicable people—even eating with them!

3, 4   So Jesus used this illustration: "If you had 100 sheep and one of them strayed away and was lost in the wilderness, wouldn't you leave the 99 others to go and search for the lost one until you found it?

5   And then you would joyfully carry it home on your shoulders.

6   When you arrived you would call together your friends and neighbors to rejoice with you because your lost sheep was found.

7   Well, in the same way heaven will be happier over one lost sinner who returns to God than over 99 others who haven't strayed away!

8   Or take another illustration: A woman has ten valuable silver coins and loses one. Won't she light a lamp and look in

---

[3]Perhaps the reference is to impure salt; when wet, the salt dissolves and drains out, leaving a tasteless residue. Matthew 5:13.

every corner of the house and sweep every nook and cranny until she finds it?

9   And then won't she call in her friends and neighbors to rejoice with her?

10   In the same way there is joy in the presence of the angels of God when one sinner repents."

To further illustrate the point, He told them this story:

11   "A man had two sons.

12 ⁃ When the younger told his father, 'I want my share of your estate now, instead of waiting until you die!' his father agreed to divide his wealth between his sons.

13   A few days later this younger son packed all his belongings and took a trip to a distant land, and there wasted all his money on parties and prostitutes.

14   About the time his money was gone a great famine swept over the land, and he began to starve.

15   He persuaded a local farmer to hire him to feed his pigs.

16   The boy became so hungry that even the pods he was feeding the swine looked good to him. And no one gave him anything.

17   When he finally came to his senses, he said to himself, 'At home even the hired men have food enough and to spare, and here I am, dying of hunger!

18   I will go home to my father and say, "Father, I have sinned against both heaven and you,

19   And am no longer worthy of being called your son. Please take me on as a hired man." '

20   So he returned home to his father. And while he was still a long distance away, his father saw him coming, and was filled with loving pity and ran and embraced him and kissed him.

21   His son said to him, 'Father, I have sinned against heaven and you, and am not worthy of being called your son—'

22   But his father said to the slaves, 'Quick! Bring the finest robe in the house and put it on him. And a jeweled ring for his finger; and shoes!

23   And kill the calf we have in the fattening pen. We must celebrate with a feast,

24   For this son of mine was dead and has returned to life. He was lost and is found.' So the party began.

25   Meanwhile, the older son was in the fields working; when he returned home, he heard dance music coming from the house,

26   And he asked one of the servants what was going on.

27   'Your brother is back,' he was told, 'and your father has killed the calf we were fattening and has prepared a great feast to celebrate his coming home again unharmed.'

28   The older brother was angry and wouldn't go in. His father came out and begged him,

29   But he replied, 'All these years I've worked hard for you and never once refused to do a single thing you told me to; and in all that time you never gave me even one young goat for a feast with my friends.

30   Yet when this son of yours comes back after spending your money on prostitutes, you celebrate by killing the finest calf we have on the place.'

31   'Look, dear son,' his father said to him, 'you and I are very close, and everything I have is yours.

32   But it is right to celebrate. For he is your brother; and he was dead and has come back to life!

He was lost and is found!' "

CHAPTER 16

JESUS now told this story to His disciples: "A rich man hired an accountant to handle his affairs, but soon a rumor went around that the accountant was thoroughly dishonest.

2   So his employer called him in and said, 'What's this I hear about your stealing from me? Get your report in order, for you are to be dismissed.'

3   The accountant thought to himself, 'Now what? I'm

through here, and I haven't the strength to go out and dig ditches, and I'm too proud to beg.

4　I know just the thing! And then I'll have plenty of friends to take care of me when I leave!'

5, 6　So he invited each one who owed money to his employer to come and discuss the situation. He asked the first one, 'How much do you owe him?' 'My debt is 850 gallons of olive oil,' the man replied. 'Yes, here is the contract you signed,' the accountant told him. 'Tear it up and write another one for half that much!'

7　'And how much do you owe him?' he asked the next man. 'A thousand bushels of wheat,' was the reply. 'Here,' the accountant said, 'take your note and replace it with one for only 800 bushels!'

8　The rich man had to admire the rascal for being so shrewd.[1] And it is true that the citizens of this world are more clever [in dishonesty![2]] than the godly[3] are.

9　But shall I tell *you* to act that way, to buy friendship through cheating? Will this ensure your entry into an everlasting home in heaven?[4]

10　NO![5] For unless you are honest in small matters, you won't be in large ones. If you cheat even a little, you won't be honest with greater responsibilities.

11　And if you are untrustworthy about worldly wealth, who will trust you with the true riches of heaven?

12　And if you are not faithful with other people's money, why should you be entrusted with money of your own?

13　For neither you nor anyone else can serve two masters. You will hate one and show loyalty to the other, or else the other way around—you will be enthusiastic about one and despise the other. You cannot serve both God and money."

14　The Pharisees, who dearly loved their money, naturally scoffed at all this.

---

[1]Or, "Do you think the rich man commended the scoundrel for being so shrewd?"
[2]Implied.
[3]Literally, "sons of the light."
[4]Literally, and probably ironically, "make to yourselves friends by means of the mammon of unrighteousness; that when it shall fail you, they may receive you into the eternal tabernacles!" Some commentators would interpret this to mean: "Use your money for good, so that it will be waiting to befriend you when you get to heaven." But this would imply the end justifies the means, an unbiblical idea.
[5]Implied.

15   Then He said to them, "You wear a noble, pious expression in public, but God knows your evil hearts. Your pretense brings you honor from the people, but it is an abomination in the sight of God.

16   Until John the Baptist began to preach, the laws of Moses and the messages of the prophets were your guides. But John introduced the Good News that the Kingdom of God would come soon. And now eager multitudes are pressing in.

17   But that doesn't mean that the Law has lost its force in even the smallest point. It is as strong and unshakable as heaven and earth.

18   So anyone who divorces his wife and marries someone else commits adultery, and anyone who marries a divorced woman commits adultery."

                    *   *   *   *   *

19   "There was a certain rich man," Jesus said, "who was splendidly clothed and lived each day in mirth and luxury.

20   One day Lazarus, a diseased beggar, was laid at his door.

21   As he lay there longing for scraps from the rich man's table, the dogs would come and lick his open sores.

22   Finally the beggar died and was carried by the angels to be with Abraham in the place of the righteous dead.[6] The rich man also died and was buried,

23   And his soul went into hell.[7] There, in torment, he saw Lazarus in the far distance with Abraham.

24   'Father Abraham,' he shouted, 'have some pity! Send Lazarus over here if only to dip the tip of his finger in water and cool my tongue, for I am in anguish in these flames.'

25   But Abraham said to him, 'Son, remember that during your lifetime you had everything you wanted, and Lazarus had nothing. So now he is here being comforted and you are in anguish.

26   And besides, there is a great chasm separating us, and anyone wanting to come to you from here is stopped at its edge; and no one over there can cross to us.'

---

[6]Literally, "into Abraham's bosom."
[7]Literally, "in Hades."

27   Then the rich man said, 'O Father Abraham, then please send him to my father's home—

28   For I have five brothers—to warn them about this place of torment lest they come here when they die.'

29   But Abraham said, 'The Scriptures have warned them again and again. Your brothers can read them any time they want to.'

30   The rich man replied, 'No, Father Abraham, they won't bother to read them. But if someone is sent to them from the dead, then they will turn from their sins.'

31   But Abraham said, 'If they won't listen to Moses and the prophets, they won't listen even though someone rises from the dead.' "[8]

CHAPTER 17

THERE will always be temptations to sin," Jesus said one day to His disciples, "but woe to the man who does the tempting.

2, 3   If he were thrown into the sea with a huge rock tied to his neck, he would be far better off than facing the punishment in store for those who harm these little children's souls. I am warning you!

Rebuke your brother if he sins, and forgive him if he is sorry.

4   Even if he wrongs you seven times a day and each time turns again and asks forgiveness, forgive him."

              *   *   *   *   *

5   One day the apostles said to the Lord, "We need more faith; tell us how to get it."

6   "If your faith were only the size of a mustard seed," Jesus answered, "it would be large enough to uproot that mulberry tree over there and send it hurtling into the sea! Your command would bring immediate results!

7, 8, 9   When a servant comes in from plowing or taking care

---

[8]Even Christ's resurrection failed to convince the Pharisees, to whom He gave this illustration.

of sheep, he doesn't just sit down and eat, but first prepares his master's meal and serves him his supper before he eats his own. And he is not even thanked, for he is merely doing what he is supposed to do.

10   Just so, if you merely obey Me, you should not consider yourselves worthy of praise. For you have simply done your duty!"

*   *   *   *   *

11   As they continued onward toward Jerusalem, they reached the border between Galilee and Samaria,

12   And as they entered a village there, ten lepers stood at a distance,

13   Crying out, "Jesus, sir, have mercy on us!"

14   He looked at them and said, "Go to the Jewish priest and show him that you are healed!" And as they were going, their leprosy disappeared!

15   One of them came back to Jesus, shouting, "Glory to God, I'm healed!"

16   He fell flat on the ground in front of Jesus, face downward in the dust, thanking Him for what He had done. This man was a despised[1] Samaritan.

17   Jesus asked, "Didn't I heal ten men? Where are the nine?

18   Does only this foreigner return to give glory to God?"

19   And Jesus said to the man, "Stand up and go; your faith has made you well."

*   *   *   *   *

20   One day the Pharisees asked Jesus, "When will the Kingdom of God begin?" Jesus replied, "The Kingdom of God isn't ushered in with visible signs.

21   You won't be able to say, 'It has begun here in this place or there in that part of the country.' For the Kingdom of God is within you."[2]

22   Later He talked again about this with His disciples. "The time is coming when you will long for Me[3] to be with you even for a single day, but I won't be here," He said.

---

[1] Implied. Samaritans were despised by Jews as being only "half-breed" Hebrews.
[2] Or, "among you."
[3] Literally, "the Son of Man."

23   "Reports will reach you that I have returned and that I am in this place or that; don't believe it or go out to look for Me.

24   For when I return, you will know it beyond all doubt. It will be as evident as the lightning that flashes across the skies.

25   But first I must suffer terribly and be rejected by this whole nation.

26   [When I return[4]] the world will be [as indifferent to the things of God[4]] as the people were in Noah's day.

27   They ate and drank and married—everything just as usual right up to the day when Noah went into the ark and the flood came and destroyed them all.

28   And the world will be as it was in the days of Lot: people went about their daily business—eating and drinking, buying and selling, farming and building—

29   Until the morning Lot left Sodom. Then fire and brimstone rained down from heaven and destroyed them all.

30   Yes, it will be 'business as usual' right up to the hour of My return.[5]

31   Those away from home that day must not return to pack; those in the fields must not return to town—

32   Remember what happened to Lot's wife!

33   Whoever clings to his life shall lose it, and whoever loses his life shall save it.

34   That night two men will be asleep in the same room, and one will be taken away, the other left.

35, 36   Two women will be working together at household tasks; one will be taken, the other left; and so it will be with men working side by side in the fields."

37   "Lord, where will they be taken?" the disciples asked. Jesus replied, "Where the body is, the vultures gather!"[6]

---

[4]Implied.
[5]Or, "the hour I am revealed."
[6]This may mean that God's people will be taken out to the execution grounds and their bodies left to the vultures.

CHAPTER 18

ONE day Jesus told His disciples a story to illustrate their need for constant prayer and to show them that they must keep praying until the answer comes.

2   "There was a city judge," He said, "a very godless man who had great contempt for everyone.

3   A widow of that city came to him frequently to appeal for justice against a man who had harmed her.

4, 5   The judge ignored her for a while, but eventually she got on his nerves. 'I fear neither God nor man,' he said to himself, 'but this woman bothers me. I'm going to see that she gets justice, for she is wearing me out with her constant coming!' "

6   Then the Lord said, "If even an evil judge can be worn down like that,

7   Don't you think that God will surely give justice to His people who plead with Him day and night?

8   Yes! He will answer them quickly! But the question is: When I, the Son of Mankind, return, how many will I find who have faith [and are praying[1]]?"

9   Then He told this story to some who boasted of their virtue and scorned everyone else:

10   "Two men went to the Temple to pray. One was a proud, self-righteous Pharisee, and the other a cheating tax collector.

11   The proud Pharisee 'prayed' this prayer: 'Thank God, I am not a sinner like everyone else, especially like that tax collector over there! For I never cheat, I don't commit adultery,

12   I go without food twice a week, and I give to God a tenth of everything I earn.'

13   But the corrupt tax collector stood at a distance and dared not even lift his eyes to heaven as he prayed, but beat upon his chest in sorrow, exclaiming, 'God, be merciful to me, a sinner.'

14   I tell you, this sinner, not the Pharisee, returned home

[1]Implied.

189

forgiven! For the proud shall be humbled, but the humble shall be honored."

*   *   *   *   *

15   One day some mothers brought their babies to Him to touch and bless. But the disciples told them to go away.

16, 17   Then Jesus called the children over to Him and said to the disciples, "Let the little children come to Me! Never send them away! For the Kingdom of God belongs to men who have hearts as trusting as these little children's. And anyone who doesn't have their kind of faith will never get within the Kingdom's gates."

*   *   *   *   *

18   Once a Jewish religious leader asked Him this question: "Good sir, what shall I do to get to heaven?"

19   "Do you realize what you are saying when you call me 'good'?" Jesus asked him. "Only God is truly good, and no one else.

20   But as to your question, you know what the ten commandments say—don't commit adultery, don't murder, don't steal, don't lie, honor your parents, and so on."

21   The man replied, "I've obeyed every one of these laws since I was a small child."

22   "There is still one thing you lack," Jesus said. "Sell all you have and give the money to the poor—it will become treasure for you in heaven—and come, follow Me."

23   But when the man heard this he went sadly away, for he was very rich.

24   Jesus watched him go and then said to His disciples, "How hard it is for the rich to enter the Kingdom of God!

25   It is easier for a camel to go through the eye of a needle than for a rich man to enter the Kingdom of God!"

26   Those who heard Him say this exclaimed, "If it is that hard, how can *anyone* be saved?"

27   He replied, "God can do what men can't!"

28   And Peter said, "We have left our homes and followed You."

29   "Yes," Jesus replied, "and everyone who has done as you have, leaving home, wife, brothers, parents, or children for the sake of the Kingdom of God,

30   Will be repaid many times over now, as well as receiving eternal life in the world to come."

*   *   *   *   *

31   Gathering the Twelve around Him He told them, "As you know, we are going to Jerusalem. And when we get there, all the predictions of the ancient prophets concerning Me will come true.

32   I will be handed over to the Gentiles to be mocked and treated shamefully and spat upon,

33   And lashed and killed. And the third day I will rise again."

34   But they didn't understand a thing He said. He seemed to be talking in riddles.

35   As they approached Jericho, a blind man was sitting beside the road, begging from travelers.

36   When he heard the noise of a crowd going past, he asked what was happening.

37   He was told that Jesus from Nazareth was going by,

38   So he began shouting, "Jesus, Son of David, have mercy on me!"

39   The crowds ahead of Jesus tried to hush the man, but he only yelled the louder, "Son of David, have mercy on me!"

40   When Jesus arrived at the spot, He stopped. "Bring the blind man over here," He said.

41   Then Jesus asked the man, "What do you want?"

"Lord," he pleaded, "I want to see!"

42   And Jesus said, "All right, begin seeing! Your faith has healed you!"

43   And instantly the man could see, and followed Jesus, praising God. And all who saw it happen praised God too.

CHAPTER 19

AS Jesus was passing through Jericho, a man named Zacchaeus, one of the most influential Jews in the Roman tax-collecting business (and, of course, a very rich man),

3 Tried to get a look at Jesus, but he was too short to see over the crowds.

4 So he ran ahead and climbed into a sycamore tree beside the road, to watch from there.

5 When Jesus came by He looked up at Zacchaeus and called him by name! "Zacchaeus," he said, "Quick! Come down! For I am going to be a guest in your home today!"

6 Zacchaeus hurriedly climbed down and took Jesus to his house in great excitement and joy.

7 But the crowds were displeased. "He has gone to be the guest of a notorious sinner," they grumbled.

8 Meanwhile, Zacchaeus stood before the Lord and said, "Sir, from now on I will give half my wealth to the poor, and if I find I have overcharged anyone on his taxes, I will penalize myself by giving him back four times as much!"

9, 10 Jesus told him, "This shows[1] that salvation has come to this home today. This man was one of the lost sons of Abraham, and I, the Son of Mankind, have come to search for and to save such souls as his."

11 And because Jesus was nearing Jerusalem, He told a story to correct the impression that the Kingdom of God would begin right away.

12 "A nobleman living in a certain province was called away to the distant capital of the empire to be crowned king of his province.

13 Before he left he called together ten assistants and gave them each $2,000 to invest while he was gone.

14 But some of his people hated him and sent him their declaration of independence, stating that they had rebelled and would not acknowledge him as their king.

15 Upon his return he called in the men to whom he had

---

[1]Implied.

192

given the money, to find out what they had done with it, and what their profits were.

16   The first man reported a tremendous gain—ten times as much as the original amount!

17   'Fine!' the king exclaimed. 'You are a good man. You have been faithful with the little I entrusted to you, and as your reward, you shall be governor of ten cities.'

18   The next man also reported a splendid gain—five times the original amount.

19   'All right!' his master said. 'You can be governor over five cities.'

20   But the third man brought back only the money he had started with. 'I've kept it safe,' he said,

21   'Because I was afraid [you would demand my profits²], for you are a hard man to deal with, taking what isn't yours and even confiscating the crops that others plant!'

22   'You vile and wicked slave,' the king roared. 'Hard, am I? That's exactly how I'll be toward you! If you knew so much about me and how tough I am,

23   Then why didn't you deposit the money in the bank so that I could at least get some interest on it?"

24   Then turning to the others standing by he ordered, 'Take the money away from him and give it to the man who earned the most.'

25   'But, sir,' they said, 'he has enough already!'

26   'Yes,' the king replied, 'but it is always true that those who have, get more, and those who have little, soon lose even that.

27   And now about these enemies of mine who revolted— bring them in and execute them before me.' "

28   After telling this story, Jesus went on towards Jerusalem, walking along ahead of His disciples.

29   As they came to the towns of Bethphage and Bethany, on the Mount of Olives, He sent two disciples ahead,

30   With instructions to go to the next village, and as they entered they were to look for a donkey tied beside the road. It

---

²Implied.

would be a colt, not yet broken for riding. "Untie him," Jesus said, "and bring him here.

31 And if anyone asks you what you are doing, just say, 'The Lord needs him.' "

32 They found the colt as Jesus said,

33 And sure enough, as they were untying it, the owners demanded an explanation. "What are you doing?" they asked. "Why are you untying our colt?"

34 And the disciples simply replied, "The Lord needs him!"

35 So they brought the colt to Jesus and threw some of their clothing across its back for Jesus to sit on.

36, 37 Then the crowds spread out their robes along the road ahead of Him, and as they reached the place where the road started down from the Mount of Olives, the whole procession began to shout and sing as they walked along, praising God for all the wonderful miracles Jesus had done.

38 "God has given us a King!" they exulted. "Long live the King! Let all heaven rejoice! Glory to God in the highest heavens!"

39 But some of the Pharisees among the crowd said, "Sir, rebuke your followers for saying things like that!"

40 He replied, "If they keep quiet, the stones along the road will burst into cheers!"

41 But as they came closer to Jerusalem and He saw the city ahead, He began to cry.

42 "Eternal peace was within your reach and you turned it down," He wept, "and now it is too late.

43 Your enemies will pile up earth against your walls and encircle you and close in on you,

44 And crush you to the ground, and your children within you; your enemies will not leave one stone upon another—for you have rejected the opportunity God offered you."

45 Then He entered the Temple and began to drive out the merchants from their stalls,

46 Saying to them, "The Scriptures declare, 'My Temple

is a place of prayer; but you have turned it into a den of thieves.' "

47 After that He taught daily in the Temple, but the chief priests and other religious leaders and the business community[3] were trying to find some way to get rid of Him.

48 But they could think of nothing, for He was a hero to the people—they hung on every word He said.

CHAPTER 20

ON one of those days when He was teaching and preaching the Good News in the Temple, He was confronted by the chief priests and other religious leaders and councilmen.

2 They demanded to know by what authority He had driven out the merchants from the Temple.

3 "I'll ask you a question before I answer," He replied.

4 "Was John sent by God, or was he merely acting under his own authority?"

5 They talked it over among themselves. "If we say his message was from heaven, then we are trapped because he will ask, 'Then why didn't you believe him?'

6 But if we say John was not sent from God, the people will mob us, for they are convinced that he was a prophet."

7 Finally they replied, "We don't know!"

8 And Jesus responded, "Then I won't answer your question either."

9 Now He turned to the people again and told them this story: "A man planted a vineyard and rented it out to some farmers, and went away to a distant land to live for several years.

10 When harvest time came, he sent one of his men to the farm to collect his share of the crops. But the tenants beat him up and sent him back empty-handed.

[3]Literally, "the leading men among the people."

11   Then he sent another, but the same thing happened; he was beaten up and insulted and sent away without collecting.

12   A third man was sent and the same thing happened. He, too, was wounded and chased away.

13   'What shall I do?' the owner asked himself. 'I know! I'll send my cherished son. Surely they will show respect for him.'

14   But when the tenants saw his son, they said, 'This is our chance! This fellow will inherit all the land when his father dies. Come on. Let's kill him, and then it will be ours.'

15   So they dragged him out of the vineyard and killed him. What do you think the owner will do?

16   I'll tell you—he will come and kill them and rent the vineyard to others."

"But they would never do a thing like that," His listeners protested.

17   Jesus looked at them and said, "Then what does the Scripture mean where it says, 'The Stone rejected by the builders was made the cornerstone'?"

18   And He added, "Whoever stumbles over that Stone shall be broken; and those on whom it falls will be crushed to dust."

19   When the chief priests and religious leaders heard about this story He had told, they wanted Him arrested immediately, for they realized that He was talking about them. They were the wicked tenants in His illustration. But they were afraid that if they themselves arrested Him there would be a riot. So they tried to get Him to say something that could be reported to the Roman governor as reason for arrest by him.

20   Watching their opportunity, they sent secret agents pretending to be honest men.

21   They said to Jesus, "Sir, we know what an honest teacher you are. You always tell the truth and don't budge an inch in the face of what others think, but teach the ways of God.

22   Now tell us—is it right to pay taxes to the Roman government or not?

23   He saw through their trickery and said,

24   "Show Me a coin. Whose portrait is this on it? And whose name?"

They replied, "Caesar's—the Roman emperor's."

25   He said, "Then give the emperor all that is his—and give to God all that is His!"

26   Thus their attempt to outwit Him before the people failed; and marveling at His answer, they were silent.

27   Then some Sadducees—men who believed that death is the end of existence, that there is no resurrection—

28   Came to Jesus with this: "The laws of Moses state that if a man dies without children, the man's brother shall marry the widow and their children will legally belong to the dead man, to carry on his name.

29   We know of a family of seven brothers. The oldest married and then died without any children.

30   His brother married the widow and he, too, died. Still no children.

31   And so it went, one after the other, until each of the seven had married her and died, leaving no children.

32   Finally the woman died also.

33   Now here is our question: Whose wife will she be in the resurrection! For all of them were married to her!"

34, 35   Jesus replied, "Marriage is for people here on earth, but when those who are counted worthy of being raised from the dead get to heaven, they do not marry.

36   And they never die again; in these respects they are like angels, and are sons of God, for they are raised up in new life from the dead.

37, 38   But as to your real question—whether or not there is a resurrection—why, even the writings of Moses himself prove this. For when he describes how God appeared to him in the burning bush, he speaks of God as 'the God of Abraham, the God of Isaac, and the God of Jacob.' To say

197

that the Lord *is*[1] some person's God means that person is *alive,* not dead! So from God's point of view, all men are living."

39 "Well said, sir!" remarked some of the experts in the Jewish law who were standing there.

40 And that ended their questions, for they dared ask no more!

41 Then He presented *them* with a question. "Why is it," He asked, "that Christ, the Messiah, is said to be a descendant of King David?

42, 43 For David himself wrote in the book of Psalms: 'God said to my Lord, the Messiah, "Sit at My right hand until I place Your enemies beneath Your feet." '

44 How can the Messiah be both David's son and David's God at the same time?"

45 Then, with the crowds listening, He turned to His disciples and said,

46 "Beware of these experts in religion, for they love to parade in dignified robes and to be bowed to by the people as they walk along the street. And how they love the seats of honor in the synagogues and at religious festivals!

47 But even while they are praying long prayers with great outward piety, they are planning schemes to cheat widows out of their property. Therefore God's heaviest sentence awaits these men."

CHAPTER 21

AS He stood in the Temple, He was watching the rich tossing their gifts into the collection box.

2 Then a poor widow came by and dropped in two small copper coins.

3 "Really," He remarked, "this poor widow has given more than all the rest of them combined.

---

[1]Otherwise the statement would be, "He *had been* that person's God."

4 For they have given a little of what they didn't need, but she, poor as she is, has given everything she has."

5 Some of His disciples began talking about the beautiful stonework of the Temple and the memorial decorations on the walls.

6 But Jesus said, "The time is coming when all these things you are admiring will be knocked down, and not one stone will be left on top of another; all will become one vast heap of rubble."

7 "Master!" they exclaimed. "When? And will there be any warning ahead of time?"

8 He replied, "Don't let anyone mislead you. For many will come announcing themselves as the Messiah,[1] and saying, 'The time has come.' But don't believe them!

9 And when you hear of wars and insurrections beginning, don't panic. True, wars must come, but the end won't follow immediately—

10 For nation shall rise against nation and kingdom against kingdom,

11 And there will be great earthquakes, and famines in many lands, and epidemics, and terrifying things happening in the heavens.

12 But before all this occurs, there will be a time of special persecution, and you will be dragged into synagogues and prisons and before kings and governors for My name's sake.

13 But as a result, the Messiah will be widely known and honored.[2]

14 Therefore, don't be concerned about how to answer the charges against you,

15 For I will give you the right words and such logic that none of your opponents will be able to reply!

16 Even those closest to you—your parents, brothers, relatives, and friends will betray you and have you arrested; and some of you will be killed.

---

[1]Literally, "will come in My Name."
[2]Literally, "It shall turn out unto you for a testimony."

17   And everyone will hate you because you are Mine and are called by My Name.

18   But not a hair of your head will perish!

19   For if you stand firm, you will win your souls.

20   But when you see Jerusalem surrounded by armies, then you will know that the time of its destruction has arrived.

21   Then let the people of Judea flee to the hills. Let those in Jerusalem try to escape, and those outside the city must not attempt to return.

22   For those will be days of God's judgment,[3] and the words of the ancient Scriptures written by the prophets will be abundantly fulfilled.

23   Woe to expectant mothers in those days, and those with tiny babies. For there will be great distress upon this nation[4] and wrath upon this people.

24   They will be brutally killed by enemy weapons, or sent away as exiles and captives to all the nations of the world; and Jerusalem shall be conquered and trampled down by the Gentiles until the period of Gentile triumph ends in God's good time.

25   Then there will be strange events in the skies—warnings, evil omens and portents in the sun, moon and stars; and down here on earth the nations will be in turmoil, perplexed by the roaring seas and strange tides.

26   The courage of many people will falter because of the fearful fate they see coming upon the earth, for the stability of the very heavens will be broken up.

27   Then the peoples of the earth shall see Me,[5] the Man from Heaven, coming in a cloud with power and great glory.

28   So when all these things begin to happen, stand straight and look up! For your salvation is near."

29   Then He gave them this illustration: "Notice the fig tree, or any other tree.

3Literally, "days of vengeance."
4Literally, "upon the land," or, "upon the earth."
5Literally, "the Son of Man."

30   When the leaves come out, you know without being told that summer is near.

31   In the same way, when you see the events taking place that I've described you can be just as sure that the Kingdom of God is near.

32   I solemnly declare to you that when these things happen, the end of this age[6] has come.

33   And though all heaven and earth shall pass away, yet My words remain forever true.

34, 35   Watch out! Don't let My sudden coming catch you unawares; don't let me find you living in careless ease, carousing and drinking, and occupied with the problems of this life, like all the rest of the world.

36   Keep a constant watch. And pray that if possible you may arrive in My presence without having to experience these horrors.[7]

37, 38   Every day Jesus went to the Temple to teach, and the crowds began gathering early in the morning to hear Him. And each evening He returned to spend the night on the Mount of Olives.

CHAPTER 22

A ND now the Passover celebration was drawing near—the Jewish festival when only bread made without yeast was used.

2   The chief priests and other religious leaders were actively plotting Jesus' murder, trying to find a way to kill Him without starting a riot—a possibility they greatly feared.

3   Then Satan entered into Judas Iscariot, who was one of the twelve disciples,

4   And he went over to the chief priests and captains of the Temple guards to discuss the best ways to betray Jesus to them.

5   They were, of course, delighted to know that he was ready to help them and promised him a reward.

6Or, "this generation."
7Or, "Pray for strength to pass safely through these coming horrors."

6   So he began to look for an opportunity for them to arrest Jesus quietly when the crowds weren't around.

7   Now the day of the Passover celebration arrived, when the Passover lamb was killed and eaten with the unleavened bread.

8   Jesus sent Peter and John ahead to find a place to prepare their Passover meal.

9   "Where do You want us to go?" they asked.

10   And He replied, "As soon as you enter Jerusalem,[1] you will see a man walking along carrying a pitcher of water. Follow him into the house he enters,

11   And say to the man who lives there, 'Our Teacher says for you to show us the guest room where He can eat the Passover meal with His disciples.'

12   He will take you upstairs to a large room all ready for us. That is the place. Go ahead and prepare the meal there."

13   They went off to the city and found everything just as Jesus had said, and prepared the Passover supper.

14   Then Jesus and the others arrived, and at the proper time all sat down together at the table;

15   And He said, "I have looked forward to this hour with deep longing, anxious to eat this Passover meal with you before My suffering begins.

16   For I tell you now that I won't eat it again until what it represents has occurred in the Kingdom of God."

17   Then He took a glass of wine, and when He had given thanks for it, He said, "Take this and share it among yourselves.

18   For I will not drink wine again until the Kingdom of God has come."

19   Then He took a loaf of bread; and when He had thanked God for it, He broke it apart and gave it to them, saying, "This is My body, given for you. Eat it in remembrance of Me."

20   After supper He gave them another glass of wine, saying, "This wine is the token of God's new agreement to save

---

[1]Literally, "the city."

you—an agreement sealed with the blood I shall pour out to purchase back your souls.[2]

21 But here at this table, sitting among us as a friend, is the man who will betray Me.

22 I[3] must die. It is part of God's plan. But, oh, the horror awaiting that man who betrays Me."

23 Then the disciples wondered among themselves which of them would ever do such a thing.

24 And they began to argue among themselves as to who would have the highest rank [in the coming Kingdom[4]].

25 Jesus told them, "In this world the kings and great men order their slaves around, and the slaves have no choice but to like it![5]

26 But among you, the one who serves you best will be your leader.

27 Out in the world the master sits at the table and is served by his servants. But not here! For I am your servant.

28 Nevertheless, because you have stood true to Me in these terrible days,[6]

29 And because My Father has granted Me a Kingdom, I, here and now, grant you the right

30 To eat and drink at My table in that Kingdom; and you will sit on thrones judging the twelve tribes of Israel.

31 Simon, Simon, Satan has asked to have you, to sift you like wheat,

32 But I have pleaded in prayer for you that your faith should not completely fail.[7] So when you have repented and turned to Me again, strengthen and build up the faith of your brothers."

33 Simon said, "Lord, I am ready to go to jail with You, and even to die with You."

34 But Jesus said, "Peter, let Me tell you something. Between now and tomorrow morning when the rooster crows, you

[2]Literally, "This cup is the new covenant in My blood, poured out for you."
[3]Literally, "the Son of Man."
[4]Implied.
[5]Literally, "they (the kings and great men) are called 'benefactors.' "
[6]Literally, "you have continued with Me in My temptation."
[7]Literally, "fail not."

will deny Me three times, declaring that you don't even know Me."

35   Then Jesus asked them, "When I sent you out to preach the Good News and you were without money, duffle bag, or extra clothing, how did you get along?"

"Fine," they replied.

36   "But now," He said, "take a duffle bag if you have one, and your money. And if you don't have a sword, better sell your clothes and buy one!

37   For the time has come for this prophecy about Me to come true: 'He will be condemned as a criminal!' Yes, everything written about Me by the prophets will come true."

38   "Master," they replied, "we have two swords among us."

"Enough!" He said.

39   Then, accompanied by the disciples, He left the upstairs room and went as usual to the Mount of Olives.

40   There He told them, "Pray God that you will not be overcome[8] by temptation."

41, 42   He walked away, perhaps a stone's throw, and knelt down and prayed this prayer: "Father, if You are willing, please take away this cup of horror from Me. But I want Your will, not Mine."

43   Then an angel from heaven appeared and strengthened Him,

44   For He was in such agony of spirit that He broke into a sweat of blood, with great drops falling to the ground as He prayed more and more earnestly.

45   At last He stood up again and returned to the disciples —only to find them asleep, exhausted from grief.

46   "Asleep!" He said. "Get up! Pray God that you will not fall when you are tempted."

47   But even as He said this, a mob approached, led by Judas, one of His twelve disciples. Judas walked over to Jesus and kissed Him on the cheek in friendly greeting.[9]

---

[8]Literally, "that you enter not into temptation."
[9]Literally, "approached Jesus to kiss Him." This is still the traditional greeting among men in eastern lands.

48   But Jesus said, "Judas, how can you do this—betray the Messiah with a kiss?"

49   When the other disciples saw what was about to happen, they exclaimed, "Master, shall we fight? We brought along the swords!"

50   And one of them slashed at the High Priest's servant, and cut off his right ear.

51   But Jesus said, "Don't resist any more." And He touched the place where the man's ear had been and restored it.

52   Then Jesus addressed the chief priests and captains of the Temple guards and the religious leaders who headed the mob. "Am I a robber," He asked, "that you have come armed with swords and clubs to get Me?

53   Why didn't you arrest Me in the Temple? I was there every day! But this is your moment—the time when Satan's power reigns supreme."

54   So they seized Him and led Him to the High Priest's residence, and Peter followed at a distance.

55   The soldiers lit a fire in the courtyard and sat around it for warmth, and Peter joined them there.

56   A servant girl noticed him in the firelight and began staring at him. Finally she spoke: "This man was with Jesus!"

57   Peter denied it! "Woman," he said, "I don't even know the man!"

58   After a while someone else looked at him and said, "You must be one of them!"

"No sir, I am not!" Peter replied.

59   About an hour later someone else flatly stated, "I know this fellow is one of Jesus' disciples, for both are from Galilee."

60   But Peter said, "Man, I don't know what you are talking about." And as he said the words, a rooster crowed.

61   At that moment Jesus turned and looked at Peter. Then Peter remembered what He had said—"Before the rooster crows tomorrow morning, you will deny Me three times."

62   And Peter walked out of the courtyard, crying bitterly.

63, 64   Now the guards in charge of Jesus began mocking

Him. They blindfolded Him and hit Him with their fists and asked, "Who hit you that time, prophet?"

65   And they threw all sorts of other insults at Him.

66   Early the next morning at daybreak the Jewish Supreme Court assembled, including the chief priests and all the top religious authorities of the nation. Jesus was led before this Council,

67, 68   And instructed to state whether or not He claimed to be the Messiah. But He replied, "If I tell you, you won't believe Me or let Me present My case.

69   But the time is soon coming when I, the Man of Glory,[10] shall be enthroned beside Almighty God."

70   They all shouted, "Then you claim you are the Son of God?"

And He replied, "Yes, I am."

71   "What need do we have for other witnesses?" they shouted, "for we ourselves have heard him say it."

CHAPTER 23

THEN the entire Council took Jesus over to Pilate, the governor.[1]

2   They began at once accusing Him: "This fellow has been leading our people to ruin by telling them not to pay their taxes to the Roman government and by claiming He is our Messiah— a King."

3   So Pilate asked Him, "Are you their Messiah—their King?"[2]

"Yes," Jesus replied, "It is as you say."

4   Then Pilate turned to the chief priests and to the mob and said, "So? That isn't a crime!"

5   Then they became desperate. "But he is causing riots against the government everywhere he goes, all over Judea, from Galilee to Jerusalem!"

---

[10]Literally, "the Son of Man."
[1]Implied.
[2]Literally, "Are you the King of the Jews?"

6 "Is He then a Galilean?" Pilate asked.

7 When they told him yes, Pilate said to take Him to King Herod, for Galilee was under Herod's jurisdiction; and Herod happened to be in Jerusalem at the time.

8 Herod was delighted at the opportunity to see Jesus, for he had heard a lot about Him and had been hoping to see Him perform a miracle.

9 He asked Jesus question after question, but there was no reply.

10 Meanwhile, the chief priests and the other religious leaders stood there shouting their accusations.

11 Now Herod and his soldiers began mocking and ridiculing Jesus; and putting a kingly robe on Him, they sent Him back to Pilate.

12 That day Herod and Pilate—enemies before—became fast friends.

13 Then Pilate called together the chief priests and other Jewish leaders, along with the people,

14 And announced his verdict: "You brought this man to me, accusing him of leading a revolt against the Roman government.[3] I have examined him thoroughly on this point and find him innocent.

15 Herod came to the same conclusion and sent him back to us—nothing this man has done calls for the death penalty.

16 I will therefore have him scourged with leaded thongs, and release him."

17,[4] 18 But now a mighty roar rose from the crowd as with one voice they shouted, "Kill him, and release Barabbas to us!"

19 (Barabbas was in prison for starting an insurrection in Jerusalem against the government, and for murder.)

20 Pilate argued with them, for he wanted to release Jesus.

21 But they shouted, "Crucify him! Crucify him!"

22 Once more, for the third time, he demanded, "Why? What crime has he committed? I have found no reason to

---

[3]Literally, "as one who perverts the people."
[4]Some ancient authorities add verse 17, "For it was necessary for him to release unto them at the feast one (prisoner)."

sentence him to death. I will therefore scourge him and let him go."

23   But they shouted louder and louder for Jesus' death, and their voices prevailed.

24   So Pilate sentenced Jesus to die as they demanded.

25   And he released Barabbas, the man in prison for insurrection and murder, at their request. But he delivered Jesus over to them to do with as they would.

26   As the crowd led Jesus away to His death, Simon of Cyrene, who was just coming into Jerusalem from the country, was forced to follow, carrying Jesus' cross.

27   Great crowds trailed along behind, and many grief-stricken women.

28   But Jesus turned and said to them, "Daughters of Jerusalem, don't weep for Me, but for yourselves and for your children.

29   For the days are coming when the women who have no children will be counted fortunate indeed.

30   Mankind will beg the mountains to fall on them and crush them, and the hills to bury them.

31   For if such things as this are done to Me, the Living Tree, what will they do to you?"[5]

*   *   *   *   *

32, 33   Two others, criminals, were led out to be executed with Him at a place called "The Skull." There all three were crucified—Jesus on the center cross, and the two criminals on either side.

34   "Father, forgive these people," Jesus said, "for they don't know what they are doing."

And the soldiers gambled for His clothing, throwing dice for each piece.

35   The crowd watched.

And the Jewish leaders laughed and scoffed. "He was so good at helping others," they said, "let's see him save himself if he is really God's Chosen One, the Messiah."

36   The soldiers mocked Him, too, by offering Him a drink —of sour wine.

---

[5]Literally, "For if they do this when the tree is green, what will happen when it is dry?"

37 And they called to Him, "If you are the King of the Jews, save yourself!"

38 A signboard was nailed to the cross above Him with these words: "THIS IS THE KING OF THE JEWS."

39 One of the criminals hanging beside Him scoffed, "So you're the Messiah, are you? Prove it by saving yourself—and us, too, while you're at it!"

40, 41 But the other criminal protested. "Don't you even fear God when you are dying? We deserve to die for our evil deeds, but this man hasn't done one thing wrong."

42 Then he said, "Jesus, remember me when You come into Your Kingdom."

43 And Jesus replied, "Today you will be with Me in Paradise. This is a solemn promise."

44 By now it was noon, and darkness fell across the whole land[6] for three hours, until 3 o'clock.

45 The light from the sun was gone—and suddenly[7] the thick veil hanging in the Temple split apart.

46 Then Jesus shouted, "Father, I commit My spirit to You," and with those words He died.[8]

47 When the captain of the Roman military unit handling the executions saw what had happened, he was stricken with awe before God and said, "Surely this man was innocent."[9]

48 And when the crowd that came to see the crucifixion saw that Jesus was dead, they went home in deep sorrow.

49 Meanwhile, Jesus' friends, including the women who had followed Him down from Galilee, stood in the distance watching.

50, 51, 52 Then a man named Joseph, a member of the Jewish Supreme Court, from the city of Arimathea in Judea, went to Pilate and asked for the body of Jesus. He was a godly man who had been expecting the Messiah's coming and had not agreed with the decision and actions of the other Jewish leaders.

---

[6]Or, "the whole world."
[7]Implied.
[8]Literally, "yielded up the spirit."
[9]Literally, "righteous."

53   So he took down Jesus' body and wrapped it in a long linen cloth and laid it in a new, unused tomb hewn into the rock [at the side of a hill[10]].

54   This was done late on Friday afternoon, the day of preparation for the Sabbath.

55   As the body was taken away, the women from Galilee followed and saw it carried into the tomb.

56   Then they went home and prepared spices and ointments to embalm Him; but by the time they were finished it was the Sabbath, so they rested all that day as required by the Jewish law.

CHAPTER 24

B UT very early on Sunday morning they took the ointments to the tomb—

2   And found that the huge stone covering the entrance had been rolled aside.

3   So they went in—but the Lord Jesus' body was gone!

4   They stood there puzzled, trying to think what could have happened to it. Suddenly two men appeared before them, clothed in shining robes so bright their eyes were dazzled.

5   The women were terrified and bowed low before them. Then the men asked, "Why are you looking in a tomb for someone who is alive?

6, 7   He isn't here! He has come back to life again! Don't you remember what He told you back in Galilee—that the Messiah[1] must be betrayed into the power of evil men and be crucified and that He would rise again the third day?"

8   Then they remembered,

9   And rushed back to Jerusalem[2] to tell His eleven disciples —and everyone else—what had happened.

10   (The women who went to the tomb were Mary Magdalene and Joanna and Mary the mother of James, and several others.)

[10]Implied.
[1]Literally, "the Son of Man."
[2]Literally, "returned from the tomb."

11   But the story sounded like a fairy tale to the men—they didn't believe it.

12   However, Peter ran to the tomb to look. Stooping, he peered in and saw the empty linen wrappings; and then he went back home again, wondering what had happened.

13   That same day, Sunday, two of Jesus' followers were walking to the village of Emmaus, seven miles out of Jerusalem.

14   As they walked along they were talking of Jesus' death,

15   When suddenly Jesus Himself came along and joined them and began walking beside them!

16   But they didn't recognize Him, for God kept them from it.

17   "You seem to be in a deep discussion about something," He said. "What are you so concerned about?" They stopped short, sadness written across their faces.

18   And one of them, Cleopas, replied, "You must be the only person in Jerusalem who hasn't heard about the terrible things that happened there last week."[3]

19   "What things?" Jesus asked.

"The things that happened to Jesus, the Man from Nazareth," they said. "He was a Prophet who did incredible miracles and was a mighty Teacher, highly regarded by both God and man.

20   But the chief priests and our religious leaders arrested Him and handed Him over to the Roman government to be condemned to death, and they crucified Him.

21   We had thought He was the glorious Messiah and that He had come to rescue Israel. And now, besides all this—which happened three days ago—

22, 23   Some women from our group of His followers were at His tomb early this morning and came back with an amazing report that His body was missing, and that they had seen some angels there who told them Jesus is alive!

24   Some of our men ran out to see, and sure enough, Jesus' body was gone, just as the women had said."

---

[3]Literally, "in these days."

25   Then Jesus said to them, "You are such foolish, foolish people! You find it so hard to believe all that the prophets wrote in the Scriptures!

26   Wasn't it clearly predicted by the prophets that the Messiah would have to suffer all these things before entering His time of glory?"

27   Then Jesus quoted them passage after passage from the writings of the prophets, beginning with the book of Genesis and going right on through the Scriptures, explaining what the passages meant and what they said about Himself.

28   By this time they were nearing Emmaus and the end of their journey. Jesus would have gone on,

29   But they begged Him to stay the night with them, as it was getting late. So He went home with them.

30   As they sat down to eat, He asked God's blessing on the food and then took a small loaf of bread and broke it and was passing it over to them,

31   When suddenly—it was as though their eyes were opened—they recognized Him! And at that moment He disappeared!

32   They began telling each other how their hearts had felt strangely warm as He talked with them and explained the Scriptures during the walk down the road.

33, 34   Within the hour they were on their way back to Jerusalem, where the eleven disciples and the other followers of Jesus greeted them with these words, "The Lord has really risen! He appeared to Peter!"

35   Then the two from Emmaus told their story of how Jesus had appeared to them as they were walking along the road and how they had recognized Him as He was breaking the bread.

36   And just as they were telling about it, Jesus Himself was suddenly standing there among them, and greeted them!

37   But the whole group was terribly frightened, thinking they were seeing a ghost!

38   "Why are you frightened?" He asked. "Why do you doubt that it is really I?

39   Look at My hands! Look at My feet! You can see that it is I, Myself! Touch Me and make sure that I am not a ghost! For ghosts don't have bodies, as you see that I do!"

40   As He spoke, He held out His hands for them to see [the marks of the nails[4]], and showed them [the wounds in[4]] His feet.

41   Still they stood there undecided, filled with joy and doubt. Then He asked them, "Do you have anything here to eat?"

42   They gave Him a piece of broiled fish,

43   And He ate it as they watched!

44   Then He said, "When I was with you before, don't you remember My telling you that everything written about Me by Moses and the prophets and in the Psalms must all come true?"

45   Then He opened their minds to understand at last these many Scriptures!

46   And He said, "Yes, it was written long ago that the Messiah must suffer and die and rise again from the dead on the third day;

47   And that this message of salvation should be taken from Jerusalem to all the nations: *There is forgiveness of sins for all who turn to Me.*

48   You have seen these prophecies come true.

49   And now I will send the Holy Spirit[5] upon you, just as My Father promised. Don't begin telling others[6] yet—stay here in the city until the Holy Spirit comes and fills you with power from heaven."

50   Then Jesus led them out along the road[7] to Bethany, and lifting His hands to heaven, He blessed them,

51   And then began rising into the sky, and went on to heaven.

52   And they worshiped Him, and returned to Jerusalem filled with mighty joy,

53   And were continually in the Temple, praising God.

---

[4]Implied.
[5]Implied. Literally, "the promise of my Father."
[6]Literally, "but wait here in the city until. . . ." The paraphrase relates this to verse 47.
[7]Implied. Bethany was a mile or so away, across the valley on the Mount of Olives.

TUNE IN!

We live in an exciting world. We who are young in the 20th Century balance atop a surfer's wave of accelerating action. This restless, pulsating action affects our lives in many ways . . . scientific advances are changing the way we shop, travel, learn and relax.

The delegate to the National Youth Conference on the Atom watching an experiment at Argonne National Laboratories is —with us—intensely interested in what's coming next and how it will affect us. Projections about flat TV's, computer-regulated traffic, air travel to anywhere in the world in 45 minutes, pocket computers, cities below the surface of the sea—all seem like science fiction, yet reputable scientists are predicting them. But as we read and hear about the widening stream of these innovations, we often get strange concepts about God's role in all these changes. One group of university students was asked, "Do you believe God fully understands the molecule and the atom?" The majority replied that they thought that He did not (the story sounds absurd, but it's true!). Somehow,

in our modern times, we get the idea that God was able to put together trees and animals and mountains, but that He really can't keep up on such things as jet travel, new cars, satellite TV, contemporary music and fantastic computer advances. Yet God set up all the principles by which our electronic age functions. In a very real sense He made (through the brains of humans whom he created) the neat sports car you've been eyeing, the chic clothes, the jet to Acapulco, just as unquestionably as He made the birds and the bees and the trees.

The magnificent truth—for each of us who really cares to find it out—is that the Person who masterminded all creation was once breathing, sleeping and eating on this planet Earth just as you and I are: and we can get acquainted with Him! Carefully read the first five verses of this book. Think them through in relation to all that's going on around you. This flesh-and-blood Jesus caused the most dramatic events that ever happened on this planet. And here, from the original documents—part of the Bible itself—you have the full story. Read this book carefully and see how the contemporary Jesus relates to *you!*

JOHN

CHAPTER 1

BEFORE anything else existed,[1] there was Christ,[2] with God. He has always[1] been alive and is Himself God.

3 He created everything there is—nothing exists that He didn't make.

4 Eternal life is in Him, and this life gives light to all mankind.

5 His life is the light that shines through the darkness—and the darkness can never extinguish it.

6, 7 God sent John the Baptist as a witness to the fact that Jesus Christ is the true Light.

8 John himself was not the Light; he was only a witness to identify it.

9 Later on, the one who is the true Light arrived to shine on everyone coming into the world.

10 But although He made the world, the world didn't recognize Him when He came.

11, 12 Even in His own land and among His own people, the Jews, He was not accepted. Only a few would welcome and receive Him. But to all who received Him, He gave the right to become children of God. All they needed to do was to trust Him to save them.[3]

13 All those who believe this are reborn!—not a physical rebirth[4] resulting from human passion or plan—but from the will of God.

[1]Literally, "In the beginning."
[2]Literally, "the Word," meaning Christ, the wisdom and power of God and the first cause of all things; God's personal expression of Himself to men.
[3]Literally, "to believe on His name."
[4]Literally, "not of blood."

214

14 And Christ[5] became a human being and lived here on earth among us and was full of loving forgiveness[6] and truth. And some of us have seen His glory[7]—the glory of the only Son of the heavenly Father![8]

15 John pointed Him out to the people, telling the crowds, "This is the one I was talking about when I said, 'Someone is coming who is greater by far than I am—for He existed long before I did!' "

16 We have all benefited from the rich blessings He brought to us—blessing upon blessing heaped upon us!

17 For Moses gave us only the Law with its rigid demands and merciless justice, while Jesus Christ brought us loving forgiveness as well.

18 No one has ever actually seen God, but, of course, His only Son has, for He is the companion of the Father and has told us all about Him.

19 The Jewish leaders[9] sent priests and assistant priests from Jerusalem to ask John whether he claimed to be the Messiah.

20 He denied it flatly. "I am not the Christ," he said.

21 "Well then, who are you?" they asked. "Are you Elijah?"

"No," he replied.

"Are you the Prophet?"

"No."

22 "Then who are you? Tell us, so we can give an answer to those who sent us. What do you have to say for yourself?"

23 He replied, "I am a voice from the barren wilderness, shouting as Isaiah prophesied, 'Get ready for the coming of the Lord!' "

24, 25 Then those who were sent by the Pharisees asked him, "If you aren't the Messiah or Elijah or the Prophet, what right do you have to baptize?"

---

[5]Literally, "the Word," meaning Christ, the wisdom and power of God and the first cause of all things; God's personal expression of Himself to men.
[6]Literally, "grace."
[7]See Matthew 17:2.
[8]Or, "His unique Son."
[9]Literally, "the Jews."
[10]See Deuteronomy 18:15.

26 John told them, "I merely baptize with[11] water, but right here in the crowd is Someone you have never met,

27 Who will soon begin His ministry among you, and I am not even fit to be His slave."

28 This incident took place at Bethany, a village on the other side of the Jordan River where John was baptizing.

29 The next day John saw Jesus coming toward him and said, "Look! There is the Lamb of God who takes away the world's sin!

30 He is the one I was talking about when I said, 'Soon a man far greater than I am is coming, who existed long before me!'

31 I didn't know He was the one, but I am here baptizing with[11] water in order to point Him out to the nation of Israel."

32 Then John told about seeing the Holy Spirit in the form of a dove descending from heaven and resting upon Jesus.

33 "I didn't know He was the one," John said again, "but at the time God sent me to baptize He told me, 'When you see the Holy Spirit descending and resting upon someone—He is the one you are looking for. He is the one who baptizes with[11] the Holy Spirit.'

34 I saw it happen to this man, and I therefore testify that He is the Son of God."

35 The following day as John was standing with two of his disciples,

36 Jesus walked by. John looked at Him intently and then declared, "See! There is the Lamb of God!"

37 Then John's two disciples turned and followed Jesus!

38 Jesus looked around and saw them following. "What do you want?" He asked them.

"Sir," they replied, "where do You live?"

39 "Come and see," He said. So they went with Him to the place where He was staying and were with Him from about four o'clock that afternoon until the evening.

40 (One of these men was Andrew, Simon Peter's brother.)

---

[11]Or, "in."

41 Andrew then went to find his brother Peter and told him, "We have found the Messiah!"

42 And he brought Peter to meet Jesus. Jesus looked intently at Peter for a moment and then said, "You are Simon, John's son—but you shall be called Peter, the rock!"

43 The next day Jesus decided to go to Galilee. He found Philip and told him, "Come with Me."

44 (Philip was from Bethsaida, Andrew and Peter's home town.)

45 Philip now went off to look for Nathanael and told him, "We have found the Messiah!—the very person Moses and the prophets told about! His name is Jesus, the son of Joseph from Nazareth!"

46 "Nazareth!" exclaimed Nathanael. "Can anything good come from there?"

"Just come and see for yourself," Philip declared.

47 As they approached, Jesus said, "Here comes an honest man—a true son of Israel."

48 "How do you know what I am like?" Nathanael demanded.

And Jesus replied, "I could see you under the fig tree before Philip found you."

49 Nathanael replied, "Sir, You are the Son of God—the King of Israel!"

50 Jesus asked him, "Do you believe all this just because I told you I had seen you under the fig tree? You will see greater proofs than this.

51 You will even see heaven open and the angels of God coming back and forth to Me, the Man of Glory."[12]

CHAPTER 2

TWO days later Jesus' mother was a guest at a wedding in the village of Cana in Galilee,

2 And Jesus and His disciples were invited too.

---

[12]Literally, "the Son of Man." This was a name of great exaltation and glory.

3 The wine supply ran out during the festivities, and Jesus' mother came to Him with the problem.

4 "I can't help you now," He said.[1] "It isn't yet My time for miracles."

5 But His mother told the servants, "Do whatever He tells you to."

6 Six stone waterpots were standing there; they were used for Jewish ceremonial purposes and held perhaps 20 to 30 gallons each.

7, 8 Then Jesus told the servants to fill them to the brim with water. When this was done He said, "Dip some out and take it to the master of ceremonies."

9 When the master of ceremonies tasted the water that was now wine, not knowing where it had come from (though, of course, the servants did), he called the bridegroom over.

10 "This is wonderful stuff!" he said, "You're different from most! Usually a host uses the best wine first, and afterwards, when everyone is full and doesn't care, then he brings out the less expensive brands. But you have kept the best for the last!"

11 This miracle at Cana in Galilee was Jesus' first public demonstration of His heaven-sent power. And His disciples believed that He really was the Messiah.[2]

12 After the wedding He left for Capernaum for a few days with His mother, brothers, and disciples.

13 Then it was time for the annual Jewish Passover celebration, and Jesus went to Jerusalem.

14 In the Temple area He saw merchants selling cattle, sheep, and doves for sacrifices, and money changers behind their counters.

15 Jesus made a whip from some ropes and chased them all out, and drove out the sheep and oxen, scattering the money changers' coins over the floor and turning over their tables!

16 Then, going over to the men selling doves, He told them, "Get these things out of here. Don't turn My Father's House into a market!"

[1] Literally, "Woman, what have I to do with you?"
[2] Literally, "His disciples believed on Him."

17 Then His disciples remembered this prophecy from the Scriptures: "Concern for God's House will be My undoing."

18 "What right have you to order them out?" the Jewish leaders[3] demanded. "If you have this authority from God, show us a miracle to prove it."

19 "All right," Jesus replied, "this is the miracle I will do for you: Destroy this sanctuary and in three days I will raise it up!"

20 "What!" they exclaimed. "It took 46 years to build this Temple, and you can do it in three days?"

21 But by "this sanctuary" He meant His body.

22 After He came back to life again, the disciples remembered His saying this and realized that what He had quoted from the Scriptures really did refer to Him, and had all come true!

23 Because of the miracles He did in Jerusalem at the Passover celebration, many people were convinced that He was indeed the Messiah.

24, 25 But Jesus didn't trust them, for He knew mankind to the core. No one needed to tell Him how changeable human nature is!

CHAPTER 3

AFTER dark one night a Jewish religious leader named Nicodemus, a member of the sect of the Pharisees, came for an interview with Jesus. "Sir," he said, "we all know that God has sent You to teach us. Your miracles are proof enough of this."

3 Jesus replied, "With all the earnestness I possess I tell you this: Unless you are born again, you can never get into the Kingdom of God."

4 "Born again!" exclaimed Nicodemus. "What do You mean? How can an old man go back into his mother's womb and be born again?"

[3]Literally, "the Jews."

5 Jesus replied, "What I am telling you so earnestly is this: Unless one is born of water[1] and the Spirit, he cannot enter the Kingdom of God.

6 Men can only reproduce human life, but the Holy Spirit gives new life from heaven;

7 So don't be surprised at My statement that you must be born again!

8 Just as you can hear the wind but can't tell where it comes from or where it will go next, so it is with the Spirit. We do not know on whom He will next bestow this life from heaven."

9 "What do You mean?" Nicodemus asked.

10, 11 Jesus replied, "You, a respected Jewish teacher, and yet you don't understand these things? I am telling you what I know and have seen—and yet you won't believe Me.

12 But if you don't even believe Me when I tell you about such things as these that happen here among men, how can you possibly believe if I tell you what is going on in heaven?

13 For only I, the Man of Heaven,[2] have come to earth and will return to heaven again.

14 And as Moses in the wilderness lifted up the bronze image of a serpent on a pole, even so I must be lifted up upon a pole,

15 So that anyone who believes in Me will have eternal life.

16 For God loved the world so much that He gave His only[3] Son so that anyone who believes in Him shall not perish but have eternal life.

17 God did not send His Son into the world to condemn it, but to save it.

18 There is no eternal doom awaiting those who trust Him to save them. But those who don't trust Him have already been tried and condemned for not believing in the only[3] Son of God.

19 Their sentence is based on this fact: that the Light from

---

[1] Or, "Physical birth is not enough. You must also be born spiritually. . . ." This alternate paraphrase interprets "born of water" as meaning the normal process observed during every human birth.
[2] Literally, "the Son of Man."
[3] Or, "the unique Son of God."

heaven came into the world, but they loved the darkness more than the Light, for their deeds were evil.

20   They hated the heavenly Light because they wanted to sin in the darkness. They stayed away from that Light for fear their sins would be exposed and they would be punished.

21   But those doing right come gladly to the Light to let everyone see that they are doing what God wants them to."

*   *   *   *   *

22   Afterwards Jesus and His disciples left Jerusalem and stayed for a while in Judea and baptized there.

*   *   *   *   *

23, 24   At this time John the Baptist was not yet in prison. He was baptizing at Aenon, near Salim, because there was plenty of water there.

25   One day someone began an argument with John's disciples, telling them that Jesus' baptism was best.[4]

26   So they came to John and said, "Master, the man you met on the other side of the Jordan River—the one you said was the Messiah—He is baptizing too, and everybody is going over there instead of coming here to us."

27   John replied, "God in heaven appoints each man's work.

28   My work is to prepare the way for that man so that everyone will go to Him. You yourselves know how plainly I told you that I am not the Messiah. I am here to prepare the way for Him—that is all.

29   The crowds will naturally go to the main attraction[5]— the bride will go where the bridegroom is! A bridegroom's friends rejoice with him. I am the Bridegroom's friend, and I am filled with joy at His success.

30   He must become greater and greater, and I must become less and less.

31   He has come from heaven and is greater than anyone else. I am of the earth, and my understanding is limited to the things of earth.

---

[4]Literally, "about purification."
[5]Implied.

32 He tells what He has seen and heard, but how few believe what He tells them!

33, 34 Those who believe Him discover that God is a fountain of truth. For this one—sent by God—speaks God's words, for God's Spirit is upon Him without measure or limit.

35 The Father loves this man because He is His Son, and God has given Him everything there is.

36 And all who trust Him—God's Son—to save them have eternal life; those who don't believe and obey Him shall never see heaven, but the wrath of God remains upon them."

CHAPTER 4

WHEN the Lord knew that the Pharisees had heard about the greater crowds coming to Him than to John to be baptized and to become His disciples—(though Jesus Himself didn't baptize them, but His disciples did)—

3 He left Judea and returned to the province of Galilee.

4 He had to go through Samaria on the way,

5, 6 And around noon as He approached the village of Sychar, He came to Jacob's Well, located on the parcel of ground Jacob gave to his son Joseph. Jesus was tired from the long walk in the hot sun and sat wearily beside the well.

7 Soon a Samaritan woman came to draw water, and Jesus asked her for a drink.

8 He was alone at the time as His disciples had gone into the village to buy some food.

9 The woman was surprised that a Jew would ask a "despised Samaritan" for anything—usually they wouldn't even speak to them!—and she remarked about this to Jesus.

10 He replied, "If you only knew what a wonderful gift God has for you, and who I am, you would ask Me for some *living* water!"

11 "But you don't have a rope or a bucket," she said, "and this is a very deep well! Where would you get this living water?

12   And besides, are you greater than our ancestor Jacob? How can you offer better water than this which he and his sons and cattle enjoyed?"

13   Jesus replied that people soon became thirsty again after drinking this water.

14   "But the water I give them," He said, "becomes a perpetual spring within them, watering them forever with eternal life."

15   "Please, sir," the woman said, "give me some of that water! Then I'll never be thirsty again and won't have to make this long trip out here every day."

16   "Go and get your husband," Jesus told her.

17, 18   "But I'm not married," the woman replied.

"All too true!" Jesus said. "For you have had five husbands, and you aren't even married to the man you're living with now. [You couldn't have spoken a truer word![1]]"

19   "Sir," the woman said, "You must be a prophet.

20   But say, tell me, why is it that you Jews insist that Jerusalem is the only place of worship, while we Samaritans claim it is here [at Mount Gerazim[1]], where our ancestors worshiped?"

21, 22, 23, 24   Jesus replied, "The time is coming, Ma'am, when we will no longer be concerned about whether to worship the Father here or in Jerusalem. For it's not *where* we worship that counts, but *how* we worship—is our worship spiritual and real? Do we have the Holy Spirit's help? For God is Spirit, and we must have His help to worship as we should. The Father wants this kind of worship from us. But you Samaritans know so little about Him, worshiping blindly, while we Jews know all about Him, for salvation comes to the world through the Jews."

25   The woman said, "Well, at least I know that the Messiah will come—the one they call Christ—and when He does, He will explain everything to us."

26   Then Jesus told her, "I am the Messiah!"

27   Just then His disciples arrived. They were surprised to find Him talking to a woman, but none of them asked Him why, or what they had been discussing.

---

[1]Implied.

28, 29   Then the woman left her waterpot beside the well and went back to the village and told everyone, "Come and meet a man who told me everything I ever did! Can this be the Messiah?"

30   So the people came streaming from the village to see Him.

31   Meanwhile, the disciples were urging Jesus to eat.

32   "No," He said, "I have some food you don't know about."

33   "Who brought it to Him?" the disciples asked each other.

34   Then Jesus explained: "My nourishment comes from doing the will of God who sent Me, and from finishing His work.

35   Do you think the work of harvesting will not begin until the summer ends four months from now? Look around you! Vast fields of human souls are ripening all around us, and are ready now for reaping.

36   The reapers will be paid good wages and will be gathering eternal souls into the granaries of heaven! What joys await the sower and the reaper, both together!

37   For it is true that one sows and someone else reaps.

38   I sent you to reap where you didn't sow; others did the work, and you received the harvest."

39   Many from the Samaritan village believed He was the Messiah because of the woman's report: "He told me everything I ever did!"

40, 41   When they came out to see Him at the well, they begged Him to stay at their village; and He did, for two days, long enough for many of them to believe in Him after hearing Him.

42   Then they said to the woman, "Now we believe because we have heard Him ourselves, not just because of what you told us. He is indeed the Savior of the world."

43, 44   At the end of the two days' stay He went on into Galilee,[2] for as Jesus used to say, "A prophet is honored everywhere except in his own country!"

---

[2] Apparently to avoid the crowds.

45   But the Galileans welcomed Him with open arms, for they had been in Jerusalem at the Passover celebration and had seen some of His miracles.[3]

46, 47   In the course of His journey through Galilee He arrived at the town of Cana, where He had turned the water into wine. While He was there, a man in the city of Capernaum, a government official, whose son was very sick, heard that Jesus had come from Judea and was traveling in Galilee. This man went over to Cana, found Jesus, and begged Him to come to Capernaum with him and heal his son, who was now at death's door.

48   Jesus asked, "Won't any of you believe in Me unless I do more and more miracles?"

49   The official pled, "Sir, please come now before my child dies."

50   Then Jesus told him, "Go back home. Your son is healed!" And the man believed Jesus and started home.

51   While he was on his way, some of his servants met him with the news that all was well—his son had recovered!

52   He asked them when the lad had begun to feel better, and they replied, "Yesterday afternoon at about one o'clock his fever suddenly disappeared!"

53   Then the father realized it was the same moment that Jesus had told him, "Your son is healed." And the officer and his entire household believed that Jesus was the Messiah.

54   This was Jesus' second miracle in Galilee after coming from Judea.

CHAPTER 5

AFTERWARDS Jesus returned to Jerusalem for one of the Jewish religious holidays.

2   Inside the city, near the Sheep Gate, was Bethesda Pool, with five covered platforms or porches surrounding it.

3   Crowds of sick folks—lame, blind, or with paralyzed

---

[3]See John 2:23.

limbs—lay on the platforms (waiting for a certain movement of the water,

4   For an angel of the Lord came from time to time and disturbed the water, and the first person to step down into it afterwards was healed).[1]

5   One of the men lying there had been sick for 38 years.

6   When Jesus saw him and knew how long he had been ill, He asked him, "Would you like to get well?"

7   "I can't," the sick man said, "for I have no one to help me into the pool at the movement of the water. While I am trying to get there, someone else always gets in ahead of me."

8   Jesus told him, "Stand up, roll up your sleeping mat and go on home!"

9   Instantly, the man was healed! He rolled up the mat and began walking! But it was on the Sabbath when this miracle was done.

10   So the Jewish leaders objected. They said to the man who was cured, "You can't work on the Sabbath! It's illegal to carry that sleeping mat!"

11   "The man who healed me told me to," was his reply.

12   "Who said such a thing as that?" they demanded.

13   The man didn't know, and Jesus had disappeared into the crowd.

14   But afterwards Jesus found him in the Temple and told him, "Now you are well; don't sin as you did before,[2] or something even worse may happen to you."

15   Then the man went to find the Jewish leaders and told them it was Jesus who had healed him.

16   So they began harassing Jesus as a Sabbath breaker.

17   But Jesus replied, "My Father constantly does good,[3] and I'm following His example."

18   Then the Jewish leaders were all the more eager to kill Him because in addition to disobeying their Sabbath laws, He had spoken of God as His Father, thereby making Himself equal with God.

---

[1] Many of the ancient manuscripts omit the material within the parentheses.
[2] Implied. Literally, "sin no more."
[3] Implied. Literally, "My Father works even until now, and I work."

19   Jesus replied, "The Son can do nothing by Himself. He does only what He sees the Father doing, and in the same way.

20   For the Father loves the Son, and tells Him everything He is doing; and the Son will do far more awesome miracles than this man's healing!

21   He will even raise from the dead anyone He wants to, just as the Father does.

22   And the Father leaves all judgment of sin to His Son,

23   So that everyone will honor the Son, just as they honor the Father. But if you refuse to honor God's Son, whom He sent to you, then you are certainly not honoring the Father.

24   I say emphatically that anyone who listens to My message and believes in God who sent Me has eternal life, and will never be damned for his sins, but has already passed out of death into life.

25   And I solemnly declare that the time is coming, in fact, it is here, when the dead shall hear My voice—the voice of the Son of God—and those who listen shall live.

26   The Father has life in Himself, and has granted His Son to have life in Himself,

27   And to judge the sins of all mankind because He is the Son of Man.

28   Don't be so surprised! Indeed the time is coming when all the dead in their graves shall hear the voice of God's Son,

29   And shall rise again—those who have done good, to eternal life; and those who have continued in evil, to judgment.

30   But I pass no judgment without consulting the Father. I judge as I am told. And My judgment is absolutely fair and just, for it is according to the will of God who sent Me and is not merely My own.

31   When I make claims about Myself they aren't believed,

32, 33   But someone else, yes, John the Baptist,[4] is making these claims for Me too. You have gone out to listen to his preaching, and I can assure you that all he says about Me is true!

[4]Implied. However, most commentators believe the reference is to the witness of His Father. See verse 37.

34   But the truest witness I have is not from a man, though I have reminded you about John's witness so that you will believe in Me and be saved.

35   John shone brightly for a while, and you benefited and rejoiced,

36   But I have a greater witness than John. I refer to the miracles I do; these have been assigned Me by the Father, and they prove that the Father has sent Me.

37   And the Father Himself has also testified about Me, though not appearing to you personally, or speaking to you directly.

38   But you are not listening to Him, for you refuse to believe Me—the one sent to you with God's message.

39   You search the Scriptures, for you believe they give you eternal life. And the Scriptures point to Me!

40   Yet you won't come to Me so that I can give you this life eternal!

41, 42   Your approval or disapproval means nothing to Me, for as I know so well, you don't have God's love within you.

43   I know, because I have come to you representing My Father and you refuse to welcome Me, though you readily enough receive those who aren't sent from Him, but represent only themselves!

44   No wonder you can't believe! For you gladly honor each other, but you don't care about the honor that comes from the only God!

45   Yet it is not I who will accuse you of this to the Father—Moses will! Moses, on whose laws you set your hopes of heaven.

46   For you have refused to believe Moses. He wrote about Me, but you refuse to believe him, so you refuse to believe in Me.

47   And since you don't believe what he wrote, no wonder you don't believe Me either."

CHAPTER 6

AFTER this, Jesus crossed over the Sea of Galilee, also known as the Sea of Tiberias.

2, 3, 4, 5   And a huge crowd, many of them pilgrims on their way to Jerusalem for the annual Passover celebration[1], were following Him wherever He went, to watch Him heal the sick. So when Jesus went up into the hills and sat down with His disciples around Him, He soon saw a great multitude of people climbing the hill, looking for Him. Turning to Philip He asked, "Philip, where can we buy bread to feed all these people?"

6   (He was testing Philip, for He already knew what He was going to do.)

7   Philip replied, "It would take a fortune[2] to begin to do it!"

8, 9   Then Andrew, Simon Peter's brother, spoke up. "There's a youngster here with five barley loaves and a couple of fish! But what good is that with all this mob?"

10   "Tell everyone to sit down," Jesus ordered. And all of them—the approximate count of the men only was 5,000—sat down on the grassy slopes.

11   Then Jesus took the loaves and gave thanks to God and passed them out to the people. Afterwards He did the same with the fish. And everyone ate until full!

12   "Now gather the scraps," Jesus told His disciples, "so that nothing is wasted."

13   And 12 baskets were filled with the leftovers!

14   When the people realized what a great miracle had happened, they exclaimed, "Surely, He is the Prophet we have been expecting!"

15   Jesus saw that they were ready to take Him by force and make Him their king, so He went higher into the mountains alone.

16   That evening His disciples went down to the shore to wait for Him.

[1] Literally, "Now the Passover, the feast of the Jews, was at hand."
[2] Literally, 200 denarii, a denarius being a full day's wage.

17   But as darkness fell and Jesus still hadn't come back, they got into the boat and headed out across the lake toward Capernaum.

18, 19   But soon a gale swept down upon them as they rowed, and the sea grew very rough. They were three or four miles out when suddenly they saw Jesus walking toward the boat! They were terrified,

20   But He called out to them and told them not to be afraid.

21   Then they were willing to let Him in, and immediately the boat was where they were going![3]

22, 23   The next morning, back across the lake, crowds began gathering on the shore [waiting to see Jesus[4]]. For they knew that He and His disciples had come over together and that the disciples had gone off in their boat, leaving Him behind. Several small boats from Tiberias were nearby,

24   So when the people saw that Jesus wasn't there, nor His disciples, they got into the boats and went across to Capernaum to look for Him.

25   When they arrived and found Him, they said, "Sir, how did You get here?"

26   Jesus replied, "The truth of the matter is that you want to be with Me because I fed you, not because you believe in Me.

27   But you shouldn't be so concerned about perishable things like food. No, spend your energy seeking the eternal life that I the Man from Heaven[5] can give you. For God the Father has sent Me for this very purpose."

28   They replied, "What should we do to satisfy God?"

29   Jesus told them, "This is the will of God, that you believe in the one He has sent."

30, 31   They replied, "You must show us more miracles if You want us to believe You are the Messiah. Give us free bread every day, like our fathers had while they journeyed

---

[3]Literally, "and straightway the boat was at the land . . . ."
[4]Implied.
[5]Literally, "the Son of Man."

through the wilderness! As the Scriptures say, 'Moses gave them bread from heaven.' "

32   Jesus said, "Moses didn't give it to them. My Father did.[6] And now He offers you true Bread from heaven.

33   The true Bread is a Person—the one sent by God from heaven, and He gives life to the world."

34   "Sir," they said, "give us that bread every day of our lives!"

35   Jesus replied, "I am the Bread of Life. No one coming to Me will ever be hungry again. Those believing in Me will never thirst.

36   But the trouble is, as I have told you before, you haven't believed even though you have seen Me.

37   But some will come to Me—those the Father has given Me—and I will never, never reject them.

38   For I have come here from heaven to do the will of God who sent Me, not to have My own way.

39   And this is the will of God, that I should not lose even one of all those He has given Me, but that I should raise them to eternal life at the Last Day.

40   For it is My Father's will that everyone who sees His Son and believes on Him should have eternal life—that I should raise him at the Last Day."

41   Then the Jews began to murmur against Him because He claimed to be the Bread from heaven.

42   "What?" they exclaimed. "Why, he is merely Jesus the son of Joseph, whose father and mother we know. What is this he is saying, that he came down from heaven?"

43   But Jesus replied, "Don't murmur among yourselves about My saying that.

44   For no one can come to Me unless the Father who sent Me draws him to Me, and at the Last Day I will bring all such back to life.

45   As it is written in the Scriptures, 'They shall all be taught of God.' Those the Father speaks to, who learn the truth from Him, will be attracted to Me.

---

[6]Implied.

46   (Not that anyone actually sees the Father, for only I have seen Him.)

47   How earnestly I tell you this—anyone who believes in Me already has eternal life!

48   Yes, I am the Bread of Life!

49   There was no real life[7] in that bread from the skies, which was given to your fathers in the wilderness, for they all died.

50, 51   But there is such a thing as Bread from heaven giving eternal life to everyone who eats it. And I am that Living Bread that came down out of heaven. Anyone eating this Bread shall live forever; My flesh is this Bread, given to redeem humanity."

52   Then the Jews began arguing with each other about what He meant. "How can this man give us his flesh to eat?" they asked.

53   So Jesus said it again, "With all the earnestness I possess I tell you this: Unless you eat the flesh of the Man of Glory[8] and drink His blood, you cannot have eternal life within you.

54   But anyone who does eat My flesh and drink My blood has eternal life, and I will raise him at the Last Day.

55   For My flesh is the true food, and My blood is the true drink.

56   Everyone who eats My flesh and drinks My blood is in Me, and I in him.

57   I live by the power of the living Father who sent Me, and in the same way those who partake of Me shall live because of Me!

58   I am the true Bread from heaven; and anyone who eats this Bread shall live forever, and not die as your fathers did—though they ate bread from heaven."

59   (He preached this sermon in the synagogue in Capernaum.)

60   Even His disciples said, "This is very hard to understand. Who can tell what He means?"

---

[7]Implied.
[8]Implied. Literally, "Son of Man."

61   Jesus knew within Himself that His disciples were complaining and said to them, "Does *this* offend you?

62   Then what will you think if you see Me, the Son of Mankind, return to heaven again?

63   Only the Holy Spirit gives eternal life.[9] Those born only once with physical birth[10] will never receive this gift. But now I have told you how to get this true spiritual life.

64   But some of you don't believe Me." (For Jesus knew from the beginning who didn't believe and knew the one who would betray Him.)

65   And He remarked, "That is what I meant when I said that no one can come to Me unless the Father attracts him to Me."

66   At this point many of His disciples turned away and deserted Him.

67   Then Jesus turned to the Twelve and asked, "Are you going too?"

68   Simon Peter replied, "Master, to whom shall we go? You alone have the words that give eternal life,

69   And we believe them and know You are the holy Son of God."

70   Then Jesus said, "I chose the twelve of you, and one is a devil."

71   He was speaking of Judas, son of Simon Iscariot, one of the Twelve, who would betray Him.

CHAPTER 7

AFTER this, Jesus went to Galilee, going from village to village, for he wanted to stay out of Judea where the Jewish leaders were plotting His death.

2   But soon it was time for the Tabernacle Ceremonies, one of the annual Jewish holidays,

3   And Jesus' brothers urged Him to go to Judea for the

---

[9]Literally, "It is the Spirit who quickens."
[10]See John 1:13. Literally, "the flesh profits nothing."

celebration. "Go where more people can see your miracles!" they scoffed.

4 "You can't be famous when you hide like this! If you're so great, prove it to the world!"

5 For even His brothers didn't believe in Him.

6 Jesus replied, "It is not the right time for Me to go now. But you can go anytime and it will make no difference,

7 For the world can't hate you; but it does hate Me, because I accuse it of sin and evil.

8 You go on, and I'll come later[1] when it is the right time."

9 So He remained in Galilee.

10 But after His brothers had left for the celebration, then He went too, though secretly, staying out of the public eye.

11 The Jewish leaders tried to find Him at the celebration and kept asking if anyone had seen Him.

12 There was a lot of discussion about Him among the crowds. Some said, "He's a wonderful man," while others said, "No, he's duping the public."

13 But no one had the courage to speak out for Him in public for fear of reprisals from the Jewish leaders.

14 Then, midway through the festival, Jesus went up to the Temple and preached openly.

15 The Jewish leaders were surprised when they heard Him. "How can he know so much when he's never been to our schools?" they asked.

16 So Jesus told them, "I'm not teaching you My own thoughts, but those of God who sent Me.

17 If any of you really determines to do God's will, then you will certainly know whether My teaching is from God or is merely My own.

18 Anyone presenting his own ideas is looking for praise for himself, but anyone seeking to honor the one who sent him is a good and true person.

19 None of *you* obeys the laws of Moses! So why pick on *Me* for breaking them? Why kill *Me* for this?"

---

[1]Literally, "I go not up (yet) unto this feast." The word "yet" is included in the text of many ancient manuscripts.

20 The crowd replied, "You're out of your mind! Who's trying to kill you?"

21, 22, 23 Jesus replied, "I worked on the Sabbath by healing a man, and you were surprised. But you work on the Sabbath, too, whenever you obey Moses' law of circumcision (actually, however, this tradition of circumcision is older than the Mosaic law); for if the correct time for circumcising your children falls on the Sabbath, you go ahead and do it, as you should. So why should I be condemned for making a man completely well on the Sabbath?

24 Think this through and you will see that I am right."

25 Some of the people who lived there in Jerusalem said among themselves, "Isn't this the man they are trying to kill?

26 But here He is preaching in public, and they say nothing to Him. Can it be that our leaders have learned, after all, that He really is the Messiah?

27 But how could He be? For we know where this man was born; when Christ comes, He will just appear and no one will know where He comes from."

28 So Jesus, in a sermon in the Temple, called out, "Yes, you know Me and where I was born and raised, but I am the representative of one you don't know, and He is Truth.

29 I know Him because I was with Him, and He sent Me to you."

30 Then the Jewish leaders sought to arrest Him; but no hand was laid on Him, for God's time had not yet come.

31 Many among the crowds at the Temple believed on Him. "After all," they said, "what miracles do you expect the Messiah to do that this man hasn't done?"

32 When the Pharisees heard that the crowds were in this mood, they and the chief priests sent officers to arrest Jesus.

33 But Jesus told them, "[Not yet![2]] I am to be here a little longer. Then I shall return to the one who sent Me.

34 You will search for Me but not find Me. And you won't be able to come where I am!"

35 The Jewish leaders were puzzled by this statement.

---

[2]Implied.

"Where is he planning to go?" they asked. "Maybe he is thinking of leaving the country and going as a missionary among the Jews in other lands, or maybe even to the Gentiles!

36   What does he mean about our looking for him and not being able to find him, and, 'You won't be able to come where I am'?"

37   On the last day, the climax of the holidays, Jesus shouted to the crowds, "If anyone is thirsty, let him come to Me and drink.

38   For the Scriptures declare that rivers of living water shall flow from the inmost being of anyone who believes in Me."

39   (He was speaking of the Holy Spirit, who would be given to everyone believing in Him; but the Spirit had not yet been given, because Jesus had not yet returned to His glory in heaven.)

40   When the crowds heard Him say this, some of them declared, "This man surely is the prophet who will come just before the Messiah."

41, 42   Others said, "He *is* the Messiah." Still others, "But he *can't* be! Will the Messiah come from *Galilee?* For the Scriptures clearly state that the Messiah will be born of the royal line of David, in *Bethlehem,* the village where David was born."

43   So the crowd was divided about Him.

44   And some wanted Him arrested, but no one touched Him.

45   The Temple police who had been sent to arrest Him returned to the chief priests and Pharisees. "Why didn't you bring Him in?" they demanded.

46   "He says such wonderful things!" they mumbled. "We've never heard anything like it."

47   "So you also have been led astray?" the Pharisees mocked.

48   "Is there a single one of us Jewish rulers or Pharisees who believes he is the Messiah?

49 These stupid crowds do, yes; but what do they know about it? A curse upon them anyway!"[3]

50 Then Nicodemus spoke up. (Remember him? He was the Jewish leader who came secretly to interview Jesus.)

51 "Is it legal to convict a man before he is even tried?" he asked.

52 They replied, "Are you a wretched Galilean too? Search the Scriptures and see for yourself—no prophets will come from Galilee!"

53[4] Then the meeting broke up and everybody went home.

CHAPTER 8

JESUS returned to the Mount of Olives,

2 But early the next morning He was back again at the Temple. A crowd soon gathered, and He sat down and talked to them.

3 As He was speaking, the Jewish leaders and Pharisees brought a woman caught in adultery and placed her out in front of the staring crowd.

4 "Teacher," they said to Jesus, "this woman was caught in the very act of adultery.

5 Moses' law says to kill her. What about it?"

6 They were trying to trap Him into saying something they could use against Him, but Jesus stooped down and wrote in the dust with His finger.

7 They kept demanding an answer, so He stood up again and said, "All right, hurl the stones at her until she dies. But only he who never sinned may throw the first!"

8 Then He stooped down again and wrote some more in the dust.

9 And the Jewish leaders slipped away one by one, beginning with the eldest, until only Jesus was left in front of the crowd with the woman.

---

[3]Literally, "This multitude is accursed."
[4]Most ancient manuscripts omit John 7:53-8:11.

10   Then Jesus stood up again and said to her, "Where are your accusers? Didn't even one of them condemn you?"

11   "No, sir," she said.

And Jesus said, "Neither do I. Go and sin no more."

12   Later, in one of His talks, Jesus said to the people, "I am the Light of the world. So if you follow Me, you won't be stumbling through the darkness, for living light will flood your path."

13   The Pharisees replied, "You are boasting—and lying!"

14   Jesus told them, "These claims are true even though I make them concerning Myself. For I know where I came from and where I am going, but you don't know this about Me.

15   You pass judgment on Me without knowing the facts. I am not judging you now;

16   But if I were, it would be an absolutely correct judgment in every respect, for I have with Me the Father who sent Me.

17   Your laws say that if two men agree on something that has happened, their witness is accepted as fact.

18   Well, I am one witness, and My Father who sent Me is the other."

19   "Where is your father?" they asked.

Jesus answered, "You don't know who I am, so you don't know who My Father is. If you knew Me, then you would know Him too."

20   Jesus made these statements while in the section of the Temple known as the Treasury. But He was not arrested, for His time had not yet run out.

21   Later He said to them again, "I am going away; and you will search for Me, and die in your sins. And you cannot come where I am going."

22   The Jews asked, "Is he planning suicide? What does he mean, 'You cannot come where I am going'?"

23   Then He said to them, "You are from below; I am from above. You are of this world; I am not.

24   That is why I said that you will die in your sins; for

unless you believe that I am the Messiah, the Son of God, you will die in your sins."

25 "Tell us who you are," they demanded.

He replied, "I am the one I have always claimed to be.

26 I could condemn you for much and teach you much, but I won't, for I say only what I am told to by the one who sent Me; and He is Truth."

27 But they still didn't understand that He was talking to them about God.[1]

28 So Jesus said, "When you have killed the Man of Glory,[2] then you will realize that I am He and that I have not been telling you My own ideas, but have spoken what the Father taught Me.

29 And He who sent Me is with Me—He has not deserted Me—for I always do those things that are pleasing to Him."

30, 31 Then many of the Jewish leaders who heard Him say these things began believing Him to be the Messiah. Jesus said to them, "You are truly My disciples if you live as I tell you to,

32 And you will know the truth, and the truth will set you free."

33 "But we are descendants of Abraham," they said, "and have never been slaves to any man on earth! What do you mean, 'set free'?"

34 Jesus replied, "You are slaves of sin, every one of you.

35 And slaves don't have rights, but the Son has every right there is!

36 So if the Son sets you free, you will indeed be free—

37 (Yes, I realize that you are descendants of Abraham!) And yet some of you are trying to kill Me because My message does not find a home within your hearts.

38 I am telling you what I saw when I was with My Father. But you are following the advice of *your* father."

39 "Our father is Abraham," they declared.

"No!" Jesus replied, "for if he were, you would follow his good example.

[1]Literally, "the Father."
[2]Literally, "when you have lifted up the Son of Man."

40   But instead you are trying to kill Me—and all because I told you the truth I heard from God. Abraham wouldn't do a thing like that!

41   No, you are obeying your *real* father when you act that way."

They replied, "We were not born out of wedlock—our true Father is God Himself."

42   Jesus told them, "If that were so, then you would love Me, for I have come to you from God. I am not here on My own, but He sent Me.

43   Why can't you understand what I am saying? It is because you are prevented from doing so!

44   For you are the children of your father the Devil and you love to do the evil things he does. He was a murderer from the beginning and a hater of truth—there is not an iota of truth in him. When he lies, it is perfectly normal; for he is the father of liars.

45   And so when I tell the truth, you just naturally don't believe it!

46   Which of you can truthfully accuse Me of one single sin? [No one!³] And since I am telling you the truth, why don't you believe Me?

47   Anyone whose Father is God listens gladly to the words of God. Since you don't, it proves you aren't His children."

48   "You Samaritan! Foreigner! Devil!" the Jewish leaders snarled. "Didn't we say all along you were possessed by a demon?"

49   "No," Jesus said, "I have no demon in Me. For I honor My Father—and you dishonor Me.

50   And though I have no wish to make Myself great, God wants this for Me and judges [those who reject Me⁴].

51   With all the earnestness I have I tell you this—no one who obeys Me shall ever die!"

52   The leaders of the Jews said, "Now we know you are possessed by a demon. Even Abraham and the mightiest

³Implied.
⁴Implied. Literally, "There is one that seeketh and judgeth."

prophets died, and yet you say that obeying you will keep a man from dying!

53   So you are greater than our father Abraham, who died? And greater than the prophets, who died? Who do you think you are?"

54   Then Jesus told them this: "If I am merely boasting about Myself, it doesn't count. But it is My Father—and you claim Him as your God—who is saying these glorious things about Me.

55   But you do not even know Him. I do. If I said otherwise, I would be as great a liar as you! But it is true—I know Him and fully obey Him.

56   Your father Abraham rejoiced to see My day. He knew I was coming and was glad."

57   *The Jewish leaders:* "You aren't even 50 years old—sure, you've seen Abraham!"

58   *Jesus:* "The absolute truth is that I was in existence before Abraham was ever born!"

59   At that point the Jewish leaders picked up stones to kill Him. But Jesus was hidden from them, and walked past them and left the Temple.

CHAPTER 9

AS He was walking along, He saw a man blind from birth.
2   "Master," His disciples asked Him, "why was this man born blind? Was it a result of his own sins or those of his parents?"

3   "Neither," Jesus answered. "But to demonstrate the power of God.

4   All of us must quickly carry out the tasks assigned us by the one who sent Me, for there is little time left before the night falls and all work comes to an end.

5   But while I am still here in the world, I give it My light."

6   Then He spat on the ground and made mud from the spittle and smoothed the mud over the blind man's eyes,

7   And told him, "Go and wash in the Pool of Siloam" (the word "Siloam" means "Sent"). So the man went where he was sent and washed and came back seeing!

8   His neighbors and others who knew him as a blind beggar asked each other, "Is this the same fellow—that beggar?"

9   Some said yes, and some said no. "It can't be the same man," they thought, "but he surely looks like him!"

And the beggar said, "I *am* the same man!"

10   Then they asked him how in the world he could see. What had happened?

11   And he told them, "A man they call Jesus made mud and smoothed it over my eyes and told me to go to the Pool of Siloam and wash off the mud. I did, and I can see!"

12   "Where is he now?" they asked.

"I don't know," he replied.

13   Then they took the man to the Pharisees.

14   Now as it happened, this all occurred on a Sabbath.[1]

15   Then the Pharisees asked him all about it. So he told them how Jesus had smoothed the mud over his eyes, and when it was washed away, he could see!

16   Some of them said, "Then this fellow Jesus is not from God, because he is working on the Sabbath."

Others said, "But how could an ordinary sinner do such miracles?" So there was a deep division of opinion among them.

17   Then the Pharisees turned on the man who had been blind and demanded, "This man who opened your eyes—who do you say he is?"

"I think He must be a prophet sent from God," the man replied.

18   The Jewish leaders wouldn't believe he had been blind, until they called in his parents

19   And asked them, "Is this your son? Was he born blind? If so, how can he see?"

---

[1] i.e., on Saturday, the weekly Jewish holy day when all work is forbidden.

20 His parents replied, "We know this is our son and that he was born blind,

21 But we don't know what happened to make him see, or who did it. He is old enough to speak for himself. Ask him."

22, 23 They said this in fear of the Jewish leaders who had announced that anyone saying Jesus was the Messiah would be excommunicated.

24 So for the second time they called in the man who had been blind and told him, "Give the glory to God, not to Jesus, for we know Jesus is an evil person."

25 "I don't know whether He is good or bad," the man replied, "but I know this: *I was blind, and now I see!*"

26 "But what did he do?" they asked. "How did he heal you?"

27 "Look!" the man exclaimed. "I told you once; didn't you listen? Why do you want to hear it again? Do you want to become His disciples too?"

28 Then they cursed him and said, "You are his disciple, but we are disciples of Moses.

29 We know God has spoken to Moses, but as for this fellow, we don't know anything about him."

30 "Why, that's very strange!" the man replied. "He can heal blind men, and yet you don't know anything about Him!

31 Well, God doesn't listen to evil men, but He has open ears to those who worship Him and do His will.

32 Since the world began there has never been anyone who could open the eyes of someone born blind.

33 If this man were not from God, He couldn't do it."

34 "You illegitimate bastard,[2] you!" they shouted. "Are you trying to teach *us?*" And they threw him out.

35 When Jesus heard what had happened, He found the man and said, "Do you believe in the Messiah?"[3]

36 The man answered, "Who is He, sir, for I want to."

37 "You have seen Him," Jesus said, "and He is speaking to you!"

---

[2]Literally, "You were altogether born in sin."
[3]Literally, "the Son of Man."

38   "Yes, Lord," the man said, "I believe!" And he worshiped Jesus.

39   Then Jesus told him, "I have come into the world to give sight to those who are spiritually blind and to show those who think they see that they are blind."

40   The Pharisees who were standing there asked, "Are you saying we are blind?"

41   "If you were blind, you wouldn't be guilty," Jesus replied. "But your guilt remains because you claim to know what you are doing."

CHAPTER 10

ANYONE refusing to walk through the gate into a sheepfold, who sneaks over the wall, must surely be a thief!

2   For a shepherd comes through the gate.

3   The gatekeeper opens the gate for him, and the sheep hear his voice and come to him; and he calls his own sheep by name and leads them out.

4   He walks ahead of them; and they follow him, for they recognize his voice.

5   They won't follow a stranger but will run from him, for they don't recognize his voice."

6   Those who heard Jesus use this illustration didn't understand what He meant,

7   So He explained it to them. "I am the Gate for the sheep," He said.

8   "All others who came before Me were thieves and robbers. But the true sheep did not listen to them.

9   Yes, I am the Gate. Those who come in by way of the Gate will be saved and will go in and out and find green pastures.

10   The thief's purpose is to steal, kill and destroy. My purpose is to give eternal life—abundantly.

11   I am the Good Shepherd. The Good Shepherd lays down His life for the sheep.

12   A hired man will run when he sees a wolf coming and will leave the sheep, for they aren't his and he isn't their shepherd. And so the wolf leaps on them and scatters the flock.

13   The hired man runs because he is hired and has no real concern for the sheep.

14   I am the Good Shepherd and know My own sheep, and they know Me,

15   Just as My Father knows Me and I know the Father; and I lay down My life for the sheep.

16   I have other sheep, too, in another fold. I must bring them also, and they will heed My voice; and there will be one flock with one Shepherd.

17   The Father loves Me because I lay down My life that I may have it back again.

18   No one can kill Me without My consent—I lay down My life voluntarily. For I have the right and power to lay it down when I want to and also the right and power to take it again. For the Father has given Me this right."

19   When He said these things, the Jewish leaders were again divided in their opinions about Him.

20   Some of them said, "He has a demon or else is crazy. Why listen to a man like that?"

21   Others said, "This doesn't sound to us like a man possessed by a demon! Can a demon open the eyes of blind men?"

*   *   *   *   *

22, 23   It was winter,[1] and Jesus was in Jerusalem at the time of the Dedication Celebration. He was at the Temple, walking through the section known as Solomon's Hall.

24   The Jewish leaders surrounded Him and asked, "How long are you going to keep us in suspense? If you are the Messiah, tell us plainly."

25   "I have already told you,[2] and you don't believe Me," Jesus replied. "The proof is in the miracles I do in the name of My Father.

---

[1]December 25 was the usual date for this celebration of the cleansing of the Temple.
[2]Chapter 5:19; 8:36, 56, 58, etc., etc.

26 But you don't believe Me because you are not part of My flock.

27 My sheep recognize My voice, and I know them, and they follow Me.

28 I give them eternal life and they shall never perish. No one shall snatch them away from Me,

29 For My Father has given them to Me, and He is more powerful than anyone else, so no one can kidnap them from Me.

30 I and the Father are one."

31 Then again the Jewish leaders picked up stones to kill Him.

32 Jesus said, "At God's direction I have done many a miracle to help the people. For which one are you killing Me?"

33 They replied, "Not for any good work, but for blasphemy; you, a mere man, have declared yourself to be God."

34, 35, 36 "In your own Law it says that men are gods!" He replied. "So if the Scripture, which cannot be untrue, speaks of those as gods to whom the message of God came, do you call it blasphemy when the one sanctified and sent into the world by the Father says, 'I am the Son of God'?

37 Don't believe Me unless I do miracles of God.

38 But if I do, believe them even if you don't believe Me. Then you will become convinced that the Father is in Me, and I in the Father."

39 Once again they started to arrest Him. But He walked away and left them,

40 And went beyond the Jordan River to stay near the place where John was first baptizing.

41 And many followed Him. "John didn't do miracles," they remarked to one another, "but all his predictions concerning this man have come true."

42 And many came to the decision that He was the Messiah.[3]

---

[3]Literally, "Many believed on Him there."

CHAPTER 11

DO you remember Mary, who poured the costly perfume on Jesus' feet and wiped them with her hair?[1] Well, her brother Lazarus, who lived in Bethany with Mary and her sister Martha, was sick.

3 So the two sisters sent a message to Jesus telling Him, "Sir, your good friend is very, very sick."

4 But when Jesus heard about it He said, "The purpose of his illness is not death, but for the glory of God. I, the Son of God, will receive glory from this situation."

5 Although Jesus was very fond of Martha, Mary, and Lazarus,

6 He stayed where He was for the next two days and made no move to go to them.

7 Finally, after the two days, He said to His disciples, "Let's go to Judea."

8 But His disciples objected. "Master," they said, "only a few days ago the Jewish leaders in Judea were trying to kill You. Are You going there again?"

9 Jesus replied, "There are 12 hours of daylight every day, and during every hour of it a man can walk safely and not stumble.

10 Only at night is there danger of a wrong step, because of the dark."

11 Then He said, "Our friend Lazarus has gone to sleep, but now I will go and waken him!"

12, 13 The disciples, thinking Jesus meant Lazarus was having a good night's rest, said, "That means he is getting better!" But Jesus meant Lazarus had died.

14 Then He told them plainly, "Lazarus is dead.

15 And for your sake, I am glad I wasn't there, for this will give you another opportunity to believe in Me. Come, let's go to him."

16 Thomas, nicknamed "The Twin," said to his fellow disciples, "Let's go too—and die with Him."

[1]See John 12:3.

247

17 When they arrived at Bethany, they were told that Lazarus had already been in his tomb for four days.

18 Bethany was only a couple of miles down the road from Jerusalem,

19 And many of the Jewish leaders had come to pay their respects and to console Martha and Mary on their loss.

20 When Martha got word that Jesus was coming, she went to meet Him. But Mary stayed at home.

21 Martha said to Jesus, "Sir, if You had been here, my brother wouldn't have died.

22 And even now it's not too late, for I know that God will bring my brother back to life again, if You will only ask Him to."

23 Jesus told her, "Your brother will come back to life again."

24 "Yes," Martha said, "when everyone else does, on Resurrection Day."

25 Jesus told her, "I am the one who raises the dead and gives them life again. Anyone who believes in Me, even though he dies like anyone else, shall live again.

26 He is given eternal life for believing in Me and shall never perish.[2] Do you believe this, Martha?"

27 "Yes, Master," she told Him. "I believe You are the Messiah, the Son of God, the one we have so long awaited."

28 Then she left Him and returned to Mary and, calling her aside from the mourners, told her, "He is here and wants to see you."

29 So Mary went to Him at once.

30 Now Jesus had stayed outside the village, at the place where Martha met Him.

31 When the Jewish leaders who were at the house trying to console Mary saw her leave so hastily, they assumed she was going to Lazarus' tomb to weep; so they followed her.

32 When Mary arrived where Jesus was, she fell down at His feet, saying, "Sir, if You had been here, my brother would still be alive."

---

[2]Literally, "Whoever lives and believes on Me shall never die."

33   When Jesus saw her weeping and the Jewish leaders wailing with her, He was moved with indignation and deeply troubled.

34   "Where is he buried?" He asked them.

They told Him, "Come and see."

35   Tears came to Jesus' eyes.

36   "They were close friends," the Jewish leaders said. "See how much he loved him."

37, 38   But some said, "This fellow healed a blind man—why couldn't he keep Lazarus from dying?" And again Jesus was moved with deep anger. Then they came to the tomb. It was a cave with a heavy stone rolled across its door.

39   "Roll the stone aside," Jesus told them.

But Martha, the dead man's sister, said, "By now the smell will be terrible, for he has been dead four days."

40   "But didn't I tell you that you will see a wonderful miracle from God if you believe?" Jesus asked her.

41   So they rolled the stone aside. Then Jesus looked up to heaven and said, "Father, thank You for hearing Me.

42   (You always hear Me, of course, but I said it because of all these people standing here, so that they will believe You sent Me.)"

43   Then He shouted, "Lazarus, come out!"

44   And Lazarus came—bound up in the gravecloth, his face muffled in a head swath. Jesus told them, "Unwrap him and let him go!"

45   And so at last many of the Jewish leaders who were with Mary and saw it happen, finally believed on Him!

46   But some went away to the Pharisees and reported it to them.

47   Then the chief priests and Pharisees convened a council to discuss the situation. "What are we going to do?" they asked each other, "for this man certainly does miracles.

48   If we let him alone the whole nation will follow him—and then the Roman army will come and kill us and take over the Jewish government."

49   And one of them, Caiaphas, who was High Priest that year, said, "You stupid idiots—

50   Let this one man die for the people—why should the whole nation perish?"

51   This prophecy that Jesus should die for the entire nation came from Caiaphas in his position as High Priest—he didn't think of it by himself, but was inspired to say it.

52   It was a prediction that Jesus' death would not be for Israel only, but for all the children of God scattered around the world.

53   So from that time on the Jewish leaders began plotting Jesus' death.

54   Jesus now stopped His public ministry and left Jerusalem; he went to the edge of the desert, to the village of Ephraim, and stayed there with His disciples.

55   The Passover, a Jewish holy day, was near, and many country people arrived in Jerusalem several days early so that they could go through the cleansing ceremony before the Passover began.

56   They wanted to see Jesus, and as they gossiped in the Temple, they asked each other, "What do you think? Will He come for the Passover?"

57   Meanwhile the chief priests and Pharisees had publicly announced that anyone seeing Jesus must report Him immediately so that they could arrest Him.

CHAPTER 12

SIX days before the Passover ceremonies began, Jesus arrived in Bethany where Lazarus was—the man He had brought back to life.

2   A banquet was prepared in Jesus' honor. Martha served, and Lazarus sat at the table with Him.

3   Then Mary took a jar of costly perfume made from essence of nard, and anointed Jesus' feet with it and wiped them with her hair. And the house was filled with fragrance.

4 But Judas Iscariot, one of His disciples—the one who would betray Him—said,

5 "That perfume was worth a fortune. It should have been sold and the money given to the poor."

6 Not that he cared for the poor, but he was in charge of the disciples' funds and often dipped into them for his own use!

7 Jesus replied, "Let her alone. She did it in preparation for My burial.

8 You can always help the poor, but I won't be with you very long."

9 When the ordinary people of Jerusalem heard of His arrival, they flocked to see Him and also to see Lazarus—the man who had come back to life again.

10 Then the chief priests decided to kill Lazarus too,

11 For it was because of him that many of the Jewish leaders had deserted and believed in Jesus as their Messiah.

12 The next day, the news that Jesus was on the way to Jerusalem swept through the city, and a huge crowd of Passover visitors

13 Took palm branches and went down the road to meet Him, shouting, "The Savior! God bless the King of Israel! Hail to God's Ambassador!"

14 Jesus rode along on a young donkey, fulfilling the prophecy that said:

15 "Don't be afraid of your King, people of Israel, for He will come to you meekly, sitting on a donkey's colt!"

16 (His disciples didn't realize at the time that this was a fulfillment of prophecy; but after Jesus returned to His glory in heaven, then they noticed how many prophecies of Scripture had come true before their eyes.)

17 And those in the crowd who had seen Jesus call Lazarus back to life were telling all about it.

18 That was the main reason why so many went out to meet Him—because they had heard about this mighty miracle.

19 Then the Pharisees said to each other, "We've lost. Look—the whole world has gone after him!"

20   Some Greeks who had come to Jerusalem to attend the Passover

21   Paid a visit to Philip,[1] who was from Bethsaida, and said, "Sir, we want to meet Jesus."

22   Philip told Andrew about it, and they went together to ask Jesus.

23, 24   Jesus replied that the time had come for Him to return to His glory in heaven, and that "I must fall and die like a kernel of wheat that falls into the furrows of the earth. Unless I die I will be alone—a single seed. But My death will produce many new wheat kernels—a plentiful harvest of new lives.

25   If you love your life down here—you will lose it. If you despise your life down here—you will exchange it for eternal glory.

26   If these Greeks[2] want to be My disciples, tell them to come and follow Me, for My servants must be where I am. And if they follow Me, the Father will honor them.

27   Now My soul is deeply troubled. Shall I pray, 'Father, save Me from what lies ahead'? But that is the very reason why I came!

28   Father, bring glory and honor to Your name."

Then a voice spoke from heaven saying, "I have already done this, and I will do it again."

29   When the crowd heard the voice, some of them thought it was thunder, while others declared an angel had spoken to Him.

30   Then Jesus told them, "The voice was for your benefit, not Mine.

31   The time of judgment for the world has come—and the time when Satan,[3] the prince of this world, shall be cast out.

32   And when I am lifted up [on the cross[4]], I will draw everyone to Me."

33   He said this to indicate how He was going to die.

34   "Die?" asked the crowd. "We understood that the

[1]Philip's name was Greek, though he was a Jew.
[2]Literally, "if any man."
[3]Implied. See 2 Corinthians 4:4, and Ephesians 2:2 and 6:12.
[4]Implied.

252

Messiah would live forever and never die. Why are you saying he will die? What Messiah are you talking about?"

35 Jesus replied, "My light will shine out for you just a little while longer. Walk in it while you can, and go where you want to go before the darkness falls, for then it will be too late for you to find your way.

36 Make use of the Light while there is still time; then you will become light bearers."[5] After saying these things, Jesus went away and was hidden from them.

37 But despite all the miracles He had done, most of the people would not believe He was the Messiah.

38 This is exactly what Isaiah the prophet had predicted: "Lord, who will believe us? Who will accept God's mighty miracles as proof?"[6]

39 But they couldn't believe, for as Isaiah also said:

40 "God[7] has blinded their eyes and hardened their hearts so that they can neither see nor understand nor turn to Me to heal them."

41 Isaiah was referring to Jesus when he made this prediction, for he had seen a vision of the Messiah's glory.

42 However, even many of the Jewish leaders believed Him to be the Messiah but wouldn't admit it to anyone because of their fear that the Pharisees would excommunicate them from the synagogue;

43 For they loved the praise of men more than the praise of God.

* * * * *

44 Jesus shouted to the crowds, "If you trust Me, you are really trusting God.

45 For when you see Me, you are seeing the one who sent Me.

46 I have come as a Light to shine in this dark world, so that all who put their trust in Me will no longer wander in the darkness.

[5]Literally, "sons of light."
[6]Literally, "To whom has the arm of the Lord been revealed?" Isaiah 53:1.
[7]Literally, "He" Isaiah 6:10. The Greek here is a very free rendering, or paraphrase, of the original Hebrew.

47   If anyone hears Me and doesn't obey Me, I am not his judge—for I have come to save the world and not to judge it.

48   But all who reject Me and My message will be judged at the Day of Judgment by the truths I have spoken.

49   For these are not My own ideas, but I have told you what the Father said to tell you.

50   And I know His instructions lead to eternal life; so whatever He tells Me to say, I say!"

CHAPTER 13

JESUS knew on the evening of Passover Day that it would be His last night on earth before returning to His Father. During supper the Devil had already suggested to Judas Iscariot, Simon's son, that this was the night to carry out his plan to betray Jesus. Jesus knew that the Father had given Him everything and that He had come from God and would return to God. And how He loved His disciples!

4   So He got up from the supper table, took off His robe, wrapped a towel around His loins,[1]

5   Poured water into a basin, and began to wash the disciples' feet and to wipe them with the towel He had around Him.

6   When He came to Simon Peter, Peter said to Him, "Master, You shouldn't be washing our feet like this!"

7   Jesus replied, "You don't understand now why I am doing it; some day you will."

8   "No," Peter protested, "You shall never wash my feet!"
"But if I don't, you can't be My partner," Jesus replied.

9   Simon Peter exclaimed, "Then wash my hands and head as well—not just my feet!"

10   Jesus replied, "One who has bathed all over needs only to have his feet washed to be entirely clean. Now you are clean —but that isn't true of everyone here."

[1]As the lowliest of slaves would dress.

254

11   For Jesus knew who would betray Him. That is what He meant when He said, "Not all of you are clean."

12   After washing their feet He put on His robe again and sat down and asked, "Do you understand what I was doing?

13   You call Me 'Master' and 'Lord,' and you do well to say it, for it is true.

14   And since I, the Lord and Teacher, have washed your feet, you ought to wash each other's feet.

15   I have given you an example to follow: do as I have done to you.

16   How true it is that a servant is not greater than his master. Nor is the messenger more important than the one who sends him.

17   You know these things—now do them! That is the path of blessing.

18   I am not saying these things to all of you; I know so well each one of you I chose. The Scripture declares, 'One who eats supper with Me will betray Me,' and this will soon come true.

19   I tell you this now so that when it happens, you will believe on Me.

*   *   *   *   *

20   Truly, anyone welcoming the Holy Spirit,² whom I will send, is welcoming Me. And to welcome Me is to welcome the Father who sent Me."

*   *   *   *   *

21   Now Jesus was in great anguish of spirit and exclaimed, "Yes, it is true—one of you will betray Me."

22   The disciples looked at each other, wondering whom He could mean.

23   Since I³ was sitting next⁴ to Jesus at the table, being His closest friend,

24   Simon Peter motioned to me to ask Him who it was who would do this terrible deed.

²Implied. Literally, "whomsoever I send."
³Literally, "There was one at the table." All commentators believe him to be John, the writer of this book.
⁴Literally, "reclining on Jesus' bosom." The custom of the period was to recline around the table, leaning on the left elbow. John, next to Jesus, was at His side.

25 So I turned[5] and asked Him, "Lord, who is it?"

26 He told me, "It is the one I honor by giving the bread dipped in the sauce."[6] And when He had dipped it, He gave it to Judas, son of Simon Iscariot.

27 As soon as Judas had eaten it, Satan entered into him. Then Jesus told him, "Hurry—do it now."

28 None of the others at the table knew what Jesus meant.

29 Some thought that since Judas was their treasurer, Jesus was telling him to go and pay for the food or to give some money to the poor.

30 Judas left at once, going out into the night.

31 As soon as Judas left the room, Jesus said, "My time has come; the glory of God will soon surround Me—and God shall receive great praise because of all that happens to Me.

32 And God shall give Me His own glory, and this so very soon.

33 Dear, dear children, how brief are these moments before I must go away and leave you! Then, though you search for Me, you cannot come to Me—just as I told the Jewish leaders.

34 And so I am giving a new commandment to you now—love each other just as much as I love you.

35 Your strong love for each other will prove to the world that you are My disciples."

36 Simon Peter said, "Master, where are You going?" And Jesus replied, "You can't go with Me now; but you will follow Me later."

37 "But why can't I come now?" he asked, "for I am ready to die for You."

38 Jesus answered, "Die for Me? No—three times before the cock crows tomorrow morning, you will deny that you even know Me!"

---

[5]Literally, "leaning back against Jesus' chest," to whisper his inquiry.
[6]Literally, "He it is for whom I shall dip the sop and give it him." The honored guest was thus singled out in the custom of that time.

CHAPTER 14

LET not your heart be troubled. You are trusting God, now trust in Me.

2, 3 There are many homes up there where My Father lives, and I am going to prepare them for your coming. When everything is ready, then I will come and get you, so that you can always be with Me where I am. If this weren't so, I would tell you plainly.

4 And you know where I am going and how to get there."

5 "No, we don't," Thomas said. "We haven't any idea where You are going, so how can we know the way?"

6 Jesus told him, "I am the Way—yes, and the Truth and the Life. No one can get to the Father except by means of Me.

7 If you had known who I am, then you would have known who My Father is. From now on you know Him—and have seen Him!"

8 Philip said, "Sir, show us the Father and we will be satisfied."

9 Jesus replied, "Don't you even yet know who I am, Philip, even after all this time I have been with you? Anyone who has seen Me has seen the Father! So why are you asking to see Him?

10 Don't you believe that I am in the Father and the Father is in Me? The words I say are not My own but are from my Father who lives in Me. And he does His work through Me.

11 Just believe it—that I am in the Father and the Father is in Me. Or else believe it because of the mighty miracles you have seen Me do.

12, 13 In solemn truth I tell you, anyone believing in Me shall do the same miracles I have done, and even greater ones, because I am going to be with the Father. You can ask Him for *anything,* using My name, and I will do it, for this will bring praise to the Father because of what I, the Son, will do for you.

14 Yes, ask *anything,* using My name, and I will do it!

257

15, 16 If you love Me, obey Me; and I will ask the Father and He will give you another Comforter, and He will never leave you.

17 He is the Holy Spirit, the Spirit who leads into all truth. The world at large cannot receive Him, for it isn't looking for Him and doesn't recognize Him. But you do, for He lives with you now and some day shall be in you.

18 No, I will not abandon you or leave you as orphans in the storm—I will come to you.

19 In just a little while I will be gone from the world, but I will still be present with you. For I will live again—and you will too.

20 When I come back to life again, you will know that I am in My Father, and you in Me, and I in you.

21 The one who obeys Me is the one who loves Me; and because he loves Me, My Father will love him; and I will too, and I will reveal Myself to him."

22 Judas, (not Judas Iscariot, but His other disciple with that name) said to Him, "Sir, why are You going to reveal Yourself only to us disciples and not to the world at large?"

23 Jesus replied, "Because I will only reveal Myself to those who love Me and obey Me. The Father will love them too, and We will come to them and live with them.

24 Anyone who doesn't obey Me doesn't love Me. And remember, I am not making up this answer to your question! It is the answer given by the Father who sent Me.

25 I am telling you these things now while I am still with you.

26 But when the Father sends the Comforter[1] to represent Me[2]—and by the Comforter I mean the Holy Spirit—He will teach you much, as well as remind you of everything I Myself have told you.

27 I am leaving you with a gift—peace of mind and heart! And the peace I give isn't fragile like the peace the world gives. So don't be troubled or afraid.[3]

28 Remember what I told you—I am going away, but I will

[1]Or, "Advocate," or, "Lawyer."
[2]Literally, "in My name."
[3]Implied.

come back to you again. If you really love Me, you will be very happy for Me, for now I can go to the Father, who is greater than I am.

29 I have told you these things before they happen so that when they do, you will believe [in Me⁴].

30 I don't have much more time to talk to you, for the evil prince of this world approaches. He has no power over Me,

31 But I will freely do what the Father requires of Me so that the world will know that I love the Father. Come, let's be going.

CHAPTER 15

I AM the true Vine, and My Father is the Gardener.

2 He lops off every branch that doesn't produce. And He prunes those branches that bear fruit for even larger crops.

3 He has already tended you by pruning you back for greater strength and usefulness by means of the commands I gave you.

4 Take care to live in Me, and let Me live in you. For a branch can't produce fruit when severed from the vine. Nor can you be fruitful apart from Me.

5 Yes, I am the Vine; you are the branches. Whoever lives in Me and I in him shall produce a large crop of fruit. For apart from Me you can't do a thing.

6 If anyone separates from Me, he is thrown away like a useless branch, withers, and is gathered into a pile with all the others and burned.

7 But if you stay in Me and obey My commands, you may ask any request you like, and it will be granted!

8 My true disciples produce bountiful harvests. This brings great glory to My Father.

9 I have loved you even as the Father has loved Me. Live within My love.

10 When you obey Me you are living in My love, just as I obey My Father and live in His love.

---

⁴Implied.

11   I have told you this so that you will be filled with My joy. Yes, your cup of joy will overflow!

12   I demand that you love each other as much as I love you.

13   And here is how to measure it—the greatest love is shown when a person lays down his life for his friends;

14   And you are My friends if you obey Me.

15   I no longer call you slaves, for a master doesn't confide in his slaves; now you are my friends, proved by the fact that I have told you everything the Father told Me.

16   You didn't choose Me! I chose you! I appointed you to go and produce lovely fruit always, so that no matter what you ask for from the Father, using My name, He will give it to you.

17   I demand that you love each other,

18   For you get enough hate from the world! But then, it hated Me before it hated you.

19   The world would love you if you belonged to it; but you don't—for I chose you to come out of the world, and so it hates you.

20   Do you remember what I told you? 'A slave isn't greater than his master!' So since they persecuted Me, naturally they will persecute you. And if they had listened to Me, they would listen to you!

21   The people of the world will persecute you because you belong to Me, for they don't know God who sent Me.

22   They would not be guilty if I had not come and spoken to them. But now they have no excuse for their sin.

23   Anyone hating Me is also hating My Father.

24   If I hadn't done such mighty miracles among them they would not be counted guilty. But as it is, they saw these miracles and yet they hated both of us—Me and My Father.

25   This has fulfilled what the prophets said concerning the Messiah, 'They hated Me without reason.'

26   But I will send you the Comforter—the Holy Spirit, the source of all truth. He will come to you from the Father and will tell you all about Me.

27   And you also must tell everyone about Me, because you have been with Me from the beginning.

CHAPTER 16

I HAVE told you these things so that you won't be staggered by all that lies ahead.[1]

2 For you will be excommunicated from the synagogues, and indeed the time is coming when those who kill you will think they are doing God a service.

3 This is because they have never known the Father or Me.

4 Yes, I'm telling you these things now so that when they happen you will remember I warned you. I didn't tell you earlier because I was going to be with you for a while longer.

5 But now I am going away to the one who sent Me; and none of you seems interested in the purpose of My going; none wonders why.[2]

6 Instead you are only filled with sorrow.

7 But the fact of the matter is that it is best for you that I go away, for if I don't, the Comforter won't come. If I do, He will—for I will send Him to you.

8 And when He has come He will convince the world of its sin, and of the availability of God's goodness, and of deliverance from judgment.[3]

9 The world's sin is unbelief in Me;

10 There is righteousness available because I go to the Father and you shall see Me no more;

11 There is deliverance from judgment because the prince of this world has already been judged.

12 Oh, there is so much more I want to tell you, but you can't understand it now.

13 When the Holy Spirit, who is truth, comes, He shall guide you into all truth, for He will not be presenting His own ideas, but will be passing on to you what He has heard. He will tell you about the future.

14 He shall praise Me and bring Me great honor by showing you My glory.

---

[1] Implied.
[2] Literally, "none of you is asking Me whither I am going." The question had been asked before (John 13:36, 14:5), but apparently not in this deeper sense.
[3] Literally, "He will convict the world of sin and righteousness and judgment."

261

15   All the Father's glory is Mine; this is what I mean when I say that He will show you My glory.

16   In just a little while I will be gone, and you will see Me no more; but just a little while after that, and you will see Me again!"

17, 18   "Whatever is He saying?" some of His disciples asked. "What is this about 'going to the Father'? We don't know what He means."

19   Jesus realized they wanted to ask Him so He said, "Are you asking yourselves what I mean?

20   The world will greatly rejoice over what is going to happen to Me, and you will weep. But your weeping shall suddenly be turned to wonderful joy [when you see Me again⁴].

21   It will be the same joy as that of a woman in labor when her child is born—her anguish gives place to rapturous joy and the pain is forgotten.

22   You have sorrow now, but I will see you again and then you will rejoice; and no one can rob you of that joy.

23   At that time you won't need to ask Me for anything, for you can go directly to the Father and ask Him, and He will give you what you ask for because you use My name.

24   You haven't tried this before, [but begin now⁴]. Ask, using My name, and you will receive, and your cup of joy will overflow.

25   I have spoken of these matters very guardedly, but the time will come when this will not be necessary and I will tell you plainly all about the Father.

26   Then you will present your petitions over My signature!⁵ And I won't need to ask the Father to grant you these requests,

27   For the Father Himself loves you dearly because you love Me and believe that I came from the Father.

28   Yes, I came from the Father into the world and will leave the world and return to the Father."

---

⁴Implied.
⁵Literally, "you shall ask *in My name*." The above paraphrase is the modern equivalent of this idea, otherwise obscure.

29 "At last You are speaking plainly," His disciples said, "and not in riddles.

30 Now we understand that You know everything and don't need anyone to tell You anything.[6] From this we believe that You came from God."

31 "Do you finally believe this?" Jesus asked.

32 "But the time is coming—in fact, it is here—when you will be scattered, each one returning to his own home, leaving Me alone. Yet I will not be alone, for the Father is with Me.

33 I have told you all this so that you will have peace of heart and mind. Here on earth you will have many trials and sorrows; but cheer up, for I have overcome the world."

CHAPTER 17

WHEN Jesus had finished saying all these things He looked up to heaven and said, "Father, the time has come. Reveal the glory of Your Son so that He can give the glory back to You.

2 For You have given Him authority over every man and woman in all the earth. He gives eternal life to each one You have given Him.

3 And this is the way to have eternal life—by knowing You, the only true God, and Jesus Christ, the one You sent to earth!

4 I brought glory to You here on earth by doing everything You told Me to.

5 And now, Father, reveal My glory as I stand in Your presence, the glory We shared before the world began.

6 I have told these men all about You. They were in the world, but then You gave them to Me. Actually, they were always Yours, and You gave them to Me; and they have obeyed You.

7 Now they know that everything I have is a gift from You,

---

[6]Literally, "and need not that anyone should ask you," i.e., discuss what is true.

8 For I have passed on to them the commands You gave Me; and they accepted them and know of a certainty that I came down to earth from You, and they believe You sent Me.

9 My plea is not for the world but for those You have given Me because they belong to You.

10 And all of them, since they are Mine, belong to You; and You have given them back to Me with everything else of Yours, and so *they are My glory!*

11 Now I am leaving the world, and leaving them behind, and coming to You. Holy Father, keep them in Your own care—all those You have given me—so that they will be united just as We are, with none missing.

12 During My time here I have kept safe within Your family[1] all of these You gave Me. I guarded them so that not one perished, except the son of hell, as the Scriptures foretold.

13 And now I am coming to You. I have told them many things while I was with them so that they would be filled with My joy.

14 I have given them Your commands. And the world hates them because they don't fit in with it, just as I don't.

15 I'm not asking You to take them out of the world, but to keep them safe from Satan's power.

16 They are not part of this world any more than I am.

17 Make them pure and holy through teaching them Your words of truth.

18 As You sent Me into the world, I am sending them into the world,

19 And I consecrate Myself to meet their need for growth in truth and holiness.

20 I am not praying for these alone but also for the future believers who will come to Me because of the testimony of these.

21 My prayer for all of them is that they will be of one heart and mind, just as You and I are, Father—that just as You are in Me and I am in You, so they will be in Us, and the world will believe You sent Me.

---

[1]Literally, "kept in Your name those whom You have given Me."

22 I have given them the glory You gave Me—the glorious unity of being one, as We are—

23 I in them and You in Me, all being perfected into one—so that the world will know You sent Me and will understand that You love them as much as You love Me.

24 Father, I want them with Me—these You've given Me —so that they can see My glory. You gave Me the glory because You loved Me before the world began!

25 O righteous Father, the world doesn't know You, but I do; and these disciples know You sent Me.

26 And I have revealed You to them, and will keep on revealing You so that the mighty love You have for Me may be in them, and I in them."

CHAPTER 18

AFTER saying these things Jesus crossed the Kidron ravine with His disciples and entered a grove of olive trees.

2 Judas, the betrayer, knew this place, for Jesus had gone there many times with His disciples.

3 The chief priests and Pharisees had given Judas a squad of soldiers and police to accompany him. Now with blazing torches, lanterns, and weapons they arrived at the olive grove.

4, 5 Jesus fully realized all that was going to happen to Him. Stepping forward to meet them He asked, "Whom are you looking for?"

"Jesus of Nazareth," they replied.

"I am He," Jesus said.

6 And as He said it, they all fell backwards to the ground!

7 Once more He asked them, "Whom are you searching for?"

And again they replied, "Jesus of Nazareth."

8 "I told you I am He," Jesus said; "and since I am the one you are after, let these others go."

9 He did this to carry out the prophecy He had just made, "I have not lost a single one of those You gave Me . . . ."

10   Then Simon Peter drew a sword and slashed off the right ear of Malchus, the High Priest's servant.

11   But Jesus said to Peter, "Put your sword away. Shall I not drink from the cup the Father has given Me?"

12   So the Jewish police, with the soldiers and their lieutenant, arrested Jesus and tied Him.

13   First they took Him to Annas, the father-in-law of Caiaphas, the High Priest that year.

14   Caiaphas was the one who told the other Jewish leaders, "Better that one should die for all."

15   Simon Peter followed along behind, as did another of the disciples who was acquainted with the High Priest. So that other disciple was permitted into the courtyard along with Jesus,

16   While Peter stood outside the gate. Then the other disciple spoke to the girl watching at the gate, and she let Peter in.

17   The girl asked Peter, "Aren't you one of Jesus' disciples?"

"No," he said, "I am not!"

18   The police and the household servants were standing around a fire they had made, for it was cold. And Peter stood there with them, warming himself.

19   Inside, the High Priest began asking Jesus about His followers and what He had been teaching them.

20   Jesus replied, "What I teach is widely known, for I have preached regularly in the synagogue and Temple; I have been heard by all the Jewish leaders and teach nothing in private that I have not said in public.

21   Why are you asking Me this question? Ask those who heard Me. You have some of them here. They know what I said."

22   One of the soldiers standing there struck Jesus with his fist. "Is that the way to answer the High Priest?" he demanded.

23   "If I lied, prove it," Jesus replied. "Should you hit a man for telling the truth?"

24   Then Annas sent Jesus, bound, to Caiaphas the High Priest.

25   Meanwhile, as Simon Peter was standing by the fire, he was asked again, "Aren't you one of His disciples?"

"Of course not," he replied.

26   But one of the household slaves of the High Priest—a relative of the man whose ear Peter had cut off—asked, "Didn't I see you out there in the olive grove with Jesus?"

27   Again Peter denied it. And immediately a rooster crowed.

28   Jesus' trial before Caiaphas ended in the early hours of the morning. Next he was taken to the palace of the Roman governor.[1] His accusers wouldn't go in themselves for that would "defile"[2] them, they said, and they wouldn't be allowed to eat the Passover lamb.

29   So Pilate, the governor, went out to them and asked, "What is your charge against this man? What are you accusing him of doing?"

30   "We wouldn't have arrested him if he weren't a criminal!" they retorted.

31   "Then take him away and judge him yourselves by your own laws," Pilate told them.

"But we want him crucified," they said, "and your approval is required."[3]

32   This fulfilled Jesus' prediction concerning the method of His execution.[4]

33   Then Pilate went back into the palace and called for Jesus to be brought to him, "Are you the King of the Jews?" he asked Him.

34   " 'King' as *you* use the word or as the *Jews* use it?" Jesus asked.[5]

35   "Am I a Jew?" Pilate retorted. "Your own people and

---

[1]Literally, "the Praetorium."
[2]By Jewish law, entering the house of a Gentile was a serious offense.
[3]Literally, "It is not lawful for us to put any man to death."
[4]This prophecy is recorded in Matthew 20:19, which indicates His death by crucifixion, a practice under Roman law.
[5]A paraphrase of this verse—that goes beyond the limits of this book's paraphrasing—would be, "Do you mean their King, or their Messiah?" If Pilate was asking as the Roman governor, he would be inquiring whether Jesus was setting up a rebel government. But the Jews were using the word "King" to mean their religious ruler, the Messiah. Literally this verse reads, "Are you saying this of yourself, or did someone else say it about me?"

their chief priests brought you here. Why? What have you done?"

36   Then Jesus answered, "I am not an earthly king. If I were, My followers would have fought when I was arrested by the Jewish leaders. But My Kingdom is not of the world."

37   Pilate replied, "But you are a king then?"

"Yes," Jesus said. "I was born for that purpose. And I came to bring truth to the world. All who love the truth are My followers."

38   "What is truth?" Pilate exclaimed. Then he went out again to the people and told them, "He is not guilty of any crime.

39   But you have a custom of asking me to release someone from prison each year at Passover. So if you want me to, I'll release the 'King of the Jews.' "

40   But they screamed back, "No! Not this man, but Barabbas!" Barabbas was a robber.

CHAPTER 19

THEN Pilate laid open Jesus' back with a leaded whip,
2   And the soldiers made a crown of thorns and placed it on His head and robed Him in royal[1] purple.

3   "Hail, 'King of the Jews!' " they mocked, and struck Him with their fists.

4   Pilate went outside again and said to the Jews, "I am going to bring him out to you now, but understand clearly that I find him NOT GUILTY."

5   Then Jesus came out wearing the crown of thorns and the purple robe. And Pilate said, "Behold the man!"

6   At sight of Him the chief priests and Jewish officials began yelling, "Crucify! Crucify!"

"*You* crucify him," Pilate said. "I find him NOT GUILTY."

7   They replied, "By our laws he ought to die because he called himself the Son of God."

[1]Implied.

8   When Pilate heard this, he was more frightened than ever.

9   He took Jesus back into the palace again and asked Him, "Where are you from?" but Jesus gave no answer.

10   "You won't talk to me?" Pilate demanded. "Don't you realize that I have the power to release you or to crucify you?"

11   Then Jesus said, "You would have no power at all over Me unless it were given to you from above. So those[2] who brought Me to you have the greater sin."

12   Then Pilate tried to release Him, but the Jewish leaders told him, "If you release this man, you are no friend of Caesar's. Anyone who declares himself a king is a rebel against Caesar."

13   At these words Pilate brought Jesus out to them again and sat down at the judgment bench on the stone-paved platform.[3]

14   It was now about noon of the day before Passover. And Pilate said to the Jews, "Here is your king!"

15   "Away with him," they yelled, "Away with him—crucify him!"

"What? Crucify your king?" Pilate asked.

"We have no king but Caesar," the chief priests shouted back.

16   Then Pilate gave Jesus to them to be crucified.

17   So they had Him at last, and He was taken out of the city, carrying His cross to the place known as "The Skull," in Hebrew, "Golgotha."

18   There they crucified Him and two others with Him, one on either side, with Jesus between them.

19   And Pilate posted a sign over Him reading, "JESUS OF NAZARETH, THE KING OF THE JEWS."

20   The place where Jesus was crucified was near the city; and the signboard was written in Hebrew, Latin, and Greek, so that many people read it.

21   Then the chief priests said to Pilate, "Change it from

---

[2] Literally, "he."
[3] Literally, "the judgment seat in a place that is called The Pavement, but in Hebrew, Gabbatha."

'The King of the Jews' to '*He said,* I am King of the Jews.'"

22   Pilate replied, "What I have written, I have written. It stays exactly as it is."

23, 24   When the soldiers had crucified Jesus, they put His garments into four piles, one for each of them. But they said, "Let's not tear up his robe," for it was seamless. "Let's throw dice to see who gets it." This fulfilled the Scripture that says,

> "They divided My clothes among them, and cast lots for My robe."[4]

25   So that is what they did.

Standing near the cross were Jesus' mother, Mary, His aunt, the wife of Cleopas, and Mary Magdalene.

26   When Jesus saw His mother standing there beside me, His close friend,[5] He said to her, "He is your son."

27   And to me[6] He said, "She is your mother!" And from then on I took her into my home.

28   Jesus knew that everything was now finished, and to fulfill the Scriptures said, "I'm thirsty."

29   A jar of sour wine was sitting there, so a sponge was soaked in it and put on a hyssop branch and held up to His lips.

30   When Jesus had tasted[7] it, He said, "It is finished," and bowed His head and dismissed His spirit.

31   The Jewish leaders didn't want the victims hanging there the next day, which was the Sabbath (and a very special Sabbath at that, for it was the Passover), so they asked Pilate to order the legs of the men broken to hasten death; then their bodies could be taken down.

32   So the soldiers came and broke the legs of the two men crucified with Jesus;

33   But when they came to Him, they saw that He was dead already, so they didn't break His.

34   However, one of the soldiers pierced His side with a spear, and blood and water flowed out.

---

[4]Psalm 22:18
[5]Literally, "standing by the disciple whom He loved."
[6]Literally, "to the disciple."
[7]Literally, "had received."

35   I saw all this myself and have given an accurate report so that you also can believe.[8]

36, 37   The soldiers did this in fulfillment of the Scripture that says, "Not one of His bones shall be broken," and, "They shall look on Him whom they pierced."

38   Afterwards Joseph of Arimathea, who had been a secret disciple of Jesus for fear of the Jewish leaders, boldly asked Pilate for permission to take Jesus' body down; and Pilate told him to go ahead. So he came and took it away.

39   Nicodemus, the man who had come to Jesus at night,[9] came too, bringing a hundred pounds of embalming ointment made from myrrh and aloes.

40   Together they wrapped Jesus' body in a long linen cloth saturated with the spices, as is the Jewish custom of burial.

41   The place of crucifixion was near a grove of trees,[10] where there was a new tomb, never used before.

42   And so, because of the need for haste before the Sabbath, and because the tomb was close at hand, they laid Him there.

CHAPTER 20

E ARLY Sunday[1] morning, while it was still dark, Mary Magdalene came to the tomb and found that the stone was rolled aside from the entrance.

2   She ran and found Simon Peter and me[2] and said, "They have taken the Lord's body out of the tomb, and I don't know where they have put Him!"

3, 4   We[3] ran to the tomb to see; I[4] outran Peter and got there first,

5   And stooped and looked in and saw the linen cloth lying there, but I didn't go in.

---

[8]Literally, "And he who has seen has borne witness, and his witness is true; and he knows what he says is true, that you also may believe."
[9]See chapter 3.
[10]Literally, "a garden."
[1]Literally, "on the first day of the week."
[2]Literally, "the other disciple whom Jesus loved."
[3]Literally, "Peter and the other disciple."
[4]Literally, "the other disciple also, who came first."

6   Then Simon Peter arrived and went on inside. He also noticed the cloth lying there,

7   While the swath that had covered Jesus' head was rolled up in a bundle and was lying at the side.

8   Then I⁵ went in too, and saw, and believed [that He had risen⁵] —

9   For until then we hadn't realized that the Scriptures said He would come to life again!

10   We⁶ went on home,

11   And by that time Mary had returned to the tomb⁷ and was standing outside crying. And as she wept, she stooped and looked in

12   And saw two white-robed angels sitting at the head and foot of the place where the body of Jesus had been lying.

13   "Why are you crying?" the angels asked her.

"Because they have taken away my Lord," she replied, "and I don't know where they have put Him."

14   She glanced over her shoulder and saw someone standing behind her. It was Jesus, but she didn't recognize Him!

15   "Why are you crying?" He asked her. "Whom are you looking for?"

She thought He was the gardener. "Sir," she said, "if you have taken Him away, tell me where you have put Him, and I will go and get Him."

16   "Mary!" Jesus said. She turned toward Him. "Master!" she exclaimed.

17   "Don't touch Me," He cautioned, "for I haven't yet ascended to the Father. But go find My brothers and tell them that I ascend to My Father and your Father, My God and your God."

18   Mary Magdalene found the disciples and told them, "I have seen the Lord!" Then she gave them His message.

19   That evening the disciples were meeting behind locked doors, in fear of the Jewish leaders, when suddenly Jesus was standing there among them! After greeting them,

⁵Implied.
⁶Literally, "the disciples."
⁷Implied.

20   He showed them His hands and side. And how wonderful was their joy as they saw their Lord!

21   He spoke to them again and said, "As the Father has sent Me, even so I am sending you."

22   Then He breathed on them and told them, "Receive the Holy Spirit.

23   If you forgive anyone's sins, they are forgiven. If you refuse to forgive them, they are unforgiven."

24   One of the disciples, Thomas, "The Twin," was not there at the time with the others.

25   When they kept telling him, "We have seen the Lord," he replied, "I won't believe it unless I see the nail wounds in His hands—and put my fingers into them—and place my hand into His side."

26   Eight days later the disciples were together again, and this time Thomas was with them. The doors were locked; but suddenly, as before, Jesus was standing among them and greeting them.

27   Then He said to Thomas, "Put your finger into My hands. Put your hand into My side. Don't be faithless any longer. Believe!"

28   "My Lord and my God!" Thomas said.

29   Then Jesus told him, "You believe because you have see Me. But blessed are those who haven't seen Me and believe anyway."

30, 31   Jesus' disciples saw Him do many other miracles besides the one told about in this book, but these are recorded so that you will believe that He is the Messiah, the Son of God, and that believing in Him you will have Life.

CHAPTER 21

L ATER Jesus appeared again to the disciples beside the Lake of Galilee. This is how it happened:

2   A group of us were there—Simon Peter, Thomas, "The

Twin," Nathanael from Cana in Galilee, my brother James and I[1] and two other disciples.

3   Simon Peter said, "I'm going fishing."

"We'll come too," we all said. We did, but caught nothing all night.

4   At dawn we saw a man standing on the beach but couldn't see who he was.

5   He called, "Any fish, boys?"[2]

"No," we replied.

6   Then He said, "Throw out your net on the right-hand side of the boat, and you'll get plenty of them!" So we did, and couldn't draw in the net because of the weight of the fish, there were so many!

7   Then I[3] said to Peter, "It is the Lord!" At that, Simon Peter put on his tunic (for he was stripped to the waist) and jumped into the water [and swam ashore[4]].

8   The rest of us stayed in the boat and pulled the loaded net to the beach, about 300 feet away.

9   When we got there, we saw that a fire was kindled and fish were frying over it, and there was bread.

10   "Bring some of the fish you've just caught," Jesus said.

11   So Simon Peter went out and dragged the net ashore. By his count there were 153 large fish; and yet the net hadn't torn!

12   "Now come and have some breakfast!" Jesus said; and none of us dared ask Him if He really was the Lord, for we were quite sure of it.

13   Then Jesus went around serving us the bread and fish.

14   This was the third time Jesus had appeared to us since His return from the dead.

15   After breakfast Jesus said to Simon Peter, "Simon, son of John, do you love Me more than these others?"[5]

[1]Literally, "the sons of Zebedee."
[2]Literally, "children."
[3]Literally, "that disciple therefore whom Jesus loved."
[4]Implied.
[5]Literally, "more than these." See Mark 14:29.

"Yes," Peter replied, "You know I am Your friend."

"Then feed My lambs," Jesus told him.

16 Jesus repeated the question: "Simon, son of John, do you *really* love Me?"

"Yes, Lord," Peter said, "You know I am Your friend."

"Then take care of My sheep," Jesus said.

17 Once more He asked him, "Simon, son of John, are you even My friend?"

Peter was grieved at the way Jesus asked the question this third time. "Lord, You know my heart;[6] You know I am," he said.

Jesus said, "Then feed My little sheep.

18 When you were young, you were able to do as you liked and go wherever you wanted to; but when you are old, you will stretch out your hands and others will direct you and take you where you don't want to go."

19 Jesus said this to let him know what kind of death he would die to glorify God. Then Jesus told him, "Follow Me."

20 Peter turned around and saw the disciple Jesus loved following, the one who had leaned around at supper that time to ask Jesus, "Master, which of us will betray You?"

21 Peter asked Jesus, "What about him, Lord? What sort of death will he die?"[7]

22 Jesus replied, "If I want him to live[8] until I return, what is that to you? *You* follow Me."

23 So the rumor spread among the brotherhood that that disciple wouldn't die! But that isn't what Jesus said at all! He only said, "If I want him to live[8] until I come, what is that to you?"

24 *I am that disciple!* I saw these events and have recorded them here. And we all know that my account of these things is accurate.

25 And I suppose that if all the other events in Jesus' life were written, the whole world could hardly contain the books!

---

[6]Literally, "all things."
[7]Implied. Literally, "and this man, what?"
[8]Literally, "tarry."

SPEAK OUT

Picture yourself: ☐ . . . getting an "A" in the roughest math course of the semester. ☐ . . . standing alone on a Rocky Mountain peak staring at breathtaking beauty ☐ . . . hitting a hole-in-one. ☐ Now, picture yourself *not* being able to share these experiences with anyone. It would kill half the pleasure! After all, what good's an exciting game or trip without friends along? ☐ In the same way, if Christ lives within you, then talking about Him should be as natural as talking about your unexpected

"A," or your winning touchdown, or that very special date you just had. ☐ Yet Speaking Out *isn't* that natural! Not at all. People say they don't want to "discuss religion." And often we over-react, thinking people are even more defensive than they actually are. We quickly lose the desire to communicate Christ beyond our small circle of Christian friends. ☐ Yet what a delight it is to share Christ with those who have never tasted the sweetness of fellowship with Him. The Lord Jesus commands us to share our faith so that their lives, too, can be filled with this new dynamic. ☐ Then why are we so often negligent and fearful? ☐ This dramatic Book of Acts can open the door to witnessing for us ordinary people with extra-ordinary Life within. These first-century Christians were quite ordinary non-supermen, yet they "turned the world upside down." ☐ God's command to speak out for Him *is* possible to obey. It doesn't have to haunt you. It can become a natural part of your Christian life.

ACTS

CHAPTER 1

DEAR Friend who loves God:
In my first letter[1] I told you about Jesus' life and teachings and how He returned to heaven after giving His chosen apostles further instructions from the Holy Spirit.

3 During the 40 days after His crucifixion He had appeared to the apostles from time to time in human form and proved to them in many ways that it was actually He Himself they were seeing. And on these occasions He talked to them about the Kingdom of God.

4 In one of these meetings He told them not to leave Jerusalem until the Holy Spirit came upon them in fulfillment of the Father's promise, a matter he had previously discussed with them.

5 "John baptized you with[2] water," He reminded them, "but you shall be baptized with[2] the Holy Spirit in just a few days."

6 And another time when He appeared to them, they asked Him, "Lord, are you going to free Israel [from Rome[3]] now and restore us as an independent nation?"

7 "The Father sets those dates," He replied, "and they are not for you to know.

8 But when the Holy Spirit has come upon you, you will receive power to preach with great effect to the people in Jerusalem, throughout Judea, in Samaria, and to the ends of the earth, about My death and resurrection."

[1]i.e., the book of Luke; see footnote chapter 1, verse 1.
[2]Or, "in."
[3]Implied.

276

9 It was not long afterwards that He rose into the sky and disappeared into a cloud, leaving them staring after Him.

10 As they were straining their eyes for another glimpse, suddenly two white-robed men were standing there among them,

11 And said, "Men of Galilee, why are you standing here staring at the sky? Jesus has gone away to heaven, and some day, just as He went, He will return!"

12 They were at the Mount of Olives when this happened, so now they walked the half mile back to Jerusalem

13, 14 And held a prayer meeting in an upstairs room of the house where they were staying. Here is the list of those who were present at the meeting:

Peter,
John,
James,
Andrew,
Philip,
Thomas,
Bartholomew,
Matthew,
James (son of Alphaeus),
Simon (also called "The Zealot"),
Judas (son of James),
And the brothers of Jesus.
Several women, including Jesus' mother, were also there.

15 This prayer meeting went on for several days. During this time, on a day when about 120 people were present, Peter stood up and addressed them as follows:

16 "Brothers, it was necessary for the Scriptures to come true concerning Judas, who betrayed Jesus by guiding the mob to Him, for this was predicted long ago by the Holy Spirit, speaking through King David.

17 Judas was one of us, chosen to be an apostle just as we were.

18 He bought a field with the money he received for his

treachery and falling headlong there, he burst open, spilling out his bowels.

19   The news of his death spread rapidly among all the people of Jerusalem, and they named the place 'The Field of Blood.'

20   King David's prediction of this appears in the Book of Psalms, where he says, 'Let his home become desolate with no one living in it.'[4] And again, 'Let his work be given to someone else to do.'[5]

21, 22   So now we must choose someone else to take Judas' place and to join us as witnesses of Jesus' resurrection. Let us select someone who has been with us constantly from our first association with the Lord—from the time He was baptized by John until the day He was taken from us into heaven."

23   The assembly nominated two men: Joseph Justus (also called Barsabbas) and Matthias.

24, 25   Then they all prayed for the right man to be chosen. "O Lord," they said, "You know every heart; show us which of these men You have chosen as an apostle to replace Judas the traitor, who has gone on to his proper place."

26   Then they drew straws,[6] and in this manner Matthias was chosen and became an apostle with the other eleven.

CHAPTER 2

SEVEN weeks[1] had now gone by since Jesus' death and resurrection, and the Day of Pentecost[2] arrived. As the believers met together that day,

2   Suddenly there was a sound like the roaring of a mighty windstorm in the skies above them and it filled the house where they were meeting.

---

[4]Psalm 69:25.
[5]Psalm 109:8.
[6]Literally, "cast lots," or, "threw dice."
[1]Implied. See Leviticus 23:16.
[2]This annual celebration came 50 days after the Passover ceremonies, when Christ was crucified.

3   Then, what looked like flames or tongues of fire appeared and settled on their heads.

4   And everyone present was filled with the Holy Spirit and began speaking in languages they didn't know,[3] for the Holy Spirit gave them this ability.

5   Many godly Jews were in Jerusalem that day for the religious celebrations, having arrived from many nations.

6   And when they heard the roaring in the sky above the house, crowds came running to see what it was all about, and were stunned to hear their own languages being spoken by the disciples.

7   "How can this be?" they exclaimed. "For these men are all from Galilee,

8   And yet we hear them speaking all the native languages of the lands where we were born!

9   Here we are—Parthians, Medes, Elamites, men from Mesopotamia, Judea, Cappadocia, Pontus, Ausia,[4]

10   Phrygia, Pamphylia, Egypt, the Cyrene language areas of Libya, visitors from Rome—both Jews and Jewish converts—

11   Cretans, and Arabians. And we all hear these men telling in our own languages about the mighty miracles of God!"

12   They stood there amazed and perplexed. "What can this mean?" they asked each other.

13   But others in the crowd were mocking. "They're drunk, that's all!" they said.

14   Then Peter stepped forward with the eleven apostles, and shouted to the crowd, "Listen, all of you, visitors and residents of Jerusalem alike!

15   Some of you are saying these men are drunk! It isn't true! It's much too early for that! People don't get drunk by 9 a.m.!

16   No! What you see this morning was predicted centuries ago by the prophet Joel—

17   'In the last days,' God said, 'I will pour out My Holy Spirit upon all mankind, and your sons and daughters shall

---

[3]Literally, "in other tongues."
[4]Literally, "Asia," a province of what is now Turkey.

prophesy, and your young men shall see visions, and your old men dream dreams.

18   Yes, the Holy Spirit shall come upon all My servants, men and women alike, and they shall prophesy.

19   And I will cause strange demonstrations in the heavens and on the earth—blood and fire and clouds of smoke;

20   The sun shall turn black and the moon blood-red before that awesome Day of the Lord arrives.

21   But anyone who asks for mercy from the Lord shall have it and shall be saved.'

22   O men of Israel, listen! God publicly endorsed Jesus of Nazareth by doing tremendous miracles through Him, as you well know.

23   But God, following His prearranged plan, let you use the Roman[5] government to nail Him to the cross and murder Him.

24   Then God released Him from the horrors of death and brought Him back to life again, for death could not keep this man within its grip.

25   King David quoted Jesus as saying:
   'I know the Lord is always with Me. He is helping Me. God's mighty power supports Me.

26   No wonder My heart is filled with joy and My tongue shouts His praises! For I know all will be well with Me in death—

27   You will not leave My soul in hell or let the body of Your Holy Son decay.

28   You will give Me back My life, and give Me wonderful joy in Your presence.'

29   Dear brothers, think! David wasn't referring to himself when he spoke these words I have quoted,[6] for he died and was buried, and his tomb is still here among us!

30   But he was a prophet, and knew God had promised with an unbreakable oath that one of David's own descendants would [be the Messiah and[6]] sit on David's throne.

---

[5]Literally, "men without the Law." See Romans 2:12.
[6]Implied from verse 31.

31 David was looking far into the future and predicting the Messiah's resurrection, and saying that the Messiah's soul would not be left in hell and His body would not decay.

32 He was speaking of Jesus, and we all are witnesses that Jesus rose from the dead.

33 And now He sits on the throne of highest honor in heaven, next to God. And just as promised, the Father has sent the Holy Spirit—with the results you are seeing and hearing today.

34 [No, David was not speaking of himself in these words of his I have quoted[7]], for he never ascended into the skies. Moreover, he further stated, 'God spoke to my Lord, the Messiah, and said to Him, Sit here in honor beside Me

35 Until I bring Your enemies into complete subjection.'

36 Therefore I clearly state to everyone in Israel that God has made this Jesus you crucified to be the Lord, the Messiah!"

37 These words of Peter's moved them deeply, and they said to him and to the other apostles, "Brothers, what should we do?"

38 And Peter replied, "Each one of you must turn from sin, return to God, and be baptized in the name of Jesus Christ for the forgiveness of your sins; then you also shall receive this gift, the Holy Spirit.

39 For Christ promised Him to each one of you who has been called by the Lord our God, and to your children and even to those in distant lands!"

40 Then Peter preached a long sermon, telling about Jesus and strongly urging all his listeners to save themselves from the evils of their nation.

41 And those who believed Peter were baptized—about 3,000 in all!

42 They joined with the other believers in regular attendance at the apostles' teaching sessions and at the Communion services[8] and prayer meetings.

43 A deep sense of awe was on them all, and the apostles did many miracles.

---

[7]Implied.
[8]Literally, "the breaking of bread," i.e., "the Lord's Supper."

44   And all the believers met together constantly and shared everything with each other,

45   Selling their possessions and dividing with those in need.

46   They worshiped together regularly at the Temple each day, met in small groups in homes for Communion, and shared their meals with great joy and thankfulness,

47   Praising God. The whole city was favorable to them, and each day God added to them all who were being saved.

CHAPTER 3

PETER and John went to the Temple one afternoon to take part in the three o'clock daily prayer meeting.

2   As they approached the Temple, they saw a man lame from birth carried along the street and laid beside the Temple gate—the one called The Beautiful Gate—as was his custom every day.

3   As Peter and John were passing by, he asked them for some money.

4   They looked at him intently, and then Peter said, "Look here!"

5   The lame man looked at them eagerly, expecting a gift.

6   But Peter said, "We don't have any money for you! But I'll give you something else! I command you in the name of Jesus Christ of Nazareth, *walk!*"

7, 8   Then Peter took the lame man by the hand and pulled him to his feet. And as he did, the man's feet and ankle-bones were healed and strengthened so that he came up with a leap, stood there a moment and began walking! Then, walking, leaping, and praising God, he went into the Temple with them.

9   When the people inside saw him walking and heard him praising God,

10   And realized he was the lame beggar they had seen so often at The Beautiful Gate, they were inexpressibly surprised!

11   They all rushed out to Solomon's Hall, where he was

holding tightly to Peter and John! Everyone stood there awed by the wonderful thing that had happened.

12 Peter saw his opportunity and addressed the crowd! "Men of Israel," he said, "what is so surprising about this? And why look at us as though we by our own power and godliness had made this man walk?

13 For it is the God of Abraham, Isaac, Jacob and of all our ancestors who has brought glory to His servant Jesus by doing this. I refer to the Jesus whom you rejected before Pilate, despite Pilate's determination to release Him.

14 You didn't want Him freed—this holy, righteous one. Instead you demanded the release of a murderer.

15 And you killed the Author of Life; but God brought Him back to life again. And John and I are witnesses of this fact, for after you killed Him we saw Him alive!

16 Jesus' name has healed this man—and you know how lame he was before. Faith in Jesus' name—faith given us from God—has caused this perfect healing.

17 Dear brothers, I realize that what you did to Jesus was done in ignorance; and the same can be said of your leaders.

18 But God was fulfilling the prophecies that the Messiah must suffer all these things.

19 Now change your mind and attitude to God and turn to Him so He can cleanse away your sins and send you wonderful times of refreshment from the presence of the Lord

20 And send Jesus your Messiah back to you again.

21, 22 For He must remain in heaven until the final recovery of all things from sin, as prophesied from ancient times. Moses, for instance, said long ago, 'The Lord God will raise up a Prophet among you, who will resemble Me![1] Listen carefully to everything He tells you.

23 Anyone who will not listen to Him shall be utterly destroyed.'[2]

24 Samuel and every prophet since have all spoken about what is going on today.

25 You are the children of those prophets; and you are

[1]Literally, "like unto Me."
[2]Literally, "destroyed from among the people."

included in God's promise to your ancestors to bless the entire world through the Jewish race—that is the promise God gave to Abraham.

26 And as soon as God had brought His servant to life again, He sent Him first of all to you men of Israel, to bless you by turning you back from your sins."

CHAPTER 4

WHILE they were talking to the people, the chief priests, the captain of the Temple police, and some of the Sadducees[1] came over to them,

2 Very disturbed that Peter and John were claiming that Jesus had risen from the dead.

3 They arrested them and since it was already evening, jailed them overnight.

4 But many of the people who heard their message believed it, so that the number of believers now reached a new high of about 5,000 men!

5 The next day it happened that the Council of all the Jewish leaders was in session in Jerusalem—

6 Annas the High Priest was there, and Caiaphas, John, Alexander, and others of the High Priest's relatives.

7 So the two disciples were brought in before them. "By what power, or by whose authority have you done this?" the Council demanded.

8 Then Peter, filled with the Holy Spirit, said to them, "Honorable leaders and elders of our nation,

9 If you mean the good deed done to the cripple, and how he was healed,

10 Let me clearly state to you and to all the people of Israel that it was done in the name and power of Jesus from Nazareth, the Messiah, the man you crucified—but God raised back to life again. It is by His authority that this man stands here healed!

11 For Jesus the Messiah is (the one referred to in the

---

[1]The Sadducees were a Jewish religious sect that denied the resurrection of the dead.

Scriptures when they speak of) a 'stone discarded by the builders which became the capstone of the arch.'[2]

12 There is salvation in no one else! Under all heaven there is no other name for men to call upon to save them."

13 When the Council saw the boldness of Peter and John, and could see that they were obviously uneducated non-professionals, they were amazed and realized what being with Jesus had done for them!

14 And the Council could hardly discredit the healing when the man they had healed was standing right there beside them!

15 So they sent them out of the Council chamber and conferred among themselves.

16 "What shall we do with these men?" they asked each other. "We can't deny that they have done a tremendous miracle, and everybody in Jerusalem knows about it.

17 But perhaps we can stop them from spreading their propaganda. We'll tell them that if they do it again we'll really throw the book at them."

18 So they called them back in, and told them never again to speak about Jesus.

19 But Peter and John replied, "You decide whether God wants us to obey you instead of Him!

20 We cannot stop telling about the wonderful things we saw Jesus do and heard Him say."

21 The Council then threatened them further, and finally let them go because they didn't know how to punish them without starting a riot. For everyone was praising God for this wonderful miracle—

22 The healing of a man who had been lame for 40 years!

23 As soon as they were freed, Peter and John found the other disciples and told them what the council had said.

24 Then all the believers united in this prayer: "O Lord, Creator of heaven and earth and of the sea and everything in them—

25, 26 You spoke long ago by the Holy Spirit through our ancestor King David, your servant, saying, 'Why do the heathen

---

[2]Implied. Literally, "became the head of the corner."

rage against the Lord, and the foolish nations plan their little plots against Almighty God? The kings of the earth unite to fight against Him, against the anointed Son of God!'

27 That is what is happening here in this city today! For Herod the king, and Pontius Pilate the governor, and all the Romans—as well as the people of Israel—are united against Jesus, Your anointed Son, Your holy servant.

28 They won't stop at anything that You in Your wise power will let them do.

29 And now, O Lord, hear their threats, and grant to Your servants great boldness in their preaching,

30 And send Your healing power, and may miracles and wonders be done by the name of Your holy servant Jesus."

31 After this prayer, the building where they were meeting shook and they were all filled with the Holy Spirit and boldly preached God's message.

32 All the believers were of one heart and mind, and no one felt that what he owned was his own; everyone was sharing.

33 And the apostles preached powerful sermons about the resurrection of the Lord Jesus, and there was warm fellowship[3] among all the believers,

34, 35 And no poverty—for all who owned land or houses sold them and brought the money to the apostles to give to others in need.

36 For instance, there was Joseph (the one the apostles nicknamed "Barny the Preacher"! He was of the tribe of Levi, from the island of Cyprus).

37 He was one of those who sold a field he owned and brought the money to the apostles for distribution to those in need.

CHAPTER 5

BUT there was a man named Ananias (with his wife Sapphira) who sold some property,

---

[3]Literally, "great grace was upon them all."

2   And brought only part of the money, claiming it was the full price. (His wife had agreed to this deception.)

3   But Peter said, "Ananias, Satan has filled your heart. When you claimed this was the full price, you were lying to the Holy Spirit.

4   The property was yours to sell or not, as you wished. And after selling it, it was yours to decide how much to give. How could you do a thing like this? You weren't lying to us, but to God."

5   As soon as Ananias heard these words, he fell to the floor, dead! Everyone was terrified,

6   And the younger men covered him with a sheet and took him out and buried him.

7   About three hours later his wife came in, not knowing what had happened.

8   Peter asked her, "Did you people sell your land for such and such a price?"

"Yes," she replied, "we did."

9   And Peter said, "How could you and your husband even think of doing a thing like this—conspiring together to test the Spirit of God's ability to know what is going on?[1] Just outside that door are the young men who buried your husband, and they will carry you out too."

10   Instantly she fell to the floor, dead, and the young men came in and, seeing that she was dead, carried her out and buried her beside her husband.

11   Terror gripped the entire church and all others who heard what had happened.

12   Meanwhile, the apostles were meeting regularly at the Temple in the area known as Solomon's Hall, and they did many remarkable miracles among the people.

13   The other believers didn't dare join them, though, but all had the highest regard for them.

14   And more and more believers were added to the Lord, crowds both of men and women.

15   Sick people were brought out into the streets on beds

---

[1] Literally, "to try the Spirit of the Lord."

and mats so that at least Peter's shadow would fall across some of them as he went by!

16   And crowds came in from the Jerusalem suburbs, bringing their sick folk and those possessed by demons; and every one of them was healed.

17   The High Priest and his relatives and friends among the Sadducees reacted with violent jealousy

18   And arrested the apostles, and put them in the public jail.

19   But an angel of the Lord came at night, opened the gates of the jail and brought them out. Then he told them,

20   "Go over to the Temple and preach about this Life!"

21   They arrived at the Temple about daybreak, and immediately began preaching! Later that morning[2] the High Priest and his courtiers arrived at the Temple, and, convening the Jewish Council and the entire Senate, they sent for the apostles to be brought for trial.

22   But when the police arrived at the jail, the men weren't there, so they returned to the Council and reported,

23   "The jail doors were locked, and the guards were standing outside, but when we opened the gates, no one was there!"

24   When the police captain[3] and the chief priests heard this, they were frantic, wondering what would happen next and where all this would end!

25   Then someone arrived with the news that the men they had jailed were out in the Temple, preaching to the people!

26, 27   The police captain went with his officers and arrested them (without violence, for they were afraid the people would kill them if they roughed up the disciples) and brought them in before the Council.

28   "Didn't we tell you never again to preach about this Jesus?" the High Priest demanded. "And instead you have filled all Jerusalem with your teaching and intend to bring the blame for this man's death on us!"

---

[2] Implied.
[3] Literally, "the captain of the Temple."

29   But Peter and the apostles replied, "We must obey God rather than men.

30   The God of our ancestors brought Jesus back to life again after you had killed Him by hanging Him on a cross.

31   Then, with mighty power, God exalted Him to be a Prince and Savior, so that the people of Israel would have an opportunity for repentance, and for their sins to be forgiven.

32   And we are witnesses of these things, and so is the Holy Spirit, who is given by God to all who obey Him."

33   At this, the Council was furious, and decided to kill them.

34   But one of their members, a Pharisee named Gamaliel, (an expert on religious law and very popular with the people), stood up and requested that the apostles be sent outside the Council chamber while he talked.

35   Then he addressed his colleagues as follows: "Men of Israel, take care what you are planning to do to these men!

36   Some time ago there was that fellow Theudas, who pretended to be someone great. About 400 others joined him, but he was killed, and his followers were harmlessly dispersed.

37   After him, at the time of the taxation, there was Judas of Galilee. He drew away some people as disciples, but he also died, and his followers scattered.

38   And so my advice is, leave these men alone. If what they teach and do is merely on their own, it will soon be overthrown.

39   But if it is of God, you will not be able to stop them, lest you find yourselves fighting even against God."

40   The Council accepted his advice, called in the apostles, had them beaten, and then told them never again to speak in the name of Jesus, and finally let them go.

41   They left the Council chamber rejoicing that God had counted them worthy to suffer dishonor for His name.

42   And every day, in the Temple and in the city,⁴ they continued to teach and preach that Jesus is the Messiah.

---

⁴Literally, "at home." Possibly, "from house to house," or perhaps, "in their meeting halls."

CHAPTER 6

B UT with the believers multiplying rapidly, there were rumblings of discontent. Those who spoke only Greek complained that their widows were being discriminated against, that they were not being given as much food, in the daily distribution, as the widows who spoke Hebrew.

2   So the Twelve called a meeting of all the believers. "We should spend our time preaching, not administering a feeding program,"[1] they said.

3   "Now look around among yourselves, dear brothers, and select seven men, wise and full of the Holy Spirit, who are well thought of by everyone; and we will put them in charge of this business.

4   Then we can spend our time in prayer, preaching, and teaching."

5   This sounded reasonable to the whole assembly, and they elected the following:

Stephen (a man unusually full of faith and the Holy Spirit),

Philip,

Prochorus,

Nicanor,

Timon,

Parmenas,

Nicolaus of Antioch (a Gentile convert to the Jewish faith, who had become a Christian).

6   These seven were presented to the apostles, who prayed for them and laid their hands on them in blessing.

*   *   *   *   *

7   God's message was preached in ever-widening circles, and the number of disciples increased vastly in Jerusalem; and many of the Jewish priests were converted too.

8   Stephen, the man so full of faith and the Holy Spirit's power,[2] did spectacular miracles among the people.

9   But one day some of the men from the Jewish cult of

[1]Literally, "it is not fit that we should forsake the Word of God and serve tables."
[2]Literally, "full of grace and power." See verse 5.

"The Freedmen" started an argument with him, and they were soon joined by Jews from Cyrene, Alexandria in Egypt, and the Turkish provinces of Cilicia, and Ausia.

10   But none of them were able to stand against Stephen's wisdom and spirit.

11   So they brought in some men to lie about him, claiming they had heard Stephen curse Moses, and even God.

12   This accusation roused the crowds to fury against Stephen, and the Jewish leaders[3] arrested him and brought him before the Council.

13   The lying witnesses testified again that Stephen was constantly speaking against the Temple and against the laws of Moses.

14   They declared, "We have heard him say that this fellow Jesus of Nazareth will destroy the Temple, and throw out all of Moses' laws."

15   At this point everyone in the Council chamber saw Stephen's face become as radiant as an angel's!

CHAPTER 7

THEN the High Priest asked him, "Are these accusations true?"

2   This was Stephen's lengthy reply:

"The glorious God appeared to our ancestor Abraham in Iraq[1] before he moved to Syria,[2]

3   And told him to leave his native land, to say good-bye to his relatives and to start out for a country that God would direct him to.

4   So he left the land of the Chaldeans and lived in Haran, in Syria, until his father died. Then God brought him here to the land of Israel,

5   But gave him no property of his own, not one little tract of land. However, God promised that eventually the whole

---

[3]Literally, "the elders and the Scribes."
[1]Literally, "Mesopotamia."
[2]Literally, "Haran," a city in the area we now know as Syria.

country would belong to him and his descendants—though as yet he had no children!

6 But God also told him that these descendants of his would leave the land and live in a foreign country and there become slaves for 400 years.

7 'But I will punish the nation that enslaves them,' God told him, 'and afterwards My people will return to this land of Israel and worship Me here.'

8 God also gave Abraham the ceremony of circumcision at that time, as evidence of the covenant between God and the people of Abraham. And so Isaac, Abraham's son, was circumcised when he was eight days old. Isaac became the father of Jacob, and Jacob was the father of the twelve patriarchs of the Jewish nation.

9 These men were very jealous of Joseph and sold him to be a slave in Egypt. But God was with him,

10 And delivered him out of all of his anguish, and gave him favor before Pharaoh, king of Egypt. God also gave Joseph unusual wisdom, so that Pharaoh appointed him governor over all Egypt, as well as putting him in charge of all the affairs of the palace.

11 But a famine developed in Egypt and Canaan and there was great misery for our ancestors. When their food was gone,

12 Jacob heard that there was still grain in Egypt, so he sent his sons[3] to buy some.

13 The second time they went, Joseph revealed his identity to his brothers, and they were introduced to Pharaoh.

14 Then Joseph sent for his father Jacob and all his brothers' families to come to Egypt, 75 persons in all.

15 So Jacob came to Egypt, where he died, and all his sons.

16 All of them were taken to Shechem and buried in the tomb Abraham bought from the sons of Hamor, Shechem's father.

17, 18 As the time drew near when God would fulfill His promise to Abraham to free his descendants from slavery, the Jewish people greatly multiplied in Egypt; but then a king was crowned who had no respect for Joseph's memory.

---

[3]Literally, "our fathers."

19   This king plotted against our race, forcing parents to abandon their children in the fields.

20   About that time Moses was born—a child of divine beauty. His parents hid him at home for three months,

21   And when at last they could no longer keep him hidden, and had to abandon him, Pharaoh's daughter found him and adopted him as her own son,

22   And taught him all the wisdom of the Egyptians, and he became a mighty prince and orator.[4]

23   One day as he was nearing his 40th birthday, it came into his mind to visit his brothers, the people of Israel.

24   During this visit he saw an Egyptian mistreating a man of Israel. So Moses killed the Egyptian.

25   Moses supposed his brothers would realize that God had sent him to help them, but they didn't.

26   The next day he visited them again and saw two men of Israel fighting. He tried to be a peacemaker, 'Gentlemen,' he said, 'you are brothers and shouldn't be fighting like this! It is wrong!'

27   But the man in the wrong told Moses to mind his own business. 'Who made *you* a ruler and judge over us?' he asked.

28   'Are you going to kill me as you killed that Egyptian yesterday?'

29   At this, Moses fled the country, and lived in the land of Midian, where his two sons were born.

30   Forty years later, in the desert near Mount Sinai, an Angel appeared to him in a flame of fire in a bush.

31   Moses saw it and wondered what it was, and as he ran to see, the voice of the Lord called out to him,

32   'I am the God of your ancestors—of Abraham, Isaac and Jacob.' Moses shook with terror and dared not look.

33   And the Lord said to him, 'Take off your shoes, for you are standing on holy ground.

34   I have seen the anguish of My people in Egypt and have heard their cries. I have come down to deliver them. Come, I will send you to Egypt.'

4Literally, "mighty in word and works."

35 And so God sent back the same man His people had previously rejected by demanding, 'Who made *you* a ruler and judge over us?' Moses was sent to be their ruler and savior.

36 And by means of many remarkable miracles he led them out of Egypt and through the Red Sea, and back and forth through the wilderness for 40 years.

37 Moses himself told the people of Israel, 'God will raise up a Prophet much like me[5] from among your brothers.'

38 How true this proved to be, for in the wilderness, Moses was the go-between—the mediator between the people of Israel and the Angel who gave them the Law of God—the Living Word—on Mount Sinai.

39 But our fathers rejected Moses and wanted to return to Egypt.

40 They told Aaron, 'Make idols for us, so that we will have gods to lead us back; for we don't know what has become of this Moses, who brought us out of Egypt.'

41 So they made a calf-idol and sacrificed to it, and rejoiced in this thing they had made.

42 Then God turned away from them and gave them up, and let them serve the sun, moon and stars as their gods! In the book of Amos' prophecies the Lord God asks, 'Was it to Me you were sacrificing during those 40 years in the desert, Israel?

43 No, your real interest was in your heathen gods— Sakkuth, and the star god Kaiway, and in all the images you made. So I will send you into captivity far away beyond Babylon.'

44 Our ancestors carried along with them a portable Temple, or Tabernacle, through the wilderness. In it they kept the stone tablets with the Ten Commandments written on them. This building was constructed in exact accordance with the plan shown to Moses by the Angel.

45 Years later, when Joshua led the battles against the

---

[5]Literally, "like unto me."

Gentile nations, this Tabernacle was taken with them into their new territory, and used until the time of King David.

46   God blessed David greatly, and David asked for the privilege of building a permanent Temple for the God of Jacob.

47   But it was Solomon who actually built it.

48, 49   However, God doesn't live in temples made by human hands. 'The heaven is My throne,' says the Lord through His prophets, 'and earth is My footstool. What kind of home could you build?' asks the Lord! 'Would I stay in it?

50   Didn't I make both heaven and earth?'

51   You stiff-necked heathen! Must you forever resist the Holy Spirit? But your fathers did, and so do you!

52   Name one prophet your ancestors didn't persecute! They even killed the ones who predicted the coming of the Righteous One—the Messiah whom you betrayed and murdered.

53   Yes, and you deliberately destroyed God's Laws, though you received them from the hands of angels."[6]

54   The Jewish leaders were stung to fury by Stephen's accusation, and ground their teeth in rage.

55   But Stephen, full of the Holy Spirit, gazed steadily upward into heaven and saw the glory of God and Jesus standing at God's right hand.

56   And he told them, "Look, I see the heavens opened and Jesus the Messiah[7] standing beside God, at His right hand!"

57   Then they mobbed him, putting their hands over their ears, and drowning out his voice with their shouts,

58   And dragged him out of the city to stone him. The official witnesses—the executioners—took off their coats and laid them at the feet of a young man named Paul.[8]

59   And as the murderous stones came hurtling at him, Stephen prayed, "Lord Jesus, receive my spirit."

60   And he fell to his knees, shouting, "Lord, don't charge them with this sin!" and with that, he died.

---

[6]Literally, "the Law as it was ordained by angels."
[7]Literally, "the Son of Man."
[8]Paul is also known as Saul.

CHAPTER 8

P AUL was in complete agreement with the killing of Stephen. And a great wave of persecution of the believers began that day, sweeping over the church in Jerusalem, and everyone except the apostles fled into Judea and Samaria.

2 (But some godly Jews[1] came and with great sorrow buried Stephen.)

3 Paul was like a wild man, going everywhere to devastate the believers, even entering private homes and dragging out men and women alike and jailing them.

4 But the believers[2] who had fled Jerusalem went everywhere preaching the Good News about Jesus!

5 Philip, for instance, went to the city of Samaria and told the people there about Christ.

6 Crowds listened intently to what he had to say because of the miracles he did.

7 Many evil spirits were cast out, screaming as they left their victims, and many who were paralyzed or lame were healed,

8 So there was much joy in that city!

9, 10, 11 A man named Simon had formerly been a sorcerer there for many years; he was a very influential, proud man because of the amazing things he could do—in fact, the Samaritan people often spoke of him as the Messiah.[3]

12 But now they believed Philip's message that Jesus was the Messiah, and his words concerning the Kingdom of God; and many men and women were baptized.

13 Then Simon himself believed and was baptized and began following Philip wherever he went, and was amazed by the miracles he did.

14 When the apostles back in Jerusalem heard that the people of Samaria had accepted God's message, they sent down Peter and John.

---

[1]Literally, "devout men." It is not clear whether these were Christians who braved the persecution, or whether they were godly and sympathetic Jews.
[2]Literally, "the church."
[3]Literally, "this man is that Power of God which is called great."

15   As soon as they arrived, they began praying for these new Christians to receive the Holy Spirit,

16   For as yet He had not come upon any of them. For they had only been baptized in the name of the Lord Jesus.

17   Then Peter and John laid their hands upon these believers, and they received the Holy Spirit.

18   When Simon saw this—that the Holy Spirit was given when the apostles placed their hands upon peoples' heads—he offered money to buy this power.

19   "Let me have this power too," he exclaimed, "so that when I lay my hands on people, they will receive the Holy Spirit!"

20   But Peter replied, "Your money perish with you for thinking God's gift can be bought!

21   You can have no part in this, for your heart is not right before God.

22   Turn from this great wickedness and pray. Perhaps God will yet forgive your evil thoughts—

23   For I can see that there is jealousy[4] and sin in your heart."

24   "Pray for me," Simon exclaimed, "that these terrible things won't happen to me."

25   After testifying and preaching in Samaria, Peter and John returned to Jerusalem, stopping at several Samaritan villages along the way to preach the Good News to them too.

26   But as for Philip, an angel of the Lord said to him, "Go over to the road that runs from Jerusalem through the Gaza Desert, arriving around noon."

27   So he did, and who should be coming down the road but the Treasurer of Ethiopia, an eunuch of great authority under Candace the queen. He had gone to Jerusalem to worship at the Temple,

28   And was now returning in his chariot, reading aloud from the book of the prophet Isaiah.

29   The Holy Spirit said to Philip, "Go over and walk along beside the chariot!"

---

[4]Literally, "the gall of bitterness."

30   Philip ran over and heard what he was reading and asked, "Do you understand it?"

31   "Of course not!" the man replied. "How can I when there is no one to instruct me?" And he begged Philip to come up into the chariot and sit with him!

32   The passage of Scripture he had been reading from was this:

"He was led as a sheep to the slaughter,
And as a lamb is silent before the shearers, so He opened not His mouth;

33   In His humiliation, justice was denied Him; and who can express the wickedness of the people of His generation?[5] For His life is taken from the earth."

34   The eunuch asked Philip, "Was Isaiah talking about himself or someone else?"

35   So Philip began with this same Scripture and then used many others to tell him about Jesus.

36   As they rode along, they came to a small body of water, and the eunuch said, "Look! Water! Why can't I be baptized?"

37[6]   "You can," Philip answered, "if you believe with all your heart."
And the eunuch replied, "I believe that Jesus Christ is the Son of God."

38   He stopped the chariot, and they went down into the water and Philip baptized him.

39   And when they came up out of the water, the Spirit of the Lord caught away Philip, and the eunuch never saw him again, but went on his way rejoicing.

40   Meanwhile, Philip discovered himself at Azotus! He preached the Good News there and in every city along the way, as he traveled to Caesarea.

---

[5]Implied. Literally, "Who can declare His generation." Alternatively, "Who will be able to speak of His posterity? For . . ."
[6]Many ancient manuscripts omit verse 37 wholly or in part.

CHAPTER 9

BUT Paul, threatening with every breath and eager to destroy every Christian, went to the High Priest in Jerusalem.

2 He requested a letter addressed to synagogues in Damascus, requiring their cooperation in the persecution of any believers he found there, both men and women, so that he could bring them in chains to Jerusalem.

3 As he was nearing Damascus on this mission, suddenly a brilliant light from heaven spotted down upon him!

4 He fell to the ground and heard a voice saying to him, "Paul! Paul! Why are you persecuting Me?"

5 "Who is speaking, sir?" Paul asked.

And the voice replied, "I am Jesus, the one you are persecuting!

6 Now get up and go into the city and await My further instructions."

7 The men with Paul stood speechless with surprise, for they heard the sound of someone's voice but saw no one!

8, 9 As Paul picked himself up off the ground, he found that he was blind. He had to be led into Damascus and was there three days, blind, going without food and water all that time.

10 Now there was in Damascus a believer named Ananias. The Lord spoke to him in a vision, calling, "Ananias!"

"Yes, Lord!" he replied.

11 And the Lord said, "Go over to Straight Street and find the house of a man named Judas and ask there for Paul of Tarsus. He is praying to Me right now, for

12 I have shown him a vision of a man named Ananias coming in and laying his hands on him so that he can see again!"

13 "But Lord," exclaimed Ananias, "I have heard about the terrible things this man has done to the believers in Jerusalem!

14 And we hear that he has arrest warrants with him from

the chief priests, authorizing him to arrest every believer in Damascus!"

15 But the Lord said, "Go and do what I say. For Paul is my chosen instrument to take My message to the nations and before kings, as well as to the people of Israel.

16 And I will show him how much he must suffer for Me."

17 So Ananias went over and found Paul and laid his hands on him and said, "Brother Paul, the Lord Jesus, who appeared to you on the road, has sent me so that you may be filled with the Holy Spirit and get your sight back."

18 Instantly (it was as though scales fell from his eyes) Paul could see, and was immediately baptized.

19 Then he ate and was strengthened. He stayed with the believers in Damascus for a few days

20 And went at once to the synagogue to tell everyone there the Good News about Jesus—that He is indeed the Son of God!

21 All who heard him were amazed. "Isn't this the same man who persecuted Jesus' followers so bitterly in Jerusalem?" they asked. "And we understand that he came here to arrest them all and take them in chains to the chief priests."

22 Paul became more and more fervent in his preaching, and the Damascus Jews couldn't withstand his proofs that Jesus was indeed the Christ.

23 After a while the Jewish leaders determined to kill him.

24 But Paul was told about their plans, that they were watching the gates of the city day and night prepared to murder him.

25 So during the night some of his converts let him down in a basket through an opening in the city wall!

26 Upon arrival in Jerusalem he tried to meet with the believers, but they were all afraid of him. They thought he was faking!

27 Then Barnabas brought him to the apostles and told them how Paul had seen the Lord on the way to Damascus,

what the Lord had said to him, and all about his powerful preaching in the name of Jesus.

28 Then they accepted him, and after that he was constantly with the believers

29 And preached boldly in the name of the Lord. But then some Greek-speaking Jews with whom he had argued plotted to murder him.

30 However, when the other believers heard about his danger, they took him to Caesarea and then sent him to his home[1] in Tarsus.

31 Meanwhile, the church had peace throughout Judea, Galilee and Samaria, and grew in strength and numbers. The believers learned how to walk in the fear of the Lord and in the comfort of the Holy Spirit.

32 Peter traveled from place to place to visit them,[1] and in his travels came to the believers in the town of Lydda.

33 There he met a man named Aeneas, paralyzed and bedridden for eight years.

34 Peter said to him, "Aeneas! Jesus Christ has healed you! Get up and make your bed!" And he was healed instantly.

35 Then the whole population of Lydda and Sharon turned to the Lord when they saw Aeneas walking around.

36 In the city of Joppa there was a woman named Dorcas ("Gazelle"), a believer who was always doing kind things for others, especially for the poor.

37 About this time she became ill and died. Her friends prepared her for burial and laid her in an upstairs room.

38 But when they learned that Peter was nearby at Lydda, they sent two men to beg him to return with them to Joppa.

39 This he did; as soon as he arrived, they took him upstairs where Dorcas lay. The room was filled with weeping widows who were showing one another the coats and other garments Dorcas had made for them.

40 But Peter asked them all to leave the room; then he knelt and prayed. Turning to the body he said, "Get up,

---

[1]Implied.

Dorcas,"[2] and she opened her eyes! And when she saw Peter, she sat up!

41   He gave her his hand and helped her up and called in the believers and widows, presenting her to them!

42   The news raced through the town, and many believed in the Lord.

43   And Peter stayed a long time in Joppa, living with Simon, the tanner.

CHAPTER 10

IN Caesarea there lived a Roman army officer, Cornelius, a captain of an Italian regiment.

2   He was a godly man, deeply reverent, as was his entire household. He gave generously to charity and was a man of prayer.

3   While wide awake one afternoon he had a vision—it was about three o'clock—and in this vision he saw an angel of God coming toward him. "Cornelius!" the angel said.

4   Cornelius stared at him in terror. "What do you want, sir?" he asked the angel.

And the angel replied, "Your prayers and charities have not gone unnoticed by God!

5, 6   Now send some men to Joppa to find a man named Simon Peter, who is staying with Simon, the tanner, down by the shore, and ask him to come and visit you."

7   As soon as the angel was gone, Cornelius called two of his household servants and a godly soldier, one of his personal bodyguard,

8   And told them what had happened and sent them off to Joppa.

9, 10   The next day, as they were nearing the city, Peter went up on the flat roof of his house to pray. It was noon and he was hungry, but while lunch was being prepared, he fell into a trance.

---

[2]Literally, "Tabitha," her name in Hebrew.

11   He saw the sky open, and a great canvas sheet,[1] suspended by its four corners, settle to the ground.

12   In the sheet were all sorts of animals, snakes and birds [forbidden to the Jews for food[2]].

13   Then a voice said to him, "Go kill and eat any of them you wish."

14   "Never, Lord," Peter declared, "I have never in all my life eaten such creatures, for they are forbidden by our Jewish laws."

15   The voice spoke again, "Don't contradict God! If He says something is kosher, then it is!"

16   The same vision was repeated three times! Then the sheet was pulled up again to heaven!

17   Peter was very perplexed. What could the vision mean? What was he supposed to do? Just then the men sent by Cornelius had found the house and were standing outside at the gate,

18   Inquiring whether this was the place where Simon Peter lived!

19   Meanwhile, as Peter was puzzling over the vision, the Holy Spirit said to him, "Three men have come to see you.

20   Go down and meet them and go with them. All is well, I have sent them."

21   So Peter went down. "I'm the man you're looking for," he said. "Now what is it you want?"

22   Then they told him about Cornelius the Roman officer, a good and godly man, well thought of by the Jews, and how an angel had instructed him to send for Peter to come and tell him what God wanted him to do.

23   So Peter invited them in and lodged them overnight. The next day he went with them, accompanied by some other believers from Joppa.

24   They arrived in Caesarea the following day, and Cornelius was waiting for him, and had called together his relatives and close friends to meet Peter.

---

[1]Implied.
[2]Implied; see Leviticus 11 for the forbidden list.

25   As Peter entered his home, Cornelius fell to the floor before him in worship.

26   But Peter said, "Stand up! I'm not a god!"

27   So he got up and they talked together for a while and then went in where the others were assembled.

28   Peter told them, "You know it is against the Jewish laws for me to come into a Gentile home like this. But God has shown me in a vision that I should never think of anyone as inferior.[3]

29   So I came as soon as I was sent for. Now tell me what you want.

30   Cornelius replied, "Four days ago I was praying as usual at this time of the afternoon, when suddenly a man was standing before me clothed in a radiant robe!

31   He told me, 'Cornelius, your prayers are heard and your charities have been noticed by God!

32   Now send some men to Joppa and summon Simon Peter, who is staying in the home of Simon, a tanner, down by the shore.'

33   So I sent for you at once, and you have done well to come so soon. Now here we are, waiting before the Lord, anxious to hear what He has told you to tell us!"

34   Then Peter replied, "I see very clearly that the Jews are not God's only favorites!

35   In every nation He has those who worship Him and do good deeds and are acceptable to Him.

36, 37   I'm sure you have heard about the Good News for the people of Israel—that there is peace with God through Jesus, the Messiah, who is Lord of all creation. This message has spread all through Judea, beginning with John the Baptist in Galilee.

38   And you no doubt know that Jesus of Nazareth was anointed by God with the Holy Spirit and with power, and He went around doing good and healing all who were possessed by demons, for God was with Him.

39   And we apostles are witnesses of all He did throughout Israel and in Jerusalem, where He was murdered on a cross.

---

[3]Literally, "that I should not call any man common or unclean."

40, 41 But God brought Him back to life again three days later and showed Him to certain witnesses God had selected beforehand—not to the general public, but to us who ate and drank with Him after He rose from the dead.

42 And He sent us to preach the Good News everywhere and to testify that Jesus is ordained of God to be the Judge of all—living and dead.

43 And all the prophets have written about Him, saying that everyone who believes in Him will have their sins forgiven through His name."

44 Even as Peter was saying these things, the Holy Spirit fell upon all those listening!

45 The Jews who came with Peter were amazed that the gift of the Holy Spirit would be given to Gentiles too!

46, 47 But there could be no doubt about it,[4] for they heard them speaking in tongues and praising God. Peter asked, "Can anyone object to my baptizing them, now that they have received the Holy Spirit just as we did?"

48 So he did,[4] baptizing them in the name of Jesus, the Messiah. Afterwards Cornelius begged him to stay with them for several days.

CHAPTER 11

S OON the news reached the apostles and other brothers in Judea that Gentiles also were being converted!

2 But when Peter arrived back in Jerusalem, the Jewish believers argued with him.

3 "You fellowshiped with Gentiles and even ate with them," they accused.

4 Then Peter told them the whole story.

5 "One day in Joppa," he said, "while I was praying, I saw a vision—a huge sheet, let down by its four corners from the sky.

6 Inside the sheet were all sorts of animals, reptiles and birds [which we are not to eat[1]].

---

[4]Implied.
[1]Implied.

7   And I heard a voice say, 'Kill and eat whatever you wish.'

8   'Never, Lord,' I replied. 'For I have never yet eaten anything forbidden by our Jewish laws!'

9   But the voice came again, 'Don't say it isn't right when God declares it is!'

10   This happened *three times* before the sheet and all it contained disappeared into heaven.

11   Just then three men who had come to take me with them to Caesarea arrived at the house where I was staying!

12   The Holy Spirit told me to go with them and not to worry about their being Gentiles! These six brothers here accompanied me, and we soon arrived at the home of the man who had sent the messengers.

13   He told us how an angel had appeared to him and told him to send messengers to Joppa to find Simon Peter!

14   'He will tell you how you and all your household can be saved!' the angel had told him.

15   Well, I began telling them the Good News, but just as I was getting started with my sermon, the Holy Spirit fell on them, just as He fell on us at the beginning!

16   Then I thought of the Lord's words when He said, 'Yes, John baptized with[2] water, but you shall be baptized with[2] the Holy Spirit.'

17   And since it was *God* who gave these Gentiles the same gift He gave us when we believed on the Lord Jesus Christ, who was I to argue?"

18   When the others heard this, all their objections were answered and they began praising God! "Yes," they said, "God has given to the Gentiles, too, the privilege of turning to Him and receiving eternal life!"

19   Meanwhile, the believers who fled from Jerusalem during the persecution after Stephen's death traveled as far as Phoenicia, Cyprus, and Antioch, scattering the Good News, but only to Jews.

20   However, some of the believers who went to Antioch

[2]Or, "in."

306

from Cyprus and Cyrene also gave their message about the Lord Jesus to some Greeks.

21   And the Lord honored this effort so that large numbers of these Gentiles became believers.

22   When the church at Jerusalem heard what had happened, they sent Barnabas to Antioch to help the new converts.

23   When he arrived and saw the wonderful things God was doing, he was filled with excitement and joy, and encouraged the believers to stay close to the Lord, whatever the cost.

24   Barnabas was a kindly person, full of the Holy Spirit and strong in faith. As a result large numbers of people were added to the Lord.

25   Then Barnabas went on to Tarsus to hunt for Paul.

26   When he found him, he brought him back to Antioch; and both of them stayed there for a full year, teaching the many new converts. (It was there at Antioch that the believers were first called "Christians.")

27   During this time some prophets came down from Jerusalem to Antioch,

28   And one of them, named Agabus, stood up in one of the meetings to predict by the Spirit that a great famine was coming upon the land of Israel.[3] (This was fulfilled during the reign of Claudius.)

29   So the believers decided to send relief to the Christians in Judea, each giving as much as he could.

30   This they did, consigning their gifts to Barnabas and Paul to take to the elders of the church in Jerusalem.

CHAPTER 12

ABOUT that time King Herod moved against some of the believers,

2   And killed the apostle[1] James (John's brother).

3   When Herod saw how much this pleased the Jewish leaders, he arrested Peter during the Passover celebration

---

[3]Literally, "upon the earth."
[1]Implied.

4 And imprisoned him, placing him under the guard of 16 soldiers. Herod's intention was to deliver Peter to the Jews for execution after the Passover.

5 But earnest prayer was going up to God from the Church for his safety all the time he was in prison.

6 The night before he was to be executed, he was asleep, double-chained between two soldiers with others standing guard before the prison gate,

7 When suddenly there was a light in the cell and an angel of the Lord stood beside Peter! The angel slapped him on the side to awaken him and said, "Quick! Get up!" And the chains fell off his wrists!

8 Then the angel told him, "Get dressed and put on your shoes." And he did. "Now put on your coat and follow me!" the angel ordered.

9 So Peter left the cell, following the angel. But all the time he thought it was a dream or vision, and didn't believe it was really happening.

10 They passed the first and second cell blocks and came to the iron gate to the street, and this opened to them of its own accord! So they passed through and walked along together for a block, and then the angel left him.

11 Peter finally realized what had happened! "It's really true!" he said to himself. "The Lord has sent His angel and saved me from Herod and from what the Jews were hoping to do to me!"

12 After a little thought he went to the home of Mary, mother of John Mark, where many were gathered for a prayer meeting.

13 He knocked at the door in the gate, and a girl named Rhoda came to open it.

14 When she recognized Peter's voice, she was so over-joyed that she ran back inside to tell everyone that Peter was standing outside in the street!

15 They didn't believe her. "You're out of your mind," they said. When she insisted they decided, "It must be his angel. [They must have killed him.[2]]"

---

[2]Implied.

16   Meanwhile Peter continued knocking! When they finally went out and opened the door, their surprise knew no bounds.

17   He motioned for them to quiet down and told them what had happened and how the Lord had brought him out of jail.
"Tell James and the others what happened," he said—and left for safer quarters.

18   At dawn, the jail was in great commotion. What had happened to Peter?

19   When Herod sent for him and found that he wasn't there, he had the 16 guards arrested, court-martialed and sentenced to death.[3] Afterwards he left to live in Caesarea for a while.

20   While he was in Caesarea, a delegation from Tyre and Sidon arrived to see him. He was highly displeased with the people of those two cities, but the delegates made friends with Blastus, the royal secretary, and asked for peace, for their cities were economically dependent upon trade with Herod's country.

21   An appointment with Herod was granted, and when the day arrived he put on his royal robes, sat on his throne and made a speech to them.

22   At its conclusion the people gave him a great ovation, shouting, "It is the voice of a god and not of a man!"

23   Instantly, an angel of the Lord struck Herod with a sickness so that he was filled with maggots and died—because he accepted the people's worship instead of giving the glory to God.

*   *   *   *   *

24   God's Good News was spreading rapidly and there were many new believers.

25   Barnabas and Paul now visited Jerusalem and, as soon as they had finished their business, returned to Antioch,[3] taking John Mark with them.

---
[3]Implied.

CHAPTER 13

AMONG the prophets and teachers of the church at Antioch were Barnabas and Symeon (also called "The Black Man"), Lucius (from Cyrene), Manaen (the foster-brother of King Herod), and Paul.

2 One day as these men were worshiping and fasting the Holy Spirit said, "Dedicate Barnabas and Paul for a special job I have for them."

3 So after more fasting and prayer, the men laid their hands on them—and sent them on their way.

4 Directed by the Holy Spirit they went to Seleucia and then sailed for Cyprus.

5 There, in the town of Salamis, they went to the Jewish synagogue and preached. (John Mark went with them as their assistant.)

6, 7 Afterwards they preached from town to town across the entire island until finally they reached Paphos where they met a Jewish sorcerer, a fake prophet named Bar-Jesus. He had attached himself to the governor, Sergius Paulus, a man of considerable insight and understanding. The governor invited Barnabas and Paul to visit him, for he wanted to hear their message from God.

8 But the sorcerer, Elymas (his name in Greek), interfered and urged the governor to pay no attention to what Paul and Barnabas said, trying to keep him from trusting the Lord.

9 Then Paul, filled with the Holy Spirit, glared angrily at the sorcerer and said,

10 "You son of the Devil, full of every sort of trickery and villainy, enemy of all that is good, will you never end your opposition to the Lord?

11 And now God has laid His hand of punishment upon you, and you will be stricken awhile with blindness." Instantly mist and darkness fell upon him, and he began wandering around begging for someone to take his hand and lead him.

310

12   When the governor saw what happened he believed and was astonished at the power of God's message.

13   Now Paul and those with him left Paphos by ship for Turkey,[1] landing at the port town of Perga. There John deserted[2] them and returned to Jerusalem.

14   But Barnabas and Paul went on to Antioch, a city in the province of Pisidia. On the Sabbath they went into the synagogue for the services.

15   After the usual readings from the Books of Moses and from the Prophets, those in charge of the service sent them this message: "Brothers, if you have any word of instruction for us come and give it!"

16   So Paul stood, waved a greeting to them[3] and began. "Men of Israel," he said, "and all others here who reverence God, [let me begin my remarks with a bit of history[4]].

17   The God of this nation Israel chose our ancestors and honored them in Egypt by gloriously leading them out of their slavery.

18   And He nursed them through 40 years of wandering around in the wilderness.

19, 20   Then He destroyed seven nations in Canaan, and gave Israel their land as an inheritance. Judges ruled for about 450 years, and were followed by Samuel the prophet.

21   Then the people begged for a king, and God gave them Saul (son of Kish), a man of the tribe of Benjamin, who reigned for 40 years.

22   But God removed him and replaced him with David as king, a man about whom God said, 'David (son of Jesse) is a man after My own heart, for he will obey Me.'

23   And it is one of King David's descendants, Jesus, who is God's promised Savior of Israel!

24   But before He came, John the Baptist preached the need for everyone in Israel to turn from sin to God.

25   As John was finishing his work he asked, 'Do you think

---

[1]Literally, "Pamphylia."
[2]Literally, "departed from them." See chapter 15, verse 38.
[3]Literally, "beckoning with the hand."
[4]Implied.

I am the Messiah? No! But He is coming soon—and in comparison with Him, I am utterly worthless.'

26   Brothers—you sons of Abraham, and also all of you Gentiles here who reverence God—this salvation is for all of us!

27   The Jews in Jerusalem and their leaders fulfilled prophecy by killing Jesus; for they didn't recognize Him, or realize that He is the one the prophets had written about, though they heard the prophets' words read every Sabbath.

28   They found no just cause to execute Him, but asked Pilate to have Him killed anyway.

29   When they had fulfilled all the prophecies concerning His death, He was taken from the cross and placed in a tomb.

30   But God brought Him back to life again!

31   And He was seen many times during the next few days by the men who had accompanied Him to Jerusalem from Galilee—these men have constantly testified to this in public witness.

32, 33   And now Barnabas and I are here to bring you this Good News—that God's promise to our ancestors has come true in our own time, in that God brought Jesus back to life again. This is what the second Psalm is talking about when it says concerning Jesus, 'Today I have honored You as My Son.'[5]

34   For God had promised to bring Him back to life again, no more to die. This is stated in the Scripture that says, 'I will do for You the wonderful thing I promised David.'

35   In another Psalm He explained more fully, saying, 'God will not let His Holy One decay.'

36   This was not a reference to David, for after David had served his generation according to the will of God, he died and was buried, and his body decayed.

37   [No, it was a reference to another[6]]—Someone God brought back to life, whose body was not touched at all by the ravages of death.[7]

---

[5]Literally, "this day have I begotten You."
[6]Implied.
[7]Literally, "saw no corruption."

38   Brothers! Listen! In this man Jesus, there is forgiveness for your sins!

39   Everyone who trusts in Him is freed from all guilt and declared righteous—something the Jewish law could never do.

40   Oh, be careful! Don't let the prophets' words apply to you! For they said,

41   'Look and perish, you despisers [of the truth[8]], for I am doing something in your day—something that you won't believe when you hear it announced.' "

42   As the people left the synagogue that day, they asked Paul to return and speak to them again the next week.

43   And many Jews and godly Gentiles who worshiped at the synagogue followed Paul and Barnabas down the street as the two men urged them to accept the mercies God was offering.

44   The following week almost the entire city turned out to hear them preach the Word of God.

45   But when the Jewish leaders[9] saw the crowds, they were jealous, and cursed[10] and argued against whatever Paul said.

46   Then Paul and Barnabas spoke out boldly and declared, "It was necessary that this Good News from God should be given first to you Jews. But since you have rejected it, and shown yourselves unworthy of eternal life—well, we will offer it to Gentiles.

47   For this is as the Lord commanded when He said, 'I have made you a light to the Gentiles, to lead them from the farthest corners of the earth[11] to My salvation.' "

48   When the Gentiles heard this, they were very glad and rejoiced in Paul's message; and as many as wanted[12] eternal life, believed.

49   So God's message spread all through that region.

50   Then the Jewish leaders stirred up both the godly women and the civic leaders of the city and incited a mob against Paul and Barnabas, and ran them out of town.

---

[8]Implied.
[9]Literally, "the Jews."
[10]Or, "blasphemed."
[11]Literally, "from the uttermost part of the earth."
[12]Or, "were disposed to," or, "ordained to."

51   But they shook off the dust of their feet against the town and went on to the city of Iconium.

52   And their converts[13] were filled with joy and with the Holy Spirit.

CHAPTER 14

AT Iconium, Paul and Barnabas went together to the synagogue and preached with such power that many—both Jews and Gentiles—believed.

2   But the Jews who spurned God's message stirred up distrust among the Gentiles against Paul and Barnabas, saying all sorts of evil things about them.

3   Nevertheless, they stayed there a long time, preaching boldly, and the Lord proved their message was from Him by giving them power to do great miracles.

4   But the people of the city were divided in their opinion about them. Some agreed with the Jewish leaders, and some backed the apostles.

5, 6   When Paul and Barnabas learned of a plot to incite a mob of Gentiles, Jews, and Jewish leaders to attack and stone them, they fled for their lives, going to the cities of Lycaonia, Lystra, Derbe, and the surrounding area,

7   And preaching the Good News there.

8   While they were at Lystra, they came upon a man with crippled feet who had been that way from birth, so he had never walked.

9   He was listening as Paul preached, and Paul noticed him and realized he had faith to be healed!

10   So Paul called to him, "Stand up!" and the man leaped to his feet and started walking!

11   When the listening crowd saw what Paul had done, they shouted (in their local dialect, of course), "These men are gods in human bodies!"

12   They decided that Barnabas was the Greek god Jupiter,

---

[13]Literally, "the disciples."

and that Paul, because he was the chief speaker, was Mercury!

13   The local priest of the Temple of Jupiter, located on the outskirts of the city, brought them cartloads of flowers and sacrificed oxen to them at the city gates before the crowds.

14   But when Barnabas and Paul saw what was happening they ripped at their clothing in dismay and ran out among the people, shouting,

15   "Men! What are you doing? We are merely human beings like yourselves! We have come to bring you the Good News that you are invited to turn from the worship of these foolish things and to pray instead to the living God who made heaven and earth and sea and everything in them.

16   In bygone days He permitted the nations to go their own ways,

17   But He never left Himself without a witness; there were always His reminders—the kind things He did such as sending you rain and good crops and giving you food and gladness."

18   But even so, Paul and Barnabas could scarcely restrain the people from sacrificing to them!

19   Yet only a few days later, some Jews arrived from Antioch and Iconium and turned the crowds into a murderous mob that stoned Paul and dragged him out of the city, apparently dead!

20   But as the believers stood around him, he got up and went back into the city! The next day he left with Barnabas for Derbe.

21   After preaching the Good News there and making many disciples, they returned again to Lystra, Iconium and Antioch,

22   Where they helped the believers to grow in love for God and each other. They encouraged them to continue in the faith in spite of all the persecution, reminding them that they must enter into the Kingdom of God through many tribulations.

23   Paul and Barnabas also appointed elders in every church and prayed for them with fasting, turning them over to the care of the Lord in whom they trusted.

24   Then they traveled back through Pisidia to Pamphylia,

25   Preached again in Perga, and went on to Attalia.

26   Finally they returned by ship to Antioch, where their
journey had begun, and where they had been committed to God
for the work now completed.

27   Upon arrival they called together the believers and
reported on their trip, telling how God had opened the door of
faith to the Gentiles too.

28   And they stayed there with the believers at Antioch for
a long while.

CHAPTER 15

WHILE Paul and Barnabas were at Antioch, some men
from Judea arrived and began to teach the believers that
unless they adhered to the ancient Jewish[1] custom of circumcision, they could not be saved.

2   Paul and Barnabas argued and discussed this with them
at length, and finally the believers sent them to Jerusalem,
accompanied by some local men, to talk to the apostles and
elders there about this question.

3   After the entire congregation had escorted them out of
the city the delegates went on to Jerusalem, stopping along the
way in the cities of Phoenicia and Samaria to visit the believers,
telling them—much to everyone's joy—that the Gentiles, too,
were being converted.

4   Arriving in Jerusalem, they met with the church leaders
—all the apostles and elders were present—and Paul and
Barnabas reported on what God had been doing through their
ministry.

5   But then some of the men who had been Pharisees before
their conversion stood to their feet and declared that all Gentile
converts must be circumcised and required to follow all the
Jewish customs and ceremonies.[2]

6   So the apostles and church elders set a further meeting
to decide this question.

---

[1]Literally, "the custom of Moses."
[2]Literally, "to charge them to keep the laws of Moses."

7 At the meeting, after long discussion, Peter stood and addressed them as follows:

"Brothers, you all know that God chose me from among you long ago to preach the Good News to the Gentiles, so that they also could believe.

8 God, who knows men's hearts, confirmed the fact that He accepts Gentiles by giving them the Holy Spirit, just as He gave Him to us.

9 He made no distinction between them and us, for He cleansed their lives through faith, just as He did ours.

10 And now are you going to correct God by burdening the Gentiles with a yoke that neither we nor our fathers were able to bear?

11 Don't you believe that all are saved the same way, by the free gift of the Lord Jesus?"

12 There was no further discussion, and everyone now listened as Barnabas and Paul told about the miracles God had done through them among the Gentiles.

13 When they had finished, James took the floor. "Brothers," he said, "listen to me.

14 Peter[3] has told you about the time God first visited the Gentiles to take from them a people to bring honor to His name.

15 And this fact of Gentile conversion agrees with what the prophets predicted. For instance, listen to this passage from the prophet Amos[4]:

16 'Afterwards' [says the Lord[4]], 'I will return and renew the broken contract with David,[5]

17 So that Gentiles, too, will find the Lord—all those marked with My name.'

18 That is what the Lord says, who reveals His plans made from the beginning.

19 And so my judgment is that we should not insist that the Gentiles who turn to God must obey our Jewish laws,

20 Except that we should write to them to refrain from

[3]Literally, "Symeon."
[4]Implied. See Amos 9:11-12.
[5]Literally, "rebuild the tabernacle of David which is fallen."

eating meat sacrificed to idols, from all fornication, and also from eating unbled meat of strangled animals.

21 For these things have been preached against in Jewish synagogues in every city on every Sabbath for many generations."

22 Then the apostles and elders and the whole congregation voted to send delegates to Antioch with Paul and Barnabas, to report on this decision. The men chosen were two of the church leaders—Judas (also called Barsabbas) and Silas.

23 This is the letter they took along with them:

"From: The apostles, elders and brothers at Jerusalem.

To: The Gentile brothers in Antioch, Syria and Cilicia. Greetings!

24 We understand that some believers from here have upset you and questioned your salvation,[6] but they had no such instructions from us.

25 So it seemed wise to us, having unanimously agreed on our decision, to send to you these two official representatives, along with our beloved Barnabas and Paul.

26 These men—Judas and Silas, who have risked their lives for the sake of our Lord Jesus Christ—will confirm orally what we have decided concerning your question.

27, 28, 29 For it seemed good to the Holy Spirit and to us to lay no greater burden of Jewish laws on you than to abstain from eating food offered to idols and from unbled meat of strangled animals,[7] and, of course, from fornication. If you do this, it is enough. Farewell."

30 The four messengers went at once to Antioch, where they called a general meeting of the Christians and gave them the letter.

31 And there was great joy throughout the church that day as they read it.

32 Then Judas and Silas, both being gifted speakers,[8] preached long sermons to the believers, strengthening their faith.

---

[6]Literally, "subverted your souls."
[7]Literally, "and from blood."
[8]Or, "prophets."

33   They stayed several days,[9] and then Judas and Silas returned to Jerusalem taking greetings and appreciation to those who had sent them.

34, 35   Paul and Barnabas stayed on at Antioch to assist several others who were preaching and teaching there.

36   Several days later Paul suggested to Barnabas that they return again to Turkey, and visit each city where they had preached before,[10] to see how the new converts were getting along.

37   Barnabas agreed, and wanted to take along John Mark.

38   But Paul didn't like that idea at all, since John had deserted them in Pamphylia.

39   Their disagreement over this was so sharp that they separated. Barnabas took Mark with him and sailed for Cyprus,

40, 41   While Paul chose Silas and, with the blessing of the believers, left for Syria and Cilicia, to encourage the churches there.

CHAPTER 16

PAUL and Silas went first to Derbe and then on to Lystra where they met Timothy, a believer whose mother was a Christian Jewess but his father a Greek.

2   Timothy was well thought of by the brothers in Lystra and Iconium,

3   So Paul asked him to join them on their journey. In deference to the Jews of the area, he circumcised Timothy before they left, for everyone knew that his father was a Greek [and hadn't permitted this before[1]].

4   Then they went from city to city, making known the decision concerning the Gentiles, as decided by the apostles and elders in Jerusalem.

5   So the church grew daily in faith and numbers.

6   Next they traveled through Phrygia and Galatia, because

---

[9]Literally, "spent some time."
[10]Implied. Literally, "return now and visit every city wherein we proclaimed the word of the Lord.
[1]Implied.

the Holy Spirit had told them not to go into the Turkish province of Ausia at that time.

7   Then going along the borders of Mysia they headed north for the province of Bithynia, but again the Spirit of Jesus said no.

8   So instead they went on through Mysia province to the city of Troas.

9   That night[2] Paul had a vision. In his dream he saw a man over in Macedonia, Greece, pleading with him, "Come over here and help us."

10   Well, that settled it. We[3] would go to Macedonia, for we could only conclude that God was sending us to preach the Good News there.

11   We went aboard a boat at Troas, and sailed straight across to Samothrace, and the next day on to Neapolis,

12   And finally reached Philippi, a Roman[4] colony just inside the Macedonian border, and stayed there several days.

13   On the Sabbath, we went a little way outside the city to a river bank where we understood some people met for prayer; and we taught the Scriptures to some women who came.

14   One of them was Lydia, a saleswoman from Thyatira, a merchant of purple cloth. She was already a worshiper of God and, as she listened to us, the Lord opened her heart and she accepted all that Paul was saying.

15   She was baptized along with all her household and asked us to be her guests. "If you agree that I am faithful to the Lord," she said, "come and stay at my home." And she urged us until we did.

16   One day as we were going down to the place of prayer beside the river, we met a demon-possessed slave girl who was a fortune-teller, and earned much money for her masters.

17   She followed along behind us shouting, "These men are servants of God and they have come to tell you how to have your sins forgiven."

18   This went on day after day until Paul, in great distress, turned and spoke to the demon within her. "I command you in

---

[2]Literally, "in the night."
[3]Luke, the writer of this book, now joined Paul and accompanied him on his journey.
[4]Implied.

the name of Jesus Christ to come out of her," he said. And instantly it left her.

19 Her masters' hopes of wealth were now shattered; they grabbed Paul and Silas and dragged them before the judges at the marketplace.

20, 21 "These Jews are corrupting our city," they shouted. "They are teaching the people to do things that are against the Roman laws."

22 A mob was quickly formed against Paul and Silas, and the judges ordered them stripped and beaten with wooden whips.

23 Again and again the rods slashed down across their bared backs, causing the blood to flow; and afterwards they were thrown into prison. The jailer was threatened with death if they escaped,[5]

24 So he took no chances, but put them into the inner dungeon and clamped their feet into the stocks.

25 Around midnight, as Paul and Silas were praying and singing hymns to the Lord—and the other prisoners were listening—

26 Suddenly there was a great earthquake; the prison was shaken to its foundations, all the doors flew open—and the chains of every prisoner fell off!

27 The jailer wakened to see the prison doors wide open, and assuming the prisoners had escaped, he drew his sword to kill himself.

28 But Paul yelled to him, "Don't do it! We are all here!"

29 Trembling with fear, the jailer called for lights and ran to the dungeon and fell down before Paul and Silas.

30 He brought them out and begged them, "Sirs, what must I do to be saved?"

31 They replied, "Believe on the Lord Jesus and you will be saved, and your entire household."

32 Then they told him and all his household the Good News from the Lord.

33 That same hour he washed their stripes and he and all his family were baptized.

---

[5]Implied.

34   Then he brought them up into his house and set a meal before them. How he and his household rejoiced because all were now believers!

35   The next morning the judges sent police officers over to tell the jailer, "Let those men go!"

36   So the jailer told Paul they were free to leave.

37   But Paul replied, "Oh, no they don't! They have publicly beaten us without trial and jailed us—and we are Roman citizens! So now they want us to leave secretly? Never! Let them come themselves and release us!"

38   The police officers reported to the judges, who feared for their lives when they heard Paul and Silas were Roman citizens.

39   So they came to the jail and begged them to go, and brought them out and pled with them to leave the city.

40   Paul and Silas then returned to the home of Lydia where they met with the believers and preached to them once more before leaving town.

CHAPTER 17

N OW they traveled through the cities of Amphipolis and Apollonia and came to Thessalonica, where there was a Jewish synagogue.

2   As was Paul's custom, he went there to preach, and for three Sabbaths in a row he opened the Scriptures to the people,

3   Explaining the prophecies about the sufferings of the Messiah and His coming back to life, and proving that Jesus is the Messiah.

4   Some who listened were persuaded and became converts—including a large number of godly Greek men, and also many important women of the city.[1]

5   But the Jewish leaders were jealous and incited some worthless fellows from the streets to form a mob and start a riot. They attacked the home of Jason, planning to take Paul and Silas to the City Council for punishment.

[1]Some manuscripts read, "many of the wives of leading men."

322

6 Not finding them there, they dragged out Jason and some of the other believers, and took them before the Council instead. "Paul and Silas have turned the rest of the world upside down, and now they are here disturbing our city," they shouted,

7 "And Jason has let them into his home. They are all guilty of treason, for they claim another king, Jesus, instead of Caesar."

8, 9 The people of the city, as well as the judges, were concerned at these reports and let them go only after they had posted bail.

10 That night the Christians hurried Paul and Silas to Beroea, and, as usual,[2] they went to the synagogue to preach.

11 But the people of Beroea were more open minded than those in Thessalonica, and gladly listened to the message. They searched the Scriptures day by day to check up on Paul and Silas' statements to see if they were really so.

12 As a result, many of them believed, including several prominent Greek women and many men also.

13 But when the Jews in Thessalonica learned that Paul was preaching in Beroea, they went over and stirred up trouble.

14 The believers acted at once, sending Paul on to the coast, while Silas and Timothy remained behind.

15 Those accompanying Paul went on with him to Athens, and then returned to Beroea with a message for Silas and Timothy to hurry and join him.

16 While Paul was waiting for them in Athens, he was deeply troubled by all the idols he saw everywhere throughout the city.

17 He went to the synagogue for discussions with the Jews and the devout Gentiles, and spoke daily in the public square to all who happened to be there.

18 He also had an encounter with some of the Epicurean and Stoic philosophers. Their reaction, when he told them about Jesus and His resurrection, was, "He's a dreamer," or, "He's pushing some foreign religion."

---

[2]Implied.

19 But they invited him to the forum at Mars Hill. "Come and tell us more about this new religion," they said,

20 "For you are saying some rather startling things and we want to hear more."

21 (I should explain that all the Athenians as well as the foreigners in Athens seemed to spend all their time discussing the latest new ideas!)

22 So Paul, standing before them at the Mars Hill forum, addressed them as follows:

"Men of Athens, I notice that you are very religious,

23 For as I was out walking I saw your many altars, and one of them had this inscription on it—'To the Unknown God.' You have been worshiping Him without knowing who He is, and now I wish to tell you about Him.

24 He made the world and everything in it, and since He is Lord of heaven and earth, He doesn't live in man-made temples;

25 And human hands can't minister to His needs—for He has no needs! He Himself gives life and breath to everything, and satisfies every need there is.

26 He created all the people of the world from one man, Adam,[3] and scattered the nations across the face of the earth. He decided beforehand which should rise and fall, and when. He determined their boundaries.

27 His purpose in all of this is that they should seek after God, and perhaps feel their way toward Him and find Him— though He is not far from any one of us.

28 For in Him we live and move and are! As one of your own poets says it, 'We are the sons of God.'

29 If this is true, we shouldn't think of God as an idol made by men from gold or silver or chipped from stone.

30 God tolerated man's past ignorance about these things, but now He commands everyone to put away idols and worship only Him.

31 For He has set a day for justly judging the world by the man He has appointed, and has pointed Him out by bringing Him back to life again."

[3]Implied.

32   When they heard Paul speak of the resurrection of a person who had been dead, some laughed, but others said, "We want to hear more about this later."

33   That ended Paul's discussion with them,

34   But a few joined him and became believers. Among them was Dionysius, a member of the City Council, and a woman named Damaris, and others.

CHAPTER 18

THEN Paul left Athens and went to Corinth.

2, 3   There he became acquainted with a Jew named Aquila, born in Pontus, who had recently arrived from Italy with his wife, Priscilla. They had been expelled from Italy as a result of Claudius Caesar's order to deport all Jews from Rome. Paul lived and worked with them, for they were tentmakers just as he was.

4   Each Sabbath found Paul at the synagogue, trying to convince the Jews and Greeks alike.

5   And after the arrival of Silas and Timothy from Macedonia, Paul spent his full time preaching and testifying to the Jews that Jesus is the Messiah.

6   But when the Jews opposed him and blasphemed, hurling abuse at Jesus, Paul shook off the dust from his robe and said, "Your blood be upon your own heads—I am innocent—from now on I will preach to the Gentiles."

7   After that he stayed with Titus Justus, a Gentile[1] who worshiped God and lived next door to the synagogue.

8   Crispus, the leader of the synagogue, and all his household believed in the Lord and were baptized—as were many others in Corinth.

9   One night the Lord spoke to Paul in a vision and told him, "Don't be afraid! Speak out! Don't quit!

10   For I am with you and no one can harm you. Many people here in this city belong to Me."

[1]Implied.

11   So Paul stayed there the next year and a half, teaching the truths of God.

12   But when Gallio became governor of Achaia, the Jews rose in concerted action against Paul and brought him before the governor for judgment.

13   They accused Paul of "persuading men to worship God in ways that are contrary to Roman law."

14   But just as Paul started to make his defense, Gallio turned to his accusers and said, "Listen, you Jews, if this were a case involving some crime, I would be obliged to listen to you,

15   But since it is merely a bunch of questions of semantics and personalities and your silly Jewish laws, you take care of it. I'm not interested and I'm not touching it."

16   And he drove them out of the courtroom.

17   Then the mob[2] grabbed Sosthenes, the new leader of the synagogue, and beat him outside the courtroom! But Gallio couldn't have cared less.

18   Paul stayed in the city several days after that and then said good-bye to the Christians and sailed for the coast of Syria, taking Priscilla and Aquila with him. At Cenchreae, Paul had his head shaved according to Jewish custom, for he had taken a vow.[3]

19   Arriving at the port of Ephesus, he left us aboard ship while he went over to the synagogue for a discussion with the Jews.

20   They asked him to stay for a few days, but he felt that he had no time to lose.[4]

21   "I must by all means be at Jerusalem for the holiday,"[5] he said. But he promised to return to Ephesus later if God permitted; and so we set sail again.

22   The next stop was at the port of Caesarea from where he visited the church [at Jerusalem[6]] and then sailed on to Antioch.

---

[2]Implied.
[3]Probably a vow to offer a sacrifice in Jerusalem in thanksgiving for answered prayer. The head was shaved 30 days before such gifts and sacrifices were given to God at the Temple.
[4]Possibly in order to arrive in Jerusalem within the prescribed 30 days.
[5]Literally, "feast." This entire sentence is omitted in many of the ancient manuscripts.
[6]Implied.

23 After spending some time there, he left for Turkey again, going through Galatia and Phrygia visiting all the believers, encouraging them and helping them grow in the Lord.

24 As it happened, a Jew named Apollos, a wonderful Bible teacher and preacher, had just arrived in Ephesus from Alexandria in Egypt.

25, 26 While he was in Egypt, someone had told him about John the Baptist and what John had said about Jesus, but that is all he knew. He had never heard the rest of the story! So he was preaching boldly and enthusiastically in the synagogue, "The Messiah is coming! Get ready to receive Him!" Priscilla and Aquila were there and heard him—and it was a powerful sermon. Afterwards they met with him and explained what had happened to Jesus since the time of John, and all that it meant![7]

27 Apollos had been thinking about going to Greece, and the believers encouraged him in this. They wrote to their fellow-believers there, telling them to welcome him. And upon his arrival in Greece, he was greatly used of God to strengthen the church,

28 For he powerfully refuted all the Jewish arguments in public debate, showing by the Scriptures that Jesus is indeed the Messiah.

CHAPTER 19

WHILE Apollos was in Corinth, Paul traveled through Turkey and arrived in Ephesus, where he found several disciples.

2 "Did you receive the Holy Spirit when you believed?" he asked them.

"No," they replied, "we don't know what you mean. What is the Holy Spirit?"

3 "Then what beliefs did you acknowledge at your baptism?" he asked.

And they replied, "What John the Baptist taught."

4 Then Paul pointed out to them that John's baptism was

---

[7]Literally, "explained to him the way of God more accurately."

to demonstrate a desire to turn from sin to God and that those receiving his baptism must then go on to believe in Jesus, the one John said would come later.

5   As soon as they heard this, they were baptized in[1] the name of the Lord Jesus.

6   Then, when Paul laid his hands upon their heads, the Holy Spirit came on them, and they spoke in other languages and prophesied.

7   The men involved were about 12 in number.

8   Then Paul went to the synagogue and preached boldly each Sabbath day[2] for three months, telling what[3] he believed and why, and persuading many to believe in Jesus.

9   But some rejected his message and publicly spoke against Christ, so he left, refusing to preach to them again. Pulling out the believers, he began a separate meeting at the lecture hall of Tyrannus and preached there daily.

10   This went on for the next two years, so that everyone in the Turkish province of Ausia—both Jews and Greeks—heard the Lord's message.

11   And God gave Paul the power to do unusual miracles,

12   So that even when his handkerchiefs or parts of his clothing were placed upon sick people, they were healed, and any demons within them came out.

13   A team of itinerant Jews who were traveling from town to town casting out demons planned to experiment by using the name of the Lord Jesus. The incantation they decided on was this: "I adjure you by Jesus, whom Paul preaches, to come out!"

14   Seven sons of Sceva, a Jewish priest, were doing this.

15   But when they tried it on a man possessed by a demon, the demon replied, "I know Jesus and I know Paul, but who are you?"

16   And he leaped on two of them and beat them up, so that they fled out of his house naked and badly injured.

17   The story of what happened spread quickly all through

---

[1]Or, "into."
[2]Implied.
[3]Literally, "concerning the Kingdom of God."

Ephesus, to Jews and Greeks alike; and a solemn fear descended on the city, and the name of the Lord Jesus was greatly honored.

18, 19   Many of the believers who had been practicing black magic confessed their deeds and brought their incantation books and charms and burned them at a public bonfire. (Someone estimated the value of the books at $10,000.[4])

20   This indicates how deeply the whole area was stirred by God's message.

21   Afterwards, Paul felt impelled by the Holy Spirit[5] to go across to Greece before returning to Jerusalem. "And after that," he said, "I must go on to Rome!"

22   He sent his two assistants, Timothy and Erastus, on ahead to Greece while he stayed awhile longer in Turkey.

23   But about that time, a big blowup developed in Ephesus concerning the Christians.

24   It began with Demetrius, a silversmith who employed many craftsmen to manufacture silver shrines of the Greek goddess Diana.

25   He called a meeting of his men, together with others employed in related trades, and addressed them as follows:

"Gentlemen, this business is our income.

26   As you know so well from what you've seen and heard, this man Paul has persuaded many, many people that handmade gods aren't gods at all. As a result, our sales volume is going down! And this trend is evident not only here in Ephesus, but throughout the entire province!

27   Of course, I am not only talking about the business aspects of this situation and our loss of income, but also of the possibility that the temple of the great goddess Diana will lose its influence, and that Diana—this magnificent goddess worshiped not only throughout this part of Turkey but all around the world—will be forgotten!"

28   At this their anger boiled and they began shouting, "Great is Diana of the Ephesians!"

29   A crowd began to gather and soon the city was filled

[4]Approximately £ 3,500.
[5]Literally, "purposed in the spirit."

with confusion. Everyone rushed to the amphitheater, dragging along Gaius and Aristarchus, Paul's traveling companions, for trial.

30   Paul wanted to go in, but the disciples wouldn't let him.

31   Some of the Roman officers of the province, friends of Paul, also sent a message to him, begging him not to risk his life by entering.

32   Inside, the people were all shouting, some one thing and some another—everything was in confusion. In fact, most of them didn't even know why they were there.

33   Alexander was spotted among the crowd by some of the Jews and dragged forward. He motioned for silence and tried to speak.

34   But when the crowd realized he was a Jew, they started shouting again and kept it up for two hours: "Great is Diana of the Ephesians! Great is Diana of the Ephesians!"

35   At last the mayor was able to quiet them down enough to speak. "Men of Ephesus," he said, "everyone knows that Ephesus is the center[6] of the religion of the great Diana, whose image fell down to us from heaven.

36   Since this is an indisputable fact, you shouldn't be disturbed no matter what is said, and should do nothing rash.

37   Yet you have brought these men here who have stolen nothing from her temple and have not defamed her.

38   If Demetrius and the craftsmen have a case against them, the courts are currently in session and the judges can take the case at once. Let them go through legal channels.

39   And if there are complaints about other matters, they can be settled at the regular City Council meetings;

40   For we are in danger of being called to account by the Roman government for today's riot, since there is no cause for it. And if Rome demands an explanation, I won't know what to say."

41   Then he dismissed them, and they dispersed.

---

[6]Literally, "is the temple-keeper."

CHAPTER 20

W HEN it was all over, Paul sent for the disciples, preached a farewell message to them, said good-bye and left for Greece,

2   Preaching to the believers along the way, in all the cities he passed through.

3   He was in Greece three months and was preparing to sail for Syria when he discovered a plot by the Jews against his life, so he decided to go north to Macedonia first.

4   Several men were traveling with him, going as far as Turkey;[1] they were Sopater of Beroea, the son of Pyrrhus; Aristarchus and Secundus, from Thessalonica; Gaius, from Derbe; and Timothy; and Tychicus and Trophimus, who were returning to their homes in Turkey,

5   And had gone on ahead and were waiting for us at Troas.

6   As soon as the Passover ceremonies ended, we boarded ship at Philippi in northern Greece and five days later arrived in Troas, Turkey, where we stayed a week.

7   On Sunday, we gathered for a communion service, with Paul preaching. And since he was leaving the next day, he talked until midnight!

8   The upstairs room where we met was lighted with many flickering lamps;

9   And as Paul spoke on and on, a young man named Eutychus, sitting on the window sill, went fast asleep and fell three stories to his death below.

10, 11, 12   Paul went down and gathered him into his arms. "Don't worry," he said, "he's all right!" And he was! What a wave of awesome joy swept through the crowd! They all went back upstairs and ate the Lord's Supper together; then Paul preached another long sermon—so it was dawn when he finally left them!

13   Paul was going by land to Assos, and we went on ahead by ship.

[1]Literally, "Asia."

14   He joined us there and we sailed together to Mitylene;

15   The next day we passed Chios; the next, we touched at Samos; and a day later we arrived at Miletus.

16   Paul had decided against stopping at Ephesus this time, as he was hurrying to get to Jerusalem, if possible, for the celebration of Pentecost.

17   But when we landed at Miletus, he sent a message to the elders of the church at Ephesus asking them to come down to the boat to meet him.

18   When they arrived he told them, "You men know that from the day I set foot in Turkey until now

19   I have done the Lord's work humbly—yes, and with tears—and have faced grave danger from the plots of the Jews against my life.

20   Yet I never shrank from telling you the truth, either publicly or in your homes.

21   I have had one message for Jews and Gentiles alike—the necessity of turning from sin to God through faith in our Lord Jesus Christ.

22   And now I am going to Jerusalem, drawn there irresistibly by the Holy Spirit,[2] not knowing what awaits me,

23   Except that the Holy Spirit has told me in city after city that jail and suffering lie ahead.

24   But life is worth nothing unless I use it for doing the work assigned me by the Lord Jesus—the work of telling others the Good News about God's mighty kindness and love.

25   And now I know that none of you among whom I went about teaching the Kingdom will ever see me again.

26   Let me say plainly that no man's blood can be laid at my door,

27   For I didn't shrink from declaring all God's message to you.

28   And now beware! Be sure that you feed and shepherd God's flock—His church, purchased with His blood—for the Holy Spirit is holding you responsible as overseers.

29   I know full well that after I leave you, false teachers,

---

[2]Or, "by an inner compulsion."

like vicious wolves, will appear among you, not sparing the flock.

30   Some of you yourselves will distort the truth in order to draw a following.

31   Watch out! Remember the three years I was with you— my constant watchcare over you night and day and my many tears for you.

32   And now I entrust you to God and His care and to His wonderful words which are able to build your faith and give you all the inheritance of those who are set apart for Himself.

33   I have never been hungry for money or fine clothing—

34   You know that these hands of mine worked to pay my own way and even to supply the needs of those who were with me.

35   And I was a constant example to you in helping the poor; for I remembered the words of the Lord Jesus, It is more blessed to give than to receive.' "

36   When he had finished speaking, he knelt and prayed with them,

37   And they wept aloud as they embraced him[3] in farewell,

38   Sorrowing most of all because he said that he would never see them again. Then they accompanied him down to the ship.

CHAPTER 21

AFTER parting from the Ephesian elders, we sailed straight to Cos. The next day we reached Rhodes and then went to Patara.

2   There we boarded a ship sailing for the Syrian province of Phoenicia.

3   We sighted the island of Cyprus, passed it on our left and landed at the harbor of Tyre, in Syria, where the ship unloaded.

4   We went ashore, found the local believers and stayed

[3]Literally, "fell on Paul's neck and kissed him."

with them a week. These disciples warned Paul—the Holy Spirit prophesying through them—not to go on to Jerusalem.

5   At the end of the week when we returned to the ship, the entire congregation including wives and children walked down to the beach with us where we prayed and said our farewells.

6   Then we went aboard and they returned home.

7   The next stop after leaving Tyre was Ptolemais where we greeted the believers, but stayed only one day.

8   Then we went on to Caesarea and stayed at the home of Philip the Evangelist, one of the first seven deacons.[1]

9   He had four unmarried[2] daughters who had the gift of prophecy.

10   During our stay of several days, a man named Agabus, who also had the gift of prophecy, arrived from Judea

11   And visited us. He took Paul's belt, bound his own feet and hands with it and said, "The Holy Spirit declares, 'So shall the owner of this belt be bound by the Jews in Jerusalem and turned over to the Romans.' "

12   Hearing this, all of us—the local believers and his traveling companions—begged Paul not to go on to Jerusalem.

13   But he said, "Why all this weeping? You are breaking my heart! For I am ready not only to be jailed at Jerusalem, but also to die for the sake of the Lord Jesus."

14   When it was clear that he wouldn't be dissuaded, we gave up and said, "The will of the Lord be done."

15   So shortly afterwards, we packed our things and left for Jerusalem.

16   Some disciples from Caesarea accompanied us, and on arrival we were guests at the home of Mnason, originally from Cyprus, one of the early believers;

17   And all the believers at Jerusalem welcomed us cordially.

18   The second day Paul took us with him to meet with James and the elders of the Jerusalem church.

19   After greetings were exchanged, Paul recounted the

[1]See Acts 6:5; 8:1-13.
[2]Literally, "virgins."

334

many things God had accomplished among the Gentiles through his work.

20 They praised God but then said, "You know, dear brother, how many thousands of Jews have also believed, and they are all very insistent that Jewish believers must continue to follow the Jewish traditions and customs.[3]

21 Our Jewish Christians here at Jerusalem have been told that you are against the laws of Moses, against our Jewish customs, and that you forbid the circumcision of their children.

22 Now what can be done? For they will certainly hear that you have come.

23 We suggest this: We have four men here who are preparing to shave their heads and take some vows.

24 Go with them to the Temple and have your head shaved too—and pay for theirs to be shaved. Then everyone will know that you approve of this custom for the Hebrew Christians and that you yourself obey the Jewish laws and are in line with our thinking in these matters.

25 As for the Gentile Christians, we aren't asking them to follow these Jewish customs at all—except for the ones we wrote to them about: not to eat food offered to idols, not to eat unbled meat from strangled animals, and not to commit fornication."

26, 27 So Paul agreed to their request and the next day went with the men to the Temple for the ceremony, thus publicizing his vow to offer a sacrifice seven[4] days later with the others. The seven days were almost ended when some Jews from Turkey saw him in the Temple and roused a mob against him. They grabbed him,

28 Yelling, "Men of Israel! Help! Help! This is the man who preaches against our people and tells everybody to disobey the Jewish laws. He even talks against the Temple and defiles it by bringing Gentiles in!"

29 (For down in the city earlier that day, they had seen him with Trophimus, a Gentile[5] from Ephesus in Turkey, and assumed that Paul had taken him into the Temple.)

---

[3]Literally, "they are all zealous for the law."
[4]Literally, "the days of purification."
[5]Implied.

30 The whole population of the city was electrified by these accusations and a great riot followed. Paul was dragged out of the Temple, and immediately the gates were closed behind him.

31 As they were killing him, word reached the commander of the Roman garrison that all Jerusalem was in an uproar.

32 He quickly ordered out his soldiers and officers and ran down among the crowd. When the mob saw the troops coming, they quit beating Paul.

33 The commander arrested him and ordered him bound with double chains. Then he asked the crowd who he was and what he had done.

34 Some shouted one thing and some another. When he couldn't find out anything in all the uproar and confusion, he ordered Paul to be taken to the armory.[6]

35 As they reached the stairs, the mob grew so violent that the soldiers lifted Paul to their shoulders to protect him,

36 And the crowd surged behind shouting, "Away with him, away with him!"

37, 38 As Paul was about to be taken inside, he said to the commander, "May I have a word with you?"

"Do you know Greek?" the commander asked, surprised. "Aren't you that Egyptian who led a rebellion a few years ago[7] and took 4,000 members of the Assassins with him into the desert?"

39 "No," Paul replied, "I am a Jew from Tarsus in Cilicia which is no small town. I request permission to talk to these people."

40 The commander agreed, so Paul stood on the stairs and motioned to the people to be quiet; soon a deep silence enveloped the crowd, and he addressed them in Hebrew as follows:

---

[6]Literally, "castle," or "fort."
[7]Literally, "before these days."

CHAPTER 22

B ROTHERS and fathers, listen to me as I offer my defense."
2 (When they heard him speaking in Hebrew, the silence was even greater.)

3 "I am a Jew," he said, "born in Tarsus, a city in Cilicia, but educated here in Jerusalem under Gamaliel, at whose feet I learned to follow our Jewish laws and customs very carefully. I became very anxious to honor God in everything I did, just as you have tried to do today.

4 And I persecuted the Christians, hounding them to death, binding and delivering both men and women to prison.

5 The High Priest or any member of the Council can testify that this is so. For I asked them for letters to the Jewish leaders in Damascus, with instructions to let me bring any Christians I found to Jerusalem in chains to be punished.

6 As I was on the road, nearing Damascus, suddenly about noon a very bright light from heaven shone around me.

7 And I fell to the ground and heard a voice saying to me, 'Saul, Saul, why are you persecuting me?'

8 'Who is it speaking to me, sir?' I asked. And He replied, 'I am Jesus of Nazareth, the one you are persecuting.'

9 The men with me saw the light but didn't understand what was said.

10 And I said, 'What shall I do, Lord?' And the Lord told me, 'Get up and go into Damascus, and there you will be told what awaits you in the years ahead.'

11 I was blinded by the intense light, and had to be led into Damascus by my companions.

12 There a man named Ananias, as godly a man as you could find for obeying the law, and well thought of by all the Jews of Damascus,

13 Came to me, and standing beside me said, 'Brother Saul, receive your sight!' And that very hour I could see him!

14 Then he told me, 'The God of our fathers has chosen

you to know His will and to see the Messiah[1] and hear Him speak.

15   You are to take His message everywhere, telling what you have seen and heard.

16   And now, why delay? Go and be baptized, and be cleansed from your sins, calling on the name of the Lord.'

17, 18   One day after my return to Jerusalem, while I was praying in the Temple, I fell into a trance and saw a vision of God saying to me, 'Hurry! Leave Jerusalem, for the people here won't believe you when you give them My message.'

19   'But Lord,' I argued, 'they certainly know that I imprisoned and beat those in every synagogue who believed on You.

20   And when Your witness Stephen was killed, I was standing there agreeing—keeping the coats they laid aside as they stoned him.'

21   But God said to me, 'Leave Jerusalem, for I will send you far away to the *Gentiles!*' "

22   The crowd listened until Paul came to that word, then with one voice they shouted, "Away with such a fellow! Kill him! He isn't fit to live!"

23   They yelled and threw their coats in the air and tossed up handfuls of dust.

24   So the commander brought him inside and ordered him lashed with whips to make him confess his crime. He wanted to find out why the crowd had become so furious!

25   As they tied Paul down to lash him, Paul said to an officer standing there, "Is it legal for you to whip a Roman citizen who hasn't even been tried?"

26   The officer went to the commander and asked, "What are you doing? This man is a Roman citizen!"

27   So the commander went over and asked Paul, "Tell me, are you a Roman citizen?"

"Yes, I certainly am."

28   "I am too," the commander muttered, "and it cost me plenty!"

"But I am a citizen by birth!"

---

[1] Literally, "Righteous One."

29   The soldiers standing ready to lash him, quickly disappeared when they heard Paul was a Roman citizen, and the
commander was frightened because he had ordered him bound
and whipped.

30   The next day the commander freed him from his chains
and ordered the chief priests into session with the Jewish
Council. He had Paul brought in before them to try to find out
what the trouble was all about.

CHAPTER 23

G AZING intently at the Council, Paul began: "Brothers, I
have always lived before God in all good conscience!"

2   Instantly Ananias the High Priest commanded those close
to Paul to slap him on the mouth.

3   Paul said to him, "God shall slap you, you whitewashed pigpen.[1] What kind of judge are you to break the law
yourself by ordering me struck like that?"

4   Those standing near Paul said to him, "Is that the way
to talk to God's High Priest?"

5   "I didn't realize he was the High Priest, brothers," Paul
replied, "for the Scriptures say, 'Never speak evil of any of
your rulers.'"

6   Then Paul thought of something! Part of the Council
were Sadducees, and part were Pharisees! So he shouted,
"Brothers, I am a Pharisee, as were all my ancestors! And I am
being tried here today because I believe in the resurrection of
the dead!"

7   This divided the Council right down the middle—the
Pharisees against the Sadducees—

8   For the Sadducees say there is no resurrection or angels
or even eternal spirit within us,[2] but the Pharisees believe in all
of these.

9   So a great clamor arose. Some of the Jewish leaders[3]
jumped up to argue that Paul was all right. "We see nothing

[1]Literally, "you whitewashed wall."
[2]Literally, "nor spirit."
[3]Literally, "scribes."

339

wrong with him," they shouted. "Perhaps a spirit or angel spoke to him [there on the Damascus road⁴]."

10   The shouting grew louder and louder, and the men were tugging at Paul from both sides, pulling him this way and that. Finally the commander, fearing they would tear him apart, ordered his soldiers to take him away from them by force and bring him back to the armory.

11   That night the Lord stood beside Paul and said, "Don't worry, Paul; just as you have told the people about Me here in Jerusalem, so you must also in Rome."

12, 13   The next morning some 40 or more of the Jews got together and bound themselves by a curse neither to eat nor drink until they had killed Paul!

14   Then they went to the chief priests and elders and told them what they had done.

15   "Ask the commander to bring Paul back to the Council again," they requested. "Pretend you want to ask a few more questions. We will kill him on the way."

16   But Paul's nephew got wind of their plan and came to the armory and told Paul.

17   Paul called one of the officers and said, "Take this boy to the commander. He has something important to tell him."

18   So the officer did, explaining, "Paul, the prisoner, called me over and asked me to bring this young man to you to tell you something."

19   The commander took the boy by the hand, and leading him aside asked, "What is it you want to tell me, lad?"

20   "Tomorrow," he told him, "The Jews are going to ask you to bring Paul before the Council again, pretending they want to get some more information.

21   But don't do it! There are more than 40 men hiding along the road ready to jump him and kill him. They have bound themselves under a curse to neither eat nor drink till he is dead. They are out there now, expecting you to agree to their request."

22   "Don't let a soul know you told me this," the commander warned the boy as he left.

⁴Implied.

23, 24   Then the commander called two of his officers and ordered, "Get 200 soldiers ready to leave for Caesarea at nine o'clock tonight! Take 200 spearmen and 70 mounted cavalry. Give Paul a horse to ride and get him safely to Governor Felix."

25   Then he wrote this letter to the governor:

26   *"From:* Claudius Lysias

To: His Excellency, Governor Felix.

Greetings!

27   This man was seized by the Jews and they were killing him when I sent the soldiers to rescue him, for I learned that he was a Roman citizen.

28   Then I took him to their Council to try to find out what he had done.

29   I soon discovered it was something about their Jewish beliefs, certainly nothing worthy of imprisonment or death.

30   But when I was informed of a plot to kill him, I decided to send him on to you and will tell his accusers to bring their charges before you."

31   So that night, as ordered, the soldiers took Paul to Antipatris.

32   They returned to the armory the next morning, leaving him with the cavalry to take him on to Caesarea.

33   When they arrived in Caesarea, they presented Paul and the letter to the governor.

34   He read it and then asked Paul where he was from. "Cilicia," Paul answered.

35   "I will hear your case fully when your accusers arrive," the governor told him, and ordered him kept in the prison at King Herod's palace.

CHAPTER 24

FIVE days later Ananias the High Priest arrived with some of the Jewish leaders[1] and the lawyer[2] Tertullus, to make their accusations against Paul.

---

[1] Literally, "elders."
[2] Literally, "orator."

2   When Tertullus was called forward, he laid charges against Paul in the following address to the governor:

"Your Excellency, you have given quietness and peace to us Jews and have greatly reduced the discrimination against us.

3   And for this we are very, very grateful to you.

4   But lest I bore you, kindly give me your attention for only a moment as I briefly outline our case against this man.

5   For we have found him to be a troublemaker, a man who is constantly inciting the Jews throughout the entire world to riots and rebellions against the Roman government. He is a ringleader of the sect known as the Nazarenes.

6   Moreover, he was trying to defile the Temple when we arrested him. We would have given him what he justly deserves,

7   But Lysias, the commander of the garrison, came and took him violently away from us,

8   Demanding that he be tried by Roman law. You can find out the truth of our accusations by examining him yourself."

9   Then all the other Jews chimed in, declaring that everything Tertullus said was true.

10   Now it was Paul's turn. The governor motioned for him to rise and speak. Paul began: "I know, sir, that you have been a judge of Jewish affairs for many years, and this gives me confidence as I make my defense.

11   You can quickly discover that it was no more than twelve days ago that I arrived in Jerusalem to worship at the Temple,

12   And you will discover that I have never incited a riot in any synagogue or on the streets of any city;

13   And these men certainly cannot prove the things they accuse me of doing.

14   But one thing I do confess, that I believe in the way of salvation, which they refer to as a sect; I follow that system of serving the God of our ancestors; I firmly believe in the Jewish law and everything written in the books of prophecy;

15   And I believe, just as these men do, that there will be a resurrection of both the righteous and ungodly.

16 Because of this I try with all my strength to always maintain a clear conscience before God and man.

17 After several years away, I returned to Jerusalem with money to aid the Jews, and to offer a sacrifice to God.

18 My accusers saw me in the Temple as I was presenting my thank offering.[3] I had shaved my head as their laws required, and there was no crowd around me, and no rioting! But some Jews from Turkey were there,

19 (Who ought to be here if they have anything against me)—

20 But look! Ask these men right here what wrongdoing their Council found in me,

21 Except that I said one thing I shouldn't[4] when I shouted out, 'I am here before the Council to defend myself for believing that the dead will rise again!' "

22 Felix, who knew Christians didn't go around starting riots,[5] told the Jews to wait for the arrival of Lysias, the garrison commander, and then he would decide the case.

23 He ordered Paul to prison but instructed the guards to treat him gently and not to forbid any of his friends from visiting him or bringing him gifts to make his stay more comfortable.

24 A few days later Felix came with Drusilla, his legal[6] wife, a Jewess. Sending for Paul, they listened as he told them about faith in Christ Jesus.

25 And as he reasoned with them about righteousness and self-control and the judgment to come, Felix was terrified. "Go away for now," he replied, "and when I have a more convenient time, I'll call for you again."

26 He also hoped that Paul would bribe him, so he sent for him from time to time and talked with him.

27 Two years went by in this way; then Felix was succeeded by Porcius Festus. And because Felix wanted to gain favor with the Jews, he left Paul in chains.

---

[3] Implied.
[4] Literally, "except it be for this one voice."
[5] Literally, "having more accurate knowledge."
[6] Literally, "his own wife."

CHAPTER 25

THREE days after Festus arrived in Caesarea to take over his new responsibilities, he left for Jerusalem,

2 Where the chief priests and other Jewish leaders got hold of him and gave him their story about Paul.

3 They begged him to bring Paul to Jerusalem at once. (Their plan was to waylay and kill him.)

4 But Festus replied that since Paul was at Caesarea and he himself was returning there soon,

5 Those with authority in this affair should return with him for the trial.

6 Eight or ten days later he returned to Caesarea and the following day opened Paul's trial.

7 On Paul's arrival in court the Jews from Jerusalem gathered around, hurling many serious accusations which they couldn't prove.

8 Paul denied the charges: "I am not guilty," he said. "I have not opposed the Jewish laws or desecrated the Temple or rebelled against the Roman government."

9 Then Festus, anxious to please the Jews, asked him, "Are you willing to go to Jerusalem and stand trial before me?"

10, 11 But Paul replied, "No! I demand my privilege of a hearing before the Emperor himself. You know very well I am not guilty. If I have done something worthy of death, I don't refuse to die! But if I am innocent, neither you nor anyone else has a right to turn me over to these men to kill me. *I appeal to Caesar.*"

12 Festus conferred with his advisors and then replied, "Very well! You have appealed to Caesar, and to Caesar you shall go!"

13 A few days later King Agrippa arrived with Bernice[1] for a visit with Festus.

14 During their stay of several days Festus discussed Paul's case with the king. "There is a prisoner here," he told him, "whose case was left for me by Felix.

[1] She was his sister.

344

15 When I was in Jerusalem, the chief priests and other Jewish leaders gave me their side of the story and asked me to have him killed.

16 Of course I quickly pointed out to them that Roman law does not convict a man before he is tried. He is given an opportunity to defend himself face to face with his accusers.

17 When they came here for the trial, I called the case the very next day and ordered Paul brought in.

18 But the accusations made against him weren't at all what I supposed they would be.

19 It was something about their religion, and about someone called Jesus who died, but Paul insists is alive!

20 I was perplexed as to how to decide a case of this kind and asked him whether he would be willing to stand trial on these charges in Jerusalem.

21 But Paul appealed to Caesar! So I ordered him back to jail until I could arrange to get him to the Emperor."

22 "I'd like to hear the man myself," Agrippa said. And Festus replied, "You shall—tomorrow!"

23 So the next day, after the king and Bernice had arrived at the courtroom with great pomp, accompanied by military officers and prominent men of the city, Festus ordered Paul brought in.

24 Then Festus addressed the audience: "King Agrippa and all present," he said, "this is the man whose death is demanded both by the local Jews and by those in Jerusalem!

25 But in my opinion he has done nothing worthy of death. However, he appealed his case to Caesar, and I have no alternative but to send him.

26 But what shall I write the Emperor? For there is no real charge against him! So I have brought him before you all, and especially you, King Agrippa, to examine him and then tell me what to write.

27 For it doesn't seem reasonable to send a prisoner to the Emperor without any charges against him!"

CHAPTER 26

THEN Agrippa said to Paul, "Go ahead. Tell us your story." So Paul, with many gestures,[1] presented his defense:

2 "I am fortunate, King Agrippa," he began, "to be able to present my answer before you,

3 For I know you are an expert on Jewish laws and customs. Now please listen patiently!

4 As the Jews are well aware, I was given a thorough Jewish training from my earliest childhood in Tarsus[2] and later at Jerusalem, and I lived accordingly.

5 If they would admit it, they know that I have always been the strictest of Pharisees when it comes to obedience to Jewish laws and customs.

6 But the real reason behind their accusations is something else—it is because I am looking forward to the fulfillment of God's promise made to our ancestors.

7 The 12 tribes of Israel strive night and day to attain this same hope I have! Yet, O King, for me it is a crime, they say!

8 But is it a crime to believe in the resurrection of the dead? Does it seem incredible to you that God can bring men back to life again?

9 I used to believe that I ought to do many horrible things to the followers[3] of Jesus of Nazareth.

10 I imprisoned many of the saints in Jerusalem, as authorized by the High Priests; and when they were condemned to death, I cast my vote against them.

11 I used torture to try to make Christians everywhere curse Christ. I was so violently opposed to them that I even hounded them in distant cities in foreign lands.

12 I was on such a mission to Damascus, armed with the authority and commission of the chief priests,

13 When one day about noon, sir, a light from heaven brighter than the sun shone down on me and my companions.

[1] Literally, "stretched forth his hand."
[2] Literally, "my own nation."
[3] Literally, "the name."

346

14   We all fell down, and I heard a voice speaking to me in Hebrew, 'Saul, Saul, why are you persecuting Me? You are only hurting yourself.'[4]

15   'Who are you, sir?' I asked. And the Lord replied, 'I am Jesus, the one you are persecuting.

16   Now stand up! For I have appeared to you to appoint you as My servant and My witness. You are to tell the world about this experience and about the many other occasions when I shall appear to you.

17   And I will protect you from both your own people and the Gentiles. Yes, I am going to send you to the Gentiles

18   To open their eyes to their true condition so that they may repent and live in the light of God instead of in Satan's darkness, so that they may receive forgiveness for their sins and God's inheritance along with all people everywhere whose sins are cleansed away, who are set apart by faith in Me.'

19   And so, O King Agrippa, I was not disobedient to that vision from heaven!

20   I preached first to those in Damascus, then in Jerusalem and through Judea, and also to the Gentiles that all must forsake their sins and turn to God—and prove their repentance by doing good deeds.

21   The Jews arrested me in the Temple for preaching this, and tried to kill me,

22   But God protected me so that I am still alive today to tell these facts to everyone, both great and small. I teach nothing except what the prophets and Moses said—

23   That the Messiah would suffer, and be the First to rise from the dead, to bring light to Jews and Gentiles alike."

24   Suddenly Festus shouted, "Paul, you are insane. Your long studying has broken your mind!"

25   But Paul replied, "I am not insane, Most Excellent Festus. I speak words of sober truth.

26   And King Agrippa knows about these things. I speak frankly for I am sure these events are all familiar to him, for they were not done in a corner!

---

[4]Literally, "it is hard for you to kick against the oxgoad!"

27 King Agrippa, do you believe the prophets? But I know you do—"

28 Agrippa interrupted him. "With trivial proofs like these,[5] you expect me to become a Christian?"

29 And Paul replied, "Would to God that whether my arguments are trivial or strong, both you and everyone here in this audience might become the same as I am, except for these chains."

30 Then the king, the governor, Bernice, and all the others stood and left.

31 As they talked it over afterwards they agreed, "This man hasn't done anything worthy of death or imprisonment."

32 And Agrippa said to Festus, "He could be set free if he hadn't appealed to Caesar!"

CHAPTER 27

ARRANGEMENTS were finally made to start us on our way to Rome by ship; so Paul and several other prisoners were placed in the custody of an officer named Julius, a member of the imperial guard.

2 We left on a boat bound for Greece,[1] which was scheduled to make several stops along the Turkish coast.[2] I should add that Aristarchus,[3] a Greek from Thessalonica, was with us.

3 The next day when we docked at Sidon, Julius was very kind to Paul and let him go ashore to visit with friends and receive their hospitality.

4 Putting to sea from there, we encountered headwinds that made it difficult to keep the ship on course, so we sailed north of Cyprus between the island and the mainland,[4]

5 And passed along the coast of the provinces of Cilicia and Pamphylia, landing at Myra, in the province of Lycia.

---

[5]Literally, "with little (persuasion)."
[1]Literally, "Adramyttium," a Greek port.
[2]Literally, "the coast of Asia."
[3]See Acts 19:29, 20:4, Philemon 24.
[4]Implied. Literally, "we sailed under the lee of Cyprus." Narratives from that period interpret this as meaning what is indicated in the paraphrase above.

6 There our officer found an Egyptian ship from Alexandria, bound for Italy, and put us aboard.

7, 8 We had several days of rough sailing, and finally neared Cnidus;[5] but the winds had become too strong, so we ran across to Crete, passing the port of Salmone. Beating into the wind with great difficulty and moving slowly along the southern coast, we arrived at Fair Havens, near the city of Lasea.

9 There we stayed for several days. The weather was becoming dangerous for long voyages by then, because it was late in the year,[6] and Paul spoke to the ship's officers about it.

10 "Sirs," he said, "I believe there is trouble ahead if we go on—perhaps shipwreck, loss of cargo, injuries, and death."

11 But the officers in charge of the prisoners listened more to the ship's captain and the owner than to Paul.

12 And since Fair Havens was an exposed[7] harbor—a poor place to spend the winter—most of the crew advised trying to go further up the coast to Phoenix, in order to winter there; Phoenix was a good harbor with only a northwest and southwest exposure.

13 Just then a light wind began blowing from the south, and it looked like a perfect day for the trip; so they pulled up anchor and sailed along close to shore.

14, 15 But shortly afterwards, the weather changed abruptly and a heavy wind of typhoon strength (a "northeaster," they called it) caught the ship and blew it out to sea. They tried at first to face back to shore but couldn't, so they gave up and let the ship run before the gale.

16 We finally sailed behind a small island named Clauda, where with great difficulty we hoisted aboard the lifeboat that was being towed behind us,

17 And then banded the ship with ropes to strengthen the hull. The sailors were afraid of being driven across to the quicksands of the African coast,[8] so they lowered the topsails and were thus driven before the wind.

---

[5]Cnidus was a port on the southeast coast of Turkey.
[6]Literally, "because the Fast was now already gone by." It came at about the time of the autumn equinox.
[7]Implied.
[8]Literally, "fearing lest they should be cast upon the Syrtis."

18   The next day as the seas grew higher, the crew began throwing the cargo overboard.

19   The following day they threw out the tackle and anything else they could lay their hands on.

20   The terrible storm raged unabated many days,[9] until at last all hope was gone.

21   No one had eaten for a long time, but finally Paul called the crew together and said, "Men, you should have listened to me in the first place and not left Fair Havens—you would have avoided all this injury and loss!

22   But cheer up! Not one of us will lose our lives, even though the ship will go down.

23   For last night an angel of the God to whom I belong and whom I serve stood beside me,

24   And said, 'Don't be afraid, Paul—for you will surely stand trial before Caesar! What's more, God has granted your request and will save the lives of all those sailing with you.'

25   So take courage! For I believe God! It will be just as He said!

26   But we will be shipwrecked on an island."

27   About midnight on the 14th night of the storm, as we were being driven to and fro on the Adriatic Sea, the sailors suspected land was near.

28   They sounded, and found 120 feet of water below them. A little later they sounded again, and found only 90 feet.

29   At this rate they knew they would soon be driven ashore; and fearing rocks along the coast, they threw out four anchors from the stern and prayed for daylight.

30   Some of the sailors planned to abandon the ship, and lowered the emergency boat as though they were going to put out anchors from the prow.

31   But Paul said to the soldiers and commanding officer, "You will all die unless everyone stays aboard."

32   So the soldiers cut the ropes and let the boat fall off.

33   As the darkness gave way to the early morning light, Paul begged everyone to eat. "You haven't touched food for two weeks," he said.

---

[9]Literally, "neither sun nor stars shone upon us."

34   "Please eat something now for your own good! For not a hair of your heads shall perish!"

35   Then he took some hardtack and gave thanks to God before them all, and broke off a piece and ate it.

36   Suddenly everyone felt better and began eating,

37   All two hundred seventy-six of us—for that is the number we had aboard.

38   After eating, the crew lightened the ship further by throwing all the wheat overboard.

39   When it was day, they didn't recognize the coastline, but noticed a bay with a beach and wondered whether they could get between the rocks and be driven up onto the beach.

40   They finally decided to try. Cutting off the anchors and leaving them in the sea, they lowered the rudders, raised the foresail and headed ashore.

41   But the ship hit a sandbar[10] and ran aground. The bow of the ship stuck fast, while the stern was exposed to the violence of the waves and began to break apart.

42   The soldiers advised their commanding officer to let them kill the prisoners lest any of them swim ashore and escape.

43   But Julius[11] wanted to spare Paul, so he told them no. Then he ordered all who could swim to jump overboard and make for land.

44   And the rest to try for it on planks and debris from the broken ship. So everyone escaped safely ashore!

CHAPTER 28

WE soon learned that we were on the island of Malta. The people of the island were very kind to us, building a bonfire on the beach to welcome and warm us in the rain and cold.

3   As Paul gathered an armful of sticks to lay on the fire, a

---

[10]Literally, "a place where two seas met."
[11]Implied.

poisonous snake, driven out by the heat, fastened itself onto his hand!

4   The people of the island saw it hanging there and said to each other, "A murderer, no doubt! Though he escaped the sea, justice will not permit him to live!"

5   But Paul shook off the snake into the fire and was unharmed.

6   The people waited for him to begin swelling or suddenly fall dead; but when they had waited a long time and no harm came to him, they changed their minds and decided he was a god.

7   Near the shore where we landed was an estate belonging to Publius, the governor of the island. He welcomed us courteously and fed us for three days.

8   As it happened, Publius' father was ill with fever and dysentery. Paul went in and prayed for him, and laying his hands on him, healed him!

9   Then all the other sick people in the island came and were cured.

10   As a result we were showered with gifts,[1] and when the time came to sail, people put on board all sorts of things we would need for the trip.

11   It was three months after the shipwreck before we set sail again, and this time it was in "The Twin Brothers" of Alexandria, a ship that had wintered at the island.

12   Our first stop was Syracuse, where we stayed three days.

13   From there we circled around to Rhegium; a day later a south wind began blowing, so the following day we arrived at Puteoli,

14   Where we found some believers! They begged us to stay with them seven days. Then, we sailed on to Rome.

15   The brothers in Rome had heard we were coming and came to meet us at the Forum[2] on the Appian Way. Others joined us at The Three Taverns[3]. When Paul saw them, he thanked God and took courage.

---

[1]Literally, "honors."
[2]About 43 miles from Rome.
[3]About 35 miles from Rome.

16   When we arrived in Rome, Paul was permitted to live wherever he wanted to, though guarded by a soldier.

17   Three days after his arrival, he called together the local Jewish leaders and spoke to them as follows:

"Brothers, I was arrested by the Jews in Jerusalem and handed over to the Roman government for prosecution, even though I had harmed no one nor violated the customs of our ancestors.

18   The Romans gave me a trial and wanted to release me, for they found no cause for the death sentence demanded by the Jewish leaders.

19   But when the Jews protested the decision, I felt it necessary, with no malice against them, to appeal to Caesar.

20   I asked you to come here today so we could get acquainted and I could tell you that it is because I believe the Messiah[4] has come that I am bound with this chain."

21   They replied, "We have heard nothing against you! We have had no letters from Judea or reports from those arriving from Jerusalem.[5]

22   But we want to hear what you believe, for the only thing we know about these Christians is that they are denounced everywhere!"

23   So a time was set and on that day large numbers came to his house. He told them about the Kingdom of God and taught them about Jesus from the Scriptures—from the five books of Moses and the books of prophecy. He began lecturing in the morning and went on into the evening!

24   Some believed, and some didn't.

25   But after they had argued back and forth among themselves, they left with this final word from Paul ringing in their ears: "The Holy Spirit was right when He said through Isaiah the prophet,

26   'Say to the Jews, "You will hear and see but not understand,

27   For your hearts are too fat and your ears don't listen

---

[4] Literally, "the hope of Israel." But perhaps he is referring here, as in his other defenses, to his belief in the resurrection of the dead.
[5] Implied.

and you have closed your eyes against understanding, for you don't want to see and hear and understand and turn to Me to heal you." [6]

28, 29[7]   So I want you to realize that this salvation from God is available to the Gentiles too, and they will accept it."

30   Paul lived for the next two years in his rented house[8] and welcomed all who visited him,

31   Telling them with all boldness about the Kingdom of God and about the Lord Jesus Christ; and no one tried to stop him.

---

[6]Isaiah 6:9, 10.
[7]Some of the ancient manuscripts add, "And when he had said these words, the Jews departed, having much dissenting among themselves."
[8]Or, "at his own expense."

HOW ?!?!

Christian students discuss how they can come alive to what God wants them to be doing in the world, in preparation for an article for CAMPUS LIFE Magazine. How can we—*really?* We read about the life of Jesus and what an impact He had. We see how the first Christians turned the world upside down. But how does all that relate to us *now?* How, personally, can I "come alive"? In this Book of Romans, set against the background of Christ's life and the exploits of the early church, Paul gets personal about what must happen within us. You may not be able to relate to all the Jewish cultural background, but you'll recognize how basically similar we humans are— and the way God will come into the life of anyone who is really serious about inviting Him to take over and make him genuinely *alive.*

JIM WHITMER

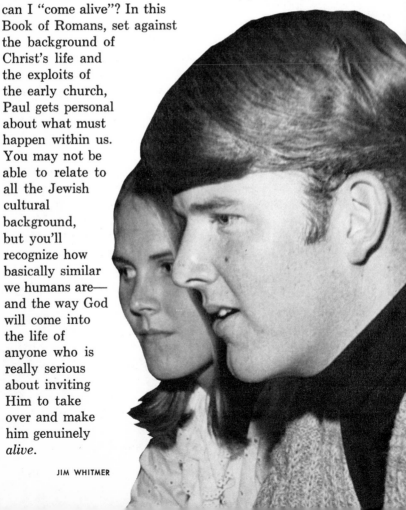

ROMANS

CHAPTER 1

D EAR Friends in Rome,
1 This letter is from Paul, Jesus Christ's slave, chosen to be a missionary, and sent out to preach God's Good News.

2 This Good News was promised long ago by God's prophets in the Old Testament.

3 It is the Good News about His Son, Jesus Christ our Lord, who came as a human baby, born into King David's royal family line;

4 And by being raised from the dead He was proved to be the mighty Son of God, with the holy nature of God Himself.

5 And now, through Christ, all the kindness of God has been poured out upon us undeserving sinners; and now He is sending us out around the world to tell all people everywhere the great things God has done for them, so that they, too, will believe and obey Him.

6, 7 And you, dear friends in Rome, are among those He dearly loves; you, too, are invited by Jesus Christ to be God's very own—yes, His holy people. May all God's mercies and peace be yours from God our Father and from Jesus Christ our Lord.

* * * * *

8 Let me say first of all that wherever I go I hear you being talked about! For your faith in God is becoming known around the world. How I thank God through Jesus Christ for this good report, and for each one of you.

9 God knows how often I pray for you. Day and night I

bring you and your needs in prayer to the one I serve with all my might, telling others the Good News about His Son.

10   And one of the things I keep on praying for is the opportunity, God willing,[1] to come at last to see you and, if possible, that I will have a safe trip.[2]

11, 12   For I long to visit you so that I can impart to you the faith[3] that will help your church grow strong in the Lord. Then, too, I need your help, for I want not only to share my faith with you but to be encouraged by yours: Each of us will be a blessing to the other.

13   I want you to know, dear brothers, that I planned to come many times before (but was prevented) so that I could work among you and see good results, just as I have among the other Gentile churches.[4]

14   For I owe a great debt to you and to everyone else, both to civilized peoples and heathen nations; yes, to the educated and uneducated alike.

15   So, to the fullest extent of my ability, I am ready to come also to you in Rome to preach God's Good News.

16   For I am not ashamed of this Good News about Christ. It is God's powerful method of bringing all who believe it to heaven. This message was preached first to the Jews alone, but now everyone is invited to come to God in this same way.

17   This Good News tells us that God makes us ready for heaven—makes us right in God's sight—when we put our faith and trust in Christ to save us. This is accomplished from start to finish by faith.[5] As the Scripture says it, "The man who finds life will find it through trusting God."[6]

18   But God shows His anger from heaven against all sinful, evil men who push away the truth from them.

19   For the truth about God is known to them instinctively[7]; God has put this knowledge in their hearts.

20   Since earliest times men have seen the earth and sky

[1]Literally, "in the will of God."
[2]Or, "that I will finally succeed in coming."
[3]Literally, "some spiritual gift . . . that is, . . . faith."
[4]Literally, "among the Gentiles."
[5]Literally: "(this) righteousness of God is *revealed* from faith to faith."
[6]Habakkuk 2:4.
[7]Literally, "is manifest in them."

and all God made, and have known of His existence and great eternal power. So they will have no excuse [when they stand before God at Judgment Day[8]].

21   Yes, they knew about Him all right, but they wouldn't admit it or worship Him or even thank Him for all His daily care. And after awhile they began to think up silly ideas of what God was like and what He wanted them to do. The result was that their foolish minds became dark and confused.

22   Claiming themselves to be wise without God, they became utter fools instead.

23   And then, instead of worshiping the glorious, ever-living God, they took wood and stone and made idols for themselves, carving them to look like mere birds and animals and snakes and puny[9] men.

24   So God let them go ahead into every sort of sex sin, and do whatever they wanted to—yes, vile and sinful things with each other's bodies.

25   Instead of believing what they knew was the truth about God, they deliberately chose to believe lies. So they prayed to the things God made, but wouldn't obey the blessed God who made these things.

26   That is why God let go of them and let them do all these evil things, so that even their women turned against God's natural plan for them and indulged in sex sin with each other.

27   And the men, instead of having a normal sex relationship with women, burned with lust for each other, men doing shameful things with other men and, as a result, getting paid within their own souls with the penalty they so richly deserved.

28   So it was that when they gave God up and would not even acknowledge Him, God gave them up to doing everything their evil minds could think of.

29   Their lives became full of every kind of wickedness and sin, of greed and hate, envy, murder, fighting, lying, bitterness, and gossip.

30   They were backbiters, haters of God, insolent, proud

---

[8]Implied. Or, "They have no excuse for saying there is no God."
[9]Literally, "mortal."

braggarts, always thinking of new ways of sinning and continually being disobedient to their parents.

31   They tried to misunderstand,[10] broke their promises, and were heartless—without pity.

32   They were fully aware of God's death penalty for these crimes, yet they went right ahead and did them anyway, and encouraged others to do them, too.

CHAPTER 2

"WELL," you may be saying, "what terrible people you have been talking about!" But wait a minute! You are just as bad. When you say they are wicked and should be punished, you are talking about yourselves, for you do these very same things.

2   And we know that God, in justice, will punish anyone who does such things as these.

3   Do you think that God will judge and condemn others for doing them and overlook you when you do them, too?

4   Don't you realize how patient He is being with you? Or don't you care? Can't you see that He has been waiting all this time without punishing you, to give you time to turn from your sin? His kindness is meant to lead you to repentance.

5   But no, you won't listen; and so you are saving up terrible punishment for yourselves because of your stubbornness in refusing to turn from your sin; for there is going to come a day of wrath when God will be the just Judge of all the world.

6   He will give each one whatever his deeds deserve.

7   He will give eternal life to those who patiently do the will of God,[1] seeking for the unseen[2] glory and honor and eternal life that He offers.[2]

8   But He will terribly punish those who fight against the truth of God and walk in evil ways—God's anger will be poured out upon them.

---

[10]Or, "were confused fools."
[1]Literally, "who patiently do good."
[2]Implied.

9 There will be sorrow and suffering for Jews and Gentiles alike who keep on sinning.

10 But there will be glory and honor and peace from God for all who obey Him,[3] whether they are Jews or Gentiles.

11 For God treats everyone the same.

12, 13, 14, 15 He will punish sin wherever it is found. He will punish the heathen when they sin, even though they never had God's written laws, for down in their hearts they know right from wrong. God's laws are written within them; their own conscience accuses them, or sometimes excuses them. And God will punish the Jews for sinning because they have His written laws but don't obey them. They know what is right but don't do it. After all, salvation is not given to those who know what to do, unless they do it.

16 The day will surely come when at God's command Jesus Christ will judge the secret lives of everyone, their inmost thought and motives; this is all part of God's great plan which I proclaim.

17 You Jews think all is well between yourselves and God because He gave His laws to you;[4] you brag that you are His special friends.

18 Yes, you know what He wants; you know right from wrong and favor the right because you have been taught His laws from earliest youth.

19 You are so sure of the way to God that you could point it out to a blind man. You think of yourselves as beacon lights, directing men who are lost in darkness to God.

20 You think that you can guide the simple and teach even children the affairs of God, for you really know His laws, which are full of all knowledge and truth.

21 Yes, you teach others—then why don't you teach yourselves? You tell others not to steal—do *you* steal?

22 You say it is wrong to commit adultery—do *you* do it? You say, "Don't pray to idols," and then make money your god instead.[5]

---

[3]Literally, "all who do good."
[4]Or, "you rely upon the law for your salvation."
[5]Literally, "do you rob temples?"

23   You are so proud of knowing God's laws, *but you dishonor Him by breaking them.*

24   No wonder the Scriptures say that the world speaks evil of God because of you.

25   Being a Jew is worth something if you obey God's laws; but if you don't, then you are no better off than the heathen.

26   And if the heathen obey God's laws, won't God give them all the rights and honors He planned to give the Jews?

27   In fact, those heathen will be much better off[6] than you Jews who know so much about God and have His promises but don't obey His laws.

28   For you are not real Jews just because you were born of Jewish parents or because you have gone through the Jewish initiation ceremony of circumcision.

29   No, a real Jew is anyone whose heart is right with God. For God is not looking for those who cut their bodies in actual body circumcision, but He is looking for those with changed hearts and minds. Whoever has that kind of change in his life will get his praise from God, even if not from you.

CHAPTER 3

THEN what's the use of being a Jew? Are there any special benefits for them from God? Is there any value in the Jewish circumcision ceremony?

2   Yes, being a Jew has many advantages. First of all, God trusted them with His laws [so that they could know and do His will[1]].

3   True, some of them were unfaithful, but just because they broke their promises to God, does that mean God will break His promises to those who love Him?

4   Of course not! Though everyone else in the world is a liar, God is not. Do you remember what the book of Psalms says about this?[2] That God's words will always prove true and right, no matter who questions them.

---

[6]Literally, "will condemn" you.
[1]Implied.
[2]Psalm 51:4.

5 "But," some say, "our breaking faith with God is good, our sins serve a good purpose, for people will notice how good God is when they see how bad we are. Is it fair, then, for Him to punish us when our sins are helping Him?" (That is the way some people talk.)

6 God forbid! Then what kind of God would He be, to overlook sin? How could He ever condemn anyone?

7 For He could not judge and condemn me as a sinner if my dishonesty brought Him glory by pointing up His honesty in contrast to my lies.

8 If you follow through with that idea you come to this: the worse we are, the better God likes it! But the damnation of those who say such things is just. Yet some claim that this is what I preach!

9 Well, then, are we Jews *better* than others? No, not at all, for we have already shown that all men alike are sinners, whether Jews or Gentiles.

10 As the Scriptures say, "No one is good—no one in all the world is innocent."[3]

11 No one has ever really followed God's paths, or even truly wanted to.

12 Every one has turned away; all have gone wrong. No one anywhere has kept on doing what is right; not one.

13 Their talk is foul and filthy like the stench from an open grave.[4] Their tongues are loaded with lies. Everything they say has in it the sting and poison of deadly snakes.

14 Their mouths are full of cursing and bitterness.

15 They are quick to kill, hating anyone who disagrees with them.[5]

16 Wherever they go they leave misery and trouble behind them,

17 And they have never known what it is to feel secure or enjoy God's blessing.

18 They care nothing about God nor what He thinks of them.

---

[3]Psalm 14:3.
[4]Literally, "Their throat is an open grave." Perhaps the meaning is "their speech injures others."
[5]Implied.

19   So the judgment of God lies very heavily upon the Jews, for they are responsible to keep God's laws instead of doing all these evil things; not one of them has any excuse; in fact, all the world stands hushed and guilty before Almighty God.

20   Now do you see it? No one can ever be made right in God's sight by doing what the law commands. For the more we know of God's laws, the clearer it becomes that we aren't obeying them; His laws serve only to make us see that we are sinners.

21, 22   But now God has shown us a different way to heaven[6]—not by "being good enough" and trying to keep His laws, but by a new way (though not new, really, for the Scriptures told about it long ago). Now God says He will accept and acquit us—declare us "not guilty"—if we trust Jesus Christ to take away our sins. And we all can be saved in this same way, by coming to Christ, no matter who we are or what we have been like.

23   Yes, all have sinned; all fall short of God's glorious ideal;

24   Yet now God declares us "not guilty" of offending Him if we trust in Jesus Christ, who in His kindness freely takes away our sins.

25   For God sent Christ Jesus to take the punishment for our sins and to end all God's anger against us. He used Christ's blood and our faith as the means of saving us from His wrath.[7] In this way He was being entirely fair, even though He did not punish those who sinned in former times. For He was looking forward to the time when Christ would come and take away those sins.

26   And now in these days also He can receive sinners in this same way, because Jesus took away their sins. But isn't this unfair for God to let criminals go free, and say that they are innocent? No, for He does it on the basis of their trust in Jesus who took away their sins.

27   Then what can we boast about doing, to earn our salvation? Nothing at all. Why? Because our acquittal is not based

---

[6]Implied. Literally, "A righteousness of God has been manifested."
[7]Literally, "to be a propitiation."

on our good deeds; it is based on what Christ has done and our faith in Him.

28   So it is that we are saved[8] by faith in Christ and not by the good things we do.

29   And does God save only the Jews in this way? No, the Gentiles, too, may come to Him in this same manner.

30   God treats us all the same; all, whether Jews or Gentiles, are acquitted if they have faith.

31   Well then, if we are saved by faith, does this mean that we no longer need obey God's laws? Just the opposite! In fact, only when we trust Jesus can we truly obey Him.

CHAPTER 4

ABRAHAM was, humanly speaking, the founder of our Jewish nation. What were his experiences concerning this question of being saved by faith? Was it because of his good deeds that God accepted him? If so, then he would have something to boast about. But from God's point of view Abraham had no basis at all for pride.

3   For the Scriptures tell us Abraham *believed God,* and that is why God canceled his sins and declared him "not guilty."

4, 5   But didn't he earn his right to heaven by all the good things he did? No, for being saved is a gift; if a person could earn it by being good, then it wouldn't be free—but it is! It is *given* to those who do *not* work for it. For God declares sinners to be good in His sight if they have faith in Christ to save them from God's wrath.[1]

6   King David spoke of this, describing the happiness of an undeserving sinner who is declared "not guilty"[2] by God.

7   "Blessed, and to be envied," he said, "are those whose sins are forgiven and put out of sight.

8   Yes, what joy there is for anyone whose sins are no longer counted against him by the Lord."[3]

[8]Literally, "justified."
[1]Literally, "Faith is reckoned for righteousness."
[2]Literally, "righteous."
[3]Psalm 32:1-2.

9   Now then, the question: Is this blessing given only to those who have faith in Christ but also keep the Jewish laws, or is the blessing also given to those who do not keep the Jewish rules, but only trust in Christ? Well, what about Abraham? We say that he received these blessings through his faith. Was it by faith alone? Or because he also kept the Jewish rules?

10   For the answer to that question, answer this one: *When did God give this blessing to Abraham? It was before he became a Jew*—before he went through the Jewish initiation ceremony of circumcision.

11   It wasn't until later on, *after* God had promised to bless him *because of his faith,* that he was circumcised. The circumcision ceremony was a sign that Abraham already had faith and that God had already accepted him and declared him just and good in His sight—before the ceremony took place. So Abraham is the spiritual father of those who believe and are saved without obeying Jewish laws. We see, then, that those who do not keep these rules are justified by God through faith.

12   And Abraham is also the spiritual father of those Jews who have been circumcised. They can see from his example that it is not this ceremony that saves them, for Abraham found favor with God by faith alone, *before he was circumcised.*

13   It is clear, then, that God's promise to give the whole earth to Abraham and his descendants was not because Abraham obeyed God's laws but because he trusted God to keep His promise.

14   So if you still claim that God's blessings go to those who are "good enough," then you are saying that God's promises to those who have faith are meaningless, and faith is foolish.

15   But the fact of the matter is this: when we try to gain God's blessing and salvation by keeping His laws we always end up under His anger, for we always fail to keep them. The only way we can keep from breaking laws is not to have any to break!

16   So God's blessings are given to us by faith, as a free

gift; we are certain to get them whether or not we follow Jewish customs if we have faith like Abraham's, for Abraham is the father of us all when it comes to these matters of faith.

17 That is what the Scriptures mean when they say that God made Abraham the father of many nations. God will accept all people in every nation who trust God as Abraham did. And this promise is from God Himself, who makes the dead live again and speaks of future events with as much certainty as though they were already past!

18 So, when God told Abraham that He would give him a son who would have many descendants and become a great nation, Abraham believed God even though such a promise just couldn't come to pass!

19 And because his faith was strong, he didn't worry about the fact that he was too old to be a father, at the age of one hundred, and that Sarah his wife, at ninety,[4] was also much too old to have a baby.

20 But Abraham never doubted. He believed God, for his faith and trust grew ever stronger, and he praised God for this blessing even before it happened.

21 He was completely sure that God was well able to do anything He promised.

22 And because of Abraham's faith God forgave his sins and declared him "not guilty."

23 Now this wonderful statement—that he was accepted and approved through his faith—wasn't just for Abraham's benefit.

24 It was for us, too, assuring us that God will accept us in the same way He accepted Abraham—when we believe the promises of God who brought back Jesus our Lord from the dead.

25 He died for our sins and rose again to make us right with God, filling us with God's goodness.[5]

---

[4]Genesis 17:17.
[5]Literally, "raised for our justification."

CHAPTER 5

S O now, since we have been made right in God's sight by faith in His promises, we can have real peace with Him because of what Jesus Christ our Lord has done for us.

2 For because of our faith, He has brought us into this place of highest privilege where we now stand, and we confidently and joyfully look forward to actually becoming all that God has had in mind for us to be.

3 We can rejoice, too, when we run into problems and trials for we know that they are good for us—they help us learn to be patient.

4 And patience develops strength of character in us and helps us trust God more each time we use it until finally our hope and faith are strong and steady.

5 Then, when that happens, we are able to hold our heads high no matter what happens and know that all is well, for we know how dearly God loves us, and we feel this warm love everywhere within us because God has given us the Holy Spirit to fill our hearts with His love.

6 When we were utterly helpless with no way of escape, Christ came at just the right time and died for us sinners who had no use for Him.

7 Even if we were good, we really wouldn't expect anyone to die for us, though, of course, that might be barely possible.

8 But God showed His great love for us by sending Christ to die for us while we were still sinners.

9 And since by His blood He did all this for us as sinners, how much more will He do for us now that He has declared us not guilty? Now He will save us from all of God's wrath to come.

10 And since, when we were His enemies, we were brought back to God by the death of His Son, what blessings He must have for us now that we are His friends, and He is living within us!

11 Now we rejoice in our wonderful new relationship with

God—all because of what our Lord Jesus Christ has done in dying for our sins—making us friends of God.

*   *   *   *   *

12 When Adam sinned, sin entered the entire human race. His sin spread death throughout all the world, so everything began to grow old and die,[1] for all sinned.

13 [We know that it was Adam's sin that caused this[2]] because although, of course, people were sinning from the time of Adam until Moses, God did not in those days judge them guilty of death for breaking His laws—because He had not yet given His laws to them, nor told them what He wanted them to do.

14 So when their bodies died it was not for their own sins[2] since they themselves had never disobeyed God's special law against eating the forbidden fruit, as Adam had.

What a contrast between Adam and Christ who was yet to come!

15 And what a difference between man's sin and God's forgiveness! For this one man, Adam, brought death to many through his *sin*. But this one man, Jesus Christ, brought forgiveness to many through God's *mercy*.

16 Adam's *one* sin brought the penalty of death to many, while Christ freely takes away *many* sins and gives glorious life instead.

17 The sin of this one man, Adam, caused *death to be king over all,* but all who will take God's gift of forgiveness and acquittal are *kings of life*[3] because of this one man, Jesus Christ.

18 Yes, Adam's *sin* brought *punishment* to all, but Christ's *righteousness* makes men *right with God,* so that they can live.

19 Adam caused many to be sinners because he *disobeyed* God, and Christ caused many to be made acceptable to God because He *obeyed*.

20 The Ten Commandments were given so that all could see the extent of their failure to obey God's laws. But the more

---

[1]Literally, "Sin entered into the world, and death through sin."
[2]Implied.
[3]Literally, "reign in life."

we see our sinfulness, the more we see God's abounding grace forgiving us.

21 Before, sin ruled over all men and brought them to death, but now God's kindness rules instead, giving us right standing with God and resulting in eternal life through Jesus Christ our Lord.

CHAPTER 6

WELL then, shall we keep on sinning so that God can keep on showing us more and more kindness and forgiveness? 2, 3 Of course not! Should we keep on sinning when we don't have to? For sin's power over us was broken when we became Christians and were baptized to become a part of Jesus Christ; through His death the power of your sinful nature was shattered.

4 Your old sin-loving nature was buried with Him by baptism when He died, and when God the Father, with glorious power, brought Him back to life again, you were given His wonderful new life to enjoy.

5 For you have become a part of Him, and so you died with Him, so to speak, when He died[1]; and now you share His new life, and shall rise as He did.

6 Your old evil desires were nailed to the cross with Him; that part of you that loves to sin was crushed and fatally wounded, so that your sin-loving body is no longer under sin's control, no longer needs to be a slave to sin;

7 For when you are deadened to sin you are freed from all its allure and its power over you.

8 And since your old sin-loving nature "died" with Christ, we know that you will share His new life.

9 Christ rose from the dead and will never die again. Death no longer has any power over Him.

10 He died once for all to end sin's power, but now He lives forever in unbroken fellowship with God.

---

[1]Literally, "united with him in the likeness of his death."

11   So look upon your old sin nature as dead and unresponsive to sin, and instead be alive to God, alert to Him, through Jesus Christ our Lord.

12   Do not let sin control your puny body any longer; do not give in to its sinful desires.

13   Do not let any part of your bodies become tools of wickedness, to be used for sinning; but give yourselves completely to God—every part of you—for you are back from death and you want to be tools in the hands of God, to be used for His good purposes.

14   Sin need[2] never again be your master, for now you are no longer tied to the law where sin enslaves you, but you are free under God's favor and mercy.

15   Does this mean that now we can go ahead and sin and not worry about it? (For our salvation does not depend on keeping the law, but on receiving God's grace!) Of course not!

16   Don't you realize that you can choose your own master? You can choose sin (with death) or else obedience (with acquittal). The one to whom you offer yourself—he will take you and be your master and you will be his slave.

17   Thank God that though you once chose to be slaves of sin, now you have obeyed with all your heart the teaching to which God has committed you.

18   And now you are free from your old master, sin; and you have become slaves to your new master, righteousness.

19   I speak this way, using the illustration of slaves and masters, because it is easy to understand: just as you used to be slaves to all kinds of sin, so now you must let yourselves be slaves to all that is right and holy.

20   In those days when you were slaves of sin you didn't bother much with goodness.

21   And what was the result? Evidently not good, since you are ashamed now even to think about those things you used to do, for all of them end in eternal doom.

22   But now you are free from the power of sin and are slaves of God, and His benefits to you include holiness and everlasting life.

---

[2]Literally, "sin will never again be your master."

369

23   For the wages of sin is death, but the free gift of God is eternal life through Jesus Christ our Lord.

CHAPTER 7

D ON'T you understand yet, dear Jewish[1] brothers in Christ, that when a person dies the law no longer holds him in its power?

2   Let me illustrate: when a woman marries, the law binds her to her husband as long as he is alive. But if he dies, she is no longer bound to him; the laws of marriage no longer apply to her.

3   Then she can marry someone else if she wants to. That would be wrong while he was alive, but it is perfectly all right after he dies.

4   Your "husband," your master, used to be the Jewish law; but you "died," as it were, with Christ on the cross; and since you are "dead," you are no longer "married to the law," and it has no more control over you. Then you came back to life again when Christ did, and are a new person. And now you are "married," so to speak, to the one who rose from the dead, so that you can produce good fruit, that is, good deeds for God.

5   When your old nature was still active, sinful desires were at work within you, making you want to do whatever God said not to, and producing sinful deeds, the rotting fruit of death.

6   But now you need no longer worry about the Jewish laws and customs[2] because you "died" while in their captivity, and now you can really serve God; not in the old way, mechanically obeying a set of rules, but in the new way, [with all of your hearts and minds[3]].

7   Well then, am I suggesting that these laws of God are evil? Of course not! No, the law is not sinful but it was the law that showed me my sin. I would never have known the sin in my heart—the evil desires that are hidden there—if the law had not said, "You must not have evil desires in your heart."

[1]Implied. Literally, "men who know (the) law."
[2]Literally, "Now we are delivered from the law."
[3]Implied.

8 But sin used this law against evil desires by reminding me that such desires are wrong and arousing all kinds of forbidden desires within me! Only if there were no laws to break would there be no sinning.

9 That is why I felt fine so long as I did not understand what the law really demanded. But when I learned the truth, I realized that I had broken the law and was a sinner, doomed to die.

10 So as far as I was concerned, the good law which was supposed to show me the way of life resulted instead in my being given the death penalty.

11 Sin fooled me by taking the good laws of God and using them to make me guilty of death.

12 But still, you see, the law itself was wholly right and good.

13 But how can that be? Didn't the law cause my doom? How then can it be good? No, it was sin, devilish stuff that it is, that used what was good to bring about my condemnation. So you can see how cunning and deadly and damnable it is. For it uses God's good laws for its own evil purposes.

14 The law is good, then, and the trouble is not there but with *me*, because I am sold into slavery with Sin as my owner.

15 I don't understand myself at all, for I really want to do what is right, but I can't. I do what I don't want to—what I hate.

16 I know perfectly well that what I am doing is wrong, and my bad conscience proves that I agree with these laws I am breaking.

17 But I can't help myself, because I'm no longer doing it. It is sin inside me that is stronger than I am that makes me do these evil things.

18 I know I am rotten through and through so far as my old sinful nature is concerned. No matter which way I turn I can't make myself do right. I want to but I can't.

19 When I want to do good, I don't; and when I try not to do wrong, I do it anyway.

20   Now if I am doing what I don't want to, it is plain where the trouble is: sin still has me in its evil grasp.

21   It seems to be a fact of life that when I want to do what is right, I inevitably do what is wrong.

22   I love to do God's will so far as my new nature is concerned;

23, 24, 25   But there is something else deep within me, in my lower nature, that is at war with my mind and wins the fight and makes me a slave to the sin that is still within me. In my mind I want to be God's willing servant but instead I find myself still enslaved to sin.

So you see how it is: my new life tells me to do right, but the old nature that is still inside me loves to sin. Oh, what a terrible predicament I'm in! Who will free me from my slavery to this deadly lower nature? Thank God! It has been done[4] by Jesus Christ our Lord. He has set me free.

CHAPTER 8

SO there is now no condemnation awaiting those who belong to Christ Jesus.

2   For the power of the life-giving Spirit—and this power is mine through Christ Jesus—has freed me from the vicious circle of sin and death.

3   We aren't saved from sin's grasp by knowing the commandments of God, because we can't and don't keep them, but God put into effect a different plan to save us. He sent His own Son in a human body like ours—except that ours are sinful—and destroyed sin's control over us by giving Himself as a sacrifice for our sins.

4   So now we can obey God's laws if we follow after the Holy Spirit and no longer obey the old evil nature within us.

5   Those who let themselves be controlled by their lower natures live only to please themselves, but those who follow after the Holy Spirit find themselves doing those things that please God.

[4]Or, "it will be done." Literally, "I thank God through Jesus Christ our Lord."

6 Following after the Holy Spirit leads to life and peace, but following after the old nature leads to death,

7 Because the old sinful nature within us is against God. It never did obey God's laws and it never will.

8 That's why those who are still under the control of their old sinful selves, bent on following their old evil desires, can never please God.

9 But you are not like that. You are controlled by your new nature if you have the Spirit of God living in you. (And remember that if anyone doesn't have the Spirit of Christ living in him, he is not a Christian at all.)

10 Yet, even though Christ lives within you, your body will die because of sin; but your spirit will live, for Christ has pardoned it.[1]

11 And if the Spirit of God, who raised up Jesus from the dead, lives in you, He will make your dying bodies live again after you die, by means of this same Holy Spirit living within you.

12 So, dear brothers, you have no obligations whatever to your old sinful nature to do what it begs you to do.

13 For if you keep on following it you are lost and will perish, but if through the power of the Holy Spirit you crush it and its evil deeds, you shall live.

14 For all who are led by the Spirit of God are sons of God.

15 And so we should not be like cringing, fearful slaves, but we should behave like God's very own children, adopted into the bosom of His family, and calling to Him, "Father, Father."

16 For His Holy Spirit speaks to us deep in our hearts, and tells us that we really are God's children.

17 And since we are His children, we will share His treasures —for all God gives to His Son Jesus is now ours too. But if we are to share His glory, we must also share His suffering.

18 Yet what we suffer now is nothing compared to the glory He will give us later.

---

[1]Or possibly, "but the Holy Spirit who lives in you will give you life, for He has already given you righteousness." Literally, "but the spirit is life because of righteousness."

19   For all creation is waiting patiently and hopefully for that future day when God will resurrect His children.[2]

20, 21   For on that day thorns and thistles, sin, death, and decay[3]—the things that overcame the world against its will at God's command—will all disappear, and the world around us will share in the glorious freedom from sin which God's children enjoy.

22   For we know that even the things of nature, like animals and plants, suffer in sickness and death as they await this great event.[4]

23   And even we Christians, although we have the Holy Spirit within us as a foretaste of future glory, also groan to be released from pain and suffering. We, too, wait anxiously for that day when God will give us our full rights as His children, including the new bodies He has promised us—bodies that will never be sick again and will never die.

24   We are saved by trusting. And trusting means looking forward to getting something we don't yet have—for a man who already has something doesn't need to hope and trust that he will get it.

25   But if we must keep trusting God for something that hasn't happened yet, it teaches us to wait patiently and confidently.

26   And in the same way—by our faith[5]—the Holy Spirit helps us with our daily problems and in our praying. For we don't even know what we should pray for, nor how to pray as we should; but the Holy Spirit prays for us with such feeling that it cannot be expressed in words.

27   And the Father who knows all hearts knows, of course, what the Spirit is saying as He pleads for us in harmony with God's own will.

28   And we know that all that happens to us is working for our good if we love God and are fitting into His plans.

29   For from the very beginning God decided that those who came to Him—and all along He knew who would—should

---

[2]Literally, "waiting for the revelation of the sons of God."
[3]Implied.
[4]Literally, "the whole creation has been groaning in travail together until now."
[5]Implied. Literally, "in like manner."

become like His Son, so that His Son would be the First, with many brothers.

30 And having chosen us, He called us to come to Him; and when we came, He declared us "not guilty," filled us with Christ's goodness, gave us right standing with Himself, and promised us His glory.

31 What can we ever say to such wonderful things as these? If God is on our side, who can ever be against us?

32 Since He did not spare even His own Son for us but gave Him up for us all, won't He also surely give us everything else?

33 Who dares accuse us whom God has chosen for His own? Will God? No! He is the one who has forgiven us and given us right standing with Himself.

34 Who then will condemn us? Will Christ? NO! For He is the one who died for us and came back to life again for us and is sitting at the place of highest honor next to God, pleading for us there in heaven.

35 Who then can ever keep Christ's love from us? When we have trouble or calamity, when we are hunted down or destroyed, is it because He doesn't love us anymore? And if we are hungry, or penniless, or in danger, or threatened with death, has God deserted us?

36 No, for the Scriptures tell us that for His sake we must be ready to face death at every moment of the day—we are like sheep awaiting slaughter;

37 But despite all this, overwhelming victory is ours through Christ who loved us enough to die for us.

38 For I am convinced that nothing can ever separate us from His love. Death can't, and life can't. The angels won't, and all the powers of hell itself cannot keep God's love away. Our fears for today, our worries about tomorrow,

39 Or where we are—high above the sky, or in the deepest ocean—nothing will ever be able to separate us from the love of God demonstrated by our Lord Jesus Christ when He died for us.

CHAPTER 9

OH, Israel, my people! Oh, my Jewish brothers! How I long for you to come to Christ. My heart is heavy within me and I grieve bitterly day and night because of you. Christ knows and the Holy Spirit knows that it is no mere pretense when I say that I would be willing to be forever damned if that would save you.

4 God has given you so much, but still you will not listen to Him. He took you as His own special, chosen people and led you along with a bright cloud of glory and told you how very much He wanted to bless you. He gave you His rules for daily life so you would know what He wanted you to do. He let you worship Him, and gave you mighty promises.

5 Great men of God were your fathers, and Christ Himself was one of you, a Jew so far as His human nature is concerned, He who now rules over all things. Praise God forever!

6 Well then, has God failed to fulfill His promises to the Jews? No! [For these promises are only to those who are truly Jews.[1]] And not everyone born into a Jewish family is truly a Jew!

7 Just the fact that they come from Abraham doesn't make them truly Abraham's children. For the Scriptures say that the promises apply only to Abraham's son Isaac and Isaac's descendants, though Abraham had other children too.

8 This means that not all of Abraham's children are children of God, but only those who believe the promise of salvation which He made to Abraham.

9 For God had promised, "Next year I will give you and Sarah a son."

10, 11, 12, 13 And years later, when this son, Isaac, was grown up and married, and Rebecca his wife was about to bear him twin children, God told her that Esau, the child born first, would be a servant to Jacob, his twin brother. In the words of the Scripture, "I chose to bless Jacob, but not Esau." And God said this before the children were even born, before they had

[1]Implied.

376

done anything either good or bad. This proves that God was doing what He had decided from the beginning; it was not because of what the children did but because of what God wanted and chose.

14   Was God being unfair? Of course not.

15   For God had said to Moses, "If I want to be kind to someone, I will. And I will take pity on anyone I want to."

16   And so God's blessings are not given just because someone decides to have them or works hard to get them. They are given because God takes pity on those He wants to.

17   Pharaoh, king of Egypt, was an example of this fact. For God told him He had given him the kingdom of Egypt for the very purpose of displaying the awesome power of God against him: so that all the world would hear about God's glorious name.[2]

18   So you see, God is kind to some just because He wants to be, and He makes some refuse to listen.

19   Well then, why does God blame them for not listening? Haven't they done what He made them do?

20   No, don't say that. Who are you to criticize God? Should the thing made say to the one who made it, "Why have you made me like this?"

21   When a man makes a jar out of clay, doesn't he have a right to use the same lump of clay to make one jar beautiful, to be used for holding flowers, and another to throw garbage into?

22   Does not God have a perfect right to show His fury and power against those who are fit only for destruction, those He has been patient with for all this time?

23, 24   And He has a right to take others such as ourselves, who have been made for pouring the riches of His glory into, whether we are Jews or Gentiles, and to be kind to us so that everyone can see how very great His glory is.

25   Remember what the prophecy of Hosea says? There God says that He will find other children for Himself (who are not from His Jewish family) and will love them, though no one had ever loved them before.

---

[2]Literally, "that My name might be published abroad in all the earth."

26   And the heathen, of whom it once was said, "You are not My people," shall be called "sons of the Living God."[3]

27   Isaiah the prophet cried out concerning the Jews that though there would be millions[4] of them, only a small number would ever be saved.

28   "For the Lord will execute His sentence upon the earth, quickly ending His dealings, justly cutting them short."[5]

29   And Isaiah says in another place that except for God's mercy all the Jews would be destroyed—all of them—just as everyone in the cities of Sodom and Gomorrah perished.[6]

30   Well then, what shall we say about these things? Just this, that God has given the Gentiles the opportunity to be acquitted by faith, even though they had not been really seeking God.

31   But the Jews, who tried so hard to get right with God by keeping His laws, never succeeded.

32   Why not? Because they were trying to be saved by keeping the law and being good instead of by depending on faith. They have stumbled over the great stumblingstone.

33   God warned them of this in the Scriptures when He said, "I have put a Rock in the path of the Jews, and many will stumble over Him (Jesus). Those who believe in Him will never be disappointed."[7]

CHAPTER 10

DEAR brothers, the longing of my heart and my prayer is that the Jewish people might be saved.

2   I know what enthusiasm you have for the honor of God, but it is misdirected zeal.

3   For you don't understand that Christ has died to make you right with God. Instead you are trying to make yourselves good enough to gain God's favor by keeping the Jewish laws and customs, but that is not God's way of salvation.

---

[3]Hosea 2:23.
[4]Literally: "as the sand of the sea," *i.e.*, numberless.
[5]Isaiah 10:22; 28:22.
[6]Isaiah 1:9.
[7]Isaiah 28:16.

4 You don't understand that Christ gives to those who trust in Him everything you are trying to get by keeping His laws. He ends all that.

5 For Moses wrote that if a person could be perfectly good and hold out against temptation all his life and never sin once, only then could he be pardoned and saved.

6 But the salvation that comes through faith says, "You don't need to search the heavens to find Christ and bring Him down to help you," and,

7 "You don't need to go among the dead to bring Christ back to life again,"

8 For salvation that comes from trusting Christ—which is what we preach—is already within easy reach of each of us; in fact, it is as near as our own hearts and mouths.

9 For if you tell others with your own mouth that Jesus Christ is your Lord, and believe in your own heart that God has raised Him from the dead, you will be saved.

10 For it is by believing in his heart that a man becomes right with God; and with his mouth he tells others of his faith, confirming his salvation.[1]

11 For the Scriptures tell us that no one who believes in Christ will ever be disappointed.

12 Jew and Gentile are the same in this respect: they all have the same Lord who generously gives His riches to all those who ask Him for them.

13 Anyone who calls upon the name of the Lord will be saved.

14 But how shall they ask Him to save them unless they believe in Him? And how can they believe in Him if they have never heard about Him? And how can they hear about Him unless someone tells them?

15 And how will anyone go and tell them unless someone sends him? That is what the Scriptures are talking about when they say, "How beautiful are the feet of those who preach the Gospel of peace with God and bring glad tidings of good

---

[1]Literally, "Confession is made unto salvation."

things."[2] In other words, how welcome are those who come preaching God's Good News!

16   But not everyone who hears the Good News has welcomed it, for Isaiah the prophet said, "Lord, who has believed me when I told them?"[3]

17   Yet faith comes from listening to this Good News—the Good News about Christ.

18   But what about the Jews? Have they heard God's Word? Yes, for it has gone wherever they are; the Good News has been told to the ends of the earth.

19   And did they understand [that God would give His salvation to others if they refused to take it[4]]? Yes, for even back in the time of Moses, God had said that He would make His people jealous and try to wake them up by giving His salvation to the foolish heathen nations.

20   And later on Isaiah said boldly that God would be found by people who weren't even looking for Him.[5]

21   In the meantime, He keeps on reaching out His hands to the Jews, but they keep arguing[6] and refusing to come.

CHAPTER 11

I ask then, has God rejected and deserted His people the Jews? Oh no, not at all. Remember that I myself am a Jew, a descendant of Abraham and a member of Benjamin's family.

2, 3   No, God has not discarded His own people whom He chose from the very beginning. Do you remember what the Scriptures say about this? Elijah the prophet was complaining to God about the Jews, telling God how they had killed the prophets and torn down God's altars; Elijah claimed that he was the only one left in all the land who still loved God, and now they were trying to kill him too.

[2]Isaiah 52:7.
[3]Isaiah 53:1.
[4]Implied.
[5]Isaiah 65:1.
[6]Literally, "disobedient, obstinate."

4   And do you remember how God replied? God said, "No, you are not the only one left. I have seven thousand others besides you who still love Me and have not bowed down to idols!"[1]

5   It is the same today. Not all the Jews have turned away from God; there are a few being saved as a result of God's kindness in choosing them.

6   And if it is by God's kindness, then it is not by their being good enough. For in that case the free gift would no longer be free—it isn't free when it is earned.

7   So this is the situation: most of the Jews have not found the favor of God they are looking for. A few have—the ones God has picked out—but the eyes of the others have been blinded.

8   This is what our Scriptures refer to when they say that God has put them to sleep, shutting their eyes and ears so that they do not understand what we are talking about when we tell them of Christ. And so it is to this very day.

9   King David spoke of this same thing when he said, "Let their good food and other blessings trap them into thinking all is well between themselves and God. Let these good things boomerang on them and fall back upon their heads to justly crush them.

10   Let their eyes be dim," he said, "so that they cannot see, and let them walk bent-backed forever with a heavy load."

11   Does this mean that God has rejected His Jewish people forever? Of course not! His purpose was to make His salvation available to the Gentiles, and then the Jews would be jealous and begin to want God's salvation for themselves.

12   Now if the whole world became rich as a result of God's offer of salvation, when the Jews stumbled over it and turned it down, think how much greater a blessing the world will share in later on when the Jews, too, come to Christ.

13   As you know, God has appointed me as a special messenger to you Gentiles. I lay great stress on this and remind the Jews about it as often as I can,

[1] I Kings 19:18.

14   So that if possible I can make them want what you Gentiles have and in that way save some of them.

15   And how wonderful it will be when they become Christians! When God turned away from them it meant that He turned to the rest of the world to offer His salvation; and now it is even more wonderful when the Jews come to Christ. It will be like dead people coming back to life.

16   And since Abraham and the prophets are God's people, their children will be too. For if the roots of the tree are holy, the branches will be too.

17   But some of these branches from Abraham's tree, some of the Jews, have been broken off. And you Gentiles who were branches from, we might say, a wild olive tree, were grafted in. So now you, too, receive the blessing God has promised Abraham and his children, sharing in God's rich nourishment of His own special olive tree.

18   But you must be careful not to brag about being put in to replace the branches that were broken off. Remember that you are important only because you are now a part of God's tree; you are just a branch, not a root.

19   "Well," you may be saying, "those branches were broken off to make room for me so I must be pretty good."

20   Watch out! Remember that those branches, the Jews, were broken off because they didn't believe God, and you are there only because you do. Do not be proud; be humble and grateful—and careful.

21   For if God did not spare the branches He put there in the first place, He won't spare you either.

22   Notice how God is both so kind and so severe. He is very hard on those who disobey, but very good to you if you continue to love and trust Him. But if you don't, you too will be cut off.

23   On the other hand, if the Jews leave their unbelief behind them and come back to God, God will graft them back into the tree again. He has the power to do it.

24   For if God was willing to take you who were so far away from Him—being part of a wild olive tree—and graft you

into His own good tree—a very unusual thing to do—don't you see that He will be far more ready to put the Jews back again, who were there in the first place?

25 I want you to know about this truth from God, dear brothers, so that you will not feel proud and start bragging. Yes, it is true that some of the Jews have set themselves against the Gospel now, but this will last only until all of you Gentiles have come to Christ—those of you who will.

26 And then all Israel will be saved. Do you remember what the prophets said about this? "There shall come out of Zion a Deliverer, and He shall turn the Jews from all ungodliness.

27 At that time I will take away their sins, just as I promised."

28 Now many of the Jews are enemies of the Gospel. They hate it. But this has been a benefit to you, for it has resulted in God's giving His gifts to you Gentiles. Yet the Jews are still beloved of God because of His promises to Abraham, Isaac, and Jacob.

29 For God's gifts and His call can never be withdrawn; He will never go back on His promises.

30 Once you were rebels against God, but when the Jews refused His gifts God was merciful to you instead.

31 And now the Jews are the rebels, but some day they, too, will share in God's mercy upon you.

32 For God has given them all up to sin[2] so that He could have mercy upon all alike.

33 Oh, what a wonderful God we have! How great are His wisdom and knowledge and riches! How impossible it is for us to understand His decisions and His methods!

34 For who among us can know the mind of the Lord? Who knows enough to be His counselor and guide?

35 And who could ever offer to the Lord enough to induce Him to act?

36 For everything comes from God alone. Everything lives by His power, and everything is for His glory. To Him be glory evermore.

---

[2]Literally, "shut up all unto disobedience."

CHAPTER 12

AND so, dear brothers, I plead with you to give your bodies to God. Let them be a living sacrifice, holy—the kind He can accept. When you think of that He has done for you, is this too much to ask?

2   Don't copy the behavior and customs of this world, but be a new and different person with a fresh newness in all you do and think. Then you will learn from your own experience how His ways will really satisfy you.

3   As God's messenger I give each of you God's warning: be honest in your estimate of yourselves, measuring your value by how much faith God has given you.

4, 5   Just as there are many parts to our bodies, so it is with Christ's body. We are all parts of it, and it takes every one of us to make it complete, for we each have different work to do. So we belong to each other, and each needs all the others.

6   God has given each of us the ability to do certain things well. So if God has given you the ability to prophesy, then prophesy whenever you can—as often as your faith is strong enough to receive a message from God.

7   If your gift is that of serving others, serve them well. If you are a teacher, do a good job of teaching.

8   If you are a preacher, see to it that your sermons are strong and helpful. If God has given you money, be generous in helping others with it. If God has given you administrative ability and put you in charge of the work of others, take the responsibility seriously. Those who offer comfort to the sorrowing should do so with Christian cheer.

9   Don't just pretend that you love others: really love them. Hate what is wrong. Stand on the side of the good.

10   Love each other with brotherly affection and take delight in honoring each other.

11   Never be lazy in your work but serve the Lord enthusiastically.

12   Be glad for all God is planning for you. Be patient in trouble, and prayerful always.

13 When God's children are in need, you be the one to help them out. And get into the habit of inviting guests home for dinner or, if they need lodging, for the night.

14 If someone mistreats you because you are a Christian, don't curse him; pray that God will bless him.

15 When others are happy, be happy with them. If they are sad, share their sorrow.

16 Work happily together. Don't try to act big. Don't try to get into the good graces of important people, but enjoy the company of ordinary folks. And don't think you know it all!

17 Never pay back evil for evil. Do things in such a way that everyone can see you are honest clear through.

18 Don't quarrel with anyone. Be at peace with everyone, just as much as possible.

19 Dear friends, never avenge yourselves. Leave that to God, for He has said that He will repay those who deserve it. [Don't take the law into your own hands.[1]]

20 Instead, feed your enemy if he is hungry. If he is thirsty give him something to drink and you will be "heaping coals of fire on his head." In other words, he will feel ashamed of himself for what he has done to you.

21 Don't let evil get the upper hand but conquer evil by doing good.

CHAPTER 13

O BEY the government, for God is the one who has put it there. There is no government anywhere that God has not placed in power.

2 So those who refuse to obey the laws of the land are refusing to obey God, and punishment will follow.

3 For the policeman does not frighten people who are doing right; but those doing evil will always fear him. So if you don't want to be afraid, keep the laws and you will get along well.

[1]Implied.

4   The policeman is sent by God to help you. But if you are doing something wrong, of course you should be afraid, for he will have you punished. He is sent by God for that very pur-pose.

5   Obey the laws, then, for two reasons: first, to keep from being punished, and second, just because you know you should.

6   Pay your taxes too, for these same two reasons. For government workers need to be paid so that they can keep on doing God's work, serving you.

7   Pay everyone whatever he ought to have: pay your taxes and import duties gladly, obey those over you, and give honor and respect to all those to whom it is due.

8   Pay all your debts except the debt of love for others—never finish paying that! For if you love them, you will be obeying all of God's laws, fulfilling all His requirements.

9   If you love your neighbor as much as you love yourself you will not want to harm or cheat him, or kill him or steal from him. And you won't sin with his wife or want what is his, or do anything else the Ten Commandments say is wrong. All ten are wrapped up in this one, to love your neighbor as you love yourself.

10   Love does no wrong to anyone. That's why it fully satis-fies all of God's requirements. It is the only law you need.

11   Another reason for right living is this: you know how late it is; time is running out. Wake up, for the coming of the Lord[1] is nearer now than when we first believed.

12, 13   The night is far gone, the day of His return[1] will soon be here. So quit the evil deeds of darkness and put on the armor of right living, as we who live in the daylight should! Be decent and true in everything you do so that all can approve your behavior. Don't spend your time in wild parties and getting drunk or in adultery and lust, or fighting, or jealousy.

14   But ask the Lord Jesus Christ to help you live as you should, and don't make plans to enjoy evil.

---

[1]Literally, "our salvation."

386

CHAPTER 14

GIVE a warm welcome to any brother who wants to join you, even though his faith is weak. Don't criticize him for having different ideas from yours about what is right and wrong.[1]

2 For instance, don't argue with him about whether or not to eat meat that has been offered to idols. You may believe there is no harm in this, but the faith of others is weaker; they think it is wrong, and will go without any meat at all and eat vegetables rather than eat that kind of meat.

3 Those who think it is all right to eat such meat must not look down on those who won't. And if you are one of those who won't, don't find fault with those who do. For God has accepted them to be His children.

4 They are God's servants, not yours. They are responsible to Him, not to you. Let Him tell them whether they are right or wrong. And God is able to make them do as they should.

5 Some think that Christians should observe the Jewish holidays as special days to worship God, but others say it is wrong and foolish to go to all that trouble, for every day alike belongs to God. On questions of this kind everyone must decide for himself.

6 If you have special days for worshiping the Lord, you are trying to honor Him; you are doing a good thing. So is the person who eats meat that has been offered to idols; he is thankful to the Lord for it; he is doing right. And the person who won't touch such meat, he, too, is anxious to please the Lord, and is thankful.

7 We are not our own bosses to live or die as we ourselves might choose.

8 Living or dying we follow the Lord. Either way we are His.

---

[1]Literally, "Receive him that is weak in faith, not for decisions of scruples." Perhaps the meaning is, "Receive those whose consciences hurt them when they do things others have no doubts about." Accepting them might cause discord in the church, but Paul says to welcome them anyway.

9 Christ died and rose again for this very purpose, so that He can be our Lord both while we live and when we die.

10 You have no right to criticize your brother or look down on him. Remember, each of us will stand personally before the Judgment Seat of God.

11 For it is written, "As I live," says the Lord, "every knee shall bow to me and every tongue confess to God."

12 Yes, each of us will give an account of himself to God.

13 So don't criticize each other any more. Try instead to live in such a way that you will never make your brother stumble by letting him see you doing something he thinks is wrong.

14 As for myself, I am perfectly sure on the authority of the Lord Jesus that there is nothing really wrong with eating meat that has been offered to idols. But if someone believes it is wrong, then he shouldn't do it because for him it is wrong.

15 And if your brother is bothered by what you eat, you are not acting in love if you go ahead and eat it. Don't let your eating ruin someone for whom Christ died.

16 Don't do anything that will cause criticism against yourself even though you know that what you do is right.

17 For, after all, the important thing for us as Christians is not what we eat or drink but stirring up goodness and peace and joy from the Holy Spirit.

18 If you let Christ be Lord in these affairs, God will be glad; and so will others.

19 In this way aim for harmony in the church and try to build each other up.

20 Don't undo the work of God for a chunk of meat. Remember, there is nothing wrong with the meat, but it is wrong to eat it if it makes another stumble.

21 The right thing to do is to quit eating meat or drinking wine or doing anything else that offends your brother or makes him sin.

22 You may know that there is nothing wrong with what you do, even from God's point of view, but keep it to yourself; don't flaunt your faith in front of others who might be hurt by

it. In this situation, happy is the man who does not sin by doing what he knows is right.

23   But anyone who believes that something he wants to do is wrong shouldn't do it. He sins if he does, for he thinks it is wrong, and so for him it *is* wrong. Anything that is done apart from what he feels is right is sin.

CHAPTER 15

EVEN if we believe that it makes no difference to the Lord whether we do these things, still we cannot just go ahead and do them to please ourselves; for we must bear the "burden" of being considerate of the doubts and fears of others—of those who feel these things are wrong. Let's please the other fellow, not ourselves, and do what is for his good and thus build him up in the Lord.

3   Christ didn't please Himself. As the Psalmist said, "He came for the very purpose of suffering under the insults of those who were against the Lord."

4   These things that were written in the Scriptures so long ago are to teach us patience and to encourage us, so that we will look forward expectantly to the time when God will conquer sin and death.

5   May God who gives patience, steadiness, and encouragement help you to live in complete harmony with each other— each with the attitude of Christ toward the other.

6   And then all of us can praise the Lord together with one voice, giving glory to God, the Father of our Lord Jesus Christ.

7   So, warmly welcome each other into the church, just as Christ has warmly welcomed you; then God will be glorified.

8   Remember that Jesus Christ came to show that God is true to His promises and to help the Jews.

9   And remember that He came also that the Gentiles might be saved and give glory to God for His mercies to them. That is what the Psalmist meant when he wrote: "I will praise You among the Gentiles, and sing to Your name."

10   And in another place, "Be glad, O you Gentiles, along with His people the Jews."

11   And yet again, "Praise the Lord, O you Gentiles, let everyone praise Him."

12   And the prophet Isaiah said, "There shall be an Heir in the house of Jesse, and He will be King over the Gentiles; they will pin their hopes on Him alone."

13   So I pray for you Gentiles that God who gives you hope will keep you happy and full of peace as you believe in Him. I pray that God will help you overflow with hope in Him through the Holy Spirit's power within you.

14   I know that you are wise and good, my brothers, and that you know these things so well that you are able to teach others all about them.

15, 16   But even so I have been bold enough to emphasize some of these points, knowing that all you need is this reminder from me; for I am, by God's grace, a special messenger from Jesus Christ to you Gentiles, bringing you the Gospel and offering you up as a fragrant sacrifice to God; for you have been made pure and pleasing to Him by the Holy Spirit.

17   So it is right for me to be a little proud of all Christ Jesus has done through me.

18   I dare not judge how effectively He has used others, but I know this: He has used me to win the Gentiles to God.

19   I have won them by my message and by the good way I have lived before them, and by the miracles done through me as signs from God—all by the Holy Spirit's power. In this way I have preached the full[1] Gospel of Christ all the way from Jerusalem clear over into Illyricum.

20   But all the while my ambition has been to go still farther, preaching where the name of Christ has never yet been heard, rather than where a church has already been started by someone else.

21   I have been following the plan spoken of in the Scriptures where Isaiah says that those who have never heard the name of Christ before will see and understand.

---

[1]Or, "I have fully accomplished my Gospel ministry."

22   In fact that is the very reason I have been so long in coming to visit you.

23   But now at last I am through with my work here, and I am ready to come after all these long years of waiting.

24   For I am planning to take a trip to Spain, and when I do, I will stop off there in Rome; and after we have had a good time together for a little while, you can send me on my way again.

25   But before I come, I must go down to Jerusalem to take a gift to the Jewish Christians there.

26   For you see, the Christians in Macedonia and Achaia have taken up an offering for those in Jerusalem who are going through such hard times.

27   They were very glad to do this, for they feel that they owe a real debt to the Jerusalem Christians. Why? Because the news about Christ came to them from the church in Jerusalem. And since they received this wonderful spiritual gift of the Gospel from them, they feel that the least they can do in return is to give them some material aid.[2]

28   As soon as I have delivered this money and completed this good deed of theirs, I will come to see you on my way to Spain.

29   And I am sure that when I come the Lord will give me a great blessing for you.

30   Will you be my prayer partners? For the Lord Jesus Christ's sake, and because of your love for me—given to you by the Holy Spirit—pray much with me for my work.

31   Pray that I will be protected in Jerusalem from those who are not Christians. Pray also that the Christians there will be willing to accept the money I am bringing them.

32   Then I will be able to come to you with a happy heart by the will of God, and we can refresh each other.

33   And now may our God, who gives peace, be with you all. Amen.

---

[2]Literally, "For if the Gentiles have come to share in their spiritual blessings, they ought also to be of service to them in material blessings."

CHAPTER 16

PHOEBE, a dear Christian woman from the town of Cenchreae, will be coming to see you soon. She has worked hard in the church there. Receive her as your sister in the Lord, giving her a warm Christian welcome. Help her in every way you can, for she has helped many in their needs, including me.

3 Tell Priscilla and Aquila "hello." They have been my fellow workers in the affairs of Christ Jesus.

4 In fact, they risked their lives for me; and I am not the only one who is thankful to them: so are all the Gentile churches.

5 Please give my greetings to all those who meet to worship in their home. Greet my good friend Epaenetus. He was the very first person to become a Christian in Asia.

6 Remember me to Mary, too, who has worked so hard to help us.

7 Then there are Andronicus and Junias, my relatives who were in prison with me. They are respected by the apostles, and became Christians before I did. Please give them my greetings.

8 Say "hello" to Ampliatus, whom I love as one of God's own children,

9 And Urbanus, our fellow worker, and beloved Stachys.

10 Then there is Apelles, a good man whom the Lord approves; greet him for me. And give my best regards to those working at the house of Aristobulus.

11 Remember me to Herodion my relative. Remember me to the Christian slaves over at Narcissus House.

12 Say "hello" to Tryphaena and Tryphosa, the Lord's workers, and to dear Persis, who has worked so hard for the Lord.

13 Greet Rufus for me, whom the Lord picked out to be His very own; and also his dear mother who has been such a mother to me.

14 And please give my greetings to Asyncritus, Phlegon, Hermes, Patrobas, Hermas, and the other brothers who are with them.

15 Give my love to Philologus, Julia, Nereus and his sister, and to Olympas, and all the Christians who are with them.

16 Shake hands warmly with each other. All the churches here send you their greetings.

17 And now there is one more thing to say before I end this letter. Stay away from those who cause divisions and are upsetting people's faith, teaching things about Christ that are contrary to what you have been taught.

18 Such teachers are not working for our Lord Jesus, but only want gain for themselves. They are good speakers, and simple-minded people are often fooled by them.

19 But everyone knows that you stand loyal and true. This makes me very happy. I want you always to remain very clear about what is right, and to stay innocent of any wrong.

20 The God of peace will soon crush Satan under your feet. The blessings from our Lord Jesus Christ be upon you.

21 Timothy my fellow-worker, and Lucius and Jason and Sosipater, my relatives, send you their good wishes.

22 I, Tertius, the one who is writing this letter for Paul, send my greetings too, as a Christian brother.

23 Gaius says to say "hello" to you for him. I am his guest, and the church meets here in his home. Erastus, the city treasurer, sends you his greetings and so does Quartus, a Christian brother.

24 Good-bye. May the grace of our Lord Jesus Christ be with you all.

25, 26, 27 I commit you to God, who is able to make you strong and steady in the Lord, just as the Gospel says, and just as I have told you. This is God's plan of salvation for you Gentiles, kept secret from the beginning of time. But now as the prophets foretold and as God commands, this message is being preached everywhere, so that people all around the world will have faith in Christ and obey Him. To God, who alone is wise, be the glory forever through Jesus Christ our Lord. Amen.

Sincerely,
Paul

HATRED

Face it. The human being enjoys hating others. Look around your world—isn't it true? The signs and placards, the anger between one group and another boils everywhere—and often boils over, with millions murdered as a result. One wonders why, with Christians, the same kind of bickering and hatefulness can sometimes be seen. It seldom boils over into bloodshed—but the evil comes from the same sources. Hatreds and viciousness, lust and shallowness—this is the kind of town Corinth was—and the

"OUR OBJECTIVE IS TH
INDEPENDENCE OF VIET NA
AND ITS FREEDOM FROM
ATTACK. "[...] THE USA

BOB COMBS

IS SUCH FUN!

church people there were so immature that their lives seldom seemed much different from those who had never met Him. And maybe you've known some church people like that yourself. Well, here is what Paul—in two lengthy letters—had to say to a group that was clearly in need of growing up and of realizing how much they needed God's power in order to become strong Christian individuals in the wild city they lived in.

A bit like our situations now?

I CORINTHIANS

CHAPTER 1

FROM: Paul, chosen by God to be Jesus Christ's missionary, and from brother Sosthenes.

2 *To:* The Christians in Corinth, invited by God to be His people and made acceptable[1] to Him by Christ Jesus. *And to:* All Christians everywhere—whoever calls upon the name of Jesus Christ, our Lord and theirs.

3 May God our Father and the Lord Jesus Christ give you all of His blessings, and great peace of heart and mind.

4 I can never stop thanking God for all the wonderful gifts He has given you, now that you are Christ's:

5 He has enriched your whole life. He has helped you speak out for Him and has given you a full understanding of the truth;

6 What I told you Christ could do for you has happened!

7 Now you have every grace and blessing; every spiritual gift and power for doing His will are yours during this time of waiting for the return of our Lord Jesus Christ.

8 And He guarantees right up to the end that you will be counted free from all sin and guilt on that day when He returns.

9 God will surely do this for you, for He always does just what He says, and He is the one who invited you into this wonderful friendship with His Son, even Christ our Lord.

10 But, dear brothers, I beg you in the name of the Lord Jesus Christ to stop arguing among yourselves. Let there be real harmony so that there won't be splits in the church. I plead with you to be of one mind, united in thought and purpose.

---

[1] Or, "chosen by Christ Jesus." Literally, "sanctified in Christ Jesus."

11   For some of those who live at Chloe's house have told me of your arguments and quarrels, dear brothers.

12   Some of you are saying, "I am a follower of Paul"; and others say that they are for Apollos or for Peter; and some that they alone are the true followers of Christ.

13   And so, in effect, you have broken Christ into many pieces. But did I, Paul, die for your sins? Were any of you baptized in my name?

14   I am so thankful now that I didn't baptize any of you except Crispus and Gaius.

15   For now no one can think that I have been trying to start something new, beginning a "Church of Paul."

16   Oh, yes, and I baptized the family of Stephanas. I don't remember ever baptizing anyone else.

17   For Christ didn't send me to baptize, but to preach the Gospel; and even my preaching sounds poor, for I do not fill my sermons with profound words and high sounding ideas, for fear of diluting the mighty power there is in the simple message of the cross of Christ.

18   I know very well how foolish it sounds to those who are[2] lost, when they hear that Jesus died to save them. But we who are[2] saved recognize this message as the very power of God.

19   For God says, "I will destroy all human plans of salvation no matter how wise they seem to be, and ignore the best ideas of men, even the most brilliant of them."

20   So what about these wise men, these scholars, these brilliant debaters of this world's great affairs? God has made them all look foolish, and shown their wisdom to be useless nonsense.

21   For God in His wisdom saw to it that the world would never find God through human brilliance, and then He stepped in and saved all those who believed His message, which the world calls foolish and silly.

22   It seems foolish to the Jews because they want a sign from heaven as proof that what is preached is true; and it is

[2]Or, "are being . . ."

foolish to the Gentiles because they believe only what agrees with their philosophy and seems wise to them.

23 So when we preach about Christ dying to save them, the Jews are offended and the Gentiles say it's all nonsense.

24 But God has opened the eyes of those called to salvation, both Jews and Gentiles, to see that Christ is the mighty power of God to save them; Christ Himself is the center of God's wise plan for their salvation.

25 This so-called "foolish" plan of God is far wiser than the wisest plan of the wisest man, and God in His weakness— Christ dying on the cross—is far stronger than any man.

26 Notice among yourselves, dear brothers, that few of you who follow Christ have big names or power or wealth.

27 Instead, God has deliberately chosen to use ideas the world considers foolish and of little worth in order to shame those people considered by the world as wise and great.

28 He has chosen a plan despised by the world, counted as nothing at all, and used it to bring down to nothing those the world considers great,

29 So that no one anywhere can ever brag in the presence of God.

30 For it is from God alone that you have your life through Christ Jesus. He showed us God's plan of salvation; He was the one who made us acceptable to God; He made us pure and holy[3] and gave Himself to purchase our salvation.[4]

31 As it says in the Scriptures, "If anyone is going to boast, let him boast only of what the Lord has done."

CHAPTER 2

D EAR brothers, even when I first came to you I didn't use lofty words and brilliant ideas to tell you God's message.

2 For I decided that I would speak only of Jesus Christ and His death on the cross.

3 I came to you in weakness—timid and trembling.

[3]Or, "He brought us near to God."
[4]Or, "to free us from slavery to sin."

4 And my preaching was very plain, not with a lot of oratory and human wisdom, but the Holy Spirit's power was in my words, proving to those who heard them that the message was from God.

5 I did this because I wanted your faith to stand firmly upon God, not on man's great ideas.

6 Yet when I am among mature Christians I do speak with words of great wisdom, but not the kind that comes from here on earth, and not the kind that appeals to the great men of this world, who are doomed to fall.

7 Our words are wise because they are from God, telling of God's wise plan to bring us into the glories of heaven. This plan was hidden in former times, though it was made for our benefit before the world began.

8 But the great men of the world have not understood it; if they had, they never would have crucified the Lord of Glory.

9 That is what is meant by the Scriptures which say that no mere man has ever seen, heard or even imagined what wonderful things God has ready for those who love the Lord.

10 But we know about these things because God has sent His Spirit to tell us, and His Spirit searches out and shows us all of God's deepest secrets.

11 No one can really know what anyone else is thinking, or what he is really like, except that person himself. And no one can know God's thoughts except God's own Spirit.

12 And God has actually given us His Spirit (not the world's spirit) to tell us about the wonderful free gifts of grace and blessing that God has given us.

13 In telling you about these gifts we have even used the very words given us by the Holy Spirit, not words that we as men might choose. So we use the Holy Spirit's words to explain the Holy Spirit's facts.[1]

14 But the man who isn't a Christian can't understand and can't accept these thoughts from God, which the Holy Spirit teaches us. They sound foolish to him, because only those who have the Holy Spirit within them can understand what the Holy Spirit means. Others just can't take it in.

---

[1]Or, "interpreting spiritual truth in spiritual language."

15   But the spiritual man has insight into everything, and that bothers and baffles the man of the world, who can't understand him at all.

16   How could he? For certainly he has never been one to know the Lord's thoughts, or to discuss them with Him, or to move the hands of God by prayer.[2] But, strange as it seems, we Christians actually do have within us a portion of the very thoughts and mind of Christ.

CHAPTER 3

DEAR brothers, I have been talking to you as though you were still just babies in the Christian life, who are not following the Lord, but your own desires; I cannot talk to you as I would to healthy Christians, who are filled with the Spirit.

2   I have had to feed you with milk and not with solid food, because you couldn't digest anything stronger. And even now you still have to be fed on milk.

3   For you are still only baby Christians, controlled by your own desires, not God's. When you are jealous of one another and divide up into quarreling groups, doesn't that prove you are still babies, wanting your own way? In fact, you are acting like people who don't belong to the Lord at all.

4   There you are, quarreling about whether I am greater than Apollos, and dividing the church. Doesn't this show how little you have grown in the Lord?[1]

5   Who am I, and who is Apollos, that we should be the cause of a quarrel? Why, we're just God's servants, each of us with certain special abilities, and with our help you believed.

6   My work was to plant the seed in your hearts, and Apollos' work was to water it, but it was God, not we, who made the garden grow in your hearts.

7   The person who does the planting or watering isn't very important, but God is important because He is the one who makes things grow.

[2]Or, "who can advise Him?"
[1]Literally, "are you not (mere) men?"

8   Apollos and I are working as a team, with the same aim, though each of us will be rewarded for his own hard work.

9   We are only God's co-workers. You are *God's* garden, not ours; you are *God's* building, not ours.

10   God, in His kindness, has taught me how to be an expert builder. I have laid the foundation and Apollos[2] has built on it. But he who builds on the foundation must be very careful.

11   For no one can ever lay any other real foundation than that one we already have—Jesus Christ.

12   But there are various kinds of materials that can be used to build on that foundation. Some use gold and silver and jewels; and some build with sticks, and hay, or even straw!

13   There is going to come a time of testing at Christ's Judgment Day to see what kind of material each builder has used. Everyone's work will be put through the fire so that all can see whether or not it keeps its value, and what was really accomplished.

14   Then every workman who has built on the foundation with the right materials, and whose work still stands, will get his pay.

15   But if the house he has built burns up, he will have a great loss. He himself will be saved, but like a man escaping through a wall of flames.

16   Don't you realize that all of you together are the house of God, and that the Spirit of God lives among you in His house?

17   If anyone defiles and spoils God's home, God will destroy him. For God's home is holy and clean, and you are that home.

18   Stop fooling yourselves. If you count yourself above average in intelligence, as judged by this world's standards, you had better put this all aside and be a fool rather than let it hold you back from the true wisdom from above.

19   For the wisdom of this world is foolishness to God. As it says in the book of Job, God uses man's own brilliance to trap him; he stumbles over his own "wisdom" and falls.

---

[2]Implied.

20 And again, in the book of Psalms, we are told that the Lord knows full well how the human mind reasons, and how foolish and futile it is.

21 So don't be proud of following the wise men of this world.[3] For God has already given you everything you need.

22 He has given you Paul and Apollos and Peter as your helpers. He has given you the whole world to use, and life and even death are your servants. He has given you all of the present and all of the future. All are yours,

23 And you belong to Christ, and Christ is God's.

CHAPTER 4

SO Apollos and I should be looked upon as Christ's servants who distribute God's blessings by explaining God's secrets.

2 Now the most important thing about a servant is that he does just what his master tells him to.

3 What about me? Have I been a good servant? Well, I don't worry over what you think about this, or what anyone else thinks. I don't even trust my own judgment on this point.

4 My conscience is clear, but even that isn't final proof. It is the Lord Himself who must examine me and decide.

5 So be careful not to jump to conclusions before the Lord returns as to whether someone is a good servant or not. When the Lord comes, He will turn on the light so that everyone can see exactly what each one of us is really like, deep down in our hearts. Then everyone will know why we have been doing the Lord's work. At that time God will give to each one whatever praise is coming to him.

6 I have used Apollos and myself as examples to illustrate what I have been saying: that you must not have favorites. You must not be proud of one of God's teachers more than another.

7 What are you so puffed up about? What do you have that God hasn't given you? And if all you have is from God,

---

[3]Literally, "Let no one glory in men."

400

why act as though you are so great, and as though you have accomplished something on your own?

8   You seem to think you already have all the spiritual food you need. You are full and spiritually contented, rich kings on your thrones, leaving us far behind! I wish you really were already on your thrones, for when that times comes you can be sure that we will be there, too, reigning with you.

9   Sometimes I think God has put us apostles at the very end of the line, like prisoners soon to be killed, put on display at the end of a victor's parade, to be stared at by men and angels alike.

10   Religion has made us foolish, you say, but of course you are all such wise and sensible Christians! We are weak, but not you! You are well thought of, while we are laughed at.

11   To this very hour we have gone hungry and thirsty, without even enough clothes to keep us warm. We have been kicked around without homes of our own.

12   We have worked wearily with our hands to earn our living. We have blessed those who cursed us. We have been patient with those who injured us.

13   We have replied quietly when evil things have been said about us. Yet right up to the present moment we are like dirt under foot, like garbage.

14   I am not writing about these things to make you ashamed, but to warn and counsel you as beloved children.

15   For although you may have ten thousand others to teach you about Christ, remember that you have only me as your father. For I was the one who brought you to Christ when I preached the Gospel to you.

16   So I beg you to follow my example, and do as I do.

17   That is the very reason why I am sending Timothy—to help you do this. For he is one of those I won to Christ, a beloved and trustworthy child in the Lord. He will remind you of what I teach in all the churches wherever I go.

18   I know that some of you will have become proud, thinking that I am afraid to come to deal with you.

19   But I will come, and soon, if the Lord will let me, and

then I'll find out whether these proud men are just big talkers or whether they really have God's power.

20   The kingdom of God is not just talking; it is living by God's power.

21   Which do you choose? Shall I come with punishment and scolding, or shall I come with quiet love and gentleness?

CHAPTER 5

EVERYONE is talking about the terrible thing that has happened there among you, something so evil that even the heathen don't do it: you have a man in your church who is living in sin with his father's wife.[1]

2   And are you still so conceited, so "spiritual"? Why aren't you mourning in sorrow and shame, and seeing to it that this man is removed from your membership?

3, 4   Although I am not there with you, I have been thinking a lot about this, and in the name of the Lord Jesus Christ I have already decided what to do, just as though I were there. You are to call a meeting of the church—and the power of the Lord Jesus will be with you as you meet, and I will be there in spirit—

5   And cast out this man from the fellowship of the church and into Satan's hands, to punish him,[2] in the hope that his soul will be saved when our Lord Jesus Christ returns.

6   What a terrible thing it is that you are boasting about your purity, and yet you let this sort of thing go on. Don't you realize that if even one person is allowed to go on sinning, soon all will be affected?

7   Remove this evil cancer—this wicked person—from among you, so that you can stay pure. Christ, God's Lamb, has been slain for us.

8   So let us feast upon Him and grow strong in the Christian life, leaving entirely behind us the cancerous old life with

---

[1]Possibly his step-mother.
[2]Literally, "for the destruction of the flesh."

402

all its hatreds and wickedness. Let us feast instead upon the pure bread of honor and sincerity and truth.

9   When I wrote to you before I said not to mix with evil people.

10   But when I said that I wasn't talking about unbelievers who live in sexual sin, or are greedy cheats and thieves and idol worshipers. For you can't live in this world without being with people like that.

11   What I meant was that you are not to keep company with anyone who claims to be a brother Christian but indulges in sexual sins, or is greedy, or is a swindler, or worships idols, or is a drunkard, or abusive. Don't even eat lunch with such a person.

12   It isn't our job to judge outsiders. But it certainly is our job to judge and deal strongly with those who are members of the church, and who are sinning in these ways.

13   God alone is the Judge of those on the outside. But you yourselves must deal with this man and put him out of your church.

CHAPTER 6

HOW is it that when you have something against another Christian, you "go to law" and ask a heathen court to decide the matter instead of taking it to other Christians to decide which of you is right?

2   Don't you know that some day we Christians are going to judge and govern the world? So why can't you decide even these little things among yourselves?

3   Don't you realize that we Christians will judge and reward the very angels in heaven? So you should be able to decide your problems down here on earth easily enough.

4   Why then go to outside judges who are not even Christians?[1]

---

[1] Or, "Even the least capable people in the church should be able to decide these things for you." Both interpretations are possible.

5   I am trying to make you ashamed. Isn't there anyone in all the church who is wise enough to decide these arguments?

6   But, instead, one Christian sues another and accuses his Christian brother in front of unbelievers.

7   To have such lawsuits at all is a real defeat for you as Christians. Why not just accept mistreatment and leave it at that? It would be far more honoring to the Lord to let yourselves be cheated.

8   But, instead, you yourselves are the ones who do wrong, cheating others, even your own brothers.

9, 10   Don't you know that those doing such things have no share in the kingdom of God? Don't fool yourselves. Those who live immoral lives, who are idol worshipers, adulterers or homosexuals—will have no share in His kingdom. Neither will thieves or greedy people, drunkards, slandermongers, or robbers.

11   There was a time when some of you were just like that but now your sins are washed away, and you are set apart for God, and He has accepted you because of what the Lord Jesus Christ and the Spirit of our God have done for you.

12   I can do anything I want to if Christ has not said no,[2] but some of these things aren't good for me. Even if I am allowed to do them, I'll refuse to if I think they might get such a grip on me that I can't easily stop when I want to.

13   For instance, take the matter of eating. God has given us an appetite for food and stomachs to digest it. But that doesn't mean we should eat more than we need. Don't think of eating as important, because some day God will do away with both stomachs and food. But sexual sin is never right: our bodies were not made for that, but for the Lord, and the Lord wants to fill our bodies with Himself.

14   And God is going to raise our bodies from the dead by His power just as He raised up the Lord Jesus Christ.

15   Don't you realize that your bodies are actually parts and members of Christ? So should I take part of Christ and join Him to a prostitute? Never!

---

[2] Literally, "all things are lawful for me." Obviously, Paul is not here permitting sins such as have just been expressly prohibited in verses 8 and 9. He is apparently quoting some in the church of lustful Corinth who were excusing their sins.

16   And don't you know that if a man joins himself to a prostitute she becomes a part of him and he becomes a part of her? For God tells us in the Scripture that in His sight the two become one person.

17   But if you give yourself to the Lord, you and Christ are joined together as one person.

18   That is why I say to run from sex sin. No other sin affects the body as this one does. When you sin this sin it is against your own body.

19   Haven't you yet learned that your body is the home of the Holy Spirit God gave you, and that He lives within you? Your own body does not belong to you.

20   For God has bought you with a great price. So use every part of your body to give glory back to God, because He owns it.

CHAPTER 7

NOW about those questions you asked in your last letter: my answer is that if you do not marry, it is good.

2   But usually it is best to be married, each man having his own wife, and each woman having her own husband, because otherwise you might fall back into sin.

3   The man should give his wife all that is her right as a married woman, and the wife should do the same for her husband:

4   For a girl who marries no longer has full right to her own body, for her husband then has his rights to it, too; and in the same way the husband no longer has full right to his own body, for it belongs also to his wife.

5   So do not refuse these rights to each other. The only exception to this rule would be the agreement of both husband and wife to refrain from the rights of marriage for a limited time, so that they can give themselves more completely to prayer. Afterwards, they should come together again so that Satan won't be able to tempt them because of their lack of self-control.

6   I'm not saying you *must* marry; but you certainly *may* if you wish.

7   I wish everyone could get along without marrying, just as I do. But we are not all the same. God gives some the gift of a husband or wife, and others He gives the gift of being able to stay happily unmarried.

8   So I say to those who aren't married, and to widows—better to stay unmarried if you can, just as I am.

9   But if you can't control yourselves, go ahead and marry. It is better to marry than to burn with lust.

10   Now, for those who are married I have a command, not just a suggestion. And it is not a command from me, for this is what the Lord Himself has said: a wife must not leave her husband.

11   But if she is separated from him, let her remain single or else go back to him. And the husband must not divorce his wife.

12   Here I want to add some suggestions of my own. These are not direct commands from the Lord, but they seem right to me: If a Christian has a wife who is not a Christian, but she wants to stay with him anyway, he must not leave her or divorce her.

13   And if a Christian woman has a husband who isn't a Christian, and he wants her to stay with him, she must not leave him.

14   For perhaps the husband who isn't a Christian may become a Christian with the help of his Christian wife. And the wife who isn't a Christian may become a Christian with the help of her Christian husband. Otherwise, if the family separates, the children might never come to know the Lord; whereas a united family may, in God's plan, result in the children's salvation.

15   But if the husband or wife who isn't a Christian is eager to leave, it is permitted. In such cases the Christian husband or wife should not insist that the other stay, for God wants His children to live in peace and harmony.

16   For, after all, there is no assurance to you wives that

your husbands will be converted if they stay; and the same may be said to you husbands concerning your wives.

17 But be sure in deciding these matters that you are living as God intended, marrying or not marrying in accordance with God's direction and help, and accepting whatever situation God has put you into. This is my rule for all the churches.

18 For instance, a man who already has gone through the Jewish ceremony of circumcision before he became a Christian shouldn't worry about it; and if he hasn't been circumcised, he shouldn't do it now.

19 For it doesn't make any difference at all whether a Christian has gone through this ceremony or not. But it makes a lot of difference whether he is pleasing God and keeping God's commandments. That is the important thing.

20 Usually a person should keep on with the work he was doing when God called him.

21 Are you a slave? Don't let that worry you—but of course, if you get a chance to be free, take it.

22 If the Lord calls you, and you are a slave, remember that Christ has set you free from the awful power of sin; and if He has called you and you are free, remember that you are now a slave of Christ.

23 You have been bought and paid for by Christ, so you belong to Him—be free now from all these earthly prides and fears.[1]

24 So, dear brothers, whatever situation a person is in when he becomes a Christian, let him stay there, for now the Lord is there to help him.

25 Now I will try to answer your other question. What about girls who are not yet married? Should they be permitted to do so? In answer to this question, I have no special command for them from the Lord. But the Lord in His kindness has given me wisdom that can be trusted, and I will be glad to tell you what I think.

26 Here is the problem: we Christians are facing great dangers to our lives at present. In times like these I think it is best for a person to remain unmarried.

---

[1]Literally, "Become not bondservants of men."

27 Of course, if you already are married, don't separate because of this. But if you aren't, don't rush into it at this time.

28 But if you men decide to go ahead anyway and get married now, it is all right; and if a girl gets married in times like these, it is no sin. However, marriage will bring extra problems that I wish you didn't have to face right now.

29 The important thing to remember is that our remaining time is very short, [and so are our opportunities for doing the Lord's work²]. For that reason those who have wives should stay as free as possible for the Lord;³

30 Happiness or sadness or wealth should not keep anyone from doing God's work.

31 Those in frequent contact with the exciting things the world offers should make good use of their opportunities without stopping to enjoy them; for the world in its present form will soon be gone.

32 In all you do, I want you to be free from worry. An unmarried man can spend his time doing the Lord's work and thinking how to please Him.

33 But a married man can't do that so well; he has to think about his earthly responsibilities and how to please his wife.

34 His interests are divided. It is the same with a girl who marries. She faces the same problem. A girl who is not married is anxious to please the Lord in all she is and does.⁴ But a married woman must consider other things such as housekeeping and the likes and dislikes of her husband.

35 I am saying this to help you, not to try to keep you from marrying. I want you to do whatever will help you serve the Lord best, with as few other things as possible to distract your attention from Him.

36 But if anyone feels he ought to marry because he has trouble controlling his passions, it is all right, it is not a sin; let him marry.

37 But if a man has the willpower not to marry and decides that he doesn't need to and won't, he has made a wise decision.

²Implied.
³Literally, "(that) those who have wives may be as though they didn't."
⁴Literally, "pure in body and in spirit."

38 So the person who marries does well, and the person who doesn't marry does even better.

39 The wife is part of her husband as long as he lives; if her husband dies, then she may marry again, but only if she marries a Christian.

40 But in my opinion she will be happier if she doesn't marry again; and I think I am giving you counsel from God's Spirit when I say this.

CHAPTER 8

NEXT is your question about eating food that has been sacrificed to idols. On this question everyone feels that only his answer is the right one! But although being a "know-it-all" makes us feel important, what is really needed to build the church is love.

2 If anyone thinks he knows all the answers, he is just showing his ignorance.

3 But the person who truly loves God is the one who is open to God's knowledge.

4 So now, what about it? Should we eat meat that has been sacrificed to idols? Well, we all know that an idol is not really a god, and that there is only one God, and no other.

5 According to some people, there are a great many gods, both in heaven and on earth.

6 But we know that there is only one God, the Father, who created all things[1] and made us to be His own; and one Lord Jesus Christ, who made everything and gives us life.

7 However, some Christians don't realize this. All their lives they have been used to thinking of idols as alive, and have believed that food offered to the idols is really being offered to actual gods. So when they eat such food it bothers them and hurts their tender consciences.

8 Just remember that God doesn't care whether we eat it or not. We are no worse off if we don't eat it, and no better off if we do.

---

[1]Literally, "of whom are all things."

9   But be careful not to use your freedom to eat it, lest you cause some Christian brother to sin whose conscience[2] is weaker than yours.

10   You see, this is what may happen: Someone who thinks it is wrong to eat this food will see you eating at a temple restaurant, for you know there is no harm in it. Then he will become bold enough to do it too, although all the time he still feels it is wrong.

11   So because you "know it is all right to do it," you will be responsible for causing great spiritual damage to a brother with a tender conscience for whom Christ died.

12   And it is a sin against Christ to sin against your brother by encouraging him to do something he thinks is wrong.

13   So if eating meat offered to idols is going to make my brother sin, I'll not eat any of it as long as I live, because I don't want to do this to him.

CHAPTER 9

I AM an apostle, God's messenger, responsible to no mere man. I am one who has actually seen Jesus our Lord with my own eyes. And your changed lives are the result of my hard work for Him.

2   If in the opinion of others, I am not an apostle, I certainly am to you, for you have been won to Christ through me.

3   This is my answer to those who question my rights.

4   Or don't I have any rights at all? Can't I claim the same privilege the other apostles have of being a guest in your homes?

5   If[1] I had a wife, and if[1] she were a believer, couldn't I bring her along on these trips just as the other disciples do, and as the Lord's brothers do, and as Peter does?

6   And must Barnabas and I alone keep working for our living, while you supply these others?

7   What soldier in the army has to pay his own expenses? And have you ever heard of a farmer who harvests his crop and

[2]Implied. Literally, "faith."
[1]Implied. Literally, "Have we no right to lead about a wife that is a believer?"

doesn't have the right to eat some of it? What shepherd takes care of a flock of sheep and goats and isn't allowed to drink some of the milk?

8   And I'm not merely quoting the opinions of men as to what is right. I'm telling you what God's law says.

9   For in the law God gave to Moses He said that you must not put a muzzle on an ox to keep it from eating when it is treading out the wheat. Do you suppose God was thinking only about oxen when He said this?

10   Wasn't He also thinking about us? Of course He was. He said this to show us that Christian workers should be paid by those they help. Those who do the plowing and threshing should expect some share of the harvest.

11   We have planted good spiritual seed in your souls. Is it too much to ask, in return, for mere food and clothing?

12   You give them to others who preach to you, and you should. But shouldn't we have an even greater right to them? Yet we have *never* used this right, but supply our own needs without your help. We have never demanded payment of any kind for fear that, if we did, you might be less interested in our message to you from Christ.

13   Don't you realize that God told those working in His temple to take for their own needs some of the food brought there as gifts to Him? And those who work at the altar of God get a share of the food that is brought by those offering it to the Lord.

14   In the same way the Lord has given orders that those who preach the Gospel should be supported by those who accept it.

15   Yet I have never asked you for one penny. And I am not writing this to hint that I would like to start now. In fact, I would rather die of hunger than lose the satisfaction I get from preaching to you without charge.

16   For just preaching the Gospel isn't any special credit to me—I couldn't keep from preaching it if I wanted to. I would be utterly miserable. Woe unto me if I don't.

17   If I were volunteering my services of my own free will,

then the Lord would give me a special reward; but that is not the situation, for God has picked me out and given me this sacred trust and I have no choice.

18 Under this circumstance, what is my pay? It is the special joy I get from preaching the Good News without expense to anyone, never demanding my rights.

19 And this has a real advantage: I am not bound to obey anyone just because he pays my salary; yet I have freely and happily become a servant of any and all so that I can win them to Christ.

20 When I am with the Jews I seem as one of them so that they will listen to the Gospel and I can win them to Christ. When I am with Gentiles who follow Jewish customs and ceremonies I don't argue, even though I don't agree, because I want to help them.

21 When with the heathen I agree with them as much as I can, except of course that I must always do what is right as a Christian. And so, by agreeing, I can win their confidence[2] and help them too.

22 When I am with those whose consciences bother them easily, I don't act as though I know it all and don't say they are foolish; the result is that they are willing to let me help them. Yes, whatever a person is like, I try to find common ground with him so that he will let me tell him about Christ and let Christ save him.

23 I do this to get the Gospel to them and also for the blessing I myself receive when I see them come to Christ.

24 In a race, everyone runs but only one person gets first prize. So run your race to win.

25 To win the contest you must deny yourselves many things that would keep you from doing your best. An athlete goes to all this trouble just to win a blue ribbon or a silver cup,[3] but we do it for a heavenly reward that never disappears.

26 So I run straight to the goal with purpose in every step. I fight to win. I'm not just shadow-boxing or playing around.

---

[2]Implied.
[3]Literally, "a wreath that quickly fades," given to the winners of the original Olympic races of Paul's time.

27   Like an athlete I punish my body, treating it roughly, training it to do what it should, not what it wants to. Otherwise I fear that after enlisting others for the race, I myself might be declared unfit and ordered to stand aside.

CHAPTER 10

FOR we must never forget, dear brothers, what happened to our people in the wilderness long ago. God guided them by sending a cloud that moved along ahead of them; and He brought them all safely through the waters of the Red Sea.

2   This might be called their "baptism"—baptized both in sea and cloud!—as followers of Moses—their commitment to him as their leader.

3, 4   And by a miracle[1] God sent them food to eat and water to drink there in the desert; they drank the water that Christ gave them.[2] He was there with them as a mighty Rock of spiritual refreshment.

5   Yet after all this most of them did not obey God, and He destroyed them in the wilderness.

6   From this lesson we are warned that we must not desire evil things as they did,

7   Nor worship idols as they did. (The Scriptures tell us, "The people sat down to eat and drink and then got up to dance" in worship of the golden calf.)

8   Another lesson for us is what happened when some of them sinned with other men's wives, and 23,000 fell dead in one day.

9   And don't try the Lord's patience—they did, and died from snake bites.

10   And don't murmur against God and His dealings with you, as some of them did, for that is why God sent His Angel to destroy them.

11   All these things happened to them as examples—as object lessons to us—to warn us against doing the same things;

---

[1]Implied. Literally, "spiritual food and drink."
[2]Literally, "For they drank of a spiritual Rock that followed them, and the Rock was Christ."

they were written down so that we could read about them and learn from them in these last days as the world nears its end.

12 <u>So be careful.</u> If you are thinking, "Oh, I would never behave like that"—let this be a warning to you. For you too may fall into sin.

13 But remember this—the wrong desires that come into your life aren't anything new and different. Many others have faced exactly the same problems before you. And no temptation is irresistible. You can trust God to keep the temptation from becoming so strong that you can't stand up against it, for He has promised this and will do what He says. He will show you how to escape temptation's power so that you can bear up patiently against it.

14 So, dear friends, carefully avoid idol-worship of every kind.

15 You are intelligent people. Look now and see for yourselves whether what I am about to say is true.

16 When we ask the Lord's blessing upon our drinking from the cup of wine at the Lord's Table, this means, doesn't it, that all who drink it are sharing together the blessing of Christ's blood? And when we break off pieces of the bread from the loaf to eat there together, this shows that we are sharing together in the benefits of His body.

17 No matter how many of us there are, we all eat from the same loaf, showing that we are all parts of the one body of Christ.

18 And the Jewish people, all who eat the sacrifices, are united by that act.

19 What am I trying to say? Am I saying that the idols to whom the heathen bring sacrifices are really alive and are real gods, and that these sacrifices are of some value? No, not at all.

20 What I am saying is that those who offer food to these idols are united together in sacrificing to demons, certainly not to God. And I don't want any of you to be partners with demons when you eat the same food, along with the heathen, that has been offered to these idols.

21   You cannot drink from the cup at the Lord's Table and at Satan's table, too. You cannot eat bread both at the Lord's Table and at Satan's table.

22   What? Are you tempting the Lord to be angry with you? Are you stronger than He is?

23   You are certainly free to eat food offered to idols if you want to; it's not against God's laws to eat such meat, but that doesn't mean that you should go ahead and do it. It may be perfectly legal, but it may not be best and helpful.

24   Don't think only of yourself. Try to think of the other fellow, too, and what is best for him.

25   Here's what you should do. Take any meat you want that is sold at the market. Don't ask whether or not it was offered to idols, lest the answer hurt your conscience.

26   For the earth and every good thing in it belongs to the Lord and is yours to enjoy.

27   If someone who isn't a Christian asks you out to dinner, go ahead; accept the invitation if you want to. Eat whatever is on the table and don't ask any questions about it. Then you won't know whether or not it had been used as a sacrifice to idols, and you won't risk having a bad conscience over eating it.

28   But if someone warns you that this meat has been offered to idols, then don't eat it for the sake of the man who told you, and of his conscience.

29   In this case *his* feeling about it is the important thing, not yours. But why, you may ask, must I be guided and limited by what someone else thinks?

30   If I can thank God for the food and enjoy it, why let someone spoil everything just because he thinks I am wrong?

31   Well, I'll tell you why. It is because you must do everything for the glory of God, even your eating and drinking.

32   So don't be a stumbling block to anyone, whether they are Jews or Gentiles or Christians.

33   That is the plan I follow, too. I try to please everyone in everything I do, not doing what I like or what is best for me, but what is best for them, so that they may be saved.

CHAPTER 11

A ND you should follow my example, just as I follow Christ's.

2 I am so glad, dear brothers, that you have been remembering and doing everything I taught you.

3 But there is one matter I want to remind you about: that a wife is responsible to her husband, her husband is responsible to Christ, and Christ is responsible to God.

4 That is why, if a man refuses to remove his hat while praying or preaching, he dishonors Christ.

5 And that is why a woman who publicly prays or prophesies without a covering on her head dishonors her husband [for her covering is a sign of her subjection to him[1]].

6 Yes, if she refuses to wear a head covering, then she should cut off all her hair. And if it is shameful for a woman to have her head shaved, then she should wear a covering.

7 But a man should not wear anything on his head [when worshiping, for his hat is a sign of subjection to men[2]]. God's glory is man made in His image, and man's glory is the woman.

8 The first man didn't come from woman, but the first woman came out of man.[3]

9 And Adam, the first man, was not made for Eve's benefit, but Eve was made for Adam.

10 So a woman should wear a covering on her head as a sign that she is under man's authority,[4] a fact for all the angels to notice and rejoice in.[5]

11 But remember that in God's plan men and women need each other.

12 For although the first woman came out of man, all men have been born from women ever since, and both men and women come from God their Creator.

---

[1]Implied, from verses 7, 10.
[2]Implied.
[3]Genesis 2:21-22.
[4]Literally, "For this cause ought the woman to have power on (her) head."
[5]Literally, "because of the angels."

416

13   What do you yourselves really think about this? Is it right for a woman to pray in public without covering her head?

14, 15   Doesn't even instinct itself teach us that women's heads should be covered? For women are proud of their long hair, while a man with long hair tends to be ashamed.

16   But if anyone wants to argue about this, all I can say is that we never teach anything else than this—that a woman should wear a covering when prophesying or praying publicly in the church, and all the churches feel the same way about it.

17   Next on my list of items to write you about is something else I cannot agree with. For it sounds as if more harm than good is done when you meet together for your communion services.

18   Everyone keeps telling me about the arguing that goes on in these meetings, and the divisions developing among you, and I can just about believe it.

19   But I suppose you feel this is necessary so that you who are always right will become known and recognized!

20   When you come together to eat, it isn't the Lord's Supper you are eating,

21   But your own. For I am told that everyone hastily gobbles all the food he can without waiting to share with the others, so that one doesn't get enough and goes hungry while another has too much to drink and gets drunk.

22   What? Is this really true? Can't you do your eating and drinking at home, to avoid disgracing the church and shaming those who are poor and can bring no food? What am I supposed to say about these things? Do you want me to praise you? Well, I certainly do not!

23   For this is what the Lord Himself has said about His Table, and I have passed it on to you before: That on the night when Judas betrayed Him, the Lord Jesus took bread,

24   And when He had given thanks to God for it, He broke it and gave it to His disciples and said, "Take this and eat it. This is My body, which is given[6] for you. Do this to remember Me."

25   In the same way, He took the cup of wine after supper, saying, "This cup is the new agreement between God and you

---

[6]Some ancient manuscripts read, "broken."

that has been established and set in motion by My blood. Do this in remembrance of Me whenever you drink it."

26 For every time you eat this bread and drink this cup you are re-telling the message of the Lord's death, that He has died for you. Do this until He comes again.

27 So if anyone eats this bread and drinks from this cup of the Lord in an unworthy manner, he is guilty of sin against the body and the blood of the Lord.

28 That is why a man should examine himself carefully before eating the bread and drinking from the cup.

29 For if he eats the bread and drinks from the cup unworthily, not thinking about the body of Christ and what it means, he is eating and drinking God's judgment upon himself; for he is trifling with the death of Christ.

30 That is why many of you are weak and sick, and some have even died.

31 But if you carefully examine yourselves before eating you will not need to be judged and punished.

32 Yet, when we are judged and punished by the Lord, it is so that we will not be condemned with the rest of the world.

33 So, dear brothers, when you gather for the Lord's Supper —the communion service—wait for each other;

34 If anyone is really hungry he should eat at home so that he won't bring punishment upon himself when you meet together.

I'll talk to you about the other matters after I arrive.

CHAPTER 12

AND now, brothers, I want to write about the special abilities the Holy Spirit gives to each of you, for I don't want any misunderstanding about them.

2 You will remember that before you became Christians you went around from one idol to another, not one of which could speak a single word.

3 But now you are meeting people who claim to speak

messages from the Spirit of God. How can you know whether they are really inspired by God or whether they are fakes? Here is the test: no one speaking by the power of the Spirit of God can curse Jesus, and no one can say, "Jesus is Lord," and really mean it, unless the Holy Spirit is helping him.

4   Now God gives us many kinds of special abilities, but it is the same Holy Spirit who is the source of them all.

5   There are different kinds of service to God, but it is the same Lord we are serving.

6   There are many ways in which God works in our lives, but it is the same God who does the work in and through all of us who are His.

7   The Holy Spirit displays God's power through each of us as a means of helping the entire church.

8   To one person the Spirit gives the ability to give wise advice; someone else may be especially good at studying and teaching, and this is his gift from the same Spirit.

9   He gives special faith to another, and to someone else the power to heal the sick.

10   He gives power for doing miracles to some, and to others power to prophesy and preach. He gives someone else the power to know whether evil spirits are speaking through those who claim to be giving God's messages—or whether it is really the Spirit of God who is speaking. Still another person is able to speak in languages he never learned; and others, who do not know the language either, are given power to understand what he is saying.

11   It is the same and only Holy Spirit who gives all these gifts and powers, deciding which each one of us should have.

12   Our bodies have many parts, but the many parts make up only one body when they are all put together. So it is with the "body" of Christ.

13   Each of us is a part of the one body of Christ. Some of us are Jews, some are Gentiles, some are slaves and some are free. But the Holy Spirit has fitted us all together into one body. We have been baptized into Christ's body by the one Spirit, and have all been given that same Holy Spirit.

14   Yes, the body has many parts, not just one part.

15   If the foot says, "I am not a part of the body becaus I am not a hand," that does not make it any less a part of th body.

16   And what would you think if you heard an ear say, am not part of the body because I am only an ear, and not eye"? Would that make it any less a part of the body?

17   Suppose the whole body were an eye—then how would you hear? Or if your whole body were just one big ear, how could you smell anything?

18   But that isn't the way God has made us. He has made many parts for our bodies and has put each part just where He wants it.

19   What a strange thing a body would be if it had only one part!

20   So He has made many parts, but still there is only one body.

21   The eye can never say to the hand, "I don't need you." The head can't say to the feet, "I don't need you."

22   And some of the parts that seem weakest and least important are really the most necessary.

23   Yes, we are especially glad to have some parts that seem rather odd! And we carefully protect from the eyes of others those parts that should not be seen,

24   While of course the parts that may be seen do not require this special care. So God has put the body together in such a way that extra honor and care are given to those parts that might otherwise seem less important.

25   This makes for happiness among the parts, so that the parts have the same care for each other that they do for themselves.

26   If one part suffers, all parts suffer with it, and if one part is honored, all the parts are glad.

27   Now here is what I am trying to say: all of you together are the one body of Christ and each one of you is a separate and necessary part of it.

28   Here is a list of some of the parts He has placed in His church, which is His body:

420

Apostles,

Prophets—those who preach God's Word,

Teachers,

Those who do miracles,

Those who have the gift of healing,

Those who can help others,

Those who can get others to work together,

Those who speak in languages they have never learned.

29 Is everyone an apostle? Of course not. Is everyone a preacher? No. Are all teachers? Does everyone have the power to do miracles?

30 Can everyone heal the sick? Of course not. Does God give all of us the ability to speak in languages we've never learned? Can just anyone understand and translate what those are saying who have that gift of foreign speech?

31 No, but try your best to have the more important of these gifts. First, however, let me tell you about something else that is better than any of them!

CHAPTER 13

IF I had the gift of being able to speak in other languages without learning them, and could speak in every language there is in all of heaven and earth, but didn't love others, I would only be making noise.

2 If I had the gift of prophecy and knew all about what is going to happen in the future, knew everything about *everything*, but didn't love others, what good would it do? Even if I had the gift of faith so that I could speak to a mountain and make it move, I would still be worth nothing at all without love.

3 If I gave everything I have to poor people, and if I were burned alive for preaching the Gospel but didn't love others, it would be of no value whatever.

4 Love is very patient and kind, never jealous or envious, never boastful or proud,

5 Never haughty or selfish or rude. Love does not demand its own way. It is not irritable or touchy. It does not hold grudges and will hardly even notice when others do it wrong.

6 It is never glad about injustice, but rejoices whenever truth wins out.

7 If you love someone you will be loyal to him no matter what the cost. You will always believe in him, always expect the best of him, and always stand your ground in defending him.

8 All the special gifts and powers from God will some day come to an end, but love goes on forever. Some day prophecy, and speaking in unknown languages, and special knowledge—these gifts will disappear.

9 Now we know so little, even with our special gifts, and the preaching of those most gifted is still so poor.

10 But when we have been made perfect and complete, then the need for these inadequate special gifts will come to an end, and they will disappear.

11 It's like this: when I was a child I spoke and thought and reasoned as a child does. But when I became a man my thoughts grew far beyond those of my childhood, and now I have put away the childish things.

12 In the same way, we can see and understand only a little about God now, as if we were peering at His reflection in a poor mirror; but someday we are going to see Him in His completeness, face to face. Now all that I know is hazy and blurred, but then I will see everything clearly, just as clearly as God sees into my heart right now.

13 There are three things that remain—faith, hope, and love—and the greatest of these is love.

CHAPTER 14

L ET love be your greatest aim; nevertheless, ask also for the special abilities the Holy Spirit gives, and especially the gift of prophecy, being able to preach the messages of God.

2 But if your gift is that of being able to "speak in tongues," that is, to speak in languages you haven't learned, you will be talking to God but not to others, since they won't be able to understand you. You will be speaking by the power of the Spirit but it will all be a secret.

3 But one who prophesies, preaching the messages of God, is helping others grow in the Lord, encouraging and comforting them.

4 So a person "speaking in tongues" helps himself grow spiritually, but one who prophesies, preaching messages from God, helps the entire church grow in holiness and happiness.

5 I wish you all had the gift of "speaking in tongues" but, even more, I wish you were all able to prophesy, preaching God's messages, for that is a greater and more useful power than to speak in unknown languages—unless, of course, you can tell everyone afterwards what you were saying, so that they can get some good out of it too.

6 Dear friends, even if I myself should come to you talking in some language you don't understand, how would that help you? But if I speak plainly what God has revealed to me, and tell you the things I know, and what is going to happen, and the great truths of God's Word—that is what you need; that is what will help you.

7 Even musical instruments—the flute, for instance, or the harp—are examples of the need for speaking in plain, simple English[1] rather than in unknown languages. For no one will recognize the tune the flute is playing unless each note is sounded clearly.

8 And if the army bugler doesn't play the right notes, how will the soldiers know that they are being called to battle?

9 In the same way, if you talk to a person in some language he doesn't understand, how will he know what you mean? You might as well be talking to an empty room.

10 I suppose that there are hundreds of different languages in the world, and all are excellent for those who understand them,

---

[1] The local language, whatever it is.

11   But to me they mean nothing. A person talking to me in one of these languages will be a stranger to me and I will be a stranger to him.

12   Since you are so anxious to have special gifts from the Holy Spirit, ask Him for the very best, for those that will be of real help to the whole church.

13   If someone is given the gift of speaking in unknown tongues, he should pray also for the gift of knowing what he has said, so that he can tell people afterwards, plainly.

14   For if I pray in a language I don't understand, my spirit is praying but I don't know what I am saying.

15   Well, then, what shall I do? I will do both. I will pray in unknown tongues and also in ordinary language that everyone understands. I will sing in unknown tongues and also in ordinary language, so that I can understand the praise I am giving;

16   For if you praise and thank God with the spirit alone, speaking in another language, how can those who don't understand you be praising God along with you? How can they join you in giving thanks when they don't know what you are saying?

17   You will be giving thanks very nicely, no doubt, but the other people present won't be helped.

18   I thank God that I "speak in tongues" privately[2] more than any of the rest of you.

19   But in public worship I would much rather speak five words that people can understand and be helped by, than ten thousand words while "speaking in tongues" in an unknown language.

20   Dear brothers, don't be childish in your understanding of these things. Be innocent babies when it comes to planning evil, but be men of intelligence in understanding matters of this kind.

21   We are told in the ancient Scriptures that God would send men from other lands to speak in foreign languages to His people, but even then they would not listen.

---

[2]Implied. See verses 19 and 28.

22   So you see that being able to "speak in tongues" is not a help to God's children, but is to interest the unsaved. However, prophecy (preaching the deep truths of God) is what the Christians need, and unbelievers aren't yet ready for it.

23   Even so, if an unsaved person, or someone who doesn't have these gifts, comes to church and hears you all talking in other languages, he is likely to think you are crazy.

24   But if you prophesy, preaching God's word, [even though such preaching is mostly for believers[3]] and an unsaved person or a new Christian comes in who does not understand about these things, all these sermons will convince him of the fact that he is a sinner, and his conscience will be pricked by everything he hears.

25   As he listens, his secret thoughts will be laid bare and he will fall down on his knees and worship God, declaring that God is really there among you.

26   Well, my brothers, let's add up what I am saying. When you meet together some will sing, another will teach, or tell some special information God has given him, or speak in an unknown language, or tell what someone else is saying who is speaking in the unknown language, but everything that is done must be useful to all, and build them up in the Lord.

27   No more than two or three should speak in an unknown language, and they must speak one at a time, and someone must be ready to interpret what they are saying.

28   But if no one is present who can interpret, they must not speak out loud. They must talk silently to themselves and to God in the unknown language but not publicly.

29, 30   Two or three may prophesy, one at a time, if they have the gift, while all the others listen. But if, while someone is prophesying, someone else receives a message or idea from the Lord, he must not interrupt. The one who is speaking should be allowed to finish before another begins.

31   In this way all who have the gift of prophecy can speak, one after the other, and everyone will learn and be encouraged and helped.

[3]Implied.

32   Remember that a person who has a message from God has the power to stop himself or wait his turn.[4]

33   God is not one who likes things to be disorderly and upset. He likes harmony, and He finds it in all the other churches.

34   Women should be silent during the church meetings. They are not to take part in the discussion, for they are subordinate to men[5] as the Scriptures also declare.

35   If they have any questions to ask, let them ask their husbands at home, for it is improper for women to express their opinions in church meetings.

36   You disagree? And do you think that the knowledge of God's will begins and ends with you Corinthians? Well, you are mistaken!

37   You who claim to have the gift of prophecy or any other special ability from the Holy Spirit should be the first to realize that what I am saying is a commandment from the Lord Himself.

38   But if anyone still disagrees—well, we will leave him in his ignorance.[6]

39   So, my fellow believers, long to be prophets so that you can preach God's message plainly; and never say it is wrong to "speak in tongues";

40   However, be sure that everything is done properly in a good and orderly way.

CHAPTER 15

N OW let me remind you, brothers, of what the Gospel really is, for it has not changed—it is the same Good News I preached to you before. You welcomed it then and still do now, for your faith is squarely built upon this wonderful message;

[4]Literally, "The spirits of the prophets are subject to the prophets."
[5]Literally, "They are not authorized to speak." They are permitted to pray and prophesy (I Cor. 11:5), apparently in public meetings, but not to teach men (I Tim. 2:12).
[6]Or, "If he disagrees, ignore his opinion."

2   And it is this Good News that saves you if you still firmly believe it, unless of course you never really believed it in the first place.

3   I passed on to you right from the first what had been told to me, that Christ died for our sins just as the Scriptures said He would,

4   And that He was buried, and that three days afterwards He arose from the grave just as the prophets foretold.

5   He was seen by Peter and later by the rest of "the Twelve."[1]

6   After that He was seen by more than five hundred Christian brothers at one time, most of whom are still alive, though some have died by now.

7   Then James saw Him and later all the apostles.

8   Last of all I saw Him too, long after the others, as though I had been born almost too late for this.

9   For I am the least worthy of all the apostles, and I shouldn't even be called an apostle at all after the way I treated the church of God.

10   But whatever I am now it is all because God poured out such kindness and grace upon me—and not without results: for I have worked harder than all the other apostles, yet actually I wasn't doing it, but God working in me, to bless me.

11   It makes no difference who worked the hardest, I or they; the important thing is that we preached the Gospel to you, and you believed it.

12   But tell me this! Since you believe what we preach, that *Christ* rose from the dead, why are some of you saying that dead people will never come back to life again?

13   For if there is no resurrection of the dead, then Christ must still be dead.

14   And if He is still dead, then all our preaching is useless and your trust in God is empty, worthless, hopeless;

15   And we apostles are all liars because we have said that God raised Christ from the grave, and of course that isn't true if the dead do not come back to life again.

---

[1]The name given to Jesus' twelve disciples, and still used after Judas was gone from among them.

16   If they don't, then Christ is still dead,

17   And you are very foolish to keep on trusting God to save you, and you are still under condemnation for your sins;

18   In that case all Christians who have died are lost!

19   And if being a Christian is of value to us only now in this life, we are the most miserable of creatures.

20   But the fact is that Christ did actually rise from the dead, and has become the first of millions[2] who will come back to life again some day.

21   Death came into the world because of what one man (Adam) did, and it is because of what this other man (Christ) has done that now there is the resurrection from the dead.

22   Everyone dies because all of us are related to Adam, being members of his sinful race, and wherever there is sin, death results. But all who are related to Christ will rise again.

23   Each, however, in his own turn: Christ rose first; then when Christ comes back, all His people will become alive again.

24   After that the end will come when He will turn the kingdom over to God the Father, having put down all enemies of every kind.

25   For Christ will be King until He has defeated all His enemies,

26   Including the last enemy—death. This too must be defeated and ended.

27   For the rule and authority over all things has been given to Christ by His Father; except, of course, Christ does not rule over the Father Himself, who gave Him this power to rule.

28   When Christ has finally won the battle against all His enemies, then He, the Son of God, will put Himself also under His Father's orders, so that God who has given Him the victory over everything else will be utterly supreme.

29   If the dead will not come back to life again, then what point is there in people being baptized for those who are gone? Why do it unless you believe that the dead will some day rise again?

---

[2]Literally, "the first-fruits of them that are asleep."

428

30   And why should we ourselves be continually risking our lives, facing death hour by hour?

31   For it is a fact that I face death daily; that is as true as my pride in your growth in the Lord.

32   And what value was there in fighting wild beasts—those men of Ephesus—if it was only for what I gain in this life down here? If we will never live again after we die, then we might as well go and have ourselves a good time: let us eat, drink, and be merry. What's the difference? For tomorrow we die, and that ends everything!

33   Don't be fooled by those who say such things. If you listen to them you will start acting like them.

34   Get some sense and quit your sinning. For to your shame I say it, some of you are not even Christians at all and have never really known God.[3]

35   But someone may ask, "How will the dead be brought back to life again? What kind of bodies will they have?"

36   What a foolish question! You will find the answer in your own garden! When you put a seed into the ground it doesn't grow into a plant unless it "dies" first.

37   And when the green shoot comes up out of the seed, it is very different from the seed you first planted. For all you put into the ground is a dry little seed of wheat, or whatever it is you are planting,

38   Then God gives it a beautiful new body—just the kind He wants it to have; a different kind of plant grows from each kind of seed.

39   And just as there are different kinds of seeds and plants, so also there are different kinds of flesh. Humans, animals, fish, and birds are all different.

40   The angels[4] in heaven have bodies far different from ours, and the beauty and the glory of their bodies is different from the beauty and the glory of ours.

41   The sun has one kind of glory while the moon and stars

[3]Or, "there are some who know nothing of God."
[4]Literally, "there are celestial bodies." This may refer to the sun, moon, planets, and stars.

have another kind. And the stars differ from each other in their beauty and brightness.

42   In the same way, our earthly bodies which die and decay are different from the bodies we shall have when we come back to life again, for they will never die.

43   The bodies we have now embarrass us for they become sick and die; but they will be full of glory when we come back to life again. Yes, they are weak, dying bodies now, but when we live again they will be full of strength.

44   They are just human bodies at death, but when they come back to life they will be superhuman bodies. For just as there are natural, human bodies, there are also supernatural, spiritual bodies.

45   The Scriptures tell us that the first man, Adam, was given a natural, human body[5] but Christ[6] is more[7] than that, for He was life-giving Spirit.

46   First, then, we have these human bodies and later on God gives us spiritual, heavenly bodies.

47   Adam was made from the dust of the earth, but Christ came from heaven above.

48   Every human being has a body just like Adam's, made of dust, but all who become Christ's will have the same kind of body as His—a body from heaven.

49   Just as each of us now has a body like Adam's, so we shall some day have a body like Christ's.

50   I tell you this, my brothers: an earthly body made of flesh and blood cannot get into God's kingdom. These perishable bodies of ours are not the right kind to live forever.

51   But I am telling you this strange and wonderful secret: we shall not all die, but we shall all be given new bodies!

52   It will all happen in a moment, in the twinkling of an eye, when the last trumpet is blown. For there will be a trumpet blast from the sky[7] and all the Christians who have died will suddenly become alive, with new bodies that will never, never

---

[5]Literally, "was made a living soul."
[6]Literally, "the last Adam."
[7]Implied.

die; and then we who are still alive shall suddenly have new bodies too.

53   For our earthly bodies, the ones we have now that can die, must be transformed into heavenly bodies that cannot perish but will live forever.

54   When this happens, then at last this Scripture will come true—"Death is swallowed up in victory."

55, 56   O death, where then your victory? Where then your sting? For sin—the sting that causes death—will all be gone; and the law, which reveals our sins, will no longer be our judge.

57   How we thank God for all of this! It is He who makes us victorious through Jesus Christ our Lord!

58   So my dear brothers, since future victory is sure, be strong and steady, always abounding in the Lord's work, for you know that nothing you do for the Lord is ever wasted as it would be if there were no resurrection.

CHAPTER 16

NOW here are the directions about the money you are collecting to send to the Christians in Jerusalem;[1] (and, by the way, these are the same directions I gave to the churches in Galatia).

2   Every Sunday each of you should put aside something from what you have earned during the week, and use it for this offering. The amount depends on how much the Lord has helped you earn. Don't wait until I get there and then try to collect it all at once.

3   When I come I will send your loving gift with a letter to Jerusalem, to be taken there by trustworthy messengers you yourselves will choose.

4   And if it seems wise for me to go along too, then we can travel together.

5   I am coming to visit you after I have been to Macedonia first, but I will be staying there only for a little while.

[1] Implied.

6 It could be that I will stay longer with you, perhaps all winter, and then you can send me on to my next destination.

7 This time I don't want to make just a passing visit and then go right on; I want to come and stay awhile, if the Lord will let me.

8 I will be staying here at Ephesus until the holiday of Pentecost,

9 For there is a wide open door for me to preach and teach here. So much is happening, but there are many enemies.

10 If Timothy comes make him feel at home, for he is doing the Lord's work just as I am.

11 Don't let anyone despise or ignore him [because he is young²], but send him back to me happy with his time among you; I am looking forward to seeing him soon, along with the others who are returning.

12 I begged Apollos to visit you along with the others, but he thought that it was not at all God's will for him to go now; he will be seeing you later on when he has the opportunity.

13 Keep your eyes open for spiritual danger; stand true to the Lord; act like men; be strong;

14 And whatever you do, do it with kindness and love.

15 Do you remember Stephanas and his family? They were the first to become Christians in Greece and they are spending their lives helping and serving Christians everywhere.

16 Please follow their instructions and do everything you can to help them as well as all others like them who work hard at your side with such real devotion.

17 I am so glad that Stephanas, Fortunatus, and Achaicus have arrived here for a visit. They have been making up for the help you aren't here to give me.

18 They have cheered me greatly and have been a wonderful encouragement to me, as I am sure they were to you, too. I hope you properly appreciate the work of such men as these.

19 The churches here in Asia send you their loving greetings. Aquila and Priscilla send you their love and so do all the others who meet in their home for their church service.

---

²Implied in I Timothy 4:12.

20   All the friends here have asked me to say "hello" to you for them. And give each other a loving handshake when you meet.

21   I will write these final words of this letter with my own hand:

22   If anyone does not love the Lord, that person is cursed. Lord Jesus, come!

23   May the love and favor of the Lord Jesus Christ rest upon you.

24   My love to all of you, for we all belong to Christ Jesus.

Sincerely,

Paul

II CORINTHIANS

CHAPTER 1

DEAR Friends,
This letter is from me, Paul, appointed by God to be Jesus Christ's messenger; and from our dear brother Timothy. We are writing to all of you Christians there in Corinth and throughout Greece.[1]

2 May God our Father and the Lord Jesus Christ mightily bless each one of you, and give you peace.

3, 4 What a wonderful God we have—He is the Father of our Lord Jesus Christ, the source of every mercy, and the one who so wonderfully comforts and strengthens us in our hardships and trials. And why does He do this? So that when others are troubled, needing our sympathy and encouragement, we can pass on to them this same help and comfort God has given us.

5 You can be sure that the more we undergo sufferings for Christ, the more He will shower us with His comfort and encouragement.

6, 7 We are in deep trouble for bringing you God's comfort and salvation. But in our trouble God had comforted us—and this, too, to help you: to show you from our personal experience how God will tenderly comfort you when you undergo these same sufferings. He will give you the strength to endure.

8 I think you ought to know, dear brothers, about the hard time we went through in Asia. We were really crushed and overwhelmed, and feared we would never live through it.

9 We felt we were doomed to die and saw how powerless

---

[1]Or, "throughout Achaia."

we were to help ourselves; but that was good, for then we put everything into the hands of God, who alone could save us, for He can even raise the dead.

10 And He did help us, and saved us from a terrible death; yes, and we expect Him to do it again and again.

11 But you must help us too, by praying for us. For much thanks and praise will go to God from you who see His wonderful answers to your prayers for our safety!

12 We are so glad that we can say with utter honesty that in all our dealings we have been pure and sincere, quietly depending upon the Lord for His help, and not on our own skills. And that is even more true, if possible, about the way we have acted toward you.

13, 14 My letters have been straightforward and sincere; nothing is written between the lines! And even though you don't know me very well (I hope someday you will), I want you to try to accept me and be proud of me, as you already are to some extent; just as I shall be of you on that day when our Lord Jesus comes back again.

15, 16 It was because I was so sure of your understanding and trust that I planned to stop and see you on my way to Macedonia, as well as afterwards when I returned, so that I could be a double blessing to you and so that you could send me on my way to Judea.

17 Then why, you may be asking, did I change my plan? Hadn't I really made up my mind yet? Or am I like a man of the world who says "yes" when he really means "no"?

18 Never! As surely as God is true, I am not that sort of person. My "yes" means "yes."

19 Timothy and Silvanus and I have been telling you about Jesus Christ the Son of God. He isn't one to say "yes" when He means "no." He always does exactly what He says.

20 He carries out and fulfills all of God's promises, no matter how many of them there are; and we have told everyone how faithful He is, giving glory to His name.

21 It is this God who has made you and me into faithful Christians and commissioned us apostles to preach the Good News.

22 He has put His brand upon us—His mark of ownership—and given us His Holy Spirit in our hearts as guarantee that we belong to Him, and as the first installment of all that He is going to give us.

23 I call upon this God to witness against me if I am not telling the absolute truth: the reason I haven't come to visit you yet is that I don't want to sadden you with a severe rebuke.

24 When I come, although I can't do much to help your faith, for it is strong already, I want to be able to do something about your joy: I want to make you happy, not sad.

CHAPTER 2

NO," I said to myself, "I won't do it. I'll not make them unhappy with another painful visit."

2 For if I make you sad, who is going to make me happy? You are the ones to do it, and how can you if I cause you pain?

3 That is why I wrote as I did in my last letter, so that you will get things straightened out before I come.[1] Then, when I do come, I will not be made sad by the very ones who ought to give me greatest joy. I felt sure that your happiness was so bound up in mine that you would not be happy either, unless I came with joy.

4 Oh, how I hated to write that letter! It almost broke my heart and I tell you honestly that I cried over it. I didn't want to hurt you, but I had to show you how very much I loved you and cared about what was happening to you.

5, 6 Remember that the man I wrote about, who caused all the trouble, has not caused sorrow to me as much as to all the rest of you—though I certainly have my share in it too. I don't want to be harder on him than I should. He has been punished enough by your united disapproval.

7 Now it is time to forgive him and comfort him. Otherwise he may become so bitter and discouraged that he won't be able to recover.

---

[1]Implied.

436

8   Please show him now that you still do love him very much.

9   I wrote to you as I did so that I could find out how far you would go in obeying me.

10   When you forgive anyone, I do too. And whatever I have forgiven (to the extent that this affected me too) has been by Christ's authority, and for your good.

11   A further reason for forgiveness is to keep from being outsmarted by Satan; for we know what he is trying to do.

12   Well, when I got as far as the city of Troas, the Lord gave me tremendous opportunities to preach the Gospel.

13   But Titus, my dear brother, wasn't there to meet me and I couldn't rest, wondering where he was and what had happened to him. So I said good-bye and went right on to Macedonia to try to find him.

14   But thanks be to God! For through what Christ has done, He has triumphed over us so that now wherever we go He uses us to tell others about the Lord and to spread the Gospel like a sweet perfume.

15   As far as God is concerned there is a sweet, wholesome fragrance in our lives. It is the fragrance of Christ within us, an aroma to both the saved and the unsaved all around us.

16   To those who are not being saved, we seem a fearful smell of death and doom, while to those who know Christ we are a life-giving perfume. But who is adequate for such a task as this?

17   Only those who, like ourselves, are men of integrity, sent by God, speaking with Christ's power, with God's eye upon us. We are not like those hucksters—and there are many of them—whose idea in getting out the Gospel is to make a good living out of it.

CHAPTER 3

ARE we beginning to be like those false teachers of yours who must tell you all about themselves and bring long letters of recommendation with them? I think you hardly need someone's letter to tell you about us, do you? And we don't need a recommendation from you, either!

2   The only letter I need is you yourselves! By looking at the good change in your hearts, everyone can see that we have done a good work among you.

3   They can see that you are a letter from Christ, written by us. It is not a letter written with pen and ink, but by the Spirit of the living God; not one carved on stone, but in human hearts.

4   We dare to say these good things about ourselves only because of our great trust in God through Christ, that He will help us to be true to what we say,

5   And not because we think we can do anything of lasting value by ourselves. Our only power and success comes from God.

6   He is the one who has helped us tell others His new agreement to save them. We do not tell them that they must obey every law of God or die; but we tell them there is life for them from the Holy Spirit. The old way, trying to be saved by keeping the Ten Commandments, ends in death; in the new way, the Holy Spirit gives them life.

7   Yet that old system of law that led to death began with such glory that people could not bear to look at Moses' face. For as he gave them God's law to obey, his face shone out with the very glory of God—though the brightness was already fading away.

8   Shall we not expect far greater glory in these days when the Holy Spirit is giving life?

9   If the plan that leads to doom was glorious, much more glorious is the plan that makes men right with God.

10   In fact, that first glory as it shone from Moses' face is worth nothing at all in comparison with the overwhelming glory of the new agreement.

11   So if the old system that faded into nothing was full of heavenly glory, the glory of God's new plan for our salvation[1] is certainly far greater, for it is eternal.

12   Since we know that this new glory will never go away, we can preach with great boldness,

[1]Implied.

438

13 And not as Moses did, who put a veil over his face so that the Israeli could not see the glory fade away.

14 Not only Moses' face was veiled, but his people's minds and understanding were veiled and blinded too. Even now when the Scripture is read it seems as though Jewish hearts and minds are covered by a thick veil, because they cannot see and understand the real meaning of the Scriptures. For this veil of misunderstanding can be removed only by believing in Christ.

15 Yes, even today when they read Moses' writings their hearts are blind and they think that obeying the Ten Commandments is the way to be saved.

16 But whenever anyone turns to the Lord from his sins, then the veil is taken away.

17 The Lord is the Spirit who gives them life, and where He is there is freedom [from trying to be saved by keeping the laws of God[2]].

18 But we Christians have no veil over our faces; we can be mirrors that brightly reflect the glory of the Lord. And as the Spirit of the Lord works within us, we become more and more like Him.

CHAPTER 4

IT is God Himself, in His mercy, who has given us this wonderful work [of telling His Good News to others[1]], and so we never give up.

2 We do not try to trick people into believing—we are not interested in fooling anyone. We never try to get anyone to believe that the Bible teaches what it doesn't. All such shameful methods we forego. We stand in the presence of God as we speak and so we tell the truth, as all who know us will agree.

3 If the Good News we preach is hidden to anyone, it is hidden from the one who is on the road to eternal death.

4 Satan, who is the god of this evil world, has made him blind, unable to see the glorious light of the Gospel that is

[2]Implied.
[1]Implied.

shining upon him, or to understand the amazing message we preach about the glory of Christ, who is God.[2]

5 We don't go around preaching about ourselves, but about Christ Jesus as Lord. All we say of ourselves is that we are your slaves because of what Jesus has done for us.

6 For God, who said, "Let there be light in the darkness," has made us understand that it is the brightness of His glory that is seen in the face of Jesus Christ.

7 But this precious treasure—this light and power that now shine within us[3]—is held in a perishable container, that is, in our weak bodies. Everyone can see that the glorious power within must be from God and is not our own.

8 We are pressed on every side by troubles, but not crushed and broken. We are perplexed because we don't know why things happen as they do, but we don't give up and quit.

9 We are hunted down, but God never abandons us. We get knocked down, but we get up again and keep going.

10 These bodies of ours are constantly facing death just as Jesus did; so it is clear to all that it is only the living Christ within [who keeps us safe[3]].

11 Yes, we live under constant danger to our lives because we serve the Lord, but this gives us constant opportunities to show forth the power of Jesus Christ within our dying bodies.

12 Because of our preaching we face death, but it has resulted in eternal life for you.

13 We boldly say what we believe [trusting God to care for us[3]], just as the Psalm writer did when he said, "I believe and therefore I speak."

14 We know that the same God who brought the Lord Jesus back from death will also bring us back to life again with Jesus, and present us to Him along with you.

15 These sufferings of ours are for your benefit. And the more of you who are won to Christ, the more there are to thank Him for His great kindness, and the more the Lord is glorified.

16 That is why we never give up. Though our bodies are dying, our inner strength in the Lord is growing every day.

---

[2]Literally, "the image of God."
[3]Implied.

17 These troubles and sufferings of ours are, after all, quite small and won't last very long. Yet this short time of distress will result in God's richest blessing upon us forever and ever!

18 So we do not look at what we can see right now, the troubles all around us, but we look forward to the joys in heaven which we have not yet seen. The troubles will soon be over, but the joys to come will last forever.

CHAPTER 5

FOR we know that when this tent we live in now is taken down—when we die and leave these bodies—we will have wonderful new bodies in heaven, homes that will be ours forevermore, made for us by God Himself, and not by human hands.

2 How weary we grow of our present bodies. That is why we look forward eagerly to the day when we shall have heavenly bodies which we shall put on like new clothes.

3 For we shall not be merely spirits without bodies.

4 These earthly bodies make us groan and sigh, but we wouldn't like to think of dying and having no bodies at all. We want to slip into our new bodies so that these dying bodies will, as it were, be swallowed up by everlasting life.

5 This is what God has prepared for us and, as a guarantee, He has given us His Holy Spirit.

6 Now we look forward with confidence to our heavenly bodies, realizing that every moment we spend in these earthly bodies is time spent away from our eternal home in heaven with Jesus.

7 We know these things are true by believing, not by seeing.

8 And we are not afraid, but are quite content to die, for then we will be at home with the Lord.

9 So our aim is to please Him always in everything we do, whether we are here in this body or away from this body and with Him in heaven.

10 For we must all stand before Christ to be judged and

have our lives laid bare—before Him. Each of us will receive whatever he deserves for the good or bad things he has done in his earthly body.

11 It is because of this solemn fear of the Lord, which is ever present in our minds, that we work so hard to win others. God knows our hearts, that they are pure in this matter, and I hope that, deep within, you really know it too.

12 Are we trying to pat ourselves on the back again? No, I am giving you some good ammunition! You can use this on those preachers of yours who brag about how well they look and preach, but don't have true and honest hearts. You can boast about us that we, at least, are well intentioned and honest.

13, 14 Are we insane [to say such things about ourselves[1]]? If so, it is to bring glory to God. And if we are in our right minds, it is for your benefit. Whatever we do, it is certainly not for our own profit, but because Christ's love controls us now. Since we believe that Christ died for all of us, we should also believe that we have died to the old life we used to live.

15 He died for all so that all who live—having received eternal life from Him—might live no longer for themselves, to please themselves, but to spend their lives pleasing Christ who died and rose again for them.

16 So stop evaluating Christians by what the world thinks about them or by what they seem to be like on the outside. Once I mistakenly thought of Christ that way, merely as a human being like myself. How differently I feel now!

17 When someone becomes a Christian he becomes a brand new person inside. He is not the same any more. A new life has begun!

18 All these new things are from God who brought us back to Himself through what Christ Jesus did. And God has given us the privilege of urging everyone to come into His favor and be reconciled to Him.

19 For God was in Christ, restoring the world to Himself, no longer counting men's sins against them but blotting them

---

[1]Implied.

442

out. This is the wonderful message He has given us to tell others.

20   We are Christ's ambassadors. God is using us to speak to you: we beg you, as though Christ Himself were here pleading with you, receive the love He offers you—be reconciled to God.

21   For God took the sinless Christ and poured into Him our sins. Then, in exchange, He poured God's goodness into us![2]

CHAPTER 6

A S God's partners we beg you not to toss aside this marvelous message of God's great kindness.

2   For God says, "Your cry came to me at a favorable time, when the doors of welcome were wide open. I helped you on a day when salvation was being offered." Right now God is ready to welcome you. Today He is ready to save you.

3   We try to live in such a way that no one will ever be offended or kept back from finding the Lord by the way we act, so that no one can find fault with us and blame it on the Lord.

4   In fact, in everything we do we try to show that we are true ministers of God. We patiently endure suffering and hardship and trouble of every kind.

5   We have been beaten, put in jail, faced angry mobs, worked to exhaustion, stayed awake through sleepless nights of watching, and gone without food.

6   We have proved ourselves to be what we claim by our wholesome lives and by our understanding of the Gospel and by our patience. We have been kind and truly loving and filled with the Holy Spirit.

7   We have been truthful, with God's power helping us in all we do. All of the godly man's arsenal—weapons of defense, and weapons of attack—have been ours.

8   We stand true to the Lord whether others honor us or

---

[2]Literally, "Him who knew no sin, He made sin on our behalf, that we might become the righteousness of God in Him."

despise us, whether they criticize us or commend us. We are honest, but they call us liars.

9 The world ignores us, but we are known to God; we live close to death, but here we are, still very much alive. We have been injured but kept from death.

10 Our hearts ache, but at the same time we have the joy of the Lord. We are poor, but we give rich spiritual gifts to others. We own nothing, and yet we enjoy everything.

11 Oh, my dear Corinthian friends! I have told you all my feelings; I love you with all my heart.

12 Any coldness still between us is not because of any lack of love on my part, but because your love is too small and does not reach out to me and draw me in.

13 I am talking to you now as if you truly were my very own children. Open your hearts to us! Return our love!

14 Don't be teamed with those who do not love the Lord, for what do the people of God have in common with the people of sin? How can light live with darkness?

15 And what harmony can there be between Christ and the devil? How can a Christian be a partner with one who doesn't believe?

16 And what union can there be between God's temple and idols? For you are God's temple, the home of the living God, and God has said of you, "I will live in them and walk among them, and I will be their God and they shall be my people."

17 That is why the Lord has said, "Leave them; separate yourselves from them; don't touch their filthy things, and I will welcome you,

18 And be a Father to you, and you will be My sons and daughters."

CHAPTER 7

HAVING such great promises as these, dear friends, let us turn away from everything wrong, whether of body or spirit, and purify ourselves, living in the wholesome fear of God, giving ourselves to Him alone.

2   Please open your hearts to us again, for not one of you has suffered any wrong from us. Not one of you was led astray. We have cheated no one nor taken advantage of anyone.

3   I'm not saying this to scold or blame you, for, as I have said before, you are in my heart forever and I live and die with you.

4   I have the highest confidence in you, and my pride in you is great. You have greatly encouraged me; you have made me so happy in spite of all my suffering.

5   When we arrived in Macedonia there was no rest for us; outside, trouble was on every hand and all around us; within us, our hearts were full of dread and fear.

6   Then God who cheers those who are discouraged refreshed us by the arrival of Titus.

7   Not only was his presence a joy, but also the news that he brought of the wonderful time he had with you. When he told me how much you were looking forward to my visit, and how sorry you were about what had happened, and about your loyalty and warm love for me, well, I overflowed with joy!

8   I am no longer sorry that I sent that letter to you, though I was very sorry for a time, realizing how painful it would be to you. But it hurt you only for a little while.

9   Now I am glad I sent it, not because it hurt you, but because the pain turned you to God. It was a good kind of sorrow you felt, the kind of sorrow God wants His people to have, so that I need not come to you with harshness.

10   For God sometimes uses sorrow in our lives to help us turn away from sin and seek eternal life. We should never regret His sending it. But the sorrow of the man who is not a Christian is not the sorrow of true repentance and does not prevent eternal death.

11   Just see how much good this grief from the Lord did for you! You no longer shrugged your shoulders, but became earnest and sincere, and very anxious to get rid of the sin that I wrote you about. You became frightened about what had happened, and longed for me to come and help. You went right to work on the problem and cleared it up [punishing the man

who sinned[1]]. You have done everything you could to make it right.

12 I wrote as I did so the Lord could show how much you really do care for us. That was my purpose even more than to help the man[1] who sinned, or his father[1] to whom he did the wrong.

13 In addition to the encouragement you gave us by your love, we were made happier still by Titus' joy when you gave him such a fine welcome and set his mind at ease.

14 I told him how it would be—told him before he left me of my pride in you—and you didn't disappoint me. I have always told you the truth and now my boasting to Titus has also proved true!

15 He loves you more than ever when he remembers the way you listened to him so willingly and received him so anxiously and with such deep concern.

16 How happy this makes me, now that I am sure all is well between us again. Once again I can have perfect confidence in you.

CHAPTER 8

NOW I want to tell you what God in His grace has done for the churches in Macedonia.

2 Though they have been going through much trouble and hard times, they have mixed their wonderful joy with their deep poverty, and the result has been an overflow of giving to others.

3 They gave not only what they could afford, but far more; and I can testify that they did it because they wanted to, and not because of nagging on my part.

4 They begged us to take the money so they could share in the joy of helping the Christians in Jerusalem.

5 Best of all, they went beyond our highest hopes, for their first action was to dedicate themselves to the Lord and to us, for whatever directions God might give to them through us.

[1]Implied.

446

6 They were so enthusiastic about it that we have urged Titus, who encouraged your giving in the first place, to visit you and encourage you to complete your share in this ministry of giving.

7 You people there are leaders in so many ways—you have so much faith, so many good preachers, so much learning, so much enthusiasm, so much love for us. Now I want you to be leaders also in the spirit of cheerful giving.

8 I am not giving you an order; I am not saying you must do it, but others are eager for it. This is one way to prove that your love is real, that it goes beyond mere words.

9 You know how full of love and kindness our Lord Jesus was: though He was so very rich, yet to help you He became so very poor, so that by being poor He could make you rich.

10 I want to suggest that you finish what you started to do a year ago, for you were not only the first to propose this idea, but the first to begin doing something about it.

11 Having started the ball rolling so enthusiastically, you should carry this project through to completion just as gladly, giving whatever you can out of whatever you have. Let your enthusiastic idea at the start be equalled by your realistic action now.

12 If you are really eager to give, then it isn't important how much you have to give. God wants you to give what you have, not what you haven't.

13 Of course, I don't mean that those who receive your gifts should have an easy time of it at your expense,

14 But you should divide with them. Right now you have plenty and can help them; then at some other time they can share with you when you need it. In this way each will have as much as he needs.

15 Do you remember what the Scriptures say about this? "He that gathered much had nothing left over, and he that gathered little had enough." So you also should share with those in need.

16 I am thankful to God that He has given Titus the same real concern for you that I have.

17   He is glad to follow my suggestion that he visit you again—but I think he would have come anyway, for he is very eager to see you!

18   I am sending another well-known brother with him, who is highly praised as a preacher of the Good News in all the churches.

19   In fact, this man was elected by the churches to travel with me to take the gift to Jerusalem. This will glorify the Lord and show our eagerness to help each other.

20   By traveling together we will guard against any suspicion, for we are anxious that no one should find fault with the way we are handling this large gift.

21   God knows we are honest, but I want everyone else to know it too. That is why we have made this arrangement.

22   And I am sending you still another brother, whom we know from experience to be an earnest Christian. He is especially interested, as he looks forward to this trip, because I have told him all about your eagerness to help.

23   If anyone asks who Titus is, say that he is my partner, my helper in helping you, and you can also say that the other two brothers represent the assemblies here and are splendid examples of those who belong to the Lord.

24   Please show your love for me to these men and do for them all that I have publicly boasted you would.

CHAPTER 9

I REALIZE that I really don't even need to mention this to you, about helping God's people.

2   For I know how eager you are to do it, and I have boasted to the friends in Macedonia that you were ready to send an offering a year ago. In fact, it was this enthusiasm of yours that stirred up many of them to begin helping.

3   But I am sending these men just to be sure that you really are ready, as I told them you would be, with your money all collected; I don't want it to turn out that this time I was wrong in my boasting about you.

4   I would be very much ashamed—and so would you—if some of these Macedonian people come with me, only to find that you still aren't ready after all I have told them!

5   So I have asked these other brethren to arrive ahead of me to see that the gift you promised is on hand and waiting. I want it to be a real gift and not look as if it were being given under pressure.

6   But remember this—if you give little, you will get little. A farmer who plants just a few seeds will get only a small crop, but if he plants much, he will reap much.

7   Every one must make up his own mind as to how much he should give. Don't force anyone to give more than he really wants to, for cheerful givers are the ones God prizes.

8   God is able to make it up to you by giving you everything you need and more, so that there will not only be enough for your own needs, but plenty left over to give joyfully to others.

9   It is as the Scriptures say: "The godly man gives generously to the poor. His good deeds will be an honor to him forever."

10   For God, who gives seed to the farmer to plant, and later on, good crops to harvest and eat, will give you more and more seed to plant and will make it grow so that you can give away more and more fruit from your harvest.

11   Yes, God will give you much so that you can give away much, and when we take your gifts to those who need them they will break out into thanksgiving and praise to God for your help.

12   So, two good things happen as a result of your gifts—those in need are helped, and they overflow with thanks to God.

13   Those you help will be glad not only because of your generous gifts to themselves and to others, but they will praise God for this proof that your deeds are as good as your doctrine.

14   And they will pray for you with deep fervor and feeling because of the wonderful grace of God shown through you.

15   Thank God for His Son—His Gift too wonderful for words.

449

CHAPTER 10

I PLEAD with you—yes, I, Paul—and I plead gently, as Christ Himself would do. Yet some of you are saying, "Paul's letters are bold enough when he is far away, but when he gets here he will be afraid to raise his voice!"

2   I hope I won't need to show you when I come how harsh and rough I can be. I don't want to carry out my present plans against some of you who seem to think my deeds and words are merely those of an ordinary man.

3   It is true that I am an ordinary, weak human being, but I don't use human plans and methods to win my battles.

4   I use God's mighty weapons, not those made by men, to knock down the devil's strongholds.

5   These weapons can break down every proud argument against God and every wall that can be built to keep men from finding Him. With these weapons I can capture rebels and bring them back to God, and change them into men whose hearts' desire is obedience to Christ.

6   I will use these weapons against every rebel who remains after I have first used them on you yourselves, and you surrender to Christ.

7   The trouble with you is that you look at me and I seem weak and powerless, but you don't look beneath the surface. Yet if anyone can claim the power and authority of Christ, I certainly can.

8   I may seem to be boasting more than I should about my authority over you—authority to help you, not to hurt you—but I shall make good every claim.

9   I say this so that you will not think I am just blustering when I scold you in my letters.

10   "Don't bother about his letters," some say. "He sounds big, but it's all noise. When he gets here you will see that there is nothing great about him, and you have never heard a worse preacher!"

11   This time my personal presence is going to be just as rough on you as my letters are!

450

12   Oh, don't worry, I wouldn't dare say that I am as wonderful as these other men who tell you how good they are! Their trouble is that they are only comparing themselves with each other, and measuring themselves against their own little ideas. What stupidity!

13   But we will not boast of authority we do not have. Our goal is to measure up to God's plan for us, and this plan includes our working there with you.

14   We are not going too far when we claim authority over you, for we were the first to come to you with the Good News concerning Christ.

15   It is not as though we were trying to claim credit for the work someone else has done among you. Instead, we hope that your faith will grow and that, still within the limits set for us, our work among you will be greatly enlarged.

16   After that, we will be able to preach the Good News to other cities that are far beyond you, where no one else is working; then there will be no question about being in someone else's field.

17   As the Scriptures say, "If anyone is going to boast, let him boast about what the Lord has done and not about himself."

18   When someone boasts about himself and how well he has done, it doesn't count for much. But when the Lord commends him, that's different!

CHAPTER 11

I HOPE you will be patient with me as I keep on talking like a fool. Do bear with me and let me say what is on my heart.

2   I am anxious for you with the deep concern of God Himself—anxious that your love should be for Christ alone, just as a pure maiden saves her love for one man only, for the one who will be her husband.

3   But I am frightened, fearing that in some way you will be

451

led away from your pure and simple devotion to our Lord, just as Eve was deceived by Satan in the Garden of Eden.

4   You seem so gullible: you believe whatever anyone tells you even if he is preaching about another Jesus than the one we preach, or a different spirit than the Holy Spirit you received, or shows you a different way to be saved. You swallow it all.

5   Yet I don't feel that these marvelous "messengers from God," as they call themselves, are any better than I am.

6   If I am a poor speaker, at least I know what I am talking about, as I think you realize by now, for we have proved it again and again.

7   Did I do wrong and cheapen myself and make you look down on me because I preached God's Good News to you without charging you anything?

8, 9   Instead I "robbed" other churches by taking what they sent me, and using it up while I was with you, so that I could serve you without cost. And when that was gone[1] and I was getting hungry I still didn't ask you for anything, for the Christians from Macedonia brought me another gift. I have never yet asked you for one cent, and I never will.

10   I promise this with every ounce of truth I possess—that I will tell everyone in Greece about it!

11   Why? Because I don't love you? God knows I do.

12   But I will do it to cut out the ground from under the feet of those who boast that they are doing God's work in just the same way we are.

13   God never sent those men at all; they are "phonies" who have fooled you into thinking they are Christ's apostles.

14   Yet I am not surprised! Satan can change himself into an angel of light,

15   So is it no wonder his servants can do it too, and seem like godly ministers. In the end they will get every bit of punishment their wicked deeds deserve.

16   Again I plead, don't think that I have lost my wits to talk like this; but even if you do, listen to me anyway—a witless man, a fool—while I also boast a little as they do.

[1]Implied.

452

17   Such bragging isn't something the Lord commanded me to do, for I am acting like a brainless fool.

18   Yet those other men keep telling you how wonderful they are, so here I go:

19, 20   (You think you are so wise—yet you listen gladly to those fools; you don't mind at all when they make you their slaves and take everything you have, and take advantage of you, and put on airs, and slap you in the face.

21   I'm ashamed to say that I'm not strong and daring like that! But whatever they can boast about—I'm talking like a fool again—I can boast about it, too.)

22   They brag that they are Hebrews, do they? Well, so am I. And they say that they are Israelites, God's chosen people? So am I. And they are descendants of Abraham? Well, I am too.

23   They say they serve Christ? But I have served Him far more! (Have I gone mad to boast like this?) I have worked harder, been put in jail oftener, been whipped times without number, and faced death again and again and again.

24   Five different times the Jews gave me their terrible thirty-nine lashes.

25   Three times I was beaten with rods. Once I was stoned. Three times I was shipwrecked. Once I was in the open sea all night and the whole next day.

26   I have traveled many weary miles and have been often in great danger from flooded rivers, and from robbers, and from my own people, the Jews, as well as from the hands of the Gentiles. I have faced grave dangers from mobs in the cities and from death in the deserts and in the stormy seas and from men who claim to be brothers in Christ but are not.

27   I have lived with weariness and pain and sleepless nights. Often I have been hungry and thirsty and have gone without food; often I have shivered with cold, without enough clothing to keep me warm.

28   Then, besides all this, I have the constant worry of how the churches are getting along:

29   Who makes a mistake and I do not feel his sadness? Who falls without my longing to help him? Who is spiritually

hurt without my fury rising against the one who hurt him?

30   But if I must brag, I would rather brag about the things that show how weak I am.

31   God, the Father of our Lord Jesus Christ, who is to be praised forever and ever, knows I tell the truth.

32   For instance, in Damascus the governor under King Aretas kept guards at the city gates to catch me;

33   But I was let down by rope and basket from a hole in the city wall, and so I got away! [What popularity!²]

CHAPTER 12

THIS boasting is all so foolish, but let me go on. Let me tell about the visions I've had, and revelations from the Lord.

2, 3   Fourteen years ago I¹ was taken up to heaven² for a visit. Don't ask me whether my body was there or just my spirit, for I don't know; only God can answer that. But anyway, there I was in paradise,

4   And heard things so astounding that they are beyond a man's power to describe or put in words (and anyway I am not allowed to tell them to others).

5   That experience is something worth bragging about, but I am not going to do it. I am going to boast only about how weak I am and how great God is to use such weakness for His glory.

6   I have plenty to boast about and would be no fool in doing it, but I don't want anyone to think more highly of me than he should from what he can actually see in my life and my message.

7   I will say this: because these experiences I had were so tremendous, God was afraid I might be puffed up by them; so I was given a sickness which has been a thorn in my flesh, a messenger from Satan to hurt and bother me, and prick my pride.

---

² Implied.
¹ Literally, "A man in Christ."
² Literally, "the third heaven."

8 Three different times I begged God to make me well again.

9 Each time He said, "No. But I am with you; that is all you need. My power shows up best in weak people." Now I am glad to boast about how weak I am; I am glad to be a living demonstration of Christ's power, instead of showing off my own power and abilities.

10 Since I know it is all for Christ's good, I am quite happy about "the thorn," and about insults and hardships, persecutions and difficulties; for when I am weak, then I am strong—the less I have, the more I depend on Him.

11 You have made me act like a fool—boasting like this—for you people ought to be writing about me and not making me write about myself. There isn't a single thing these other marvelous fellows have that I don't have too, even though I am really worth nothing at all.

12 When I was there I certainly gave you every proof that I was truly an apostle, sent to you by God Himself: for I patiently did many wonders and signs and mighty works among you.

13 The only thing I didn't do for you, that I do everywhere else in all other churches, was to become a burden to you—I didn't ask you to give me food to eat and a place to stay. Please forgive me for this wrong!

14 Now I am coming to you again, the third time; and it is still not going to cost you anything, for I don't want your money. I want *you!* And anyway, you are my children, and little children don't pay for their father's and mother's food—it's the other way around; parents supply food for their children.

15 I am glad to give you myself and all I have for your spiritual good, even though it seems that the more I love you, the less you love me.

16 Some of you are saying, "It's true that his visits didn't seem to cost us anything, but he is a sneaky fellow, that Paul, and he fooled us. As sure as anything he must have made money from us some way."

17 But how? Did any of the men I sent to you take advantage of you?

18   When I urged Titus to visit you, and sent our other brother with him, did they make any profit? No, of course not. For we have the same Holy Spirit, and walk in each other's steps, doing things the same way.

19   I suppose you think I am saying all this to get back into your good graces. That isn't it at all. I tell you, with God listening as I say it, that I have said this to help *you*, dear friends—to build you up spiritually and not to help myself.[3]

20   For I am afraid that when I come to visit you I won't like what I find, and then you won't like the way I will have to act. I am afraid that I will find you quarreling, and envying each other, and being angry with each other, and acting big, and saying wicked things about each other and whispering behind each other's backs, filled with conceit and disunity.

21   Yes, I am afraid that when I come God will humble me before you and I will be sad and mourn because many of you who have sinned became sinners and don't even care about the wicked, impure things you have done: your lust and immorality, and the taking of other men's wives.

CHAPTER 13

THIS is the third time I am coming to visit you. The Scriptures tell us that if two or three have seen a wrong, it must be punished. [Well, this is my third warning, as I come now for this visit.[1]]

2   I have already warned those who had been sinning when I was there last; now I warn them again, and all others, just as I did then, that this time I come ready to punish severely and I will not spare them.

3   I will give you all the proof you want that Christ speaks through me. Christ is not weak in His dealings with you, but is a mighty power within you.

4   His weak, human body died on the cross, but now He lives by the mighty power of God. We, too, are weak in our

[3]Implied.
[1]Implied.

bodies, as He was, but now we live and are strong, as He is, and have all of God's power to use in dealing with you.

5 Check up on yourselves. Are you really Christians? Do you pass the test? Do you feel Christ's presence and power more and more within you? Or are you just pretending to be Christians when actually you aren't at all?

6 I hope you can agree that I have stood that test and truly belong to the Lord.

7 I pray that you will live good lives, not because that will be a feather in our caps[2], proving that what we teach is right; no, for we want you to do right even if we ourselves are despised.

8 Our responsibility is to encourage the right at all times, not to hope for evil.[3]

9 We are glad to be weak and despised if you are really strong. Our greatest wish and prayer is that you will become mature Christians.

10 I am writing this to you now in the hope that I won't need to scold and punish when I come; for I want to use the Lord's authority which He has given me, not to punish you but to make you strong.

11 I close my letter with these last words:

Be happy.

Grow in Christ.

Pay attention to what I have said.

Live in harmony and peace.

And may the God of love and peace be with you.

12 Greet each other warmly in the Lord.

13 All the Christians here send you their best regards.

14 May the grace of our Lord Jesus Christ be with you all. May God's love and the Holy Spirit's friendship be yours.

Paul

---

[2]Literally, "not that we may appear approved."
[3]Literally, "For we can do nothing against the truth, but for the truth."

UP, UP AND

Cheerleaders in a practice session leap in exuberance and precision. Humans too seldom feel what these girls express—the freedom and the joy of life. More often, we have soiled consciences that fear the future, fear God, fear others. Paul, in

AWAY!!!!

this book, tells of a new freedom we have—a freedom which opens the way to a life of such sweeping fullness that anything compared to it is flat
and tasteless. How can this be? Read on . . . .

GALATIANS

CHAPTER 1

FROM: Paul the missionary and all the other Christians here.

To: The churches of Galatia.[1]

I was not called to be a missionary by any group or agency. My call is from Jesus Christ Himself, and from God the Father who raised Him from the dead.

3 May peace and blessing be yours from God the Father and from the Lord Jesus Christ.

4 He died for our sins just as God our Father planned, and rescued us from this evil world in which we live.

5 All glory to God through all the ages of eternity. Amen.

6 I am amazed that you are turning away so soon from God who, in His love and mercy, invited you to share the eternal life He gives through Christ; you are already following a different "way to heaven," which really doesn't go to heaven at all.

7 For there is no other way than the one we showed you; you are being fooled by those who twist and change the truth concerning Christ.

8 Let God's curses fall on anyone, including myself, who preaches any other way to be saved than the one we told you about; yes, if an angel comes from heaven and preaches any other message, let him be forever cursed.

9 I will say it again: if anyone preaches any other Gospel than the one you welcomed, let God's curse fall upon him.

[1]Galatia was a city in what is now called Turkey.

10 You can see that I am not trying to please you by sweet talk and flattery; no, I am trying to please God. If I were still trying to please men I could not be Christ's servant.

11 Dear friends, I solemnly swear that the way to heaven which I preach is not based on some mere human whim or dream.

12 For my message comes from no less a person than Jesus Christ Himself, who told me what to say. No one else has taught me.

13 You know what I was like when I followed the Jewish religion—how I went after the Christians mercilessly, hunting them down and doing my best to get rid of them all.

14 I was one of the most religious Jews of my own age in the whole country, and tried as hard as I possibly could to follow all the old, traditional rules of my religion.

15 But then something happened! For even before I was born God had chosen me to be His, and called me—what kindness and grace—

16 To reveal His Son within me so that I could go to the Gentiles and show them the Good News about Jesus. When all this happened to me I didn't go at once and talk it over with anyone else;

17 I didn't go up to Jerusalem to consult with those who were apostles before I was. No, I went away into the deserts of Arabia, and then came back to the city of Damascus.

18 It was not until three years later that I finally went to Jerusalem for a visit with Peter, and stayed there with him for fifteen days.

19 And the only other apostle I met at that time was James, our Lord's brother.

20 (Listen to what I am saying, for I am telling you this in the very presence of God. This is exactly what happened—I am not lying to you.)

21 Then after this visit I went to Syria and Cilicia.

22 And still the Christians in Judea didn't even know what I looked like.

23 All they knew was what people were saying, that "our

459

former enemy is now preaching the very faith he tried to wreck."

24   And they gave glory to God because of me.

CHAPTER 2

THEN fourteen years later I went back to Jerusalem again, this time with Barnabas; and Titus came along too.

2   I went there with definite orders from God to confer with the brothers there about the message I was preaching to the Gentiles. I talked privately to the leaders of the church so that they would all understand just what I had been teaching and, I hoped, agree that it was right.

3   And they did agree; they did not even demand that Titus, my companion, should be circumcised, though he was a Gentile.

4   Even that question wouldn't have come up except for some so-called "Christians" there—false ones, really—who came to spy on us and see what freedom we enjoyed in Christ Jesus, as to whether we obeyed the Jewish laws or not. They tried to get us all tied up in their rules, like slaves in chains.

5   But we did not listen to them for a single moment, for we did not want to confuse you into thinking that salvation can be earned by being circumcised and by obeying Jewish laws.

6   And the great leaders of the church who were there had nothing to add to what I was preaching. (By the way, their being great leaders made no difference to me, for all are the same to God.)

7, 8, 9   In fact, when Peter, James, and John, who were known as the pillars of the church, saw how greatly God had used me in winning the Gentiles, just as Peter had been blessed so greatly in his preaching to the Jews—for the same God gave us each our special gifts—they shook hands with Barnabas and me and encouraged us to keep right on with our preaching to the Gentiles while they continued their work with the Jews.

10   The only thing they did suggest was that we must always remember to help the poor, and I, too, was eager for that.

11   But when Peter came to Antioch I had to oppose him publicly, speaking strongly against what he was doing for it was very wrong.

12   For when he first arrived he ate with the Gentile Christians [who don't bother with circumcision and the many other Jewish laws[1]]. But afterwards when some Jewish friends of James came, he wouldn't eat with the Gentiles anymore because he was afraid of what these Jewish legalists, who insisted that circumcision was necessary for salvation, would say;

13   And then all the other Jewish Christians and even Barnabas became hypocrites too, following Peter's example, though they certainly knew better.

14   When I saw what was happening and that they weren't being honest about what they really believed, and weren't following the truth of the Gospel, I said to Peter in front of all the others, "Though you are a Jew by birth, you have long since discarded the Jewish laws; so why, all of a sudden, are you trying to make these Gentiles obey them?

15   You and I are Jews by birth, not mere Gentile sinners,

16   And yet we Jewish Christians know very well that we cannot become right with God by obeying our Jewish laws, but only by faith in Jesus Christ to take away our sins. And so we, too, have trusted Jesus Christ, that we might be accepted by God because of faith—and not because we have obeyed the Jewish laws. For no one will ever be saved by obeying them."

17   But what if we trust Christ to save us and then find that we are wrong, and that we cannot be saved without being circumcised and obeying all the other Jewish laws? Wouldn't we need to say that faith in Christ had ruined us? God forbid that anyone should dare to think such things about our Lord.

18   Rather, we are sinners if we start rebuilding the old systems I have been destroying, of trying to be saved by keeping Jewish laws,

19   For it was through reading the Scripture that I came to

[1]Implied.

realize that I could never find God's favor by trying—and failing—to obey the laws. I came to realize that acceptance with God comes by believing in Christ.[2]

20 I have been crucified with Christ: and I myself no longer live, but Christ lives in me. And the real life I now have within this body is a result of my trusting in the Son of God, who loved me and gave Himself for me.

21 I am not one of those who treats Christ's death as meaningless. For if we could be saved by keeping Jewish laws, then there was no need for Christ to die.

CHAPTER 3

OH, foolish Galatians! What magician has hypnotized you and cast an evil spell upon you? For you used to see the meaning of Jesus Christ's death as clearly as though I had waved a placard before you with a picture on it of Christ dying on the cross.

2 Let me ask you this one question: Did you receive the Holy Spirit by trying to keep the Jewish laws? Of course not, for the Holy Spirit came upon you only after you heard about Christ and trusted Him to save you.

3 Then have you gone completely crazy? For if trying to obey the Jewish laws never gave you spiritual life in the first place, why do you think that trying to obey them now will make you stronger Christians?

4 You have suffered so much for the Gospel. Now are you going to just throw it all overboard? I can hardly believe it!

5 I ask you again, does God give you the power of the Holy Spirit and work miracles among you as a result of your trying to obey the Jewish laws? No, of course not. It is when you believe in Christ and fully trust Him.

6 Abraham had the same experience—God declared him fit for heaven only because he believed God's promises.

7 You can see from this that the real children of Abraham are all the men of faith who truly trust in God.

---

[2]Literally, "For I through the law died unto the law, that I might live unto God."

8, 9 What's more, the Scriptures looked forward to this time when God would save the Gentiles also, through their faith. God told Abraham about this long ago when He said, "I will bless those in every nation who trust in Me as you do." And so it is: all who trust in Christ share the same blessing Abraham received.

10 Yes, and those who depend on the Jewish laws to save them are under God's curse, for the Scriptures point out very clearly, "Cursed is everyone who at any time breaks a single one of these laws that are written in God's Book of the Law."

11 Consequently, it is clear that no one can ever win God's favor by trying to keep the Jewish laws, because God has said that the only way we can be right in His sight is by faith. As the prophet Habakkuk says it, "The man who finds life will find it through trusting God."

12 How different from this way of faith is the way of law which says that a man is saved by obeying every law of God, without one slip.

13 But Christ has bought us out from under the doom of that impossible system by taking the curse for our wrongdoing upon Himself. For it is written in the Scripture, "Anyone who is hanged on a tree is cursed" [as Jesus was hung upon a wooden cross[1]].

*   *   *   *   *

14 Now God can bless the Gentiles, too, with this same blessing He promised to Abraham; and all of us as Christians can have the promised Holy Spirit through this faith.

15 Dear brothers, even in everyday life a promise made by one man to another, if it is written down and signed, cannot be changed. He cannot decide afterward to do something else instead.

16 Now, God gave some promises to Abraham and his Child. And notice that it doesn't say the promises were to his *children,* as it would if all his sons—all the Jews—were being spoken of, but to his *Child*—and that, of course, means Christ.

17 Here's what I am trying to say: God's promise to save

---

[1]Implied.

through faith—and God wrote this promise down and signed it—could not be canceled or changed four hundred and thirty years later when God gave the Ten Commandments.

18　If *obeying those laws* could save us, then it is obvious that this would be a different way of gaining God's favor than Abraham's way, for he simply accepted God's promise.

19　Well then, why were the laws given? They were added after the promise was given, to show men how guilty they are of breaking God's laws. But this system of law was to last only until the coming of Christ, the Child to whom God's promise was made. (And there is this further difference. God gave His laws to angels to give to Moses, who then gave them to the people;

20　But when God gave His promise to Abraham, He did it by Himself alone, without angels or Moses as go-betweens.)

21, 22　Well then, are God's laws and God's promises against each other? Of course not! If we could be saved by His laws, then God would not have had to give us a different way to get out of the grip of sin—for the Scriptures insist we are all its prisoners. The only way out is through faith in Jesus Christ; the way of escape is open to all who believe Him.

23　Until Christ came we were guarded by the law, kept in protective custody, so to speak, until we could believe in the coming Savior.

24　Let me put it another way. The Jewish laws were our teacher and guide until Christ came to give us right standing with God through our faith.

25　But now that Christ has come, we don't need those laws any longer to guard us and lead us to Him.

26　For now we are all children of God through faith in Jesus Christ,

27　And we who have been baptized into union with Christ are enveloped by Him.

28　We are no longer Jews or Greeks or slaves or free men or even merely men or women, but we are all the same—we are Christians; we are one in Christ Jesus.

29　And now that we are Christ's we are the true

descendants of Abraham, and all of God's promises to him belong to us.

CHAPTER 4

BUT remember this, that if a father dies and leaves great wealth for his little son, that child is not much better off than a slave until he grows up, even though he actually owns everything his father had.

2 He has to do what his guardians and managers tell him to, until he reaches whatever age his father set.

3 And that is the way it was with us before Christ came. We were slaves to Jewish laws and rituals for we thought they could save us.

4 But when the right time came, the time God decided on, He sent His Son, born of a woman, born as a Jew,

5 To buy freedom for us who were slaves to the law so that He could adopt us as His very own sons.

6 And because we are His sons God has sent the Spirit of His Son into our hearts, so now we can rightly speak of God as our dear Father.

7 Now we are no longer slaves, but God's own sons. And since we are His sons, everything He has belongs to us, for that is the way God planned.

8 Before you Gentiles knew God you were slaves to so-called gods that did not even exist.

9 And now that you have found God (or I should say, now that God has found you) how can it be that you want to go back again and become slaves once more to another poor, weak, useless religion of trying to get to heaven by obeying God's laws?

10 You are trying to find favor with God by what you do or don't do on certain days or months or seasons or years.

11 I fear for you. I am afraid that all my hard work for you was worth nothing.

*   *   *   *   *

12 Dear brothers, please feel as I do about these things, for

I am as free from these chains as you used to be. You did not despise me then when I first preached to you,

13 Even though I was sick when I first brought you the Good News of Christ.

14 But even though my sickness was revolting to you, you didn't reject me and turn me away. No, you took me in and cared for me as though I were an angel from God, or even Jesus Christ Himself.

15 Where is that happy spirit that we felt together then? For in those days I know you would gladly have taken out your own eyes and given them to replace mine[1] if that would have helped me.

16 And now have I become your enemy because I tell you the truth?

17 Those false teachers who are so anxious to win your favor are not doing it for your good. What they are trying to do is to shut you off from me so that you will pay more attention to them.

18 It is a fine thing when people are nice to you with good motives and sincere hearts, especially if they aren't doing it just when I am with you!

19 Oh, my children, how you are hurting me. I am once again suffering for you the pains of a mother waiting for her child to be born—longing for the time when you will finally be filled with Christ.

20 How I wish I could be there with you right now and not have to reason with you like this, for at this distance I frankly don't know what to do.

21 Listen to me, you friends who think you have to obey the Jewish laws to be saved: Why don't you find out what those laws really mean?

22 For it is written that Abraham had two sons, one from his slave-wife and one from his freeborn wife.

23 There was nothing unusual about the birth of the slave-wife's baby. But the baby of the freeborn wife was born only after God had especially promised he would come.

---

[1] It is traditional to suppose that Paul was handicapped by a disease of the eyes.

24, 25 Now this true story is an illustration of God's two ways of helping people. One way was by giving them His laws to obey. He did this on Mount Sinai, when He gave the Ten Commandments to Moses. Mount Sinai, by the way, is called "Mount Hagar" by the Arabs—and in my illustration Abraham's slave-wife Hagar represents Jerusalem, the mother-city of the Jews, the center of that system of trying to please God by trying to obey the Commandments; and the Jews, who try to follow that system, are her slave children.

26 But our mother-city is the heavenly Jerusalem, and she is not a slave to Jewish laws.

27 That is what Isaiah meant when he prophesied, "Now you can rejoice, O childless woman; you can shout with joy though you never before had a child. For I am going to give you many children—more children than the slave-wife has."

28 You and I, dear brothers, are the children that God promised, just as Isaac was.

29 And so we who are born of the Holy Spirit are persecuted now by those who want us to keep the Jewish laws, just as Isaac the child of promise was persecuted by Ishmael the slave-wife's son.

30 But the Scriptures say that God told Abraham to send away the slave-wife and her son, for the slave-wife's son could not inherit Abraham's home and lands along with the free woman's son.

31 Dear brothers, we are not slave children, obligated to the Jewish laws, but children of the free woman, acceptable to God because of our faith.

CHAPTER 5

SO Christ has made us free. Now make sure that you stay free and don't get all tied up again in the chains of slavery to Jewish laws and ceremonies.

2 Listen to me, for this is serious: *if you are counting on circumcision and keeping the Jewish laws to make you right with God, then Christ cannot save you.*

3   I'll say it again. Anyone trying to find favor with God by being circumcised must always obey every other Jewish law or perish.

4   Christ is useless to you if you are counting on clearing your debt to God by keeping those laws; you are lost from God's grace.

5   But we by the help of the Holy Spirit are counting on Christ's death to clear away our sins and make us right with God.

6   And we to whom Christ has given eternal life don't need to worry about whether we have been circumcised or not, or whether we are obeying the Jewish ceremonies or not; for all we need is faith working through love.

7   You were getting along so well. Who has interfered with you to hold you back from following the truth?

8   It certainly isn't God who has done it, for He is the one who has called you to freedom in Christ.

9   But it takes only one wrong person among you to infect all the others.

10   I am trusting the Lord to bring you back to believing as I do about these things. God will deal with that person, whoever he is, who has been troubling and confusing you.

11   Some people even say that I myself am preaching that circumcision and Jewish laws are necessary to the plan of salvation. Well, if I preached that, I would be persecuted no more— for that message doesn't offend anyone. The fact that I am still being persecuted proves that I am still preaching salvation through faith in the cross of Christ alone.

12   I only wish these teachers who want you to cut yourselves by being circumcised would cut themselves off from you and leave you alone!

13   For, dear brothers, you have been given freedom: not freedom to do wrong, but freedom to love and serve each other.

14   For the whole Law can be summed up in this one command: "Love others as you love yourself."

15   But if instead of showing love among yourselves you

are always critical and catty, watch out! Beware of ruining each other.

16   I advise you to obey only the Holy Spirit's instructions. He will tell you where to go and what to do, and then you won't always be doing the wrong things your evil nature wants you to.

17   For we naturally love to do evil things that are just the opposite from the things that the Holy Spirit tells us to do; and the good things we want to do when the Spirit has His way with us are just the opposite of our natural desires. These two forces within us are constantly fighting each other to win control over us and our wishes are never free from their pressures.

18   When you are guided by the Holy Spirit you need no longer force yourself to obey Jewish laws.

19   But when you follow your own wrong inclinations your lives will produce these evil results: impure thoughts, eagerness for lustful pleasure,

20   Idolatry, spiritism (that is, encouraging the activity of demons), hatred and fighting, jealousy and anger, constant effort to get the best for yourself, complaints and criticisms, the feeling that everyone else is wrong except those in your own little group —and there will be wrong doctrine,

21   Envy, murder, drunkenness, wild parties, and all that sort of thing. Let me tell you again as I have before, that anyone living that sort of life will not inherit the kingdom of God.

22   But when the Holy Spirit controls our lives He will produce this kind of fruit in us: love, joy, peace, patience, kindness, goodness, faithfulness,

23   Gentleness and self-control; and here there is no conflict with Jewish laws.

24   Those who belong to Christ have nailed their natural evil desires to His cross and crucified them there.

25   If we are living now by the Holy Spirit's power, let us follow the Holy Spirit's leading in every part of our lives.

26   Then we won't need to look for honors and popularity, which lead to jealousy and hard feelings.

CHAPTER 6

DEAR brothers, if a Christian is overcome by some sin, you who are godly should gently and humbly help him back onto the right path, remembering that next time it might be one of you who is in the wrong.

2 Share each other's troubles and problems, and so obey our Lord's command.

3 If anyone thinks he is too great to stoop to this, he is fooling himself. He is really a nobody.

4 Let everyone be sure that he is doing his very best, for then he will have the personal satisfaction of work well done, and won't need to compare himself with someone else.

5 Each of us must bear some faults and burdens of his own. For none of us is perfect!

6 Those who are taught the Word of God should help their teachers by paying them.

7 Don't be misled; remember that you can't ignore God and get away with it: a man will always reap just the kind of crop he sows!

8 If he sows to please his own wrong desires, he will be planting seeds of evil and he will surely reap a harvest of spiritual decay and death; but if he plants the good things of the Spirit, he will reap the everlasting life which the Holy Spirit gives him.

9 And let us not get tired of doing what is right, for after a while we will reap a harvest of blessing if we don't get discouraged and give up.

10 That's why whenever we can we should always be kind to everyone, and especially to our Christian brothers.

11 I will write these closing words in my own handwriting. See how large I have to make the letters!

12 Those teachers of yours who are trying to convince you to be circumcised are doing it for just one reason: so that they can be popular and avoid the persecution they would get if they admitted that the cross of Christ alone can save.

13   And even those teachers who submit to circumcision don't try to keep the other Jewish laws; but they want you to be circumcised in order that they can boast that you are their disciples.

14   As for me, God forbid that I should boast about anything except the cross of our Lord Jesus Christ. Because of that cross my interest in all the attractive things of the world was killed long ago, and the world's interest in me is also long dead.

15   It doesn't make any difference now whether we have been circumcised or not; what counts is whether we really have been changed into new and different people.

16   May God's mercy and peace be upon all of you who live by this principle and upon those everywhere who are really God's own.

17   From now on please don't argue with me about these things, for I carry on my body the scars of the whippings and wounds from Jesus' enemies that mark me as His slave.

18   Dear brothers, may the grace of our Lord Jesus Christ be with you all.

Sincerely,
Paul

TWO GRIM

A South Vietnamese soldier, almost starved, pauses to stare at the Viet Cong prison which he survived for two years until liberated by U.S. paratroopers . . .

. . . two U.S. infantrymen stop during a major battle to assess the situation and wonder where the next action will erupt . . .

PAUSES...

In the horror of war, men have many moments to pause for reflection, to wonder . . . why all the cruelties, the starvation and tortures, the insane kill kill kill? In this Book of Ephesians, Paul talks about the basic hatred behind all of this in the world and goes on to describe the only cure and the only weapons which will really change planet earth.

EPHESIANS

CHAPTER 1

D EAR Christian friends at Ephesus, ever loyal to the Lord: This is Paul writing to you, chosen by God to be Jesus Christ's messenger.

2   May His blessings and peace be yours, sent to you from God our Father and Jesus Christ our Lord.

3   How we praise God, the Father of our Lord Jesus Christ, who has blessed us with every blessing in heaven because we belong to Christ.

4   Long ago, even before He made the world, God chose us to be His very own, through what Christ would do for us; He decided then to make us holy in His eyes, without a single fault—we who stand before Him covered with His love.

5   His unchanging plan has always been to adopt us into His own family by sending Jesus Christ to die for us. And He did this because He wanted to!

6   Now all praise to God for His wonderful kindness to us and His favor that He has poured out upon us, because we belong to His dearly loved Son.

7   So overflowing is His kindness towards us that He took away all our sins through the blood of His Son, by whom we are saved;

8   And He has showered down upon us the richness of His grace—for how well He understands us and knows what is best for us at all times.

9   God has told us His secret reason for sending Christ, a plan He decided on in mercy long ago;

10 And this was His purpose: that when the time is ripe He will gather us all together from wherever we are—in heaven or on earth—to be with Him in Christ, forever.

11 Moreover, because of what Christ has done we have become gifts to God that He delights in, for as part of God's sovereign plan we were chosen from the beginning to be His, and all things happen just as He decided long ago.

12 God's purpose in this was that we should praise God and give glory to Him for doing these mighty things for us, who were the first to trust in Christ.

13 And because of what Christ did, all you others too, who heard the Good News about how to be saved, and trusted Christ, were marked as belonging to Christ by the Holy Spirit, who long ago had been promised to all of us Christians.

14 His presence within us is God's guarantee that He really will give us all that He promised; and the Spirit's seal upon us means that God has already purchased us and that He guarantees to bring us to Himself. This is just one more reason for us to praise our glorious God.

15 That is why, ever since I heard of your strong faith in the Lord Jesus and of the love you have for Christians everywhere,

16, 17 I have never stopped thanking God for you. I pray for you constantly, asking God, the glorious Father of our Lord Jesus Christ, to give you wisdom to see clearly and really understand who Christ is and all that He has done for you.

18 I pray that your hearts will be flooded with light so that you can see something of the future He has called you to share. I want you to realize that God has been made rich because we who are Christ's have been given to Him!

19 I pray that you will begin to understand how incredibly great His power is to help those who believe Him. It is that same mighty power

20 That raised Christ from the dead and seated Him in the place of honor at God's right hand in heaven,

21 Far, far above any other king or ruler or dictator or

leader. Yes, His honor is far more glorious than that of anyone else either in this world or in the world to come.

22 And God has put all things under His feet and made Him the supreme Head of the church—

23 Which is His body, filled with Himself, the Author and Giver of everything everywhere.

CHAPTER 2

ONCE you were under God's curse, doomed forever for your sins.

2 You went along with the crowd and were just like all the others, full of sin, obeying Satan, the mighty prince of the power of the air, who is at work right now in the hearts of those who are against the Lord.

3 All of us used to be just as they are, our lives expressing the evil within us, doing every wicked thing that our passions or our evil thoughts might lead us into. We started out bad, being born with evil natures, and were under God's anger just like everyone else.

4 But God is so rich in mercy; He loved us so much

5 That even though we were spiritually dead and doomed by our sins, He gave us back our lives again[1] when He raised Christ from the dead—only by His undeserved favor have we ever been saved—

6 And lifted us up from the grave into glory along with Christ, where we sit with Him in the heavenly realms—all because of what Christ Jesus did. *put us on display*

7 And now God can always point to us as examples of how very, very rich His kindness is, as shown in all He has done for us through Jesus Christ.

8 Because of His kindness you have been saved through trusting Christ. And even trusting[2] is not of yourselves; it too is a gift from God.

---

[1] Literally, "He made us alive."
[2] Or, "Salvation is not of yourselves."

474

9   Salvation is not a reward for the good we have done, so none of us can take any credit for it.

10   It is God Himself who has made us what we are and given us new lives from Christ Jesus; and long ages ago He planned that we should spend these lives in helping others.

11   Never forget that once you were heathen, and that you were called godless and "unclean" by the Jews. (But their hearts, too, were still unclean, even though they were going through the ceremonies and rituals of the godly, for they circumcised themselves as a sign of godliness.)

12   Remember that in those days you were living utterly apart from Christ; you were enemies of God's children and He had promised you no help. You were lost, without God, without hope.

13   But now you belong to Christ Jesus, and though you once were far away from God, now you have been brought very near to Him because of what Jesus Christ has done for you with His blood.

14   For Christ Himself is our way of peace. He has made peace between us Jews and you Gentiles by making us all one family,³ breaking down the wall of contempt⁴ that used to separate us.

15   By His death He ended the angry resentment between us, caused by the Jewish laws which favored the Jews and excluded the Gentiles, for He died to annul that whole system of Jewish laws. Then He took the two groups that had been opposed to each other and made them parts of Himself; thus He fused us together to become one new person, and at last there was peace.

16   As parts of the same body, our anger against each other has disappeared, for both of us have been reconciled to God. And so the feud ended at last at the cross.

17   And He has brought this Good News of peace to you Gentiles who were very far away from Him, and to us Jews who were near.

18   Now all of us, whether Jews or Gentiles, may come to

³Literally, "by making us one."
⁴Implied.

God the Father with the Holy Spirit's help because of what Christ has done for us.

19   Now you are no longer strangers to God and foreigners to heaven, but you are members of God's very own family, citizens of God's country, and you belong in God's household with every other Christian.

20   What a foundation you stand on now: the apostles and the prophets; and the cornerstone of the building is Jesus Christ Himself!

21   We who believe are carefully joined together with Christ as parts of a beautiful, constantly growing temple for God.

22   And you also are joined with Him and with each other by the Spirit, and are part of this dwelling place of God.

CHAPTER 3

I PAUL, the servant of Christ, am here in jail because of you—for preaching that you Gentiles are a part of God's house.

2, 3   No doubt you already know that God has given me this special work of showing God's favor to you Gentiles, as I briefly mentioned before in one of my letters. God Himself showed me this secret plan of His, that the Gentiles, too, are included in His kindness.

4   I say this to explain to you how I know about these things.

5   In olden times God did not share this plan with His people, but now He has revealed it by the Holy Spirit to His apostles and prophets.

6   And this is the secret: that the Gentiles will have their full share with the Jews in all the riches inherited by God's sons; both are invited to belong to His church, and all of God's promises of mighty blessings through Christ apply to them both when they accept the Good News about Christ and what He has done for them.

476

7 God has given me the wonderful privilege of telling everyone about this plan of His; and He has given me His power and special ability to do it well.

8 Just think! Though I did nothing to deserve it, and though I am the most useless Christian there is, yet I was the one chosen for this special joy of telling the Gentiles the Glad News of the endless treasures available to them in Christ;

9 And to explain to everyone that God is the Savior of the Gentiles too, just as He who made all things had secretly planned from the very beginning.

10 And His reason? To show to all the powers of heaven how perfectly wise God is when they see all of His family—Jews and Gentiles—joined together in His church,

11 Just as He had always planned to do through Jesus Christ our Lord.

12 Now we can come fearlessly right into God's presence, assured of His glad welcome when we come with Christ and trust in Him.

13 So please don't lose heart at what they are doing to me here. It is for you I am suffering and you should feel honored and encouraged.

14, 15 When I think of the wisdom and scope of His plan I fall down on my knees and pray to the Father of all the great family of God—some of them already in heaven and some down here on earth—

16 That out of His glorious, unlimited resources He will give you the mighty inner strengthening of His Holy Spirit.

17 And I pray that Christ will be more and more at home in your hearts, living within you as you trust in Him. May your roots go down deep into the soil of God's marvelous love;

18, 19 And may you be able to feel and understand, as all God's children should, how long, how wide, how deep, and how high His love really is; and to experience this love for yourselves, though it is so great that you will never see the end of it or fully know or understand it. And so at last you will be filled up with God Himself.

20 Now glory be to God who by His mighty power at work

within us is able to do far more than we would ever dare to ask or even dream of—infinitely beyond our highest prayers, desires, thoughts, or hopes.

21   May He be given glory forever and ever through endless ages because of His master plan of salvation for the church through Jesus Christ.

CHAPTER 4

I BEG you—I, a prisoner here in jail for serving the Lord— to live and act in a way worthy of those who have been chosen for such wonderful blessings as these.

2   Be humble and gentle. Be patient with each other, making allowance for each other's faults because of your love.

3   Try always to be led along together by the Holy Spirit, and so be at peace with one another.

4   We are all parts of one body, we have the same Spirit, and we have all been called to the same glorious future.

5   For us there is only one Lord, one faith, one baptism,

6   And we all have the same God and Father who is over us all and in us all, and living through every part of us.

7   However, Christ has given each of us special abilities— whatever He wants us to have out of His rich storehouse of gifts.

8   The Psalmist tells about this, for he says that when Christ returned triumphantly to heaven after His resurrection and victory over Satan, He gave generous gifts to men.

9   Notice that it says He returned to heaven. This means that He had first come down from the heights of heaven, far down to the lowest parts of the earth.

10   The same one who came down is the one who went back up, that He might fill all things everywhere with Himself, from the very lowest to the very highest.[1]

11   Some of us have been given special ability as apostles; to others He has given the gift of being able to preach well;

---

[1]Literally, "that He might fill all things."

some have special ability in winning people to Christ, helping them to trust Him as their Savior; still others have a gift for caring for God's people as a shepherd does his sheep, leading and teaching them in the ways of God.

12 Why is it that He gives us these special abilities to do certain things best? It is that God's people will be equipped to do better work for Him, building up the church, the body of Christ, to a position of strength and maturity;

13 Until finally we all believe alike about our salvation and about our Savior, God's Son, and all become full-grown in the Lord—yes, to the point of being filled full with Christ.

14 Then we will no longer be like children, forever changing our minds about what we believe because someone has told us something different, or has cleverly lied to us and made the lie sound like the truth.

15, 16 Instead we will lovingly follow the truth at all times— speaking truly, dealing truly, living truly[2]—and so become more and more in every way like Christ who is the Head of His body, the church. Under His direction the whole body is fitted together perfectly, and each part in its own special way helps the other parts, so that the whole body is healthy and growing and full of love.

17, 18 Let me say this, then, speaking for the Lord: live no longer as the unsaved do, for they are blinded and confused. Their closed hearts are full of darkness; they are far away from the life of God because they have shut their minds against Him, and they cannot understand His ways.

19 They don't care anymore about right and wrong and have given themselves over to impure ways. They stop at nothing, being driven by their evil minds and reckless lusts.

20 But that isn't the way Christ taught you!

21 If you have really heard His voice and learned from Him the truths concerning Himself,

22 Then throw off your old evil nature—the old you that was a partner in your evil ways—rotten through and through, full of lust and sham.

---

[2]Amplified New Testament.

23   Now your attitudes and thoughts must all be constantly changing for the better.

24   Yes, you must be a new and different person, holy and good. Clothe yourself with this new nature.

25   Stop lying to each other; tell the truth, for we are parts of each other and when we lie to each other we are hurting ourselves.

26   If you are angry, don't sin by nursing your grudge. Don't let the sun go down with you still angry—get over it quickly;

27   For when you are angry you give a mighty foothold to the devil.

28   If anyone is stealing he must stop it and begin using those hands of his for honest work so he can give to others in need.

29   Don't use bad language. Say only what is good and helpful to those you are talking to, and what will give them a blessing.

30   Don't cause the Holy Spirit sorrow by the way you live. Remember, He is the one who marks you to be present[3] on that day when salvation from sin will be complete.

31   Stop being mean, bad-tempered and angry. Quarreling, harsh words, and dislike of others should have no place in your lives.

32   Instead, be kind to each other, tenderhearted, forgiving one another, just as God has forgiven you because you belong to Christ.

CHAPTER 5

FOLLOW God's example in everything you do just as a much loved child imitates his father.

2   Be full of love for others, following the example of Christ who loved you and gave Himself to God as a sacrifice to take

---

[3]Literally, "in whom you were sealed unto the day of redemption."

away your sins. And God was pleased, for Christ's love for you was like sweet perfume to Him.

3 Let there be no sex sin, impurity or greed among you. Let no one be able to accuse you of any such things.

4 Dirty stories, foul talk and coarse jokes—these are not for you. Instead, remind each other of God's goodness and be thankful.

5 You can be sure of this: the kingdom of Christ and of God will never belong to anyone who is impure or greedy, for a greedy person is really an idol worshiper—he loves and worships the good things of this life more than God.

6 Don't be fooled by those who try to excuse these sins, for the terrible wrath of God is upon all those who do them.

7 Don't even associate with such people.

8 For though once your heart was full of darkness, now it is full of light from the Lord, and your behavior should show it!

9 Because of this light within you, you should do only what is good and right and true.

10 Learn as you go along what pleases the Lord.[1]

11 Take no part in the worthless pleasures of evil and darkness, but instead, rebuke and expose them.

12 It would be shameful even to mention here those pleasures of darkness which the ungodly do.

13 But when you expose them, the light shines in upon their sin and shows it up, and when they see how wrong they really are, some of them may even become children of light!

14 That is why God says in the Scriptures, "Awake, O sleeper, and rise up from the dead; and Christ shall give you light."

15, 16 So be careful how you act; these are difficult days. Don't be fools; be wise: make the most of every opportunity you have for doing good.

17 Don't act thoughtlessly, but try to find out and do whatever the Lord wants you to.

18 Don't drink too much wine, for many evils lie along

---

[1]Or, "your lives should be an example."

that path; be filled instead with the Holy Spirit, and controlled by Him.

19   Talk with each other much about the Lord, quoting psalms and hymns and singing sacred songs, making music in your hearts to the Lord.

20   Always give thanks for everything to our God and Father in the name of our Lord Jesus Christ.

21   Honor Christ by submitting to each other.

22   You wives must submit to your husband's leadership in the same way you submit to the Lord.

23   For a husband is in charge of his wife in the same way Christ is in charge of His body the church. (He gave His very life to take care of it and be its Savior!)

24   So you wives must willingly obey your husbands in everything, just as the church obeys Christ.

25   And you husbands, show the same kind of love to your wives as Christ showed to the church when He died for her,

26   To make her holy and clean, washed by baptism[2] and God's Word;

27   So that He could give her to Himself as a glorious church without a single spot or wrinkle or any other blemish, being holy and without a single fault.

28   That is how husbands should treat their wives, loving them as parts of themselves. For since a man and his wife are now one, a man is really doing himself a favor and loving himself when he loves his wife!

29, 30   No one hates his own body but lovingly cares for it, just as Christ cares for His body the church, of which we are parts.

31   (That the husband and wife are one body is proved by the Scripture which says, "A man must leave his father and mother when he marries, so that he can be perfectly joined to his wife, and the two shall be one.")

32   I know this is hard to understand, but it is an illustration of the way we are parts of the body of Christ.

33   So again I say, a man must love his wife as a part of

---

[2]Literally, "having cleansed it by washing of water with the word."

himself; and the wife must see to it that she deeply respects her husband—obeying, praising and honoring him.

CHAPTER 6

CHILDREN, obey your parents; this is the right thing to do because God has placed them in authority over you.

2   Honor your father and mother. This is the first of God's Ten Commandments that ends with a promise.

3   And this is the promise: that if you honor your father and mother, yours will be a long life, full of blessing.

4   And now a word to you parents. Don't keep on scolding and nagging your children, making them angry and resentful. Rather, bring them up with the loving discipline the Lord Himself approves, with suggestions and godly advice.

5   Slaves, obey your masters; be eager to give them your very best. Serve them as you would Christ.

6, 7   Don't work hard only when your master is watching and then shirk when he isn't looking; work hard and with gladness all the time, as though working for Christ, doing the will of God with all your hearts.

8   Remember, the Lord will pay you for each good thing you do, whether you are slave or free.

9   And you slave owners must treat your slaves right, just as I have told them to treat you. Don't keep threatening them; remember, you yourselves are slaves to Christ; you have the same Master they do, and He has no favorites.

10   Last of all I want to remind you that your strength must come from the Lord's mighty power within you.

11   Put on all of God's armor so that you will be able to stand safe against all strategies and tricks of Satan.

12   For we are not fighting against people made of flesh and blood, but against persons without bodies—the evil rulers of the unseen world, those mighty satanic beings and great evil princes of darkness who rule this world; and against huge numbers of wicked spirits in the spirit world.

13 So use every piece of God's armor to resist the enemy whenever he attacks, and when it is all over, you will still be standing up.

14 But to do this, you will need the strong belt of truth and the breastplate of God's approval.

15 Wear shoes that are able to speed you on as you preach the Good News of peace with God.

16 In every battle you will need faith as your shield to stop the fiery arrows aimed at you by Satan.

17 And you will need the helmet of salvation and the sword of the Spirit—which is the Word of God.

18 Pray all the time. Ask God for anything in line with the Holy Spirit's wishes. Plead with Him, reminding Him of your needs, and keep praying earnestly for all Christians everywhere.

19 Pray for me, too, and ask God to give me the right words as I boldly tell others about the Lord, and as I explain to them that His salvation is for the Gentiles too.

20 I am in chains now for preaching this message from God. But pray that I will keep on speaking out boldly for Him even here in prison, as I should.

21 Tychicus, who is a much loved brother and faithful helper in the Lord's work, will tell you all about how I am getting along.

22 I am sending him to you for just this purpose, to let you know how we are and be encouraged by his report.

23 May God give peace to you, my Christian brothers, and love, with faith from God the Father and the Lord Jesus Christ.

24 May God's grace and blessing be upon all who sincerely love our Lord Jesus Christ.

Sincerely,
Paul

GRIT
AND STRAIN!!!

"I'm gonna win!" That thought is uppermost in the
mind of each of these teens competing for top honors

in the Sun Valley meet. After months and months of gruelling training, they give it all they've got to win that top prize. Yet even the exhilaration of winning it—even the flush of emotion, the *Wow!* that comes from getting the top trophy—can't be compared with what is talked about in the following letter. "*Nothing* can be compared to it," the writer says. And, as we enjoy the excitement of sports competition or anything else in which we can excel, we know deep down that these thrills of victory God allows us to enjoy are only small fragments of the deeper victories this letter communicates.

PHILIPPIANS

CHAPTER 1

FROM: Paul and Timothy, slaves of Jesus Christ.

To: The pastors and deacons and all the Christians in the city of Philippi.

2 May God bless you all. Yes, I pray that God our Father and the Lord Jesus Christ will give each of you His fullest blessings, and His peace in your hearts and your lives.

3 All my prayers for you are full of praise to God!

4 When I pray for you, my heart is full of joy,

5 Because of all your wonderful help in making known the Good News about Christ from the time you first heard it until now.

6 And I am sure that God who began the good work within you will keep right on helping you grow in His grace until His task within you is finally finished on that day when Jesus Christ returns.

7 How natural it is that I should feel as I do about you, for you have a very special place in my heart. We have shared together the blessings of God, both when I was in prison and when I was out, defending the truth and telling others about Christ.

8 Only God knows how deep is my love and longing for you—with the tenderness of Jesus Christ.

9 My prayer for you is that you will overflow more and more with love for others, and at the same time keep on growing in spiritual knowledge and insight,

10 For I want you always to see clearly the difference

between right and wrong, and to be inwardly clean, no one being able to criticize you from now until our Lord returns.

11 May you always be doing those good, kind things which show that you are a child of God, for this will bring much praise and glory to the Lord.

* * * * *

12 And I want you to know this, dear brothers: Everything that has happened to me here has been a great boost in getting out the Good News concerning Christ.

13 For everyone around here, including all the soldiers over at the barracks, knows that I am in chains simply because I am a Christian.

14 And because of my imprisonment many of the Christians here seem to have lost their fear of chains! Somehow my patience has encouraged them and they have become more and more bold in telling others about Christ.

15 Some, of course, are preaching the Good News because they are jealous of the way God has used me. They want reputations as fearless preachers! But others have purer motives,

16, 17 Preaching because they love me, for they know that the Lord has brought me here to use me to defend the Truth. And some preach to make me jealous, thinking that their success will add to my sorrows here in jail!

18 But whatever their motive for doing it, the fact remains that the Good News about Christ is being preached and I am glad.

19 I am going to keep on being glad, for I know that as you pray for me, and as the Holy Spirit helps me, this is all going to turn out for my good.

20 For I live in eager expectation and hope that I will never do anything that will cause me to be ashamed of myself but that I will always be ready to speak out boldly for Christ while I am going through all these trials here, just as I have in the past; and that I will always be an honor to Christ, whether I live or whether I must die.

* * * * *

21 For to me, living means opportunities for Christ, and dying—well, that's better yet!

22   But if living will give me more opportunities to win people to Christ, then I really don't know which is better, to live or die!

23   Sometimes I want to live and at other times I don't, for I long to go and be with Christ. How much happier for *me* than being here!

24   But the fact is that I can be of more help to *you* by staying!

25   Yes, I am still needed down here and so I feel certain I will be staying on earth a little longer, to help you grow and become happy in your faith;

26   My staying will make you glad and give you reason to glorify Christ Jesus for keeping me safe, when I return to visit you again.

*   *   *   *   *

27   But whatever happens to me, remember always to live as Christians should, so that, whether I ever see you again or not, I will keep on hearing good reports that you are standing side by side with one strong purpose—to tell the Good News

28   Fearlessly, no matter what your enemies may do. They will see this as a sign of their downfall, but for you it will be a clear sign from God that He is with you, and that He has given you eternal life with Him.

29   For to you has been given the privilege not only of trusting Him but also of suffering for Him.

30   We are in this fight together. You have seen me suffer for Him in the past; and I am still in the midst of a great and terrible struggle now, as you know so well.

CHAPTER 2

IS there any such thing as Christians cheering each other up? Do you love me enough to want to help me? Does it mean anything to you that we are brothers in the Lord, sharing the same Spirit? Are your hearts tender and sympathetic at all?

2   Then make me truly happy by loving each other and

agreeing wholeheartedly with each other, working together with one heart and mind and purpose.

3   Don't be selfish; don't live to make a good impression on others. Be humble, thinking of others as better than yourself.

4   Don't just think about your own affairs, but be interested in others, too, and in what they are doing.

5   Your attitude should be the kind that was shown us by Jesus Christ,

6   Who, though He was God, did not demand and cling to His rights as God,

7   But laid aside His mighty power and glory, taking the disguise of a slave and becoming like men.[1]

8   And He humbled Himself even further, going so far as actually to die a criminal's death on a cross.[2]

9   Yet it was because of this that God raised Him up to the heights of heaven and gave Him a name which is above every other name,

10   That at the name of Jesus every knee shall bow in heaven and on earth and under the earth,

11   And every tongue shall confess that Jesus Christ is Lord, to the glory of God the Father.

*   *   *   *   *

12   Dearest friends, when I was there with you, you were always so careful to follow my instructions. And now that I am away you must be even more careful to do the good things that result from being saved, obeying God with deep reverence, shrinking back from all that might displease Him.

13   For God is at work within you, helping you want to obey Him, and then helping you do what He wants.

14   In everything you do, stay away from complaining and arguing,

15   So that no one can speak a word of blame against you. You are to live clean, innocent lives as children of God in a dark world full of people who are crooked and stubborn. Shine out among them like beacon lights,

16   Holding out to them the Word of Life. Then when

[1] Literally, "was made in the likeness of men."
[2] Literally, "became obedient unto death, even the death of the cross."

Christ returns how glad I will be that my work among you was so worthwhile.

17 And if my lifeblood is, so to speak, to be poured out over your faith which I am offering up to God as a sacrifice— that is, if I am to die for you—even then I will be glad, and will share my joy with each of you.

18 For you should be happy about this, too, and rejoice with me for having this privilege of dying for you.

*   *   *   *   *

19 If the Lord is willing, I will send Timothy to see you soon. Then when he comes back he can cheer me up by telling me all about you and how you are getting along.

20 There is no one like Timothy for having a real interest in you;

21 Everyone else seems to be worrying about his own plans and not those of Jesus Christ.

22 But you know Timothy. He has been just like a son to me in helping me preach the Good News.

23 I hope to send him to you just as soon as I find out what is going to happen to me here.

24 And I am trusting the Lord that soon I myself may come to see you.

25 Meanwhile, I thought I ought to send Epaphroditus back to you. You sent him to help me in my need; well, he and I have been real brothers, working and battling side by side.

26 Now I am sending him home again, for he has been homesick for all of you and upset because you heard that he was ill.

27 And he surely was; in fact, he almost died. But God had mercy on him, and on me too, not allowing me to have this sorrow on top of everything else.

28 So I am all the more anxious to get him back to you again, for I know how thankful you will be to see him, and that will make me happy and lighten all my cares.

29 Welcome him in the Lord with great joy, and show your appreciation,

30 For he risked his life for the work of Christ and was at

the point of death while trying to do for me the things you couldn't do because you were far away.

CHAPTER 3

WHATEVER happens, dear friends, be glad in the Lord. I never get tired of telling you this and it is good for you to hear it again and again.

* * * * *

2 Watch out for those wicked men—dangerous dogs, I call them—who say you must be circumcised to be saved.

3 For it isn't the *cutting of our bodies* that makes us children of God; it is *worshiping Him with our spirits*. That is the only true "circumcision." We Christians glory in what Christ Jesus has done for us and realize that we are helpless to save ourselves.

4 Yet if anyone ever had reason to hope that he could save himself, it would be I. If others could be saved by what they are, certainly I could!

5 For I went through the Jewish initiation ceremony when I was eight days old, having been born into a pure-blooded Jewish home that was a branch of the old original Benjamin family. So I was a real Jew if there ever was one! What's more, I was a member of the Pharisees who demand the strictest obedience to every Jewish law and custom.

6 And sincere? Yes, so much so that I greatly persecuted the church; and I tried to obey every Jewish rule and regulation right down to the very last point.

7 But all these things that I once thought very worthwhile— now I've thrown them all away so that I can put my trust and hope in Christ alone.

8 Yes, everything else is worthless when compared with the priceless gain of knowing Christ Jesus my Lord. I have put aside all else, counting it worth less than nothing, in order that I can have Christ,

9 And become one with Him, no longer counting on being

saved by being good enough or by obeying God's laws, but by trusting Christ to save me; for God's way of making us right with Himself depends on faith—counting on Christ alone.

10   Now I have given up everything else—I have found it to be the only way to really know Christ and to experience the mighty power that brought Him back to life again, and to find out what it means to suffer and to die with Him,

11   So, whatever it takes, I will be one who lives in the fresh newness of life of those who are alive from the dead.

12   I don't mean to say I am perfect. I haven't learned all I should even yet, but I keep working toward that day when I will finally be all that Christ saved me for and wants me to be.

13   No, dear brothers, I am still not all I should be but I am bringing all my energies to bear on this one thing: Forgetting the past and looking forward to what lies ahead,

14   I strain to reach the end of the race and receive the prize for which God is calling us up to heaven because of what Christ Jesus did for us.

*   *   *   *   *

15   I hope all of you who are mature Christians will see eye-to-eye with me on these things, and if you disagree on some point I believe that God will make it plain to you—

16   If you fully obey the truth you have.

*   *   *   *   *

17   Dear brothers, pattern your lives after mine and notice who else lives up to my example.

18   For I have told you often before, and I say it again now with tears in my eyes, there are many who walk along the Christian road who are really enemies of the cross of Christ.

19   Their future is eternal loss, for their god is their appetite: they are proud of what they should be ashamed of; and all they think about is this life here on earth.

20   But our homeland is in heaven, with our Savior the Lord Jesus Christ; and we are looking forward to His return from there.

*   *   *   *   *

21   When He comes back He will take these dying bodies of ours and change them into glorious bodies like His own, using

491

the same mighty power that He will use to conquer all else everywhere.

CHAPTER 4

DEAR brother Christians, I love you and long to see you, for you are my joy and my reward for my work. My beloved friends, stay true to the Lord.

*   *   *   *   *

2   And now I want to plead with those two dear women, Euodias and Syntyche. Please, please, with the Lord's help, quarrel no more—be friends again.

3   And I ask you, my true teammate, to help these women, for they worked side by side with me in telling the Good News to others; and they worked with Clement, too, and the rest of my fellow workers whose names are written in the Book of Life.

*   *   *   *   *

4   Always be full of joy in the Lord; I say it again, rejoice!

5   Let everyone see that you are unselfish and considerate in all you do. Remember that the Lord is coming soon.

6   Don't worry about anything; instead, pray about everything; tell God your needs and don't forget to thank Him for His answers.

7   If you do this you will experience God's peace, which is far more wonderful than the human mind can understand. His peace will keep your thoughts and your hearts quiet and at rest as you trust in Christ Jesus.

*   *   *   *   *

8   And now, brothers, as I close this letter let me say this one more thing: Fix your thoughts on what is true and good and right. Think about things that are pure and lovely, and dwell on the fine, good things in others. Think about all you can praise God for and be glad about.

9   Keep putting into practice all you learned from me and saw me doing, and the God of peace will be with you.

*   *   *   *   *

10   How grateful I am and how I praise the Lord that you

are helping me again. I know you have always been anxious to send what you could, but for a while you didn't have the chance.

11 Not that I was ever in need, for I have learned how to get along happily whether I have much or little.

12 I know how to live on almost nothing or with everything. I have learned the secret of contentment in every situation, whether it be a full stomach or hunger, plenty or want;

13 For I can do everything God asks me to with the help of Christ who gives me the strength and power.

14 But even so, you have done right in helping me in my present difficulty.

15 As you well know, when I first brought the Gospel to you and then went on my way, leaving Macedonia, only you Philippians became my partners in giving and receiving. No other church did this.

16 Even when I was over in Thessalonica you sent help twice.

17 But though I appreciate your gifts, what makes me happiest is the well-earned reward you will have because of your kindness.

18 At the moment I have all I need—more than I need! I am generously supplied with the gifts you sent me when Epaphroditus came. They are a sweet-smelling sacrifice that pleases God well.

19 And it is He who will supply all your needs from His riches in glory, because of what Christ Jesus has done for us.

20 Now unto God our Father be glory forever and ever. Amen.

Sincerely,
Paul

P.S.

21 Say "hello" for me to all the Christians there; the brothers with me send their greetings too.

22 And all the other Christians here want to be remembered to you, especially those who work in Caesar's palace.

23 The blessings of our Lord Jesus Christ be upon your spirits.

TO MAKE A

Five high schoolers on tour of a Detroit automaker watch as a front seat is installed. Throughout the plant they saw hundreds of different cars and models—many not yet available to the pub-

CAR

lic. Understandably, they wouldn't have minded driving off with one! If "clothes make the man," then "a car makes the teen." Yet as we consider cars and clothes and all the better things of life, how can Paul's comment in this next letter—"You have everything when you have Christ"—be relevant for today? Isn't looking toward the next world a bit naive? Think it through. . . .

BENYAS-KAUFMAN

COLOSSIANS

CHAPTER 1

FROM: Paul, chosen by God to be Jesus Christ's messenger, and from Brother Timothy.

2   *To:* The faithful Christian brothers—God's people—in the city of Colosse.

May God our Father shower you with blessings and fill you with His great peace.

3   Whenever we pray for you we always begin by giving thanks to God the Father of our Lord Jesus Christ,

4   For we have heard how much you trust the Lord, and how much you love His people.

5   And you are looking forward to the joys of heaven, and have been ever since the Gospel first was preached to you.

6   The same Good News that came to you is going out all over the world and changing lives everywhere, just as it changed yours that very first day you heard it and understood about God's great kindness to sinners.

7   Epaphras our much-loved fellow worker was the one who brought you this Good News. He is Jesus Christ's slave, here to help us in your stead.

8   And he is the one who has told us about the great love for others which the Holy Spirit has given you.

9   So ever since we first heard about you we have kept on praying and asking God to help you understand what He wants you to do, and to make you wise about spiritual things,

10   That the way you live will always please the Lord and honor Him, that you will always be doing good, kind things for

others, all the time learning to know God better and better.

11 We are praying, too, that you will be filled with His mighty, glorious strength so that you can keep going no matter what happens—always full of the joy of the Lord,

12 And always thankful to the Father who has made us fit to share all the wonderful things that belong to those who live in the kingdom of light.

13 For He has rescued us out of the darkness and gloom of Satan's kingdom and brought us into the kingdom of His dear Son,

14 Who bought our freedom with His blood and forgave us all our sins.

* * * * *

15 Christ is the exact likeness of the unseen God. He existed before God made anything at all,[1] and, in fact,

16 Christ Himself is the Creator who made everything in heaven and earth, the things we can see and the things we can't; the spirit world with its kings and kingdoms, its rulers and authorities; all were made by Christ for His own use and glory.

17 He was before all else began and it is His power that holds everything together.

18 He is the Head of the body made up of His people— that is, His church—which He began; and He is the Leader of all who arise from the dead,[2] so that He is first in everything;

19 For God wanted all of Himself to be in His Son.

20 It was through what His Son did that God cleared a path for everything to come to Him—all things in heaven and on earth—for Christ's death on the cross has made peace with God for all by His blood.

21 This includes you who were once so far away from God. You were His enemies and hated Him and were separated from Him by your evil thoughts and actions, yet now He has brought you back as His friends.

22 He has done this through the death on the cross of His own human body, and now as a result Christ has brought you

[1]Literally, "the firstborn of all creation."
[2]Literally, "He is the Beginning, the firstborn from the dead."

into the very presence of God, and you are standing there before Him with nothing left against you—nothing left that He could even chide you for;

23   The only condition is that you fully believe the Truth, standing in it steadfast and firm, strong in the Lord, convinced of the Good News that Jesus died for you, and never shifting from trusting Him to save you. This is the wonderful news that came to each of you and is now spreading all over the world. And I, Paul, have the joy of telling it to others.

*   *   *   *   *

24   But part of my work is to suffer for you; and I am glad, for I am helping to finish up the remainder of Christ's sufferings for His body, the church.

*   *   *   *   *

25   God has sent me to help His church and to tell His secret plan to you Gentiles.

26, 27   He has kept this secret for centuries and generations past, but now at last it has pleased Him to tell it to those who love Him and live for Him, and the riches and glory of His plan are for you Gentiles too. And this is the secret: *that Christ in your hearts is your only hope of glory.*

28   So everywhere we go we talk about Christ to all who will listen, warning them and teaching them as well as we know how. We want to be able to present each one to God, perfect because of what Christ has done for each of them.

29   This is my work, and I can do it only because Christ's mighty energy is at work within me.

CHAPTER 2

I WISH you could know how much I have struggled in prayer for you and for the church at Laodicea, and for my many other friends who have never known me personally.

2   This is what I have asked of God for you: that you will be encouraged and knit together by strong ties of love, and that you will have the rich experience of knowing Christ with real

certainty and clear understanding. *For God's secret plan, now at last made known, is Christ Himself.*

3 In Him lie hidden all the mighty, untapped treasures of wisdom and knowledge.

4 I am saying this because I am afraid that someone may fool you with smooth talk.

5 For though I am far away from you my heart is with you, happy because you are getting along so well, happy because of your strong faith in Christ.

6 And now just as you trusted Christ to save you, trust Him, too, for each day's problems; live in vital union with Him.

7 Let your roots grow down into Him and draw up nourishment from Him. See that you go on growing in the Lord, and become strong and vigorous in the truth. Let your lives overflow with joy and thanksgiving for all He has done.

8 Don't let others spoil your faith and joy with their philosophies, their wrong and shallow answers built on men's thoughts and ideas, instead of on what Christ has said.

9 For in Christ there is all of God in a human body;

10 *So you have everything when you have Christ,* and you are filled with God through your union with Christ. He is the highest ruler, with authority over every other power.

*   *   *   *   *

11 When you came to Christ He set you free from your evil desires, not by a bodily operation of circumcision but by a spiritual operation, the baptism of your souls.

12 For in baptism you see how your old, evil nature died with Him and was buried with Him; and then you came up out of death with Him into a new life because you trusted the Word of the mighty God who raised Christ from the dead.

13 You were dead in sins, and your sinful desires were not yet cut away. Then He gave you a share in the very life of Christ, for He forgave all your sins,

14 And blotted out the charges proved against you, the list of His commandments which you had not obeyed. He took this list of sins and destroyed it by nailing it to Christ's cross.

15 In this way God took away Satan's power to accuse you

of sin, and God openly displayed to the whole world Christ's triumph at the cross where your sins were all taken away.

16   So don't let anyone criticize you for what you eat or drink, or for not celebrating Jewish holidays and feasts or new moon ceremonies or Sabbaths.

17   For these were only temporary rules that ended when Christ came. They were only shadows of the real thing—of Christ Himself.

18   Don't let anyone declare you lost when you refuse to worship angels, as they say you must. They have seen a vision, they say, and know you should. These proud men have a very clever imagination.

19   But they are not connected to Christ, the Head to which all of us who are His body are joined; for we are joined together by His strong sinews and we grow only as we get our nourishment and strength from Him.

20   Since you died, as it were, with Christ and this has set you free from following the world's ideas of how to be saved— by doing good and obeying various rules[1]—why do you keep right on following them anyway, still bound by such rules as

21   Not eating, tasting, or even touching certain foods?

22   Such rules are mere human teachings, for food was made to be eaten and used up.

23   These rules may seem good, for rules of this kind require strong devotion and are humiliating and hard on the body, but they have no effect when it comes to conquering a person's evil thoughts and desires. They only make him proud.

CHAPTER 3

SINCE you became alive again, so to speak, when Christ arose from the dead, now set your sights on the rich treasures and joys of heaven where He sits beside God in the place of honor and power.

2   Let heaven fill your thoughts; don't spend your time worrying about things down here.

[1]Literally, "If you died with Christ from the rudiments of the world."

3 You should have as little desire for this world as a dead person does. Your real life is in heaven with Christ and God.

4 And when Christ who is our real life comes back again, you will shine with Him and share in all His glories.

5 Away then with sinful, earthly things; deaden the evil desires lurking within you; have nothing to do with sexual sin, impurity, lust and shameful desires; don't worship the good things of life, for that is idolatry.

6 God's terrible anger is upon those who do such things.

7 You used to do them when your life was still part of this world;

8 But now is the time to cast off and throw away all these rotten garments of anger, hatred, cursing, and dirty language.

9 Don't tell lies to each other; it was your old life with all its wickedness that did that sort of thing; now it is dead and gone.

10 You are living a brand new kind of life that is continually learning more and more of what is right, and trying constantly to be more and more like Christ who created this new life within you.

11 In this new life one's nationality or race or education or social position is unimportant; such things mean nothing. Whether a person has Christ is what matters, and He is equally available to all.

12 Since you have been chosen by God who has given you this new kind of life, and because of His deep love and concern for you, you should practice tenderhearted mercy and kindness to others. Don't worry about making a good impression on them but be ready to suffer quietly and patiently.

13 Be gentle and ready to forgive; never hold grudges. Remember, the Lord forgave you, so you must forgive others.

14 Most of all, let love guide your life for then the whole church will stay together in perfect harmony.

15 Let the peace of heart which comes from Christ be always present in your hearts and lives, for this is your responsibility and privilege as members of His body. And always be thankful.

16   Remember what Christ taught and let His words enrich your lives and make you wise; teach them to each other and sing them out in psalms and hymns and spiritual songs, singing to the Lord with thankful hearts.

17   And whatever you do or say, let it be as a representative of the Lord Jesus, and come with Him into the presence of God the Father to give Him your thanks.

18   You wives, submit yourselves to your husbands, for that is what the Lord has planned for you.

19   And you husbands must be loving and kind to your wives and not bitter against them, nor harsh.

20   You children must always obey your fathers and mothers, for that pleases the Lord.

21   Fathers, don't scold your children so much that they become discouraged and quit trying.

22   You slaves must always obey your earthly masters, not only trying to please them when they are watching you but all the time; obey them willingly because of your love for the Lord and because you want to please Him.

23   Work hard and cheerfully at all you do, just as though you were working for the Lord and not merely for your masters,

24   Remembering that it is the Lord Christ who is going to pay you, giving you your full portion of all He owns. He is the one you are really working for.

25   And if you don't do your best for Him, He will pay you in a way that you won't like—for He has no special favorites who can get away with shirking.

CHAPTER 4

YOU slave owners must be just and fair to all your slaves. Always remember that you, too, have a Master in heaven who is closely watching you.

*   *   *   *   *

2   Don't be weary in prayer; keep at it; watch for God's answers and remember to be thankful when they come.

3   Don't forget to pray for us too, that God will give us many chances to preach the Good News of Christ for which I am here in jail.

4   Pray that I will be bold enough to tell it freely and fully, and make it plain, as, of course, I should.

5   Make the most of your chances to tell others the Good News. Be wise in all your contacts with them.

6   Let your conversation be gracious as well as sensible, for then you will have the right answer for everyone.

*   *   *   *   *

7   Tychicus, our much loved brother, will tell you how I am getting along. He is a hard worker and serves the Lord with me.

8   I have sent him on this special trip just to see how you are, and to comfort and encourage you.

9   I am also sending Onesimus, a faithful and much loved brother, one of your own people. He and Tychicus will give you all the latest news.

10   Aristarchus, who is with me here as a prisoner, sends you his love, and so does Mark, a relative of Barnabas. And as I said before, give Mark a hearty welcome if he comes your way.

11   Jesus Justus also sends his love. These are the only Jewish Christians working with me here, and what a comfort they have been!

12   Epaphras, from your city, a servant of Christ Jesus, sends you his love. He is always earnestly praying for you, asking God to make you strong and perfect and to help you know His will in everything you do.

13   I can assure you that he has worked hard for you with his prayers, and also for the Christians in Laodicea and Hierapolis.

14   Dear doctor Luke sends his love, and so does Demas.

15   Please give my greeting to the Christian friends at Laodicea, and to Nymphas, and to those who meet in his home.

16   By the way, after you have read this letter will you pass it on to the church at Laodicea? And read the letter I wrote to them.

17   And say to Archippus, "Be sure that you do all the Lord has told you to."

18   Here is my own greeting in my own handwriting: Remember me here in jail. May God's blessings surround you.

Sincerely,

Paul

WHAT'S SHE SAYING ABOUT ME?

When a person looks at another and asks that question, the immediate reaction we get is that it's probably not complimentary! As we talk about others we seem to delight in tearing them down, but we get few kicks out of praising someone. □ Paul complimented the people to whom he addressed these next two letters. Others were saying *good* things about them—and this was the kind of spirit shown in the fellowship of those "Christ-ones." □ Why shouldn't we *enjoy* saying good things about others? Why aren't we more wrapped up in good feelings of loving others? *How* can we start to live this way instead of enjoying "sweet nastiness." These two letters go a long way toward answering that.

I THESSALONIANS

CHAPTER 1

F ROM: Paul, Silas and Timothy.

To: The Church at Thessalonica—to you who belong to God the Father and the Lord Jesus Christ: May blessing and peace of heart be your rich gifts from God our Father, and from Jesus Christ our Lord.

2   We always thank God for you and pray for you constantly.

3   We never forget your loving deeds as we talk to our God and Father about you, and your strong faith and steady looking forward to the return of our Lord Jesus Christ.

4   We know that God has chosen you, dear brothers, much beloved of God.

5   For when we brought you the Good News, it was not just meaningless chatter to you; no, you listened with great interest. What we told you produced a powerful effect upon you, for the Holy Spirit gave you great and full assurance that what we said was true. And you know how our very lives were further proof to you of the truth of our message.

6   So you became our followers and the Lord's; for you received our messages with joy from the Holy Spirit in spite of the trials and sorrows it brought you.

7   Then you yourselves became an example to all the other Christians in Macedonia and Achaia.

8   And now the Word of the Lord has spread out from you to others everywhere, far beyond the boundaries of Macedonia and Achaia, for wherever we go we find people telling us about

your remarkable faith in God. We don't need to tell *them* about it,

9　For *they* keep telling *us* about the wonderful welcome you gave us, and how you turned away from your idols to God so that now the living and true God only is your master.

10　And they speak of how you are looking forward to the return of God's Son from heaven—Jesus, whom God brought back to life—and He is our only Savior from God's terrible anger against sin.

CHAPTER 2

YOU yourselves know, dear brothers, how worthwhile that visit was.

2　You know how badly we had been treated at Philippi just before we came to you, and how much we suffered there. Yet God gave us the courage to boldly repeat the same message to you, even though we were surrounded by enemies.

3　So you can see that we were not preaching with any false motives or evil purposes in mind; we were perfectly straightforward and sincere.

4　For we speak as messengers from God, trusted by Him to tell the truth; we change His message not one bit to suit the taste of those who hear it; for we serve God alone, who examines our hearts' deepest thoughts.

5　Never once did we try to win you with flattery, as you very well know, and God knows we were not just pretending to be your friends so that you would give us money!

6　As for praise, we have never asked for it from you or anyone else, although as apostles of Christ we certainly had a right to some honor from you.

7　But we were as gentle among you as a mother feeding and caring for her own children.

8　We loved you dearly—so dearly that we gave you not only God's message, but our own lives too.

9　Don't you remember, dear brothers, how hard we

504

worked among you? Night and day we toiled and sweated to earn enough to live on so that our expenses would not be a burden to anyone there, as we preached God's Good News among you.

10   You yourselves are our witnesses—as is God—that we have been pure and honest and faultless toward every one of you.

11   We talked to you as a father to his own children—don't you remember?—pleading with you, encouraging you and even demanding

12   That your daily lives should not embarrass God, but bring joy to Him who invited you into His kingdom to share His glory.

13   And we will never stop thanking God for this: that when we preached to you, you didn't think of the words we spoke as being just our own, but you accepted what we said as the very Word of God—which, of course, it was—and it changed your lives when you believed it.

14   And then, dear brothers, you suffered what the churches in Judea did, persecution from your own countrymen, just as they suffered from their own people the Jews.

15   After they had killed their own prophets, they even executed the Lord Jesus; and now they have brutally persecuted us and driven us out. They are against both God and man,

16   Trying to keep us from preaching to the Gentiles for fear some might be saved; and so their sins continue to grow. But the anger of God has caught up with them at last.

17   Dear brothers, after we left you and had been away from you but a very little while (though our hearts never left you), we tried hard to come back to see you once more.

18   We wanted very much to come and I, Paul, tried again and again, but Satan stopped us.

19   For what is it we live for, that gives us hope and joy and is our proud reward and crown? It is you! Yes, you will bring us much joy as we stand together before our Lord Jesus Christ when He comes back again.

20   For you are our trophy and joy.

CHAPTER 3

FINALLY, when I could stand it no longer, I decided to stay alone in Athens

2, 3 And send Timothy, our brother and fellow worker, God's minister, to visit you to strengthen your faith and encourage you, and to keep you from becoming fainthearted in all the troubles you were going through. (But of course you know that such troubles are a part of God's plan for us Christians.

4 Even while we were still with you we warned you ahead of time that suffering would soon come—and it did.)

5 As I was saying, when I could bear the suspense no longer I sent Timothy to find out whether your faith was still strong. I was afraid that perhaps Satan had gotten the best of you and that all our work had been useless.

6 And now Timothy has just returned and brings the welcome news that your faith and love are as strong as ever, and that you remember our visit with joy and want to see us just as much as we want to see you.

7 So we are greatly comforted, dear brothers, in all of our own crushing troubles and suffering here, now that we know you are standing true to the Lord.

8 We can bear anything as long as we know that you remain strong in Him.

9 How can we thank God enough for you and for the joy and delight you have given us in our praying for you?

10 For night and day we pray on and on for you, asking God to let us see you again, to fill up any little cracks there may yet be in your faith.

11 May God our Father Himself and our Lord Jesus send us back to you again.

12 And may the Lord make your love to grow and overflow to each other and to everyone else, just as our love does toward you.

13 This will result in your hearts' being made strong, sinless

and holy by God our Father, so that you may stand before Him guiltless on that day when our Lord Jesus Christ returns with all those who belong to Him.[1]

CHAPTER 4

LET me add this, dear brothers: you already know how to please God in your daily living, for you know the commands we gave you from the Lord Jesus Himself. Now we beg you—yes, we demand of you in the name of the Lord Jesus—that you live more and more closely to that ideal.

3, 4   For God wants you to be holy and pure, and to keep clear of all sexual sin so that each of you will marry in holiness and honor—

5   Not in lustful passion as the heathen do, in their ignorance of God and His ways.

6   And this also is God's will: that you never cheat in this matter by taking another man's wife, because the Lord will punish you terribly for this, as we have solemnly told you before.

7   For God has not called us to be dirty-minded and full of lust, but to be holy and clean.

8   If anyone refuses to live by these rules he is not disobeying the rules of men but of God who gives His *Holy* Spirit to you.

9   But concerning the pure brotherly love that there should be among God's people, I don't need to say very much, I'm sure! For God Himself is teaching you to love one another.

10   Indeed, your love is already strong toward all the Christian brothers throughout your whole nation. Even so, dear friends, we beg you to love them more and more.

11   This should be your ambition: to live a quiet life, minding your own business and doing your own work, just as we told you before.

12   As a result, people who are not Christians will trust and

[1]Literally, "with all His saints. Amen."

respect you, and you will not need to depend on others for enough money to pay your bills.

*   *   *   *   *

13 And now, dear brothers, I want you to know what happens to a Christian when he dies so that when it happens, you will not be full of sorrow, as those are who have no hope.

14 For since we believe that Jesus died and then came back to life again, we can also believe that when Jesus returns, God will bring back with Him all the Christians who have died.

15 I can tell you this directly from the Lord: that we who are still living when the Lord returns will not rise to meet Him ahead of those who are in their graves.

16 For the Lord Himself will come down from heaven with a mighty shout and with the soul-stirring cry of the archangel and the great trumpet-call of God. And the Christians who are dead will be the first to rise to meet the Lord.

17 Then we who are still alive and remain on the earth will be caught up with them in the clouds to meet the Lord in the air and remain with Him forever.

18 So comfort and encourage each other with this news.

CHAPTER 5

WHEN is all this going to happen? I really don't need to say anything about that, dear brothers,

2 For you know perfectly well that no one knows. That day of the Lord will come unexpectedly like a thief in the night.

3 When people are saying, "All is well, everything is quiet and peaceful"—then, all of a sudden, disaster will fall upon them as suddenly as a woman's birth pains begin when her child is born. And these people will not be able to get away anywhere—there will be no place to hide.

4 But dear brothers, you are not in the dark about these things, and you won't be surprised as by a thief when that day of the Lord comes.

5 For you are all children of the light and of the day, and do not belong to darkness and night.

6 So be on your guard, not asleep like the others. Watch for His return and stay sober.

7 Night is the time for sleep and the time when people get drunk.

8 But let us who live in the light keep sober, protected by the armor of faith and love, and wearing as our helmet the happy hope of salvation.

9 For God has not chosen to pour out His anger upon us, but to save us through our Lord Jesus Christ;

10 He died for us so that we can live with Him forever, whether we are dead or alive at the time of His return.

11 So encourage each other to build each other up, just as you are already doing.

12 Dear brothers, honor the officers of your church who work hard among you and warn you against all that is wrong.

13 Think highly of them and give them your wholehearted love because they are straining to help you. And remember, no quarreling among yourselves.

14 Dear brothers, warn those who are lazy or wild; comfort those who are frightened; take tender care of those who are weak; and be patient with everyone.

15 See that no one pays back evil for evil, but always try to do good to each other and to everyone else.

16 Always be joyful.

17 Always keep on praying.

18 Always be thankful no matter what happens, for that is God's will for you who belong to Christ Jesus.

19 Do not smother the Holy Spirit.

20 Do not scoff at those who prophesy,

21 But test everything that is said to be sure it is true, and if it is, then accept it.

22 Keep away from every kind of evil.

23 May the God of peace Himself make you entirely clean; and may your spirit and soul and body be kept strong and blameless until that day when our Lord Jesus Christ comes back again.

24   God, who called you to become His child, will do all this for you, just as He promised.

25   Dear brothers, pray for us.

26   Shake hands for me with all the brothers there.

27   I command you in the name of the Lord to read this letter to all the Christians.

28   And may rich blessings from our Lord Jesus Christ be with you, every one.

Sincerely,

Paul

II THESSALONIANS

CHAPTER 1

FROM: Paul, Silas and Timothy.

To: The church of Thessalonica—kept safe in God our Father and in the Lord Jesus Christ.

2 May God the Father and the Lord Jesus Christ give you rich blessings and peace-filled hearts and minds.

3 Dear brothers, giving thanks to God for you is not only the right thing to do, but it is our duty to God, because of the really wonderful way your faith has grown, and because of your growing love for each other.

4 We are happy to tell other churches about your patience and complete faith in God, in spite of all the crushing troubles and hardships you are going through.

5 This is only one example of the fair, just way God does things, for He is using your sufferings to make you ready for His kingdom,

6 While at the same time He is preparing judgment and punishment for those who are hurting you.

7 And so I would say to you who are suffering, God will give you rest along with us when the Lord Jesus appears suddenly from heaven in flaming fire with His mighty angels,

8 Bringing judgment on those who do not wish to know God, and who refuse to accept His plan to save them through our Lord Jesus Christ.

9 They will be punished in everlasting hell, forever separated from the face of the Lord, never to see the glory of His power

10   When He comes to receive praise and admiration because of all He has done for His people, His saints. And you will be with Him, because you have believed God's word which we gave you.

11   And so we keep on praying for you that our God will make you the kind of children He wants to have—will make you as good as you wish you could be!—rewarding your faith with His power.

12   Then everyone will be praising the name of the Lord Jesus Christ because of the results they see in you; and your greatest glory will be that you belong to Him. The tender mercy of our God and of the Lord Jesus Christ have made all this possible for you.

CHAPTER 2

A ND now, what about the coming again of our Lord Jesus Christ, and our being gathered together to meet Him? Please don't be upset and excited, dear brothers, by the rumor that this day of the Lord has already begun.[1] If you hear of people having visions and special messages from God about this, or letters that are supposed to have come from me, don't believe them.

3   Don't be carried away and deceived regardless of what they say. For that day will not come until two things happen: first, there will be a time of great rebellion against God, and then the man of rebellion will come—the son of hell.

4   He will defy every god there is, and tear down every other object of adoration and worship. He will go in and sit as God in the temple of God, claiming that he himself is God.

5   Don't you remember that I told you this when I was with you?

6   And you know who is keeping him from being here already; for he can come only when his time is ready.

7   As for the work this man of rebellion and hell will do when he comes, it is already going on,[2] but he himself will not

[1]Literally, "is just at hand."
[2]Literally, "the mystery of lawlessness is already at work."

512

come until the one who is holding him back steps out of the way.

8   Then this wicked one will appear, whom the Lord Jesus will burn up with the breath of His mouth and destroy by His presence when He returns.

9   This man of sin will come as Satan's tool, full of Satanic power, and will trick everyone with strange demonstrations, and will pretend to do great miracles.

10   He will completely fool those who are on their way to hell because they have said "no" to the Truth; they have refused to believe it and love it, and let it save them,

11   So God will allow them to believe lies with all their hearts,

12   And all of them will be justly judged for believing falsehood, refusing the Truth, and enjoying their sins.

13   But we must forever give thanks to God for you, our brothers loved by the Lord, because God chose from the very first to give you salvation, cleansing you by the work of the Holy Spirit and by your trusting in the Truth.

14   Through us He told you the Good News. Through us He called you to share in the glory of our Lord Jesus Christ.

15   With all these things in mind, dear brothers, stand firm and keep a strong grip on the truth that we taught you in our letters and during the time we were with you.

16   May our Lord Jesus Christ Himself and God our Father, who has loved us and given us everlasting comfort and hope which we don't deserve,

17   Comfort your hearts with all comfort, and help you in every good thing you say and do.

CHAPTER 3

FINALLY, dear brothers, as I come to the end of this letter I ask you to pray for us. Pray first that the Lord's message will spread rapidly and triumph wherever it goes, winning converts everywhere as it did when it came to you.

2   Pray too that we will be saved out of the clutches of evil men, for not everyone loves the Lord.

3   But the Lord is faithful; He will make you strong and guard you from Satanic attacks of every kind.

4   And we trust the Lord that you are putting into practice the things we taught you, and that you always will.

5   May the Lord bring you into an ever deeper understanding of the love of God and of the patience that comes from Christ.

6   Now here is a command, dear brothers, given in the name of our Lord Jesus Christ by His authority: stay away from any Christian who spends his days in laziness and does not follow the ideal of hard work we set up for you.

7   For you well know that you ought to follow our example: you never saw us loafing;

8   We never accepted food from anyone without buying it; we worked hard day and night for the money we needed to live on, in order that we would not be a burden to any of you.

9   It wasn't that we didn't have the right to ask you to feed us, but we wanted to show you, firsthand, how you should work for your living.

10   Even while we were still there with you we gave you this rule: "He who does not work shall not eat."

11   Yet we hear that some of you are living in laziness, refusing to work, and wasting your time in gossiping.

12   In the name of the Lord Jesus Christ we appeal to such people—we command them—to quiet down, get to work, and earn their own living.

13   And to the rest of you I say, dear brothers, never be tired of doing right.

14   If anyone refuses to obey what we say in this letter, notice who he is and stay away from him, that he may be ashamed of himself.

15   Don't think of him as an enemy, but speak to him as you would to a brother who needs to be warned.

16   May the Lord of peace Himself give you His peace no matter what happens. The Lord be with you all.

17 Now here is my greeting which I am writing with my own hand, as I do at the end of all my letters, for proof that it really is from me. This is in my own handwriting.

18 May the blessing of our Lord Jesus Christ be upon you all.

Sincerely,

Paul

Bob Seagren with fiberglass pole whips up and over successfully. In the '68 Olympics he toppled the old world record by vaulting 17' 8½". In the following two letters, Paul challenges the young man Timothy to reach for the very top—giving everything to reach the goal. Bob Seagren, with the world's eyes on him, strained every molecule of his body to clear that bar. Timothy and those who want to reach the same goals have the eyes of Someone more awesome than three billion people watching! You'll find throughout these letters how keeping this far more important "Audience" in mind is the way to the good life!

OLYMPIC
RECORD
SMASHER

I TIMOTHY

CHAPTER 1

FROM: Paul, a missionary of Jesus Christ, sent out by God our Savior and by Jesus Christ our Lord—our only hope.

2   *To:* Timothy.

Timothy, you are like a son to me in the things of the Lord. May God our Father and Jesus Christ our Lord show you His kindness and mercy and give you great peace of heart and mind.

3, 4   As I said when I left for Macedonia, please stay there in Ephesus and try to stop the men who are teaching such wrong doctrine. Put an end to their myths and fables, and their idea of being saved by finding favor with an endless chain of angels leading up to God—wild ideas that stir up questions and arguments instead of helping people accept God's plan of faith.

5   What I am eager for is that all the Christians there will be filled with love that comes from pure hearts, and that their minds will be clean and their faith strong.

6   But these teachers have missed this whole idea and spend their time arguing and talking foolishness.

7   They want to become famous as teachers of the laws of Moses when they haven't the slightest idea what those laws really show us.

8   Those laws are good when used as God intended.

9   But they were not made for us, whom God has saved; they are for sinners who hate God, have rebellious hearts, curse and swear, attack their fathers and mothers, and murder.

516

10, 11   Yes, these laws are made to identify as sinners all who are immoral and impure: homosexuals, kidnappers, liars, and all others who do things that contradict the glorious Good News of our blessed God, whose messenger I am.

12   How thankful I am to Christ Jesus our Lord for choosing me as one of His messengers, and giving me the strength to be faithful to Him,

13   Even though I used to scoff at the name of Christ. I hunted down His people, harming them in every way I could. But God had mercy on me because I didn't know what I was doing, for I didn't know Christ at that time.

14   Oh, how kind our Lord was, for He showed me how to trust Him and become full of the love of Christ Jesus.

15   How true it is, and how I long that everyone should know it, that Christ Jesus came into the world to save sinners— and I was the greatest of them all.

16   But God had mercy on me so that Christ Jesus could use me as an example to show everyone how patient He is with even the worst sinners, so that others will realize that they, too, can have everlasting life.

17   Glory and honor to God for ever and ever. He is the King of the ages, the unseen one who never dies; He alone is God, and full of wisdom. Amen.

18   Now, Timothy, my son, here is my command to you: fight well in the Lord's battles, just as the Lord told us through His prophets that you would.

19   Cling tightly to your faith in Christ and always keep your conscience clear, doing what you know is right. For some people have disobeyed their consciences and have deliberately done what they knew was wrong. It isn't surprising that soon they lost their faith in Christ after defying God like that.

20   Hymenaeus and Alexander are two examples of this. I had to give them over to Satan to punish them until they could learn not to bring shame to the name of Christ.

CHAPTER 2

HERE are my directions: pray much for others; plead for God's mercy upon them; give thanks for all He is going to do for them.

2   Pray in this way for kings and all others who are in authority over us, or are in places of high responsibility, so that we can live in peace and quietness, spending our time in godly living and thinking much about the Lord.[1]

3   This is good and pleases God our Savior,

4   For He longs for all to be saved and to understand this truth:

5   *That God is on one side and all the people on the other side, and Christ Jesus, Himself man, is between them to bring them together,*

6   *By giving His life for all mankind.* This is the message which at the proper time God gave to the world.

7   And I have been chosen—this is the absolute truth—as God's minister and missionary to teach this truth to the Gentiles, and to show them God's plan of salvation through faith.

8   So I want men everywhere to pray with holy hands lifted up to God, free from sin and anger and resentment.

9, 10   And the women should be the same way, quiet and sensible in manner and clothing. Christian women should be noticed for being kind and good, not for the way they fix their hair or because of their jewels or fancy clothes.

11   Women should listen and learn quietly and humbly.

12   I never let women teach men or lord it over them. Let them be silent in your church meetings.

13   Why? Because God made Adam first, and afterwards He made Eve.

14   And it was not Adam who was fooled by Satan, but Eve, and sin was the result.

15   So God sent pain and suffering to women when their children are born, but He will save their souls if they trust in Him, living quiet, good, and loving lives.

---

[1] Literally, "in gravity."

518

CHAPTER 3

I T is a true saying that if a man wants to be a pastor,[1] he has a good ambition.

2 For a pastor must be a good man whose life cannot be spoken against. He must have only one wife, and he must be hard working and thoughtful, orderly, and full of good deeds. He must enjoy having guests in his home, and must be a good Bible teacher.

3 He must not be a drinker or quarrelsome, but he must be gentle and kind, and not be one who loves money.

4 He must have a well-behaved family, with children who obey quickly and quietly.

5 For if a man can't make his own little family behave, how can he help the whole church?

6 The pastor must not be a new Christian, because he might be proud of being chosen so soon, and pride comes before a fall. (Satan's downfall is an example.)

7 Also, he must be well spoken of by people outside the church—those who aren't Christians—so that Satan can't trap him with many accusations, and leave him without freedom to lead his flock.

8 The deacons must be the same sort of good, steady men as the pastors. They must not be heavy drinkers and must not be greedy for money.

9 They must be earnest, wholehearted followers of Christ who is the hidden Source of their faith.

10 Before they are asked to be deacons they should be given other jobs in the church as a test of their character and ability, and if they do well, then they may be chosen as deacons.

11 Their wives must be thoughtful, not heavy drinkers, not gossipers, but faithful in everything they do.

12 Deacons should have only one wife and they should have happy, obedient families.

---

[1]More literally, "church leader" or "presiding elder."

13   Those who do well as deacons will be well rewarded both by respect from others and also by developing their own confidence and bold trust in the Lord.

14   I am writing these things to you now, even though I hope to be with you soon,

15   So that if I don't come for awhile you will know what kind of men you should choose as officers for the church of the living God, which contains and holds high the truth of God.

16   It is quite true that the way to live a godly life is not an easy matter. But the answer lies in Christ, who came to earth as a man, was proved spotless and pure in His Spirit, was served by angels, was preached among the nations, was accepted by men everywhere and was received up again to His glory in heaven.

CHAPTER 4

BUT the Holy Spirit tells us clearly that in the last times some in the church will turn away from Christ and become eager followers of teachers with devil-inspired ideas.

2   These teachers will tell lies with straight faces and do it so often that their consciences won't even bother them.

3   They will say it is wrong to be married and wrong to eat meat, even though God gave these things to well-taught Christians to enjoy and be thankful for.

4   For everything God made is good, and we may eat it gladly if we are thankful for it,

5   And if we ask God to bless it, for it is made good by the Word of God and prayer.

6   If you explain this to the others you will be doing your duty as a worthy pastor who is fed by faith and by the true teaching you have followed.

7   Don't waste time arguing over foolish ideas and silly myths and legends. Spend your time and energy in the exercise of keeping spiritually fit.

8   Bodily exercise is all right, but spiritual exercise is much

more important and is a tonic for all you do. So exercise yourself spiritually and practice being a better Christian, because
that will help you not only now in this life, but in the next
life too.

9, 10   This is the truth and everyone should accept it. We
work hard and suffer much in order that people will believe it,
for our hope is in the living God who died for all, and particularly for those who have accepted His salvation.

11   Teach these things and make sure everyone learns them
well.

12   Don't let anyone think little of you because you are
young. Be their ideal; let them follow the way you teach and
live; be a pattern for them in your love, your faith, and your
clean thoughts.

13   Until I get there, read and explain the Scriptures to the
church; preach God's Word.

14   Be sure to use the abilities God has given you through
His prophets when the elders of the church laid their hands
upon your head.

15   Put these abilities to work; throw yourself into your
tasks so that everyone may notice your improvement and
progress.

16   Keep a close watch on all you do and think. Stay true to
what is right and God will bless you and use you to help
others.

CHAPTER 5

NEVER speak sharply to an older man, but plead with him
respectfully just as though he were your own father. Talk
to the younger men as you would to much loved brothers.

2   Treat the older women as mothers, and the girls as your
sisters, thinking only pure thoughts about them.

3   The church should take loving care of women whose husbands have died if they don't have anyone else to help them.

4   But if they have children or grandchildren, these are the

ones who should take the responsibility, for kindness should begin at home, supporting needy parents. This is something that pleases God very much.

5 The church should care for widows who are poor and alone in the world if they are looking to God for His help, and spending much time in prayer;

6 But not if they are spending their time running around gossiping, seeking only pleasure and thus ruining their souls.

7 This should be your church rule so that the Christians will know and do what is right.

8 But anyone who won't care for his own relatives when they need help, especially those living in his own family, has no right to say he is a Christian. Such a person is worse than the heathen.

9 A widow who wants to become one of the special church workers[1] should be at least sixty years old and have been married only once.

10 She must be well thought of by everyone because of the good she has done. Has she brought up her children well? Has she been kind to strangers as well as to other Christians? Has she helped those who are sick and hurt? Is she always ready to show kindness?

11 The younger widows should not become members of this special group because after awhile they are likely to disregard their vow to Christ and marry again.

12 And so they will stand condemned because they broke their first promise.

13 Besides, they are likely to be lazy and spend their time gossiping around from house to house, getting into other people's business.

14 So I think it is better for these younger widows to marry again and have children, and take care of their own homes; then no one will be able to say anything against them.

15 For I am afraid that some of them have already turned away from the church and been led astray by Satan.

16 Let me remind you again that a widow's relatives must take care of her, and not leave this to the church to do. Then

---

[1]Literally, "enrolled as a widow."

the church can spend its money for the care of widows who are all alone and have nowhere else to turn.

17   Pastors who do their work well should be paid well and should be highly appreciated, especially those who work hard at both preaching and teaching.

18   For the Scriptures say, "Never tie up the mouth of an ox when it is treading out the grain—let him eat as he goes along!" And in another place, "Those who work deserve their pay!"

19   Don't listen to complaints against the pastor unless there are two or three witnesses to accuse him.

20   If he has really sinned, then he should be rebuked in front of the whole church so that no one else will follow his example.

21   I solemnly command you in the presence of God and the Lord Jesus Christ and of the holy angels to do this whether the pastor is a special friend of yours or not. All must be treated exactly the same.

22   Never be in a hurry about choosing a pastor; you may overlook his sins and it will look as if you approve of them. Be sure that you yourself stay away from all sin.

23   (By the way, this doesn't mean you should completely give up drinking wine. You ought to take a little sometimes as medicine for your stomach because you are sick so often.)

24   Remember that some men, even pastors, lead sinful lives and everyone knows it. In such situations you can do something about it. But in other cases only the judgment day will reveal the terrible truth.

25   In the same way, everyone knows how much good some pastors do, but sometimes their good deeds aren't known until long afterward.

CHAPTER 6

CHRISTIAN slaves should work hard for their owners and respect them; never let it be said that Christ's people are poor workers. Don't let the name of God or His teaching be laughed at because of this.

2   If their owner is a Christian, that is no excuse for slowing down; rather they should work all the harder because a brother in the faith is being helped by their efforts. Teach these truths, Timothy, and encourage all to obey them.

3   Some may deny these things, but they are the sound, wholesome teachings of the Lord Jesus Christ and are the foundation for a godly life.

4   Anyone who says anything different is both proud and stupid. He is quibbling over the meaning of Christ's words and stirring up arguments ending in jealousy and anger, which only lead to name-calling, accusations, and evil suspicions.

5   These arguers—their minds warped by sin—don't know how to tell the truth; to them the Good News is just a means of making money. Keep away from them.

6   Do you want to be truly rich? You already are if you are happy and good.

7   After all, we didn't bring any money with us when we came into the world, and we can't carry away a single penny when we die.

8   So we should be well satisfied without money if we have enough food and clothing.

9   But people who long to be rich soon begin to do all kinds of wrong things to get money, things that hurt them and make them evil-minded and finally send them to hell itself.

10   For the love of money is the first step toward all kinds of sin. Some people have even turned away from God because of their love for it, and as a result have pierced themselves with many sorrows.

11   Oh, Timothy, you are God's man. Run from all these evil things and work instead at what is right and good, learning to trust Him and love others, and to be patient and gentle.

12   Fight on for God. Hold tightly to the eternal life which

God has given you, and which you have confessed with such a ringing confession before many witnesses.

13 I command you before God who gives life to all, and before Christ Jesus who gave a fearless testimony before Pontius Pilate,

14 That you fulfill all He has told you to do, so that no one can find fault with you from now until our Lord Jesus Christ returns.

15 For in due season Christ will be revealed from heaven by the blessed and only Almighty God, the King of Kings and Lord of Lords,

16 Who alone can never die, who lives in light so terrible that no human being can approach Him. No mere man has ever seen Him, nor ever will. Unto Him be honor and everlasting power and dominion forever and ever. Amen.

17 Tell those who are rich not to be proud and not to trust in their money, which will soon be gone, but their pride and trust should be in the living God who always richly gives us all we need for our enjoyment.

18 Tell them to use their money to do good. They should be rich in good works and should give happily to those in need, always being ready to share with others whatever God has given them.

19 By doing this they will be storing up real treasure for themselves in heaven—it is the only safe investment for eternity! And they will be living a fruitful Christian life down here as well.

20 Oh, Timothy, don't fail to do these things that God entrusted to you. Keep out of foolish arguments with those who boast of their "knowledge" and thus prove their lack of it.

21 Some of these people have missed the most important thing in life—they don't know God. May God's mercy be upon you.

Sincerely,

Paul

II TIMOTHY

CHAPTER 1

FROM: Paul, Jesus Christ's missionary, sent out by God to tell men and women everywhere about the eternal life He has promised them through faith in Jesus Christ.

2 *To:* Timothy, my dear son. May God the Father and Christ Jesus our Lord shower you with His kindness, mercy and peace.

3 How I thank God for you, Timothy. I pray for you every day, and many times during the long nights I beg my God to bless you richly. He is my fathers' God, and mine, and my only purpose in life is to please Him.

4 How I long to see you again. How happy I would be, for I remember your tears as we left each other.

5 I know how much you trust the Lord, just as your mother Eunice and your grandmother Lois do; and I feel sure you are still trusting Him as much as ever.

6 This being so, I want to remind you to stir into flame the strength and boldness[1] that is in you, that entered into you when I laid my hands upon your head and blessed you.

7 For the Holy Spirit, God's gift, does not want you to be afraid of people, but to be wise and strong, and to love them and enjoy being with them.

8 If you will stir up this inner power, you will never be afraid to tell others about our Lord, or to let them know that I am your friend even though I am here in jail for Christ's sake. You will be ready to suffer with me for the Lord, for He will give you strength in suffering.

---

[1] Implied. Literally, "stir up the gift of God."

9 It is He who saved us and chose us for His holy work, not because we deserved it but because that was His plan long before the world began—to show His love and kindness to us through Christ.

10 And now He has made all of this plain to us by the coming of our Savior Jesus Christ, who broke the power of death and showed us the way of everlasting life through trusting Him.

11 And God has chosen me to be His missionary, to preach to the Gentiles and teach them.

12 That is why I am suffering here in jail and I am certainly not ashamed of it, for I know the one in whom I trust, and I am sure that He is able to safely guard all that I have given Him until the day of His return.

13 Hold tightly to the pattern of truth I taught you, especially concerning the faith and love Christ Jesus offers you.[2]

14 Guard well the splendid, God-given ability you received as a gift from the Holy Spirit who lives within you.

15 As you know, all the Christians who came here from Asia have deserted me; even Phygellus and Hermogenes are gone.

16 May the Lord bless Onesiphorus and all his family, because he visited me and encouraged me often. His visits revived me like a breath of fresh air, and he was never ashamed of my being in jail.

17 In fact, when he came to Rome he searched everywhere trying to find me, and finally did.

18 May the Lord give him a special blessing at the day of Christ's return. And you know better than I can tell you how much he helped me at Ephesus.

CHAPTER 2

OH, Timothy, my son, be strong with the strength Christ Jesus gives you.

2 For you must teach others those things you and many

[2]Literally, "that is in Christ Jesus."

others have heard me speak about. Teach these great truths to trustworthy men who will, in turn, pass them on to others.

3 Take your share of suffering as a good soldier of Jesus Christ, just as I do,

4 And as Christ's soldier do not let yourself become tied up in worldly affairs, for then you cannot satisfy the one who has enlisted you in His army.

5 Follow the Lord's rules for doing His work, just as an athlete either follows the rules or is disqualified and wins no prize.

6 Work hard, like a farmer who gets paid well if he raises a large crop.

7 Think over these three illustrations, and may the Lord help you to understand how they apply to you.

8 Don't ever forget the wonderful fact that Jesus Christ was a Man, born into King David's family; and that He was God, as shown by the fact that He rose again from the dead.

9 It is because I have preached these great truths that I am in trouble here and have been put in jail like a criminal. But the Word of God is not chained, even though I am.

10 I am more than willing to suffer if that will bring salvation and eternal glory in Christ Jesus to those God has chosen.

11 I am comforted by this truth, that when we suffer and die for Christ it only means that we will begin living with Him in heaven.

12 And if we think that our present service for Him is hard, just remember that some day we are going to sit with Him and rule with Him. But if we give up when we suffer, and turn against Christ, then He must turn against us.

13 Even when we are too weak to have any faith left, He remains faithful to us and will help us, for He cannot disown us who are part of Himself, and He will always carry out His promises to us.

14 Remind your people of these great facts, and command them in the name of the Lord not to argue over unimportant things. Such arguments are confusing and useless, and even harmful.

528

15 Work hard so God can say to you, "Well done." Be a good workman, one who does not need to be ashamed when God examines your work. Know what His Word says and means.

16 Steer clear of foolish discussions which lead people into the sin of anger with each other.

17 Things will be said that will burn and hurt for a long time to come. Hymenaeus and Philetus, in their love of argument, are men like that.

18 They have left the path of truth, preaching the lie that the resurrection of the dead has already occurred; and they have weakened the faith of some who believe them.

19 But God's truth stands firm like a great rock, and nothing can shake it. It is a foundation stone with these words written on it: "The Lord knows those who are really His," and "A person who calls himself a Christian should not be doing things that are wrong."

20 In a wealthy home there are dishes made of gold and silver as well as some made from wood and clay. The expensive dishes are used for guests, and the cheap ones are used in the kitchen or to put garbage in.

21 If you stay away from sin you will be like one of these dishes made of purest gold—the very best in the house—so that Christ Himself can use you for His highest purposes.

22 Run from anything that gives you the evil thoughts that young men often have, but stay close to anything that makes you want to do right. Have faith and love, and enjoy the companionship of those who love the Lord and have pure hearts.

23 Again I say, don't get involved in foolish arguments which only upset people and make them angry.

24 God's people must not be quarrelsome; they must be gentle, patient teachers of those who are wrong.

25 Be humble when you are trying to teach those who are mixed up concerning the truth. For if you talk meekly and courteously to them they are more likely, with God's help, to turn away from their wrong ideas and believe what is true.

26   Then they will come to their senses and escape from Satan's trap of slavery to sin which he uses to catch them whenever he likes, and then they can begin doing the will of God.

CHAPTER 3

YOU may as well know this too, Timothy, that in the last days it is going to be very difficult to be a Christian.

2   For people will love only themselves and their money; they will be proud and boastful, sneering at God, disobedient to their parents, ungrateful to them, and thoroughly bad.

3   They will be hardheaded and never give in to others; they will be constant liars and troublemakers and will think nothing of immorality. They will be rough and cruel, and sneer at those who try to be good.

4   They will betray their friends; they will be hotheaded, puffed up with pride, and prefer good times to worshiping God.

5   They will go to church,[1] yes, but they won't really believe anything they hear. Don't be taken in by people like that.

6   They are the kind who craftily sneak into other people's homes and make friendships with silly, sin-burdened women and teach them their new doctrines.

7   Women of that kind are forever following new teachers, but they never understand the truth.

8   And these teachers fight truth just as Jannes and Jambres fought against Moses. They have dirty minds, warped and twisted, and have turned against the Christian faith.

9   But they won't get away with all this forever. Some day their deceit will be well known to everyone, as was the sin of Jannes and Jambres.

10   But you know from watching me that I am not that kind of person. You know what I believe and the way I live and what I want. You know my faith in Christ and how I have suffered. You know my love for you, and my patience.

---

[1] Literally, "having a form of godliness."

530

11   You know how many troubles I have had as a result of my preaching the Good News. You know about all that was done to me while I was visiting in Antioch, Iconium and Lystra, but the Lord delivered me.

12   Yes, and suffering will come to all who decide to live godly lives to please Christ Jesus, from those who hate Him.

13   In fact, evil men and false teachers will become worse and worse, deceiving many, they themselves having been deceived by Satan.

14   But you must keep on believing the things you have been taught. You know they are true for you know that you can trust those of us who have taught you.

15   You know how, when you were a small child, you were taught the holy Scriptures; and it is these that make you wise to accept God's salvation by trusting in Christ Jesus.

16   The whole Bible[2] was given to us by inspiration from God and is useful to teach us what is true and to make us realize what is wrong in our lives; it straightens us out and helps us do what is right.

17   It is God's way of making us well prepared at every point, fully equipped to do good to everyone.

CHAPTER 4

AND so I solemnly urge you before God and before Christ Jesus—who will some day judge the living and the dead when He appears to set up His kingdom—

2   To preach the Word of God urgently at all times, whenever you get the chance, in season and out, when it is convenient and when it is not. Correct and rebuke your people when they need it, encourage them to do right, and all the time be feeding them patiently with God's Word.

3   For there is going to come a time when people won't listen to the truth, but will go around looking for teachers who will tell them just what they want to hear.

---

[2]Literally, "every Scripture."

4 They won't listen to what the Bible says but will blithely follow their own misguided ideas.

5 You must stay awake and watch out for all these dangers. And don't be afraid of suffering for the Lord. Bring others to Christ. Leave nothing undone that you ought to do.

6 I say this because I won't be around to help you very much longer. My time has almost run out. Very soon now I will be on my way to heaven.

7 I have fought long and hard for my Lord, and through it all I have kept true to Him. And now the time has come for me to stop fighting and rest.

8 In heaven a crown is waiting for me which the Lord, the righteous Judge, will give me on that great day of His return. And not just to me, but to all those whose lives show that they are eagerly looking forward to His coming back again.

9 Please come as soon as you can,

10 For Demas has left me. He loved the good things of this life and went to Thessalonica. Crescens has gone to Galatia, Titus to Dalmatia.

11 Only Luke is with me. Bring Mark with you when you come, for I need him.

12 (Tychicus is gone too, as I sent him to Ephesus.)

13 When you come, be sure to bring the coat I left at Troas with Brother Carpus, and also the books, but especially the parchments.

14 Alexander the coppersmith has done me much harm. The Lord will punish him,

15 But be careful of him, for he fought against everything we said.

16 The first time I was brought before the judge no one was here to help me. Everyone had run away. I hope that they will not be blamed for it.

17 But the Lord stood with me and gave me the opportunity to boldly preach a whole sermon for all the world to hear. And He saved me from being thrown to the lions.[1]

18 Yes, and the Lord will always deliver me from all evil

[1]Literally, "I was delivered out of the mouth of the lion."

and will bring me into His heavenly kingdom. To God be the glory for ever and ever. Amen.

19   Please say "hello" for me to Priscilla and Aquila and those living at the home of Onesiphorus.

20   Erastus stayed at Corinth, and I left Trophimus sick at Miletus.

21   Do try to be here before winter. Eubulus sends you greetings, and so do Pudens, Linus, Claudia, and all the others.

22   May the Lord Jesus Christ be with your spirit.

Farewell,

Paul

MEANWHILE, OFF

Fred Davis of Central High in Jackson, Miss. (in photos he's Number 11 and the lead runner) not only filled student leadership and athletic positions in his school, but shared with many others what Christ meant to him. As a result, Number 55—Dave Roberts—and the runner behind Fred, Doug Frazier—came to Him, as did numerous others. As you read this next letter, note that Paul points out that Titus was left on Crete to do a job. Fred was put by God into Central High to do a job. Each of us is placed in some situation—not only to talk about what it means to be involved with Jesus Christ, but to live with Him in charge. Notice how Paul refers to phonies who mouth it but don't live it—yet depicts a way of "enthusiasm for doing kind things for others" and "the purity of mind and heart" that can make our youth a time for meaning and reality instead of frustration.

THE FIELD...

TITUS

CHAPTER 1

FROM: Paul, the slave of God and the messenger of Jesus Christ. I have been sent to bring faith to those God has chosen and to teach them to know God's truth—the kind of truth that changes lives—so that they can have eternal life, which God promised them before the world began—and He cannot lie.

3 And now in His own good time He has revealed this Good News and permits me to tell it to everyone. By command of God our Savior I have been trusted to do this work for Him.

4 *To:* Titus, who is truly my son in the affairs of the Lord. May God the Father and Christ Jesus our Savior give you His blessings and His peace.

5 I left you there on the island of Crete so that you could do whatever was needed to help strengthen each of its churches, and I asked you to appoint pastors[1] in every city who would follow the instructions I gave you.

6 The men you choose must be well thought of for their good lives; they must have only one wife and their children must love the Lord and not have a reputation for being wild or disobedient to their parents.

7 These pastors[1] must be men of blameless lives because they are God's ministers. They must not be proud or impatient; they must not be drunkards or fighters or greedy for money.

8 They must enjoy having guests in their homes and must

---

[1]More literally, "elders."

love all that is good. They must be sensible men, and fair. They must be clean minded and level headed.

9 Their belief in the truth which they have been taught must be strong and steadfast, so that they will be able to teach it to others and show those who disagree with them where they are wrong.

10 For there are many who refuse to obey; this is especially true among those who say that all Christians must obey the Jewish laws. But this is foolish talk; it blinds people to the truth,

11 And it must be stopped. Already whole families have been turned away from the grace of God. Such teachers are only after your money.

12 One of their own men, a prophet from Crete, has said about them, "These men of Crete are all liars; they are like lazy animals, living only to satisfy their stomachs."

13 And this is true. So speak to the Christians there as sternly as necessary to make them strong in the faith,

14 And to stop them from listening to Jewish folk tales and the demands of men who have turned their back on the truth.

15 A person who is pure of heart sees goodness and purity in everything; but a person whose own heart is evil and untrusting finds evil in everything, for his dirty mind and rebellious heart color all he sees and hears.

16 Such persons claim they know God, but from seeing the way they act, one knows they don't. They are rotten and disobedient, worthless so far as doing anything good is concerned.

CHAPTER 2

B UT as for you, speak up for the right living that goes along with true Christianity.

2 Teach the older men to be serious and unruffled; they must be sensible, knowing and believing the truth and doing everything with love and patience.

3 Teach the older women to be quiet and respectful in

everything they do. They must not go around speaking evil of others and must not be heavy drinkers, but they should be teachers of goodness.

4   These older women must train the younger women to live quietly, to love their husbands and their children,

5   And to be sensible and clean minded, spending their time in their own homes, being kind and obedient to their husbands, so that the Christian faith can't be spoken against by those who know them.

6   In the same way, urge the young men to behave carefully, taking life seriously.

7   And here you yourself must be an example to them of good deeds of every kind. Let everything you do reflect your love of the truth and the fact that you are in dead earnest about it.

8   Your conversation should be so sensible and logical that anyone who wants to argue will be ashamed of himself because there won't be anything to criticize in anything you say!

9   Urge slaves to obey their masters and to try their best to satisfy them. They must not talk back,

10   Nor steal, but must show themselves to be entirely trustworthy. In this way they will make people want to believe in our Savior and God.

11   For the free gift of eternal salvation is now being offered to everyone;

12   And along with this gift comes the realization that God wants us to turn from godless living and sinful pleasures and to live good, God-fearing lives day after day,

13   Looking forward to that time when His glory shall be seen—the glory of our great God and Savior Jesus Christ,

14   Who died under God's judgment against our sins, so that He could rescue us from constant falling into sin and make us His very own people, with cleansed hearts and real enthusiasm for doing kind things for others.

15   You must teach these things and encourage your people to do them, correcting them when necessary as one who has every right to do so. Don't let anyone think that what you say is not important.

CHAPTER 3

REMIND your people to obey the government and its officers, and always to be obedient and ready for any honest work.

2 They must not speak evil of anyone, nor quarrel, but be gentle and truly courteous to all.

3 Once we, too, were foolish and disobedient; we were misled by others and became slaves to many evil pleasures and wicked desires. Our lives were full of resentment and envy. We hated others and they hated us.

4 But when the time came for the kindness and love of God our Savior to appear,

5 Then He saved us—not because we were good enough to be saved, but because of His kindness and pity—by washing away our sins and giving us the new joy of the indwelling Holy Spirit

6 Whom He poured out upon us with wonderful fullness—and all because of what Jesus Christ our Savior did

7 So that He could declare us good in God's eyes—all because of His great kindness; and now we can share in the wealth of the eternal life He gives us, and we are eagerly looking forward to receiving it.

8 These things I have told you are all true. Insist on them so that Christians will be careful to do good deeds all the time, for this is not only right, but it brings results.

9 Don't get involved in arguing over unanswerable questions and controversial theological ideas; keep out of arguments and quarrels about obedience to Jewish laws, for this kind of thing isn't worthwhile; it only does harm.

10 If anyone is causing divisions among you, he should be given a first and second warning. After that have nothing more to do with him,

11 For such a person has a wrong sense of values. He is sinning, and he knows it.

12   I am planning to send either Artemas or Tychicus to you. As soon as one of them arrives, please try to meet me at Nicopolis as quickly as you can, for I have decided to stay there for the winter.

13   Do everything you can to help Zenas the lawyer and Apollos with their trip; see that they are given everything they need.

14   For our people must learn to help all who need their assistance, that their lives will be fruitful.

15   Everybody here sends greetings. Please say "hello" to all of the Christian friends there. May God's blessings be with you all.

Sincerely,

Paul

CHRISTIANS HAVE PREJUDICE TOO!

Students discuss the subject
"On Being a Negro in Chicago" and come to
the conclusion that even genuine Christians can

PHIL LANDRUM

be prejudiced, and that Christians must apply themselves
to cracking racial tensions through understanding,
concern and love—Christ-love. In this very
short, dramatic
letter to Philemon,
we see some
principles the
Bible lays out
about class
systems and what
our attitudes
should be toward
people different
from us. And
those who feel
others are "lower"
than they obviously
need to look deep
down inside. . . .

PHILEMON

CHAPTER 1

FROM: Paul, in jail for preaching the Good News about Jesus Christ, and from Brother Timothy.

To: Philemon, our much loved fellow worker, and to the church that meets in your home, and to Apphia our sister, and to Archippus who like myself is a soldier of the cross.

3 May God our Father and the Lord Jesus Christ give you His blessings and His peace.

4 I always thank God when I am praying for you, dear Philemon,

5 Because I keep hearing of your love and trust in the Lord Jesus and in His people.

6 And I pray that as you share your faith with others it will grip their lives too, as they see the wealth of good things in you that come from Christ Jesus.

7 I myself have gained much joy and comfort from your love, my brother, because your kindness has so often refreshed the hearts of God's people.

8, 9 Now I want to ask a favor of you. I could demand it of you in the name of Christ because it is the right thing for you to do, but I love you and prefer just to ask you—I, Paul, an old man now, here in jail for the sake of Jesus Christ.

10 My plea is that you show kindness to my child Onesimus, whom I won to the Lord while here in my chains.

11 Onesimus (whose name means "Useful") hasn't been of much use to you in the past, but now he is going to be of real use to both of us.

12   I am sending him back to you, and with him comes my own heart.

13   I really wanted to keep him here with me while I am in these chains for preaching the Good News, and you would have been helping me through him,

14   But I didn't want to do it without your consent. I didn't want you to be kind because you had to but because you wanted to.

15   Perhaps you could think of it this way: that he ran away from you for a little while so that now he can be yours forever,

16   No longer only a slave, but something much better—a beloved brother, especially to me. Now he will mean much more to you too, because he is not only a servant but also your brother in Christ.

17   If I am really your friend, give him the same welcome you would give to me if I were the one who was coming.

18   If he has harmed you in any way or stolen anything from you, charge me for it.

19   I will pay it back (I, Paul, personally guarantee this by writing it here with my own hand) but I won't mention how much you owe me! The fact is, you even owe me your very soul!

20   Yes, dear brother, give me joy with this loving act and my weary heart will praise the Lord.

21   I've written you this letter because I am positive that you will do what I ask and even more!

22   Please keep a guest room ready for me, for I am hoping that God will answer your prayers and let me come to you soon.

23   Epaphras my fellow prisoner, who is also here for preaching Christ Jesus, sends you his greetings.

24   So do Mark, Aristarchus, Demas and Luke, my fellow workers.

25   The blessings of our Lord Jesus Christ be upon your spirit.

                                                                    Paul

A GUY COULD GET
A HEADACHE!

Books, tests, studies, philosophies, everybody's believing different things, and a thousand shades of meanings. How does it all fit? How can we piece it all together? Consider this first chapter which indicates where we can get authoritative answers. This Book explained to the Jews of that day underlying granite-boulders of truth, which are just as valid today—as are the comments about putting this truth into action.

HEBREWS

CHAPTER 1

LONG ago God spoke in many different ways to our fathers through the prophets [in visions, dreams, and even face to face[1]], telling them little by little about His plans.

2 But now in these days He has spoken to us through His Son to whom He has given everything, and through whom He made the world and everything there is.

3 God's Son shines out with God's glory, and all that God's Son is and does marks Him as God. He regulates the universe by the mighty power of His command. He is the one who died to cleanse us and clear our record of all sin, and then sat down in highest honor beside the great God of heaven.

4 Thus He became far greater than the angels, as proved by the fact that His name "Son of God," which was passed on to Him from His Father, is far greater than the names and titles of the angels.

5, 6 For God never said to any angel, "You are My Son, and today I have given You the honor that goes with that name."[2] But God said it about Jesus. Another time He said, "I am His Father and He is My Son." And still another time— when His firstborn Son came to earth—God said, "Let all the angels of God worship Him."

7 God speaks of His angels as messengers swift as the wind and as servants made of flaming fire;

8 But of His Son He says, "Your kingdom, O God, will last forever and ever; its commands are always just and right.

---

[1]Implied.
[2]Literally, "this day I have begotten You."

9   You love right and hate wrong; so God, even Your God, has poured out more gladness upon You than on anyone else."

10   God also called Him "Lord" when He said, "Lord, in the beginning You made the earth, and the heavens are the work of Your hands.

11   They will disappear into nothingness, but You will remain forever. They will become worn out like old clothes,

12   And some day You will fold them up and replace them. But You Yourself will never change, and Your years will never end."

13   And did God ever say to an angel, as He does to His Son, "Sit here beside Me in honor until I crush all Your enemies beneath Your feet"?

14   No, for the angels are only spirit-messengers sent out to help and care for those who are to receive His salvation.

CHAPTER 2

S O we must listen very carefully to the truths we have heard, or we may drift away from them.

2   For since the messages from angels have always proved true and people have always been punished for disobeying them,

3   What makes us think that we can escape if we are indifferent to this great salvation announced by the Lord Jesus Himself, and passed on to us by those who heard Him speak?

4   God always has shown us that these messages are true by signs and wonders and various miracles and by giving certain special abilities from the Holy Spirit to those who believe; yes, God has assigned such gifts to each of us.

5   And the future world we are talking about will not be controlled by angels.

6   No, for in the book of Psalms David says to God, "What is mere man that You are so concerned about him? And who is this Son of Man You honor so highly?

7   For though You made Him lower than the angels for a little while, now You have crowned Him with glory and honor.

8   And You have put Him in complete charge of everything there is. Nothing is left out." We have not yet seen all of this take place,

9   But we do see Jesus—who for awhile was a little lower than the angels—crowned now by God with glory and honor because He suffered death for us. Yes, because of God's great kindness, Jesus tasted death for everyone in all the world.

10   And it was right and proper that God, who made everything for His own glory, should allow Jesus to suffer, for in doing this He was bringing vast multitudes of God's people to heaven; for His suffering made Jesus a perfect Leader, one fit to bring them into their salvation.

11   We who have been made holy by Jesus, now have the same Father He has. That is why Jesus is not ashamed to call us His brothers.

12   For He says in the book of Psalms, "I will talk to My brothers about God My Father, and together we will sing His praises."

13   At another time He said, "I will put My trust in God along with My brothers." And at still another time, "See, here am I and the children God gave Me."

14   Since we, God's children, are human beings—made of flesh and blood—He became flesh and blood too by being born in human form; for only as a human being could He die and in dying break the power of the devil who had the power of death.

15   Only in that way could He deliver those who through fear of death have been living all their lives as slaves to constant dread.

16   We all know He did not come as an angel but as a human being—yes, a Jew.

17   And it was necessary for Jesus to be like us, His brothers, so that He could be our merciful and faithful High Priest before God, a Priest who would be both merciful to us and faithful to God in dealing with the sins of the people.

18   For since He Himself has now been through suffering

and temptation, He knows what it is like when we suffer and are tempted, and He is wonderfully able to help us.

* * * * *

CHAPTER 3

THEREFORE, dear brothers whom God has set apart for Himself—you who are chosen for heaven—I want you to think now about this Jesus who is God's Messenger and the High Priest of our faith.

2 For Jesus was faithful to God who appointed Him High Priest, just as Moses also faithfully served in God's house.

3 But Jesus has far more glory than Moses, just as a man who builds a fine house gets more praise than his house does.

4 And many people can build houses, but only God made everything.

5 Well, Moses did a fine job working in God's house, but he was only a servant; and his work was mostly to illustrate and suggest those things that would happen later on.

6 But Christ, God's faithful Son, is in complete charge of God's house. And we Christians are God's house—He lives in us!—if we keep up our courage firm to the end, and our joy and our trust in the Lord.

7, 8 And since Christ is so much superior, the Holy Spirit warns us to listen to Him, to be careful to hear His voice today and not let our hearts become set against Him, as the people of Israel did. They steeled themselves against His love and complained against Him in the desert while He was testing them.

9 But God was patient with them forty years, though they tried His patience sorely; He kept right on doing His mighty miracles for them to see.

10 "But," God says, "I was very angry with them, for their hearts were always looking somewhere else instead of up to Me, and they never found the paths I wanted them to follow."

11 Then God, full of this anger against them, bound Him-

self with an oath that He would never let them come to His place of rest.

12   Beware then of your own hearts, dear brothers, lest you find that they, too, are evil and unbelieving and are leading you away from the living God.

13   Speak to each other about these things every day while there is still time, so that none of you will become hardened against God, being blinded by the glamor[1] of sin.

14   For if we are faithful to the end, trusting God just as we did when we first became Christians, we will share in all that belongs to Christ.

15   But *now* is the time. Never forget the warning, *"Today* if you hear God's voice speaking to you, do not harden your hearts against Him, as the people of Israel did when they rebelled against Him in the desert."

16   And who were those people I speak of, who heard God's voice speaking to them but then rebelled against Him? They were the ones who came out of Egypt with Moses their leader.

17   And who was it who made God angry for all those forty years? These same people who sinned and as a result died in the wilderness.

18   And to whom was God speaking when He swore with an oath that they could never go into the land He had promised His people? He was speaking to all those who disobeyed Him.

19   And why couldn't they go in? Because they didn't trust Him.

CHAPTER 4

ALTHOUGH God's promise still stands—His promise that all may enter His place of rest—we ought to tremble with fear because some of you may be on the verge of failing to get there after all.

2   For this wonderful news—the message that God wants to save us—has been given to us just as it was to those who lived

---

[1]Literally, "deceitfulness."

in the time of Moses. But it didn't do them any good because they didn't believe it. They didn't mix it with faith.

3   For only we who believe God can enter into His place of rest. He has said, "I have sworn in My anger that those who don't believe Me will never get in," even though He has been ready and waiting for them since the world began.

4   We know He is ready and waiting because it is written that God rested on the seventh day of creation, having finished all that He had planned to make.

5   Even so they didn't get in, for God finally said, "They shall never enter my rest."

6   Yet the promise remains and some get in—but not those who had the first chance, for they disobeyed God and failed to enter.

7   But He has set another time for coming in, and that time is now. He announced this through King David long years after man's first failure to enter, saying in the words already quoted, "Today when you hear Him calling, do not harden your hearts against Him."

8   This new place of rest He is talking about does not mean the land of Israel that Joshua led them into. If that were what God meant, He would not have spoken long afterwards about "today" being the time to get in.

9   So there is a full complete rest *still waiting* for the people of God.

10   Christ has already entered there. He is resting from his work, just as God did after the creation.

11   Let us do our best to go into that place of rest, too, being careful not to disobey God as the children of Israel did, thus failing to get in.

12   For whatever God says to us is full of living power: it is sharper than the sharpest dagger, cutting swift and deep into our innermost thoughts and desires with all their parts, exposing us for what we really are.

13   He knows about everyone, everywhere. Everything about us is bare and wide open to the all-seeing eyes of our living

God; nothing can be hidden from Him to whom we must explain all that we have done.

14   But Jesus the Son of God is our great High Priest who has gone to heaven itself to help us; therefore let us never stop trusting Him.

15   This High Priest of ours understands our weaknesses, since He had the same temptations we do, though He never once gave way to them and sinned.

16   So let us come boldly to the very throne of God and stay there to receive His mercy and to find grace to help us in our times of need.

CHAPTER 5

THE Jewish high priest is merely a man like anyone else, but he is chosen to speak for all other men in their dealings with God. He presents their gifts to God and offers to Him the blood of animals that are sacrificed to cover the sins of the people and his own sins too. And because he is a man he can deal gently with other men, though they are foolish and ignorant, for he, too, is surrounded with the same temptations and understands their problems very well.

4   Another thing to remember is that no one can be a high priest just because he wants to be. He has to be called by God for this work in the same way God chose Aaron.

5   That is why Christ did not elect Himself to the honor of being High Priest; no, He was chosen by God. God said to Him, "My Son, today I have honored[1] You."

6   And another time God said to Him, "You have been chosen to be a priest forever, with the same rank as Melchizedek."

7   Yet while Christ was here on earth He pleaded with God, praying with tears and agony of soul to the only one who

---

[1]Literally, "begotten You." Probably the reference is to the day of Christ's resurrection.

would save Him from [premature²] death. And God heard His prayers because of His strong desire to obey God at all times.

8   And even though Jesus was God's Son, He had to learn from experience what it was like to obey, when obeying meant suffering.

9   It was after He had proved Himself perfect in this experience that Jesus became the Giver of eternal salvation to all those who obey Him.

10   For remember that God had chosen Him to be a High Priest with the same rank as Melchizedek.

*   *   *   *   *

11   There is much more I would like to say along these lines, but you don't seem to listen, so it's hard to make you understand.

12, 13   You have been Christians a long time now, and you ought to be teaching others, but instead you have dropped back to the place where you need someone to teach you all over again the very first principles in God's Word. You are like babies who can drink only milk, not old enough for solid food. And when a person is still living on milk it shows he isn't very far along in the Christian life, and doesn't know much about the difference between right and wrong. He is still a baby-Christian!

14   You will never be able to eat solid spiritual food and understand the deeper things of God's Word until you become better Christians and learn right from wrong by practicing doing right.

---

²Implied. Christ's longing was to live until He could die on the cross for all mankind. There is a strong case to be made that Satan's great desire was that Christ should die prematurely, before the mighty work at the cross could be performed. Christ's body, being human, was frail and weak like ours (except that His was sinless). He had said just a few moments before, "My soul is exceeding sorrowful *unto death*." And can a human body live long under such pressure of spirit as He underwent in the Garden, that caused sweating of great drops of blood? But God graciously heard and answered His anguished cry in Gethsemane ("Let this cup pass from me") and preserved Him from seemingly imminent and premature death: for an angel was sent to strengthen Him so that He could live to accomplish God's perfect will at the cross. . . . But some readers may prefer the explanation that Christ's plea was that He be saved *out from* death, at the Resurrection.

CHAPTER 6

LET us stop going over the same old ground again and again, always teaching those first lessons about Christ. Let us go on instead to other things and become mature in our understanding, as strong Christians ought to be. Surely we don't need to speak further about the foolishness of trying to be saved by being good, or about the necessity of faith in God;

2 You don't need further instruction about baptism and spiritual gifts[1] and the resurrection of the dead and eternal judgment.

3 The Lord willing, we will go on now to other things.

4 There is no use trying to bring you back to the Lord again if you have once understood the Good News and tasted for yourself the good things of heaven and shared in the Holy Spirit,

5 And know how good the Word of God is, and felt the mighty powers of the world to come,

6 And then have turned against God. You cannot bring yourself to repent again if you have nailed the Son of God to the cross again by rejecting Him, holding Him up to mocking and to public shame.

7 When a farmer's land has had many showers upon it and good crops come up, that land has experienced God's blessing upon it.

8 But if it keeps on having crops of thistles and thorns, the land is considered no good and is ready for condemnation and burning off.

9 Dear friends, even though I am talking like this I really don't believe that what I am saying applies to you. I am confident you are producing the good fruit that comes along with your salvation.

10 For God is not unfair. How can He forget your hard work for Him, or forget the way you used to show your love for Him—and still do—by helping His children?

[1] Literally, "the laying on of hands."

11   And we are anxious that you keep right on loving others as long as life lasts, so that you will get your full reward.

12   Then, knowing what lies ahead for you, you won't become bored with being a Christian, nor become spiritually dull and indifferent, but you will be anxious to follow the example of those who receive all that God has promised them because of their strong faith and patience.

*   *   *   *   *

13   For instance, there was God's promise to Abraham: God took an oath in His own name, since there was no one greater to swear by,

14   That He would bless Abraham again and again, and give him a son and make him the father of a great nation of people.

15   Then Abraham waited patiently until finally God gave him a son, Isaac, just as He had promised.

16   When a man takes an oath, he is calling upon someone greater than himself to force him to do what he has promised, or to punish him if he later refuses to do it; the oath ends all argument about it.

17   God also bound Himself with an oath, so that those He promised to help would be perfectly sure and never need to wonder whether He might change His plans.

18   He has given us both His promise and His oath, two things we can completely count on, for it is impossible for God to tell a lie. Now all those who flee to Him to save them can take new courage when they hear such assurances from God; now they can know without doubt that He will give them the salvation He has promised them.

19   This certain hope of being saved is a strong and trustworthy anchor for our souls, connecting us with God Himself behind the sacred curtains of heaven,

20   Where Christ has gone ahead to plead for us from His position as² our High Priest, with the honor and rank of Melchizedek.

---

²Literally, "having become."

CHAPTER 7

THIS Melchizedek was king of the city of Salem, and also a priest of the Most High God. When Abraham was returning home after winning a great battle against many kings, Melchizedek met him and blessed him;

2 Then Abraham took a tenth of all he had won in the battle and gave it to Melchizedek. Melchizedek's name means "Justice," so he is the King of Justice; and he is also the King of Peace because of the name of his city, Salem, which means "Peace."

3 Melchizedek had no father or mother[1] and there is no record of any of his ancestors. He was never born and he never died but his life is like that of the Son of God—a priest forever.

4 See then how great this Melchizedek is:

(a) Even Abraham, the first and most honored of all God's chosen people, gave Melchizedek a tenth of the spoils he took from the kings he had been fighting.

5 One could understand why Abraham would do this if Melchizedek had been a Jewish priest, for later on God's people were required by law to give gifts to help their priests because the priests were their relatives.

6 But Melchizedek was not a relative, and yet Abraham paid him.

(b) Melchizedek placed a blessing upon mighty Abraham,

7 And as everyone knows, a person who has the power to bless is always greater than the person he blesses.

8 (c) The Jewish priests, though mortal, received tithes; but we are told that Melchizedek lives on.

9 (d) One might even say that Levi himself (the ancestor of all Jewish priests, of all who receive tithes), paid tithes to Melchizedek through Abraham.

10 For although Levi wasn't born yet, the seed from which

---

[1]No one can be sure whether this means that Melchizedek was Christ appearing to Abraham in human form, or simply that there is no *record* of who Melchizedek's father or mother were, no *record* of his birth or death.

he came was in Abraham when Abraham paid the tithes to Melchizedek.

11   (e) If the Jewish priests and their laws had been able to save us, why then did God need to send Christ as a priest with the rank of Melchizedek, instead of sending someone with the rank of Aaron—the same rank all other priests had?

12, 13, 14   And when God sends a new kind of priest, His law must be changed to permit it. As we all know, Christ did not belong to the priest-tribe of Levi, but came from the tribe of Judah, which had not been chosen for priesthood; Moses had never given them that work.

15   So we can plainly see that God's method changed, for Christ, the new High Priest who came with the rank of Melchizedek,

16   Did not become a priest by meeting the old requirement of belonging to the tribe of Levi, but on the basis of power flowing from a life that cannot end.

17   And the Psalmist points this out when he says of Christ, "You are a priest forever with the rank of Melchizedek."

18   Yes, the old system of priesthood based on family lines was canceled because it didn't work. It was weak and useless for saving people.

19   It never made anyone really right with God. But now we have a far better hope, for Christ makes us acceptable to God, and now we may draw near to Him.

20   God took an oath that Christ would always be a Priest,

21   Although He never said that of other priests. Only to Christ He said, "The Lord has sworn and will never change His mind: You are a Priest forever, with the rank of Melchizedek."

22   Because of God's oath, Christ can guarantee forever the success of this new and better arrangement.

23   Under the old arrangement there had to be many priests, so that when the older ones died off, the system could still be carried on by others who took their places.

24   But Jesus lives forever and continues to be a Priest so that no one else is needed.

25   He is able to save completely all who come to God

through Him. Since He will live forever, He will always be there to remind God that He has paid for their sins with His blood.

26 He is, therefore, exactly the kind of High Priest we need; for He is holy and blameless, unstained by sin, undefiled by sinners, and to Him has been given the place of honor in heaven.

27 He never needs the daily blood of animal sacrifices, as other priests did, to cover over first their own sins and then the sins of the people; for He finished all sacrifices, once and for all, when He sacrificed Himself on the cross.

28 Under the old system, even the high priests were weak and sinful men who could not keep from doing wrong, but later God appointed by His oath His Son who is perfect forever.

CHAPTER 8

WHAT we are saying is this: Christ, whose priesthood we have just described, is our High Priest, and is in heaven at the place of greatest honor next to God Himself.

2 He ministers in the temple in heaven, the true place of worship built by the Lord and not by human hands.

3 And since every high priest is appointed to offer gifts and sacrifices, Christ must make an offering too.

4 The sacrifice He offers is far better than those offered by the earthly priests. (But even so, if He were here on earth He wouldn't even be permitted to be a priest, because down here the priests still follow the old Jewish system of sacrifices.)

5 Their work is connected with a mere earthly model of the real tabernacle in heaven; for when Moses was getting ready to build the tabernacle, God warned him to follow exactly the pattern of the heavenly tabernacle as shown to him on Mount Sinai.

6 But Christ, as a Minister in heaven, has been rewarded with a far more important work than those who serve under the

old laws, because the new agreement which He passes on to us from God contains far more wonderful promises.

7   The old agreement didn't even work. If it had, there would have been no need for another to replace it.

8   But God Himself found fault with the old one, for He said, "The day will come when I will make a new agreement with the people of Israel and the people of Judah.

9   This new agreement will not be like the old one I gave to their fathers on the day when I took them by the hand to lead them out of the land of Egypt; they did not keep their part in that agreement, so I had to cancel it.

10   But this is the new agreement I will make with the people of Israel, says the Lord: I will write My laws in their minds so that they will know what I want them to do without My even telling them, and these laws will be in their hearts so that they will want to obey them, and I will be their God and they shall be My people.

11   And no one then will need to speak to his friend or neighbor or brother, saying, 'You, too, should know the Lord,' because everyone, great and small, will know Me already.

12   And I will be merciful to them in their wrongdoings, and I will remember their sins no more."

13   God speaks of these new promises, of this new agreement, as taking the place of the old one; for the old one is out of date now and has been put aside forever.

CHAPTER 9

NOW in that first agreement between God and His people there were rules for worship and there was a sacred tent down here on earth. Inside this place of worship there were two rooms. The first one contained the golden candlestick and a table with special loaves of holy bread upon it; this part was called the Holy Place.

3   Then there was a curtain and behind the curtain was a room called the Holy of Holies.

554

4 In that room there were a golden incense-altar and the golden chest, called the ark of the covenant, completely covered on all sides with pure gold. Inside the ark were the tablets of stone with the Ten Commandments written on them, and a golden jar with some manna in it, and Aaron's wooden cane that budded.

5 Above the golden chest were statues of angels called the cherubim—the guardians of God's glory—with their wings stretched out over the ark's golden cover, called the mercy seat. But enough of such details.

6 Well, when all was ready the priests went in and out of the first room whenever they wanted to, doing their work.

7 But only the high priest went into the inner room, and then only once a year, all alone, and always with blood which he sprinkled on the mercy seat as an offering to God to cover his own mistakes and sins, and the mistakes and sins of all the people.

8 And the Holy Spirit uses all this to point out to us that under the old system the common people could not go into the Holy of Holies as long as the outer room and the entire system it represents were still in use.

9 This has an important lesson for us today. For under the old system, gifts and sacrifices were offered, but these failed to cleanse the hearts of the people who brought them.

10 For the old system dealt only with certain rituals—what foods to eat and drink, rules for washing themselves, and rules about this and that. The people had to keep these rules to tide them over until Christ came with God's new and better way.

11 He came as High Priest of this better system which we now have. He went into that greater, perfect tabernacle in heaven, not made by men nor part of this world,

12 And once for all took blood into that inner room, the Holy of Holies, and sprinkled it on the mercy seat; but it was not the blood of goats and calves. No, He took His own blood, and with it He, by Himself, made sure of our eternal salvation.

13 And if under the old system the blood of bulls and

555

goats and the ashes of young cows could cleanse men's bodies from sin,

14   Just think how much more surely the blood of Christ will transform our lives and hearts. His sacrifice frees us from the worry of having to obey the old rules, and makes us want to serve the living God. For by the help of the eternal Holy Spirit, Christ willingly gave Himself to God to die for our sins—He being perfect, without a single sin or fault.

15   Christ came with this new agreement so that all who are invited may come and have forever all the wonders God has promised them. For Christ died to rescue them from the penalty of the sins they had committed while still under that old system.

16   Now, if someone dies and leaves a will—a list of things to be given away to certain people when he dies—no one gets anything until it is proved that the person who wrote the will is dead.

17   The will goes into effect only after the death of the person who wrote it. While he is still alive no one can use it to get any of those things he has promised them.

18   That is why blood was sprinkled [as proof of Christ's death[1]] before even the first agreement could go into effect.

19   For after Moses had given the people all of God's laws, he took the blood of calves and goats, along with water, and sprinkled the blood over the book of God's laws and over all the people, using branches of hyssop bushes and scarlet wool to sprinkle with.

20   Then he said, "This is the blood that marks the beginning of the agreement between you and God, the agreement God commanded me to make with you."

21   And in the same way he sprinkled blood on the sacred tent and on whatever instruments were used for worship.

22   In fact we can say that under the old agreement almost everything was cleansed by sprinkling it with blood, and without the shedding of blood there is no forgiveness of sins.

23   That is why the sacred tent down here on earth, and everything in it—all copied from things in heaven—all had to

---

[1]Implied.

be made pure by Moses in this way, by being sprinkled with the blood of animals. But the real things in heaven, of which these down here are copies, were made pure with far more precious offerings.

24 For Christ has entered into heaven itself, to appear now before God as our Friend. It was not in the earthly place of worship that He did this, for that was merely a copy of the real temple in heaven.

25 Nor has He offered Himself again and again, as the high priest down here on earth offers animal blood in the Holy of Holies each year.

26 If that had been necessary, then He would have had to die again and again, ever since the world began. But no! He came once for all, at the end of the age, to put away the power of sin forever by dying for us.

27 And just as it is destined that men die only once, and after that comes judgment,

28 So also Christ died only once as an offering for the sins of many people; and He will come again, but not to deal again with our sins. This time He will come bringing salvation to all those who are eagerly and patiently waiting for Him.

CHAPTER 10

THE old system of Jewish laws gave only a dim foretaste of the good things Christ would do for us. The sacrifices under the old system were repeated again and again, year after year, but even so they could never save those who lived under their rules.

2 If they could have, one offering would have been enough; the worshipers would have been cleansed once for all, and their feeling of guilt would be gone.

3 But just the opposite happened: those yearly sacrifices reminded them of their disobedience and guilt instead of relieving their minds.

4   For it is not possible for the blood of bulls and goats to really take away sins.[1]

5   That is why Christ said, as He came into the world, "O God, the blood of bulls and goats cannot satisfy You, so You have made ready this body of Mine for Me to lay as a sacrifice upon Your altar.

6   You were not satisfied with the animal sacrifices, slain and burnt before You as offerings for sin.

7   Then I said, 'See, I have come to do Your will, to lay down My life, just as the Scriptures said that I would.'"

8   After Christ said this, about not being satisfied with the various sacrifices and offerings required under the old system,

9   He then added, "Here I am. I have come to give My life." He cancels the first system in favor of a far better one.

10   Under this new plan we have been forgiven and made clean by Christ's dying for us once and for all.

11   Under the old agreement the priests stood before the altar day after day offering sacrifices that could never take away our sins.

12   But Christ gave Himself to God for our sins as one sacrifice for all time, and then sat down in the place of highest honor at God's right hand,

13   Waiting for His enemies to be laid under His feet.

14   For by that one offering He made forever perfect in the sight of God all those whom He is making holy.

15   And the Holy Spirit testifies that this is so, for He has said,

16   "This is the agreement I will make with the people of Israel, though they broke their first agreement: I will write My laws into their minds so that they will always know My will, and I will put My laws in their hearts so that they will want to obey them."

17   And then He adds, "I will never again remember their sins and lawless deeds."

18   Now, when sins have once been forever forgiven and

---

[1]The blood of bulls and goats merely covered over the sins, taking them out of sight for hundreds of years until Jesus Christ came to die on the cross. There He gave His own blood which forever took those sins away.

forgotten, there is no need to offer more sacrifices to get rid of them.

19 And so, dear brothers, now we may walk right into the very Holy of Holies where God is, because of the blood of Jesus.

20 This is the fresh, new, life-giving way which Christ has opened up for us by tearing the curtain—His human body—to let us into the holy presence of God.

21 And since this great High Priest of ours rules over God's household,

22 Let us go right in, to God Himself, with true hearts fully trusting Him to receive us, because we have been sprinkled with Christ's blood to make us clean, and because our bodies have been washed with the pure water.

23 Now we can look forward to the salvation God has promised us. There is no longer any room for doubt, and we can tell others that salvation is ours, for there is no question that He will do what He says.

24 In response to all He has done for us, let us outdo each other in being helpful and kind to each other and in doing good.

25 Let us not neglect our church duties and meetings, as some people do, but encourage and warn each other, especially now that the day of His coming back again is drawing near.

26 If anyone sins deliberately by rejecting the Savior after knowing the truth of forgiveness, this sin is not covered by Christ's death; there is no way to get rid of it.

27 There will be nothing to look forward to but the terrible punishment of God's awful anger which will consume all His enemies.

28 A man who refused to obey the laws given by Moses was killed without mercy if there were two or three witnesses to his sin.

29 Think how much more terrible the punishment will be for those who have trampled underfoot the Son of God and

treated His cleansing blood as though it were common and unhallowed, and insulted and outraged the Holy Spirit who brings God's mercy to His people.

30 For we know Him who said, "Justice belongs to Me; I will repay them"; who also said, "The Lord Himself will handle these cases."

31 It is a fearful thing to fall into the hands of the living God.

*   *   *   *   *

32 Don't ever forget those wonderful days when you first learned about Christ. Remember how you kept right on with the Lord even though it meant terrible suffering.

33 Sometimes you were laughed at and beaten, and sometimes you watched and sympathized with others suffering the same things.

34 You suffered with those thrown into jail, and you were actually joyful when all you owned was taken from you, knowing that better things were awaiting you in heaven, things that would be yours forever.

35 Do not let this happy trust in the Lord die away, no matter what happens. Remember your reward!

36 You need to keep on patiently doing God's will if you want Him to do for you all that He has promised.

37 His coming will not be delayed much longer.

38 And those whose faith has made them good in God's sight must live by faith, trusting Him in everything. Otherwise, if they shrink back, God will have no pleasure in them.

39 But we have never turned our backs on God and sealed our fate. No, our faith in Him assures our souls' salvation.

CHAPTER 11

WHAT is faith? It is the confident assurance that something we want is going to happen. It is the certainty that what we hope for is waiting for us, even though we cannot see it up ahead.

2   Men of God in days of old were famous for their faith.

3   By faith—by believing God—we know that the world and the stars—in fact, all things—were made at God's command; and that they were made from nothing![1]

4   It was by faith that Abel obeyed God and brought an offering that pleased God more than Cain's offering did. God accepted Abel and proved it by accepting his gift; and though Abel is long dead, we can still learn lessons from him about trusting God.

5   Enoch trusted God too, and that is why God took him away to heaven without dying; suddenly he was gone because God took him. Before this happened God had said[1] how pleased He was with Enoch.

6   You can never please God without faith, without depending on Him. Anyone who wants to come to God must believe that there is a God and that He rewards those who sincerely look for Him.

7   Noah was another who trusted God. When he heard God's warning about the future, Noah believed Him even though there was then no sign of a flood, and wasting no time, he built the ark and saved his family. Noah's belief in God was in direct contrast to the sin and disbelief of the rest of the world—which refused to obey—and because of his faith he became one of those whom God has accepted.

8   Abraham trusted God, and when God told him to leave home and go far away to another land which He promised to give him, Abraham obeyed. Away he went, not even knowing where he was going.

9   And even when he reached God's promised land, he lived in tents like a mere visitor, as did Isaac and Jacob, to whom God gave the same promise.

10   Abraham did this because he was confidently waiting for God to bring him to that strong heavenly city whose designer and builder is God.

11   Sarah, too, had faith, and because of this she was able to become a mother in spite of her old age, for she realized that

---

[1]Implied.

God, who gave her His promise, would certainly do what He said.

12 And so a whole nation came from Abraham, who was too old to have even one child—a nation with so many millions of people that, like the stars of the sky and the sand on the ocean shores, there is no way to count them.

13 These men of faith I have mentioned died without ever receiving all that God had promised them; but they saw it all awaiting them on ahead and were glad, for they agreed that this earth was not their real home but that they were just strangers visiting down here.

14 And quite obviously when they talked like that, they were looking forward to their real home in heaven.

15 If they had wanted to, they could have gone back to the good things of this world.

16 But they didn't want to. They were living for heaven. And now God is not ashamed to be called their God, for He has made a heavenly city for them.

17 While God was testing him, Abraham still trusted in God and His promises, and so he offered up his son Isaac, and was ready to slay him on the altar of sacrifice;

18 Yes, to slay even Isaac, through whom God had promised to give Abraham a whole nation of descendants!

19 He believed that if Isaac died God would bring him back to life again; and that is just about what happened, for as far as Abraham was concerned, Isaac was doomed to death, but he came back again alive!

20 It was by faith that Isaac knew God would give future blessings to his two sons, Jacob and Esau.

21 By faith Jacob, when he was old and dying, blessed each of Joseph's two sons as he stood and prayed, leaning on the top of his cane.

22 And it was by faith that Joseph, as he neared the end of his life, confidently spoke of God bringing the people of Israel out of Egypt; and he was so sure of it that he made them promise to carry his bones with them when they left!

23 Moses' parents had faith too. When they saw that God had given them an unusual child, they trusted that God would

save him from the death the king commanded, and they hid him for three months, and were not afraid.

24, 25 It was by faith that Moses, when he grew up, refused to be treated as the grandson of the king, but chose to share ill-treatment with God's people instead of enjoying the fleeting pleasures of sin.

26 He thought that it was better to suffer for the promised Christ than to own all the treasures of Egypt, for he was looking forward to the great reward that God would give him.

27 And it was because he trusted God that he left the land of Egypt and wasn't afraid of the king's anger. Moses kept right on going; it seemed as though he could see God right there with him.

28 And it was because he believed God would save His people that he commanded them to kill a lamb as God had told them to and sprinkle the blood on the doorposts of their homes, so that God's terrible Angel of Death could not touch the oldest child in those homes, as he did among the Egyptians.

29 The people of Israel trusted God and went right through the Red Sea as though they were on dry ground. But when the Egyptians chasing them tried it, they all were drowned.

30 It was faith that brought the walls of Jericho tumbling down after the people of Israel had walked around them seven days, as God had commanded them.

31 By faith—because she believed in God and His power—Rahab the harlot did not die with all the others in her city when they refused to obey God, for she gave a friendly welcome to the spies.

32 Well, how much more do I need to say? It would take too long to recount the stories of the faith of Gideon and Barak and Samson and Jephthah and David and Samuel and all the prophets.

33 These people all trusted God and as a result won battles, overthrew kingdoms, ruled their people well, and received what God had promised them; they were kept from harm in a den of lions,

34 And in a fiery furnace. Some, through their faith, escaped death by the sword. Some were made strong again after they

had been weak or sick. Others were given great power in battle; they made whole armies turn and run away.

35 And some women, through faith, received their loved ones back again from death.

But others trusted God and were beaten to death, preferring to die rather than turn from God and be free—trusting that they would rise to a better life afterwards.

36 Some were laughed at and their backs cut open with whips, and others were chained in dungeons.

37, 38 Some died by stoning and some by being sawed in two; others were promised freedom if they would renounce their faith, then were killed with the sword. Some went about in skins of sheep and goats, wandering over deserts and mountains, hiding in dens and caves. They were hungry and sick and ill treated—too good for this world.

39 And these men of faith, though they trusted God and won His approval, none of them received all that God had promised them;

40 For God wanted them to wait and share the even better rewards that were prepared for us.

CHAPTER 12

SINCE we have such a huge crowd of men of faith watching us from the grandstands, let us strip off anything that slows us down or holds us back, and especially those sins that wrap themselves so tightly around our feet and trip us up; and let us run with patience the particular race that God has set before us.

2 Keep your eyes on Jesus, our leader and instructor. He was willing to die a shameful death on the cross because of the joy He knew would be His afterwards; and now He sits in the place of honor by the throne of God.

3 If you want to keep from becoming fainthearted and weary, think about His patience as sinful men did such terrible things to Him.

564

4 After all, you have never yet struggled against sin and temptation until you sweat great drops of blood.

5 And have you quite forgotten the encouraging words God spoke to you, His child? He said, "My son, don't be angry when the Lord punishes you. Don't be discouraged when He has to show you where you are wrong.

6 For when He punishes you, it proves that He loves you. When He whips you it proves you are really His child."

7 Let God train you, for He is doing what any loving father does for his children. Whoever heard of a son who was never corrected?

8 If God doesn't punish you when you need it, as other fathers punish their sons, then it means that you aren't really God's son at all—that you don't really belong in His family.

9 Since we respect our fathers here on earth, though they punish us, should we not all the more cheerfully submit to God's training so that we can begin to really live?

10 Our earthly fathers trained us for a few brief years, doing the best for us that they knew how, but God's correction is always right and for our best good, that we may share His holiness.

11 Being punished isn't enjoyable while it is happening—it hurts! But afterwards we can see the result, a quiet growth in grace and character.

12 So take a new grip with your tired hands, stand firm on your shaky legs,

13 And mark out a straight, smooth path for your feet so that those who follow you, though weak and lame, will not fall and hurt themselves, but become strong.

*   *   *   *   *

14 Try to stay out of all quarrels and seek to live a clean and holy life, for one who is not holy will not see the Lord.

15 Look after each other so that not one of you will fail to find God's best blessings. Watch out that no bitterness takes root among you, for as it springs up it causes deep trouble, hurting many in their spiritual lives.

16 Watch out that no one becomes involved in sexual sin

or becomes careless about God as Esau did: he traded his rights as the oldest son for a single meal.

17   And afterwards, when he wanted those rights back again, it was too late, even though he wept bitter tears of repentence. So remember, and be careful.

*   *   *   *   *

18   You have not had to stand face to face with terror, flaming fire, gloom, darkness and a terrible storm, as the Israelites did at Mount Sinai when God gave them His laws.

19   For there was an awesome trumpet blast, and a voice with a message so terrible that the people begged God to stop speaking.

20   They staggered back under God's command that if even an animal touched the mountain it must die.

21   Moses himself was so frightened at the sight that he shook with terrible fear.

22   But you have come right up into Mount Zion, to the city of the living God, the heavenly Jerusalem, and to the gathering of countless happy angels;

23   And to the church, composed of all those registered in heaven; and to God who is Judge of all; and to the spirits of the redeemed in heaven, already made perfect;

24   And to Jesus Himself, who has brought us His wonderful new agreement; and to the sprinkled blood which graciously forgives instead of crying out for vengeance as the blood of Abel did.

25   So see to it that you obey Him who is speaking to you. For if the people of Israel did not escape when they refused to listen to Moses, the earthly messenger, how terrible our danger if we refuse to listen to God who speaks to us from heaven!

26   When He spoke from Mount Sinai His voice shook the earth, but, "Next time," He says, "I will not only shake the earth, but the heavens too."

27   By this He means that He will sift out everything without solid foundations, so that only unshakable things will be left.

28   Since we have a kingdom nothing can destroy, let us

please God by serving Him with thankful hearts, and with holy fear and awe.

29   For our God is a consuming fire.

CHAPTER 13

CONTINUE to love each other with true brotherly love.
    2   Don't forget to be kind to strangers, for some who have done this have entertained angels without realizing it!

3   Don't forget about those in jail. Suffer with them as though you were there yourself. Share the sorrow of those being mistreated, for you know what they are going through.

*   *   *   *   *

4   Honor your marriage and its vows, and be pure; for God will surely punish all those who are immoral or commit adultery.

*   *   *   *   *

5   Stay away from the love of money; be satisfied with what you have. For God has said, "I will never, *never* fail you nor forsake you."

6   That is why we can say without any doubt or fear, "The Lord is my Helper and I am not afraid of anything that mere man can do to me."

7   Remember your leaders who have taught you the Word of God. Think of all the good that has come from their lives, and try to trust the Lord as they do.

*   *   *   *   *

8   Jesus Christ is the same yesterday, today, and forever.

9   So do not be attracted by strange, new ideas. Your spiritual strength comes as a gift from God, not from ceremonial rules about eating certain foods—a method which, by the way, hasn't helped those who have tried it!

*   *   *   *   *

10   We have an altar—the cross where Christ was sacrificed—where those who continue to seek salvation by obeying Jewish laws can never be helped.

11   Under the system of Jewish laws the high priest brought

the blood of the slain animals into the sanctuary as a sacrifice for sin, and then the bodies of the animals were burned outside the city.

12   That is why Jesus suffered and died outside the city, where His blood washed our sins away.

13   So let us go out to Him beyond the city walls [that is, outside the interests of this world, being willing to be despised[1]] to suffer with him there, bearing His shame.

14   For this world is not our home; we are looking forward to our everlasting home in heaven.

*   *   *   *   *

15   With Jesus' help we will continually offer our sacrifice of praise to God by telling others of the glory of His name.

16   Don't forget to do good and to share what you have with those in need, for such sacrifices are very pleasing to Him.

*   *   *   *   *

17   Obey your spiritual leaders and be willing to do what they say. For their work is to watch over your souls, and God will judge them on how well they do this. Give them reason to report joyfully about you to the Lord and not with sorrow, for then you will suffer for it too.

18   Pray for us, for our conscience is clear and we want to keep it that way.

19   I especially need your prayers right now so that I can come back to you sooner.

*   *   *   *   *

20, 21   And now may the God of peace who brought again from the dead our Lord Jesus, the great Shepherd of the sheep, equip you with all you need for doing His will, through the blood of the everlasting agreement between God and you. And may He produce in you through the power of Christ all that is pleasing to Him, to whom be glory forever and ever. Amen.

*   *   *   *   *

22   Brethren, please listen patiently to what I have said in this letter, for it is a short one.

---

[1]Implied.

568

23   I want you to know that Brother Timothy is now out of jail; if he comes here soon, I will come with him to see you.

24, 25   Give my greetings to all your leaders and to the other believers there. The Christians from Italy who are here with me send you their love. God's grace be with you all. Goodbye.

YOUCH!!!

A cowgirl in Phoenix hangs on in rip-snorting competition by riding a hunk of cowhide to the end of the rodeo arena. Whichever girl makes the fastest trip without falling off wins the event. Rough and rugged! But a lot of girls—and pretty ones at that—seem quite happy to try it. Rugged times can be like that—appealing, if you have a goal. In fact, they can teach one a lot of things, as this Book of James points out in such practical, down-to-bootstrap ways that it's impossible to avoid its meaning—though sometimes we'd like to.

JAMES

CHAPTER 1

FROM: James, a servant of God and of the Lord Jesus Christ.

To: Jewish Christians scattered everywhere. Greetings!

2 Dear brothers, is your life full of difficulties and temptations? Then be happy,

3 For when the way is rough, your patience has a chance to grow.

4 So let it grow, and don't try to squirm out of your problems. For when your patience is finally in full bloom, then you will be ready for anything, strong in character, full and complete.

5 If you want to know what God wants you to do, ask Him, and He will gladly tell you, for He is always ready to give a bountiful supply of wisdom to all who ask Him; He will not resent it.

6 But when you ask Him, be sure that you really expect Him to tell you, for a doubtful mind will be as unsettled as a wave of the sea that is driven and tossed by the wind;

7, 8 And every decision you then make will be uncertain, as you turn first this way, and then that. If you don't ask with faith, don't expect the Lord to give you any solid answer.

9 A Christian who doesn't amount to much in this world should be glad, for he is great in the Lord's sight.

10, 11 But a rich man should be glad that his riches mean nothing to the Lord, for he will soon be gone, like a flower that has lost its beauty and fades away, withered—killed by the scorching summer sun. So it is with rich men. They will soon die and leave behind all their busy activities.

12   Happy is the the man who doesn't give in and do wrong when he is tempted, for afterwards he will get as his reward the crown of life that God has promised those who love Him.

13   And remember, when someone wants to do wrong it is never God who is tempting him, for God never wants to do wrong and never tempts anyone else to do it.

14   Temptation is the pull of man's own evil thoughts and wishes.

15   These evil thoughts lead to evil actions and afterwards to the death penalty from God.

16   So don't be misled, dear brothers.

17   But whatever is good and perfect comes to us from God, the Creator of all light, and He shines forever without change or shadow.

18   And it was a happy day for Him[1] when He gave us our new lives, through the truth of His Word, and we became, as it were, the first children in His new family.

19   Dear brothers, don't ever forget that it is best to listen much, speak little, and not become angry;

20   For anger doesn't make us good, as God demands that we must be.

21   So get rid of all that is wrong in your life, both inside and outside, and humbly be glad for the wonderful message we have received, for it is able to save our souls as it takes hold of our hearts.

22   And remember, it is a message to obey, not just to listen to. So don't fool yourselves.

23   For if a person just listens and doesn't obey, he is like a man looking at his face in a mirror;

24   As soon as he walks away, he can't see himself anymore or remember what he looks like.

25   But if anyone keeps looking steadily into God's law for free men, he will not only remember it but he will do what it says, and God will greatly bless him in everything he does.

---

[1]Literally: "Of His own free will He gave us, etc."

26   Anyone who says he is a Christian but doesn't control his sharp tongue is just fooling himself, and his religion isn't worth much.

27   The Christian who is pure and without fault, from God the Father's point of view, is the one who takes care of orphans and widows, and whose soul remains true to the Lord—not soiled and dirtied by its contacts with the world.

CHAPTER 2

DEAR brothers, how can you claim that you belong to the Lord Jesus Christ, the Lord of glory, if you show favoritism to rich people and look down on poor people?

2   If a man comes into your church dressed in expensive clothes and with valuable gold rings on his fingers, and at the same moment another man comes in who is poor and dressed in threadbare clothes,

3   And you make a lot of fuss over the rich man and give him the best seat in the house and say to the poor man, "You can stand over there if you like, or else sit on the floor"—well,

4   This kind of action casts a question mark across your faith—are you really a Christian at all?—and shows that you are guided by wrong motives.

5   Listen to me, dear brothers: God has chosen poor people to be rich in faith, and the kingdom of heaven is theirs, for that is the gift God has promised to all those who love Him.

6   And yet, of the two strangers, you have despised the poor man. Don't you realize that it is usually the rich men who pick on you and drag you into court?

7   And all too often they are the ones who laugh at Jesus Christ, whose noble name you bear.

8   Yes indeed, it is good when you truly obey our Lord's command, "You must love and help your neighbors just as much as you love and take care of yourself."

9   But you are breaking this law of our Lord's when you favor the rich and fawn over them; it is sin.

572

10   And the person who keeps every law of God, but makes one little slip, is just as guilty as the person who has broken every law there is.

11   For the God who said you must not marry a woman who already has a husband, also said you must not murder, so even though you have not broken the marriage laws by committing adultery, but have murdered someone, you have entirely broken God's laws and stand utterly guilty before Him.

12   You will be judged on whether or not you are doing what Christ wants you to. So watch what you do and what you think;

13   For there will be no mercy to those who have shown no mercy. But if you have been merciful, then God's mercy toward you will win out over His judgment against you.

14   Dear brothers, what's the use of saying that you have faith and are Christians if you aren't proving it by helping others? Will *that* kind of faith save anyone?

15   If you have a friend who is in need of food and clothing,

16   And you say to him, "Well, good-bye and God bless you; stay warm and eat hearty," and then don't give him clothes or food, what good does that do?

17   So you see, it isn't enough just to have faith. You must also do good to prove that you have it. Faith that doesn't show itself by good works is no faith at all—it is dead and useless.

18   But someone may well argue, "You say the way to God is by faith alone, plus nothing; well, I say that good works are important too, for without good works you can't prove whether you have faith or not; but anyone can see that I have faith by the way I act."

19   Are there still some among you who hold that "only believing" is enough? Believing in one God? Well, remember that the devils believe this too—so strongly that they tremble in terror!

20   Dear foolish man! When will you ever learn that "believing" is useless without *doing* what God wants you to? Faith that does not result in good deeds is not real faith.

21   Don't you remember that even our father Abraham was

declared good because of what he *did*, when he was willing to obey God, even if it meant offering his son Isaac to die on the altar?

22 You see, he was trusting God so much that he was willing to do whatever God told him to; his faith was made complete by what he did, by his actions, his good deeds.

23 And so it happened just as the Scriptures say, that Abraham trusted God, and the Lord declared him good in God's sight, and he was even called "the friend of God."

24 So you see, a man is saved by what he does, as well as by what he believes.

25 Rahab, the prostitute, is another example of this. She was saved because of what she did when she hid those messengers and sent them safely away by a different road.

26 Just as the body is dead when there is no spirit in it, so faith is dead if it is not the kind that results in good deeds.

CHAPTER 3

DEAR brothers, don't be too eager to tell others their faults,[1] for we all make many mistakes; and when we teachers, who should know better, do wrong, our punishment will be greater than it would be for others. If anyone can control his tongue, it proves that he has perfect control over himself in every other way.

3 We can make a large horse turn around and go wherever we want by means of a small bit in his mouth.

4 And a tiny rudder makes a huge ship turn wherever the pilot wants it to go, even though the winds are strong.

5 So also the tongue is a small thing, but what enormous damage it can do. A great forest can be set on fire by one tiny spark.

6 And the tongue is a flame of fire. It is full of wickedness and poisons every part of the body. And the tongue is set on fire by hell itself, and can turn our whole lives into a blazing flame of destruction and disaster.

[1]Literally: "Not many (of you) should become masters (teachers)."

7   Men have trained, or can train, every kind of animal or bird that lives and every kind of reptile and fish,

8   But no human being can tame the tongue. It is always ready to pour out its deadly poison.

9   Sometimes it praises our heavenly Father, and sometimes it breaks out into curses against men who are made like God.

10   And so blessing and cursing come pouring out of the same mouth. Dear brothers, surely this is not right!

11   Does a spring of water bubble out first with fresh water and then with bitter water?

12   Can you pick olives from a fig tree, or figs from a grape vine? No, and you can't draw fresh water from a salty pool.

13   If you are wise, live a life of steady goodness, so that only good deeds will pour forth. And if you don't brag about them, then you will be truly wise!

14   And by all means don't brag about being wise and good if you are bitter and jealous and selfish; that is the worst sort of lie.

15   For jealousy and selfishness are not God's kind of wisdom. Such things are earthly, unspiritual, inspired by the devil.

16   For wherever there is jealousy or selfish ambition, there will be disorder and every other kind of evil.

17   But the wisdom that comes from heaven is first of all pure and full of quiet gentleness. Then it is peace-loving and courteous. It allows discussion and is willing to yield to others; it is full of mercy and good deeds. It is wholehearted and straightforward and sincere.

18   And those who are peacemakers will plant seeds of peace and reap a harvest of goodness.

CHAPTER 4

WHAT is causing the quarrels and fights among you? Isn't it because there is a whole army of evil desires within you?

2   You want what you don't have so you kill to get it. You

long for what others have, and can't afford it, so you start a fight to take it away from them. And yet the reason you don't have what you want is that you don't ask God for it.

3 And even when you do ask you don't get it because your whole aim is wrong—you want only what will give *you* pleasure.

4 You are like an unfaithful wife who loves her husband's enemies. Don't you realize that making friends with God's enemies—the evil pleasures of this world—makes you an enemy of God? I say it again, that if your aim is to enjoy the evil pleasure of the unsaved world, you cannot also be a friend of God.

5 Or what do you think the Scripture means when it says that the Holy Spirit, whom God has placed within us, watches over us with tender jealousy?

6 But He gives us more and more strength to stand against all such evil longings. As the Scripture says, God gives strength to the humble, but sets Himself against the proud and haughty.

7 So give yourselves humbly to God. Resist the devil and he will flee from you.

8 And when you draw close to God, God will draw close to you. Wash your hands, you sinners, and let your hearts be filled with God alone to make them pure and true to Him.

9 Let there be tears for the wrong things you have done. Let there be sorrow and sincere grief. Let there be sadness instead of laughter, and gloom instead of joy.

10 Then when you feel your worthlessness before the Lord, He will lift you up, encourage and help you.

11 Don't criticize and speak evil about each other, dear brothers. If you do, you will be fighting against God's law of loving one another, declaring it is wrong. But your job is not to decide whether this law is right or wrong, but to obey it.

12 Only He who made the law can rightly judge among us. He alone decides to save us or destroy. So what right do you have to judge or criticize others?

13 Look here, you people who say, "Today or tomorrow we are going to such and such a town, stay there a year, and open up a profitable business."

576

14   How do you know what is going to happen tomorrow? For the length of your lives is as uncertain as the morning fog—now you see it; soon it is gone.

15   What you ought to say is, "If the Lord wants us to, we shall live and do this or that."

16   Otherwise you will be bragging about your own plans, and such self-confidence never pleases God.

17   Remember, too, that knowing what is right to do and then not doing it is sin.

CHAPTER 5

L OOK here, you rich men, now is the time to cry and groan with anguished grief because of all the terrible troubles ahead of you.

2   Your wealth is even now rotting away, and your fine clothes are becoming mere moth-eaten rags.

3   The value of your gold and silver is dropping fast, yet it will stand as evidence against you, and eat your flesh like fire. That is what you have stored up for yourselves, to receive on that coming day of judgment.

4   For listen! Hear the cries of the field workers whom you have cheated of their pay. Their cries have reached the ears of the Lord of Hosts.

5   You have spent your years here on earth having fun, satisfying your every whim, and now your fat hearts are ready for the slaughter.

6   You have condemned and killed good men who had no power to defend themselves against you.

7   Now as for you, dear brothers who are waiting for the Lord's return, be patient, like a farmer who waits until the autumn for his precious harvest to ripen.

8   Yes, be patient. And take courage, for the coming of the Lord is near.

9   Don't grumble about each other, brothers. Are you yourselves above criticism? For see! the great Judge is coming. He is

almost here [let Him do whatever criticizing must be done[1]].

10 For examples of patience in suffering, look at the Lord's prophets.

11 We know how happy they are now because they stayed true to Him then, even though they suffered greatly for it. Job is an example of a man who continued to trust the Lord in sorrow; from his experiences we can see how the Lord's plan finally ended in good, for He is full of tenderness and mercy.

12 But most of all, dear brothers, do not swear either by heaven or earth or anything else; just say a simple yes or no, so that you will not sin and receive God's curse.

13 Is anyone among you suffering? He should keep on praying about it. And those who have reason to be thankful should continually be singing praises to the Lord.

14 Is anyone sick? He should call for the elders of the church and they should pray over him and pour a little oil upon him, calling on the Lord to heal him.

15 And their prayer, if offered in faith, will heal him, for the Lord will make him well; and if his sickness was caused by some sin, the Lord will forgive him.

16 Admit your faults to one another and pray for each other so that you may be healed. The earnest prayer of a righteous man has great power and wonderful results.

17 Elijah was as completely human as we are, and yet when he prayed earnestly that no rain would fall, none fell for the next three and one-half years!

18 Then he prayed again, this time that it *would* rain, and down it poured and the grass turned green and the gardens began to grow again.

19 Dear brothers, if anyone has slipped away from God and no longer trusts the Lord, and someone helps him understand the Truth again,

20 That person who brings him back to God will have saved a wandering soul from death, bringing about the forgiveness of his many sins.

Sincerely,
James

---

[1]Implied.

IS SHE FOR REAL ? ?

Sometimes a girl is so beautiful she seems almost make-believe. Wouldn't it be nice if we were all as attractive as this perky model? If there were a chance of someone's making each of us this attractive, most of us would be lining up outside the door. Yet, if Peter (who wrote the next two letters) had this choice, he would have chosen something entirely different.

He refers to a kind of attractiveness available to each of us, with no necessity for skin grafts or new faces —just some close observation and action when it comes to yielding to God.

I PETER

CHAPTER 1

FROM: Peter, Jesus Christ's missionary.

To: The Jewish Christians driven out of Jerusalem and scattered throughout Pontus, Galatia, Cappadocia, Ausia, and Bithynia.

2 Dear friends, God the Father chose you long ago and knew you would become His children. And the Holy Spirit has been at work in your hearts, cleansing you with the blood of Jesus Christ and making you to please Him. May God bless you richly and grant you increasing freedom from all anxiety and fear.

3 All honor to God, the God and Father of our Lord Jesus Christ; for it is His boundless mercy that has given us the privilege of being born again, so that we are now members of God's own family. Now we live in the hope of eternal life because Christ rose again from the dead.

4 And God has reserved for His children the priceless gift of eternal life; it is kept in heaven for you, pure and undefiled, beyond the reach of change and decay.

5 And God, in His mighty power, will make sure that you get there safely to receive it, because you are trusting Him. It will be yours in that coming last day for all to see.

6 So be truly glad! There is wonderful joy ahead, even though the going is rough for a while down here.

7 These trials are only to test your faith, to see whether or not it is strong and pure. It is being tested as fire tests gold and purifies it—and your faith is far more precious to God than

mere gold; so if your faith remains strong after being tried in the test tube of fiery trials, it will bring you much praise and glory and honor on the day of His return.

8 You love Him even though you have never seen Him; though not seeing Him, you trust Him; and even now you are happy with the inexpressible joy that comes from heaven itself.

9 And your further reward for trusting Him will be the salvation of your souls.

10 This salvation was something the prophets did not fully understand. Though they wrote about it, they had many questions as to what it all could mean.

11 They wondered what the Spirit of Christ within them was talking about, for He told them to write down the events which, since then, have happened to Christ: His suffering, and His great glory afterwards. And they wondered when and to whom all this would happen.

12 They were finally told that these things would not occur during their lifetime, but long years later, during yours. And now at last this Good News has been plainly announced to all of us. It was preached to us in the power of the same heaven-sent Holy Spirit who spoke to them; and it is all so strange and wonderful that even the angels in heaven would give a great deal to know more about it.

13 So now you can look forward soberly and intelligently to more of God's kindness to you when Jesus Christ returns.

14 Obey God because you are His children; don't slip back into your old ways—doing evil because you knew no better.

15 But be holy now in everything you do, just as the Lord is holy, who invited you to be His child.

16 He Himself has said, "You must be holy, for I am holy."

17 And remember that your heavenly Father to whom you pray has no favorites when He judges. He will judge you with perfect justice for everything you do; so act in reverent fear of Him from now on until you get to heaven.

18 God paid a ransom to save you from the impossible

road to heaven which your fathers tried to take, and the ransom He paid was not mere gold or silver, as you very well know.

19   But He paid for you with the precious lifeblood of Christ, the sinless, spotless Lamb of God.

20   God chose Him for this purpose long before the world began, but only recently was He brought into public view, in these last days, as a blessing to you.

21   Because of this your trust can be in God who raised Christ from the dead and gave Him great glory. Now your faith and hope can rest in Him alone.

22   Now you can have real love for everyone because your souls have been cleansed from selfishness and hatred when you trusted Christ to save you; so see to it that you really do love each other warmly, with all your hearts.

23   For you have a new life. It was not passed on to you from your parents, for the life they gave you will fade away. This new one will last forever, for it comes from Christ, God's ever-living Message to men.

24   Yes, our natural lives will fade as grass does when it becomes all brown and dry. All our greatness is like a flower that droops and falls;

25   But the Word of the Lord will last forever. And His message is the Good News that was preached to you.

CHAPTER 2

SO get rid of your feelings of hatred. Don't just pretend to be good! Be done with dishonesty and jealousy and talking about others behind their backs.

2, 3   If you have tasted the Lord's goodness and kindness, cry for more, as a baby cries for milk. Eat God's Word—read it, think about it—and grow strong in the Lord and be saved.

4   Come to Christ, who is the living Foundation of Rock upon which God builds; though men have spurned Him, He is very precious to God who has chosen Him above all others.

5   And now you have become living building-stones for

God's use in building His house. What's more, you are His holy priests; so come to Him [you are acceptable to Him because of Jesus Christ[1]] and offer to God those things that please Him.

6   As the Scriptures express it, "See, I am sending Christ to be the carefully chosen, precious Cornerstone of My church, and I will never disappoint those who trust in Him."

7   Yes, He is very precious to you who believe; and to those who reject Him, well—"The same Stone that was rejected by the builders has become the Cornerstone, the most honored and important part of the building."

8   And the Scriptures also say, "He is the Stone that some will stumble over, and the Rock that will make them fall." They will stumble because they will not listen to God's Word, nor obey it, and so this punishment must follow—that they will fall.

9   But you are not like that, for you have been chosen by God Himself—you are priests of the King, you are holy and pure, you are God's very own—all this so that you may show to others how God called you out of the darkness into His wonderful light.

10   Once you were less than nothing; now you are God's own. Once you knew very little of God's kindness; now your very lives have been changed by it.

11   Dear brothers, you are only visitors here. Since your real home is in heaven I beg you to keep away from the evil pleasures of this world; they are not for you, for they fight against your very souls.

12   Be careful how you behave among your unsaved neighbors; for then, even if they are suspicious of you and talk against you, they will end up praising God for your good works when Christ returns.

13   For the Lord's sake, obey every law of your government: those of the king as head of the state,

14   And those of the king's officers, for he has sent them to punish all who do wrong, and to honor those who do right.

15   It is God's will that your good lives should silence those

[1]Implied.

who foolishly condemn the Gospel without knowing what it can do for them, having never experienced its power.

16 You are free from the law, but that doesn't mean you are free to do wrong. Live as those who are free to do only God's will at all times.

17 Show respect for everyone. Love Christians everywhere. Fear God and honor the government.

18 Servants, you must respect your masters and do whatever they tell you—not only if they are kind and reasonable, but even if they are tough and cruel.

19 Praise the Lord if you are punished for doing right!

20 Of course, you get no credit for being patient if you are beaten for doing wrong; but if you do right and suffer for it, and are patient beneath the blows, God is well pleased.

21 This suffering is all part of the work God has given you. Christ, who suffered for you, is your example. Follow in His steps:

22 He never sinned, never told a lie,

23 Never answered back when insulted; when He suffered He did not threaten to get even; He left His case in the hands of God who always judges fairly.

24 He personally carried the load of our sins in His own body when He died on the cross, so that we can be finished with sin and live a good life from now on. For His wounds have healed ours!

25 Like sheep you wandered away from God, but now you have returned to your Shepherd, the Guardian of your souls who keeps you safe from all attacks.

CHAPTER 3

WIVES, fit in with your husbands' plans; for then if they refuse to listen when you talk to them about the Lord, they will be won by your respectful, pure behavior. Your godly lives will speak to them better than any words.

3 Don't be concerned about the outward beauty that depends on jewelry, or beautiful clothes, or hair arrangement.

4 Be beautiful inside, in your hearts, with the lasting charm of a gentle and quiet spirit which is so precious to God.

5 That kind of deep beauty was seen in the saintly women of old, who trusted God and fitted in with their husbands' plans.

6 Sarah, for instance, obeyed her husband Abraham, honoring him as head of the house. And if you do the same, you will be following in her steps like good daughters and doing what is right; then you will not need to fear [offending your husbands[1]].

7 You husbands must be careful of your wives, being thoughtful of their needs and honoring them as the weaker sex. Remember that you and your wife are partners in receiving God's blessings, and if you don't treat her as you should, your prayers will not get ready answers.

8 And now this word to all of you: You should be like one big happy family, full of sympathy toward each other, loving one another with tender hearts and humble minds.

9 Don't repay evil for evil. Don't snap back at those who say unkind things about you. Instead, pray for God's help for them, for we are to be kind to others, and God will bless us for it.

10 If you want a happy, good life, keep control of your tongue, and guard your lips from telling lies.

11 Turn away from evil and do good. Try to live in peace even if you must run after it to catch and hold it!

12 For the Lord is watching His children, listening to their prayers; but the Lord's face is hard against those who do evil.

13 Usually no one will hurt you for wanting to do good.

14 But even if they should, you are to be envied, for God will reward you for it.

15 Quietly trust yourself to Christ your Lord and if anybody asks why you believe as you do, be ready to tell him, and do it in a gentle and respectful way.

16 Do what is right; then if men speak against you, calling you evil names, they will become ashamed of themselves for falsely accusing you when you have only done what is good.

---

[1]Implied.

584

17 Remember, if God wants you to suffer, it is better to suffer for doing good than for doing wrong!

18 Christ also suffered. He died once for the sins of all us guilty sinners, although He Himself was innocent of any sin at any time, that He might bring us safely home to God. But though His body died, His spirit lived on,

19 And it was in the spirit that He visited the spirits in prison, and preached to them—

20 Spirits of those who, long before in the days of Noah, had refused to listen to God, though He waited patiently for them while Noah was building the ark. Yet only eight persons were saved from drowning in that terrible flood.

21 (That, by the way, is what baptism pictures for us: in baptism we show that we have been saved from death and doom by the resurrection of Christ;[2] not because our bodies are washed clean by the water, but because in being baptized we are turning to God and asking Him to cleanse our *hearts* from sin.)

22 And now Christ is in heaven, sitting in the place of honor next to God the Father, with all the angels and powers of heaven bowing before Him and obeying Him.

CHAPTER 4

SINCE Christ suffered and underwent pain, you must have the same attitude He did; you must be ready to suffer, too. For remember, when your body suffers, sin loses its power,

2 And you won't be spending the rest of your life chasing after evil desires, but will be anxious to do the will of God.

3 You have had enough in the past of the evil things the godless enjoy—sex sin, lust, getting drunk, wild parties, drinking bouts, and the worship of idols, and other terrible sins.[1]

4 Of course, your former friends will be very surprised when you don't eagerly join them any more in the wicked

---

[2]Or, "Baptism, which corresponds to this, now saves you through the Resurrection."
[1]Literally, "lawless idolatries."

things they do, and they will laugh at you in contempt and scorn.

5　But just remember that they must face the Judge of all, living and dead; they will be punished for the way they have lived.

6　That is why the Good News was preached even to those who were dead[2]—killed by the flood[3]—so that although their bodies were punished with death, they could still live in their spirits as God lives.

7　The end of the world is coming soon. Therefore be earnest, thoughtful men of prayer.

8　Most important of all, continue to show deep love for each other, for love makes up for many of your faults.[4]

9　Cheerfully share your home with those who need a meal or a place to stay for the night.

10　God has given each of you some special abilities; be sure to use them to help each other, passing on to others God's many kinds of blessings.

11　Are you called to preach? Then preach as though God Himself were speaking through you. Are you called to help others? Do it with all the strength and energy that God supplies, so that God will be glorified through Jesus Christ—to Him be glory and power forever and ever. Amen.

12　Dear friends, don't be bewildered or surprised when you go through the fiery trials ahead, for this is no strange, unusual thing that is going to happen to you.

13　Instead, be really glad—because these trials will make you partners with Christ in His suffering, and afterwards you will have the wonderful joy of sharing His glory in that coming day when it will be displayed.

14　Be happy if you are cursed and insulted for being a

---

[2]Peter's meaning is unclear to all commentators. God's program for the unsaved today is, "the wages of sin is death and after that the judgment." The Bible does not teach that those who are alive today' will have a second chance to hear and accept the Gospel. For this reason some believe that verse 6 would be more accurately interpreted: "And that is why the Good News of salvation was preached (in their lifetime) to those who were going to die. For though their bodies would be given the death penalty, like anyone else, they could still be alive in the spirit, as God is."
[3]Implied. See I Peter 3:19, 20.
[4]Or, "love overlooks each other's many faults."

Christian, for when that happens the Spirit of God will come upon you with great glory.[5]

15   Don't let me hear of your suffering for murdering or stealing or making trouble or being a busybody and prying into other people's affairs.

16   But it is no shame to suffer for being a Christian. Praise God for the privilege of being in Christ's family and being called by His wonderful name!

17   For the time has come for judgment, and it must begin first among God's own children. And if even we who are Christians must be judged, what terrible fate awaits those who have never believed in the Lord?

18   If the righteous are barely saved, what chance will the godless have?

19   So if you are suffering according to God's will, keep on doing what is right and trust yourself to the God who made you, for He will never fail you.

CHAPTER 5

AND now, a word to you elders of the church. I, too, am an elder; with my own eyes I saw Christ dying on the cross; and I, too, will share His glory and His honor when He returns. Fellow elders, this is my plea to you:

2   Feed the flock of God; care for it willingly, not grudgingly; not for what you will get out of it, but because you are eager to serve the Lord.

3   Don't be tyrants, but lead them by your good example,

4   And when the Head Shepherd comes, your reward will be a never-ending share in His glory and honor.

5   You younger men, follow the leadership of those who are older. And all of you serve each other with humble spirits, for God gives special blessings to those who are humble, but sets Himself against those who are proud.

6   If you will humble yourselves under the mighty hand of God, in His good time He will lift you up.

[5]Or, "the glory of the Spirit of God is being seen in you."

7 Let Him have all your worries and cares, for He is always thinking about you and watching everything that concerns you.

8 Be careful—watch out for attacks from Satan, your great enemy. He prowls around like a hungry, roaring lion, looking for some victim to tear apart.

9 Stand firm when he attacks. Trust the Lord; and remember that other Christians all around the world are going through these sufferings too.

10 After you have suffered a little while, our God, who is full of kindness through Christ, will give you His eternal glory. He personally will come and pick you up, and set you firmly in place, and make you stronger than ever.

11 To Him be all power over all things, forever and ever. Amen.

12 I am sending this note to you through the courtesy of Silvanus who is, in my opinion, a very faithful brother. I hope I have encouraged you by this letter for I have given you a true statement of the way God blesses. What I have told you here should help you to stand firmly in His love.

13 My wife[1] here in Rome—she is your sister in the Lord—sends you her greetings; so does my son Mark.

14 Give each other the handshake of Christian love. Peace be to all of you who are in Christ.

Peter

---

[1] Literally: "She who is at Babylon is likewise chosen"; but Babylon was the Christian nickname for Rome, and the "she" is thought by many to be Peter's wife to whom reference is made in Matthew 8:14, I Corinthians 9:5, etc. Others believe this should read: "Your sister church here in Babylon salutes you, and so does my son Mark."

II PETER

CHAPTER 1

FROM: Simon Peter, a servant and missionary of Jesus Christ.

To: All of you who have our kind of faith. The faith I speak of is the kind that Jesus Christ our God and Savior gives to us. How precious it is, and how just and good He is to give this same faith to each of us.

2 Do you want more and more of God's kindness and peace? Then learn to know Him better and better.

3 For as you know Him better, He will give you, through His great power, everything you need for living a truly good life: He even shares His own glory and His own goodness with us!

4 And by that same mighty power He has given us all the other rich and wonderful blessings He promised; for instance, the promise to save us from the lust and rottenness all around us, and to give us His own character.

5 But to obtain these gifts, you need more than faith; you must also work hard to be good, and even that is not enough. For then you must learn to know God better and discover what He wants you to do.

6 Next, learn to put aside your own desires so that you will become patient and godly, gladly letting God have His way with you.

7 This will make possible the next step, which is for you to enjoy other people and to like them, and finally you will grow to love them deeply.

8   The more you go on in this way, the more you will grow
strong spiritually and become fruitful and useful to our Lord
Jesus Christ.

9   But anyone who fails to go after these additions to faith
is blind indeed, or at least very shortsighted, and has forgotten
that God delivered him from the old life of sin so that now he
can live a strong, good life for the Lord.

10   So, dear brothers, work hard to prove that you really
are among those God has called and chosen, and then you will
never stumble or fall away.

11   And God will open wide the gates of heaven for you to
enter into the eternal kingdom of our Lord and Savior Jesus
Christ.

12   I plan to keep on reminding you of these things even
though you already know them and are really getting along
quite well!

13, 14   But the Lord Jesus Christ has showed me that my
days here on earth are numbered, and I am soon to die. As
long as I am still here I intend to keep sending these reminders
to you,

15   Hoping to impress them so clearly upon you that you
will remember them long after I have gone.

16   For we have not been telling you fairy tales when we
explained to you the power of our Lord Jesus Christ and His
coming again. My own eyes have seen His splendor and His
glory:

17, 18   I was there on the holy mountain when He shone
out with honor given Him by God His Father; I heard that
glorious, majestic voice calling down from heaven, saying, "This
is My much-loved Son; I am well pleased with Him."

19   So we have seen and proved that what the prophets said
came true. You will do well to pay close attention to everything
they have written, for, like lights shining into dark corners, their
words help us to understand many things that otherwise would
be dark and difficult. But when you consider the wonderful
truth of the prophets' words, then the light will dawn in your
souls and Christ the Morning Star will shine in your hearts.

20, 21   For no prophecy recorded in Scripture was ever thought up by the prophet himself. It was the Holy Spirit within these godly men who gave them true messages from God.

CHAPTER 2

BUT there were false prophets, too, in those days, just as there will be false teachers among you. They will cleverly tell their lies about God, turning against even their Master who bought them; but theirs will be a swift and terrible end.

2   Many will follow their evil teaching that there is nothing wrong with sexual sin. And because of them Christ and His way will be scoffed at.

3   These teachers in their greed will tell you anything to get hold of your money. But God condemned them long ago and their destruction is on the way.

4   For God did not spare even the angels who sinned, but threw them into hell, chained in gloomy caves and darkness until the judgment day.

5   And He did not spare any of the people who lived in ancient times before the flood except Noah, the one man who spoke up for God, and his family of seven. At that time God completely destroyed the whole world of ungodly men with the vast flood.

6   Later, He turned the cities of Sodom and Gomorrah into heaps of ashes and blotted them off the face of the earth, making them an example for all the ungodly in the future to look back upon and fear.

7, 8   But at the same time the Lord rescued Lot out of Sodom because he was a good man, sick of the terrible wickedness he saw everywhere around him day after day.

9   So also the Lord can rescue you and me from the temptations that surround us, and continue to punish the ungodly until the day of final judgment comes.

10   He is especially hard on those who follow their own evil, lustful thoughts, and those who are proud and willful, daring

even to scoff at the Glorious Ones[1] without so much as trembling,

11   Although the angels in heaven who stand in the very presence of the Lord, and are far greater in power and strength than these false teachers, never speak out disrespectfully against these evil Mighty Ones.

12   But false teachers are fools—no better than animals. They do whatever they feel like; born only to be caught and killed, they laugh at the terrifying powers of the underworld[2] which they know so little about; and they will be destroyed along with all the demons and powers of hell.[3]

13   That is the pay these teachers will have for their sin. For they live in evil pleasures day after day. They are a disgrace and a stain among you, deceiving you by living in foul sin on the side while they join your love feasts as though they were honest men.

14   No woman can escape their sinful stare, and of adultery they never have enough. They make a game of luring unstable women. They train themselves to be greedy; and are doomed and cursed.

15   They have gone off the road and become lost like Balaam, the son of Beor, who fell in love with the money he could make by doing wrong;

16   But Balaam was stopped from his mad course when his donkey spoke to him with a human voice, scolding and rebuking him.

17   These men are as useless as dried-up springs of water, promising much and delivering nothing; they are as unstable as clouds driven by the storm winds. They are doomed to the eternal pits of darkness.

18   They proudly boast about their sins and conquests, and, using lust as their bait, they lure back into sin those who have just escaped from such wicked living.

19   "You aren't saved by being good," they say, "so you might as well be bad. Do what you like, be free." But these very teachers who offer this "freedom" from law are themselves

---

[1]Or, "the glories of the unseen world."
[2]Literally, "the things they do not understand."
[3]Implied. Literally, "will be destroyed in the same destruction with them."

slaves to sin and destruction. For a man is a slave to whatever controls him.

20   And when a person has escaped from the wicked ways of the world by learning about our Lord and Savior Jesus Christ, and then gets tangled up with sin and becomes its slave again, he is worse off than he was before.

21   It would be better if he had never known about Christ at all than to learn of Him and then afterwards turn his back on the holy commandments that were given to him.

22   There is an old saying that "A dog comes back to what he has vomited, and a pig is washed only to come back and wallow in the mud again." That is the way it is with those who turn again to their sin.

CHAPTER 3

THIS is my second letter to you, dear brothers, and in both of them I have tried to remind you—if you will let me—about facts you already know: facts you learned from the holy prophets and from us apostles who brought you the words of our Lord and Savior.

3   First, I want to remind you that in the last days there will come scoffers who will do every wrong they can think of, and laugh at the truth.

4   This will be their line of argument: "So Jesus promised to come back, did he? Then where is He? He'll never come! Why, as far back as anyone can remember everything has remained exactly as it was since the first day of creation."

5, 6   They deliberately forget this fact: that God did destroy the world with a mighty flood, long after He had made the heavens by the word of His command, and had used the waters to form the earth and surround it.

7   And God has commanded that the earth and the heavens be stored away for a great bonfire at the judgment day, when all ungodly men will perish.

8   But don't forget this, dear friends, that a day or a thousand years from now is like tomorrow to the Lord.

9 He isn't really being slow about His promised return, even though it sometimes seems that way. But He is waiting, for the good reason that He is not willing that any should perish, and He is giving more time for sinners to repent.

10 The day of the Lord is surely coming, as unexpectedly as a thief, and then the heavens will pass away with a terrible noise and the heavenly bodies will disappear in fire, and the earth and everything on it will be burned up.

11 And so since everything around us is going to melt away, what holy, godly lives we should be living!

12 You should look forward to that day and hurry it along —the day when God will set the heavens on fire, and the heavenly bodies will melt and disappear in flames.

13 But we are looking forward to God's promise of new heavens and a new earth afterwards, where there will be only goodness.[1]

14 Dear friends, while you are waiting for these things to happen and for Him to come, try hard to live without sinning; and be at peace with everyone so that He will be pleased with you when He returns.

15, 16 And remember why He is waiting. He is giving us time to get His message of salvation out to others. Our wise and beloved brother Paul has talked about these same things in many of his letters. Some of his comments are not easy to understand, and there are people who are deliberately stupid, and always demand some unusual interpretation—they have twisted his letters around to mean something quite different from what he meant, just as they do the other parts of the Scripture—and the result is disaster for them.

17 I am warning you ahead of time, dear brothers, so that you can watch out and not be carried away by the mistakes of these wicked men, lest you yourselves become mixed up too.

18 But grow in spiritual strength and become better acquainted with our Lord and Savior Jesus Christ. To Him be all glory and splendid honor, both now and forevermore. Good-bye.

Peter

[1]Literally, "wherein righteousness dwells."

594

I'M COMFY HERE...

Each of us has his own group he feels at home with. These students, relaxed, casual, know they belong. Yet even in a group like this, arguments come up, friendships splinter, emptiness deepens, frustration at people's lack of understanding boils inside. We depend on our friends to provide something we deeply need. Why does it get spoiled so often? John, now an old, warmhearted man filled with love, shows us in these three letters the path to the kind of camaraderie that gives us what we need to live quality lives with those around us.

I JOHN

CHAPTER 1

C HRIST was alive when the world began, yet I myself have seen Him with my own eyes and listened to Him speak. I have touched Him with my own hands. He is God's message of Life.

2   This one who is Life from God has been shown to us and we guarantee that we have seen Him; I am speaking of Christ, who is eternal Life. He was with the Father and then was shown to us.

3   Again I say, we are telling you about what we ourselves have actually seen and heard, so that you may share the fellowship and the joys we have with the Father and with Jesus Christ His Son.

4   And if you do as I say in this letter, then you, too, will be full of joy, and so will we.

5   This is the message God has given us to pass on to you: that God is Light and in Him is no darkness at all.

6   So if we say we are His friends, but go on living in spiritual darkness and sin, we are lying.

7   But if we are living in the light of God's presence, just as Christ does, then we have wonderful fellowship and joy with each other, and the blood of Jesus His Son cleanses us from every sin.

8   If we say that we have no sin, we are only fooling ourselves, and refusing to accept the truth.

9   But if we confess our sins to Him,[1] He can be depended on to forgive us and to cleanse us from every wrong. [And it is

---

[1] Implied. Literally, "if we confess our sins."

perfectly proper for God to do this for us because Christ died to wash away our sins.[2]]

10 If we claim we have not sinned, we are lying and calling God a liar, *for He says we have sinned.*

CHAPTER 2

MY little children, I am telling you this so that you will stay away from sin. But if you sin, there is Someone to plead for you before the Father. His name is Jesus Christ, the one who is all that is good and who pleases God completely.

2 He is the one who took God's wrath against our sins upon Himself, and brought us into fellowship with God; and He is the forgiveness[1] for our sins, and not only ours but all the world's.

3 And how can we be sure that we belong to Him? By looking within ourselves: are we really trying to do what He wants us to?

4 Someone may say, "I am a Christian; I am on my way to heaven; I belong to Christ." But if he doesn't do what Christ tells him to, he is a liar.

5 But those who do what Christ tells them to will learn to love God more and more. That is the way to know whether or not you are a Christian.

6 Anyone who says he is a Christian should live as Christ did.

7 Dear brothers, I am not writing out a new rule for you to obey, for it is an old one you have always had, right from the start. You have heard it all before.

8 Yet it is always new, and works for you just as it did for Christ; and as we obey this commandment, *to love one another,* the darkness in our lives disappears and the new light of life in Christ shines in.

9 Anyone who says he is walking in the light of Christ but hates his brother Christian is still in darkness.

---

[2]Literally, "He is . . . just."
[1]Or, "atoning sacrifice."

10   But whoever loves his brother Christian is "walking in the light" and can see his way without stumbling around in darkness and sin.

11   For he who hates his Christian brother is wandering around in spiritual darkness and doesn't know where he is going, for the darkness has made him blind so that he cannot see the way.

12   I am writing these things to all of you, my little children, because your sins have been forgiven in the name of Jesus our Savior.

13   I am saying these things to you older men because you really know Christ, the one who has been alive from the beginning. And you young men, I am talking to you because you have won your battle with Satan. And I am writing to you younger boys and girls because you, too, have learned to know God our Father.

14   And so I say to you fathers who know the eternal God, and to you young men who are strong, with God's Word in your hearts, and have won your struggle against Satan:

15   Stop loving this evil world and all that it offers you, for when you love these things you show that you do not really love God;

16   For all these worldly things, these evil desires—the craze for sex, the ambition to buy everything that appeals to you, and the pride that comes from wealth and importance—these are not from God. They are from this evil world itself.

17   And this world is fading away, and these evil, forbidden things will go with it, but whoever keeps doing the will of God will live forever.

18   Dear children, this world's last hour has come. You have heard about the Antichrist who is coming—the one who is against Christ—and already many such persons have appeared. This makes us all the more certain that the end of the world is near.

19   These "against-Christ" people used to be members of our churches, but they never really belonged with us or else they would have stayed. When they left us it proved that they were not of us at all.

20 But you are not like that, for the Holy Spirit has come upon you, and you know the truth.

21 So I am not writing to you as to those who need to know the truth, but I warn you as those who can discern the difference between true and false.

22 And who is the greatest liar? The one who says that Jesus is not Christ. Such a person is antichrist, for he does not believe in God the Father and in His Son.

23 For a person who doesn't believe in Christ, God's Son, can't have God the Father either. But he who has Christ, God's Son, has God the Father also.

24 So keep on believing what you have been taught from the beginning. If you do, you will always be in close fellowship with both God the Father and His Son.

25 And He Himself has promised us this: *eternal life*.

26 These remarks of mine about the Antichrist are pointed at those who would dearly love to blindfold you and lead you astray.

27 But you have received the Holy Spirit and He lives within you, in your hearts, so that you don't need anyone to teach you what is right. For He teaches you all things, and He is the Truth, and no liar; and so, just as He has said, you must live in Christ, never to depart from Him.

28 And now, my little children, stay in happy fellowship with the Lord so that when He comes you will be sure that all is well, and will not have to be ashamed and shrink back from meeting Him.

29 Since we know that God is always good and does only right, we may rightly assume that all those who do right are His children.

CHAPTER 3

SEE how very much our heavenly Father loves us, for He allows us to be called His children—think of it—and we really *are!* But since most people don't know God, naturally they don't understand that we are His children.

2   Yes, dear friends, we are already God's children, right now, and we can't even imagine what it is going to be like later on. But we do know this, that when He comes we will be like Him, as a result of seeing Him as He really is.

3   And everyone who really believes this will try to stay pure because Christ is pure.

4   But those who keep on sinning are against God, for every sin is done against the will of God.

5   And you know that He became a man so that He could take away our sins, and that there is no sin in Him, no missing of God's will at any time in any way.

6   So if we stay close to Him, obedient to Him, we won't be sinning either; but as for those who keep on sinning, they should realize this: they sin because they have never really known Him or become His.

7   Oh, dear children, don't let anyone deceive you about this: if you are constantly doing what is good, it is because you *are* good, even as He is.

8   But if you keep on sinning, it shows that you belong to Satan, who since he first began to sin has kept steadily at it. But the Son of God came to destroy these works of the devil.

9   The person who has been born into God's family does not make a practice of sinning, because now God's life is in him; so he can't keep on sinning, for this new life has been born into him and controls him—he has been *born again.*

10   So now we can tell who is a child of God and who belongs to Satan. Whoever is living a life of sin and doesn't love his brother shows that he is not in God's family;

11   For the message to us from the beginning has been that we should love one another.

12   We are not to be like Cain, who belonged to Satan and killed his brother. Why did he kill him? Because Cain had been doing wrong and he knew very well that his brother's life was better than his.

13   So don't be surprised, dear friends, if the world hates you.

14   If we love other Christians it proves that we have been

599

delivered from hell and given eternal life. But a person who doesn't have love for others is headed for eternal death.

15 Anyone who hates his Christian brother is really a murderer at heart; and you know that no one wanting to murder has eternal life within.

16 We know what real love is from Christ's example in dying for us. And so we also ought to lay down our lives for our Christian brothers.

17 But if someone who is supposed to be a Christian has money enough to live well, and sees a brother in need, and won't help him—how can God's love be within *him?*

18 Little children, let us stop just *saying* we love people; let us *really* love them, and *show it* by our *actions.*

19 Then we will know for sure, by our actions, that we are on God's side, and our consciences will be clear, even when we stand before the Lord.

20 But if we have bad consciences and feel that we have done wrong, the Lord will surely feel that way about us even more,[1] for He knows everything we do.

21 But, dearly loved friends, if our consciences are clear, we can come to the Lord with perfect assurance and trust,

22 And get whatever we ask for because we are obeying Him and doing the things that please Him.

23 And this is what God says we must do: believe on the name of His Son Jesus Christ, and love one another.

24 Those who do what God says—they are living with God and He with them. We know this is true because the Holy Spirit He has given us tells us so.

CHAPTER 4

D EARLY loved friends, don't always believe everything you hear just because someone says it is a message from God: test it first to see if it really is. For there are many false teachers around,

---

[1]Or, perhaps, "The Lord will be merciful anyway." Literally, "If our heart condemns us, God is greater than our heart."

2   And the way to find out if their message is from the Holy Spirit is to ask: Does it really agree that Jesus Christ, God's Son, actually became man with a human body? If so, then the message is from God.

3   If not, the message is not from God but from one who is against Christ, like the "Antichrist" you have heard about who is going to come, and his attitude of enmity against Christ is already abroad in the world.

4   Dear young friends, you belong to God and have already won your fight with those who are against Christ, because there is Someone in your hearts who is stronger than any evil teacher in this wicked world.

5   These men belong to this world, so, quite naturally, they are concerned about worldly affairs and the world pays attention to them.

6   But we are children of God; that is why only those who have walked and talked with God will listen to us. Others won't. That is another way to know whether a message is really from God; for if it is, the world won't listen to it.

7   Dear friends, let us practice loving each other, for love comes from God and those who are loving and kind show that they are the children of God, and that they are getting to know Him better.

8   But if a person isn't loving and kind, it shows that he doesn't know God—for God is love.

9   God showed how much He loved us by sending His only Son into this wicked world to bring to us eternal life through His death.

10   In this act we see what real love is: it is not our love for God, but His love for us when He sent His Son to satisfy God's anger against our sins.

11   Dear friends, since God loved us as much as that, we surely ought to love each other too.

12   For though we have never yet seen God, when we love each other God lives in us and His love within us grows ever stronger.

13   And He has put His own Holy Spirit into our hearts as a proof to us that we are living with Him and He with us.

14   And furthermore, we have seen with our own eyes and now tell all the world that God sent His Son to be their Savior.

15   Anyone who believes and says that Jesus is the Son of God has God living in him, and he is living with God.

16   We know how much God loves us because we have felt His love and because we believe Him when He tells us that He loves us dearly. God is love, and anyone who lives in love is living with God and God is living in Him.

17   And as we live with Christ, our love grows more perfect and complete; so we will not be ashamed and embarrassed at the day of judgment, but can face Him with confidence and joy, because He loves us and we love Him too.

18   We need have no fear of someone who loves us perfectly; His perfect love for us eliminates all dread of what He might do to us. If we are afraid, it is for fear of what He might do to us, and shows that we are not fully convinced that He really loves us.

19   So you see, our love for Him comes as a result of His loving us first.

20   If anyone says "I love God," but keeps on hating his brother, he is a liar; for if he doesn't love his brother who is right there in front of him, how can he love God whom he has never seen?

21   And God Himself has said that one must love not only God, but his brother too.

CHAPTER 5

IF you believe that Jesus is the Christ—that He is God's Son and your Savior—then you are a child of God. And all who love the Father love His children too.

2   So you can find out how much you love God's children—your brothers and sisters in the Lord—by how much you love and obey God.

3   Loving God means doing what He tells us to do, and really, that isn't hard at all;

4   For every child of God can obey Him, defeating sin and evil pleasure by trusting Christ to help him.

5   But who could possibly fight and win this battle except by believing that Jesus is truly the Son of God?

6, 7, 8   And we know He is, because God said so with a voice from heaven when Jesus was baptized, and again as He was facing death[1]—yes, not only at His baptism but also as He faced death.[2] And the Holy Spirit, forever truthful, says it too. So we have these three witnesses: the voice of the Holy Spirit in our hearts, the voice from heaven at Christ's baptism, and the voice before He died.[3] And they all say the same thing: that Jesus Christ is the Son of God.[4]

9   We believe men who witness in our courts, and so surely we can believe whatever God declares. And God declares that Jesus is His Son.

10   All who believe this know in their hearts that it is true. If anyone doesn't believe this, he is actually calling God a liar, because he doesn't believe what God has said about His Son.

11   And what is it that God has said? That He has given us eternal life, and that this life is in His Son.

12   So whoever has God's Son has life; whoever does not have His Son, does not have life.

13   I have written this to you who believe in the Son of God so that you may know you have eternal life.

14   And we are sure of this, that He will listen to us whenever we ask Him for anything in line with His will.

15   And if we really know He is listening when we talk to Him and make our requests, then we can be sure that He will answer us.

16   If you see a Christian sinning in a way that does not end in death, you should ask God to forgive him and God will give him life, unless he has sinned that one fatal sin. But there is that one sin which ends in death and if he has done that, there is no use praying for him.

---

[1]Literally, "This is He who came by water and blood." See Matthew 3:16, 17; Luke 9:31, 35; John 12:27, 28, 32, 33. Other interpretations of this verse are equally possible.
[2]Literally, "not by water only, but by water and blood."
[3]Literally, "the Spirit, and the water, and the blood."
[4]Implied.

17   Every wrong is a sin, of course. I'm not talking about these ordinary sins; I am speaking of that one that ends in death.[5]

18   No one who has become part of God's family makes a practice of sinning, for Christ, God's Son, holds him securely and the devil cannot get his hands on him.

19   We know that we are children of God and that all the rest of the world around us is under Satan's power and control.

20   And we know that Christ, God's Son, has come to help us understand and find the true God. And now we are in God because we are in Jesus Christ His Son, who is the only true God; and He is eternal Life.

21   Dear children, keep away from anything that might take God's place in your hearts. Amen.

Sincerely,
John

---

[5]Commentators differ widely in their thoughts about what sin this is, and whether it causes physical death or spiritual death. Blasphemy against the Holy Spirit results in spiritual death (Mark 3:29) but can a Christian ever sin in such a way? Impenitence at the Communion Table sometimes ends in physical death (I Cor. 11:30). And Hebrews 6:4-8 speaks of the terrible end of those who fall away.

II JOHN

CHAPTER 1

FROM: John, the old Elder of the church.

To: That dear woman Cyria, one of God's very own, and to her children whom I love so much, as does everyone else in the church.

2 Since the Truth is in our hearts forever,

3 God the Father and Jesus Christ His Son will bless us with great mercy and much peace, and with truth and love.

4 How happy I am to find some of your children here, and to see that they are living as they should, following the Truth, obeying God's command.

5 And now I want to urgently remind you, dear friends, of the old rule God gave us right from the beginning, that Christians should love one another.

6 If we love God, we will do whatever He tells us to. And He has told us from the very first to love each other.

7 Watch out for the false leaders—and there are many of them around—who don't believe that Jesus Christ came to earth as a human being with a body like ours. Such people are against the truth and against Christ.

8 Beware of being like them, and losing the prize that you and I have been working so hard to get. See to it that you win your full reward from the Lord.

9 For if you wander beyond the teaching of Christ, you will leave God behind; while if you are loyal to Christ's teachings, you will have God too. Then you will have both the Father and the Son.

10   If anyone comes to teach you, and he doesn't believe what Christ taught, don't even invite him into your home. Don't encourage him in any way.

11   If you do you will be a partner with him in his wickedness.

12   Well, I would like to say much more, but I don't want to say it in this letter, for I hope to come to see you soon and then we can talk over these things together and have a joyous time.

13   Greetings from the children of your sister—another choice child of God.

Sincerely,
John

III JOHN

CHAPTER 1

FROM: John, the Elder.

To: Dear Gaius, whom I truly love.

2 Dear friend, I am praying that all is well with you and that your body is as healthy as I know your soul is.

3 Some of the brothers traveling by have made me very happy by telling me that your life stays clean and true, and that you are living by the standards of the Gospel.

4 I could have no greater joy than to hear such things about my children.

5 Dear friend, you are doing a good work for God in taking care of the traveling teachers and missionaries who are passing through.

6 They have told the church here of your friendship and your loving deeds. I am glad when you send them on their way with a generous gift.

7 For they are traveling for the Lord, and take neither food, clothing, shelter, nor money from those who are not Christians, even though they have preached to them.

8 So we ourselves should take care of them in order that we may become partners with them in the Lord's work.

9 I sent a brief letter to the church about this, but proud Diotrephes, who loves to push himself forward as the leader of the Christians there, does not admit my authority over him and refuses to listen to me.

10 When I come I will tell you some of the things he is doing and what wicked things he is saying about me and what

insulting language he is using. He not only refuses to welcome the missionary travelers himself, but tells others not to, and when they do he tries to put them out of the church.

11 Dear friend, don't let this bad example influence you. Follow only what is good. Remember that those who do what is right prove that they are God's children; and those who continue in evil prove that they are far from God.

12 But everyone, including Truth itself, speaks highly of Demetrius. I myself can say the same for him, and you know I speak the truth.

13 I have much to say but I don't want to write it,

14 For I hope to see you soon and then we will have much to talk about together.

15 So good-bye for now. Friends here send their love, and please give each of the folks there a special greeting from me.

Sincerely,

John

WHAT NOW, BRIGITTE?

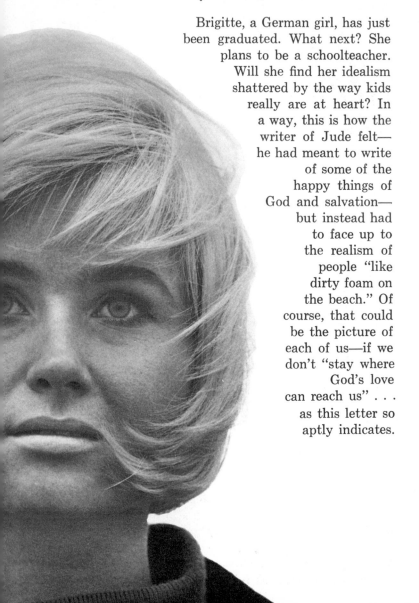

Brigitte, a German girl, has just been graduated. What next? She plans to be a schoolteacher. Will she find her idealism shattered by the way kids really are at heart? In a way, this is how the writer of Jude felt— he had meant to write of some of the happy things of God and salvation— but instead had to face up to the realism of people "like dirty foam on the beach." Of course, that could be the picture of each of us—if we don't "stay where God's love can reach us" . . . as this letter so aptly indicates.

JUDE

CHAPTER 1

FROM: Jude, a servant of Jesus Christ, and a brother of James.

To: Christians everywhere, for God the Father has chosen you and Jesus Christ has kept you safe.

2 May you be given more and more of God's kindness, peace, and love.

3 Dearly loved friends, I had been planning to write you some thoughts about the salvation God has given us, but now I find I must write of something else instead, urging you to stoutly defend the truth which God gave, once for all, to His people to keep without change through the years.

4 I say this because some godless teachers have wormed their way in among you, saying that after we become Christians we can do just as we like without fear of God's punishment. The fate of such people was written long ago, for they have turned against our only Master and Lord, Jesus Christ.

5 My answer to them is: remember this fact—which you know already—that the Lord saved a whole nation of people out of the land of Egypt, and then killed every one of them who did not trust and obey Him.

6 And I remind you of those angels who were once pure and holy, but willingly turned to a life of sin. Now God has them chained up in prisons of darkness, waiting for the judgment day.

7 And don't forget the cities of Sodom and Gomorrah and their neighboring towns, all full of lust of every kind including

lust of men for other men. Those cities were destroyed by fire and continue to be a warning to us that there is a hell in which sinners are punished.

8   Yet these false teachers go on living their evil, immoral lives, degrading their bodies and laughing at those in authority over them, even scoffing at the Glorious Ones [those mighty powers of awful evil who left their first estate[1]].

9   Yet Michael, one of the mightiest of the angels, when he was arguing with Satan about Moses' body, did not dare to accuse Satan, or jeer at him, but simply said, "The Lord rebuke you."

10   But these men mock and curse at anything they do not understand, and, like animals, they do whatever they feel like, thereby ruining their souls.

11   Woe upon them! For they follow the example of Cain who killed his brother; and, like Balaam, they will do anything for money; and like Korah, they have disobeyed God in the hope of gain and will die under His curse.

12   When these men join you at the love feasts of the church, they are evil smears among you, laughing and carrying on, gorging and stuffing themselves without a thought for others. They are like clouds blowing over dry land without giving rain, promising much, but producing nothing. They are like fruit trees without any fruit at picking time. They are not only dead, but doubly dead, for they have been pulled out, roots and all, to be burned.

13   All they leave behind them is shame and disgrace like the dirty foam left along the beach by the wild waves. They wander around looking as bright as stars, but ahead of them is the everlasting gloom and darkness that God has prepared for them.

14   Enoch, who lived long ago, soon after Adam, knew about these men and said this about them: "See, the Lord is coming with millions of His holy ones.

15   He will bring the people of the world before Him in

---

[1]Implied.

610

judgment, to receive just punishment, and to prove the terrible things they have done in rebellion against God, revealing all they have said against Him."

16 These men are constant gripers, never satisfied, doing whatever evil they feel like; they are loud-mouthed "show-offs," and when they show respect for others, it is only to get something from them in return.

17 Dear friends, remember what the apostles of our Lord Jesus Christ told you,

18 That in the last times there would come these scoffers whose whole purpose in life is to enjoy themselves in every evil way imaginable.

19 They stir up arguments; they love the evil things of the world; they do not have the Holy Spirit living in them.

20 But you, dear friends, must build up your lives ever more strongly upon the foundation of our holy faith, learning to pray in the power and strength of the Holy Spirit.

21 Stay always within the boundaries where God's love can reach and bless you. Wait patiently for the eternal life that our Lord Jesus Christ in His mercy is going to give you.

22 Try to help those who argue against you. Be merciful to those who doubt.

23 Save some by snatching them as from the very flames of hell itself. And as for others, help them to find the Lord by being kind to them, but be careful that you yourselves aren't pulled along into their sins. Hate every trace of their sin while being merciful to them as sinners.

24, 25 And now—all glory to Him who alone is God, who saves us through Jesus Christ our Lord; yes, splendor and majesty, all power and authority are His from the beginning; His they are and His they evermore shall be. And He is able to keep you from slipping and falling away, and to bring you, sinless and perfect, into His glorious presence with mighty shouts of everlasting joy. AMEN.

Jude

TO THE ONE WHO GRABS

goes the ball—and possibly the basket. To the winners go the spoils and to the interceptor goes the touchdown. It's a fact of life—and the incredible Person who appears to John in this Book tells what is given to the one who "overcomes." This Person whose "eyes were like flames of fire and voice like waves against the shore" holds out greatness to those willing to reach for it through Him. This is the same Person you read of all through the Gospels. How does this Jesus Christ of Nazareth fit into this regal pattern and the harsh destruction as well as the joys and exuberance of those aligned with Him? He is the power behind all that exists—by Him everything is held together—and in this picture of future and past events, you see His stamp of authority. You may not understand all you read here, but one factor is certain—if you are involved with Jesus Christ, He is obviously in charge of *whatever* will happen, and for you, it will be good. . . .

THE REVELATION

CHAPTER 1

THIS book unveils some of the future activities soon to occur in the life of Jesus Christ.[1] God permitted Him to reveal these things to His servant John in a vision; and then an angel was sent from heaven to explain the vision's meaning.

2 John wrote it all down—the words of God and Jesus Christ and everything he heard and saw.

3 If you read this prophecy aloud to the church, you will receive a special blessing from the Lord. Those who listen to it being read and do what it says will also be blessed. For the time is near when these things will all come true.

* * * * *

4 *From:* John

To: The seven churches in Turkey.[2]

Dear Friends:

May you have grace and peace from God who is, and was, and is to come! and from the seven-fold Spirit[3] before His throne;

5 And from Jesus Christ who faithfully reveals all truth to us. He was the first to rise from death, to die no more.[4] He is far greater than any king in all the earth. All praise to Him who always loves us and who set us free from our sins by pouring out His life blood for us.

---

[1]Literally, "the revelation of (concerning, or, from) Jesus Christ.
[2]Literally, "in Asia."
[3]Literally, "the seven spirits." But see Isaiah 11:2, where various aspects of the Holy Spirit are described, and Zech. 4:2-6, giving probability to the paraphrase; also see Revelation 2:7.
[4]Literally, "the First-born from the dead." Others (Lazarus, etc.) rose to die again. As used here the expression therefore implies "to die no more."

6   He has gathered us into His kingdom and made us priests of God His Father. Give to Him everlasting glory! He rules forever! Amen!

7   See! He is arriving, surrounded by clouds; and every eye shall see Him—yes, and those who pierced Him.[5] And the nations will weep in sorrow and in terror when He comes. Yes! Amen! Let it be so!

8   "I am the A and the Z,[6] the Beginning and the Ending of all things," says God, who is the Lord, the All Powerful One who is, and was, and is coming again![7]

9   It is I, your brother John, a fellow sufferer for the Lord's sake, who is writing this letter to you. I, too, have shared the patience Jesus gives, and we shall share His kingdom!

I was on the island of Patmos, exiled there for preaching the Word of God, and for telling what I knew about Jesus Christ.

10   It was the Lord's Day and I was worshiping, when suddenly I heard a loud voice behind me, a voice that sounded like a trumpet blast,

11   Saying, "I am A and Z, the First and Last!" And then I heard Him say, "Write down everything you see, and send your letter to the seven churches in Turkey:[8] to the church in Ephesus, the one in Smyrna, and those in Pergamos, Thyatira, Sardis, Philadelphia, and Laodicea."

12   When I turned to see who was speaking, there behind me were seven candlesticks of gold.

13   And standing among them was one who looked like Jesus who called himself the Son of Man,[9] wearing a long robe circled with a golden band across His chest.

14   His hair[10] was white as wool or snow, and His eyes penetrated like flames of fire.

15   His feet gleamed like burnished bronze, and His voice thundered like the waves against the shore.

---

[5]John saw this happen with his own eyes—the piercing of Jesus—and never forgot the horror of it.
[6]Literally, "I am Alpha and Omega"; these are the first and last letters of the Greek alphabet.
[7]Literally, "who comes" or "who is to come."
[8]"The seven churches in Asia."
[9]Literally, "like unto a Son of Man"; John recognizes Him from having lived with Him for three years, and from seeing Him in glory at the Transfiguration.
[10]Literally, "His head—the hair—was white like wool."

16   He held seven stars in His right hand and a sharp, double-bladed sword in His mouth,[11] and His face shone like the power of the sun in unclouded brilliance.

17, 18   When I saw Him, I fell at His feet as dead; but He laid His right hand on me and said, "Don't be afraid! Though I am the First and Last, the Living One who died, who is now alive forevermore, who has the keys of hell and death—don't be afraid!

19   Write down what you have just seen, and what will soon be shown to you.

20   This is the meaning of the seven stars you saw in My right hand, and the seven golden candlesticks: The seven stars are the leaders[12] of the seven churches, and the seven candlesticks are the churches themselves.

CHAPTER 2

WRITE *a letter to the leader[1] of the church at Ephesus and tell him this:*

I write to inform you of a message from Him who walks among the churches[2] and holds their leaders in His right hand. He says to you:

2   I know how many good things you are doing. I have watched your hard work and your patience; I know you don't tolerate sin among your members, and you have carefully examined the claims of those who say they are apostles but aren't. You have found out how they lie.

3   You have patiently suffered for Me without quitting.

4   Yet there is one thing wrong; you don't love Me as at first!

5   Think about those times of your first love (how different now!) and turn back to Me again and work as you did before;

---

[11]Literally, "coming out from His mouth."
[12]Literally, "angels." Some expositors (Origen, Jerome, etc.) believe from this that an angelic being is appointed by God to oversee each local church.
[1]Literally, "angel," as in 1:20.
[2]Literally, "from Him who holds the seven stars in His right hand and walks among the golden candlesticks."

or else I will come and remove your candlestick from its place among the churches.

6 But there is this about you that is good: you hate the deeds of the licentious Nicolaitans,[3] just as I do.

7 Let this message sink into the ears of anyone who listens to what the Spirit is saying to the churches: To everyone who is victorious, I will give fruit from the Tree of Life in the Paradise of God.

*   *   *   *   *

8 *To the leader[4] of the church in Smyrna write this letter:*
This message is from Him who is the First and Last, who was dead and then came back to life.

9 I know how much you suffer for the Lord, and I know all about your poverty (but you have heavenly riches!). I know the slander of those opposing you, who say that they are Jews— the children of God—but they aren't, for they support the cause of Satan.

10 Stop being afraid of what you are about to suffer—for the Devil will soon throw some of you into prison to test you. You will be persecuted for 'ten days.' Remain faithful even when facing death and I will give you the crown of life—an unending, glorious future.[5]

11 Let everyone who can hear, listen to what the Spirit is saying to the churches: He who is victorious shall not be hurt by the Second Death.

*   *   *   *   *

12 *Write this letter to the leader[4] of the church in Pergamos:*
This message is from Him who wields the sharp and double-bladed sword.

13 I am fully aware that you live in the city where Satan's throne is, at the center of Satanic worship; and yet you have remained loyal to Me, and refused to deny Me, even when Antipas, My faithful witness, was martyred among you by Satan's devotees.

---

[3]Nicolaitans, when translated from Greek to Hebrew, becomes Balaamites; followers of the men who induced the Israelites to fall by lust. (See Rev. 2:14 and Numbers 31:15, 16.)
[4]Literally, "angel." See note on 1:20.
[5]Implied.

14 And yet I have a few things against you. You tolerate some among you who do as Balaam did when he taught Balak how to ruin the people of Israel by involving them in sexual sin and encouraging them to go to idol feasts.

15 Yes, you have some of these very same followers of Balaam[6] among you!

16 Change your mind and attitude, or else I will come to you suddenly and fight against them with the sword of My mouth.

17 Let everyone who can hear, listen to what the Spirit is saying to the churches: Every one who is victorious shall eat of the hidden manna, the secret nourishment from heaven; and I will give to each a white stone, and on the stone will be engraved a new name that no one else knows except the one receiving it.

* * * * *

18 *Write this letter to the leader[7] of the church in Thyatira:*
This is a message from the Son of God, whose eyes penetrate like flames of fire, whose feet are like glowing brass.

19 I am aware of all your good deeds—your kindness to the poor, your gifts and service to them; also I know your love and faith and patience, and I can see your constant improvement in all these things.

20 Yet I have this against you: You are permitting that woman Jezebel, who calls herself a prophetess, to teach My servants that sex sin is not a serious matter; she urges them to practice immorality and to eat meat that has been sacrificed to idols.

21 I gave her time to change her mind and attitude, but she refused.

22 Pay attention now to what I am saying: I will lay her upon a sickbed of intense affliction, along with all her immoral followers,[8] unless they turn again to Me, repenting of their sin with her;

---

[6]Literally, "Nicolaitans," Greek form of "Balaamites."
[7]Literally, "angel." See note on 1:20.
[8]Literally, "together with all those who commit adultery with her."

23   And I will strike her children dead. And all the churches shall know that I am He who searches deep within men's hearts, and minds; I will give to each of you whatever you deserve.

24, 25   As for the rest of you in Thyatira who have not followed this false teaching ("deeper truths," as they call them —depths of Satan, really), I will ask nothing further of you; only hold tightly to what you have until I come.

26   To every one who overcomes—who to the very end keeps on doing things that please Me—I will give power over the nations.

27   You will rule them with a rod of iron just as My Father gave Me the authority to rule them; they will be shattered like a pot of clay that is broken into tiny pieces.

28   And I will give you the Morning Star!

29   Let all who can hear, listen to what the Spirit says to the churches.

CHAPTER 3

T O *the leader*[1] *of the church in Sardis write this letter:*
This message is sent to you by the one who has the seven-fold Spirit[2] of God and the seven stars.

I know your reputation as a live and active church, but you are dead.

2   Now wake up! Strengthen what little remains—for even what is left is at the point of death. Your deeds are far from right in the sight of God.

3   Go back to what you heard and believed at first; hold to it firmly and turn to Me again. Unless you do, I will come suddenly upon you, unexpected as a thief, and punish you.

4   Yet even there in Sardis some haven't soiled their garments with the world's filth; they shall walk with Me in white, for they are worthy.

5   Everyone who conquers will be clothed in white, and I

[1]Literally, "angel." See note on 1:20.
[2]Literally, "the seven spirits of God." See note on 1:4.

will not erase his name from the Book of Life, but I will announce before My Father and His angels that he is Mine.

6   Let all who can hear, listen to what the Spirit is saying to the churches.

*   *   *   *   *

7   *Write this letter to the leader*[3] *of the church in Philadelphia.*

This message is sent to you by the one who is holy and true, and has the key of David to open what no one can shut and to shut what no one can open.

8   I know you well: you aren't strong, but you have tried to obey[4] and have not denied My Name. Therefore I have opened a door to you that no one can shut.

9   Note this: I will force those supporting the causes of Satan while claiming to be Mine[5] (but they aren't—they are lying) to fall at your feet and acknowledge that you are the ones I love.

10   Because you have patiently obeyed Me despite the persecution, therefore I will protect you from[6] the time of Great Tribulation and temptation, which will come upon the world to test everyone alive.

11   Look, I am coming soon![7] Hold tightly to the little strength you have—so that no one will take away your crown.

12   As for the one who conquers, I will make him a pillar in the temple of My God; he will be secure, and will go out no more; and I will write My God's Name on him, and he will be a citizen in the city of My God—the New Jerusalem, coming down from heaven from My God; and he will have My new Name inscribed upon him.

13   Let all who can hear, listen to what the Spirit is saying to the churches.

*   *   *   *   *

14   *Write this letter to the leader*[8] *of the church in Laodicea:*

[3]Literally, "angel." See note on 1:20.
[4]Literally, "you have kept My word."
[5]Literally, "say they are Jews but are not."
[6]Or, "I will keep you from failing in the hour of testing . . ." The inference is not clear in the Greek as to whether this means "kept from" or "kept through" the coming horror.
[7]Or, "suddenly," "unexpectedly."
[8]Literally, "angel." See note on 1:20.

This message is from the one who stands firm,[9] the faithful and true Witness [of all that is or was or evermore shall be[10]], the primeval source of God's creation:

15 I know you well—you are neither hot nor cold; I wish you were one or the other!

16 But since you are merely lukewarm, I will spit you out of My mouth!

17 You say, 'I am rich, with everything I want; I don't need a thing!' And you don't realize that spiritually you are wretched and miserable and poor and blind and naked.

18 My advice to you is to buy pure gold from Me, gold purified by fire—only then will you truly be rich. And to purchase from Me white garments, clean and pure, so you won't be naked and ashamed; and to get medicine from Me to heal your eyes and give you back your sight.

19 I continually discipline and punish everyone I love; so I must punish you, unless you turn from your indifference and become enthusiastic about the things of God.

20 Look! I have been standing at the door and I am constantly knocking. If anyone hears Me calling him and opens the door, I will come in and fellowship with him and he with Me.

21 I will let every one who conquers sit beside Me on My throne, just as I took My place with My Father on His throne when I had conquered.

22 Let those who can hear, listen to what the Spirit is saying to the churches."

CHAPTER 4

THEN as I looked, I saw a door standing open in heaven, and the same voice I had heard before, that sounded like a mighty trumpet blast, spoke to me and said,

[9]Literally, "from the Amen."
[10]Implied.

"Come up here and I will show you what must happen in the future!"

2   And instantly I was, in spirit, there in heaven and saw—oh, the glory of it!—a throne and Someone sitting on it!

3   Great bursts of light flashed forth from Him as from a glittering diamond, or from a shining ruby, and a rainbow glowing like an emerald encircled His throne.

4   Twenty-four smaller thrones surrounded His, with twenty-four Elders sitting on them; all were clothed in white, with golden crowns upon their heads.

5   Lightning and thunder issued from the throne, and there were voices in the thunder. Directly in front of His throne were seven lighted lamps representing the seven-fold Spirit[1] of God.

6   Spread out before it was a shiny crystal sea. Four Living Beings, dotted front and back with eyes, stood at the throne's four sides.

7   The first of these Living Beings was in the form of a lion; the second looked like an ox; the third had the face of a man; and the fourth, the form of an eagle, with wings spread out as though in flight.

8   Each of these Living Beings had six wings, and the central sections of their wings were covered with eyes. Day after day and night after night they kept on saying, "Holy, holy, holy, Lord God Almighty—the one who was, and is, and is to come."

9   And when the Living Beings gave glory and honor and thanks to the one sitting on the throne, who lives forever and ever,

10   The twenty-four Elders fell down before Him and worshiped Him, the Eternal Living One, and cast their crowns before the throne, singing,

11   "O Lord, You are worthy to receive the glory and the honor and the power, for You have created all things. They were created and called into being by Your act of will."

---

[1]Literally, "the seven spirits of God." But see Zech. 4:2-6, where the lamps are equated with the one Spirit.

CHAPTER 5

A ND I saw a scroll in the right hand of the one who was sitting on the throne, a scroll with writing on the inside and on the back, and sealed with seven seals.

2   A mighty angel with a loud voice was shouting out this question: "Who is worthy to break the seals on this scroll, and to unroll it?"

3   But no one in all heaven or earth or from among the dead was permitted to open and read it.

4   Then I wept with disappointment[1] because no one anywhere was worthy; no one could tell us what it said.

5   But one of the twenty-four Elders said to me, "Cease weeping, for look! The Lion of the tribe of Judah, the Root of David, has conquered, and proved Himself worthy to open the scroll and to break its seven seals."

6   I looked and saw a Lamb standing there before the twenty-four Elders, in front of the throne and the Living Beings, and on the Lamb were wounds that once had caused His death. He had seven horns and seven eyes, which represent the seven-fold Spirit[2] of God, sent out into every part of the world.

7   He stepped forward and took the scroll from the right hand of the one sitting upon the throne.

8   And as He took the scroll, the twenty-four Elders fell down before the Lamb, each with a harp and golden vials filled with incense—the prayers of God's people!

9   They were singing[3] Him a new song with these words: "You are worthy to take the scroll and break its seals and open it; for you were slain, and Your blood has bought people from every nation as gifts for God.

10   And You have gathered them into a kingdom and made

---

[1]Implied.
[2]Literally, "the seven spirits of God"; but see Zechariah 4:2-6, 10, where the seven eyes are equated with the seven lamps and the one Spirit.
[3]Literally, "saying" or "said."

them priests of our God; they shall reign upon the earth."

11   Then in my vision I heard the singing[4] of millions of angels surrounding the throne and the Living Beings and the Elders:

12   "The Lamb is worthy" (loudly they sang[4] it!) "—the Lamb who was slain. He is worthy to receive the power, and the riches, and the wisdom, and the strength, and the honor, and the glory, and the blessing."

13   And then I heard everyone in heaven and earth, and from the dead beneath the earth and in the sea, exclaiming, "The blessing and the honor and the glory and the power belong to the one sitting on the throne, and to the Lamb forever and ever."

14   And the four Living Beings kept saying, "Amen!" And the twenty-four Elders fell down and worshiped Him.

CHAPTER 6

A S I watched, the Lamb broke the first seal and began to unroll the scroll. Then one of the four Living Beings, with a voice that sounded like thunder, said, "Come!"

2   I looked, and there in front of me was a white horse. Its rider carried a bow, and a crown was placed upon his head; he rode out to conquer in many battles and win the war.

3   Then He unrolled the scroll to the second seal, and broke it open too. And I heard the second Living Being say, "Come!"

4   This time a red horse rode out. Its rider was given a long sword and the authority to banish peace and bring anarchy to the earth; war and killing broke out everywhere.

5   When He had broken the third seal, I heard the third Living Being say, "Come!" And I saw a black horse, with its rider holding a pair of balances in his hand.

6   And a voice from among the four Living Beings said, "A

---

[4]Literally, "saying" or "said."

loaf of bread for a dollar, or three pounds of barley flour,[1] but there is no olive oil or wine."[2]

7   And when the fourth seal was broken, I heard the fourth Living Being say, "Come!"

8   And now I saw a pale horse, and its rider's name was Death. And there followed after him another horse whose rider's name was Hell. They were given control of one-fourth of the earth, to kill with war and famine and disease and wild animals.

9   And when He broke open the fifth seal, I saw an altar, and underneath it all the souls of those who had been martyred for preaching the Word of God and for being faithful in their witnessing.

10   They called loudly to the Lord and said, "O Sovereign Lord, holy and true, how long will it be before You judge the people of the earth for what they've done to us? When will You avenge our blood against those living on the earth?"

11   White robes were given to each of them, and they were told to rest a little longer until their other brothers, fellow servants of Jesus, had been martyred on the earth and joined them.

12   I watched as He broke the sixth seal, and there was a vast earthquake; and the sun became dark like black cloth, and the moon was blood-red.

13   Then the stars of heaven appeared to be falling to earth[3]—like green fruit from fig trees buffeted by mighty winds.

14   And the starry heavens disappeared[4] as though rolled up like a scroll and taken away; and every mountain and island shook and shifted.

15   The kings of the earth, and world leaders and rich men, and high-ranking military officers, and all men great and small, slave and free, hid themselves in the caves and rocks of the mountains,

---

[1]Literally, "A choenix of wheat for a denarius, and three choenix of barley for a denarius. . . ."
[2]Literally, "do not damage the oil and wine."
[3]Literally, "the stars of heaven fell to the earth."
[4]Literally, "the sky departed."

16   And cried to the mountains to crush them. "Fall on us," they pleaded, "and hide us from the face of the one sitting on the throne, and from the anger of the Lamb,

17   Because the great day of Their anger has come, and who can survive it?"

CHAPTER 7

THEN I saw four angels standing at the four corners of the earth, holding back the four winds from blowing, so that not a leaf rustled in the trees, and the ocean became as smooth as glass.

2   And I saw another angel coming from the east, carrying the Great Seal of the Living God. And he shouted out to those four angels who had been given power to injure earth and sea,

3   "Wait! Don't do anything yet—hurt neither earth nor sea nor trees—until we have placed the Seal of God upon the foreheads of His servants."

4, 5, 6, 7, 8   How many were given this mark? I heard the number—it was 144,000, out of all twelve tribes of Israel, as listed here:

Judah	12,000
Reuben	12,000
Gad	12,000
Asher	12,000
Naphtali	12,000
Manasseh	12,000
Simeon	12,000
Levi	12,000
Issachar	12,000
Zebulun	12,000
Joseph	12,000
Benjamin	12,000

9   After this I saw a vast crowd, too great to count, from all nations and provinces and languages, standing in front of the throne and before the Lamb, clothed in white, with palm branches in their hands.

10   And they were shouting with a mighty shout, "Salvation comes from our God upon the throne, and from the Lamb."

11   And now all the angels were crowding around the throne and around the Elders and the four Living Beings, and falling face down before the throne and worshiping God.

12   "Amen!" they said. "Blessing, and glory, and wisdom, and thanksgiving, and honor, and power, and might, be to our God forever and forever. Amen!"

13   Then one of the twenty-four Elders asked me, "Do you know who these are, who are clothed in white, and where they come from?"

14   "No, sir," I replied. "Please tell me."

"These are the ones coming out of the Great Tribulation," he said; "they washed their robes and whitened them by the blood of the Lamb.

15   That is why they are here before the throne of God, serving Him day and night in His temple. The one sitting on the throne will shelter them;

16   They will never be hungry again, nor thirsty, and they will be fully protected from the scorching noontime heat.

17   For the Lamb standing in front of[1] the throne will feed them and be their Shepherd and lead them to the springs of the Water of Life. And God will wipe their tears away."

CHAPTER 8

WHEN the Lamb had broken the seventh seal, there was silence throughout all heaven for what seemed like half an hour.

2   And I saw the seven angels that stand before God, and they were given seven trumpets.

3   Then another angel with a golden censer came and stood at the altar; and a great quantity of incense was given to him to mix with the prayers of God's people, to offer upon the golden altar before the throne.

---

[1]Literally, "in the center of the throne"; i.e., directly in front, not to one side. An alternate rendering might be, "at the heart of the throne."

4   And the perfume of the incense mixed with prayers ascended up to God from the altar where the angel had poured them out.

5   Then the angel filled the censer with fire from the altar and threw it down upon the earth; and thunder crashed and rumbled, lightning flashed, and there was a terrible earthquake.

6   Then the seven angels with the seven trumpets prepared to blow their mighty blasts.

7   The first angel blew his trumpet, and hail and fire mixed with blood were thrown down upon the earth. One-third of the earth was set on fire so that one-third of the trees were burned, and all the green grass.

8, 9   Then the second angel blew his trumpet, and what appeared to be a huge burning mountain was thrown into the sea, destroying a third of all the ships; and a third of the sea turned red as[1] blood; and a third of the fish were killed.

10   The third angel blew, and a great flaming star fell from heaven upon a third of the rivers and springs.

11   The star was called "Bitterness"[2] because it poisoned a third of all the water on the earth and many people died.

12   The fourth angel blew his trumpet and immediately a third of the sun was blighted and darkened, and a third of the moon and the stars, so that the daylight was dimmed by a third, and the nighttime darkness deepened.

13   As I watched, I saw a solitary eagle flying through the heavens crying loudly, "Woe, woe, woe to the people of the earth because of the terrible things that will soon happen when the three remaining angels blow their trumpets."

CHAPTER 9

THEN the fifth angel blew his trumpet and I saw one[1] who was fallen to earth from heaven, and to him was given the key to the bottomless pit.

---

[1]Literally, "became blood."
[2]Literally, "Wormwood."
[1]Literally, "a star fallen from heaven"; it is unclear whether this person is of Satanic origin, as most commentators believe, or whether the reference is to Christ.

2   When he opened it, smoke poured out as though from some huge furnace, and the sun and air were darkened by the smoke.

3   Then locusts came from the smoke and descended onto the earth and were given power to sting like scorpions.

4   They were told not to hurt the grass or plants or trees, but to attack those people who did not have the mark of God on their foreheads.

5   They were not to kill them, but to torture them for five months with agony like the pain of scorpion stings.

6   In those days men will try to kill themselves but won't be able to—death will not come. They will long to die—but death will flee away!

7   The locusts looked like horses armored for battle. They had what looked like golden crowns on their heads, and their faces looked like men's.

8   Their hair was long like women's, and their teeth were those of lions.

9   They wore breastplates that seemed to be of iron, and their wings roared like an army of chariots rushing into battle.

10   They had stinging tails like scorpions, and their power to hurt, given to them for five months, was in their tails.

11   Their king is the Prince of the bottomless pit whose name in Hebrew is Abaddon, and in Greek, Apollyon [and in English, the Destroyer[2]].

12   One terror now ends, but there are two more coming!

13   The sixth angel blew his trumpet and I heard a voice speaking from the four horns of the golden altar that stands before the throne of God,

14   Saying to the sixth angel, "Release the four mighty demons[3] held bound at the great River Euphrates."

15   They had been kept in readiness for that year and month and day and hour, and now they were turned loose to kill a third of all mankind.

---

[2]Implied.
[3]Literally, "(fallen) angels."

16   They led an army of 200,000,000[4] warriors[5]—I heard an announcement of how many there were.

17, 18   I saw their horses spread out before me in my vision; their riders wore fiery-red breastplates, though some were sky-blue and others yellow. The horses' heads looked much like lions', and smoke and fire and flaming sulphur billowed from their mouths, killing one-third of all mankind.

19   Their power of death was not only in their mouths, but in their tails as well, for their tails were similar to serpents' heads that struck and bit with fatal wounds.

20   But the men left alive after these plagues *still refused to worship God!* They would not renounce their demon-worship, nor their idols made of gold and silver, brass, stone, and wood —which neither see nor hear nor walk!

21   Neither did they change their mind and attitude about all their murders and witchcraft, their immorality and theft.

CHAPTER 10

THEN I saw another mighty angel coming down from heaven, surrounded by a cloud, with a rainbow over his head; his face shone like the sun and his feet flashed with fire.

2   And he held open in his hand a small scroll. He set his right foot on the sea and his left foot on the earth,

3   And gave a great shout—it was like the roar of a lion— and the seven thunders crashed their reply.

4   I was about to write what the thunders said when a voice from heaven called to me, "Don't do it. Their words are not to be revealed."

5   Then the mighty angel standing on the sea and land lifted his right hand to heaven,

6   And swore by Him who lives forever and ever, who created heaven and everything in it and the earth and all that it

---

[4]If this is a literal figure, it is no longer incredible, in view of a world population of 6,000,000,000 in the near future. In China alone, in 1961, there were an "estimated 200,000,000 armed and organized militiamen" (Associated Press Release, April 24, 1964).
[5]Literally, "horsemen."

contains and the sea and its inhabitants, that there should be no more delay,

7 But that when the seventh angel blew his trumpet, then God's veiled plan—mysterious through the ages ever since it was announced by His servants the prophets—would be fulfilled.

8 Then the voice from heaven spoke to him again, "Go and get the unrolled scroll from the mighty angel standing there upon the sea and land."

9 So I approached him and asked him to give me the scroll. "Yes, take it and eat it," he said. "At first it will taste like honey, but when you swallow it, it will make your stomach sour!"

10 So I took it from his hand, and ate it! and just as he had said, it was sweet in my mouth but it gave me a stomach ache when I swallowed it.

11 Then he told me, "You must prophesy further about many peoples, nations, tribes, and kings."

CHAPTER 11

NOW I was given a measuring stick and told to go and measure the temple of God, including the inner court where the altar stands, and to count the number of worshipers.[1]

2 "But do not measure the outer court," I was told, "for it has been turned over to the nations. They will trample the Holy City for forty-two months.[2]

3 And I will give power to My two witnesses to prophesy 1,260 days[2] clothed in sackcloth."

4 These two prophets are the two olive trees,[3] and two candlesticks standing before the God of all the earth.

5 Anyone trying to harm them will be killed by bursts of fire shooting from their mouths.

6 They have power to shut the skies so that no rain will fall

---

[1]Literally, "Rise and measure the temple of God, and the altar, and them that worship therein."
[2]3½ years, as in Daniel 12:7.
[3]Zechariah 4:3, 4, 11.

during the three and a half years they prophesy, and to turn rivers and oceans to blood, and to send every kind of plague upon the earth as often as they wish.

7 When they complete the three and a half years of their solemn testimony, the tyrant who comes out of the bottomless pit[4] will declare war against them and conquer and kill them;

8, 9 And for three and a half days their bodies will be exposed in the streets of Jerusalem (the city fittingly described as "Sodom" or "Egypt")—the very place where their Lord was crucified. No one will be allowed to bury them, and people from many nations will crowd around to gaze at them.

10 And there will be a worldwide holiday—people everywhere will rejoice and give presents to each other and throw parties to celebrate the death of the two prophets who had tormented them so much!

11 But after three and a half days, the spirit of life from God will enter them and they will stand up! And great fear will fall on everyone.

12 Then a loud voice will shout from heaven, "Come up!" And they will rise to heaven in a cloud as their enemies watch.

13 The same hour there will be a terrible earthquake that levels a tenth of the city, leaving 7,000 dead. Then everyone left will, in their terror, give glory to the God of heaven.

14 The second woe is past, but the third quickly follows:

15 For just then the seventh angel blew his trumpet, and there were loud voices shouting down from heaven, "The kingdom of this world now belongs to our Lord, and to His Christ; and He shall reign forever and ever."[5]

16 And the twenty-four Elders sitting on their thrones before God threw themselves down in worship, saying,

17 "We give thanks, Lord God Almighty, who is and was, for now You have assumed Your great power and have begun to reign.

18 The nations were angry with You, but now it is Your turn to be angry with them. It is time to judge the dead, and reward Your servants—prophets and people alike, all who fear

[4]Revelation 9:11.
[5]Or, "The Lord and His Anointed shall now rule the world from this day to eternity."

Your Name, both great and small—and to destroy those who have caused destruction upon the earth."

19   Then, in heaven, the temple of God was opened and the ark of His covenant could be seen inside. Lightning flashed and thunder crashed and roared, and there was a great hailstorm and the world was shaken by a mighty earthquake.

CHAPTER 12

THEN a great pageant appeared in heaven, portraying things to come. I saw a woman clothed with the sun, with the moon beneath her feet, and a crown of twelve stars on her head.

2   She was pregnant and screamed in the pain of her labor, awaiting her delivery.

3   Suddenly a red Dragon appeared, with seven heads and ten horns, and seven crowns on his heads.

4   His tail drew along behind him a third of the stars, which he plunged to the earth. He stood before the woman as she was about to give birth to her child, ready to eat the baby as soon as it was born.

5   She gave birth to a boy who was to rule all nations with a heavy hand, and He was caught up to God and to His throne.

6   The woman fled into the wilderness, where God had prepared a place for her, to take care of her for 1,260 days.

7   Then there was war in heaven; Michael and the angels under his command fought the Dragon and his hosts of fallen angels.

8   And the Dragon lost the battle and was forced from heaven.

9   This great Dragon—the ancient serpent called the Devil, or Satan, the one deceiving the whole world—was thrown down onto the earth with all his army.

10   Then I heard a loud voice shouting across the heavens, "It has happened at last! God's salvation and the power and the rule, and the authority of His Christ are finally here; for the

Accuser of our brothers has been thrown down from heaven onto earth—he accused them day and night before our God.

11   They defeated him by the blood of the Lamb, and by their testimony; for they did not love their lives but laid them down for Him.

12   Rejoice, O heavens! you citizens of heaven, rejoice! be glad! But woe to you people of the world, for the Devil has come down to you in great anger, knowing that he has little time."

13   And when the Dragon found himself cast down to earth, he persecuted the woman who had given birth to the child.

14   But she was given two wings like those of a great eagle, to fly into the wilderness to the place prepared for her, where she was cared for and protected from the Serpent, the Dragon, for three and a half years.[1]

15   And from the Serpent's mouth a vast flood of water gushed out and swept toward the woman in an effort to get rid of her;

16   But the earth helped her by opening its mouth and swallowing the flood!

17   Then the furious Dragon set out to attack the rest of her children—all who were keeping God's commandments and confessing that they belong to Jesus. He stood waiting on an ocean beach.

CHAPTER 13

AND now, in my vision, I saw a strange Creature rising up out of the sea. It had seven heads and ten horns, and ten crowns upon its horns. And written on each head were blasphemous names, each one defying and insulting God.

2   This Creature looked like a leopard but had bear's feet and a lion's mouth! And the Dragon gave him his own power and throne and great authority.

[1]Literally, "a time and times and half a time."

3   I saw that one of his heads seemed wounded beyond recovery—but the fatal wound was healed! All the world marveled at this miracle and followed the Creature in awe.

4   They worshiped the Dragon for giving him such power, and they worshiped the strange Creature. "Where is there anyone as great as he?" they exclaimed. "Who is able to fight against him?"

5   Then the Dragon encouraged the Creature to speak great blasphemies against the Lord; and gave him authority to control the earth for forty-two months.

6   All that time he blasphemed God's Name and His temple and all those living in heaven.

7   The Dragon gave him power to fight against God's people[1] and to overcome them, and to rule over all nations and language groups throughout the world.

8   And all mankind—whose names were not written down before the founding of the world in the slain[2] Lamb's Book of Life—worshiped the evil Creature.

9   Anyone who can hear, listen carefully:

10   The people of God who are destined for prison will be arrested and taken away; those destined for death will be killed.[3] But do not be dismayed, for here is your opportunity for endurance and confidence.

11   Then I saw another strange animal, this one coming up out of the earth, with two little horns like those of a lamb but a fearsome voice like the Dragon's.

12   He exercised all the authority of the Creature whose death-wound had been healed, whom he required all the world to worship.

13   He did unbelievable miracles such as making fire flame down to earth from the skies while everyone was watching.

14   By doing these miracles, he was deceiving people everywhere. He could do these marvelous things whenever the first Creature was there to watch him. And he ordered the people of

---

[1]Literally, "It was permitted to fight against God's people."
[2]Or, "those whose names were not written in the Book of Life of the Lamb slain before the founding of the world." That is, regarded as slain in the eternal plan and knowledge of God.
[3]Or, "If anyone imprisons you, he will be imprisoned! If anyone kills you, he will be killed!"

the world to make a great statue of the first Creature, who was fatally wounded and then came back to life.

15   He was permitted to give breath to this statue and even make it speak! Then the statue ordered that anyone refusing to worship it must die!

16   He required everyone—great and small, rich and poor, slave and free—to be tattooed with a certain mark on the right hand or on the forehead.

17   And no one could get a job or even buy in any store without the permit of that mark, which was either the name of the Creature or the code number of his name.

18   Here is a puzzle that calls for careful thought to solve it. Let those who are able, interpret this code: the numerical values of the letters in his name add to 666![4]

CHAPTER 14

T HEN I saw a Lamb standing on Mount Zion in Jerusalem, and with Him were 144,000 who had His Name and His Father's Name written on their foreheads.

2   And I heard a sound from heaven like the roaring of a great waterfall or the rolling of mighty thunder. It was the singing of a choir accompanied by harps.

3   This tremendous choir—144,000 strong—sang a wonderful new song in front of the throne of God and before the four Living Beings and the twenty-four Elders; and no one could sing this song except those 144,000 who had been redeemed from the earth.

4   For they are spiritually undefiled, pure as virgins,[1] following the Lamb wherever He goes. They have been purchased from among the men on the earth as a consecrated offering to God and the Lamb.

5   No falsehood can be charged against them; they are blameless.

[4]Some manuscripts read "616."
[1]Literally, "They have not defiled themselves with women, for they are virgins."

6   And I saw another angel flying through the heavens, carrying the everlasting Good News to preach to those on earth —to every nation, tribe, language and people.

7   "Fear God," he shouted, "and extol His greatness. For the time has come when He will sit as Judge. Worship Him who made the heaven and the earth, the sea and all its sources."

8   Then another angel followed him through the skies, saying, "Babylon is fallen, is fallen—that great city—because she seduced the nations of the world and made them share the wine of her intense impurity and sin."

9   Then a third angel followed them shouting, "Anyone worshiping the Creature from the sea[2] and his statue and accepting his mark on the forehead or the hand,

10   Must drink the wine of the anger of God; it is poured out undiluted into God's cup of wrath. And they will be tormented with fire and burning sulphur in the presence of the holy angels and the Lamb.

11   The smoke of their torture rises forever and ever, and they will have no relief day or night, for they have worshiped the Creature and his statue, and have been tattooed with the code of his name.

12   Let this encourage God's people to endure patiently every trial and persecution, for they are His saints who remain firm to the end in obedience to His commands and trust in Jesus."

13   And I heard a voice in the heavens above me saying, "Write this down: At last the time has come for His martyrs[3] to enter into their full reward. Yes, says the Spirit, they are blest indeed, for now they shall rest from all their toils and trials; for their good deeds follow them to heaven!"

14   Then the scene changed and I saw a white cloud, and Someone sitting on it who looked like Jesus, who was called "The Son of Man,"[4] with a crown of solid gold upon His head and a sharp sickle in His hand.

---

[2]Implied.
[3]Literally, "those who die in the faith of Jesus." Verse 12 implies death from persecution for Christ's sake.
[4]Literally, "one like a Son of Man."

15   Then an angel came from the temple and called out to Him, "Begin to use the sickle, for the time has come for You to reap; the harvest is ripe on the earth."

16   So the one sitting on the cloud swung His sickle over the earth, and the harvest was gathered in.

17   After that another angel came from the temple in heaven, and he also had a sharp sickle.

18   Just then the angel who has power to destroy the world with fire,[5] shouted to the angel with the sickle, "Use your sickle now to cut off the clusters of grapes from the vines of the earth, for they are fully ripe for judgment."

19   So the angel swung his sickle on the earth and loaded the grapes into the great winepress of God's wrath.

20   And the grapes were trodden in the winepress outside the city, and blood flowed out in a stream 200 miles long and as high as a horse's bridle.

CHAPTER 15

AND I saw in heaven another mighty pageant showing things to come: seven angels were assigned to carry down to earth the seven last plagues—and then at last God's anger will be finished.

2   Spread out before me was what seemed to be an ocean of fire and glass, and on it stood all those who had been victorious over the Evil Creature and his statue and his mark and number. All were holding harps of God,

3   And they were singing the song of Moses, the servant of God, and the song of the Lamb:

> "Great and marvelous
> Are Your doings,
> Lord God Almighty.
> Just and true
> Are Your ways,
> O King of Ages.[1]

---

[5]Literally, "who has power over fire."
[1]Some manuscripts read, "King of the Nations."

4   Who shall not fear,
           O Lord,
           And glorify Your Name?
           For You alone are holy.
           All nations will come
           And worship before You,
           For Your righteous deeds
           Have been disclosed."

5   Then I looked and saw that the Holy of Holies of the temple in heaven was thrown wide open!

6   The seven angels who were assigned to pour out the seven plagues then came from the temple, clothed in spotlessly white linen, with golden belts across their chests.

7   And one of the four Living Beings handed each of them a golden flask filled with the terrible wrath of the Living God who lives forever and forever.

8   The temple was filled with smoke from His glory and power; and no one could enter until the seven angels had completed pouring out the seven plagues.

CHAPTER 16

AND I heard a mighty voice shouting from the temple to the seven angels, "Now go your ways and empty out the seven flasks of the wrath of God upon the earth."

2   So the first angel left the temple and poured out his flask over the earth, and horrible, malignant sores broke out on everyone who had the mark of the Creature and was worshiping his statue.

3   The second angel poured out his flask upon the oceans, and they became like the watery blood of a dead man; and everything in all the oceans died.

4   The third angel poured out his flask upon the rivers and springs and they became blood.

5   And I heard this angel of the waters declaring, "You are just in sending this judgment, O Holy One, who is and was,

6   For Your saints and prophets have been martyred and

their blood poured out upon the earth; and now, in turn, You have poured out the blood of those who murdered them; it is their just reward."

7   And I heard the angel of the altar[1] say, "Yes, Lord God Almighty, Your punishments are just and true."

8   Then the fourth angel poured out his flask upon the sun, causing it to scorch all men with its fire.

9   Everyone was burned by this blast of heat, and they cursed the name of God who sent the plagues—they did not change their mind and attitude to give Him glory.

10   Then the fifth angel poured out his flask upon the throne of the Creature from the sea,[2] and his kingdom was plunged into darkness. And his subjects gnawed their tongues in anguish,

11   And cursed the God of heaven for their pains and sores, but they refused to repent of all their evil deeds.

12   The sixth angel poured out his flask upon the great River Euphrates and it dried up so that the kings from the east could march their armies westward without hindrance.

13   And I saw three evil spirits disguised as frogs leap from the mouth of the Dragon, the Creature, and his False Prophet.[3]

14   These miracle-working demons conferred with all the rulers of the world to gather them for battle against the Lord on that great coming Judgment Day of God Almighty.

15   "Take note: I will come as unexpectedly as a thief! Blessed are all who are awaiting Me, who keep their robes in readiness and will not need to walk naked and ashamed."

16   And they gathered all the armies of the world near a place called, in Hebrew, Armageddon—the Mountain of Megiddo.

17   Then the seventh angel poured out his flask into the air; and a mighty shout came from the throne of the temple in heaven, saying, "It is finished!"[4]

18   Then the thunder crashed and rolled, and lightning

---

[1]Literally, "I heard the altar cry. . . ."
[2]Implied.
[3]Described in Chap. 13:11-15 and 19:20.
[4]Literally, "it has happened." An epoch of human history has come to an end.

flashed; and there was a great earthquake of a magnitude unprecedented in human history.

19   The great city of "Babylon" split into three sections, and cities around the world fell in heaps of rubble; and so all of "Babylon's" sins were remembered in God's thoughts, and she was punished to the last drop of anger in the cup of the wine of the fierceness of His wrath.

20   And islands vanished, and mountains flattened out,

21   And there was an incredible hailstorm from heaven; hailstones weighing a hundred pounds fell from the sky onto the people below, and they cursed God because of the terrible hail.

CHAPTER 17

ONE of the seven angels who had poured out the plagues came over and talked with me. "Come with me," he said, "and I will show you what is going to happen to the Notorious Prostitute, who sits upon the many waters of the world.

2   The kings of the world have had immoral relations with her, and the people of the earth have been made drunk by the wine of her immorality."

3   So the angel took me in spirit into the wilderness. There I saw a woman sitting on a scarlet animal that had seven heads and ten horns,[1] written all over with blasphemies against God.

4   The woman wore purple and scarlet clothing and beautiful jewelry made of gold and precious gems and pearls, and held in her hand a golden goblet full of obscenities.

5   A mysterious caption was written on her forehead: "Babylon the Great, Mother of Prostitutes and of Idol Worship Everywhere around the World."

6   I could see that she was drunk—drunk with the blood of the martyrs of Jesus she had killed. I stared at her in horror.

7   "Why are you so surprised?" the angel asked. "I'll tell you who she is and what the animal she is riding represents.

[1]As the Dragon—Satan—and the Creature from the sea are also described in 12:3, 9 and 13:1.

8   He was alive but isn't now. And yet, soon he will come up out of the bottomless pit and go to eternal destruction;[2] and the people of earth, whose names have not been written in the Book of Life before the world began, will be dumbfounded at his reappearance after being dead.[3]

9   And now think hard: his seven heads represent a certain city[4] built on seven hills where this woman has her residence.

10   They also represent seven kings. Five have already fallen, the sixth now reigns, and the seventh is yet to come, but his reign will be brief.

11   The scarlet animal that died is the eighth king, having reigned before as one of the seven; after his second reign, he, too, will go to his doom.[5]

12   His ten horns are ten kings who have not yet risen to power; they will be appointed to their kingdoms for one brief moment, to reign with him.

13   They will all sign a treaty giving their power and strength to him.

14   Together they will wage war against the Lamb, and the Lamb will conquer them; for He is Lord over all lords, and King of kings, and His people are the called and chosen and faithful ones.

15   The oceans, lakes and rivers that the woman is sitting on represent masses of people of every race and nation.

16   The scarlet animal and his ten horns—which represent ten kings who will reign with him—all hate the woman, and will attack her and leave her naked and ravaged by fire.

17   For God will put a plan into their minds, a plan that will carry out His purposes: they will mutually agree to give their authority to the scarlet animal, so that the words of God will be fulfilled.

18   And this woman you saw in your vision represents the great city that rules over the kings of the earth."

[2]Literally, "go to perdition."
[3]Literally, "dumbfounded at the ruler who was, and is not, and will be present."
[4]Implied in verse 18.
[5]Literally, "go to perdition."

CHAPTER 18

A FTER all this I saw another angel come down from heaven with great authority, and the earth grew bright with his splendor.

2   He gave a mighty shout, "Babylon the Great is fallen, is fallen; she has become a den of demons, a haunt of devils and every kind of evil spirit.[1]

3   For all the nations have drunk the fatal wine of her intense immorality. The rulers of earth have enjoyed themselves[2] with her, and businessmen throughout the world have grown rich from all her luxurious living."

4   Then I heard another voice calling from heaven, "Come away from her, My people; do not take part in her sins, or you will be punished with her.

5   For her sins are piled as high as heaven and God is ready to judge her for her crimes.

6   Do to her as she has done to you, and more—give double penalty for all her evil deeds. She brewed many a cup of woe for others—give twice as much to her.

7   She has lived in luxury and pleasure—match it now with torments and with sorrows. She boasts, 'I am queen upon my throne. I am no helpless widow. I will not experience sorrow.'

8   Therefore the sorrows of death and mourning and famine shall overtake her in a single day, and she shall be utterly consumed by fire; for mighty is the Lord who judges her."

9   And the world leaders, who took part in her immoral acts and enjoyed her favors, will mourn for her as they see the smoke rising from her charred remains.

10   They will stand far off, trembling with fear and crying out, "Alas, Babylon, that mighty city! In one moment her judgment fell."

11   The merchants of the earth will weep and mourn for her, for there is no one left to buy their goods.

12   She was their biggest customer for gold and silver,

[1]Literally, "of every foul and hateful bird."
[2]Literally, "have committed fornication with her."

precious stones, pearls, finest linens, purple silks, and scarlet; and every kind of perfumed wood, and ivory goods and most expensive wooden carvings, and brass and iron and marble;

13   And spices and perfumes and incense, ointment and frankincense, wine, olive oil, and fine flour; wheat, cattle, sheep, horses, chariots, and slaves—and even the souls of men.

14   "All the fancy things you loved so much are gone," they cry. "The dainty luxuries and splendor that you prized so much will never be yours again. They are gone forever."

15   And so the merchants who have become wealthy by selling her these things shall stand at a distance, fearing danger to themselves, weeping and crying,

16   "Alas, that great city, so beautiful—like a woman clothed in finest purple and scarlet linens, decked out with gold and precious stones and pearls!

17   In one moment, all the wealth of the city is gone!" And all the shipowners and captains of the merchant ships and crews will stand a long way off,

18   Crying as they watch the smoke ascend, and saying, "Where in all the world is there another city such as this?"

19   And they will throw dust on their heads in their sorrow and say, "Alas, alas, for that great city! She made us all rich from her great wealth. And now in a single hour all is gone . . . ."

20   But you, O heaven, rejoice over her fate; and you, O children of God and the prophets and the apostles! For at last God has given judgment against her for you.

21   Then a mighty angel picked up a boulder shaped like a millstone and threw it into the ocean and shouted, "Babylon, that great city, shall be thrown away as I have thrown away this stone, and she shall disappear forever.

22   Never again will the sound of music be there—no more pianos, saxophones, and trumpets.[3] No industry of any kind will ever again exist there, and there will be no more milling of the grain.

23   Dark, dark will be her nights; not even a lamp in a window will ever be seen again. No more joyous wedding bells

---

[3]Literally, "harpers . . . pipers . . . and trumpeters."

and happy voices of the bridegrooms and the brides. Her businessmen were known around the world and she deceived all nations with her sorceries.

24   And she was responsible for the blood of all the martyred prophets and the saints."

CHAPTER 19

AFTER this I heard the shouting of a vast crowd in heaven, "Hallelujah! Praise the Lord! Salvation is from our God. Honor and authority belong to Him alone;

2   For His judgments are just and true. He has punished the Great Prostitute who corrupted the earth with her sin;[1] and He has avenged the murder of His servants."

3   Again and again their voices rang, "Praise the Lord! The smoke from her burning ascends forever and forever!"

4   Then the twenty-four Elders and four Living Beings fell down and worshiped God, who was sitting upon the throne, and said, "Amen! Hallelujah! Praise the Lord!"

5   And out of the throne came a voice that said, "Praise our God, all you His servants, small and great, who fear Him."

6   Then I heard again what sounded like the shouting of a huge crowd, or like the waves of a hundred oceans crashing on the shore, or like the mighty rolling of great thunder, "Praise the Lord. For the Lord our God, the Almighty, reigns.

7   Let us be glad and rejoice and honor Him; for the time has come for the wedding banquet of the Lamb, and His bride has prepared herself.

8   She is permitted to wear the cleanest and whitest and finest of linens." (Fine linen represents the good deeds done by the people of God.)

9   And the angel[2] dictated this sentence to me: "Blessed are those who are invited to the wedding feast of the Lamb." And he added, "God Himself has stated this."[3]

---

[1]Literally, "fornication," the word used symbolically through the prophets for the worship of false gods.
[2]Literally, "he"; the exact antecedent is unclear.
[3]Literally, "These are the true words of God."

10   Then I fell down at his feet to worship him, but he said, "No! Don't! For I am a servant of God just as you are, and as your brother Christians are, who testify of their faith in Jesus. The purpose of all prophecy and of all I have shown you is to tell about Jesus."[4]

11   Then I saw heaven opened and a white horse standing there; and the one sitting on the horse was named "Faithful and True"—the one who justly punishes and makes war.

12   His eyes were like flames, and on His head were many crowns. A name was written on His forehead,[5] and only He knew its meaning.

13   He was clothed with garments dipped in blood, and His title was "The Word of God."[6]

14   The armies of heaven, dressed in finest linen, white and clean, followed Him on white horses.

15   In His mouth He held a sharp sword to strike down the nations; He ruled them with an iron grip; and He trod the winepress of the fierceness of the wrath of Almighty God.

16   On His robe and thigh were written this title: "KING OF KINGS AND LORD OF LORDS."

17   Then I saw an angel standing in the sunshine, shouting loudly to the birds, "Come! Gather together for the supper of the Great God!

18   Come and eat the flesh of kings, and captains, and great generals; of horses and riders; and of all humanity, both great and small, slave and free."

19   Then I saw the Evil Creature gathering the governments of the earth and their armies to fight against the one sitting on the horse and His army.

20   And the Evil Creature was captured, and with him the False Prophet,[7] who could do mighty miracles when the Evil Creature was present—miracles that deceived all who had accepted the Evil Creature's mark, and who worshiped his statue. Both of them—the Evil Creature and his False Prophet

---

[4]Literally, "The testimony of Jesus is the spirit of prophecy."
[5]Implied.
[6]Literally, "The Logos," as in John 1:1—the ultimate method of God's revealing Himself to man.
[7]See chapter 13, verses 11-16.

644

—were thrown alive into the Lake of Fire that burns with sulphur.

21   And their entire army was killed with the sharp sword in the mouth of the one riding the white horse, and all the birds of heaven were gorged with their flesh.

CHAPTER 20

THEN I saw an angel come down from heaven with the key to the bottomless pit and a heavy chain in his hand.

2   He seized the Dragon—that old Serpent, the Devil, Satan —and bound him in chains for 1,000 years,

3   And threw him into the bottomless pit, which he then shut and locked, so that he could not fool the nations any more until the thousand years were finished. Afterwards he would be released again for a little while.

4   Then I saw thrones, and sitting on them were those who had been given the right to judge. And I saw the souls of those who had been beheaded for their testimony about Jesus, for proclaiming the Word of God, and who had not worshiped the Creature or his statue, nor accepted his mark on their foreheads or their hands. They had come to life again and now they reigned with Christ for a thousand years.

5   This is the First Resurrection. (The rest of the dead did not come back to life until the thousand years had ended.)

6   Blessed and holy are those who share in the First Resurrection. For them the Second Death holds no terrors, for they will be priests of God and of Christ, and shall reign with Him a thousand years.

7   When the thousand years end, Satan will be let out of his prison.

8   He will go out to deceive the nations of the world and gather them together, with Gog and Magog, for battle—a mighty host, numberless as sand along the shore.

9   They will go up across the broad plain of the earth and surround God's people and the beloved city of Jerusalem[1] on

---

[1]Implied.

every side. But fire from God in heaven will flash down on the attacking armies and consume them.

10   Then the Devil who had betrayed them will again[2] be thrown into the Lake of Fire burning with sulphur where the Creature and False Prophet are, and they will be tormented day and night forever and ever.

11   And I saw a great white throne and the one who sat upon it, from whose face the earth and sky fled away, but they found no place to hide.[3]

12   I saw the dead, great and small, standing before God; and The Books were opened, including the Book of Life. And the dead were judged according to the things written in The Books, each according to the deeds he had done.

13   The oceans surrendered the bodies buried in them; and the earth and the underworld gave up the dead in them. Each was judged according to his deeds.

14   And Death and Hell were thrown into the Lake of Fire. This is the Second Death—the Lake of Fire.

15   And if anyone's name was not found recorded in the Book of Life, he was thrown into the Lake of Fire.

CHAPTER 21

X   THEN I saw a new earth (with no oceans!) and a new sky, for the present earth and sky had disappeared.

2   And I, John, saw the Holy City, the new Jerusalem, coming down from God out of heaven. It was a glorious sight, beautiful as a bride at her wedding.

3   I heard a loud shout from the throne saying, "Look, the home of God is now among men, and He will live with them and they will be His people; yes, God Himself will be among them.[1]

4   He will wipe away all tears from their eyes, and there shall be no more death, nor sorrow, nor crying, nor pain. All of that has gone forever."

[2]Implied; Revelation 20:3.
[3]Literally, "There was no longer any place for them."
[1]Some manuscripts add, "and be their God."

5 And the one sitting on the throne said, "See, I am making all things new!" And then He said to me, "Write this down, for what I tell you is trustworthy and true:

6 It is finished! I am the A and the Z—the Beginning and the End. I will give to the thirsty the springs of the Water of Life—as a gift!

7 Everyone who conquers will inherit all these blessings, and I will be his God and he will be My son.

8 But cowards who turn back from following Me, and those who are unfaithful to Me, and the corrupt, and murderers, and the immoral, and those conversing with demons, and idol worshipers and all liars—their doom is in the Lake that burns with fire and sulphur. This is the Second Death."

9 Then one of the seven angels, who had emptied the flasks containing the seven last plagues came and said to me, "Come with me and I will show you the bride, the Lamb's wife."

10 In a vision he took me to a towering mountain peak and from there I watched that wondrous city, the holy Jerusalem, descending out of the skies from God.

11 It was filled with the glory of God, and flashed and glowed like a precious gem, crystal clear like jasper.

12 Its walls were broad and high, with twelve gates guarded by twelve angels. And the names of the twelve tribes of Israel were written on the gates.

13 There were three gates on each side—north, south, east, and west.

14 The walls had twelve foundation stones, and on them were written the names of the twelve apostles of the Lamb.

15 The angel held in his hand a golden measuring stick to measure the city and its gates and walls.

16 When he measured it, he found it was a square as wide as it was long; in fact, it was in the form of a cube, for its height was exactly the same as its other dimensions—1,500 miles each way.

17 Then he measured the thickness of the walls and found

them to be 216 feet across (the angel called out these measurements to me, using standard units).[2]

18, 19   The city itself was pure, transparent gold like glass! The wall as made of jasper, and was built on twelve layers of foundation stones inlaid with gems:

The first layer[3] with jasper;
The second with sapphire;
The third with chalcedony;
The fourth with emerald;
The fifth with sardonyx;
20   The sixth layer with sardus;
The seventh with chrysolite;
The eighth with beryl;
The ninth with topaz;
The tenth with chrysoprase;
The eleventh with jacinth;
The twelfth with amethyst.

21   The twelve gates were made of pearls—each gate from a single pearl! And the main street was pure transparent gold, like glass.

22   No temple could be seen in the city, for the Lord God Almighty and the Lamb are worshiped in it everywhere.[4]

23   And the city has no need of sun or moon to light it, for the glory of God and of the Lamb illuminate it.

24   Its light will light the nations of the earth, and the rulers of the world will come and bring their glory to it.

25   Its gates never close: they stay open all day long—and there is no night!

26   And the glory and honor of all the nations shall be brought into it.

27   Nothing evil will be permitted in it—no one immoral or dishonest—but only those whose names are written in the Lamb's Book of Life.

---

[2]Literally, "144 cubits by human measurements." A cubit was the average length of a man's arm—not an angel's! The angel used normal units of measurement that John could understand.
[3]Implied.
[4]Literally, "are its temple."

CHAPTER 22

X   AND he pointed out to me a river of pure Water of Life, clear as crystal, flowing from the throne of God and the Lamb,

2   Coursing down the center of the main street. On each side of the river grew Trees[1] of Life, bearing twelve crops of fruit, with a fresh crop each month; the leaves were used for medicine to heal the nations.

3   There shall be nothing in the city which is evil; for the throne of God and of the Lamb will be there, and His servants will worship Him.

4   And they shall see His face; and His name shall be written on their foreheads.

5   And there will be no night there—no need for lamps or sun—for the Lord God will be their light; and they shall reign forever and ever.

*   *   *   *   *

6, 7   Then the angel said to me, "These words are trustworthy and true: 'I am coming soon!'[2] God, who tells His prophets what the future holds, has sent His angel to tell you this will happen soon. Blessed are those who believe it and all else written in the scroll."

8   I, John saw and heard all these things, and fell down to worship the angel who showed them to me;

9   But again he said, "No, don't do anything like that. I, too, am a servant of Jesus as you are, and as your brothers the prophets are, as well as all those who heed the truth stated in this Book. Worship God alone."

10   Then he instructed me, "Do not seal up what you have written, for the time of fulfillment is near.

11   And when that time comes, all doing wrong will do it more and more; the vile will become more vile; good men will

---

[1]Literally, "the tree of life"—used here as a collective noun, implying plurality.
[2]Or, "suddenly," "unexpectedly."

be better; those who are holy will continue on in greater holiness."

* * * * *

12 "See, I am coming soon,[3] and My reward is with Me, to repay everyone according to the deeds he has done.

13 I am the A and the Z, the Beginning and the End, the First and Last.

14 Blessed forever are all who are washing their robes, to have the right to enter in through the gates of the city, and to eat the fruit from the Tree of Life.

15 Outside the city are those who have strayed away from God, and the sorcerers and the immoral and murderers and idolaters, and all who love to lie, and do so.

16 I, Jesus, have sent My angel to you to tell the churches all these things. I am both David's Root and his Descendant. I am the bright Morning Star.

17 The Spirit and the bride say, 'Come.' Let each one who hears them say the same, 'Come.' Let the thirsty one come— anyone who wants to; let him come and drink the Water of Life without charge.

18 And I solemnly declare to everyone who reads this book: If anyone adds anything to what is written here, God shall add to him the plagues described in this book.

19 And if anyone subtracts any part of these prophecies, God shall take away his share in the Tree of Life, and in the Holy City just described.

20 He who has said all these things declares: Yes, I am coming soon!"[3]

Amen! Come, Lord Jesus!

21 The grace of our Lord Jesus Christ be with you all. Amen!

---

[3]Or, "suddenly," "unexpectedly."